# Fodor's

# VIENNA & THE BEST OF AUSTRIA

# WELCOME TO VIENNA & THE BEST OF AUSTRIA

From Vienna to the Alps, Austria celebrates the elegance of the past yet also embraces the pleasures of contemporary culture and the outdoors. Sophisticated Vienna buzzes with former imperial palaces and striking modern structures, traditional coffeehouses and chic locavore restaurants. Beyond the capital, you can hike the Salzkammergut with its cool blue lakes, ski the fashionable slopes of Innsbruck, or soak in the enduring charms of Salzburg's classical music scene. In this fascinating intersection of old and new, you'll find plenty to savor.

## TOP REASONS TO GO

★ **Vienna:** Baroque and art nouveau architecture, cool boutiques, top-tier concert halls.

★ **Scenery:** Stunning views of alpine passes, the Danube Valley, and lowland vineyards.

★ **Music:** The land of Mozart and Strauss entertains fans with performances galore.

★ **Historic Palaces:** From Mirabell to Schönbrunn, Austria flaunts its imperial past.

★ **Museums:** The Kunsthistorisches, MuseumsQuartier, and Museum der Moderne, for a start.

★ **Skiing:** Posh resorts and world-class runs at Kitzbühel, St. Anton, and more.

# 12
## TOP EXPERIENCES

Vienna offers terrific experiences that should be on every traveler's list. Here are Fodor's top picks for a memorable trip.

## 1 Schönbrunn Palace

Play royalty for a day in Vienna by visiting the summer residence of the Habsburgs with its elegant gardens, fountains, fake Roman ruins, a hilltop café, and Europe's oldest zoo. *(Ch.2)*

## 2 Sachertorte

Indulge in a slice of Sachertorte, a dense chocolate cake layered with apricot jam. It was invented in the early 19th century by one of Austria's court confectioners. *(Ch. 3)*

## 3 Grossglockner High Alpine Highway

In the Alps, you can ascend to Austria's tallest peak and view the Pasterze glacier from 12,470 feet. See it while you can; it shrinks 30 feet every year. *(Ch. 9)*

# 4 The Ringstrasse

Streetcars travel full circle along Vienna's best-known avenue, lined with monumental buildings that recall the city's imperial splendor. *(Ch. 2)*

# 5 Thermal Spas

Soak in hot springs at one of several thermal spas that dot small towns throughout Austria. Then brag that you've experienced the country's unofficial leisure sport. *(Ch. 11)*

# 6 Heurigen

Visit a wine tavern where owners serve new wines from their own vineyards. In September, sample *Sturm*, a drink made from the first pressing of the grapes. *(Ch. 3)*

# 7 MAK Museum

In Vienna, this gorgeous collection of Austrian art objects and contemporary works also includes a fascinating display devoted to the Wiener Werkstätte. *(Ch. 2)*

# 8 The Salzkammergut

Enjoy a hike in this rural paradise in Upper Austria with 76 lakes and the Dachstein Mountain range. The opening scenes from *The Sound of Music* were filmed here. *(Ch. 10)*

# 9 The Viennese Ball

As many as 400 black-tie balls are held every year during Vienna's *Fasching*, or carnival season, which lasts from New Year's Eve through Mardi Gras. *(Ch. 5)*

## 10 Fortress Hohensalzburg

Evening classical music concerts take place in the prince's chamber of this mighty castle overlooking Salzburg's skyline. *(Ch. 8)*

## 11 Hofbibliothek

Browse the stacks at Vienna's National Library, a cathedral of books and one of the world's most ornate Baroque libraries. *(Ch. 2)*

## 12 Kitzbühel

This 16th-century village with a medieval town center has carved out a reputation as one of Europe's most fashionable winter ski resorts. *(Ch. 12)*

# CONTENTS

# CONTENTS

# ABOUT
# THIS GUIDE

## Fodor's Ratings
Everything in this guide is worth doing—
we don't cover what isn't—but exceptional sights, hotels, and restaurants are
recognized with additional accolades.
**Fodor's Choice★** indicates our top recom-
mendations; highlights places we deem
highly recommended. Care to nominate
a new place? Visit Fodors.com/contact-us.

## Trip Costs
We list prices wherever possible to help
you budget well. Hotel and restaurant
price categories from **$** to **$$$$** are noted
alongside each recommendation. For
hotels, we include the lowest cost of a
standard double room in high season.
For restaurants, we cite the average price
of a main course at dinner or, if dinner
isn't served, at lunch. For attractions,
we always list adult admission fees; dis-
counts are usually available for children,
students, and senior citizens.

## Hotels
Our local writers vet every hotel to recom-
mend the best overnights in each price cat-
egory, from budget to expensive. Unless
otherwise specified, you can expect pri-
vate bath, phone, and TV in your room.

| Top Picks | Hotels & |
|---|---|
| ★ Fodor's Choice | Restaurants |
| | ⌂ Hotel |
| **Listings** | ⇘ Number of |
| ✉ Address | rooms |
| ✉ Branch address | ❍ Meal plans |
| ☎ Telephone | ✕ Restaurant |
| ⊕ Website | ▭ No credit cards |
| ✎ E-mail | $ Price |
| ▦ Admission fee | |
| ⊙ Open/closed | **Other** |
| times | ⇨ See also |
| Ⓜ Subway | ☞ Take note |
| ✛ Directions or | ⅃ Golf facilities |
| Map coordinates | |

## Restaurants
Unless we state otherwise, restaurants
are open for lunch and dinner daily. We
mention dress code only when there's a
specific requirement and reservations only
when they're essential or not accepted.

## Credit Cards
The hotels and restaurants in this guide
typically accept credit cards. If not, we'll
say so.

# EUGENE FODOR

Hungarian-born Eugene Fodor (1905–91) began his travel career as an
interpreter on a French cruise ship. The experience inspired him to write
*On the Continent* (1936), the first guidebook to receive annual updates and
discuss a country's way of life as well as its sights. Fodor later joined the
U.S. Army and worked for the OSS in World War II. After the war, he kept up
his intelligence work while expanding his guidebook series. During the Cold
War, many guides were written by fellow agents who understood the value
of insider information. Today's guides continue Fodor's legacy by providing
travelers with timely coverage, insider tips, and cultural context.

# EXPERIENCE
# VIENNA AND THE
# BEST OF AUSTRIA

# VIENNA AND AUSTRIA TODAY

In today's Austria, the old exists alongside the new. Austria has, at various times, been the seat of an empire, the hub of artistic expression, an occupied territory during wartime, and the lone neutral ground of the Cold War. All of Vienna's distinctive eras, from the 18th-century age of the great composers to the Vienna Secession Art Nouveau period at the turn of the 20th century to the present day—with skyscrapers like the DC Towers soaring above the banks of the Danube—can be found in this remarkable city of 1.9 million residents. For centuries, the country has attracted artists, musicians, writers, athletes, actors, and doctors hoping to make a name for themselves.

Austria has been under the control of emperors, kings, dictators, presidents, and Caesars. At its height over a century ago, the Austro-Hungarian Empire covered most of central and eastern Europe with about 53 million people living under the rule of the House of Habsburg. The country's present-day boundaries put it at roughly the size of South Carolina with a population of 8.8 million, comparable to that of New Jersey.

## Politics

Like much of Europe, Austria has been shifting to the right in recent years, a direction that picked up speed in the 2017 elections, when the long-dominant center-left Social Democratic Party lost to the traditionally conservative People's Party. Led by charismatic Sebastian Kurz, the People's Party picked up more than 30% of the vote. The campaign focused on limiting immigration and strengthening the social welfare system, especially for Austria's aging population. Kurz is in his 30s, so you could say the torch of leadership has been passed to a new generation—both in age and policy. The Social Democrats, led by Chancellor Christian Kern, continue to wield political clout, but will have to adjust to sharing power in a coalition government with the right-wing, nationalist Austrian Freedom Party (FPO), led by the simultaneously charismatic and reviled Heinz-Christian Strache, a controversial figure who participated in neo-Nazi activities in his youth. With the country's president, Alexander Van der Bellen, from yet a fourth party, the Green Party, Austrians should be buckling their seat belts for a rocky political decade.

## Music

Austria is synonymous with classical music almost to the point of obsession; therefore, changes in the musical landscape often take time. After more than 500 years in existence, the famed Vienna Boys' Choir only received their first theater all to themselves in 2012: the 400-seat MuTh (Music & Theater) concert hall, where classical enthusiasts can hear this world-renowned choir, founded in 1498 by Holy Roman Emperor Maximillian I, perform music by Mozart, Schubert, and more. The theater mixes Baroque and contemporary architecture enriched with distinctive seating and panels to create some of the best acoustics in Vienna. In addition to calling on MuTh, classical devotees can listen to music (free in many cases) at Vienna's often overlooked University of Music and Performing Arts, where students from across the globe come to study.

Perhaps more than any other genre except for Austria's beloved classical, electronic music has grabbed national—and, increasingly, international—attention. Since the 1990s when Austrian duo Kruder & Dorfmeister began popularizing downtempo, which is more mellow than house or trance, Vienna has been the unofficial international capital of the cozy groove genre; visitors will find it playing in clubs, bars, and cafés throughout the city. Popular techno lounges frequently change up their playlists to keep things fresh for eager crowds, while more and more outdoor parties like the aptly named Kein Sonntag ohne Techno (No Sunday Without Techno) dot the city's new musical terrain. Record stores are also filled with electronic music produced by small labels, which have helped fuel the movement. Beyond Vienna, the Ars Electronica Festival, held every September in the northern city of Linz, focuses on digital culture with the final day devoted to electronic music, while the southeastern city of Graz—a UNESCO World Heritage Site—hosts the urban electronic arts and music Springfestival in May, drawing international crowds that bear witness to the growing popularity of electronica.

## The Economy

While other economies in the European Union might be stagnant, or even floundering, Austria's GDP has been increasing steadily each year since the early 2010s, due in part to strong exports of many home-grown products like chocolate, pistachios, and marzipan "Mozart balls," (originally produced by Salzburg confectioner Paul Furst in 1890). In 1892, Konrad Doppelmeyr invented the motorized ski lift, and his little company has grown into a conglomerate that now powers much of the international winter sports industry with its chairlifts and cable cars. The name Dietrich Mateschitz is not recognizable to most of us, but the Red Bull energy drink he invented certainly is; the €5 billion empire is still run out of the tiny village of Fuschi am See. And finally,

the Swarovski empire still exports high-fashion crystal as well as precision optical glass for telescopes and binoculars from its original family headquarters in Wattens, near Innsbruck.

## Food

The modern sustainable food movement commonly called "farm-to-table" didn't begin in Austria, but it may as well have. The country's small size, distinct seasons, aversion to processed food, and varied growing areas from mountains to vineyards to grassy flatlands provide the perfect setting for getting food quickly from its source, something that has been normal practice in Austria since the years immediately following World War II, when the country struggled to provide enough food within its borders for its citizens. Only recently has farm-to-table been promoted as such. Austrian farms and vineyards have been known to practice "biodynamic agriculture," a holistic approach that treats the farm as an entire organism, a concept developed by Austrian thinker Rudolf Steiner. Austria is considered one of the pioneers of organic farming with one-fifth of the agricultural land in the country being farmed organically, the highest percentage in the European Union. The country also has more organic farmers than all of the other EU countries together. Many restaurants have gotten into the habit of publishing the source of each ingredient, both to appease picky diners and excite foodies, with products derived from organic farming and humane animal keeping.

# WHAT'S WHERE

**1 Vienna.** Vienna mixes old-world charm with elements of a modern metropolis. The city's neighborhoods offer a journey thick with history and architecture, and the famous coffeehouses are havens for an age-old coffee-drinking ritual.

**2 Vienna Woods, Lake Neusiedl, and the Danube Valley.** Vienna is surrounded with enticing options such as hiking in the Vienna Woods and exploring the nearby towns of Marchegg and Carnuntum. The famously blue Danube courses through Austria past medieval abbeys, fanciful Baroque monasteries, verdant pastures, and compact riverside villages. A convenient base is Linz, Austria's third-largest city, and probably its most underrated.

**3 Salzburg.** Salzburg is an elegant city with a rich musical heritage that also draws visitors for its museums and architecture, the Trapp family history, old-fashioned cafés, and glorious fountains.

**4 The Eastern Alps.** Farther south and into the Alps, panoramic little towns, spas, and an array of sports highlight this section of Austria. No road in Europe matches the Grossglockner High Alpine Highway, the most spectacular pass through the Alps.

**5 Salzkammergut.** The Salzkammergut stretches across three states—from Salzburg through Styria to Upper Austria—and includes Austria's Lake District. Hallstatt is touted as one of the world's prettiest lakeside villages.

**6 Carinthia and Graz.** Carinthia is the country's sunniest (and southernmost) province. Here you'll find the Austrian Riviera, a blend of mountains, valleys, and placid blue-green lakes with lovely resorts, while Graz, the capital of Styria, is the country's second-largest city.

**7** Innsbruck, Tyrol, and Vorarlberg. The Tyrol is a region graced with cosmopolitan cities and monuments, but with the glorious Alps playing the stellar role, Nature steals every scene. Nearby, Vorarlberg's big draw is its powdery skiing regions.

CZECH REPUBLIC

SLOVAKIA

Waidhofen
Gmünd
Zwettl
Horn
Poysdorf

LOWER AUSTRIA
(NIEDERÖSTERREICH)

Schärding
Freistadt
Krems
Stockerau

Linz
**2**
Vienna
Danube (Donau)
Enns
Danube
Marchegg

Eferding
Ried
Wels
Enns
Molk
St. Pölten
**1**
Mödling
Carnuntum

UPPER AUSTRIA
(OBERÖSTERREICH)
Steyr
Scheibbs
Baden
Bruck

Vöcklabruck
Enns
Wiener
Neustadt
Neusiedler
See

**3**
**5**
Gmunden
Mariazell
Neunkirchen
Eisenstadt

St. Wolfgang
Bad Ischl
Bad Aussee
Mürzzuschlag

Hallstatt
Liezen
Kapfenberg
Bischofshofen
Bruck a. d. Mur
BURGENLAND

Radstadt
Leoben
Hartberg

St. Johann
Knittelfeld
STYRIA
(STEIERMARK)

Badgastein
Judenburg
Graz
Fürstenfeld

Feldbach
HUNGARY

CARINTHIA
(KÄRNTEN)
**6**
Bad
Gleichenberg

Spittal
St. Veit
Bad
Radkersburg

Feldkirchen
Mura

Drau
Villach
Klagenfurt
Drava

SLOVENIA

# NEED TO KNOW

## AT A GLANCE

**Capital:** Vienna

**Population:** 8,739,000

**Currency:** Euro

**Money:** ATMs are common; credit cards are widely accepted

**Language:** German

**Country Code:** 43

**Emergencies:** 112

**Driving:** On the right

**Electricity:** 230v/50 cycles; electrical plugs have two round prongs

**Time:** Six hours ahead of New York

**Documents:** Up to 90 days with valid passport; Schengen rules apply

**Mobile Phones:** GSM (900 and 1800 bands)

**Major Mobile Companies:** A1, Hutchison Drei, T-Mobile

## WEBSITES

**Austrian Tourist Office:** ⊕ www.austria.info

**Vacation Guide Austria:** ⊕ www.tiscover.com

**Vienna Tourist Information Guide:** ⊕ www.wien.info/en

## GETTING AROUND

✈ **Air Travel:** Vienna's Schwechat Airport is the largest, followed by Salzburg and Graz.

🚌 **Bus Travel:** Terminals are outside main railway stations. Buses are extensive, punctual, and clean.

🚗 **Car Travel:** In the countryside, a car rental is useful, but most major cities have traffic-free historic centers. Gas is expensive, and prepaid vignette stickers are required for motorways.

🚆 **Train Travel:** Trains in Austria are fast and efficient. Most of Vienna's train traffic comes via the Hauptbahnhof or Westbahnhof stations.

## PLAN YOUR BUDGET

|  | HOTEL ROOM | MEAL | ATTRACTIONS |
|---|---|---|---|
| Low Budget | €80 | €15 | Stairs to Cathedral Tower, €4 |
| Mid Budget | €160 | €25 | Ticket to Kunsthistorisches Museum, €14 |
| High Budget | €250 | €120 | Opera ticket, €185 |

## WAYS TO SAVE

**Eat at open-air markets.** A huge variety of foods stalls offer inexpensive hot and cold dishes throughout the day. Sausage stands are a cheap and popular alternative too.

**Book a rental apartment.** For more spacious accommodations and a kitchen, consider a furnished rental—a great option for families or groups.

**Travel with public transport.** Buy daily or weekly passes. For cheaper, off-peak rail travel, see the Austrian railway website (⊕ www.oebb.at).

**Look for concessions in museums.** Seniors over 60 get reduced admission, and under-19s are usually free.

| Hassle Factor | Low. Flights to Vienna are frequent, and Austria has great transport elsewhere. |
|---|---|
| 3 days | You can see Vienna and take a half-day trip out to Abbey of Klosterneuburg and the northern Vienna Woods. |
| 1 week | Combine a longer trip to Vienna with a one-day trip to the impressive Melk Abbey, the medieval town of Dürnstein and historic Krems, and another half-day trip to Mayerling, Heiligenkreuz, and the southern Vienna Woods. |
| 2 weeks | You have time to spend in the provincial capitals, Vienna, Salzburg, and Innsbruck, and more time to discover "off the road" highlights, including trips to some of the most picturesque lakes and mountain valleys. |

## WHEN TO GO

**High Season:** May, June, and September are busy and expensive but offer major festivals and better weather. July and August are the hottest months in the east (less so to the west) but this is also when most Viennese take their own vacations.

**Low Season:** Late January and February are the best times for airfares and hotel deals—and to escape the crowds. But unless you are skiing, winter offers the least appealing weather. Snowfall, icy winds, and freezing temperatures can cause travel disruptions (more so in the mountainous west than in the dryer east).

**Value Season:** October is gorgeous, with temperate weather, good hotel deals, and lots of cultural events. By November temperatures start to drop. Late March and April are good months to visit, before the masses arrive and when snows are nearly gone and springtime activities are abuzz.

### BIG EVENTS

**April:** Salzburg's Easter Festival offers great classical music off-season. ⊕ www.osterfestspiele-salzburg.at

**May:** Expect glamour at Vienna's fantastic Life Ball. ⊕ www.lifeball.org.

**December:** Advent is magical; town squares are transformed into glittering fairy-tale scenes.

**January and February:** Fasching (carnival) offers glitzy balls in Vienna.

## READ THIS

■ *A Nervous Splendor,* Frederic Morton. Portrays significant moments in Austria's history.

■ *The Story of the Trapp Family Singers,* Maria Augusta Trapp. The *Sound of Music* memoir.

■ *The Hare with Amber Eyes,* Edmund De Waal. A memoir/detective story.

## WATCH THIS

■ *Amadeus.* Rivals Mozart and Salieri both try to catch the ear of the Austrian emperor.

■ *Before Sunrise.* A couple meet on a train and have a brief romantic adventure in Vienna.

■ *The Third Man.* Carol Reed's timeless film noir thriller in postwar Vienna.

## EAT THIS

■ *Tafelspitz:* boiled beef, served with apple and horseradish sauce

■ *Wiener schnitzel:* panfried, breaded veal cutlet

■ *Goulash:* paprika-spiced beef stew

■ *Kaiserschmarrn:* dessert made of potato pancakes, with stewed plum sauce

■ *Salzburger nockerln:* sweet, light, and fluffy soufflé dessert

■ *Käsespätzle:* macaroni-and-cheese, mountain-style

# FLAVORS OF AUSTRIAN CUISINE

The phrase "meat and potatoes" describes the bare essentials, as well as the core components of Austrian cuisine. Nearly every typical dish in the country consists of some variation of pork, beef, or chicken with the go-to hearty vegetable, though Austrian food is frequently so much more.

The focus on "just the basics" can be seen in breakfasts that usually feature a roll topped with butter and jam alongside coffee and slices of cheese and meat and sometimes a hard-boiled egg. Lighter, lunchtime meals consisting of crusty bread, holey Alpine cheese, and ham resemble the British ploughman's lunch.

Thanks to Austria's small size, it's not hard to find fresh, local food. Most neighborhoods in cities big and small will have some sort of outdoor market full of produce, cheeses, and meats alongside small restaurants and fast-food stands. Chief among these is Vienna's *Naschmarkt* (literally: snack market), an outdoor food extravaganza that stretches for nearly a mile.

## New Trends

Of course, not all Austrian food boils down to meat and potatoes. Influences from nearby former imperial holdings like Hungary and Poland pepper the palate (goulash from the east, Mediterranean spices from the south, and pastries from Poland helped shape those found in Austria). The influx of immigrants from Turkey over the last few decades helped the *doner* kebab, a sandwich of sorts similar to a Greek gyro that features meat sliced from a rotating vertical spit, rise to the level of fast food usually reserved for pizza and french fries.

In the world of haute cuisine, you can find several restaurants in Vienna and Salzburg boasting Michelin stars and menus that are anything but traditional. At Steirereck in Vienna's Stadtpark, you'll see Austrian ingredients like Alpine beef, locally grown citrus, and vegetables mixed with French cheese and South American herbs. A six-course meal at Restaurant Konstantin Filippou will expose you to foods as varied as lamb's tongue, mackerel, and pigeon.

Austria has also seen a growing "bread trend." A few years ago, Josepf Brot von Pheinsten boutique bakery expanded from its single location in Vienna's center to an elegant bistro on one of the city's popular shopping streets. Not to be outdone, the country's chain bakeries are rebranding themselves as hipper and homier.

## Sausage

A good portion of the country's pork consumption comes in the form of the ever-present *Wurstelstand,* where sausages of all varieties can be found. The lowly hot dog is called a frankfurter here (just don't call it wiener, the name for a Viennese person) and usually served sliced on its own with a side of mustard and bread or stuffed lengthwise into a bun for easier carrying. There is also *Burenwurst,* a pork sausage similar to kielbasa, and *Bosna,* a wurst served with onions. For those who like smoked meat, there's the *Waldviertler,* which is smoked wurst, and the more elaborate *Beinwurst,* made of smoked pork, a selection of herbs, and wine. *Bockwurst* is a pork sausage, and *Weisswurst* is a veal sausage, boiled (not broiled or grilled), and often eaten for breakfast. The *Nürnberger* is a small spicy pork wurst, and the *Blutwurst* is—are you sitting down?—a sausage with congealed blood. Other varieties include the paprika-spiced *Debreziner* and the cheese-filled *Käsekrainer.*

## Coffee

Austrian writer Stefan Zweig called the Viennese coffeehouse "a sort of democratic club, open to everyone for the price of a cheap cup of coffee." The types of drinks available are as varied as the coffeehouses that serve them. Most common is the *Melange,* the Austrian version of the cappuccino featuring steamed milk and milk foam. A *Kleiner Brauner* consists of a shot of dark coffee with a bit of milk mixed in. The *Einspänner* is a strong black coffee served in a glass and topped with whipped cream. Ask for a *Maria Theresa* and your drink will come with a shot of orange liqueur inside. The *Schwarzer Mokka* is a straight espresso while *Schale Gold* is coffee with a small shot of cream, and *Kapuziner* is coffee with a splash of sweet cream (though not a cappuccino, despite the similar-sounding name).

## Cakes

*Naschkatze,* or those with a sweet tooth, have their choice of cakes and sweets to go with their many coffee options. There is *Sachertorte,* the famous chocolate cake with a layer of apricot jam and dark chocolate icing that is associated with Vienna so much that it was featured as a lyric in a Beatles song. Developed in the 18th century, the Hotel Sacher lays claim to the "original" recipe, supposedly known only to a few individuals and kept under lock and key.

*Linzer torte* is the famous Austrian torte with a lattice design made of pastry, cinnamon, hazelnuts, and red currant jam, often served at Christmastime. Often served with a dollop of whipped cream, the Austrian *apfelstrudel* gained popularity in the 1700s throughout many of the areas under the empire's control and is today considered a national dish.

Literally meaning "emperor's folly," *kaiserschmarrn* are shredded pancakes served with fruit, nuts, and whipped cream. The dish took its name from Emperor Franz Josef, who took such a liking to it that people joked it would be his folly.

## Traditional dishes

*Wiener schnitzel* is veal, pork, or sometimes turkey hammered flat, breaded, and deep-fried. A spritz of freshly squeezed lemon and a side of potato salad or french fries complete this quintessential Austrian meal.

Boiled beef in broth, *Tafelspitz* is served with horseradish and sliced and fried potatoes. Ever the foodie, it was Emperor Franz Josef who popularized the dish, which became so synonymous with Austrian cuisine that one famous restaurant hands patrons a card detailing the proper way Tafelspitz should be eaten.

*Leberknödel* is a spiced, boiled beef-liver dumpling normally served in a consommé or thin vegetable soup. Some varieties feature spleen mixed in with the dumpling.

*Fiedermaus* (pork) is another cut that Austrian butchers supply, named after the batlike shape of the cut. And then, of course, there is *Speck,* which is essentially Austrian bacon, and *Leberkäse,* which is a loaf of corned beef, pork, and bacon, often sliced as a sandwich meat.

# GREAT ITINERARIES

## VIENNA TO VORARLBERG

This itinerary travels the country from end to end, hitting the heights and seeing the sights—all in a one-week to 14-day trip.

### Days 1–3: Vienna

Austria's glorious past is evident everywhere, but especially where this tour begins, in Vienna. Get to know the city by trolley with a sightseeing tour of the Ringstrasse. Take in the Kunsthistoriches Museum, where the incredible details of the famous Brueghel paintings could keep you fascinated for hours, and then walk along Kärntnerstrasse, the city's Fifth Avenue, to magnificent St. Stephen's Cathedral, and spend an afternoon in one of the city's cozy coffeehouses. Devote a half day to Schönbrunn Palace, and set aside an evening for a visit to a jovial *Heurige* wine tavern. You should also keep an afternoon open for a slice of Sachertorte, the famous Viennese chocolate cake with layers separated by apricot jam, at the Hotel Sacher Wien, where it was invented. Be sure to visit the Judenplatz Museum, built over the remains of a 13th-century synagogue, for exhibits about life in Vienna from medieval times through World War II. Finally, make a stop at Spanische Reitschule (Spanish Riding School) to watch the stark white Lippizzaner horses who will dance their way into your heart.

### Day 4: Danube River from Vienna to Linz

To zoom from Vienna to Linz by autobahn would be to miss out on one of Austria's most treasured sights, the blue Danube. To tour some quaint wine villages, follow the "Austrian Romantic Road" (Route 3), along the north bank of the river, instead of the speedier A1 autobahn. Cross to the south side of the Danube to

the breathtaking Baroque abbey at Melk, and along the way visit the 1,000-year-old town of Krems and picture-perfect towns of Spitz and Dürnstein, in the heart of the Wachau wine region.

### Days 5 and 6: Linz

Fast-forward into Austria's future with a stop in progressive Linz, the country's third-largest city. Linz is a busy port on the Danube and an important center for trade and business. Techno-music geeks will enjoy the Ars Electronica Museum; others can wander the beautifully restored medieval courtyards of the Altstadt (Old Town). For great views, ride the city's Pöstlingbergbahn, the world's steepest mountain railway, or opt for a Danube steamer cruise to Enns. Be sure to take time to visit the Schlossmuseum Linz (Linz Castle Museum), built in the 1400s, with a vast collection of art and weaponry.

### Days 7 and 8: Salzkammergut

For Austria in all its Hollywood splendor, head to the idyllic Salzkammergut, better known as the Lake District, where *The*

*Sound of Music* was filmed. The town of Bad Ischl—famous for its operetta festival and pastries—makes a good base. Travel south on Route 145 to Hallstatt, one of Austria's most photographed lakeside villages. Return to Bad Ischl, then head west to St. Wolfgang for swimming and sailing.

### Days 9 and 10: Salzburg

This is a city made for pedestrians, with an abundance of churches, palaces, mansions, and—as befits the birthplace of Mozart—music festivals. Stroll through the old city center with its wrought-iron shop signs, tour the medieval Fortress Hohensalzburg, and relax in the Mirabell Gardens (where the von Trapp children "Do-Re-Mi"-ed). Children of all ages will adore the famed Marionettentheater.

### Days 11 and 12: Innsbruck and Tyrol

Tour Innsbruck's treasures—including the famous Golden Roof mansion and the Hofburg—but do as the Tyroleans do and spend time reveling in the high-mountain majesty. After all, Innsbruck is the only major city in the Alps. For a splendid panorama, take the cable railway to the Hafelekar, high above the Inn Valley. For a trip through the quaint villages around Innsbruck, ride the Stubaitalbahn, a charming old-time train, or head by bus to the Stubai Glacier for year-round skiing. You can also take the train to Wattens, 30 minutes away, to visit Swarovski Kristalwelten (Crystal World), a kind of Disneyland for crystalware that adjoins the company's headquarters.

### Days 13 and 14: Bregenz

Taking the Arlberg Pass (or the much more scenic Silvretta High Alpine Road), head to the city of Bregenz, capital of Vorarlberg. Bregenz owes its character as much to neighboring Switzerland and Germany as to Austria, and is most appealing in summer, when sun worshippers crowd the shores of Lake Constance to enjoy an opera festival set on the world's largest outdoor floating stage. Take a lake excursion and explore Bregenz's medieval streets.

# THE MOUNTAINS OF AUSTRIA

This is a trip where Alpine glory is all around you: meadows and forests set against a backdrop of towering craggy peaks, and gentle wooded rambles that lead to clear mountain lakes and storybook castles. Let go of your worries and let the natural beauty of the countryside work its magic.

## Days 1 and 2: Bad Ischl/St. Wolfgang

The villages and lakes of the Salzkammergut region extend south from Salzburg. Base yourself in Bad Ischl, a first-class spa in the heart of the Lake District and a favorite of Austrian Emperor Franz Josef a century ago. A walk through the village passes several locations that honor Austria's operetta tradition and composers such as Franz Lehar. From there, head west to St. Wolfgang, one of the most photo-friendly villages in Austria. For the most scenic surroundings, park in nearby Strobl and hop one of the lake ferries to the pedestrian-only village, where you can marvel at the 16th-century Michael Pacher altarpiece in the parish church and take the railway up the 5,800-foot Schafberg peak for gasp-inducing vistas.

## Day 3: Hallstatt

Set on fjordlike Hallstättersee, this jewel is an optical illusion perched between water and mountain—a tight grouping of terraced fishermen's cottages and churches offering, at first glance, no apparent reason why it doesn't tumble into the lake. On a sunny day the views of the lake and village, considered the oldest settlement in Austria, are spectacular, and on a misty morning they are even more so. Consider a canoe outing, or tour the Hallstatt salt mine, the oldest in the world and a UNESCO World Heritage Site.

## Day 4: Werfen

Take in the birds-of-prey show at the formidable Burg Hohenwerfen, a castle built in the 11th century; tour the Eisriesenwelt ("World of the Ice Giants"), the largest collection of ice caves in Europe; and cap the day with dinner at Obauer, one of Austria's finest restaurants.

---

### TIPS

Although it is much simpler to travel this route by car, it can also be undertaken using public transportation (note that many trains do not run on Sunday). Trains link Salzburg, Bad Ischl, Hallstatt, and Kitzbühel; travel to St. Wolfgang by postbus. From Hallstatt, hop the train to Bad Aussee and on to Irdning, where you may have to change trains to Bischofshofen before reaching Zell am See. Travel to and from Heiligenblut by bus.

---

## Day 5: Zell am See

Southwest of Werfen, the charming lake resort of Zell am See is nestled under the 6,000-foot Schmittenhöhe mountain. Ride the cable car from the center of town for a bird's-eye view, then take the narrow-gauge Pinzgauer railroad through the Salzach river valley to famous Krimmler waterfalls.

## Day 6: Heiligenblut

Head skyward over the dizzying Grossglockner High Alpine Highway to one of Austria's loveliest villages, Heiligenblut, which fans out across the upper Möll Valley with fabulous views of the Grossglockner, at 12,470 feet the highest mountain in Austria.

## Day 7: Kitzbühel

Travel to the glamorous resort town of Kitzbühel for a bit of window-shopping and celebrity spotting, or avoid the crowds to explore nearby Kufstein and its 13th-century mountaintop fortress. On the road headed west, the sunny valley has plenty of snow in winter and golf in summer. End your trip in Innsbruck, 91 km (57 miles) west.

# FESTIVALS IN AUSTRIA

Austria's changing seasons and countless holidays mean something is always afoot. Check out ⊕ *www.austria.info*, the website for the Austrian Tourism Office, for a comprehensive list of festivals and events.

## Winter

**Ball season** (⊕ *www.austria.info Dec.– Feb.*). What better place to dance the waltz than in the country where it was invented? Nearly 500 balls are staged throughout the city for those who need to satisfy their inner Cinderella.

**Christkindlmarkt** (⊕ *www.christkindl-maerkte.at Nov. and Dec.*). Practically every open space in cities and towns across the country is devoted to end-of-the year Christmas markets. Sweets, meats, gifts, and trinkets are available at these pop-up festivals that also feature mulled wine and the fruit-and-liquor-infused *punsch.*

**Silent Night Celebration** (⊕ *www.visit-salz-burg.net/surroundings/silentnightchapel. htm*). On Christmas Eve, join locals to celebrate at the chapel in the village of Obendorf, near Salzburg, where the timeless Christmas song was written in 1818.

## Spring

**Fasnacht** (⊕ *www.fasnacht-nassereith. at Feb. and Mar.*). Venice has its Carnival, Tyrol has its Fasnacht. Arriving just before Ash Wednesday, this Alpine festival features costumes, parades, and hand-carved masks. One of the most famous is the Schellerlaufen pageant in the small Tyrolean town of Nassereith, which depicts the symbolic fight between a bear and his keeper.

**Oestermarkt** (⊕ *www.austria.info Mar. and Apr.*). Like the Christmas markets before it, Easter markets pop up in public plazas everywhere and feature a range of regional meats, cheeses, butter, and, of course, decorative eggs.

**Festwochen** (⊕ *festwochen.at May and June*). Theaters, museums, galleries, and concert spaces across Vienna offer special programs over the course of five weeks to celebrate the city's "will to survive" after World War II.

## Summer

**Bregenz Festival** (⊕ *www.bregenzerfest-spiele.com/en Mid-July and mid-Aug.*). A highlight of this monthlong music and arts festival is the floating stage on the lake.

**Salzburg Festival** (⊕ *www.salzburgerfest-spiele.at July and Aug.*). Opera's elite flock to Salzburg for six weeks of opera, concerts, and stage plays in one of the world's premiere events of the art form.

**Donauinselfest** (*June*). For three days, thousands of fans pack a 4-mile stretch of Vienna's Danube Island for the annual music festival billed as the largest open-air event in Europe.

## Fall

**Long Night of the Museums** (⊕ *www.wien. info Oct.*). More than 100 museums in Vienna and other parts of Austria open their doors from 6 pm until 1 the next morning in a cultural free-for-all that attracts thousands each year. Comfortable shoes not included.

**National Day** (*Oct. 26*). Marking the day in 1955 when Austria declared its neutrality, the city takes a day off to take a tour of the parliament, see a free museum or two, or to check out the military's giant display on Heldenplatz in the center of Vienna.

# AUSTRIA THROUGH THE AGES

While Austria today is best known for its stunning natural beauty like its Alpine peaks and the Danube River, classical music culture, German-inspired cuisine, and an array of famous citizens from Freud to Kafka, it also has a rich and complicated social and political history.

## The Celts and the Roman Empire (circa 800 BC to AD 976)

Like much of Europe, Austria has been inhabited since the Paleolithic Age, and invaded by a parade that included the Romans, who built the settlements now known as Vienna, Salzburg, and Innsbruck. The Romans were ousted in the 4th century by Germanic and Hunnic invaders, who began converting the pagan population to Christianity. In turn, they were expelled by Charlemagne in the 7th century, who made the territory part of his French empire. After his death in 814, Charlemagne's lands were carved up and Germany took the eastern portion, which became known as Oestrreich, or Eastern Lands.

## The House of Babenberg (976 to 1273)

In 962, Pope John XII crowned Otto, the German king of Austria, as emperor of the Holy Roman Empire, which at that point was no longer holy, nor Roman, nor an Empire. Otto named Leopold of Babenberg as Austria's ruler. His descendent, Leopold III, was later canonized and declared the patron saint of Austria. In 1156, the Holy Roman Empire reclassified Austria as a duchy to be ruled over by dukes and duchessess. One of the first dukes, Heinrich II, made Vienna his capital, and built his castle on what today is the city's oldest square, Am Hof. In 1192, Leopold V imprisoned King Richard the Lion-Hearted on his way back to England from the Crusades.

Leopold used the ransom money to build fortifications around Vienna.

## The House of Habsburg (1273 to 1914)

The origins of modern Austria date to the Middle Ages and the ascension of the powerful Habsburg dynasty, which ruled the country for 640 years, turning Austria into one of the most dynamic states in Europe by expanding land holdings via acquisition and through marriage. When the future Maximilian I wed Mary of Burgundy in 1477, her dowry included the French region of Burgundy and the land now known as the Netherlands. In 1492, their son, Philip, married the daughter of Ferdinand and Isabella of Spain, aligning the two countries politically. When Philip's son Charles became king of Spain in 1519, his realm included Austria, Burgundy, and the Netherlands. A few years later, Charles was elected Holy Roman Emperor, and gave Austria to his brother, Ferdinand, to rule as archduke. When Charles abdicated in 1556, Ferdinand ascended to the throne of Holy Roman Emperor, and thus began the height of the Reformation, an unsettled time in Europe, including for Catholic Austria and its small Protestant population.

In 1618, the Thirty Years' War broke out; it was essentially a duel between the two ruling families of Europe, the Habsburgs and the Bourbons, and turned much of Europe into a battlefield, and eventually left the House of Habsburg much weaker. The death of the last male Habsburg in 1740 ushered in the golden age of Maria Theresa, when a young Mozart first performed at Schoenbrunn Palace, and Vienna became the European capital of music and culture. Her daughter, Marie

Antoinette, was famously married off to French king Louis XVI.

In 1814, the Congress of Vienna redrew the map of Europe after the French Revolution and the defeat of Napoléon, who had conquered much of Austria. When revolutionary movements threatened the Habsburg throne, they were stopped via censorship and police force. In 1866, Bismark's Prussia defeated Austria in a disastrous seven-week war, which fatally weakened Austria's position as a world power. Next-door Hungary then demanded more recognition and power, and the new nation of Austria-Hungary was created, with one parliament for each member nation, and Austria's Franz Josef as emperor. The vast new empire also included parts of northern Italy and what is now Czech Republic, Croatia, Bosnia, Serbia, and Poland. Unfortunately, uniting so many factions under a single flag caused ethnic and political tensions to simmer and eventually boil over. Despite the political unrest, music and art flourished from the 1850s to the 1890s. Music's so-called Waltz Kings, the father-and-son duo both named Johann Strauss, became Austria's darlings. Expressionist art blossomed, and Sigmund Freud made world headlines for his research on the human psyche.

### World War I, World War II, and the Modern Day (1914 to present)

The political tensions of the Austro-Hungarian empire boiled over in 1914 with the assassination of Archduke Franz Ferdinand, nephew and heir to the emperor, by a Serbian terrorist. Austria responded by declaring war against Serbia, setting off World War I. The end of the war in 1917 also brought an end to Austria-Hungary, the official end of the 640-year Habsburg dynasty, and the beginning of the Republic of Austria. Throughout the 1920s, the young nation suffered massive inflation and unemployment, and its near economic collapse in the 1930s made it powerless to defend itself against the invasion of Hitler in 1938. During this time, known as the Anschluss, Austria was incorporated into the Third Reich. In 1945, Austria was restored to its prewar boundaries, and declared itself "perpetually" neutral in 1955, when it became a member of the European Union. Austria has largely remained out of the world politics spotlight over the last few decades, instead focusing on its contributions to culture, tourism, and its high standard of living for its residents. Recent famous Austrians include actor Christoph Waltz, filmmaker Fritz Lang, actor and politician Arnold Schwarzenneger, and Red Bull founder Dietric Mateschitz.

# SKIING IN AUSTRIA

In Austria, skiing is much more than just a popular pastime; it's a national obsession, a way of life. Images of Alpine ski villages conjure fairy-tale fantasies of heavily timbered houses, onion-domed churches, welcoming locals, schnapps, and glühwein. Add to the mix some of the world's highest, treeless slopes, glaciers, and a lively après-ski scene, and you have a winter sport destination of extraordinary allure.

American skiers are often amazed to find how big European skiing is, in every sense of the word. The entire country embraces skiing, and the sport is deeply woven into the patterns of daily life in the Austrian countryside. In most cases, Alpine ski resorts are the result of the evolution of an Alpine village, where individual ski areas are linked together with a common ski pass and a spiderweb network of lifts spanning and connecting different valleys and multiple mountains. The trend of late has been resorts joining forces, creating "ski circuses" of stunning size.

## GUIDES, LIFTS, AND COSTS

To take full advantage of the promise of so much snowy terrain, American skiers should consider hiring a ski instructor–guide for a day or two. Private instructors are less expensive in Austria than in the United States, and the upper levels of Austrian ski-school classes are more about guiding than actual teaching.

It's often possible to ski the whole day without using the same lift twice, but care must be taken so you don't end your day at a village miles away from your hotel, or even the next country (some resorts are close to the German border). Lift systems in Austria are astonishingly sophisticated, and include double-decker cable cars and eight-person chairlifts. Many chairlifts have a weather protection bubble, and even heated seats. Magic-carpet loading aids efficiency, and nearly every lift has electronic entry, so you'll rarely see an attendant checking a ticket or marshalling the lineups. In addition, there are no ski-area boundaries, so you may see experienced skiers going *off-piste* (the French term for off-trail), skiing until they reach a village in the valley or the snow runs out.

Expect costs to balance out with those in the United States. Lift tickets and rental equipment in Austria are generally cheaper than in the United States, while eating out is more expensive. Lunch isn't a quick refueling stop here, but a leisurely midday break, and the slopes abound with unique huts welcoming skiers with hearty Austrian fare. As with skiing anywhere else in the world, you'll save money with multiday passes. Most resorts offer choices from 4 to 14 days.

## BEST SLOPES

There are so many choices when it comes to Austrian skiing that you're not going to see it all, or ski it all, in one lifetime. Foreign ski enthusiasts and newcomers to Austrian slopes would do well to focus first on the biggest ski regions of the Arlberg, Tyrol, and Land Salzburg. These megaski regions showcase what makes Alpine skiing so special: an astonishing variety of slopes and lifts that allow the visitor to ski, day after day, often from one village to the next. True, there are many tiny and delightful ski villages in Austria, real discoveries for adventurous skiers, but it makes more sense to sample the feast of a major *Skigebiet* (interconnected ski region, sometimes called a ski arena) first. Here, to get you started, are some of the finest.

## The Arlberg

This is a capital of Austrian skiing: a double constellation of ski-resort towns—Zürs, Lech, and Oberlech, in the Vorarlberg; and, just across the Arlberg Pass to the east and thus technically in the Tyrol, St. Anton, St. Christoph, and Stuben. These classic Arlberg resorts are interconnected by ski lifts and trails and share more than 260 km (160 miles) of groomed slopes (and limitless off-piste possibilities), 83 ski lifts, snowboard parks, carving areas and permanent race courses, and, significantly, a common ski pass.

St. Anton, part of the fabulous Arlberg area, is the cradle of skiing, where ski pioneer Hannes Schneider opened the world's first ski school back in 1921. A skier here can feel like a character out of a 1930s Luis Trenker ski film: from enjoying Jaeger tea after skiing to dinner at the Post Hotel. St. Anton links with elegant Lech in Vorarlberg (once a favorite of Princess Diana) and secretive Zurs, where royalty and celebrities discreetly vacation. In turn, Lech has recently been linked by lift with the villages of Warth and Schrocken in the next valley. St. Christoph is a spartan resort for skiing purists, a handful of handsome hotels lost in a sea of white, high above timberline, and the permanent home of the Austrian National Ski School's training and certification courses.

The pièce de résistance of Arlberg skiing is the all-day round-trip, on skis, from Zürs to Lech, Oberlech, and back. This ski epic starts with a 5-km (3-mile) off-piste run from the Madloch down to Zug and ends, late in the afternoon, many lifts and many thousands of vertical feet later, high on the opposite side of Zürs, swinging down the slopes of the Trittkopf.

## The Tyrol/Innsbruck

Austria boasts resorts throughout the country, but the western province of Tyrol is the heart of Austrian skiing, chock-full of world-class skiing—about a third of all Austrian ski resorts are found here.

After St. Anton and the Arlberg, Kitzbühel, in the heart of the Tyrol, is Austria's best-known ski destination, and although not as exclusive as Lech or Zürs, certainly one of Austria's most elegant. "Kitz" is picture-perfect and posh—all medieval, cobbled streets, wrought-iron signs, and candles flickering in the windows of charming restaurants.

For an altogether different sort of ski vacation, especially for groups of skiers and nonskiers, consider staying in downtown Innsbruck and making day trips to the six ski areas of Olympia Ski World Innsbruck. Innsbruck has twice hosted the Winter Olympics, and boasts a stunning collection of medium-size ski areas with grand views.

In ever-increasing numbers, skiers are attracted by the excellent snow conditions and nightlife of Ischgl, in the Paznaun (Valley) southwest of Innsbruck, where you can cross-border ski into the village of Samnaun, Switzerland. Kufstein, northwest of Innsbruck, is in the center of 70 peaks more than 9,000 feet high, with more than 300 miles of skiable terrain.

In Salzburgerland, serene Zell am See overlooks a lake, and Bad Gastein dramatically sits astride a raging torrent. In Carinthia, mystical Heiligenblut broods at the foot of the Grossglockner, Austria's highest mountain, and Nassfeld extends into Italy.

# EXPLORING VIENNA

Updated
by Patti
McCracken

One of the great European capitals, Vienna was for centuries the stomping ground of the Habsburg rulers of the Austro-Hungarian Empire. The empire is long gone, but reminders have been carefully preserved by the tradition-loving Viennese. Past artistic glories live on, thanks to the cultural legacy of the many artistic geniuses nourished here—including Mozart, Beethoven, Schubert, Strauss, and Gustav Klimt.

Gilt-covered, halcyon decades of symphonies and sonatas, concertos and operas marked the imperial heyday of the city. Mozart, Haydn, and Beethoven were soon followed by Schubert, Strauss, Brahms, and Mahler, all of whom lived in the city during the peaks of their careers. Their music resounded in the grand halls of newly built Baroque edifices, where flamboyant facades were ornamented with madonnas and cherubs, and soaring columns reached upward to graceful domes perched atop like an elegant gentleman's hat. It was a time of wealth and enlightenment. Literati crowded the coffeehouses, and the ballroom became the centerpiece of culture, both patrician and peasant, as all took to a waltzing craze that would forever define the capital city. Vienna was a stage for opulence and cheer, the air stirred by zephyrs of refinement and joy.

Vienna had been founded as a Roman military encampment around AD 50, and remained so for some 300 years. By the 13th century new city walls encompassed further development to the south. According to legend, the walls were financed by the huge ransom paid by the English for their king, Richard the Lion-Hearted, who was kidnapped by a local duke while on his way home from the Third Crusade in 1192.

Vienna's third set of walls dates from 1544, courtesy of the Habsburg dynasty, which ruled the Austro-Hungarian Empire for an astonishing 645 years. These walls stood until 1857, when Emperor Franz Josef decreed that they be replaced by the series of boulevards that now make up the Ringstrasse. Outlying villages were brought into Vienna's fold, and Vienna's urban planning was revolutionized, becoming a model for other European cities.

Vienna's heyday as a European capital did not begin until 1683, after a huge force of invading Turks laid siege to the city for two months before being ousted. Among the supplies they left behind were sacks of coffee beans, and, so the story goes, this gave birth to the coffeehouse culture that remains one of the city's most prized customs.

The 19th century brought with it a somber sky. Napoléon twice captured the city, denting what seemed an invincible empire. This mood was reflected in the more subdued and stately Biedermeier architecture, but the era also ushered in a splash of cutting-edge artists and architects—Gustav Klimt, Egon Schiele, Oskar Kokoschka, Joseph Hoffmann, Otto Wagner, and Adolf Loos ("form follows function") among them. They brought an unprecedented artistic revolution that set the stage for the radically experimental art of the 20th century.

Today's Vienna, with a multicultural population of 1.7 million, is as vibrant and stunning as was Maria Theresa's Baroque wonderland. Side streets teem with buskers playing to appreciative crowds. Churches and halls resound with the famous strains of Strauss on summer days, while the city's nightlife (and the fabulous music scene it nurtures) is one of Europe's best-kept secrets. A few years ago, *Fast Company* magazine recognized Vienna as the World's Smartest City, for its innovation and sustainability. All these are among the reasons why Vienna has, year after year, been declared the world's most livable city in a variety of studies and surveys, pitting it against hundreds of international rivals.

# ORIENTATION AND PLANNING

## GETTING ORIENTED

**The Eastern City Center: Stephansdom and Medieval Vienna.** Time seems to stand still in this part of Vienna, where hidden architectural treasures await discovery down narrow lanes and cobbled streets. One of the quaintest parts of town, it is a mythical place where the city's legends originated.

**The Inner City Center.** Sip a *Melange* from a splendid café while admiring the rich facades of the palatial homes of former Viennese aristocrats. Waiters, dressed as if they're off to a ball, serve coffee and cakes to the regulars.

**The Hofburg: An Imperial City.** The huge former Habsburg winter abode for seven centuries now houses many of the belongings the family left behind. The Imperial Treasury advertises with the slogan "We don't have the emperors, but we do have their jewels."

**The Western City Center: Burgtheater and Beyond.** Hobnob with the city's most celebrated thespians at Café Landtmann after catching a performance at one of Europe's largest and oldest theaters; or stroll past the Mölker Bastei, where Beethoven wrote his one and only opera, *Fidelio*.

**Across the Danube: The 2nd District.** Situated on a stretch of land between the Danube and the Danube Canal, "Leopoldstadt" is home to a burgeoning Jewish community—one which thrived here before World War II—and is one of the most up-and-coming areas in the city. The much-loved Prater amusement park is also here.

**East of the Ringstrasse: Stadtpark and Karlsplatz.** Home to the Musikverein, the city's top concert hall, and the modernist Wien Museum, dedicated to the city's history, Karlsplatz is a destination on its own. Relax in the manicured green expanses of the Stadtpark, or take the tram up to Belvedere Palace to marvel at Klimt's *Kiss*.

**South of the Ringstrasse: the MuseumsQuartier.** The MuseumsQuartier is on the site of former Habsburg stables and is among Europe's most respected museum complexes. Visit the Naturhistorisches Museum to view the

## TOP REASONS TO GO

**Ride the Ringstrasse:** Hop on streetcar No. 1 or No. 2 and travel full circle along Vienna's best-known avenue. No. 1 will take you from Staatsoper to Schwedenplatz, No. 2 from Schwedenplatz to Staatsoper. Those monumental buildings along the tree-lined boulevard reflect the imperial splendor of yesteryear.

**World of Music:** Delight your eyes and ears with a night out at the State Opera or Musikverein to experience what secured Vienna the title "heart of the music world."

**Kunsthistorisches Museum:** Enjoy the classic collection of fine art, including the best of Breughel, Titian, Rembrandt, and Rubens, at Austria's leading museum.

**Schönbrunn Palace:** Rococo romantics and Habsburg acolytes should step back in time and spend a half day experiencing the Habsburgs' former summer home.

**An extended coffee break:** Savor the true flavor of Vienna at some of its great café landmarks. Every afternoon around 3 the coffee-and-pastry ritual of *Kaffeejause* takes place from one end of the city to the other, a tradition so storied that UNESCO recognizes it as an "intangible cultural heritage." For historical overtones, head for the Café Central or the opulent Café Landtmann. Intellectuals flock to Café Bräunerhof, known for its free chamber music concerts on weekends..

world's largest meteorite collection, and the Kunsthistorisches Museum to see the Habsburg's sizable collection of Flemish and Italian paintings.

**West of the Ringstrasse: Parliament and City Hall.** The Rathaus, the Ringstrasse's most photographed building, beckons with free outdoor concert recordings throughout the summer and an ice-skating rink and sprawling Christmas market in the winter.

**Schönbrunn Palace, Park, and Zoo.** Rococo romantics and Habsburg acolytes should step back in time and spend a few hours experiencing the imperial family's former summer home.

## PLANNING

### WHEN TO GO

Vienna is warm and sunny in spring and autumn; July and August can be hot and stormy, with temperatures reaching well above 32°C (90°F). From November through March, winter can get cold, with snow falling in January and February; lows of -12°C (10°F) are frequent. Culturally, high season in Vienna is May, June, and September, when festivals, marathons, concerts, and operas are in full swing. In winter, the glittering Christmas markets attract international crowds. During the Ball Season, which starts New Year's Day and ends when Catholic Lent begins (usually late February), more than 400 balls take place, hosted by nearly every profession or trade; the Coffee House Owners Ball is the biggest, the Opera Ball the most internationally famous. Many Viennese leave the city in July and August, so the city tones down some, though it fills with tourists.

**FESTIVALS**

**Christkindlmarkt (Christmas Market).** In Vienna the biggest Christmas market goes up in mid-November in the plaza in front of the city's Rathaus (town hall); there are more than 30 smaller ones dotted around town, including outside Schönbrunn and the Belvedere Palace, in the Spittelberg Quarter on the Freyung square, and in front of Karlkirche on Karlsplatz.

**Donauinselfest (Danube Island Festival).** Held in late June, this is Europe's largest open-air music fest, attracting 3 million visitors each year. Entrance is free. ⊠ *Donauinsel* ⊕ *www.donauinselfest.at.*

**Fasching.** In February, Fasching (or Fasnacht, as it's called in the western part of the country), the Carnival period before Lent, can get very wild, with huge processions of costumed figures and the occasional unwilling participation by spectators.

**Hofburg New Year's Ball.** Vienna's Ball Season kicks off on New Year's Eve with this glittering—and expensive—event (formerly known as Kaiserball), held in the elegant rooms of the Hofburg. ☎ *01/58736–66214* ⊕ *www.hofburg.com.*

**Wiener Festwochen.** This festival of theater, music, film, and exhibitions takes over Vienna from mid-May to mid-June. ☎ *01/589–220* ⊕ *www.festwochen.at.*

**Wiener Opernball** (*Vienna Opera Ball*). Perhaps the year's biggest society event, the Vienna Opera Ball is held the Thursday before Ash Wednesday at the magnificent Staatsoper. ☎ *01/5144–42250.*

**Wiener Philharmoniker.** The New Year in Vienna is greeted with a concert by the Vienna Philharmonic. Reserve a year, or even more, in advance. ☎ *01/505–6525* ⊕ *www.musikverein.at.*

**Volksoper.** The opera season runs from September through June. If you can't get into the Philharmonic concert, try for one of the performances of the Franz Lehar operetta *Die lustige Witwe*, or another light delight. ☎ *01/5144–43670* ⊕ *www.volksoper.at.*

## GETTING HERE AND AROUND
**AIR TRAVEL**

Vienna International Airport is at Schwechat, about 19 km (12 miles) southeast of the city. Austrian Airlines flies nonstop from several cities in North America. Many other major carriers make a change in Europe.

The fastest way into Vienna from Schwechat Airport is the sleek, double-decker **City Airport Train.** From the airport to the center of the city, the CAT takes only 16 minutes, and trains operate daily every 30 minutes between 6 am and 11 pm. The cost is €12 one way and €19 round-trip. Tickets can also be purchased online at ⊕ *www.cityairporttrain. com* for a reduced price. But the cheapest way to get into town from the airport is the **S7 train**, called the *Schnellbahn*, which shuttles twice an hour between the station beneath the airport and the Wien-Mitte/ Landstrasse station; the one-way fare is €4.40, and it takes about 20 minutes (only four minutes longer than the CAT train). Plus, your ticket is also good for an immediate transfer to your destination within the city on streetcar, bus, or U-Bahn.

Another cheap option is the fleet of buses operated by **Vienna Airport Lines,** which has separate routes to the city center at Schwedenplatz (20 minutes) and to the Westbahnhof (45 minutes). Buses operate every 30 minutes between 5 am and 12:30 am, and the fare is €8 each way and €13 round-trip.

If convenience is your priority, **Airport Driver** has private cars to the airport; one way is €35, and you must reserve at the Tourist Info desk, open 7 am to 10 pm. A regular taxi between the airport and the city center will charge around €40.

**Airport Contacts Airport Driver.** 🕾 *01/22822* ⊕ *www.airportdriver.at.* **City Airport Train.** 🕾 *01/25250* ⊕ *www.cityairporttrain.com.* **Vienna Airport Lines.** 🕾 *01/7007-32300* ⊕ *www.postbus.at.* **Vienna International Airport** (*VIE*). 🕾 *01/7007-22233 for flight information* ⊕ *www.viennaairport.at.*

## BICYCLE TRAVEL

Citybike rents bicycles at public stations. Payment is by credit card, with a €1 registration fee. The first hour is free; the second is €1, third €2, and fourth €4. Bikes can be picked up or returned to any of the 110 locations around town. A flat fee for exceeding the maximum 120-hour time limit or loss of the bike is a hefty €600. Bicycle Rental Pedal Power offers a special service for tourists in which several bikes can be rented at the same time.

## BOAT AND FERRY TRAVEL

When you arrive in Vienna via the Danube, the Blue Danube Steamship Company/DDSG will leave you at Praterlände near Mexikoplatz. It's a two-block walk to the U1/Vorgartenstrasse subway station, or you can take a taxi directly into town.

## CAR TRAVEL

Vienna is 300 km (187 miles) east of Salzburg, 200 km (125 miles) north of Graz. Main routes leading into the city are the A1 Westautobahn from Germany, Salzburg, and Linz and the A2 Südautobahn from Graz and points south. Rental cars can be arranged at the airport or in town.

On highways from points south or west or from Vienna's airport, "Zentrum" signs clearly mark the route to the center of Vienna. From there, however, finding your way to your hotel is a challenge, because traffic planners have installed a devious scheme limiting through traffic in the city core. Traffic congestion within Vienna is not as bad as in some places, but driving to in-town destinations generally takes longer than does public transportation.

The entire 1st through 9th Districts, and most of the rest of the city, are limited-parking zones and require a Parkschein, a paid-parking chit that can be purchased at tobacconists (AustriaTabak), gas stations, and, oddly, from cigarette machines. They must be filled out and displayed on the dash during the day, and the procedure is maddening and laborious. At this writing, a Parkscheine costs €1 for 30 minutes, €2 for one hour, €3 for 90 minutes, and €4 for two hours. These are required from 8 am until 10 pm in Districts 1 to 9, and a maximum parking time of two hours is permitted, at which point the procedure must be repeated in full. You can park for 15 minutes free of charge, but you must get a violet "gratis" sticker to put in your windshield. However, there is a remarkably handy app called HandyParken that lets you avoid the Park-scheine puzzle and pay through your phone; be sure to have your license plate number and cell-phone number near you to input the information. You can also park free in the 1st District from noon on Saturday until Monday at 8 am, but be very careful about parking illegally. Chances are that you will be towed, and fines are typically hefty.

**PUBLIC TRANSIT TRAVEL**

Overseen by Wiener Linien, Vienna's public transportation system is fast, clean, safe, and easy to use. Vienna's subway system, called the U-Bahn, services the core of the inner city. Several apps are available to ease travel, offering timetables, ticket purchase, information about service disruptions, and more. Visit ⊕ *www.wieninfo.at* and look under "Public Transport & Taxis" for a list and links.

Five subway lines, whose stations are prominently marked with blue "U" signs, crisscross the city. Track the main lines of the U-Bahn system by their color codes on subway maps: U1 is red; U2 purple, U3 orange, U4 green, and U6 brown. The last subway runs at about 12:30 am.

The main city-center subway stops in the 1st District are Stephansplatz, Karlsplatz, Herrengasse, Schottenring, and Schwedenplatz. Stephans-platz is the very heart of the city, at St. Stephen's cathedral. You can reach the amusement park of the Prater from Stephansplatz by taking the U1 to Praterstern. Near the southern edge of the Ringstrasse, the major Karlsplatz stop is right next to the Staatsoper, the pedestrian Kärntnerstrasse, and the Ringstrasse, with an easy connection to Belvedere Palace via the D Tram. You can also take the U4 from Karlsplatz to Schönbrunn Palace (Schönbrunn stop). Schottenring is on the Ringstrasse, offering quick tram connections. Schwedenplatz is a 10-minute walk to St. Stephen's through some of Vienna's oldest streets. Karlsplatz is serviced by the train lines U1, U2, and U4, while U3 goes to Herrengasse. There are handy U-Bahn stops along the rim of the city core, such as Stadtpark, MuseumsQuartier, Volkstheater, and Rathaus.

Streetcars (*Strassenbahnen*) run from about 5:15 am until about midnight. Where streetcars don't run, buses—*Autobusse*—do. Should you miss the last streetcar or bus, special night buses with an "N" designation operate at half-hour intervals over several key routes; the starting (and transfer) points are the Opera House and Schwedenplatz. These night-owl buses accept all normal tickets.

Tickets are valid for all public transportation—buses, trams, and the subway. Although there are ticket machines on trams and buses, there is a surcharge of €0.50. You'll need to punch your ticket before entering the boarding area at U-Bahn stops, but for buses and trams you punch it on board. If you're caught without a ticket you'll pay a hefty fine.

Buy single tickets for €2.20 from dispensers on the streetcar or bus, from ticket machines in subway stations, or online at ⊕ *shop.wienerlinien.at*. At tobacco shops, newsstands, or U-Bahn offices you can buy a 24-hour ticket for €7.60, a three-day ticket for €16.50, or a monthly ticket for €48.20. An inexpensive option is the €16.20 *Wochenkarte* (week card), valid from Monday to Sunday. Children under six travel free on public transit, and children under 15 travel free on Sunday and public holidays.

The Vienna Card, in addition to providing an array of deep discounts at sites, can also be used on all public transportation. You can buy them for periods of 24 hours, 48 hours, or 72 hours, with prices starting from €13.90.

**Public Transporation Contacts Wiener Linien.** ☎ *01/790–9100* ⊕ *www. wienerlinien.at.*

### TAXI TRAVEL

Taxis in Vienna are relatively reasonable. The initial charge is €2.50, and about 5% more from 11 pm until 6 am. They also may charge for each piece of luggage in the trunk. It's customary to round up the fare to cover the tip. Several companies offer chauffeured limousines.

**Taxi Companies 40100 Taxi.** ☎ *01/40100.* **60160 Taxi.** ☎ *01/60160.* **31300 Taxi.** ☎ *01/31300.*

### TRAIN TRAVEL

In 2015, Vienna's railroad system completed an extensive and much-needed overhaul. The former Südbahnhof station was converted into the city's main train station, Hauptbahnhof Wien (or Vienna Central Station) for national and international travel.

**Train Contacts Central Train Station (Hauptbahnhof).** ☎ *05/1717* ⊕ *www. hauptbahnhof-wien.at.* **Franz-Josef Bahnhof.** ✉ *Julius-Tandler-Platz 3, 9th District/Alsergrund.* **Meidling Bahnhof.** ✉ *Eichenstrasse 27, 12th District/ Meidling.* **Westbahnhof.** ✉ *Europaplatz 2, 15th District/Rudolfsheim–Fünfhaus.* **Wien-Mitte.** ✉ *Landstrasser Hauptstrasse 1c, 3rd District/Landstrasse* ☎ *01/05711.* **Wien Praterstern Bahnhof.** ✉ *Lassallestrasse, 2nd District/ Leopoldstadt* ☎ *05/1717 ÖEBB.*

## TOURS
### BUS TOURS

When you're pressed for time, a good way to see the highlights of Vienna is through a sightseeing bus tour, which gives you a speedy tour around the heart of the city and allows a closer look at the Schönbrunn and Belvedere palaces. You can cover almost the same territory on your own by taking either streetcar No. 1 or No. 2 around the Ring. The Yellow Ring Tram is a semiguided tour; it departs from Schwedenplatz and makes a 25-minute lap around the Rings (no stops) for a cost of €9. For full tours, there are a few reputable firms: Vienna Sightseeing Tours, Big Bus Tours, and Red Bus Tours are some of the best. They each run daily "get-acquainted" tours lasting about three hours, including visits to the Schönbrunn and Belvedere palace grounds.

You can tour at your own pace with Vienna Sightseeing Hop-On, Hop-Off, which offers a number of options, including ones that go farther afield to Neusiedle Lake or Carnuntum. The most popular is the short city tour for €25, which allows up to 50 stops in 24 hours. There are also two-day and three-day tours available. All tickets can be purchased at hotels, bus stops, and on the bus. The first bus leaves the Opera stop at 9:30 am, with buses leaving every 15 minutes until 7 pm.

### FIAKER (HORSE CARRIAGE) TOURS

A *Fiaker,* or horse carriage, will trot you around to whatever destination
you specify, but this is an expensive way to see the city. A short tour
of the inner city takes about 30 minutes and costs €40; a longer one
including the inner city and all of the Ringstrasse lasts about 60 minutes and costs €70. The carriages accommodate four (five if someone
sits next to the coachman). Starting points are Heldenplatz in front of
the Hofburg, Stephansplatz beside the cathedral, and across from the
Albertina, all in the 1st District.

### WALKING TOURS

Guided walking tours are a great way to see the city highlights. The tourist office offers around 40 tour topics, ranging from "Unknown Underground Vienna" to "Hollywood in Vienna" to "Jewish Families and
Their Past in Vienna." Vienna Walks and Talks offers informative walks
through the old Jewish Quarter and a *Third Man* tour about the classic
film starring Orson Welles. Tours take about 1½ hours, are held in any
weather provided at least three people turn up (which usually happens;
in fact, they are often sold out). Ask for the monthly brochure "Walks in
Vienna," which details the tours, days, times, and starting points.

**Tour Contacts Big Bus Tours.** ☎ *1/905–910* ⊕ *www.bigbustours.com.* **Red Bus
Tours.** ☎ *1/512–4030* ⊕ *www.redbuscitytours.at.* **Vienna Sightseeing Tours.**
✉ *Weyringergasse 28A, 4th District/Wieden* ☎ *01/7124–6830* ⊕ *www.vienna-
sightseeing.at.* **Vienna Walks and Talks.** ✉ *Werdertorgasse 9/2, 1st District*
☎ *01/774–8901* ⊕ *www.viennawalks.com.*

### VISITOR INFORMATION

The main center for information is the Vienna City Tourist Office, open
daily 9–7 and centrally located on Albertinaplatz between the Hofburg
and Kärntnerstrasse. Ask about a Vienna Card that combines the use of
public transportation and more than 210 discounts at museums, galleries, theaters, and concert halls, as well as bars, cafés, and restaurants.
The cards are also available at hotel and train stations.

**Tourist Information Vienna City Tourist Office.** ✉ *Am Albertinaplatz 1, at
Maysedergasse, 1st District* ☎ *01/24555* ⊕ *www.wien.info.*

# EXPLORING VIENNA

Most of Vienna lies roughly within an arc of a circle with the straight
line of the Danube Canal as its chord. The most prestigious address of
the city's 23 *Bezirke,* or districts, is its heart, the **Innere Stadt** ("Inner
City"), or 1st District, bounded by the Ringstrasse (Ring). It's useful to
note that the fabled 1st District holds the vast majority of sightseeing
attractions and once comprised the entire city. In 1857 Emperor Franz
Josef decided to demolish the ancient wall surrounding the city to create the more cosmopolitan Ringstrasse, the multilane avenue that still
encircles the expansive heart of Vienna. At that time several small villages bordering the inner city were given district numbers and incorporated into Vienna. Today the former villages go by their official district
numbers, but sometimes they are also referred to by their old village
or neighborhood names.

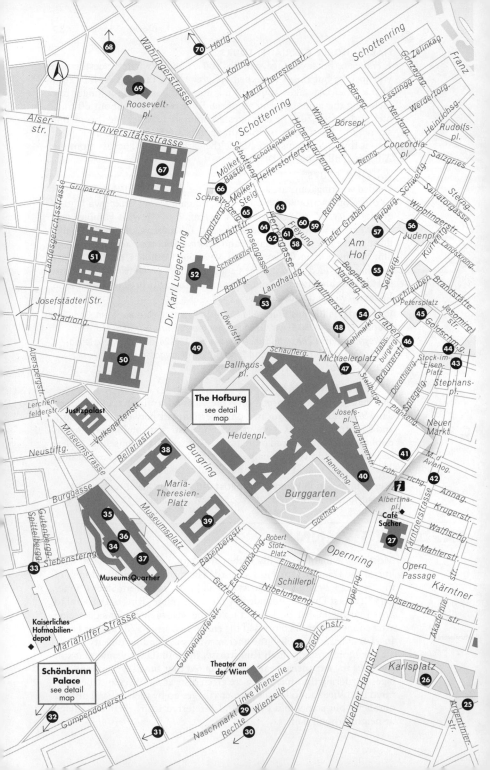

# Exploring Vienna: The Historic Heart

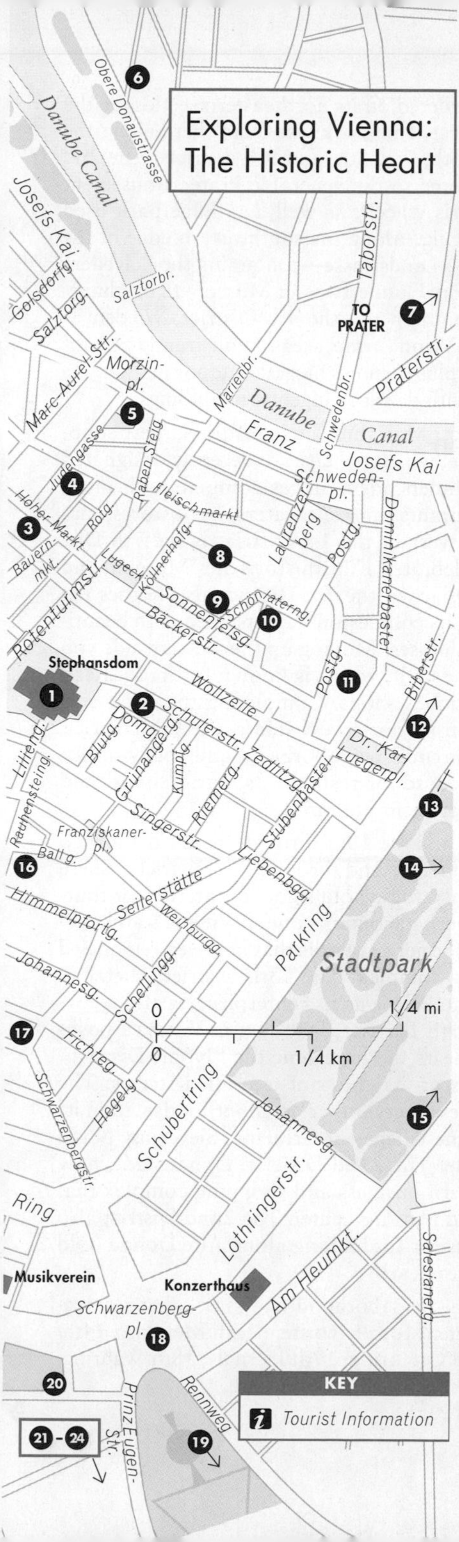

TO PRATER

Stadtpark

0 ——— 1/4 mi

0 ——— 1/4 km

Musikverein

Konzerthaus

**KEY**

*i* Tourist Information

The circular 1st District is bordered on its northeastern section by the Danube Canal and 2nd District, and clockwise from there along the Ringstrasse by the 3rd, 4th, 6th, 7th, 8th, and 9th districts. The 2nd District—Leopoldstadt—is home to the venerable Prater amusement park with its *Riesenrad* (Ferris wheel), as well as a huge park used for horseback riding and jogging. Along the southeastern edge of the 1st District is the 3rd District—Landstrasse—containing the Belvedere Palace and the fabulously quirky Hundertwasser Museum (Kunsthauswien). Extending from its southern tip, the 4th District, Wieden, is firmly established as one of Vienna's hip areas, with trendy restaurants, art galleries, and shops, plus Vienna's biggest outdoor market, the Naschmarkt, which is lined with dazzling Jugendstil buildings.

The southwestern 6th District, Mariahilf, includes the largest shopping street, Mariahilferstrasse, which the city has recently designated a pedestrian-friendly zone. Independent stores compete with international chains, smart restaurants, movie theaters, bookstores, and department stores. Directly west of the 1st District is the 7th District, Neubau. Besides the celebrated Kunsthistorisches Museum and headline-making MuseumsQuartier, the 7th District also houses the charming Spittelberg quarter, its cobblestone streets lined with beautifully preserved 18th-century houses. Moving up the western side you come to the 8th District, Josefstadt, which is known for its theaters, upscale restaurants, and antiques shops. Completing the circle surrounding the Innere Stadt on its northwest side is the 9th District, Alsergrund, once Sigmund Freud's neighborhood and today a nice residential area with lots of outdoor restaurants, curio shops, and lovely early-20th-century apartment buildings.

The other districts—the 5th, and the 10th through the 23rd—form a concentric second circle around the 2nd through 9th Districts. These are mainly residential and only a few hold sights of interest for tourists. The 11th District, Simmering, contains one of Vienna's architectural wonders, Gasometer, a former gasworks that has been remodeled into a housing and shopping complex. The 13th District, Hietzing, with the fabulous Schönbrunn Palace as its centerpiece, is also a coveted residential area. The 19th District, Döbling, is Vienna's poshest neighborhood and also bears the nickname the "Noble District" because of all the embassies on its chestnut-tree-lined streets. The 19th District also incorporates several other neighborhoods within its borders, in particular the wine villages of Grinzing, Sievering, Nussdorf, and Neustift am Walde. The 22nd District, Donaustadt, now called Donau City, is a modern business and shopping complex that has grown around the United Nations center. The 22nd District also has several fantastic stretches for sunbathing along Alte Donau (Old Danube), with waterside cafés nearby.

It may be helpful to know the neighborhood names of other residential districts: the 5th/Margareten; 10th/Favoriten; 12th/Meidling; 14th/Penzing; 15th/Fünfhaus; 16th/Ottakring; 17th/Hernals; 18th/Währing; 20th/Brigittenau; 21st/Floridsdorf; and 23rd/Liesing.

# THE EASTERN CITY CENTER: STEPHANSDOM AND MEDIEVAL VIENNA

For more than eight centuries, the commanding Stephansdom cathedral has remained the nucleus around which the city has grown. Vienna of the Middle Ages is encapsulated behind it, and you could easily spend half a day or more just prowling the narrow streets and passageways. Stephansplatz is the logical starting point from which to explore Vienna's past and present. Streets here are named after medieval trades: Bäckerstrasse was the street of the bakers, and weavers peddled their wares on Wollzeile. Legend has it that several Knights Templar were murdered in Blutgasse, or "Blood Alley."

## TOP ATTRACTIONS

FAMILY
Fodor'sChoice
★

**Haus der Musik** (*House of Music*). You could spend an entire day at this ultra-high-tech museum, housed on several floors of an early-19th-century palace near Schwarzenbergplatz. This is a highly interactive experience; in "Facing Mozart," visitors animate a Mozart portrait using a technology called facetracking. Assuming the role of virtual conductor, you can conduct the Vienna Philharmonic (or a video projection of it, anyway) and have the orchestra follow your every command; the conductor's baton is hooked to a computer, which allows you to have full control over the simulated orchestra. For added fun, the stairs at the beginning of the tour are musical; each step produces a note. Other exhibits trace the evolution of sound (from primitive noises to the music of the classical masters) and illustrate the mechanics of the human ear (you can even measure your own frequency threshold). ⊠ *Seilerstätte 30, 1st District* ☎ *01/513–4850* ⊕ *www.hdm.at* ⦷ *€13* Ⓜ *U1, U2, or U4/Karlsplatz, then Tram D/Schwarzenbergplatz.*

**Himmelpfortgasse.** The maze of tiny streets surrounding Himmelpfortgasse (literally, "Gates of Heaven Street") conjures up the Vienna of the 19th century. The most impressive house on the street is the Ministry of Finance. The rear of the Steffl department store on Rauhensteingasse now marks the site of the house in which Mozart died in 1791. There's a commemorative plaque that once identified the streetside site, together with a small memorial corner devoted to Mozart memorabilia, which can be found on the sixth floor of the store. ⊠ *1st District* Ⓜ *U1 or U3/Stephansplatz.*

NEED A BREAK

✕ **Kleines Cafe.** This landmark café is on one of the most charming squares in Vienna. The "Little Cafe" is open daily for coffee, cocktails, and light snacks, and few places are more delightful to sit in and relax on a warm afternoon or evening. ⊠ *Franziskanerplatz 3, 1st District.*

Fodor'sChoice
★

**Mozarthaus.** This is Mozart's only still-existing abode in Vienna, with three floors of displays about his life and the masterworks that he composed here. Equipped with an excellent audio guide and starting out on the third floor of the building, you can hear about Mozart's time in Vienna: where he lived and performed, who his friends and supporters were, and his passion for expensive attire—he spent more money on clothes than most royals at that time. The second floor deals with Mozart's operatic works. The first floor focuses on the 2½ years that

Mozart lived at this address (he moved around a lot in Vienna), when he wrote dozens of piano concertos, as well as *The Marriage of Figaro* and the six quartets dedicated to Joseph Haydn (who once called on Mozart here, saying to Mozart's father, "your son is the greatest composer that I know in person or by name"). For two weeks in April 1787, Mozart took on a 16-year-old pupil from Germany named Ludwig van Beethoven. Concerts are staged here, and there are activities for children. ■ TIP→ Save on the entrance fee by purchasing a combined ticket for **Mozarthaus Vienna and Haus der Musik for €18.** ⊠ *Domgasse 5, 1st District* ☎ *01/512–1791* ⊕ *www.mozarthausvienna.at* ⌨ *€11* Ⓜ *U1 or U3/Stephansplatz.*

**Schönlaterngasse** (*Street of the Beautiful Lantern*). Once part of Vienna's medieval Latin Quarter, Schönlaterngasse is the main artery of a historic neighborhood that has blossomed in recent years, thanks in part to government *Kulturschillinge*—or renovation loans. Streets are lined with beautiful Baroque town houses (often with colorfully painted facades), now distinctive showcases for art galleries, boutiques, and coffeehouses. At No. 5 you'll find a covered passage that leads to the historic **Heiligenkreuzerhof** courtyard. The picturesque street is named for the ornate wrought-iron wall lantern at Schönlaterngasse 6. Note the Baroque courtyard at Schönlaterngasse 8—one of the city's prettiest.

The quarter's most famous house is the **Basiliskenhaus.** According to legend, on June 26, 1212, a foul-smelling basilisk (half rooster, half toad, with a glance that could kill) took up residence in the courtyard well, poisoning the water. An enterprising apprentice dealt with the problem by climbing down the well armed with a mirror; when the basilisk saw its own reflection, it turned to stone. The petrified creature can still be seen in a niche on the building's facade. Be sure to peek into the house's miniature courtyard for a trip back to medieval Vienna. ⊠ *1st District* Ⓜ *U3/Stubentor, U3/Stephansplatz, U4/Schwedenplatz.*

Fodor'sChoice
★

**Stephansdom** (*St. Stephen's Cathedral*). Vienna's soaring centerpiece, this beloved cathedral enshrines the heart of the city—although when first built in the 12th century it stood outside the city walls. Vienna can thank a period of hard times for the Catholic Church for the cathedral's distinctive silhouette. Originally the structure was to have had matching 445-foot-high spires, a standard design of the era, but funds ran out, and the north tower to this day remains a happy reminder of what gloriously is not. The lack of symmetry creates an imbalance that makes the cathedral instantly identifiable from its profile alone. Like the Staatsoper and some other major buildings, it was very heavily damaged in World War II, but reconstruction loans have been utilized to restore the cathedral's former beauty. Decades of pollution have blackened the exterior, which is being painstakingly cleaned using only brushes and water, so as not to destroy the facade with chemicals.

It's difficult now to tell what was original and which parts of the walls and vaults were reconstructed. No matter: its history-rich atmosphere is dear to all Viennese. That noted, St. Stephen's has a fierce presence that is blatantly un-Viennese. It's a stylistic jumble ranging from 13th-century Romanesque to 15th-century Gothic. Like the exterior, St.

Stephen's interior lacks the soaring unity of Europe's greatest Gothic cathedrals, much of its decoration dating from the later Baroque era.

One particularly masterly work should be seen by everyone: the stone pulpit attached to the second freestanding pier on the left of the central nave, carved by Anton Pilgram between 1510 and 1550. The delicacy of its decoration would in itself set the pulpit apart, but even more intriguing are its five sculpted figures. Carved around the outside of the pulpit proper are the four Church Fathers (from left to right: St. Augustine, St. Gregory, St. Jerome, and St. Ambrose), and each is given an individual personality so sharply etched as to suggest satire, perhaps of living models. There is no satire suggested by the fifth figure, however; below the pulpit's stairs Pilgram sculpted a fine self-portrait, showing himself peering out a half-open window.

As you stroll through the aisles, remember that many notable events occurred here, including Mozart's marriage in 1782 and his funeral in December 1791.

The bird's-eye views from the cathedral's beloved **Alter Steffl** (Old Stephen Tower) will be a highlight for some. The south tower is 450 feet high and was built between 1359 and 1433. The climb up the 343 steps is rewarded with vistas that extend to the rising slopes of the Wienerwald. The north steeple houses the big Pummerin bell and a lookout terrace (access by elevator). For a special treat, take the 90-minute Saturday-evening tour including a roof walk. ⊠ *Stephansplatz, 1st District* ☎ *01/515–52–3054* ⊕ *www.stephanskirche.at* 🖃 *€17.90; elevator to Pummerin: €5.50; South Tower climb: €4.50; catacombs: €5.50* Ⓜ *U1 or U3/Stephansplatz.*

**NEED A BREAK** ✕ **Zanoni & Zanoni.** Between Rotenturmstrasse and Bäckerstrasse, this place dishes up 25 or more flavors of smooth, Italian-style gelato, including mango, caramel, and chocolate chip, and has frozen yogurt and vegan ice cream, too. ⊠ *Am Lugeck 7, 1st District* ☎ *01/512–7979.*

**Universitätskirche** (*Jesuit Church*). The church was built around 1630. Its flamboyant Baroque interior contains a fine trompe-l'oeil ceiling fresco by Andrea Pozzo, the master of visual trickery, who was imported from Rome in 1702 for the job. You might hear a Mozart or Haydn mass sung here in Latin on many Sundays. ⊠ *Dr.-Ignaz-Seipl-Platz, 1st District* ☎ *01/5125–2320* Ⓜ *U3 Stubentor/Dr.-Karl-Lueger-Platz.*

**WORTH NOTING**

**Dominikanerkirche (St. Maria Rotunda)** (*Dominican Church*). The Postgasse, to the east of Schönlaterngasse, introduces this unexpected visitor from Rome, built in the 1630s, some 50 years before the Viennese Baroque building boom. Its facade is modeled after the Roman churches of the 16th century. The interior illustrates why the Baroque style came to be considered the height of bad taste during the 19th century (and it still has many detractors today). "Sculpt till you drop" seems to have been the motto here, and the viewer's eye is given no respite. This sort of Roman architectural orgy never really gained a foothold in Vienna, and when the great Viennese architects did pull out all the decorative stops at the Belvedere Palace, they did it in a very different style and with far greater success. ⊠ *Postgasse 4, 1st District* ☎ *01/512–9174* Ⓜ *U3/Stubentor/Dr.-Karl-Lueger-Platz.*

**Heiligenkreuzerhof** (*Holy Cross Court*). Off the narrow streets and alleys behind the Stephansdom is this peaceful spot, approximately ½ km (¼ mile) from the cathedral. The beautiful Baroque courtyard has the distinct feeling of a retreat into the 18th century. Visit on a Sunday morning and you'll find a craft fair in full swing. ⊠ *1st District* Ⓜ *U1 or U3/Stephansplatz.*

## THE INNER CITY CENTER

The compact area bounded roughly by the back side of the Hofburg palace complex and Staatsoper, the Kohlmarkt, the Graben, and Kärntnerstrasse belongs to the oldest core of the city. Remains of the Roman city are just below the present-day surface. This was and still is the city's commercial heart, dense with shops and markets for various commodities. Today, the Kohlmarkt and Graben in particular offer the choicest luxury shops.

The area is marvelous for its visual treats, from the decorated squares to the varied art-drenched architecture to shop windows. The evening view down Kohlmarkt from the Graben is an inspiring classic, and the gilded dome of Michael's Gate, illuminated at night, shines its light into the palace complex, creating a glittering backdrop. Sights in this area range from the sacred—the Baroque Peterskirche—to the more profane pleasures of Demel, Vienna's beloved pastry shop, and the modernist masterwork of the Looshaus.

> ### BIRD'S-EYE VIEW
>
> A good introduction to Vienna is from a view high above it, and the city's preeminent panoramic lookout point is the observation platform of Vienna's mother cathedral, the Stephansdom. The young and agile will make it up the 343 steps of the south tower in 8 to 10 minutes; the rest will make it in closer to 20. There's also an elevator to the terrace of the north tower, which gives pretty much the same view. From atop, you can see that St. Stephen's is the veritable hub of the city's wheel.

### TOP ATTRACTIONS

**Albertina Museum.** One of the largest of the Habsburg residences, the Albertina rests on one of the last remaining fortresses of the Old City. The must-see collection of nearly 65,000 drawings and almost a million prints is one of the most prized graphic collections in the world. All the Old Masters are showcased here: Leonardo da Vinci, Michelangelo, Raphael, Rembrandt. The Batliner Collection includes excellent examples of French and German Impressionism and Russian avant-garde. The mansion's early-19th-century salons—all gilt boiserie and mirrors—provide a jewel-box setting. The excellent Do & Co restaurant, with a patio long enough for an empress's promenade, offers splendid vistas of the historical center, and the Burggarten is the perfect place to take a break. ⊠ *Augustinerstrasse 1, 1st District* ☎ *01/534–830* ⊕ *www. albertina.at* ☑ *€12.90* Ⓜ *U3/Herrengasse.*

**Am Hof.** In the Middle Ages, the ruling Babenberg family built its castle on what is today's Vienna's oldest square, the Am Hof (which translates to "at court"). The **Mariansäule**—or Maria's column—was erected in 1667 to mark victory in the Thirty Years' War. The one-time Civic Armory at the northwest corner has been used as a fire station since 1685 (the high-spirited facade, with its Habsburg eagle, was "Baroqued" in 1731). The complex includes a firefighting museum that's open on Sunday morning. Presiding over the east side of the square is the noted **Kirche Am Hof,** formerly a Jesuit monastery and now a Croatian church. At No.13 is the fairly stolid 17th-century **Palais Collalto,** famous as the setting for Mozart's first public engagement at the age of six. In Bognergasse, to the right of the church, is the **Engel Apotheke** (pharmacy) at No. 9, with a Jugendstil mosaic depicting winged women collecting the elixir of life in outstretched chalices. At the turn of the 20th century, the inner city was dotted with storefronts decorated in a similar manner; today this is the sole survivor. A fantastic permanent light installation became a fixture on the Am Hof in 2017; every day, for an hour at sundown, you can witness Olafur Eliasson's "Yellow Fog" transform the square into a supernatural wonder.

From March through November, there is an art and antiques market every Friday and Saturday from 10 to 6. Am Hof also hosts one of Vienna's celebrated Christmas markets as well as an Easter Market. ⊠ *Am Hof, 1st District* Ⓜ *U3/Herrengasse.*

**The Graben.** One of Vienna's major crossroads, the Graben's unusual width gives it the presence and weight of a city square. Its shape is due to the Romans, who chose this spot for the city's southwestern moat (Graben literally means "moat" or "ditch"). The Graben's centerpiece is the effulgently Baroque **Pestsäule,** or Plague Column. Erected by Emperor Leopold I between 1687 and 1693 as thanks to God for delivering the city from a particularly virulent plague, today the representation looks more like a host of cherubs doing their best to cope with the icing of a wedding cake wilting under a hot sun. Protestants may be disappointed to learn that the foul figure of the Pest also stands for the heretic plunging away from the "true faith" into the depths of hell. ⊠ *Between Kärntnerstrasse and Kohlmarkt, 1st District* Ⓜ *U1 or U3/Stephansplatz.*

**Jewish Museum of Vienna.** The former Eskeles Palace, once an elegant private residence, now houses the Jewish Museum Vienna. Permanent exhibits tell of the momentous role Viennese Jews have played in everything from music and medicine to art and philosophy, both in Austria and in the world at large. A permanent exhibition called "Our City" shows Jewish life in Vienna up to the present day. The museum complex includes a café and bookstore. ⊠ *Dorotheergasse 11, 1st District* ☎ *01/535–0431* ⊕ *www.jmw.at* 🎟 *€12 (includes admission to the Judenplatz museum)* ⊘ *Closed Sat.* Ⓜ *U1 or U3/Stephansplatz.*

**Judenplatz Museum.** In what was once the old Jewish ghetto, construction workers discovered the fascinating remains of a 13th-century synagogue while digging for a new parking garage. Simon Wiesenthal (a former Vienna resident) helped to turn it into a museum dedicated to the Austrian Jews who died in World War II. Marking the outside is a concrete cube whose faces are casts of library shelves, signifying a love of learning. Downstairs are three exhibition rooms devoted to medieval Jewish life and the synagogue excavations. Also in Judenplatz is a statue of the 18th-century playwright Gotthold Ephraim Lessing, erected after World War II. ✉ *Judenplatz 8, 1st District* ☏ *01/535–0431* ⊕ *www.jmw.at/museum-judenplatz* ⊒ *€12 (includes admission to Jewish Museum of Vienna)* ☉ *Closed Sat.*

**Kärntnerstrasse.** Vienna's leading central shopping street is much maligned—too commercial, too crowded, too many tasteless signs—but when the daytime tourist crowds dissolve, the Viennese arrive regularly for their evening promenade, and it is easy to see why. The street comes alive with outdoor cafés, wonderfully decorated shop windows, buskers, and well-dressed citizens walking their small, manicured dogs. Despite tourists, it has an energy that the more tasteful Graben and the impeccable Kohlmarkt lack. ✉ *1st District* Ⓜ *U1, U4/ Karlsplatz, or U1, U3/Stephansplatz.*

**Kohlmarkt.** Aside from its classic view of the domed entryway to the imperial palace complex of the Hofburg, the Kohlmarkt is best known as Vienna's most elegant shopping street, and fronts the area being refashioned the Goldenes Quartier (Golden Quarter). All the big brand names are represented here: Gucci, Louis Vuitton, Tiffany, Chanel, and Armani, to name a few. The shops, not the buildings, are remarkable, although there is an entertaining odd-couple pairing: No. 11 (early 18th century) and No. 9 (early 20th century). The mixture of architectural styles is similar to that of the Graben, but the general atmosphere is low-key, as if the street were consciously deferring to the showstopper dome at the west end. The composers Haydn and Chopin lived in houses on the street. ✉ *Between Graben and Michaelerplatz, 1st District* Ⓜ *U3/Herrengasse.*

**Looshaus.** In 1911 Adolf Loos built the Looshaus on imposing Michaelerplatz, facing the Imperial Palace, and it was considered nothing less than an architectural declaration of war. After 200 years of Baroque and neo-Baroque exuberance, the first generation of 20th-century architects had had enough. Loos led the revolt; *Ornament and Crime* was the title of his famous manifesto, in which he inveighed against the conventional architectural wisdom of the 19th century. He advocated buildings that were plain, honest, and functional. The city was scandalized by Looshaus. Emperor Franz Josef, who lived across the road, was so offended that he ordered the curtains of his windows to remain permanently shut. Today the building has lost its power to shock, and the facade seems quite innocuous. The interior remains a breathtaking surprise; the building now houses a bank, and you can go inside to see the stylish chambers and staircase. To really get up close and personal with Loos, head to the splendor of his Loos American Bar, about six blocks east at No. 10 Kärntnerdurchgang. ✉ *Michaelerplatz 3, 1st District* Ⓜ *U3/Herrengasse.*

**Michaelerplatz.** One of Vienna's most historic squares, this small plaza is now the site of an excavation that took place from 1989–91. Some remarkable Roman ruins were discovered, including what some believe was a brothel for soldiers. The excavations are a latter-day distraction from the Michaelerplatz's most noted claim to fame—the eloquent entryway to the palace complex of the Hofburg.

Mozart's *Requiem* debuted in the **Michaelerkirche** on December 10, 1791. More people stop in today due to a discovery American soldiers made in 1945, when they forced open the crypt doors, which had been sealed for 150 years. Found lying undisturbed for centuries were the mummified remains of former wealthy parishioners of the church—even the finery and buckled shoes worn at their burial had been preserved by the perfect temperatures contained within the crypt.

Bilingual tours are offered from Easter to October, Monday through Saturday, at 11 am and 1 pm. The cost is €7. You're led down into the shadowy gloom and through a labyrinth of passageways, pausing at several tombs (many of which are open so you can view the remains) for a brief explanation of the cause of death. On Wednesday at 3 pm free tours of the church are held in English. ⊠ *Herrengasse, Reitschulgasse, and Schauflergasse, 1st District* ☎ *0676/503–4164* Ⓜ *U3/Herrengasse.*

**Peterskirche** (*St. Peter's Church*). One of Vienna's most well-known churches, St. Peter's Church stands on what was once the site of a church built in the latter half of the 4th century, making this spot the oldest Christian sacred site in the city. A few centuries later, Charlemagne built another church here, and finally St. Peter's Church was constructed between 1702 and 1708 by Lucas von Hildebrandt, who also built the Belvedere Palace. The facade has angled towers, graceful turrets (said to have been inspired by the tents of the Turks during the siege of 1683), and an unusually fine entrance portal. Inside, the Baroque decoration is elaborate, with some fine touches (particularly the glass-crowned galleries high on the walls on either side of the altar and the amazing tableau of the martyrdom of St. John Nepomuk). Just before Christmas each year the basement crypt is filled with a display of nativity scenes. The church is shoehorned into tiny Petersplatz, just off the Graben. ⊠ *Petersplatz, 1st District* Ⓜ *U1 or U3/Stephansplatz.*

**Ruprechtskirche** (*St. Ruprecht's Church*). North of the Kornhäusel Tower, this is the city's most venerable church, believed to have been founded in 740; the oldest part of the present structure (the lower half of the tower) dates from the 11th century. Set on the ancient ramparts overlooking the Danube Canal, it is serene and unpretentious. ⊠ *Ruprechtsplatz, 1st District* Ⓜ *U1 or U4/Schwedenplatz.*

**Fodor'sChoice** **★** **Staatsoper** (*State Opera House*). Vying with St. Stephen's Cathedral for the honor of the emotional heart of the city, the opera house is a focus for Viennese life and one of the chief symbols of resurgence after World War II. Its directorship is one of the top jobs in Austria, almost as important as that of the country's president, and one that draws even more public attention. The first of the Ringstrasse projects to be completed (in 1869), the opera house suffered disastrous bomb damage in the last days of World War II—only the outer walls, the front facade, and the main staircase survived. The auditorium is plain when compared to the red-and-gold eruptions of London's Covent Garden or some of the Italian opera houses, but it has an elegant individuality that it shows off beautifully when the stage and auditorium are turned into a ballroom for the great Opera Ball.

The construction of the opera house is the stuff of legend. When the foundation was laid, the plans for the Opernring were not yet complete, and in the end the avenue turned out to be several feet higher than originally planned. As a result, the opera house lacked the commanding prospect that its architects, Eduard van der Nüll and August Sicard von Sicardsburg, had intended. Even Emperor Franz Josef pronounced the building a bit low to the ground. For the sensitive van der Nüll (and here the story becomes a bit suspect), failing his beloved emperor was the last straw. In disgrace and despair, he committed suicide. Sicardsburg died of grief shortly thereafter. And the emperor, horrified at the deaths his innocuous remark had caused, limited all his future artistic pronouncements to a single immutable formula: *"Es war sehr schön, es hat mich sehr gefreut"* ("It was very nice, it pleased me very much").

Renovation could not avoid a postwar look, for the cost of fully restoring the 19th-century interior was prohibitive. The original design was followed in the 1945–55 reconstruction, meaning that sight lines from some of the front boxes are poor at best. These disappointments hardly detract from the fact that this is one of the world's half-dozen greatest opera houses, and experiencing a performance here can be the highlight of a trip to Vienna. If tickets are sold out, some performances are shown live on a huge screen outside on Karajanplatz. Tours of the opera house are given regularly, but starting times vary according to rehearsals; the current schedule is posted under the arcades on both sides of the building. Under the arcade on the Kärntnerstrasse side is an information office that also sells tickets to the main opera and the Volksoper. ⊠ *Opernring 2, 1st District* ☎ *01/514–44–2606* ⊕ *www.staatsoper.at* ⌨ *€9* Ⓜ *U1, U2, or U4 Karlsplatz.*

## WORTH NOTING

**Haas-Haus.** Designed by the late Hans Hollein, one of Austria's best-known contemporary architects, who died in 2014, the Haas-Haus is one of Vienna's more controversial buildings. The modern lines contrast sharply with the venerable walls of St. Stephen's just across the way, which can be seen in the mirrored facade of the Haas-Haus. ⊠ *Stephansplatz 12, 1st District* Ⓜ *U1 or U3/Stephansplatz.*

**Hoher Markt.** Crowds gather at noon each day to see the huge mechanical Anker Clock strike the hour. That's when the full panoply of mechanical figures of Austrian historical personages parades by; see if you can spot Marcus Aurelius, Joseph Haydn, and Maria Theresa. The Anker Clock (named for the Anker Insurance Company, which financed it) took six years (1911–17) to build. It managed to survive the World War II artillery fire that badly damaged much of the square. The graceless buildings erected around the square since 1945 do little to show off the square's lovely Baroque centerpiece, the St. Joseph Fountain (portraying the marriage of Joseph and Mary), designed in 1729 by Joseph Emanuel Fischer von Erlach, son of the great Johann Bernhard Fischer von Erlach. ⊠ *1st District* Ⓜ *U1 or U4/Schwedenplatz.*

**Kaisergruft** (*Imperial Burial Vault*). On the southwest corner of the Neuer Markt, the Kapuzinerkirche, or Capuchin Church, is home to one of the more intriguing sights in Vienna: the Kaisergruft, or Imperial Burial

Vault. The crypts contain the partial remains of some 140 Habsburgs (most of the hearts are in the Augustinerkirche and the entrails in St. Stephen's) plus one non-Habsburg governess ("She was always with us in life," said Maria Theresa, "why not in death?"). Perhaps starting with their tombs is the wrong way to approach the Habsburgs in Vienna, but on the upside, at least it gives you a chance to get their names in sequence, as they lie in rows, their pewter coffins ranging from the simplest explosions of funerary conceit—with decorations of skulls, snakes, and other morbid symbols—to the huge and distinguished tomb of Maria Theresa and her husband. Designed while the couple still lived, their monument shows the empress in bed with her husband—awaking to the Last Judgment as if it were just another morning, while the remains of her son (the ascetic Josef II) lie in a simple copper casket at the foot of the bed. In 2011, 98-year-old Otto Habsburg, the eldest son of the last emperor, was laid to rest here with as much pomp as was permissible in a republic. ✉ *Tegetthofstrasse 2, 1st District* ☎ *01/512–6853* 💶 *€5* Ⓜ *U1, U3/Stephansplatz; U1, U4/Karlsplatz.*

**Kirche Am Hof.** On the east side of the Am Hof, the Church of the Nine Choirs of Angels is identified by its sprawling Baroque facade designed by Carlo Carlone in 1662. The somber interior lacks appeal, but the checkerboard marble floor may remind you of Dutch churches. ✉ *Am Hof 1, 1st District* Ⓜ *U3/Herrengasse.*

**Römermuseum.** The Hoher Markt harbors one wholly unexpected attraction: underground ruins of a Roman military camp dating from the 2nd and 3rd centuries. You'll see fragments of buildings, pieces of pottery, children's toys, and statues, idols, and ornaments. Kids can learn about everyday life with interactive games. ✉ *Hoher Markt 3, 1st District* ☎ *01/535–5606* 🌐 *www.wienmuseum.at* 💶 *€7* ⊘ *Closed Mon.* Ⓜ *U1 or U4/Schwedenplatz.*

**Stock-im-Eisen.** Set into the building on the west side of Kärntnerstrasse is one of the city's odder relics, an ancient tree trunk studded with blacksmiths' nails. Researchers in the 1970s identified the trunk as a 600-year-old spruce. Since the Middle Ages, any apprentice metalworker who came to Vienna to learn his trade hammered a nail into the trunk for good luck. During World War II, when there was talk of moving the relic to a museum in Munich, it mysteriously disappeared (and then reappeared perfectly preserved after the threat of removal had passed). ✉ *Stock-im-Eisen-Platz, Kärntnerstrasse and Singerstrasse, 1st District* Ⓜ *U1 or U3/Stephansplatz.*

## THE HOFBURG: AN IMPERIAL CITY

A walk through the Imperial Palace, called the Hofburg, brings you back to the days when Vienna was the capital of a mighty empire. You can still find in Viennese shops vintage postcards and prints that show the revered and bewhiskered Emperor Franz Josef leaving his Hofburg palace for a drive in his carriage. Today you can walk in his footsteps, gaze at the old tin bath the emperor kept under his simple iron bedstead, marvel at his bejeweled christening robe, and, along the way, feast your eyes on great works of art, impressive armor, and some of the finest Baroque interiors in Europe.

Until 1918 the Hofburg was the home of the Habsburgs, rulers of the Austro-Hungarian Empire. Now it is a vast smorgasbord of sightseeing attractions, including the Imperial Apartments, two imperial treasuries, six museums, the National Library, and the famous Winter Riding School. One of the latest Hofburg attractions is a museum devoted to "Sisi," the beloved Empress Elisabeth, wife of Franz Josef, whose beauty was the talk of Europe and whose tragic assassination (the murder weapon is one of the various exhibits) was mourned by all. The entire complex takes a minimum of a full day to explore in detail.

■ TIP→ **If your time is limited (or if you want to save most of the interior sightseeing for a rainy day), omit all the museums mentioned below except for the Imperial Apartments and the Schatzkammer.** An excellent multilingual, full-color booklet, describing the palace in detail, is for sale at most ticket counters within the complex; it gives a complete list of attractions, and maps out the palace's complicated ground plan and building history wing by wing.

Vienna took its imperial role seriously, as evidenced by the sprawling Hofburg complex, which is still today the seat of government. While the buildings cover a considerable area, the treasures lie within, discreet. Franz Josef was beneficent—witness the broad Ringstrasse he ordained and the panoply of museums and public buildings it hosts. With few exceptions (Vienna City Hall and the Votive Church), rooflines are on an even level, creating an ensemble effect that helps integrate the palace complex and its parks into the urban landscape without overwhelming it. Diplomats still bustle in and out of high-level international meetings along the elegant halls. Horse-drawn carriages still traverse the Ring and the roadway that cuts through the complex. Ignore the cars and tour buses, and you can easily imagine yourself in a Vienna of a hundred or more years ago.

Architecturally, the Hofburg—like St. Stephen's—is far from refined. It grew up over a period of 700 years (its earliest mention in court documents is from 1279, at the very beginning of Habsburg rule), and its spasmodic, haphazard growth kept it from attaining a unified identity. But many individual buildings are fine, and the National Library is a tour de force. ■ TIP→ **Want to see it all without breaking the bank? A €23 Sisi Ticket includes admission to the Kaiserappartements, the Silberkammer, the Imperial Furniture Depot, Vienna Furniture Museum, and a Grand Tour of the Schönbrunn Palace.**

### TOP ATTRACTIONS

**Augustinerkirche** (*Augustinian Church*). Built during the 14th century and presenting the most unified Gothic interior in the city, the church is something of a fraud—the interior dates from the late 18th century, not the early 14th—though the view from the entrance doorway is stunning: a soaring harmony of vertical piers, ribbed vaults, and hanging chandeliers that makes Vienna's other Gothic interiors look earthbound by comparison. Napoléon was wed here, as were Emperor Franz Josef and his beloved Sisi. Note on the right the magnificent **Tomb of the Archduchess Maria-Christina,** sculpted by the great Antonio Canova in 1805, with mourning figures trooping into a

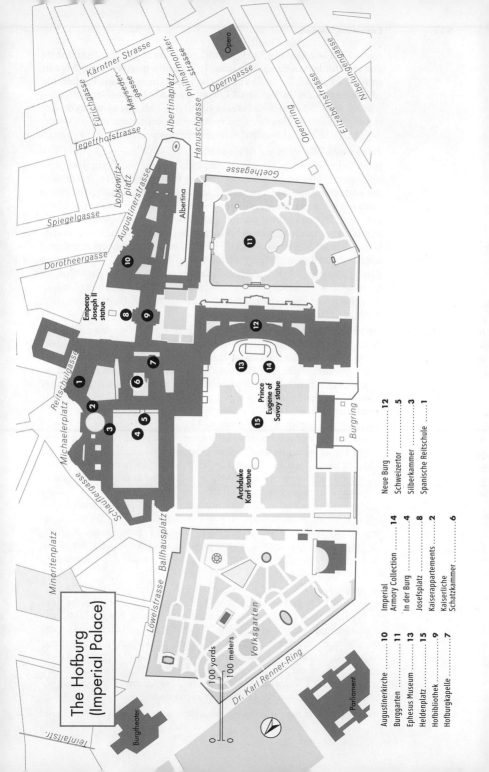

# The Hofburg (Imperial Palace)

Augustinerkirche ......**10**
Burggarten ......**11**
Ephesus Museum ......**13**
Heldenplatz ......**15**
Hofbibliothek ......**9**
Hofburgkapelle ......**7**

Imperial
Armory Collection ......**14**
In der Burg ......**4**
Josefsplatz ......**8**
Kaiserappartements ......**2**
Kaiserliche
Schatzkammer ......**6**

Neue Burg ......**12**
Schweizertor ......**5**
Silberkammer ......**3**
Spanische Reitschule ......**1**

Emperor Joseph II statue

Prince Eugene of Savoy statue

Archduke Karl statue

Albertina

Opera

Volksgarten

Parliament

Burgtheater

Kärntner Strasse
Fürichgasse
Maysedergasse
Tegetthofstrasse
Spiegelgasse
Lobkowitzplatz
Dorotheergasse
Augustinerstrasse
Reitschulgasse
Michaelerplatz
Schauflergasse
Minoritenplatz
Löwelstrasse
Ballhausplatz
Dr. Karl Renner-Ring
Teinfaltstr.
Albertinaplatz
Hanuschgasse
Philharmonikerstrasse
Operngasse
Goethegasse
Opernring
Operngasse
Elizabethstrasse
Nibelungengasse
Burgring

0 100 yards
0 100 meters

pyramid. The imposing Baroque organ sounds as heavenly as it looks, and the Sunday-morning high mass (frequently with works by Mozart or Haydn) sung here at 11 can be the highlight of a trip. To the right of the main altar, in the small Loreto Chapel, stand silver urns containing some 54 hearts of Habsburg rulers. This rather morbid sight is viewable after mass on Sunday or by appointment. ⊠ *Josefsplatz, 1st District* ☎ *01/533-7099* Ⓜ *U3/Herrengasse.*

**Burggarten.** The intimate Burggarten in back of the Neue Burg is a quiet oasis that includes a statue of a contemplative Franz Josef and an elegant statue of Mozart, moved here from the Albertinaplatz after the war, when the city's charred ruins were being rebuilt. Today the park is a favored time-out spot for the Viennese; an alluring backdrop is formed by the striking former greenhouses, now the gorgeous Palmenhaus restaurant and the **Schmetterlinghaus.** Enchantment awaits you at Vienna's unique Butterfly House. Inside are towering tropical trees, waterfalls, a butterfly nursery, and more than 150 species on display (usually 400 winged jewels are in residence). The park also has entrances on Hanuschgasse and Goethegasse. ⊠ *Opernring, 1st District* ⊕ *www.schmetterlinghaus.at* 🎟 *€6.50* Ⓜ *U2/MuseumsQuartier; Tram: 1, 2, and D/Burgring.*

Fodor's Choice    **Hofbibliothek** (*National Library*). This is one of the grandest Baroque
★    libraries in the world, a cathedral of books, its centerpiece the spectacular Prunksaal—the Grand Hall—which probably contains more book treasures than any comparable collection outside the Vatican. The main entrance to the ornate reading room is in the left corner of Josefsplatz. Designed by Fischer von Erlach the Elder just before his death in 1723 and completed by his son, the Grand Hall is full-blown high Baroque, with trompe-l'oeil ceiling frescoes by Daniel Gran. Twice a year, special exhibits highlight some of the finest and rarest tomes, well documented in German and English. From 1782, Mozart performed here regularly at the Sunday matinees of Baron Gottfried van Swieten, who lived in a suite of rooms in the grand, palacelike library. Four years later the baron founded the Society of Associated Cavaliers, which set up oratorio performances with Mozart acting as conductor. Across the street at Palais Palffy Mozart reportedly first performed *The Marriage of Figaro* before a select, private audience to see if it would pass the court censor. ⊠ *Josefsplatz 1, 1st District* ☎ *01/534-100* ⊕ *www.onb.ac.at* 🎟 *€7* ⊘ *Closed Sun.* Ⓜ *U3/Herrengasse.*

**Hofburgkapelle** (*Chapel of the Imperial Palace*). Fittingly, this is the main venue for the beloved Vienna Boys' Choir, since the group has its roots in the Hofmusikkapelle choir founded by Emperor Maximilian I five centuries ago (Haydn and Schubert were both participants as young boys). The choir sings mass here at 9:15 on Sunday from mid-September to June (tickets are €37). Be aware that you *hear* the choirboys but don't see them; soprano and alto voices peal forth from a gallery behind the seating area. ⊠ *Hofburg, Schweizer Hof, 1st District* ☎ *01/533-9927* ⊕ *www.hofmusikkapelle.gv.at* Ⓜ *U3/Herrengasse.*

**2**

**In der Burg.** This prominent courtyard of the Hofburg complex focuses on a statue of Francis II and the noted **Schweizertor** gateway. Note the **clock** on the far upper wall at the north end of the courtyard: it tells time by a sundial, also gives the time mechanically, and even, above the clockface, indicates the phase of the moon. ✉ *1st District* ✛ *Off Löwelstrasse* Ⓜ *U3/Herrengasse.*

**Josefsplatz.** Many consider this Vienna's loveliest courtyard and, indeed, the beautifully restored imperial style adorning the roof of the buildings forming Josefsplatz is one of the few visual demonstrations of Austria's onetime widespread power and influence. The square's namesake is represented in the equestrian **statue of Emperor Josef II** (1807) in the center. ✉ *Herrengasse, 1st District* Ⓜ *U3/Herrengasse.*

**Kaiserappartements** (*Imperial Apartments*). From the spectacular portal gate of the Michaelertor—you can't miss the four gigantic statues of Hercules and his labors—you climb the marble Kaiserstiege (Emperor's Staircase) to begin a tour of a long, repetitive suite of 18 conventionally luxurious state rooms. The red-and-gold decoration (19th-century imitation of 18th-century Rococo) tries to look regal, but much like the empire itself in its latter days, it's only going through the motions, and ends up looking merely official. Still, these are the rooms where the ruling family of the Habsburg empire ate, slept, and dealt with family tragedy—in the emperor's study on January 30, 1889, Emperor Franz Josef was told about the tragic death of his only son, Crown Prince Rudolf, who had shot himself and his soulmate, 17-year-old Baroness Vetsera, at the hunting lodge at Mayerling. Among the few signs of life are Emperor Franz Josef's spartan, iron field bed, on which he slept every night, and Empress Elisabeth's wooden gymnastics equipment (obsessed with her looks, Sisi suffered from anorexia and was fanatically devoted to exercise). In the Sisi Museum, part of the regular tour, five rooms display many of her treasured possessions, including her jewels, the gown she wore the night before her marriage, her dressing gown, and the opulent court salon railroad car she used. There is also a death mask made after her assassination by an anarchist in Geneva in 1898, as well as the murder weapon that killed her: a wooden-handled file. ✉ *Hofburg, Schweizer Hof, 1st District* ☎ *01/533–7570* ⊕ *www.hofburg-wien.at* ✑ *€13.90, includes admission to Silberkammer; €16.90 for a guided tour* Ⓜ *U3/Herrengasse.*

Fodor'sChoice
★ **Kaiserliche Schatzkammer** (*Imperial Treasury*). The entrance to the Schatzkammer, with its 1,000 years of treasures, is tucked away at ground level behind the staircase to the Hofburgkapelle. The elegant display is a welcome antidote to the rather staid Imperial Apartments, and the crowns and relics glow in their surroundings. Here you'll find such marvels as the Holy Lance (reputedly the lance that pierced Jesus's side), the Imperial Crown (a sacred symbol of sovereignty once stolen on Hitler's orders), and the Saber of Charlemagne. Don't miss the Burgundian Treasure, connected with that most romantic of medieval orders of chivalry, the Order of the Golden Fleece. ■TIP→ **The €20 combined ticket that includes admission to the Kunsthistorisches is a great deal.** ✉ *Hofburg, Schweizer Hof, 1st District* ☎ *01/525–240* ⊕ *www. kaiserliche-schatzkammer.at* ✑ *€12* ☉ *Closed Tues.* Ⓜ *U3/Herrengasse.*

**Silberkammer** (*Museum of Court Silver and Tableware*). Fascinating for its behind-the-scenes views of state banquets and other elegant affairs, there are more than forks and finger bowls here. Stunning decorative pieces vie with glittering silver and gold for your attention. Highlights include Emperor Franz Josef's vermeil banqueting service, the jardinière given to Empress Elisabeth by Queen Victoria, and gifts from Marie Antoinette to her brother Josef II. The fully set tables give you a view of court life. ⊠ *Hofburg, Michaelertrakt, 1st District* ☎ *01/533-7570* ⌨ *€13.90, includes admission to Kaiserappartements and Sisi Museum* Ⓜ *U3/Herrengasse.*

**Spanische Reitschule** (*Spanish Riding School*). The world-famous Spanish Riding School has been a favorite for centuries, and no wonder; who can resist the sight of the white Lipizzaner horses going through their masterful paces? For the last 300 years they have been perfecting their *haute école* riding demonstrations to the sound of Baroque music in a ballroom that seems to be a crystal-chandeliered stable. The interior of the riding school, the 1735 work of Fischer von Erlach the Younger, makes it Europe's most elegant sports arena.

The performance schedule is fairly consistent throughout the year. From August to June, evening performances are held mostly on weekends and morning exercises with music are held mostly on weekdays. Booking months ahead is good idea. If you do so, pick up tickets at the office under the Michaelerplatz rotunda dome. Otherwise tickets are available at the visitor center in Michaelerplatz (Tuesday–Saturday 9–4), and at Josefsplatz on the day of the morning exercise, 9–5. ⊠ *Michaelerplatz 1, 1st District* ☎ *01/533-9031* ⊕ *www.srs.at* ⌨ *€25-€135; morning training €15* ☉ *Closed July* Ⓜ *U3/Herrengasse.*

## WORTH NOTING

**Ephesus Museum.** One of the museums in the Neue Burg, the Ephesus Museum contains exceptional Roman antiquities unearthed by Austrian archaeologists in Turkey at the turn of the 20th century. ⊠ *Neue Burg, Heldenplatz, 1st District* ⊕ *www.khm.at* ⌨ *€15, includes admission to the Kunsthistorisches Museum and collections at the Neue Burg* ☉ *Closed Mon. and Tues.* Ⓜ *Tram: 1, 2, and D/Burgring.*

**Heldenplatz.** The Neue Burg was never completed and so the Heldenplatz was left without a discernible shape, but the space is punctuated by two superb equestrian statues depicting Archduke Karl and Prince Eugene of Savoy. The older section on the north includes the offices of the federal president. ⊠ *Hofburg, 1st District* Ⓜ *Tram: 1, 2, and D/Burgring.*

**Imperial Armory Collection.** Rivaling the armory in Graz, this is one of the most extensive arms and armor collections in the world. It's located within the Neue Burg museum complex, and you can enter at the triumphal arch set into the middle of the curved portion of the facade. ⊠ *Neue Burg, Heldenplatz, 1st District* ⊕ *www. khm.at* ⌨ *€15, includes admission to Kunsthistorisches Museum and collections at the Neue Burg* ☉ *Closed Mon. and Tues.* Ⓜ *U2/ MuseumsQuartier.*

**Neue Burg.** Standing today as a symbol of architectural overconfidence, the Neue Burg was designed for Emperor Franz Josef in 1869 as a "new château" that was part of a much larger scheme meant to make the Hofburg rival the Louvre, if not Versailles. The German architect Gottfried Semper planned a twin of the present Neue Burg on the opposite side of the Heldenplatz, with arches connecting the two with the other pair of twins on the Ringstrasse, the Kunsthistorisches Museum (Museum of Art History) and the Naturhistorisches Museum (Museum of Natural History). But World War I intervened, and with the empire's collapse the Neue Burg became the last in a long series of failed attempts to bring architectural order to the Hofburg. Today the Neue Burg houses four specialty museums: the **Imperial Armor Collection**, the **Collection of Historical Musical Instruments** (currently closed for renovations), the **Ephesus Museum**, and the **Ethnological Museum**. For details on these museums, see separate listings. ⊠ *Heldenplatz, 1st District* ☎ *01/525–240* ⊕ *www.khm.at* ⌨ *€15* Ⓜ *U2/MuseumsQuartier.*

**Schweizertor** (*Swiss Gate*). Dating from 1552 and decorated with some of the earliest classical motifs in the city, the Schweizertor leads from In der Burg through to the oldest section of the palace, a small courtyard known as the Schweizer Hof. The gateway is painted maroon, black, and gold, giving a fine Renaissance flourish to the building's facade. ⊠ *Hofburg, 1st District* Ⓜ *U3/Herrengasse.*

## ACROSS THE DANUBE: THE 2ND DISTRICT

Walk across the Danube Canal on Schwedenbrücke or Marienbrücke and you'll reach the 2nd District, the home of Vienna's famous Prater amusement park.

**Kriminalmuseum** (*Crime Museum*). This might be the strangest museum in the city, and it's certainly the most macabre. The vast collection is entirely devoted to Viennese murders of the most gruesome kind, with the most grisly displays situated, appropriately, in the cellar. Murderers and their victims are depicted in photos and newspaper clippings, and many of the actual instruments used in the killings are displayed, axes seeming to be the most popular. The Criminal Museum (housed in the "soap-boiler house," one of the oldest buildings in Leopoldstadt) is across the Danube Canal from Schwedenplatz, about a 15-minute walk from the Ruprechtskirche, the Hoher Markt, and the Heiligenkreuzerhof. ⊠ *Grosse Sperlgasse 24, 2nd District/Leopoldstadt* ☎ *01/664–300–5677* ⊕ *www.kriminalmuseum.at* ⌨ *€6* ⊙ *Closed Mon.–Wed.* Ⓜ *U2/Taborstrasse.*

**Fodor's**Choice ★ **Prater.** In 1766, to the dismay of the aristocracy, Emperor Josef II decreed that the vast expanse of imperial parklands known as the Prater would henceforth be open to the public. East of the inner city between the Danube Canal and the Danube proper, the Prater is a public park to this day, notable for its long promenade (the Hauptallee, more than 4½ km [3 miles] in length); the traditional amusement-park rides; a planetarium; and a small but interesting museum devoted to the Prater's long history. If you look carefully, you can discover a handful of children's rides dating from the '20s and '30s that survived the fire that consumed most of the Volksprater in 1945.

At the amusement park there are 250 rides, many of which will make thrill-ride enthusiasts happy, and on hot days, there is a water park to splash around in. For little ones, there is an interactive ride featuring polar bears and penguins. Madame Tussauds is also on-site if you want a photo with famous Austrian native sons and daughters (Arnold Schwarzenegger comes to mind). The best-known attraction is the 200-foot Ferris wheel that figured so prominently in the 1949 film *The Third Man*. It was one of three built in Europe at the end of the 19th century (the others were in England and France, but have long since been dismantled); the wheel was badly damaged during World War II, but restored shortly thereafter. Its progress is slow and stately (a revolution takes 10 minutes), and the views from its cars are magnificent, particularly toward dusk. ✉ *Riesenradplatz, 2nd District/Leopoldstadt* 🚇 *Park free, Ferris wheel €10* Ⓜ *U1/Praterstern*.

**NEED A BREAK**

**Schweizerhaus.** When you're at the Prater, try to eat at Schweizerhaus, which has been serving frothy mugs of beer, roast chicken, and *Stelze* (a huge hunk of crispy roast pork on the bone) for more than 100 years. The informal setting, with wood-plank tables indoors or in the garden in summer, adds to the fun. ✉ *Strasse des 1. Mai 116, 2nd District/Leopold-stadt* ☎ *01/728–0152* ☾ *Closed Nov.–Feb.*

---

# THE WESTERN CITY CENTER: BURGTHEATER AND BEYOND

Hailed as one of the most prestigious stages in the German-speaking world, the Burgtheater is home to a highly venerated ensemble of 80 actors. Always keen on stargazing, the Viennese flock to the elegant Café Landmann to observe thespians eating linzer torte. In the warmer months, students from Vienna University across the Ringstrasse stroll through Volksgarten to smell its fragrant rose garden. From here it's a short walk to the Freyung, a sumptuous square graced by the neo-Renaissance Palais Ferstel and its 19th-century shopping arcade.

## TOP ATTRACTIONS

**Burgtheater** (*National Theater*). One of the most important theaters in the German-speaking world, the Burgtheater was built between 1874 and 1888 in the Italian Renaissance style, replacing the old court theater at Michaelerplatz. Emperor Franz Josef's mistress, Katherina Schratt, was once a star performer here, and famous Austrian and German actors still stride across this stage. The opulent interior, with its 60-foot relief *Worshippers of Bacchus* by Rudolf Wyer and lobby ceiling frescoes by Ernst and Gustav Klimt, makes it well worth a visit. ✉ *Dr. Karl Lueger-Ring 2, 1st District* ☎ *01/514–4441–40* ⊕ *www.burgtheater.at* 🚇 *€7* Ⓜ *Tram: 1, 2, and D/Burgtheater, Rathaus*.

**The Freyung.** This square, whose name means "freeing"—so called, according to lore, because for many centuries monks at the adjacent Schottenkirche had the privilege of offering sanctuary for three days to anyone on the lam. In the center of the square stands the allegorical **Austria Fountain** (1845), notable because its Bavarian designer, Ludwig Schwanthaler, had the statues cast in Munich and then supposedly filled

# Mozart, Mozart, Mozart!

The composer Wolfgang Amadeus Mozart (1756–91) crammed a prodigious number of compositions into the last 10 years of his life, many of which he spent in Vienna. Here, he experienced many of the high points of his life, both personal and artistic. He wed his beloved Constanze Weber (with whom he would have six children) at St. Stephen's Cathedral in August 1782, and led the premieres of several of his greatest operas. But knowing his troubled relations with his home city of Salzburg makes his Vienna sojourn even more poignant.

From the beginning of Mozart's career, his father, frustrated in his own musical ambitions at the archbishopric in Salzburg, looked beyond the boundaries of the Austro-Hungarian Empire to promote the boy's fame. At the age of six, his son caused a sensation in the royal courts of Europe with his skills as an instrumentalist and impromptu composer. As Mozart grew up, however, his virtuosity lost its power to amaze and he was forced to make his way as an "ordinary" musician, which then meant finding a position at court. Not much more successful in Salzburg than his father had been, he was never able to rise beyond the level of organist (allowing him, as he noted with sarcasm, to sit above the cooks at table). In disgust, he relocated to Vienna, where despite the popularity of his operas he was able to obtain only an unpaid

appointment as assistant Kapellmeister at St. Stephen's mere months before his death. By then, patronage subscriptions had been taken up in Hungary and the Netherlands that would have paid him handsomely. But it was too late. Whatever the truth about the theories still swirling around his untimely death, the fact remains that he was not given the state funeral he deserved, and he was buried in an unmarked grave (as were most Viennese at the time) after a hasty, sparsely attended funeral.

Only the flint hearted can stand in Vienna's Währingerstrasse and look at the windows behind which Mozart wrote those last three symphonies in just six weeks in the summer of 1788 and not be touched. For this was the time when the Mozart fortunes had slumped to their lowest. "If you, my best of friends, forsake me, I am unhappily and innocently lost with my poor sick wife and my child," he wrote. And if one is inclined to accuse Mozart's fellow countrymen of neglect, they seem to have made up for it with a vengeance. Visitors to Vienna and Salzburg cannot escape the barrage of Mozart candies, wine, beer, coffee mugs, T-shirts, baseball caps—not to mention the gilt statues and other knickknacks. Mozart, always one to appreciate a joke, would surely see the irony in the belated veneration. Today, places with which he is associated are all reverently marked with memorial plaques.

them with cigars to be smuggled into Vienna for black-market sale. Around the sides of the square are some of Vienna's greatest patrician residences, including the Ferstel, Harrach, and Kinsky palaces. ⊠ *Am Hof and Herrengasse, 1st District* Ⓜ *U3/Herrengasse.*

**Palais Ferstel.** Not really a palace, this commercial complex dating from 1856 is named for its architect, Heinrich Ferstel. The facade is Italianate, harking back in its 19th-century way to the Florentine palazzi of the early Renaissance. The interior is unashamedly eclectic: vaguely Romanesque in feel and Gothic in decoration, with a bit of Renaissance or Baroque sculpted detail thrown in for good measure. Such eclecticism is sometimes dismissed as derivative, but here the architectural details are so respectfully and inventively combined that the interior is a pleasure to explore. The 19th-century stock-exchange rooms upstairs are now gloriously restored and used for conferences, concerts, and balls. ✉ *Freyung 2, 1st District* ⊕ *www.palaisevents.at* Ⓜ *U3/Herrengasse.*

**Schottenhof.** This shaded courtyard typifies the change that came over Viennese architecture during the Biedermeier era (1815–48). The Viennese, according to the traditional view, were so relieved to be rid of the upheavals of the Napoleonic Wars that they accepted without protest the iron-handed repression of Prince Metternich, chancellor of Austria. Restraint also ruled in architecture; Baroque license was rejected in favor of a new and historically "correct" style that was far more controlled and reserved. Kornhäusel led the way in establishing this trend in Vienna; his Schottenhof facade is all sober organization and frank repetition. But in its marriage of strong and delicate forces it still pulls off the great Viennese-waltz trick of successfully merging seemingly antithetical characteristics. ✉ *Freyung, 1st District* Ⓜ *U2/Schottentor.*

**Schottenkirche** (*Scots Church*). From 1758 to 1761, Bernardo Bellotto did paintings of the Freyung looking north toward the Schottenkirche; the pictures, which hang in the Kunsthistorisches Museum, are remarkably similar to the view you see today. A church has stood on the site of the Schottenkirche since 1177, when the monastery was established by monks from Ireland—Scotia Minor, in Latin, hence the name "Scots Church." The present edifice dates from the mid-1600s, when it replaced its predecessor, which had collapsed because of weakened foundations. The interior, with its ornate ceiling and a surplus of cherubs and angels' faces, is in stark contrast to the plain exterior. The adjacent **Museum im Schottenstift** includes the celebrated late-Gothic high altar dating from about 1470. The winged altar is fascinating for its portrayal of the Holy Family in flight into Egypt—with the city of Vienna clearly identifiable in the background. ✉ *Freyung 6, 1st District* ☎ *01/534–98–600* ⊕ *www.schottenstift.at* ✆ *Church free, museum €8* ⊗ *Closed Sun. and Mon.* Ⓜ *U2/Schottentor.*

## WORTH NOTING

**Beethoven Pasqualatihaus.** Beethoven lived in the Pasqualatihaus multiple times between 1804 and 1815, including while he was composing his only opera, *Fidelio*. He also composed his Seventh Symphony and Fourth Piano Concerto when this was his home. Today this small apartment houses a commemorative museum (in distressingly modern style). After navigating the narrow and twisting stairway, you might well ask how he maintained the jubilant spirit of the works he wrote there. Note particularly the prints that show what the window view out over the Mölker bastion was like when Beethoven lived here, and the current view too—it's a fantastic fourth-floor look out onto the Ringstrasse. ✉ *8 Mölker Bastei, 1st District* ☎ *01/535–8905* ⊕ *www.wienmuseum. at* ✆ *€5* ⊗ *Closed Mon.* Ⓜ *U2/Schottentor.*

**Globe Museum.** Across the street from the Café Central, the beautifully renovated Palais Mollard has a rare collection of more than 240 terrestrial and celestial globes on display in its second-floor museum—the only one of its kind in the world open to the public. The oldest is a globe of the Earth dating from 1536, produced by Gemma Frisius, a Belgian doctor and cosmographer. On the ground floor is a small but fascinating Esperanto museum, which explores the history of Esperanto and other planned languages. Both museums are run by the Austrian National Library. ⊠ *Herrengasse 9, 1st District* ☎ *01/534–10–710* ⊕ *www.onb. ac.at/museen/globenmuseum* ⊠ *€3, includes entrance into Esperanto and Papyrus museums* ⊙ *Closed Mon. in Oct.–Mar.* Ⓜ *U3/Herrengasse.*

**Minoritenkirche** (*Minorite Church*). Minoritenplatz is named after its centerpiece, the Minoritenkirche, a Gothic affair with a strange stump of a tower, built mostly in the 14th century. The front is brutally ugly, but the back is a wonderful, if predominantly 19th-century, surprise. The interior contains the city's most imposing piece of kitsch: a large mosaic reproduction of Leonardo da Vinci's *Last Supper,* commissioned by Napoléon in 1806 and later purchased by Emperor Franz Josef. ⊠ *Minoritenplatz 2A, 1st District* ☎ *01/533–4162* Ⓜ *U3/Herrengasse.*

**Palais Harrach.** Mozart and his sister Nannerl performed here as children for Count Ferdinand during their first visit to Vienna in 1762. The palace, next door to Palais Ferstel, was altered after 1845 and severely damaged during World War II. Many of the state rooms have lost their historical luster, but the Marble Room, set with gilt boiseries, and the Red Gallery, topped with a spectacular ceiling painting, still provide grand settings for receptions. ⊠ *Freyung 3, 1st District* Ⓜ *U3/ Herrengasse.*

**Palais Kinsky.** Just one of the architectural treasures that comprise the urban set piece of the Freyung, the Palais Kinsky is the square's best-known palace, and is one of the most sophisticated pieces of Baroque architecture in the whole city. Built between 1713 and 1716 by Hildebrandt—and returned to its former glory in the 1990s—it now houses Wiener Kunst Auktionen, a public auction business offering artwork and antiques. If there's an auction viewing, try to see the palace's spectacular 18th-century staircase, all marble goddesses and crowned with a trompe-l'oeil ceiling painted by Marcantonio Chiarini. ⊠ *Freyung 4, 1st District* ☎ *01/532–4200* ⊕ *www.palaisevents.at* Ⓜ *U3/Herrengasse.*

**Third Man Portal.** This doorway (up the incline) was made famous in 1949 by the classic film *The Third Man.* It was here that Orson Welles, as the malevolently knowing Harry Lime, stood hiding in the dark, only to have his smiling face illuminated by a sudden light from the upper-story windows of the house across the alley. To get to this apartment building from the nearby Schottenkirche, follow Teinfaltstrasse one block west to Schreyvogelgasse on the right. ⊠ *Schreyvogelgasse 8, 1st District* Ⓜ *U2/Schottentor.*

**Volksgarten.** Just opposite the Hofburg is a green oasis with a rose garden, a shining white 19th-century Greek temple, and a rather wistful white-marble monument to Empress Elisabeth, Franz Josef's Bavarian wife, who died of a dagger wound inflicted by an Italian anarchist in

## VIENNA IN FILM: THE THIRD MAN

Nothing has done more to create the myth of postwar Vienna than Carol Reed's classic 1949 film *The Third Man*. The bombed-out ruins of this proud, imperial city created an indelible image of devastation and corruption in the war's aftermath. Vienna was then divided into four sectors, each commanded by one of the victorious armies—American, Russian, French, and British. But their attempts at rigid control could not prevent a thriving black market.

Reed's film version of the Graham Greene thriller features Vienna as a leading player, from the top of its Ferris wheel to the depth of its lowest sewers—"which run right into the Blue Danube." It was the first British film to be shot entirely on location. The film is screened on Tuesday, Friday, and Sunday in the Burg Kino, and a memorabilia museum open on Saturday is near the Naschmarkt.

Geneva in 1898. If not overrun with latter-day hippies, these can offer spots to sit for a few minutes while contemplating Vienna's most ambitious piece of 19th-century city planning: the Ringstrasse. ⊠ *Burgring 1, 1st District* Ⓜ *Tram: 1, 2, or D/Rathausplatz, Burgtheater.*

## EAST OF THE RINGSTRASSE: STADTPARK AND KARLSPLATZ

Next to Stephansplatz, Karlsplatz is the inner city's busiest hub. It sprawls across the Ringstrasse to encompass the magnificent Baroque Karlskirche and an exquisite Jugendstil pavilion designed by Otto Wagner, the architect of the partly elevated tram system to the outer boroughs (now part of the U4 and U6 subway lines). From Karlsplatz, you can travel eastward on the Ringstrasse to visit the stunning Museum for Applied Arts and the romantic Stadtpark with its gilded statue of Johann Strauss, or head in the other direction to Prince Eugene's Belvedere Palace, a treasure trove of art spanning the centuries.

### TOP ATTRACTIONS

Fodor's Choice ★ **Belvedere Palace.** One of the most splendid pieces of Baroque architecture anywhere, the Belvedere Palace—actually two imposing palaces separated by a 17th-century French-style garden parterre—is one of the masterpieces of architect Lucas von Hildebrandt. Built outside the city fortifications between 1714 and 1722, the complex originally served as the summer palace of Prince Eugene of Savoy. Much later it became the home of Archduke Franz Ferdinand, whose assassination in 1914 precipitated World War I. Though the lower palace is impressive in its own right, it is the much larger upper palace, used for state receptions, banquets, and balls, that is acknowledged as Hildebrandt's masterpiece. The upper palace displays a wealth of architectural invention in its facade, avoiding the main design problems common to palaces: monotony on the one hand and pomposity on the other.

Hildebrandt's decorative manner here approaches the Rococo, that final style of the Baroque era when traditional classical motifs all but disappeared in a whirlwind of seductive asymmetric fancy. The main interiors of the palace go even further: columns are transformed into muscle-bound giants, pilasters grow torsos, capitals sprout great piles of symbolic imperial paraphernalia, and the ceilings are aswirl with ornately molded stucco. The result is the finest Rococo interior in the city.

Both the upper and lower palaces of the Belvedere are museums devoted to Austrian painting. The Belvedere's main attraction is the collection of 19th- and 20th-century Austrian paintings, centering on the work of Vienna's three preeminent early-20th-century artists: Gustav Klimt, Egon Schiele, and Oskar Kokoschka. Klimt was the oldest, and by the time he helped found the Secession movement he had forged an idiosyncratic painting style that combined realistic and decorative elements in a way that was revolutionary. *The Kiss*—his greatest painting—is here on display. Schiele and Kokoschka went even further, rejecting the decorative appeal of Klimt's glittering abstract designs and producing works that ignored conventional ideas of beauty.

An ambitious 2016 European Union initiative brought 3-D technology to the Belvedere. The project, entitled AMBAVis (Access to Museums for Blind and Visually-Impaired Persons), transformed Klimt's *The Kiss* into a remarkable and unprecedented interactive experience. Finger-tracking technology allows viewers to scan the relief, prompting audio to play. ⊠ *Prinz-Eugen-Strasse 27, 3rd District/Landstrasse* ☎ *01/795-57–134* ⊕ *www.belvedere.at* ⊠ *€20* Ⓜ *U1, U2, or U4/Karlsplatz; then Tram D or Tram 71.*

**Fodor's Choice**
★

**Karlskirche.** Dominating the Karlsplatz is one of Vienna's greatest buildings, the Karlskirche, dedicated to St. Charles Borromeo. Before you is a giant Baroque church framed by enormous freestanding columns, mates to Rome's famous Trajan's Column. These columns may be out of keeping with the building as a whole, but were conceived with at least two functions in mind: one was to portray scenes from the life of the patron saint, carved in imitation of Trajan's triumphs, and thus help to emphasize the imperial nature of the building; and the other was to symbolize the Pillars of Hercules, suggesting the right of the Habsburgs to their Spanish dominions, which the emperor had been forced to renounce. The end result is an architectural tour de force.

The Karlskirche was built in the early 18th century on what was then the bank of the River Wien. The church had its beginnings in a disaster. In 1713 Vienna was hit by a brutal outbreak of plague, and Emperor Charles VI made a vow: if the plague abated, he would build a church dedicated to his namesake, St. Charles Borromeo, the 16th-century Italian bishop who was famous for his ministrations to Milanese plague victims. In 1715 construction began, using an ambitious design by Johann Bernhard Fischer von Erlach that combined architectural elements from ancient Greece (the columned entrance porch), ancient Rome (the Trajanesque columns), contemporary Rome (the Baroque dome), and contemporary Vienna (the Baroque towers at either end). When it was finished, the church received decidedly mixed press. History, too, delivered a negative verdict: the Karlskirche spawned no imitations, and it went on to become one of European architecture's curiosities. Still, when seen lighted at night, the building is magical in its setting.

The main interior of the church utilizes only the area under the dome and is conventional despite the unorthodox facade. The space and architectural detailing are typical High Baroque; the fine vault frescoes, by J. M. Rottmayr, depict St. Charles Borromeo imploring the Holy Trinity to end the plague. If you are not afraid of heights take the panorama elevator up into the sphere of the dome and climb the top steps to enjoy an unrivaled view to the heart of the city. ☒ *Karlsplatz, 4th District/Wieden* ☎ *01/504–6187* ⊕ *www.karlskirche.at* ☜ *€8* Ⓜ *U1, U2, or U4 Karlsplatz.*

**Karlsplatz.** As with the Naschmarkt, Karlsplatz was formed when the River Wien was covered over at the turn of the 20th century. At the time, architect Otto Wagner expressed his frustration with the result—too large a space for a formal square and too small a space for an informal park—and the awkwardness is felt to this day. The buildings surrounding the Karlsplatz, however, are quite sure of themselves; the area is dominated by the classic Karlskirche, made less dramatic by the unfortunate reflecting pool with its Henry Moore sculpture, wholly out of place, in front. On the south side of the Resselpark, that part of Karlsplatz named for the inventor of the screw propeller for ships, stands the Technical University (1816–18). In a house that occupied the space closest to the church, Italian composer Antonio Vivaldi died in 1741; a plaque marks the spot. On the north side, across the heavily traveled roadway, are the Künstlerhaus (built in 1881 and still in use as an exhibition hall) and the Musikverein. The latter, finished in 1869, is now home to the Vienna Philharmonic. The downstairs lobby and the two halls upstairs have been restored and glow with fresh gilding. The main hall has what may be the world's finest acoustics.

Some of Wagner's finest Secessionist work can be seen two blocks east on the northern edge of Karlsplatz. In 1893 Wagner was appointed architectural supervisor of the new Vienna City Railway, and the matched pair of small pavilions he designed, the Otto Wagner Stadtbahn Pavilions, at No. 1 Karlsplatz, in 1898 are among the city's most ingratiating buildings. Their structural framework is frankly exposed (in keeping with Wagner's belief in architectural honesty), but they are also lovingly decorated (in keeping with the Viennese fondness for architectural finery). The result is Jugendstil at its very best, melding plain and fancy with grace and insouciance. ☒ *4th District/Wieden* Ⓜ *U1, U2, or U4/Karlsplatz.*

**Museum für Angewandte Kunst (MAK)** (*Museum of Applied Arts*). This fascinating museum contains a large collection of Austrian furniture, porcelain, art objects, and priceless Oriental carpets. The Jugendstil display devoted to Josef Hoffman and his Secessionist followers at the Wiener Werkstätte is particularly well done. The newest permanent collection is based on Asian design, showcasing Japanese woodcuts, lacquer work, color stencil plates, and Chinese porcelain. The MAK also showcases changing exhibitions of contemporary works, and the museum shop sells furniture and other objects (including great bar accessories) designed by young local artists. ☒ *Stubenring 5, 1st District* ☎ *01/711–36–0* ⊕ *www.mak.at* ☜ *€9.90* ⊘ *Closed Mon.* Ⓜ *U3/Stubentor.*

**Schwarzenbergplatz.** The center of this square is marked by an oversize equestrian sculpture of Prince Schwarzenberg—he was a 19th-century field marshal for the imperial forces. See if you can guess which building is the newest—it's the one on the northeast corner (No. 3) at Lothringerstrasse, an exacting reproduction of a building destroyed by war damage in 1945 and dating only from the 1980s. The military monument occupying the south end of the square behind the fountain is the **Russian War Memorial,** set up at the end of World War II by the Soviets; the Viennese, remembering the Soviet occupation, call its unknown soldier the "unknown plunderer." South of the memorial is the stately **Schwarzenberg Palace,** designed as a summer residence by Johann Lukas von Hildebrandt in 1697 and completed by Fischer von Erlach, father and son. ⊠ *3rd District/Landstrasse* Ⓜ *Tram: Schwarzenbergplatz.*

**Wien Museum Karlsplatz** (*Museum of Viennese History*). Housed in an incongruously modern building at the east end of the Karlsplatz, this museum possesses Viennese historical artifacts and treasures: everything from 16th-century armor to paintings by Schiele and Klimt to the preserved facade of Otto Wagner's *Die Zeit* offices. ⊠ *Karlsplatz, 4th District/Wieden* ☏ *01/505–8747–0* ⊕ *www.wienmuseum.at* ☐ *€10* ⊙ *Closed Mon.* Ⓜ *U1, U2, or U4 Karlsplatz.*

## WORTH NOTING

**Fälschermuseum** (*Museum of Art Fakes*). This museum is a must-see for those who like a bit of cunning cloak and dagger—an utterly unique collection that includes a myriad of magnificent forgeries in both arts and letters, and offers captivating backstories on how the faked pieces came to be. On display are fakes of Chagall and Rembrandt, as well as the infamous "Hitler Diaries" that were front-page news in the 1980s. ⊠ *Löwengasse 28, 3rd District/Landstrasse* ⊕ *www.faelschermuseum. com* ☐ *€5.70* ⊙ *Closed Mon.* Ⓜ *Tram 1 to Hetzgasse.*

**Hundertwasserhaus.** To see one of Vienna's most architecturally intriguing buildings, travel eastward from Schwedenplatz or Julius-Raab-Platz along Radetzkystrasse. Here you'll find the Hundertwasserhaus, a 52-apartment public-housing complex designed by the late Austrian avant-garde artist Friedensreich Hundertwasser, arguably Austria's most significant postmodernist artist. The complex looks like a colorful patchwork of gingerbread houses strung precariously together, and was highly criticized when it opened in 1985. Time heals all wounds, even imaginary assaults to the senses, and now the structure is a beloved thread of the Viennese architectural tapestry. It is across the street from the city's beloved Kunsthaus Wien, which also sprang from Hundertwasser's imagination. ⊠ *Löwengasse and Kegelgasse, 3rd District/ Landstrasse* Ⓜ *U1 or U4/Schwedenplatz, then Tram N to Hetzgasse.*

**Kunsthaus Wien.** This art museum mounts outstanding international exhibits in addition to showings of the vibrant works by avant-garde artist Friedensreich Hundertwasser. He designed this building, along with the nearby apartment building called Hundertwasserhaus. The building itself is pure Hundertwasser, a crayon box of colors, irregular floors, windows with trees growing out of them, and sudden architectural surprises, all of which make a wholly appropriate setting for modern art. ⊠ *Untere Weissgerberstrasse 13, 3rd District/Landstrasse* ☎ *01/712–0491–0* ⊕ *www.kunsthauswien.com* ☎€12 Ⓜ *U1 or U4/ Schwedenplatz, then Tram N or O to Radetzkyplatz.*

**21er Haus.** Vienna's newest museum of contemporary art is housed in the structure originally built for the 1958 World Expo, the design of which won architect Karl Schwanzer the Grand Prix d'Architecture that year. The structure was modified and reopened in 2011 as a space to show-case the best of Austrian modern art. The museum houses the largest collection and archive of renowned Austrian sculptor Fritz Wotruba. ⊠ *Arsenalstrasse 1, 3rd District/Landstrasse* ⊕ *www.21erhaus.at* ☎ €7 ⊙ *Closed Mon. and Tues.* Ⓜ *U1/ Südtirolerplatz; Tram D, 18 or O (station Quartier Belvedere).*

## SOUTH OF THE RINGSTRASSE: THE MUSEUMSQUARTIER

Late in 1857 Emperor Franz Josef issued a decree announcing the most ambitious piece of urban redevelopment Vienna had ever seen. The inner city's centuries-old walls were to be torn down, and the *glacis*—the wide expanse of open field that acted as a protective buffer between inner city and abutting villages—was to be filled in. A wide, tree-lined, circular boulevard was to be constructed in the open field, and an imposing collection of new buildings reflecting Vienna's status as the political, economic, and cultural heart of the Austro-Hungarian Empire would be erected. During the 50 years of building that followed, many factors combined to produce the Ringstrasse as it now stands, but the most important was the gradual rise of liberalism after the failed Revolution of 1848. By the latter half of the Ringstrasse era, support for constitutional government, democracy, and equality—all the con-cepts that liberalism traditionally equates with progress—was steadily increasing. As the Ringstrasse went up, it became the definitive symbol of this liberal progress; as Carl E. Schorske put it in his *Fin-de-Siècle Vienna,* it celebrated "the triumph of constitutional *Recht* (right) over imperial *Macht* (might), of secular culture over religious faith. Not pal-aces, garrisons, and churches, but centers of constitutional government and higher culture dominated the Ring."

As an ensemble, the collection is astonishing in its architectural pre-sumption: it is nothing less than an attempt to assimilate and summarize the entire architectural history of Europe. The centerpiece of Ringstrasse is Heldenplatz, the huge square in front of the Hofburg. Emperor Franz Josef had two monumental museums built as an extension of Helden-platz: the Kunsthistorisches Museum (filled with centuries of art) and Naturhistorisches Museum (focusing on natural history). Vienna's most cutting-edge art complex lies just beyond the two sandstone giants. The MuseumsQuartier is made up of several galleries showing art ranging from Expressionist to modern art to avant-garde. There's even a breath-taking museum for children. Hipsters flock to the cafés and restaurants in and around the former 18th-century riding stables.

When you exit MuseumsQuartier, walk up Burggasse to Spittelberg-gasse, where you will find the Spittelberg Quarter and its Baroque and Biedermeier buildings. Emperor Josef II supposedly frequented the neighborhood's "houses of pleasure." A plaque at the Witwe Bolte restaurant on Gutenberggasse reminds strollers that his majesty was thrown out of one establishment during a clandestine visit.

## TOP ATTRACTIONS

Fodor's Choice ★ **Kunsthistorisches Museum** (*Museum of Fine Art*). Even if you're planning on a short stay in Vienna, you'll want to come here to visit one of the greatest art collections in the world, standing in the same class as the Louvre, the Prado, and the Vatican. This is no dry-as-dust museum illustrating the history of art, as its name might imply, but rather the collections of Old Master paintings that reveal the royal taste and style of many members of the mighty House of Habsburg, which ruled over the greater part of the Western world in the 16th and 17th centuries.

The museum is most famous for the largest collection of paintings under one roof by the Netherlandish 16th-century master Pieter Brueghel the Elder. Many art historians say that seeing his sublime *Hunters in the Snow* is itself worth the trip to Vienna. Brueghel's depictions of peasant scenes, often set in magnificent landscapes, distill the poetry and magic of the 16th century as few other paintings have done. The Flemish wing also includes masterful works by Rogier van der Weyden, Holbein, Rembrandt, and Vermeer, while the Italian wing features Titian, Giorgione, Raphael, and Caravaggio. The large-scale works concentrated in the main galleries shouldn't distract you from the equal share of masterworks in the more intimate side wings.

There is also the remarkable but less-visited **Kunstkammer**, displaying priceless objects created for the Habsburg emperors. These include curiosities made of gold, silver, and crystal (including Cellini's famous salt cellar "La Saliera"), and more exotic materials such as ivory, horn, and gemstones. In addition, there are rooms devoted to Egyptian antiquities, Greek and Roman art, sculpture, and numerous other collections.

One of the best times to visit the Kunsthistorisches Museum is Thursday, when you can enjoy a sumptuous gourmet dinner (€55) in the cupola rotunda. Just across from the seating area, take a leisurely stroll through the almost-empty gallery chambers. Seating starts at 6:30 pm and the guided tour, part of the evening festivities, starts at 8 pm. ⊠ *Maria-Theresien-Platz, 7th District/Neubau* ☎ *01/525–240* ⊕ *www.khm.at* ☜ *€15* ⊙ *Closed Mon. in Sept.–May* Ⓜ *U2/MuseumsQuartier; U2 or U3/Volkstheater.*

**Leopold Museum.** Filled with pieces amassed by Rudolf and Elizabeth Leopold, the Leopold contains one of the world's greatest collections of Austrian painter Egon Schiele, as well as impressive works by Gustav Klimt and Oskar Kokoschka. Other artists worth noting are Josef Dobrowsky, Anton Faistauer, and Richard Gerstl. Center stage is held by Schiele (1890–1918), who died young, along with his wife and young baby, in the Spanish flu pandemic of 1918. His colorful, appealing landscapes are here, but all eyes are invariably drawn to the artist's tortured depictions of nude mistresses, orgiastic self-portraits, and provocatively sexual couples, all elbows and organs. ⊠ *MuseumsQuartier, Museumsplatz 1, 7th District/Neubau* ☎ *01/525–700* ⊕ *www.leopoldmuseum.org* ☜ *€13* ⊙ *Closed Tues. in Sept.–May* Ⓜ *U2 MuseumsQuartier; U2 or U3/Volkstheater.*

FAMILY **MuseumsQuartier** (*Museum Quarter*). The MQ—as many call it—is a
Fodor'sChoice sprawling collection of galleries housed in what was once the Imperial
★ Court Stables, the 260-year-old Baroque complex designed by Fischer
von Erlach. Where once 900 cavalry horses were housed, now thousands of masterworks of the 20th and 21st centuries are exhibited, all
in a complex that is architecturally an expert and subtle blending of
historic and cutting-edge: the original structure (adorned with pastry-
white stuccoed ceilings and Rococo flourishes) was retained, while
ultramodern wings were added to house five museums, most of which
showcase modern art at its best.

The Architekturzentrum, Kunsthalle, Leopold Museum, Museum
Moderner Kunst Stiftung Ludwig, and the ZOOM Kinder Museum
are all part of the MuseumsQuartier complex. In addition, the Quart-
ier21 showcases up-and-coming artists and musicians in the huge
Fischer von Erlach wing facing the Museumsplatz. Lovers of modern
art will find it easy to spend at least an entire day at MuseumsQuartier,
and with several cafés, restaurants, gift shops, and bookstores, you
won't even need to venture outside. ⊠ *Museumsplatz 1, 7th District/
Neubau* ☎ *01/523–5881* ⊕ *www.mqw.at* 🎫 *€15 to €32* Ⓜ *U2/Muse-
umsQuartier; U2 or U3/Volkstheater*.

**MUMOK** (*Museum Moderner Kunst Stiftung Ludwig*). In a sleek edifice constructed of dark stone, the MUMOK houses the national
collection of 20th-century art. Spread over eight floors, the collection is largely a bequest of Peter Ludwig, a billionaire industrialist
who collected top-notch modern art. The top works here are of the
American pop-art school, but all the trends of the last century, from
Nouveau Réalisme to Viennese Actionism, vie for your attention.
Names include René Magritte, Max Ernst, Andy Warhol, Jackson
Pollock, Cy Twombly, and Nam June Paik, to name a few. Kids will
make a beeline for Claes Oldenburg's walk-in sculpture in the shape
of Mickey Mouse. ⊠ *MuseumsQuartier, Museumsplatz 1, 7th Dis-
trict/Neubau* ☎ *01/525–000* ⊕ *www.mumok.at* 🎫 *€11* Ⓜ *U2/Muse-
umsQuartier; U2 or U3/Volkstheater*.

**Naschmarkt.** The area between Linke and Rechte Wienzeile is home to
the Naschmarkt, Vienna's largest and most famous outdoor produce
market. It's certainly one of Europe's—if not the world's—great open-air
markets, where packed rows of polished and stacked fruits and vegetables
compete for visual appeal with braces of fresh pheasant in season. Also
here are fragrant spices, redolent of Asia or the Middle East. In winter,
many stalls shorten their hours. On Saturday, a lively flea market takes
place at the tail end of the market. Be sure you get the correct change
and watch the scales when your goods are weighed. ⊠ *Between Linke
and Rechte Wienzeile, 4th District/Wieden* ⊕ *www.wienernaschmarkt.
eu* Ⓜ *U1, U2, or U4/Karlsplatz (follow signs to Secession)*.

## The Neue City

CLOSE UP

Early one day in 1911, Emperor Franz Josef started out on a morning drive from the Hofburg, when he was stunned to come upon the defiantly plain Looshaus, constructed just opposite the Michaelerplatz entrance to the imperial palace. Never again, it was said, did the royal carriage use the route, so offensive was this modernist building to His Imperial Highness. One can only imagine the emperor's reaction to the Haas-Haus, built in 1985 on Stephansplatz. Here, across from the Gothic cathedral of St. Stephen's, famed architect Hans Hollein designed a complex whose elegant curved surfaces and reflecting glass interact beautifully with its environment. The architecture proved an intelligent alternative to the demands of historicism on the one hand and aggressive modernism on the other.

This balancing act has always been a particular challenge in Vienna. For a few critics, the Gaudíesque eccentricities of the late Friedensreich Hundertwasser did the trick (besides the Kunsthaus museum he is also responsible for the multicolor, golden-globe-top central heating tower that has become almost as much a part of the skyline as St. Stephen's spire). But for all their charm, they have now been overshadowed by the Viennese modernism of today. By far the most exciting urban undertaking has to be the Spittelau Viaducts, just across from the Hundertwasser power plant. This revitalization plan for the Wiener Gürtel, perhaps Vienna's busiest thoroughfare, includes public-housing apartments, offices, and artists'

studios that interact with the arched bays of the viaduct, a landmarked structure built by Otto Wagner. Responsible for the staggering three-part complex, partly perched on stilts, is star architect Zaha Hadid. A pedestrian and bicycle bridge connects the whole project to the University of Business, the North Railway Station, and the Danube Canal.

A discreet example of Vienna's new architecture is the vast MuseumsQuartier. Hidden behind the Baroque facade of the former imperial stables, the design by Laurids and Manfred Ortner uses its enclosed space to set up a counterpoint between Fischer von Erlach's riding school and the imposing new structures built to house the Leopold Museum and the Modern Art Museum. From the first, old and new collide: to enter the complex's Halle E + G, you pass below the Emperor's Loge, whose double-headed imperial eagles now form a striking contrast to a silver-hue steel double staircase. Other important projects—notably the underground Jewish history museum on Judenplatz (look for a stark cube memorial by English sculptor Rachel Whiteread); the Gasometer complex, a planned community recycled from the immense brick drums of 19th-century gasworks; the ellipse-shape Uniqa Tower on the Danube Canal designed by Heinz Neumann, and the ecologically responsible Donau City—are among the architectural highlights on tours now organized by the Architecture Center (AZW) of the MuseumsQuartier; its maps and brochures can be used for self-guided tours.

2

**NEED A BREAK**

There are so many enticing snack stands in the Naschmarkt that it's hard to choose. A host of Turkish stands offer juicy *döner* sandwiches—thinly sliced, pressed lamb, turkey, or veal with onions and a yogurt sauce in a freshly baked roll. A number of Asian noodle and sushi stalls offer quick meals, and many snack bars offer Viennese dishes. At the Karlsplatz end of the Naschmarkt is the Nordsee glass-enclosed seafood hut.

FAMILY   **Naturhistorisches Museum** (*Natural History Museum*). The palatial 19th-century museum, twin of the celebrated Kunsthistorisches Museum, is the home of the *Venus of Willendorf*, a tiny statuette (actually, a replica—the original is in a vault) thought to be some 20,000 years old. This symbol of the Stone Age was originally unearthed in the Wachau Valley, not far from Melk. The reconstructed dinosaur skeletons draw the most attention, especially among kids. Also not to be missed is the Meteorite Room, which holds the largest and oldest collection of meteorites on the planet. A 3-D simulator allows you to stage a powerful meteor strike. The digital planetarium, with its state-of-the-art Fulldome technology, offers shows several times a day on biology, astronomy, prehistory, and the deep sea. ✉ *Maria-Theresien-Platz, 1st District* ☎ *01/52177* ⊕ *www.nhm-wien.ac.at* 💶 *€10; €5 for the planetarium* ⊘ *Closed Tues.* Ⓜ *U2 or U3/Volkstheater.*

**Secession Building.** If the Academy of Fine Arts represents the conservative attitude toward the arts in the late 1800s, then its antithesis can be found in the building immediately behind it to the southeast: the Secession Pavilion, one of Vienna's preeminent symbols of artistic rebellion. Rather than looking to the architecture of the past, like the revivalist Ringstrasse, it looked to a new antihistoricist future. In its heyday, it was a riveting trumpet-blast of a building and is today considered by many to be Europe's first example of full-blown 20th-century architecture.

The Secession began in 1897, when 20 dissatisfied Viennese artists, headed by Gustav Klimt, "seceded" from the Künstlerhausgenossenschaft, the conservative artists' society associated with the Academy of Fine Arts. The movement promoted the radically new kind of art known as Jugendstil, which found its inspiration in both the organic, fluid designs of Art Nouveau and the related but more geometric designs of the English Arts and Crafts movement. The Secession building, designed by the architect Joseph Olbrich and completed in 1898, was the movement's exhibition hall. The lower story, crowned by the entrance motto *Der Zeit Ihre Kunst, Der Kunst Ihre Freiheit* ("To Every Age Its Art, To Art Its Freedom"), is classic Jugendstil: the restrained but assured decoration (by Koloman Moser) complements the facade's pristine flat expanses of cream-color wall. Above the entrance motto sits the building's most famous feature, the gilded openwork dome that the Viennese were quick to christen "the golden cabbage" (Olbrich wanted it to be seen as a dome of laurel, a subtle classical reference meant to celebrate the triumph of art). The plain white interior was also revolutionary; its most unusual feature was movable walls, allowing the galleries to be reshaped and redesigned for every show. One early show, in 1902, was a temporary exhibition devoted to art celebrating the genius of Beethoven; Klimt's *Beethoven*

*Frieze* was painted for the occasion, and the fragments that survived can be admired in the basement. Guided tours are given Saturday at 11. ⊠ *Friedrichstrasse 12, 1st District* ☎ *01/587–53–070* ⊕ *www. secession.at* 🖃 *€9.50* ⊗ *Closed Mon.* Ⓜ *U4/Karlsplatz.*

FAMILY **ZOOM Kinder Museum** (*ZOOM Children's Museum*). Kids of all ages enjoy this outstanding museum, where they can experience the fine line between the real and virtual worlds, making screenplays come to life by becoming directors, sound technicians, authors, and actors. For the little ones there's an "ocean" where kids and parents enter a play area inhabited by magical underwater creatures. The museum operates like little workshops, with the staff very hands-on and available to the children. You must book your tickets for a specific admission time, so reserve via the website before you go. ⊠ *MuseumsQuartier, Museumsplatz 1, 7th District/Neubau* ☎ *01/524–7908* ⊕ *www.kindermuseum.at* 🖃 *€15 for family ticket* ⊗ *Closed Mon.* Ⓜ *U2/MuseumsQuartier; U2 or U3/Volkstheater.*

## WORTH NOTING

**Architekturzentrum Wien** (*Vienna Architecture Center*). Besides the permanent show of Austrian architecture in the 20th and 21st centuries, the center holds major exhibitions presenting the breadth of architecture history and visions of what is to come. ⊠ *MuseumsQuartier, Museumsplatz 1, 7th District/Neubau* ☎ *01/522–3115* ⊕ *www.azw.at* 🖃 *€9* Ⓜ *U2/MuseumsQuartier; U2 or U3/Volkstheater.*

**Dritte Mann Museum** (*Third Man Museum*). Close to the Naschmarkt, this shrine for film-noir aficionados offers an extensive private collection of memorabilia dedicated to the classic film, *The Third Man*, directed by Carol Reed and shot entirely on location in Vienna. Authentic exhibits include cinema programs, autographed cards, movie and sound recordings, and first editions of Graham Greene's novel, which was the basis of the screenplay. Also here is the original zither used by Anton Karas to record the film's music, which started a zither boom in the '50s. In the reading corner, you can browse through historic newspaper articles about the film. Note that the museum is only open on Saturday, from 2 to 6. ⊠ *Pressgasse 25, 4th District/Wieden* ☎ *01/586–4872* ⊕ *www.3mpc. net* 🖃 *€8.90* ⊗ *Closed Sun.–Fri.* Ⓜ *U4/Kettenbrückengasse.*

**Joseph Haydn House.** In commemoration of the 200th anniversary of Joseph Haydn's death, his last residence was completely renovated and now holds an exhibition worthy of the great master. Haydn bought the house—which was then considered to be in the suburbs—and added another floor, where his valet stayed. Napoléon, who happened to be occupying Vienna at the time, so admired Haydn that he hired a guard to stand outside the dying composer's house. ⊠ *Haydngasse 19, 6th District/ Mariahilf* ☎ *01/596–1307* 🖃 *€4* Ⓜ *U4/Pilgramgasse or U3/Zieglergasse.*

**Kunsthalle Wien** (*Vienna Art Gallery*). The gigantic rooms here are used for temporary exhibitions of avant-garde art, including photography, video, film, and new-media projects. The museum prides itself on finding artists who break down the borders between the genres. ⊠ *MuseumsQuartier, Museumsplatz 1, 7th District/Neubau* ☎ *01/521–8933* ⊕ *www.kunsthallewien.at* 🖃 *€8* Ⓜ *U2 MuseumsQuartier; U2 or U3/Volkstheater.*

**Spittelberg Quarter.** The Spittelberg is like a slice of Old Vienna, a perfectly preserved little enclave that allows you to experience the 18th century by strolling along cobblestone pedestrian streets lined with pretty Baroque town houses. The quarter—one block northwest of Maria-Theresien-Platz off the Burggasse—offers a fair visual idea of the Vienna that existed outside the city walls a century ago. Most buildings have been replaced, but the engaging 18th-century survivors at Burggasse 11 and 13 are adorned with religious and secular decorative sculpture, the latter with a niche statue of St. Joseph, the former with cherubic work-and-play bas-reliefs. Around holidays, particularly Easter and Christmas, the Spittelberg quarter, known for arts and handicrafts, hosts seasonal markets offering unique and interesting wares. Promenaders will also find art galleries and lots of restaurants. ⊠ *Off Burggasse, 7th District/Neubau* Ⓜ *U2 or U3/Volkstheater.*

# WEST OF THE RINGSTRASSE: PARLIAMENT AND CITY HALL

From her pedestal in front of Austria's National Parliament, Athena, the gold-helmeted Greek goddess of wisdom, looks sternly over the Ringstrasse. Locals hope that her good judgment rubs off on the legislators inside the templelike building. Nearby is the Rathaus, or City Hall, a masterpiece that's one of the city's most photographed buildings. During the summer months, the surrounding park is the setting for an international food and film festival; in winter there's a delightful Christmas market. The mood is a little more somber at the Votivkirche, an imposing cathedral that the royal family built after a thwarted assassination attempt on Emperor Franz Josef. Travel up Währingerstrasse and Liechtensteinstrasse to visit Sigmund Freud's apartment.

## TOP ATTRACTIONS

**Freud Haus.** Not far from the historic Hofburg district, the marvels and pains of the 20th century come into focus here at the Freud Haus. This was Sigmund Freud's residence for nearly half a century; it was where he lived with his wife, Martha, and where the couple raised their six children. The apartment has five rooms of memorabilia and an exhibit highlighting the personal life of the father of psychoanalysis with private letters and biographical details. The waiting-room furniture is the real deal, but the consulting room and study furniture (including the famous couch) can be seen only in photographs. The collection of telegrams (photocopies of the originals) from the State Department is chilling; they chronicle frantic efforts to help the Freud family escape Austria after the Nazi Anschluss in 1938. The apartment is one flight up, which is well marked with signs. ⊠ *Berggasse 19, Apt. 6, 9th District/Alsergrund* ☎ *01/319–1596* ⊕ *www.freud-museum.at* ⚑ *€12* Ⓜ *U2/Schottentor.*

**OFF THE BEATEN PATH**

**Kirche Am Steinhof.** Also known as the Church of St. Leopold, Otto Wagner's most exalted piece of Jugendstil architecture lies in the suburbs: the church on the grounds of the old Vienna City Psychiatric Hospital. Wagner's design here unites functional details (rounded edges on the pews to prevent injury to the patients) with a soaring, airy dome, with stained glass by Koloman Moser. ⊠ *Baumgartner Höhe 1, 14th District/Penzing* 🕾 *01/91060* 🎫 *€8* Ⓜ *U4/Unter-St.- Veit; then Bus 47A to Psychiatrisches Krankenhaus. U2/Volkstheater; then Bus 48A.*

**Parlament** (*Parliament*). Reminiscent of an ancient Greek temple, this sprawling building is the seat of the country's elected representative assembly. An embracing, heroic ramp on either side of the main structure is lined with carved marble figures of ancient Greek and Roman historians. Its centerpiece is the Pallas-Athene-Brunnen, a fountain designed by Theophil Hansen that is crowned by the Greek goddess of wisdom and surrounded by water nymphs symbolizing the executive and legislative powers governing the country. The interior of the building is currrently being refurbished and will not be open to the public until 2020. ⊠ *Dr. Karl Renner-Ring 3, 1st District* 🕾 *01/401–1024–00* ⊕ *www.parlament.gv.at* Ⓜ *Trams 1, 2, or D/Stadiongasse, Parlament.*

**Rathaus** (*City Hall*). Designed by Friedrich Schmidt and resembling a Gothic fantasy castle with its many spires and turrets, the Rathaus took more than 10 years to build and was completed in 1883. The facade holds a lavish display of standard-bearers brandishing the coats of arms of the city of Vienna and the monarchy. Guided tours include the banqueting hall and various committee rooms. Nearly 10 acres of regally landscaped park grace the front of the building, and the area is usually brimming with activity. In winter it's the scene of the most famous Christmas market in Vienna, and after the New Year, it is transformed into a gigantic ice-skating rink. In summer, folks can watch movies outside. The building is open by guided tour only. ⊠ *Rathausplatz 1, 1st District* 🕾 *01/52550* 🎫 *Free* Ⓜ *Trams 1, 2, or D/Rathaus.*

## WORTH NOTING

**Schubert's Birthplace.** Unlike most of Vienna's composers, Schubert was a native of Vienna. The modest but charming two-story house was not as idyllic then as it is today. When Schubert was born, it was home to 16 families who were crammed into as many studio apartments within the house. Many of the composer's personal items are displayed here, including his spectacles, which he allegedly didn't remove to sleep, as he was so anxious to begin composing as soon as he woke up. ⊠ *Nussdorferstrasse 54, 9th District/Alsergrund* 🕾 *01/317–3601* ⊕ *www.wienmuseum.at* 🎫 *€2* ⊙ *Closed Mon.* Ⓜ *Streetcar 37 or 38 to Canisiusgasse.*

**Universität** (*University of Vienna*). The oldest university in the German-speaking world (founded in 1365), the main section of the university is a massive block in Italian Renaissance style designed by Heinrich Ferstel and built between 1873 and 1884. Statues representing 38 important men of letters decorate the front of the building, while the rear, which encompasses the library (with nearly 2 million volumes), is adorned with sgraffito. ⊠ *Dr. Karl Lueger-Ring 1, 1st District* ☎ *01/4277–17676, 01/4277–176–01 guided tours* ⊕ *www.univie. ac.at* ⊠ *€5* Ⓜ *U2/Schottentor.*

**Votivkirche** (*Votive Church*). When Emperor Franz Josef was a young man, he was strolling along the Mölker Bastei, one of the few remaining portions of the old city wall, when he was taken unawares and stabbed in the neck by a Hungarian revolutionary. He survived, and in gratitude his family ordered that a church be built exactly on the spot he was looking at when he was struck down. The neo-Gothic church was built of gray limestone with two openwork turrets and was finally completed in 1879, after 23 years of construction. ⊠ *Rooseveltplatz, 9th District/ Alsergrund* ☎ *01/406–1192* ⊙ *Closed Mon.* Ⓜ *U2/Schottentor.*

# SCHÖNBRUNN PALACE, GARDENS, AND THE ZOO

The glories of imperial Austria are nowhere brought together more convincingly than in the Schloss Schönbrunn (Schönbrunn Palace) complex. Imperial elegance, interrupted only by tourist traffic, flows unbroken throughout the grounds. This is Vienna's primary tourist site, although few stay long enough to discover the real Schönbrunn (including the fountain with the little maiden carrying the water jar, after whom the complex is named). The outbuildings served as entertainment centers when the court moved to Schönbrunn in summer, accounting for the zoo, the theater, the fake Roman ruins, the greenhouses, and the walkways. In Schönbrunn you step back three centuries into the heart of a powerful and growing empire and follow it through to defeat and demise in 1918.

## TOP ATTRACTIONS

**Gloriette.** At the crest of the hill, topping off the Schönbrunn Gardens, sits a Baroque masterstroke: Johann Ferdinand von Hohenberg's Gloriette, now restored to its original splendor. Perfectly scaled, the Gloriette—a palatial pavilion that once offered royal guests a place to rest and relax on their tours of the palace grounds and that now houses a welcome café—holds the vast garden composition together and at the same time crowns the ensemble with a brilliant architectural tiara. This was a favorite spot of Maria Theresa's, though in later years she grew so obese—not surprising, given that she bore 16 children in 20 years—it took six men to carry her in her palanquin to the summit. ⊠ *Schönbrunn Palace, Schönbrunner-Schloss-Strasse, 13th District/ Hietzing* ⊕ *www.schoenbrunn.at* Ⓜ *U4/Schönbrunn.*

**Hofpavillon.** The restored imperial subway station known as the Hofpavillon is just outside the palace grounds (at the northwest corner, a few yards east of the Hietzing subway station). Designed by Otto Wagner in conjunction with Joseph Olbrich and Leopold Bauer, the Hofpavillon was built in 1899 for the exclusive use of Emperor Franz Josef and his entourage. Exclusive it was: the emperor used the station only once. The exterior, with its proud architectural crown, is Wagner at his best, and the lustrous interior is one of the finest examples of Jugendstil

## CLOSE UP

# A Hop Through Hip Vienna

Paris has the Latin Quarter, London has Notting Hill, and the bohemian district in Vienna is the **Freihaus** sector in the 4th District (Wieden), Vienna's trendiest neighborhood.

In the 17th century, Freihaus provided free housing to the city's poor, hence the name "Freihaus," which means Free House. The complex was destroyed in the Turkish siege of 1683, then rebuilt on a much larger scale, becoming arguably the largest housing project in Europe at the time. It was a city within a city, including shops and the old Theater auf der Wieden, in which Mozart's *The Magic Flute* premiered. A slow decline followed, spanning Franz Josef's reign from the mid-19th century to the early 20th century, with some of the area razed before World War I. During World War II, bombing raids practically finished it off.

But in the late 1990s a group of savvy local merchants revitalized the area, opening funky art galleries, antiques shops, espresso bars, trendy restaurants, and fashion boutiques. Freihaus is small, stretching from Karlsplatz to Kettenbrückengasse, which encompasses part of the Naschmarkt, the city's largest open-air market. Two of the best streets are Operngasse and Schleifmühlgasse.

What do you do with four immense gasometers more than 100 years old? Turn them into a cool, urban complex combining living and shopping. Looming large on the Vienna horizon,

the **Gasometers** have generated a lot of publicity. Just to give an idea of their size, Vienna's giant Ferris wheel (the Riesenrad) at the Prater Amusement Park would fit easily inside each one. Top architects were hired to accomplish the sleek interior renovations, creating more than 600 modern apartments and a huge shopping mall with movie theaters and restaurants. It's in Simmering, Vienna's 11th District, just eight minutes from the heart of the city on the U3 subway.

A visit to Vienna during the summer would not be complete without a few hours spent on the Donauinsel (Danube Island), more popularly known as the **Copa Kagrana.** ("Kagrana" is taken from the name of the nearby area known as Kagran.) It was originally built as a safeguard against flooding, but now this 13-square-mile island is where the Viennese head for bicycling, skateboarding, jogging, swimming, or just a leisurely stroll and dinner by the water. There are dozens of stalls and restaurants, offering grilled steaks, fried chicken, or fresh fish to go along with a mug of ice-cold draft beer or Austrian wine. Every year, 2 million visitors converge on the island for three days in June for an admission-free summer festival, the Donauinselfest (⊕ *www.donauinselfest.at*). The Copa Kagrana can be reached by subway: either the U1 to Donauinsel or the U6 to Handelskai.

decoration in the city. ⊠ *Schönbrunner-Schloss-Strasse, 13th District/ Hietzing* ☎ *01/877–1571* ☜ *€4* Ⓜ *U4/Hietzing.*

**Palmenhaus.** On the grounds of Schönbrunn Palace is this huge greenhouse filled with exotic trees and plants. ⊠ *Schönbrunn Palace, Schönbrunner-Schloss-Strasse, 13th District/Hietzing* ☎ *01/877–5087* ⊕ *www. schoenbrunn.at* ☜ *€4* Ⓜ *U4/Schönbrunn.*

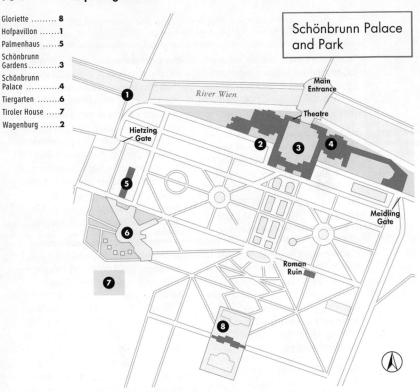

Schönbrunn Palace and Park

**Schönbrunn Gardens** (*Palace Park*). The palace grounds entice with a bevy of splendid divertissements, including a grand zoo (the Tiergarten) and a carriage museum (the Wagenburg). Climb to the Gloriette for a panoramic view out over the city as well as of the palace complex. If you're exploring on your own, seek out the intriguing Roman ruin. The marble *schöner Brunnen* ("beautiful fountain") gave its name to the palace complex. Then head over the other side of the gardens to the playground and the newly grown maze. ⊠ *Schönbrunner-Schloss-Strasse, 13th District/Hietzing* ⊕ *www. schoenbrunn.at* Ⓜ *U4/Schönbrunn.*

**Fodor's** Choice   **Schönbrunn Palace.** Originally designed by Johann Bernhard Fischer von
★   Erlach in 1696 and altered considerably for Maria Theresa 40 years later, Schönbrunn Palace, the huge Habsburg summer residence, lies within the city limits, just a few metro stops west of Karlsplatz on the U4. Bus trips to Schönbrunn offered by the city's tour operators cost several times what you'd pay if you traveled by subway; the one advantage is that they get you there with a bit less effort. Travel independently if you want time to wander through the grounds, which are open dawn to dusk.

The most impressive approach to the palace and its gardens is through the front gate, set on Schönbrunner-Schloss-Strasse halfway between the Schönbrunn and Hietzing metro stations. The vast main courtyard is ruled by a formal design of impeccable order and rigorous symmetry: wing nods at wing, facade mirrors facade, and every part stylistically complements every other. The courtyard, however, turns out to be a mere appetizer; the feast lies beyond. The breathtaking view that unfolds on the other side of the palace is one of the finest set pieces in all Europe and one of the supreme achievements of Baroque planning. Formal *Allées* (promenades) shoot off diagonally, the one on the right toward the zoo, the one on the left toward a rock-mounted obelisk and a fine false Roman ruin. But these, and the woods beyond, are merely a frame for the composition in the center: the sculpted marble fountain; the carefully planted screen of trees behind; the sudden, almost vertical rise of the grass-covered hill beyond, with the **Gloriette** a fitting crown.

Within the palace, the state salons are quite up to the splendor of the gardens, but note the contrast between these chambers and the far more modest rooms in which the rulers—particularly Franz Josef—lived and spent most of their time. Of the 1,441 rooms, 40 are open to the public on the regular tour, of which two are of special note: the Hall of Mirrors, where the six-year-old Mozart performed for Empress Maria Theresa in 1762 (and where he met seven-year-old Marie Antoinette), and the Grand Gallery, where the Congress of Vienna (1815) danced at night after carving up Napoléon's collapsed empire during the day. Ask about viewing the ground-floor living quarters (Berglzimmer), where the walls are painted with palm trees, exotic animals, and tropical views.

As you go through the palace, glance occasionally out the windows; you'll be rewarded by a better impression of the formal gardens, punctuated by hedgerows and fountains. These window vistas were enjoyed by rulers from Maria Theresa and Napoléon to Franz Josef. ⊠ *Schönbrunner-Schloss-Strasse, 13th District/Hietzing* ☎ *01/811–13–239* ⊕ *www.schoenbrunn.at* ⌨ *€14.50 for Imperial Tour (Franz Josef's rooms); €17.50 Grand Tour (includes Maria Theresa's rooms)* Ⓜ *U4/Schönbrunn.*

FAMILY **Tiergarten.** The world's oldest zoo has retained its original Baroque design, but new settings have been created for both the animals and the public. In one case, you gaze out over a natural habitat from inside one of the former animal houses. The zoo is also constantly adding new attractions and undergoing renovations, so there's plenty to see. In 2017, a giraffe enclosure was built to house two-year-olds Fleur and Sofie, the zoo's young darlings. The year before, giant panda twins Fu Fen and Fu Ban were born by natural means at the only zoo in Europe that can claim such an accomplishment. ⊠ *Schönbrunner Schlosspark, Schönbrunner-Schloss-Strasse, 13th District/Hietzing* ☎ *01/877–92–940* ⊕ *www.zoovienna.at* ⌨ *€18.50* Ⓜ *U4/Schönbrunn.*

**Tiroler House.** This Tyrolean-style building to the west of the Gloriette was a favorite retreat of Empress Elisabeth; it now includes a restaurant. ⊠ *Schönbrunner Schlosspark, Schönbrunner-Schloss-Strasse, 13th District/Hietzing* Ⓜ *U4/Schönbrunn.*

**Wagenburg** (*Imperial Carriage Museum*). Most of the carriages on display here are still roadworthy, and in fact Schönbrunn dusted off the black royal funeral carriage for the burial ceremony of Empress Zita in 1989. There are also a number of sleighs in the collection, including one upholstered in leopard skin. Today a special Sisi trail leads through the museum; on show are some of her famous gowns, carriages, personal objects, and paintings, highlighting the empress's life from marriage to her tragic death. ✉ *Schönbrunner Schlosspark, Schönbrunner-Schloss-Strasse, 13th District/Hietzing* ☎ *01/877–3244* ⊕ *www.khm.at* ☜ *€9.50* Ⓜ *U4/Schönbrunn.*

# WHERE TO EAT

Updated
by Patti
McCracken

Vienna has tried hard to shed its image of a town locked in the 19th century, and nowhere is that more evident than in the kitchens of the top-notch Austrian chefs who dominate the culinary scene here. They have turned dining from a mittel- europäisch sloshfest of Schweinsbraten, Knödeln, and Kraut (pork, dumplings, and cabbage), into an exquisite feast of international flavors.

No one denies that such courtly delights as *Tafelspitz*—the blush-pink boiled beef famed as Emperor Franz Josef's favorite dish—is delicious, but these traditional carb-loaded meals tend to leave you stuck to your seat like a suction cup.

The dining scene of today's Vienna has transformed itself, thanks in part to a new generation of chefs, such as Heinz Reitbauer Jr. and celebrity-chef Christian Petz, who've worked hard to establish an international brand of Viennese cooking known as *Neue Wiener Küche* (New Vienna cuisine). They have stepped onto the stage, front and center, to create signature dishes, such as fish soup with red curry, which have rocketed to fame; they have fan clubs, host television shows, and publish top-selling cookbooks, such as *Neue Cuisine: The Elegant Tastes of Vienna*; there are star Austrian chefs the way there are in New York and Hollywood, and these chefs want to delight an audience hungry for change.

Schmaltzy schnitzels have been replaced by prized Styrian beef—organic meat from local, farm-raised cattle—while soggy *Nockerl* (small dumplings) are traded in for seasonal delights like Carinthian asparagus, Styrian wild garlic, or the zingy taste of common garden stinging nettle. Wisely, Vienna has also warmly welcomed into its kitchens chefs from around the world, who give exotic twists to old favorites.

# DINING PLANNER

## CUSTOMS

In Vienna, the basket of bread put on your table is not free. Most of the older-style Viennese restaurants charge €0.70–€1.70 for each roll that is eaten.

## DISCOUNTS

In Vienna, dining out doesn't always have to break the bank. For lunch, look for cafés and *beisl* (bistros) offering a *Mittagsmenü*, which is the special of the day. Two courses will usually cost about €13. For a quick bite when you're on the go, the bakery chains Anker, Mann, Ströck, and Felber are found everywhere in the city. Grab a pastry filled with jam or *Topfen* (a rich ricotta cheese) to tide you over until dinner.

In late February and early March, a few dozen restaurants offer reduced-price lunches and dinners during Restaurantwoche (Restaurant Week). For more details, see ⊕ *www.restaurantwoche.at*.

## DRESS

The Viennese are keenly aware of how people are dressed. As a general rule, people try to look their best in public. Showing up at a restaurant wearing jogging pants, T-shirts, baseball caps, or other extremely casual clothing is a definite no-no. That said, jeans and a nice shirt will be fine at most places. A jacket and tie for men would be necessary in only the most formal establishments.

## FOOD FESTIVALS

Taking place over a weekend in May, the **Genuss Festival** (Gourmet Festival) is held in the Stadtpark on the Ringstrasse. The event aims at preserving Austria's rich and varied culinary traditions by highlighting delicacies from different regions. Food producers from all over the country present their creations, from poppy-seed oil to ox sausage.

In April, the province of Styria, known for its dishes involving pumpkinseed oil, showcases its culinary skills in Rathausplatz during **Steiermarkdorf** (⊕ *www.steiermarkdorf.at*). At the end of August, Austria's northernmost region of Waldviertel draws many visitors to Heldenplatz for **Waldviertelpur** (⊕ *www.waldviertelpur.at*). Servers wearing traditional dirndls serve dumplings to the sounds of brass music.

## MEALTIMES

Lunch typically starts at 11:30 or noon, and dinner service begins around 5:30 or 6. Many restaurants close between lunch and dinner (roughly 2:30 to 5:30). On weekdays, kitchens usually close around 11 pm.

## RESERVATIONS

Reservations are always a good idea; book as far ahead as you can if you know a place is particularly popular. Large parties should always call to check the reservations policy.

## SMOKING

Smoking is still allowed in the city's restaurants, but smokers are required to be in separate rooms. Smaller restaurants are not required to make special provisions for nonsmokers, so it's a good idea to check ahead.

## TIPPING AND TAXES

In Austria, tipping is customary. In cafés, bistros, and other less expensive eateries, the Viennese usually round up to the nearest euro. If they are very happy with the service in a fancier restaurant, they will give the waiter anywhere from €1 to €3. They never tip 15% to 20% of the total bill, as is customary in the United States. Tipping so much can be insulting to the waitstaff.

| WHAT IT COSTS IN EUROS | | | |
| --- | --- | --- | --- |
| $ | $$ | $$$ | $$$$ |
| under €18 | €18–€23 | €24–€31 | over €31 |

AT DINNER

Prices are the average cost of a main course at dinner or, if dinner is not served, at lunch.

# RESTAURANT REVIEWS

*Listed alphabetically within neighborhoods. Restaurant reviews have been shortened. For full information, visit Fodors.com.*

## THE EASTERN CITY CENTER: STEPHANSDOM AND MEDIEVAL VIENNA

**$**
AUSTRIAN
✕**Café Bellaria.** Located steps from the Volkstheater, the Bellaria is beloved by locals for its Monday-evening singing nights (and for its great desserts and other café cuisine). Some of the city's best singers stay for hours and take turns belting out tunes from a lengthy playlist that includes everything from opera to Elvis. **Known for:** one of Vienna's premier concert cafés; terrific desserts; warm and familial atmosphere. $ *Average main: €7* ✉ *Bellariastrasse 6, 1st District* ☎ *1/523–5320* ⊕ *www.cafebellaria.at* Ⓜ *U2/U3 Volkstheater.*

**$**
CAFÉ
✕**Café Frauenhuber.** You can retreat to Café Frauenhuber, billed as Vienna's oldest café, to find some peace and quiet away from the busy shoppers on Kärntnerstrasse. Breakfast is a go-for-broke affair, and might include a pot of tea (or coffee), a glass of prosecco, fresh-squeezed orange juice, toast, and fresh salmon with a dash of horseradish. **Known for:** extravagant breakfast buffet; local hangout with few tourists; traditional velvet-seat decor. $ *Average main: €14* ✉ *Himmelpfortgasse 6, 1st District* ☎ *01/512–5323* ⊕ *www.cafe-frauenhuber.at* Ⓜ *U1 or U3/Stephansplatz.*

**$**
CAFÉ
✕**Café Schwarzenberg.** Located near the Hotel Imperial, this is an ideal spot for a coffee and cake after a performance at the Musikverein or Konzerthaus, both just a couple of minutes away. Open until midnight, it has a good choice of food and pastries. **Known for:** large outdoor terrace; live piano music Wednesday, Friday, and weekends; late-night hours. $ *Average main: €15* ✉ *Kärntnerring 17, 1st District* ☎ *01/512–8998* ⊕ *www.cafe-schwarzenberg.at/en* Ⓜ *U2/Schottentor.*

**$**
BAKERY
Fodor's Choice
★
✕**Demel.** The display cases are filled to the brim at the world-renowned Demel, a 200-year-old pastry shop and chocolatier, famous for sweetmeats. Chocolate lovers will want to try the Viennese Sachertorte (two layers of dense chocolate cake, with apricot jam sandwiched between, and chocolate icing on top) and compare it with its competition at Café Sacher. **Known for:** famous Sachertorte; crowds of tourists; elegant decor. $ *Average main: €10* ✉ *Kohlmarkt 14, 1st District* ☎ *01/535–1717* ⊕ *www.demel.at.*

**$$**
AUSTRIAN
✕**Figlmüller.** This Wiener schnitzel institution is known for breaded veal and pork cutlets so large they overflow the plate. The cutlet is hammered—you can hear the mallets pounding from a block away—so that the schnitzel winds up wafer-thin. **Known for:** huge schnitzel; delicious potato salad; second location at Bäckerstrasse 6. $ *Average main: €17* ✉ *Wollzeile 5, 1st District* ☎ *01/512–6177* ⊕ *www.figlmueller.at* Ⓜ *U1 or U3/Stephansplatz.*

**$$**
AUSTRIAN
✕**Gasthaus zur Oper.** In case its name doesn't give it away, the proximity to the opera house should be a clue that among the dinner guests will be many of the city's regular operagoers, sitting for a meal before the show. Located on a side street near Kärntnerstrasse, this restaurant focuses on traditional Austrian dishes. **Known for:** beef from small Austrian farms; top-notch comfort foods; the "best schnitzel in Vienna". $ *Average main: €20* ✉ *Walfischgasse 5–7, 1st District* ☎ *01/512–2251* ⊕ *www.plachutta-oper.at.*

$$ AUSTRIAN

🍴 **Griechenbeisl.** Neatly tucked away in a quiet and quaint area of the Old City, this ancient inn goes back half a millennium (Mozart, Beethoven, and Schubert all dined here). Yes, it's touristy, yet the food, including all the classic hearty dishes like goulash soup, Wiener schnitzel, and *Apfelstrudel,* is as good as in many other beisl. **Known for:** old-world charm; classic Austrian dishes; famous patrons. [$] *Average main: €22* ✉ *Fleischmarkt 11, 1st District* ☎ *01/533–1977* 🌐 *www.griechenbeisl.at* [M] *U1 or U4/Schwedenplatz.*

$ INTERNATIONAL Fodor's Choice ★

🍴 **Haas & Haas Teahouse.** Situated in the courtyard of the Stephansplatz, with a direct view of stunning St. Stephen's Cathedral, this teahouse is a rare find in a city steeped in the tradition of coffeehouses. It is a cozy tea parlor, indeed, with a selection of more than 200 brews and a particularly splendid afternoon tea menu. **Known for:** English-style afternoon tea served daily; extensive menu of international dishes; extensive menu of international dishes. [$] *Average main: €15* ✉ *Stephansplatz 4, 1st District* ☎ *01/5129770* 🌐 *www.haas-haas.at* [M] *U1 or U3 Stephansplatz.*

$$$$ INTERNATIONAL Fodor's Choice ★

🍴 **Konstantin Filippou.** In a stunningly short time, Filippou has made a remarkable impression on the Vienna dining elite, evident from its Michelin star and its Gault Millau Chef of the Year award. A seat at the prized kitchen table allows a view into the kitchen to watch the chef preparing the meal, including the famous escargot seasoned with horseradish and watercress. **Known for:** frequently changing, six-course tasting menu with wine pairing; outdoor garden dining in spring and summer; one of the top restaurants in Vienna (and most expensive). [$] *Average main: €140* ✉ *Dominikanerbastei 17, 1st District* ☎ *01/51–22–229* 🌐 *www.konstantinfilippou.com* ⏲ *Closed weekends and last 3 wks of Aug.*

$$ CONTEMPORARY

🍴 **Motto am Fluss.** Even though night owls flock to the bar at Motto am Fluss until the wee hours, this sleek eatery serves an inspired selection of dishes when the sun is up, too, like tuna steak with creamy avocado sauce. Breakfast delights at the sister café include the "Full Speed Ahead" (scrambled eggs on whole-wheat bread, with slices of ham and salami and a selection of cheeses, including Camembert). **Known for:** sprawling dining room with great river views; 1950s retro decor; creative breakfast fare. [$] *Average main: €20* ✉ *Franz-Josefs Kai, 1st District* ☎ *01/25255* 🌐 *www.mottoamfluss.at.*

$ BAKERY

🍴 **Oberlaa.** Popular with the locals and a great value, you'll find irresistible confections such as the Oberlaa Kurbad cake, truffle cake, and chocolate-mousse cake here. The lemon torte is filled with a light, fruity lemon cream and a thin layer of almond paste. **Known for:** lots of tasty desserts and cakes; gift-wrapped candy options; gluten- and lactose-free treats. [$] *Average main: €8* ✉ *Neuer Markt 16, 1st District* ☎ *01/513–2936* 🌐 *www.oberlaa-wien.at.*

$ FAST FOOD

🍴 **Pizza Bizi.** Most people are drawn in by the thick aroma of buttered garlic wafting down the street; though for some, the attraction is watching the bakers toss the pizza pies into the air before popping them into the oven. Pizza Bizi is arguably one of the best slices of New York–style pizza you'll find anywhere in Europe. **Known for:** amazing pizza and pasta buffet; standing-room only seating; cash-only policy. [$] *Average main: €4* ✉ *Rotenturmstrasse 4, 1st District* ☎ *01/513–3705* 🌐 *www.pizzabizi.at.*

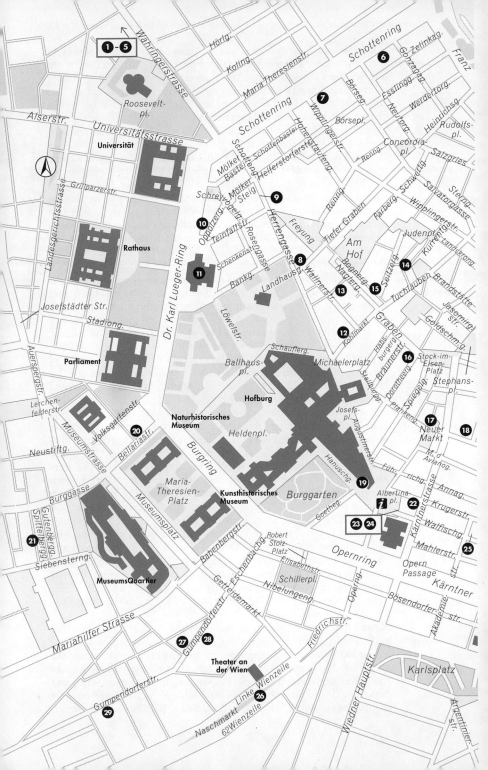

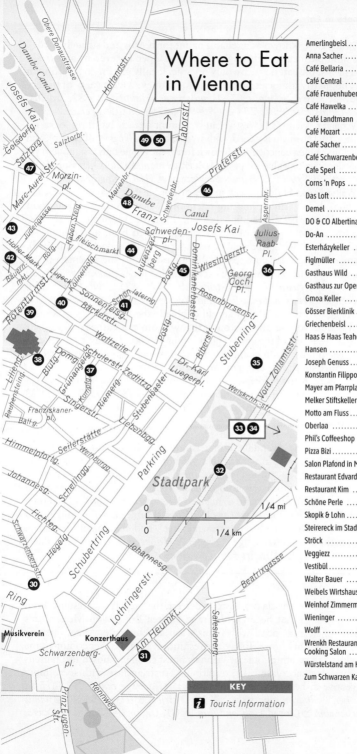

# Where to Eat in Vienna

**KEY**

🛈 *Tourist Information*

$ AUSTRIAN
🍴 **Ströck.** Long known as a reliable haunt for breads and strudels, Ströck has multiple locations throughout the city. Open for evening and weekend meals, the eateries serve only organic, locally grown goods. **Known for:** popular with locals; good value for money; wide variety of bakery options. [$] *Average main: €5* ✉ *Landstrasser Hauptstrasse 82, 3rd District/Landstrasse* ☎ *01/204-39-99-93-057* 🌐 *www.stroeck.at.*

$ VEGETARIAN
🍴 **Veggiezz.** Vienna's newest vegan restaurant already has three locations in the city. The menu is varied, with wraps, burgers (veggie, of course), and delicious quinoa concoctions. **Known for:** great veggie burgers; modern yet cozy decor; good value for price. [$] *Average main: €12* ✉ *Opernring 6, 1st District* ☎ *1/890–0032* 🌐 *www.veggiezz.at* [M] *U1/U2 Karlsplatz.*

$$$$ AUSTRIAN
🍴 **Walter Bauer.** Hidden away in one of the quietest quarters of historic Vienna, this charming and unpretentious Michelin-starred restaurant serves the very best in traditional cuisine. Even the everyman Leberkäse—an artery-blocking loaf of pork, bacon, corned beef, and onions—is turned into a delectable delight (and served with a dash of mustard). **Known for:** Austrian cuisine with the highest-quality ingredients; revolving door of Austria's top chefs; excellent wine list. [$] *Average main: €60* ✉ *Sonnenfelsgasse 17, 1st District* ☎ *01/512–9871* 🕒 *No lunch Mon. Closed weekends and mid-July–mid-Aug.* [M] *U1 or U3/Stephansplatz.*

$$ AUSTRIAN
🍴 **Weibels Wirtshaus.** Down an old cobbled lane between Singerstrasse and Schulerstrasse and a stone's throw from the cathedral, Weibels Wirtshaus is one of the coziest places to have a lazy lunch or a quiet dinner. The dinner menu changes with the season; in summer try the cold cucumber soup with cilantro shrimp, and strawberry-rhubarb mousse for dessert. **Known for:** seasonally changing menu; delightful garden terrace; intimate and romantic seating upstairs. [$] *Average main: €23* ✉ *Kumpfgasse 2, 1st District* ☎ *01/512–3986* 🌐 *www.weibel.at* [M] *U1 or U3/Stephansplatz.*

$ FAST FOOD
🍴 **Würstelstand am Hohen Markt.** Hot on the trail of the "Best Sausage" designation, the legendary Würstelstand am Hohen Markt serves the best *Bürenwurst* and American-style hot dogs. As with most of the Würstelstands, or "imbiss" kiosks, there is a surprising amount of food on offer. Fried sausage is a popular choice for locals, as is a *Bosna,* a bratwurst with onions and a mustard-ketchup concoction served on a roll. **Known for:** local favorites like Käiserkrainer (fried sausage) and Bosna (bratwurst with onions); wine, beer, and champagne available; late-night hours. [$] *Average main: €3* ✉ *Hoher Markt, corner of Marc-Aurel-Strasse, 1st District* 💳 *No credit cards.*

## THE INNER CITY CENTER

$$$$ AUSTRIAN
Fodor's Choice ★
🍴 **Anna Sacher.** The classic Austrian dessert, the Sachertorte, resulted from a family saga that began with Franz Sacher, Prince von Metternich's pastry chef, and ended with Franz's son and his wife, Anna, opening the 19th-century hotel. Today, the restaurant Anna Sacher continues the tradition of creating some of Vienna's finest cuisine. **Known for:** famous Sachertorte chocolate cake; traditional Austrian fare with some more inventive dishes; lots of Vienna history. [$] *Average main: €37* ✉ *Hotel Sacher, Philharmonikerstrasse 4, 1st District* ☎ *01/514–56840* 🌐 *www.sacher.com* 🕒 *Closed Mon. and Aug.* [M] *U1, U2, or U4/Karlsplatz/Opera.*

3

$    ✗ **Café Hawelka.** Practically a shrine—indeed, almost a museum—the
CAFÉ    Hawelka was the hangout of most of Vienna's modern artists, and
the café has acquired an admirable art collection over the years. The
Hawelka is most famous for its *Buchteln,* a baked bun with a sweet
filling, served fresh from the oven after 10 pm. **Known for:** Buchtleln,
a baked sweet bun with a sweet filling; famous former guests (check
out the guest book); impressive art collection. *$ Average main: €10*
✉ *Dorotheergasse 6, 1st District* ☎ *01/512–8230* ⊕ *www.hawelka.at*
Ⓜ *U1 or U3/Stephansplatz.*

$    ✗ **Café Mozart.** The café, named after the monument to Mozart (now
CAFÉ    in the Burggarten) that once stood outside, is overrun with sightseers,
but the waiters manage to remain calm even when customers run them
ragged. Crystal chandeliers, a brass-and-oak interior, comfortable seating, and delicious food—the Tafelspitz is excellent—add to its popularity. **Known for:** Tafelspitz that locals love; fabulous decor; role in the
classic movie The Third Man. *$ Average main: €10* ✉ *Albertinaplatz
2, 1st District* ☎ *01/24–100–200* ⊕ *www.cafe-mozart.at* Ⓜ *U1, U2, or
U4/Karlsplatz/Opera.*

$    ✗ **Café Sacher.** Arguably the most famous café in Vienna, it is the
CAFÉ    home of the legendary Sachertorte, a dense chocolate torte with fresh
Fodor's Choice    aprioct jam in the center. This legend began as a *Delikatessen* opened
★    by Sacher, court confectioner to Prince von Metternich, the most
powerful prime minister in early-19th-century Europe. **Known for:**
alleged origin of the famous Sachertorte cake; tasty savory options;
live piano music daily. *$ Average main: €12* ✉ *Hotel Sacher, Phil-
harmonikerstrasse 4, 1st District* ☎ *01/514560* ⊕ *www.sacher.com*
Ⓜ *U1, U2, or U4/Karlsplatz/Opera.*

$$    ✗ **DO & CO Albertina.** When you're ready to collapse after taking in all
INTERNATIONAL    the art at the fabulous Albertina, take a break at the museum's on-site
eatery. For something exotic, try the sushi platter or the tasty gazpacho.
**Known for:** lovely terrace with a view of the Burggarten; bar seating
for snacks and other light fare; sushi and gazpacho. *$ Average main:
€20* ✉ *Albertina Museum, Albertinaplatz 1, 1st District* ☎ *01/532–9669*
⊕ *www.doco.com/en/restaurants/do-co-restaurants/albertina-vienna*
Ⓜ *U1, U2, or U4/Karlsplatz/Opera.*

$    ✗ **Esterházykeller.** The origins here go back to 1683, when this spot
WINE BAR    opened as one of the city's official *Stadtheuriger* (wine taverns), to
provide Turk-fighting soldiers with wine before going off to battle.
Below the Esterházy palace, the atmosphere is like that of a cozy
cave, with the maze of rooms offering some of the best wines of
any cellar in town, plus a typical Viennese menu noontime and eve-
nings. **Known for:** history as one of the city's official wine taverns;
great wine list (duh); meat-heavy food menu. *$ Average main: €10*
✉ *Haarhof 1, 1st District* ☎ *01/533–3482* ⊕ *www.esterhazykeller.at*
Ⓜ *U1 or U4/Stephansplatz.*

$    ✗ **Gösser Bierklinik.** Dating back four centuries, this engaging old-world
AUSTRIAN    house sits in the heart of Old Vienna. It is one of the country's top
addresses for beer connoisseurs and serves brews, both draft and bot-
tled, *Dunkeles* (dark) and *Helles* (light), from the Gösser brewery in
Styria. **Known for:** covered courtyard; authentically Austrian beer and

cheese; sandwiches and schnitzel. $ *Average main: €15* ⊠ *Steindlgasse 4, 1st District* ☎ *01/533–7598* ⊕ *www.goesser-bierklinik.at* ⊘ *Closed Sun. No lunch weekdays July and Aug.* Ⓜ *U3/Herrengasse.*

**$**
**INTERNATIONAL**

✕ **Wrenkh Restaurant and Cooking Salon.** Vienna's vegetarian pioneer extraordinaire Christian Wrenkh prefers teaching evening cooking classes to standing in the kitchen every day. His two sons run the show, and roughly two-thirds of the menu is vegetarian, with delightful dishes like wild-rice risotto with mushrooms, Greek fried rice with vegetables, or tofu, tomato, and basil tarts. **Known for:** best vegetarian menu in Vienna; culinary classes taught by master chef; reasonable prices. $ *Average main: €15* ⊠ *Bauernmarkt 10, 1st District* ☎ *01/533–1526* ⊕ *www.wrenkh-wien.at* ⊘ *Closed Sun.* Ⓜ *U1 or U3/Stephansplatz.*

**$$$$**
**AUSTRIAN**
**Fodor's Choice**
**★**

✕ **Zum Schwarzen Kameel.** Back when Beethoven dined at the Black Camel, it was already a foodie landmark. Since then, it has been renovated (but only in 1901), and more recently split into a Delikatessen and a restaurant. **Known for:** house specialty Beinschinken; deli sandwiches from family recipe; elegant dining room. $ *Average main: €35* ⊠ *Bognergasse 5, 1st District* ☎ *01/533–8125* ⊕ *www.kameel.at* ⊘ *Closed Sun.* Ⓜ *U3/Herrengasse.*

## ACROSS THE DANUBE: THE 2ND DISTRICT

**$$$$**
**INTERNATIONAL**
**Fodor's Choice**
**★**

✕ **Das Loft.** Dine at Vienna's poshest restaurant while taking in the stunning, 360-degree panoramic vistas of the city's skyline from the 18th floor of the Sofitel Stephansdom. The gourmet meals are just as fabulous as the view, offering Vienna's finest in French cuisine. **Known for:** topnotch cuisine from Austria's premier chefs; gorgeous views especially at sunset; dress code after 6 pm. $ *Average main: €70* ⊠ *Praterstrasse 1, 2nd District/Leopoldstadt* ☎ *1/906168110* ⊕ *www.dasloftwien.at.*

**$**
**AUSTRIAN**
**FAMILY**

✕ **Schöne Perle.** This "beautiful pearl" is one of the most popular dining spots for locals in Leopoldstadt. It offers traditional Austrian comfort food, including Tafelspitz—boiled beef, the favored dish of Emperor Franz Josef—and Wiener schnitzel, but its real palate pleasers are the wide selection of vegetarian dishes on the menu. **Known for:** Austrian comfort food; cash-only policy; crowds at dinner, so make a reservation. $ *Average main: €17* ⊠ *Grosse Pfarrgasse 2, 2nd District/Leopoldstadt* ☎ *664-2433-593* ⊕ *www.schoene-perle.at* ⊟ *No credit cards.*

**$$**
**AUSTRIAN**

✕ **Skopik & Lohn.** Many restaurants have set up shop in former stalls on the market square in the artsy neighborhood that has sprung up around Karmelitermarkt, just across the Donaukanal, including Skopik & Lohn. The menu features international fare, such as roast chicken with figs and chestnuts, and linguine with fresh chanterelle mushrooms (which only grow two months out of the year). **Known for:** wide selection of international fare; artist Otto Zitko's massive doodling spree on the ceiling; hip neighborhood hangout. $ *Average main: €19* ⊠ *Leopoldsgasse 17, 2nd District/Leopoldstadt* ☎ *01/219-8977* ⊕ *www. skopikundlohn.at* ⊘ *Closed Sun. and Mon.* Ⓜ *U2/Taborstrasse.*

# Coffeehouse 101

The coffeehouse culture is as much a part of the Austrian soul as Mozart is. There are more than 1,600 coffeehouses in Vienna, and its café culture has spread throughout Europe, even all the way to western Ukraine. The *Wiener Kaffeehäuser*—the cafés known for centuries as "Vienna's parlors," might be facing competition from places like Starbucks in recent years, but nothing will ever diminish the place coffeehouses hold with Austrians. Newspapers were started and run from them; revolutions started within them. Nothing else can replace the traditonal coffehouse experience: their sumptuous, red-velvet-padded booths; the marble-top tables; the rickety yet indestructible Thonet bentwood chairs; the coffee served on small silver platters, and, with it, a shot-sized glass of water; the waiters, dressed in Sunday-best outfits; the pastries, cakes, strudels, and rich tortes; the newspapers, magazines, and journals; and a sense that here time stands still. Set aside a morning or an afternoon, and settle down in the one you've chosen. Read awhile, catch up on your letter writing, or plan tomorrow's itinerary: there's no need to worry about overstaying your welcome, even over a single small cup of coffee.

In Austria coffee is never merely coffee. It comes in countless forms and under many names. Ask a waiter for *ein Kaffee* and you'll get a vacant stare. If you want a black coffee, you must ask for a *kleiner* or *grosser Schwarzer* (small or large black coffee, small being the size of a demitasse cup). If you want it strong, add the word *gekürzt* (shortened); if you want it weaker, *verlängert* (stretched). If you want your coffee with cream, ask for a *Brauner* (again *gross* or *klein*); say *Kaffee Creme* if you wish to add the cream yourself (or *Kaffee mit Milch extra, bitte,* if you want to add milk, not cream). Others opt for a *Melange,* a mild roast with steamed milk (which you can even get *mit Haut,* with skin, or *Verkehrter,* with more milk than coffee). The usual after-dinner drink is espresso. Most delightful are the coffee-and-whipped-cream concoctions, universally cherished as *Kaffee mit Schlag.* A customer who wants more whipped cream than coffee asks for a *Doppelschlag.* Hot black coffee in a glass with one knob of whipped cream is an *Einspänner* (literally, "one-horse coach"—as coachmen needed one hand free to hold the reins). Or you can go to town on a *Mazagran,* black coffee with ice and a tot of rum, or *Eiskaffee,* cold coffee with ice cream and whipped cream. Or you can simply order *eine Portion Kaffee* and have an honest pot of coffee and jug of hot milk. Most coffeehouses offer hot food until about an hour before closing time.

3

## THE WESTERN CITY CENTER: BURGTHEATER AND BEYOND

$

CAFÉ

Fodor'sChoice

★

✕ **Café Central.** Made famous by its illustrious guests, the Café Central is one of the most famous cafés in all of Vienna. The soaring ceiling and gigantic columns are hallmarks of the landmark, which was home to Viennese literati as well as world game changers at the turn of the last century, including Leon Trotsky, who mapped out the Russian Revolution here beneath portraits of the Imperial family. **Known for:** Leon Trotsky hangout; standard café fare and desserts; crowds of tourists.

$ *Average main: €14* ⊠ *Herrengasse 14, at Strauchgasse, 1st District* ☎ *01/533–3764–24* ⊕ *www.cafecentral.wien* Ⓜ *U3/Herrengasse.*

$ ✕ **Café Landtmann.** A favorite of politicians and theater stars (the Burg is

CAFÉ next door, the Rathaus across the street) since 1873, this was Sigmund

**Fodor's Choice** Freud's favorite café (he lived within walking distance). If you want

★ a great meal at almost any time of day, there are few places that can beat this one. **Known for:** house specialty "Franz Landtmann," mix of espresso, brandy, and whipped cream; lots of history and famous guests; glass-enclosed veranda. $ *Average main: €16* ⊠ *Dr.-Karl-Lueger-Ring 4, 1st District* ☎ *01/24–100–100* ⊕ *www.landtmann.at* Ⓜ *U2/Schottenring.*

$$$ ✕ **Hansen.** This fashionable establishment is in the basement of the 19th-

MEDITERRANEAN century Vienna Stock Exchange and shares an enormous space with the flower shop Lederleitner. The chef creates a new menu of Mediterranean specialties each week. **Known for:** weekly changing menu; excellent Sunday brunch; superb contemporary art. $ *Average main: €25* ⊠ *Wipplingerstrasse 34, 1st District* ☎ *01/532–0542* ⊕ *www.hansen.co.at/en/restaurant* ☉ *Closed Sun. No dinner Sat.* Ⓜ *U2/Schottenring.*

$ ✕ **Melker Stiftskeller.** Down and down you go, into one of the friendliest

WINE BAR cellars in town, where *Stelze* (roast pork) is a popular feature, along with outstanding regional wines—Grüner Veltliner among them—by the glass or, rather, mug. This was originally the storehouse for wines from the Melk Abbey in the Danube Valley and dates from 1438, but was rebuilt in the 18th century. **Known for:** fantastic wine cellar; several centuries of history; roast pork and other Austrian classics. $ *Average main: €17* ⊠ *Schottengasse 3, 1st District* ☎ *01/533–5530* ⊕ *www.melkerstiftskeller.at* ☉ *Closed Sun. and Mon. No lunch* Ⓜ *U2/Schottentor.*

$$$ ✕ **Vestibül.** Attached to the Burgtheater, this was once the carriage ves-

AUSTRIAN tibule of the emperor's court theater. Today, the dining room is full of splendor and a menu that changes frequently, but diners can expect the best from one of Austria's most celebrated chefs. **Known for:** frequently changing menu; welcoming and friendly chef; Hummerkrautfleisch, a cabbage and lobster dish. $ *Average main: €30* ⊠ *Universitätsring 2, 1st District* ☎ *01/532–49–99–10* ⊕ *www.vestibuel.at* ☉ *Closed Sun. and 3 wks in Aug. No lunch Sat.* Ⓜ *Tram: 1 or 2.*

## EAST OF THE RINGSTRASSE: STADTPARK AND KARLSPLATZ

$ ✕ **Gasthaus Wild.** The best place for a bite near the Kunsthaus Wien and

AUSTRIAN the Hundertwasser House is Gasthaus Wild. Formerly a wine tavern, it's now a down-to-earth beisl (the equivalent of a pub, also called a *gasthaus*), where the menu changes regularly but almost always features local dishes. **Known for:** wild game when in season; great wine list; extensive dessert menu. $ *Average main: €15* ⊠ *Radetzkyplatz 1, 3rd District/Landstrasse* ☎ *01/920–9477* ⊕ *www.gasthaus-wild.at* Ⓜ *Tram: O/Radetzkyplatz.*

$ ✕ **Gmoa Keller.** One of the friendliest places in Vienna, this wonderful

AUSTRIAN old cellar—just across the street from the Konzert Haus—offers some of the heartiest home cooking in town. Come here to enjoy dishes that hail from Carinthia, one of the best being the *Kas'nudeln* (potatoes and spinach pasta filled with cheese and onion), best served with green leaf salad. **Known for:** dishes from the Carinthia region of the country; cozy and gregarious atmosphere. [$] *Average main: €12* ✉ *Am Heumarkt 25, 3rd District/Landstrasse* ☎ *01/712–5310* 🌐 *www.gmoakeller.at* ⏲ *Closed Sun.* [M] *U4/Stadtpark.*

$ AUSTRIAN 🍴 **Joseph Genuss.** Each morning, the bread here is baked fresh—kneaded by hand—using what the owners call an ancient recipe that uses only organic ingredients. All of the breads are whole grain, and include varieties such as honey lavender, sourdough walnut, and sourdough pumpkinseed. **Known for:** amazing flavors of bread including honey lavender and sourdough walnut; Old World–meets-contemporary ambience; ancient bread recipe. [$] *Average main: €6* ✉ *Landstrasser-Hauptstrasse 4, 3rd District/Landstrasse* ☎ *1710–2881* 🌐 *www.joseph.co.at.*

$$$ AUSTRIAN 🍴 **Salon Plafond in MAK.** Within the Museum of Applied Arts (MAK), you'll find this restaurant that offers fresh, locally grown fare. Everything is either made on-site or commissioned from independent local enterprises. **Known for:** fresh and locally grown cuisine; large terrace overlooking green space. [$] *Average main: €25* ✉ *Museum of Applied Arts, Stubenring 5, 1st District* ☎ *01/226–0046* 🌐 *www.salonplafond.wien* [M] *U3/Stubentor.*

$$$$ AUSTRIAN Fodor's Choice ★ 🍴 **Steirereck im Stadtpark.** Considered one of the world's 50 best restaurants, this eatery is definitely the most raved-about place in Austria. Winning dishes include delicate wild boar's head with "purple haze" carrots, turbot in an avocado crust, or char in beeswax, yellow turnips, and cream. **Known for:** buzzy dishes using herbs from on-site rooftop garden; the more casual Meierei on the lower floor; selection of more than 120 cheeses. [$] *Average main: €65* ✉ *Stadtpark, Am Heumarkt 2A, 3rd District/Landstrasse* ☎ *01/713–3168* 🌐 *steirereck.at* ⏲ *Closed weekends* [M] *U4/Stadtpark.*

## SOUTH OF THE RINGSTRASSE: THE MUSEUMSQUARTIER

$ AUSTRIAN 🍴 **Amerlingbeisl.** If you're lucky, you can snag a table in the idyllic garden of this low-key pub, hidden away inside a delightful Biedermeyer cobbled courtyard. The staff is young, hip, and carefee, and will gladly serve you breakfast—both traditional Viennese-style and vegetarian—until 3 pm. **Known for:** hip and young crowds; large breakfast buffet on Sunday; weekly cocktail specials. [$] *Average main: €12* ✉ *Stiftgasse 8, 7th District/Neubau* ☎ *1/526–1660.*

$ CAFÉ Fodor's Choice ★ 🍴 **Cafe Sperl.** Coffee in Vienna is designed to be savored and enjoyed, and one of the most splendid places in Vienna to do just that is at the Sperl. Featured in Hollywood films *A Dangerous Method* and *Before Sunrise,* the venerable café—commandeered way back when as the café for artists—is more than just a fantastically pretty face. **Known for:** the go-to café for artists; live music on Sunday; great people-watching at the window tables. [$] *Average main: €12* ✉ *Gumpendorferstrasse 11, 6th District/Mariahilf* ☎ *01/586–4158* 🌐 *www.cafesperl.at* ⏲ *Closed Sun. in July and Aug.*

$ INTERNATIONAL FAMILY 🍴 **Corns 'n Pops.** This breakfast nook—which also offers takeout—serves up an abundance of healthy cold cereal, or "muesli," which can be topped with fresh fruit. Bagels (still a rarity in Vienna) are also available, as are various hot breakfasts including scrambled eggs with tomatoes and feta cheese. **Known for:** great breakfasts, including the rare Vienna bagel; pastas and salads for lunch; trendy, diner-esque decor. [$] *Average main: €7* ✉ *Gumpendorferstrasse 37, 2nd District/Leopoldstadt* ☎ *664/131–2005* 🌐 *www.cornsnpops.com* 🕒 *Closed Sun.*

$ INTERNATIONAL

✕ **Do-An.** This bustling restaurant in a stall along the Naschmarkt is a prime place to stop for a bite and watch the crowds go by. The menu is as diverse as the customers, and includes various Turkish mainstays, such as tzatziki and falafel, and a variety of international choices. **Known for:** mostly Turkish cuisine, including falafel and tzatziki; fun market atmosphere; affordable prices. [$] *Average main: €10* ✉ *Naschmarkt Stand 412–415, 6th District/Mariahilf* ☎ *01/585–8253* 🌐 *www.doan.at.*

$ AUSTRIAN

✕ **Phil's Coffeeshop.** Cozy yet vast, this place near the Naschmarkt bucks the trend of the grand, old-school Vienna coffeehouses and becomes a café, shop, and salon all in one. Inside you'll find shelves with a constant rotation of books, DVDs, and vinyl records, all for sale. **Known for:** unique take on the Vienna coffeehouse; everything from books to furniture available to buy; evening lectures and films. [$] *Average main: €7* ✉ *Gumpendorferstrasse 10* ☎ *1/581–0489* 🌐 *www.phil.info.*

## WEST OF THE RINGSTRASSE: PARLIAMENT AND CITY HALL

$$$$ INTERNATIONAL Fodor's Choice ★

✕ **Restaurant Edvard.** This gourmet establishment at the Palais Hansen Kempinski Hotel earned a Michelin star within months after opening. Now chef Norman Etzold has taken over the kitchen, continuing to prepare masterpieces for Vienna diners. **Known for:** three-course dinners served family-style and prepared tableside by the chef; daily afternoon teas; plenty of local patrons. [$] *Average main: €50* ✉ *Schottenring 24, 1st District* ☎ *01/2361000* 🌐 *www.kempinski.com* 🕒 *Closed Sun. and Mon.*

$$$$ ASIAN FUSION

✕ **Restaurant Kim.** Since establishing herself as Austria's most inventive Asian chef, Korean-born Sohyi Kim continues to impress with her celebrated Asian-fusion cuisine. Every night, she dreams up "lite surprise" lunches for her guests, and 10-course "full surprise" dinners; yes, that means diners have no idea what exactly they are going to get. **Known for:** surprise full-course dinners and lunches featuring Asian-fusion dishes; reservations needed weeks in advance; small, intimate space. [$] *Average main: €70* ✉ *Währinger Strasse 46, 9th District/Alsergrund* ☎ *0664/4258866* 🌐 *www.kim.wien* 🕒 *Closed Sun.–Tues.* [M] *U6 Währinger Straße-Volksoper.*

## OUTSIDE THE CITY CENTER

$$ AUSTRIAN FAMILY

✕ **Mayer am Pfarrplatz.** Heiligenstadt is home to this *heurige* in one of Beethoven's former abodes; he composed his 6th Symphony, as well as parts of his 9th Symphony ("Ode to Joy") while staying in this part of town. The à la carte offerings and buffet are plentiful, and include traditional Viennese dishes, such as Wiener schnitzel and Tafelspitz (with roasted chive potatoes). **Known for:** generous buffet of regional Austrian classics; Beethoven history; great

CLOSE UP

# Wine in Vienna

For a memorable experience, sit at the edge of a vineyard in the outskirts of the city with a tankard of young white wine and listen to the *Schrammel* quartet playing sentimental Viennese songs. The wine taverns in this region sprang up in 1784 when Josef II decreed that owners of vineyards could establish their own private wine taverns, with the provision that the vintners rotate their opening times among them; soon the Viennese discovered it was cheaper to go out to the wine than to bring it inside the city walls, where taxes were levied.

These taverns in the wine-growing districts vary from the simple front room of a vintner's house to ornate settings. Named after the "new" wine, the true *Heurige* is open for only a few weeks a year to allow vintners to sell a certain quantity of their production, tax-free, when consumed on their own premises. The choice is usually between a "new" and an "old" wine, but you can also ask for a milder or sharper wine according to your taste. Most *Heurigen* are happy to let you sample the wines before you order. You can also order a *Gespritzter*, half wine and half soda water. If you visit in the fall, be sure to order a glass of *Sturm*, a cloudy drink halfway between grape juice and wine, with a delicious yeasty fizz. Don't be fooled by its sweetness; it goes right to your head.

Tourist traps still abound in Grinzing, where for years busloads descended on the picturesque wine village on Vienna's outskirts to drink new wine, but there are also worthy Heurigen destinations in Stammersdorf, Sievering, Nussdorf, or Neustift. And these days you can usually find fine dinners to accompany the excellent wine.

3

wine. $ *Average main: €19* ⊠ *Pfarrplatz 2, 19th District/Döbling* 🕾 *01/370–7373* ⊕ *www.pfarrplatz.at* ☉ *No lunch weekdays* Ⓜ *Tram: D/Nussdorf from the Ring.*

$ ✕ **Weinhof Zimmermann.** A winding walk up a tree-lined lane brings

AUSTRIAN you to the garden of one of the city's most well-known heuriger. Here

**Fodor's** Choice you will find one of the finest, most peaceful views around along with

★ specialty wine like the Grüner Veltliner. **Known for:** buffet of traditional dishes, including schnitzel and strudels; excellent Austrian wines in a cozy space; great views of both the countryside and city. $ *Average main: €14* ⊠ *Mitterwurzergasse 20, 19th District/Döbling* 🕾 *01/440– 1207* ⊕ *www.weinhof-zimmermann.at* ☉ *Closed Mon. and Nov.–mid-Mar.* Ⓜ *U2/Schottentor; Tram: 38/Grinzing.*

$ ✕ **Wieninger.** The driving force behind the WienWein group, pioneer

WINE BAR Fritz Wieninger is a masterful vintner. He exports to the United States and elsewhere, but luckily there are some bottles left to be savored in this pleasant, tree-shaded inner courtyard and tavern. **Known for:** biodynamic wines; contemporary fare; standard heurige atmosphere. $ *Average main: €14* ⊠ *Stammersdorferstrasse 78, 21st District/Floridsdorf* 🕾 *01/290–1012* ⊕ *www.wieninger.at* ☉ *Closed late Dec.–Apr. No lunch Thurs. and Fri.* Ⓜ *U2, U4/Schottenring; Tram: 31/Stammersdorf.*

$ AUSTRIAN FAMILY 🍴 **Wolff.** In the heart of the vine village of Neustift am Walde, this inn dating from 1609 sticks to tradition. The selection of white wine includes Grüner Veltliner, Riesling, and Chardonnay, and reds of Blauburger and Zweigelt. **Known for:** historical wine tavern; traditional Viennese dishes; hosted weekly singalongs. [$] *Average main: €14* ✉ *Rathstrasse 44–46, 19th District/Döbling* ☎ *01/440–2335* 🌐 *www.wienerheuriger.at* [M] *U4/U6/Spittelau; Bus: 35A/Neustift am Walde.*

# WHERE TO STAY

Updated by
Jacy Meyer

The luxury hotel market has surged in Vienna in recent years, bringing top rivals to the revered landmark lodgings that have dominated the city for well over a century. The grand old five-star dames of the Ringstrasse still stand supreme with their gilt mirrors, red velvet, and crystal-chandelier opulence. The service, as ever, tends toward impeccable, bringing to mind the valets who served the medley of Imperial Highnesses who once lived in these palaces.

For those with more modest requirements and purses, ample rooms are available in less costly but no less alluring hotels. A number of new hotels have opened in this category as well, making for an array of affordable and enticing choices.

Our lower-price options offer the best in location, value, and, in many instances, a quaint echo of Alt Wien (Old Vienna) atmosphere.

If you have only a short time to spend in Vienna, you'll probably choose to stay in the inner city (the 1st District, or 1010 postal code), to be within walking distance of the most important sights, restaurants, and shops. Outside the 1st District, though, there are many other delightful neighborhoods in which to rest your head. The "Biedermeier" quarter of Spittelberg, in the 7th District of Neubau, has cobblestone streets, rows of 19th-century houses, a wonderful array of art galleries and restaurants, and, increasingly, some good hotel options. Just to its east is the fabulous MuseumsQuartier, an area that has some very nice hotel finds. Schwedenplatz is the area fronted by the Danube Canal—a neighborhood that is one of the most happening in the city, although just a stroll from the centuries-old lanes around Fleischmarkt. Other sweet hotel options can be found in the 8th District of Josefstadt, an area noted for antiques shops, good local restaurants, bars, and theater.

Because of the Christmas markets, the weeks leading up to the holidays are a popular time to visit, as is the week around New Year's (*Silvester*), with its orchestral concerts. Expect to pay accordingly, and, at the very top hotels, a lot (around €300–€600 a night). Summer months are not as busy, perhaps because the opera is not in season. You'll find good bargains at this time of year, especially in August. Vienna also hosts a number of conventions in April, May, and September, causing hotel prices to rise and vacancy rates to drop. Air-conditioning is customary in the top-category hotels only, so don't be surprised if you have to do without. On the plus side, nights are generally cool.

# PLANNING

Where should you stay? With hundreds of Vienna hotels, it may seem like a daunting question. But fret not—our expert writers and editors have done most of the legwork. The selections here represent the best the city has to offer—from the best budget B&Bs to the sleekest boutique hotels.

## RESERVATIONS

Hotel reservations are a necessity—rooms fill up quickly, so book as far in advance as possible. WienTourismus (⊕ *www.wien.info/en/travel-info*), the Viennese Tourist Board, lets you reserve accommodations in all categories online.

## FACILITIES

Unless otherwise noted in individual descriptions, all the hotels listed have private baths, central heating, and private phones. All hotels have Wi-Fi and most have phones with voice mail.

Bringing a car to Vienna can be a headache unless your hotel provides free parking. Considering the city's parking restrictions and the intricate web of one-way streets, it makes more sense to rely on public transportation.

## WITH KIDS

Many hotels offer free stays for kids under 12, but make sure to inquire when making reservations. In the listings, look for the family icon, which indicates a property that we recommend for when you're traveling with children.

## DISCOUNTS AND DEALS

When booking, remember first to ask about discounts and packages. Even the most expensive properties regularly reduce their rates during low-season lulls and on weekends. If you're a member of a group (senior citizen, student, auto club, or the military), you may also get a deal.

■TIP→ **Vienna hotels are very proactive about encouraging guests to book on their websites, with many promising the best rates as well as offering little extras like a welcome drink or free breakfast.**

## COSTS

The lodgings we list are the cream of the crop in each price category. Properties are assigned price categories based on the price of a standard double room during high season, which in Vienna runs from September to June, when the Staatsoper is in season.

| WHAT IT COSTS IN EUROS | | | |
|---|---|---|---|
| $ | $$ | $$$ | $$$$ |
| FOR TWO PEOPLE | under €120 | €120–€170 | €171–€270 | over €270 |

Hotel prices are the average cost of a stanard double room in high season.

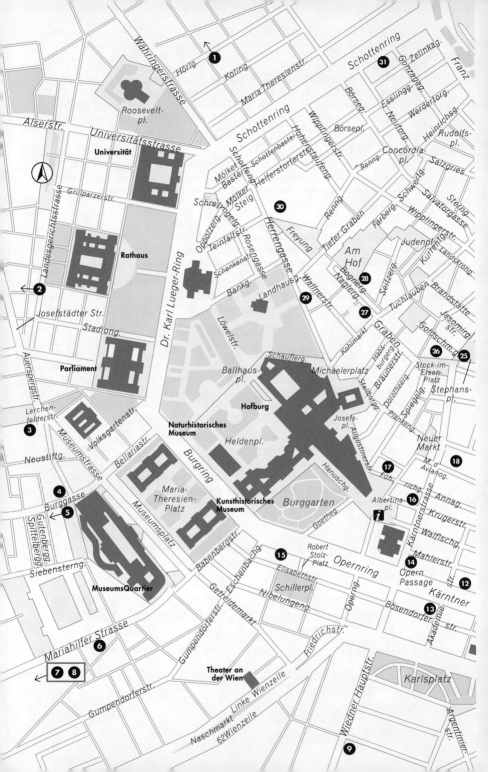

# Where to Stay in Vienna

KEY

🛈 Tourist Information

# HOTEL REVIEWS

*Listed alphabetically within neighborhoods. Hotel reviews have been shortened. For more information, visit Fodors.com.*

## THE EASTERN CITY CENTER: STEPHANSDOM AND MEDIEVAL VIENNA

$$$ HOTEL 🏨 **Ambassador.** Franz Lehár, Marlene Dietrich, the Infanta Isabel of Spain, and Mick Jagger are just a few of the celebrities who have stayed at this old dowager (from 1866). **Pros:** good value for location; great area for shopaholics and casino lovers; apartments available. **Cons:** very busy neighborhood; rooms feel outdated; elevator doesn't reach all floors. [$] *Rooms from: €225* ✉ *Kärntner Strasse 22, 1st District* ☎ *01/961–610* 🌐 *www.ambassador.at* 🛏 *89 rooms.*

$$$ HOTEL 🏨 **Grand Hotel Wien.** With one of the great locations on the Ringstrasse, just across from the Musikverein and a minute on foot from the Staatsoper, the Grand oozes old-world splendor. **Pros:** three superb restaurants; good shopping next door; larger-than-average rooms. **Cons:** desk staff can seem haughty; check-in can be slow; some rooms could use freshening up. [$] *Rooms from: €215* ✉ *Kärntner Ring 9, 1st District* ☎ *01/515–800* 🌐 *www.grandhotelwien.com* 🛏 *205 rooms.*

$$$ HOTEL 🏨 **Hollmann Beletage.** Tucked away in the center of town just a short walk from the cathedral, this intimate boutique hotel has a quiet but convenient location. **Pros:** in the heart of the city; marvelous staff; great breakfast. **Cons:** hotel entrance is hard to find; no restaurant; no views. [$] *Rooms from: €189* ✉ *Köllnerhofgasse 6, 1st District* ☎ *01/961–1960* 🌐 *www.hollmann-beletage.at* 🛏 *26 rooms* 🍴 *Breakfast.*

$$$ HOTEL Fodor's Choice ★ 🏨 **Hotel Lamée.** Guests here are transported back to the 1930s Vienna of the imagination, a glamorous center for café culture that longed to be the European Hollywood. **Pros:** very friendly staff; triple-glazing keeps street noise at street level; great rooftop bar. **Cons:** not all rooms have cathedral views; busy due to popular café and bar; area can be noisy at night. [$] *Rooms from: €215* ✉ *Lichtensteg 2, 1st District* ☎ *01/532–2240* 🌐 *hotellamee.com* 🛏 *32 rooms.*

$$$ HOTEL 🏨 **König von Ungarn.** In a 16th-century house in the shadow of St. Stephen's Cathedral, this dormered hotel began catering to court nobility in 1746 and today lets you choose between "classicism" and "designer" rooms. **Pros:** staff very helpful, accommodating, and friendly; charming hotel with a great location; nice restaurant. **Cons:** a tad old-fashioned; tour buses pass regularly; some rooms may feel cramped. [$] *Rooms from: €235* ✉ *Schulerstrasse 10, 1st District* ☎ *01/515–840* 🌐 *www.kvu.at* 🛏 *44 rooms.*

$$$$ HOTEL 🏨 **Palais Coburg.** In this 19th-century regal residence, the lobby is sleek white stone and plate glass, embodying the hotel's philosophy of "preserving the past—shaping the future." Suites are in modern or imperial style, and many of them are spectacular, two-story showpieces, the best done in gilded-yellow Biedermeier or Empire style. **Pros:** luxurious atmosphere; Michelin-starred restaurant; wine cellar. **Cons:** interior design can feel a bit over the top; pricey room rates; not in the center. [$] *Rooms from: €695* ✉ *Coburgbastei 4, 1st District* ☎ *01/518–180* 🌐 *www.palais-coburg.com* 🛏 *33 rooms.*

$$$ HOTEL 🏨 **Pension Nossek.** A family-run establishment on the upper floors of a 19th-century apartment building, the Nossek lies at the heart of Vienna's pedestrian and shopping area. **Pros:** perfect location; family oriented; friendly staff. **Cons:** a little drab in appearance; entrance can be hard to find; street is noisy with the windows open. [$] *Rooms from: €175* ✉ *Graben 17, 1st District* ☎ *01/533–704–111* 🌐 *www.pension-nossek.at* 🛏 *31 rooms* 🍴 *Breakfast.*

$ HOTEL 🏨 **Ruby Lissi.** Thanks to the rather stark decor, you may feel like you're going to the office, but all visions of work will be forgotten when you enter the wide-open breakfast-lounge-bar space; there's no formal reception area, just a self-check-in spot. **Pros:** great location with good restaurants and nightlife nearby; interesting design mix of retro and modern; music lovers can rent a guitar and jam on their own in-room Marshall box. **Cons:** the unembellished white rooms can seem cold; there's no restaurant, but the well-regarded Kendys is in the same building; basic rooms are on the small side. [$] *Rooms from: €104* ✉ *Fleischmarkt 19, 1st District* ☎ *01/205–551–80* 🌐 *www.ruby-hotels.com* 🛏 *107 rooms.*

$$$ HOTEL Fodor's Choice ★ 🏨 **Topazz.** The Topazz is an extraordinary homage to the Wiener Werkstätte style that took Vienna by storm in the early 1900s. **Pros:** a designer's dream; "green" sustainability is the rule here; oval window seats in rooms with oval windows. **Cons:** some rooms on the snug side; street can be noisy at night; no restaurant on-site. [$] *Rooms from: €259* ✉ *Lichtensteg 3, 1st District* ☎ *01/532–2250* 🌐 *www.hoteltopazz.com* 🛏 *32 rooms.*

## THE INNER CITY CENTER

$$$ HOTEL 🏨 **Am Stephansplatz.** You aren't likely to find a better location than this serene hotel, which sits directly across from the front entrance of St. Stephen's Cathedral. **Pros:** top location; great breakfast-bar views; excellent staff. **Cons:** busy location; noisy area at night; not very local. [$] *Rooms from: €239* ✉ *Stephansplatz 9, 1st District* ☎ *01/534–050* 🌐 *www.hotelamstephansplatz.at* 🛏 *56 rooms* 🍴 *Breakfast.*

$$$$ HOTEL 🏨 **Bristol.** For those wanting an Old Austria feel with modern conveniences, look no further than the Bristol. **Pros:** across the street from the Staatsoper; service is impeccable; historic charm. **Cons:** location is very busy; some rooms could use a redo; period style may not be to everyone's tastes. [$] *Rooms from: €300* ✉ *Kärntner Ring 1, 1st District* ☎ *01/515–160* 🌐 *www.bristolvienna.com* 🛏 *150 rooms.*

$$$ HOTEL 🏨 **Do&Co.** Inside the glass-and-stone Haas House, which reflects St. Stephen's Cathedral in its facade, you'll discover this unique boutique hotel. **Pros:** elegant ambience; most lavish breakfast in town; well-stocked minibar. **Cons:** glass walls in bathroom might bother more modest guests; hotel is in a pedestrian-only zone so can be a hassle with a car; staff sometimes isn't the most friendly. [$] *Rooms from: €269* ✉ *Stephansplatz 12, 1st District* ☎ *01/241–880* 🌐 *www.doco.com* 🛏 *43 rooms.*

4

$$$
HOTEL
Fodor's Choice
★

**The Guesthouse.** Smack behind the Albertina and the Staatsoper, this authentically Austrian boutique hotel is an absolutely delightful addition to the Vienna lodging scene, with fabulous views of the heart of the Innere Stadt. **Pros:** peaceful, invigorating atmosphere; staff is top-notch; pet-friendly. **Cons:** standard rooms are a tad small; parking in the area is difficult; busy area. *$ Rooms from: €255 ⊠ Fuehrichgasse 10-a, 1st District ☎ 01/512–1320 ⊕ www.theguesthouse.at ↝ 39 rooms.*

$$$$
HOTEL
FAMILY
Fodor's Choice
★

**Hotel Sacher.** One of Europe's legends, originally founded by Franz Sacher, chef to Prince Metternich—for whom the famous chocolate cake was invented—this hotel dates from 1876 but has delightfully retained its old-world atmosphere-mit-Schlag while also providing luxurious, modern-day comfort. **Pros:** special Sacher Kids' program; location directly behind the Opera House could hardly be more central; ratio of staff to guests is more than two to one. **Cons:** cramped elevator; located on a very busy street; popular dining options mean public areas aren't always restful. *$ Rooms from: €535 ⊠ Philharmonikerstrasse 4, 1st District ☎ 01/514–560 ⊕ www.sacher.com ↝ 149 rooms.*

$$$$
HOTEL
Fodor's Choice
★

**Palais Hansen Kempinski Vienna.** This Renaissance Revival–style structure, built in 1873 as an exhibition hall, was transformed 140 years later into a luxe hotel, which pays homage to the grand beginnings while also incorporating modern-day amenities. **Pros:** extensive spa; historic site; central location. **Cons:** posh prices; breakfast can lack variety; some staff can seem dismissive. *$ Rooms from: €350 ⊠ Schottenring 24, 1st District ☎ 01/236–1000 ⊕ www.kempinski.com/en/ vienna/palais-hansen ↝ 152 rooms.*

$$$
HOTEL
Fodor's Choice
★

**Radisson Blu Style Hotel.** Behind the hotel's Art Nouveau facade, London interior designer Maria Vafiadis has paid tribute to Viennese Art Deco, and the result is überstylish yet comfortable. **Pros:** design lovers will love the look; central location; quiet area of old city. **Cons:** small reception area (with oddly low reception desks); not all room rates include breakfast; staff can sometimes seem unaccommodating. *$ Rooms from: €220 ⊠ Herrengasse 12, 1st District ☎ 01/227–803–214 ⊕ www.radissonblu.com/stylehotel-vienna ↝ 78 rooms.*

## ACROSS THE DANUBE: THE SECOND DISTRICT

$
HOTEL
FAMILY

**Meininger Hotel Vienna Downtown Franz.** Brother hotel to its sister "Sissi"—six blocks away—this member of the Meininger budget hotel chain offers the same hip style and out-for-fun clientele, but has room rates that are slightly higher (these can be bargained lower, depending on daily availability). **Pros:** rare underground parking on-site; options for family or group travel; easy to make new friends. **Cons:** not a very quiet or peaceful atmosphere; with no air-conditioning, rooms can be very hot in summer; depending on dates there is a minimum stay. *$ Rooms from: €110 ⊠ Rembrandtstrasse 21, 2nd District/Leopoldstadt ☎ 01/720–882–065 ⊕ www.meininger-hotels.com/en/hotels/ vienna/downtown-franz/ ↝ 131 rooms.*

$
HOTEL
FAMILY

**Meininger Hotel Vienna Downtown Sissi.** Part of the popular Meininger chain of budget hotels, this was the first of three to open in Vienna, all offering hip design, plugged-in clientele, and some of the best deals in town. **Pros:** kitchen available to guests; decent breakfast bar; sociable atmosphere. **Cons:** only one elevator; 15-minute walk to city center; no air-conditioning. $ *Rooms from: €100* ✉ *Schiffamtsgasse 15, 2nd District/Leopoldstadt* ☎ *01/720–882–066* ⊕ *www.meininger-hotels. com/en/hotels/vienna/downtown-sissi/* ⇆ *102 rooms.*

**$**
**B&B/INN**
🏠 **The Rooms.** With no two rooms alike, this tranquil, tiny guesthouse north of the Danube—it's in the 22nd District, beyond the 2nd District on the U1 metro line—exudes an exotic aura, and the charming, friendly, and ever-so-helpful owners are ready to assist when needed. **Pros:** excellent breakfast; friendly vibe; beautiful hospitality. **Cons:** outside center; accomodations differ greatly in size; no real public spaces. $ *Rooms from: €110* ✉ *Schlenthergasse 17, 22nd District/ Donaustadt* ☎ *01/664–431–6830* ⊕ *www.therooms.at* ⇆ *4 rooms* ⦿ *Breakfast* Ⓜ *U1/Kagran.*

**$$$**
**HOTEL**
**Fodor's Choice**
★
🏠 **Sofitel Vienna Stephansdom.** Minimalist luxury can be a contradiction, but at the Sofitel it's pulled off with supreme elegance, and here, on the border of the 2nd District, it's paired with outstanding city skyline views. **Pros:** outstanding views; incredible restaurant; amazing spa. **Cons:** monochromatic palate can feel cold to some; deep bathtubs could be difficult to maneuver; some rooms could use freshening up. $ *Rooms from: €255* ✉ *Praterstrasse 1, 2nd District/Leopoldstadt* ☎ *01/906–160* ⊕ *www.sofitel.com/Vienna* ⇆ *182 rooms* Ⓜ *U4 or U1/Schwedenplatz.*

**4**

# THE WESTERN CITY CENTER: BURGTHEATER AND BEYOND

**$$$**
**B&B/INN**
🏠 **Benediktushaus.** You can stay in this guesthouse of a monastery, in the heart of Vienna, without following the dictum *ora et labora* (pray and work), though you will get to see how the monks live by the credo. **Pros:** superb location; good value; excellent breakfast spread. **Cons:** reception hours limited; church bells start ringing early; no air-conditioning. $ *Rooms from: €180* ✉ *Freyung 6a, 1st District* ☎ *01/534–989–00* ⊕ *www.benediktushaus.at* ⇆ *21 rooms* ⦿ *Breakfast.*

**$$$**
**HOTEL**
**FAMILY**
🏠 **Harmonie.** Located on a quiet street in Vienna's Serviten quarter, the peaceful Harmonie has a dancing concept designed by Peruvian artist Luis Casanova Sorolla that begins with dance performances shown on a flat-screen TV at reception. **Pros:** tea is served free every day from 3 pm; excellent breakfast; small fitness area. **Cons:** not in the center; residential area might not appeal to everyone; no restaurant in the hotel. $ *Rooms from: €200* ✉ *Harmoniegasse 5–7, 9th District/Alsergrund* ☎ *01/317–6604* ⊕ *www.harmonie-vienna.at* ⇆ *66 rooms* ⦿ *Breakfast.*

**$$$$**
**HOTEL**
🏠 **Park Hyatt.** Much care was taken to preserve the integrity and historical significance of the elegant building that houses one of Vienna's newer luxury hotels. **Pros:** fabulous ambience; remarkable location; excellent fitness area. **Cons:** restaurant staff can be off-putting; concierge advice hit-or-miss; any room issues may not be resolved quickly. $ *Rooms from: €520* ✉ *Am Hof 2, 1st District* ☎ *01/227–401–234* ⊕ *www.vienna.park.hyatt.com* ⇆ *178 rooms.*

## EAST OF THE RINGSTRASSE: STADTPARK AND KARLSPLATZ

$$$ HOTEL [H] **Das Triest.** Transformed by Sir Terence Conran into an ultrasleek ocean liner, this design hotel was once a postal-coach station on the route between Vienna and the Italian port city of Trieste; the original cross vaulting remains in the lounges and in some suites. **Pros:** lovely courtyard garden; famed bar; decent breakfast. **Cons:** not all rooms have air-conditioning; street-facing rooms may be noisy due to trams; street not very attractive. [$] *Rooms from: €200* ✉ *Wiedner Hauptstrasse 12, 4th District/Wieden* ☎ *01/589–180* 🌐 *www.dastriest.at* 🛏 *72 rooms.*

$$ HOTEL [H] **Hotel Daniel.** For a decidedly unchainlike hotel experience, try the urban Daniel, which is decked out in industrial decor and puts the shower right in the room (the toilet has a separate space.) The hotel is good for those who like a casual vibe and minimalistic look. **Pros:** excellent access to the Belvedere; popular restaurant serving all day; Vespas and bicycles available to rent. **Cons:** no closet: just a bench for your luggage; not in the center; may not be best for those looking for a high level of service. [$] *Rooms from: €160* ✉ *Landstrasser Gürtel 5, 3rd District/Landstrasse* ☎ *01/901–310* 🌐 *www.hoteldaniel.com* 🛏 *116 rooms.*

$$$$ HOTEL [H] **Hotel Imperial.** One of the landmarks of the Ringstrasse, this hotel has exemplified the grandeur of imperial Vienna ever since it was built. **Pros:** discreet, unpretentious staff; excellent restaurant and café; palatial. **Cons:** some rooms are on the small side; bathrooms can be tiny; restaurant and bar staff sometimes seem untrained. [$] *Rooms from: €399* ✉ *Kärntner Ring 16, 1st District* ☎ *01/501–100* 🌐 *www.luxurycollection.com/imperial* 🛏 *128 rooms.*

$$$ HOTEL [H] **The Ring.** Following the trend toward smaller boutique properties, this luxury lodging takes its place alongside some of Vienna's opulent grand hotels. **Pros:** helpful staff; most rooms well sized; casual ambience, but luxurious treatment. **Cons:** breakfast isn't the best value; Wi-Fi can be slow; trams frequently thunder around the block. [$] *Rooms from: €250* ✉ *Kärntner Ring 8, 1st District* ☎ *01/221–22* 🌐 *www.theringhotel.com* 🛏 *68 rooms.*

$ HOTEL [H] **Schani.** The German word *schani* means "friendly servant," and everything about this relaxed hotel exudes the sociable style of schani. **Pros:** there's a tram stop outside the front door; good for technology lovers; nice for independent workers who like to get out of their room. **Cons:** very residential; no nearby nightlife or restaurants; the shower and sink are separated from the room by a curtain. [$] *Rooms from: €100* ✉ *Karl-Popper-Strasse 22, 10th District/Favoriten* ☎ *01/955–0715* 🌐 *www.hotelschani.com* 🛏 *135 rooms.*

$$ B&B/INN Fodor's Choice ★ [H] **Spiess & Spiess.** Considered by many to be the best B&B in Vienna, this small, family-run inn offers comfortable, spacious, and exquisitely furnished rooms. **Pros:** suites great for families; spacious rooms; easy access to public transportation. **Cons:** not in the city center; residential neighborhood lacks the flair of downtown; flight of stairs to climb to reception. [$] *Rooms from: €150* ✉ *Hainburgerstrasse 19, 3rd District/Landstrasse* ☎ *01/714–8505* 🌐 *www.spiess-vienna.at* 🛏 *22 rooms* 🍴 *Breakfast.*

## SOUTH OF THE RINGSTRASSE: THE MUSEUMSQUARTIER

**$$$**
**HOTEL**
⊡ **Altstadt.** When contemporary-arts patron Otto E. Wiesenthal hired premier Italian architect Matteo Thun to revamp this lodging, the results were exquisitely decorated, sensuous chambers oozing atmosphere from the Vienna era of Freud and Klimt. **Pros:** breakfast and afternoon tea included in room rate; amazing private art collection; excellent staff. **Cons:** small reception area; outside the city center; building is not exclusive to the hotel. $ *Rooms from: €175* ⊠ *Kirchengasse 41, 7th District/Neubau* ☎ *01/522–6666* ⊕ *www.altstadt.at* ↩ *45 rooms* ❍❘ *Breakfast.*

**$$$$**
**HOTEL**
⊡ **Das Tyrol.** On a bustling Mariahilferstrasse corner, this small, luxurious hotel is a good choice for those who want to be next door to the MuseumsQuartier and near some fun shopping, too. **Pros:** plentiful breakfast; good location for shoppers; lots to see for art lovers. **Cons:** rooms differ greatly in size; busy street not so attractive; no restaurant. $ *Rooms from: €295* ⊠ *Mariahilferstrasse 15, 6th District/Mariahilf* ☎ *01/587–5415* ⊕ *www.das-tyrol.at* ↩ *30 rooms* ❍❘ *Breakfast.*

**$**
**HOTEL**
⊡ **Hotel am Brillantengrund.** The eclectic hotel—picture a 1950s theme in a 19th-century building—is a popular hangout for local creatives who mingle seamlessly with guests, making it difficult to distinguish between who's staying and those who come for breakfast or a drink. **Pros:** excellent Filipino restaurant on-site; local feel; characterful and charming design. **Cons:** no air-conditioning; minimal toiletries; small bathrooms. $ *Rooms from: €99* ⊠ *Bandgasse 4, 7th District/Neubau* ☎ *01/523–3662* ⊕ *www.brillantengrund.com* ↩ *35 rooms.*

**$$$**
**HOTEL**
⊡ **Le Méridien Vienna.** The supercool "art and tech" lobby here, adorned with Mies van der Rohe–style sofas and ottomans and nouvelle fluorescent-light panels, is a fine introduction to a stylish and pampering stay in the heart of the city. **Pros:** next door to the museums; complimentary minibar; great shower. **Cons:** lacks "Vienna" character; housekeeping can be erratic; the popular bar can be disruptive. $ *Rooms from: €205* ⊠ *Robert-Stolz-Platz 1, 1st District* ☎ *01/588–900* ⊕ *www.lemeridien-vienna.com* ↩ *294 rooms.*

**$**
**HOTEL**
⊡ **Ruby Marie.** Located just off the lively Mariahilferstrasse, the Ruby Marie is one of three Ruby hotel properties in Vienna. **Pros:** a variety of public spaces; funky vibe; good shopping location. **Cons:** neighborhood isn't relaxing; staff might be too laid-back for some; no separate shower space. $ *Rooms from: €84* ⊠ *Kaiserstrasse 2–4, 7th District/Neubau* ☎ *01/205–639–700* ⊕ *www.ruby-hotels.com* ↩ *186 rooms.*

**$$$**
**HOTEL**
⊡ **Sans Souci Hotel.** Hip trying to outdo hip is the force behind this recent boutique addition to the hotel scene. **Pros:** nice summer terrace; great location near Mariahilferstrasse's trendy shops and within the MuseumsQuartier; wonderful staff. **Cons:** beige-and-wood color schemes are a bit bland; minimum six nights for apartments; rooms on the lower floors may have tram noise. $ *Rooms from: €265* ⊠ *Burggasse 2, 7th District/Neubau* ☎ *01/522–2520* ⊕ *www.sanssouci-wien.com* ↩ *63 rooms* ❍❘ *Breakfast.*

$$$ HOTEL Fodor's Choice ★ 25hours Hotel Wien. A circus theme predominates at this bohemian addition to the city's lodging scene, each room containing exceptionally illustrated wallpaper of old-time big-top themes by German artist Olaf Hajek and quirky vintage furnishings. **Pros:** fun atmosphere; excellent staff; killer views. **Cons:** rooftop area gets overcrowded; may not appeal to those looking for a more conservative stay; standard rooms can feel cramped. [$] *Rooms from: €200* ⊠ *Lerchenfelder Strasse 1–3, 7th District/Neubau* ☎ *01/521–510* ⊕ *www.25hours-hotels.com/hotels/wien/museumsquartier* ⤳ *217 rooms.*

## WEST OF THE RINGSTRASSE: PARLIAMENT AND CITY HALL

$$$ HOTEL Rathaus Wine & Design. The friendliest staff and what might be the best breakfast buffet in town—see to it that your schedule allows you to savor the spread—make this exclusive boutique hotel a worthwhile choice. **Pros:** top-notch staff; unbeatable breakfast (served until 11 weekdays, noon weekends); penthouse has its own terrace—book way ahead. **Cons:** no restaurant; off the tourist track; breakfast isn't included. [$] *Rooms from: €190* ⊠ *Langegasse 13, 8th District/Josefstadt* ☎ *01/400–1122* ⊕ *www.hotel-rathaus-wien.at* ⤳ *39 rooms.*

$$$$ HOTEL Ritz-Carlton. From a Ringstrasse Palace to a Ritz-Carlton, all the fineries you'd expect from the brand are here, including ceiling frescoes and open fireplaces in the poshest of its suites. **Pros:** rooftop terrace is a choice spot to watch the sun set over the city; professional staff; good location. **Cons:** amenities at the club lounge here may not be as good as other Ritz-Carlton's; building's layout sometimes requires random stair climbing; some rooms look a little worn. [$] *Rooms from: €430* ⊠ *Schubertring 5–7, 1st District* ☎ *01/311–88, 01/311–88111* ⊕ *www.ritzcarlton.com/en/hotels/europe/vienna* ⤳ *245 rooms.*

# NIGHTLIFE AND PERFORMING ARTS

Updated
by Patti
McCracken

The arts in Vienna are not just for tourists. Locals enthusiastically partake of their city's rich cultural offerings, and there are many tantalizing choices, so it's always a good idea to plan ahead.

Do you want to time warp back to the 18th century at Mozart concerts featuring bewigged musicians in the opulent surroundings at Schönbrunn Palace? Or perhaps you'd like to cheer the divas at the grandest of grand opera at the Staatsoper, dive into the splendor of an evening concert of Strauss waltzes, or enjoy a trombone troupe at a *Jazzkeller*? Maybe a Baroque opera in a stunning avant-garde setting at the Theater an der Wien (where Beethoven's *Fidelio* premiered in 1805)? The choices are endless during the regular season, which runs from September to June.

But Austria is not only about the classics; it is as proud of Falco as it is of Haydn. In summer, Vienna turns into a festival town. ImPulsTanz for modern dance enthusiasts has a rich variety of performances and venues, and for some the chamber music festival, held amid 18th-century frescoes at the Laudon Water Palace, is too enticing to pass up. The abundance of choices will leave you feeling spoiled. While the upper crust discuss opera singer Anna Netrebko's most recent performance, hipsters will flock to Fluc for some of the city's best live acts.

One word of caution: the city's culture vultures dress for the occasion. Never take your coat inside the theater or the opera. (Vienna's performance halls do have coat checks.)

## PLANNING

### WHAT'S ON NOW?

A monthly printed program, the *Wien-Programm,* distributed by the city tourist board and available at any travel agency or hotel, gives an overview of what's going on in the worlds of opera, concerts, jazz, theater, and galleries, and similar information is posted on billboards and advertising columns around the city.

The film schedules in the daily newspapers *Der Standard* and *Die Presse* list foreign-language film showings; *Der Falter,* a weekly paper issued every Wednesday, publishes a comprehensive listing of events and films, while *OmU* lists showings for films in their original language with German subtitles.

### LATE-NIGHT TRANSPORTATION

During the week, subways and trams run until about midnight. On Friday and Saturday nights, U-Bahn subway lines run 24 hours a day at 15-minute intervals.

### TOP EXPERIENCES

**Catch an avant-garde opera.** Anybody can go to the Staatsoper. Theater an der Wien bills itself as a "new opera house" and lives up to this claim with daring performances of 20th- and 21st-century works.

**Put on your ball gown.** There is no other place on earth where people can live out their Cinderella fantasies in such a spectacular way. The "Ball Season" starts on New Year's Eve and runs up to the start of the Catholic period of Lent (usually the end of February). Don't be surprised if you see people donning fur coats and ball gowns on their extravagant evenings out.

**Enjoy a musical extravaganza.** Over the past three decades, Vienna has garnered a reputation as a top spot for musicals, with local talent bringing Habsburg melodrama alive to the sounds of pop tunes.

**Explore the smaller theaters.** Scan the listings of *Wien Programm* to find performances of kitsch-free Viennese music by Die Strottern at Theater am Spittelberg, or a monologue by Nobel Prize-winner Elfriede Jelinek at Burgtheater's small stage at Kasino am Schwarzenbergplatz.

**Hit the festivals.** Vienna serves as a musical gateway to the East. Get a taste of Eastern European and Middle Eastern music at festivals such as Salam Orient and the annual KlezMore showdown, or attend Europe's largest open-air music festival in June, the Donauinselfest.

## TICKETS

With a city as music mad and opera crazy as Vienna, it's not surprising to learn that the bulk of major performances are sold out in advance, but with thousands of seats to be filled every night, you may luck out.

**Albertinaplatz Tourist Information.** Last-minute tickets for theater, musicals, or cabaret are available on a first-come, first-served basis daily between 2 and 5 inside the main tourist information office on Albertinaplatz. Here the theater-ticket company Jirsa sells same-day tickets for up to half off. Note that it's cash only. ⊠ *Albertinaplatz, corner of Maysedergasse, 1st District.*

**Bundestheaterkassen.** The State Theater Booking Office (Bundestheaterkassen) sells tickets for the Akademietheater, Staatsoper, Volksoper, and Burgtheater. Tickets for the Staatsoper go on sale two months in advance, and Volksoper tickets are available one month before the date of performance. You can visit the box office or call the (frequently busy) phone line, but you can also purchase tickets online, where you have the added advantage of putting your name on the waiting list for "standby" tickets to sold-out performances. ⊠ *Operngasse 2, 1st District* ☎ *01/514–44–7810* ⊕ *www.bundestheater.at.*

# NIGHTLIFE

With its swanky bars and clubs, Vienna is humming with nighttime activity. Teenagers congregate at the Bermuda Triangle south of St. Stephen's Cathedral, while hipsters meet in cafés and bars around MuseumsQuartier and the Naschmarkt. In recent years, the viaducts underneath the U6 subway line between Thaliastrasse and Nussdorferstrasse have been transformed into restaurants, bars, and clubs. A lively bar and club scene has also taken root at the Donaukanal across from Schwedenplatz, and Motto am Fluss is still holding its own against the competition.

## BALLS

Have you ever wondered why Vienna's young people still sway to melodies composed 150 years ago? The city's ball culture is carefully nurtured, and almost everybody between the ages of 16 and 19 attends a dancing school (some even learn to waltz as part of the official high school curriculum). On your strolls through the inner city, peek in at Elmayer's on Bräunerstrasse to see young couples practice the quadrille for the next Carnival extravaganza.

Ever since the 19th-century Congress of Vienna—when pundits joked "The city dances, but it never gets anything done"—Viennese extravagance and gaiety have been world-famous. Fasching, the season of Carnival, was given over to court balls, opera balls, masked balls, chambermaids' and bakers' balls, and a hundred other gatherings, many held within the glittering interiors of Baroque theaters and palaces. Presiding over the dazzling evening gowns and gilt-encrusted uniforms was the baton of the waltz emperor, Johann Strauss. White-gloved women and men in white tie would glide over marble floors to his heavenly melodies. They still do. Now, as in the days of Franz Josef, Vienna's old three-quarter-time rhythm strikes up anew at the stroke of the clock on New Year's Day and continues through Carnival, or Fasching.

During the Ball Season, as many as 40 balls may be held in a single evening. Many events are organized by a professional group, including the Kaiserball (Imperial Ball), Philharmonikerball (Ball of the Philharmonic Orchestra), Kaffeesiederball (Coffee Brewers' Ball), the Zuckerbaeckerball (Confectioners' Ball), or the Opernball (Opera Ball). The latter is the most famous; this event transforms the Vienna Opera House into the world's most beautiful ballroom (and transfixes all of Austria when shown live on national television). The invitation reads *"Frack mit Dekorationen,"* which means that ball gowns and tails are usually required for most events (you can always get your tux from a rental agency) and women mustn't wear white (reserved for debutantes). But there's something for everyone these days, including the "Ball of Bad Taste" or "Wallflower Ball." The zaniest might be the Life Ball, sponsored by a charity raising funds for people with HIV. After your gala evening, finish off the morning with a *Katerfrühstuck*—hangover breakfast—of goulash soup.

Among the 400 balls that are held each winter, the majority are open to the public. Ticket prices vary widely, and can go as high as €600. Starting at 8 or 9 pm, these "full dress" events last until 3 or 4 am.

## BARS, LOUNGES, AND NIGHTCLUBS

Nightlife has blossomed with a profusion of vibrant and sophisticated bars, clubs, and lounges. Many of the trendy people head to the clubs around the Naschmarkt area, then move on to nearby Mariahilferstrasse for dancing. The Freihaus Quarter buzzes with cafés and shops.

Fodor's Choice ★ **Babenberger Passage.** In a former underground walkway between the Hofburg Palace and the Kunsthistorisches Museum, Passage is one of the poshest clubs in Vienna. A state-of-the-art lighting system and futuristic interior come together in a blush-hued bar and a sizzling-blue dance room. Try to spot the celebrities while sipping superbly mixed cocktails. Club, dance, and house music is played nightly. ⊠ *Ringstrasse at Babenbergerstrasse, 1st District* ☎ *01/961–66770* ⊕ *www.club-passage. at* Ⓜ *U2/MuseumsQuartier.*

**Café Carina.** In a cavernous subway station, Café Carina is dazzling in its dinginess. It's offbeat, artistic, and action packed—you get the sense that anything can happen here, from an air-guitar competition to an evening of 1980s hits. On weekends expect it to be packed. It's also one of the few completely nonsmoking venues in the city. ⊠ *Josefstädterstrasse 84 at Stadtbahnbogen, 8th District/Josefstadt* ☎ *01/4064322* ⊕ *www. cafe-carina.at* Ⓜ *U6/Josefstädterstrasse.*

**Johnnys.** Near the Naschmarkt, Johnny's brings a little Irish flair to the area. Good beer, inexpensive meals, quiz nights, and live music make this pub a popular hangout. Note that it's cash only, and often filled with smokers. ⊠ *Schleifmühlgasse 11, 4th District/Wieden* ☎ *01/587– 1921* ⊕ *www.johnnys-pub.at* Ⓜ *U4/Kettenbrückengasse.*

**Motto am Fluss.** In a nod to its location, this hip place resembles a sleek ocean liner gliding down the Danube Canal (the location is also the mooring station for the *Twin City Liner,* which regularly cruises between Vienna and Bratislava). The bar is all glass and chrome, lending it an ultramodern feel. Silver spheres dangle from the ceiling like drops of mercury. The outdoor terrace is the perfect spot to enjoy the breezes off the water. ⊠ *Schwedenplatz 2, 1st District* ☎ *01/25–225–11* ⊕ *www.mottoamfluss.at.*

**Volksgarten Club.** Back in 1870, Viennese used to come to the Volksgarten to waltz, drink champagne, and enjoy the night air in a candlelit garden. Today it's a *diskothek,* where glammed-up locals flock to go clubbing, mostly to house and party music. ⊠ *Burgring 1, 1st District* ☎ *01/532–4241* ⊕ *www.volksgarten.at* Ⓜ *U2/3 MuseumsQuartier.*

## DANCE CLUBS

**Café Leopold.** In the MuseumsQuartier, this café is hidden inside the large, white cube that is the Leopold Museum. Tables are scattered outside on the plaza at night while a regular lineup of DJs spins tunes. ⊠ *Leopold Museum, Museumsplatz 1, 1st District* ☎ *01/522–2391* ⊕ *www.cafeleopold.wien* Ⓜ *U2 or U3/MuseumsQuartier.*

**Club Schikaneder.** In the middle of the Freihaus Quarter, the Schikaneder serves as both an independent, experimental movie theater and a very popular bar filled with the city's artists. It screens one or two films daily (many in English), hosts art exhibits, and offers first-class DJ lineups regularly. ⊠ *Margaretenstrasse 22–24, 4th District/Wieden* ☎ *01/585– 2867* ⊕ *www.schikaneder.at* Ⓜ *U1, U2, or U4/Karlsplatz.*

**Fodor's**Choice **Club U.** "U" stands for underground, and fittingly, Club U is located
★ below one of the two Jugendstil pavilions that Otto Wagner built when designing Vienna's subway. One of the best dance halls for alternative music in the city, it has outdoor seating, live music, a great atmosphere, and excellent DJs who turn this place into a real Soul City most nights. ⊠ *Karlsplatz, Künstlerhauspassage, 1st District* ☎ *01/505–9904* ⊕ *www.club-u.at* Ⓜ *U1, U2, or U4/Karlsplatz.*

**Fluc.** One of the leaders in the resurgence of nightlife in Vienna's 2nd District, the Fluc attracts world-famous DJs, who praise the small venue as one of the best in Europe. It is on the site of a converted passageway, so its thick, soundproof walls mean DJs can max out the volume. ⊠ *Praterstern 5, 2nd District/Leopoldstadt* ☎ *01/218–28–24* ⊕ *www.fluc.at.*

## JAZZ CLUBS

In the last few decades, Austria has produced some great jazz talents. World-renowned saxophonist Wolfgang Puschnig, for example, holds a professorship at Vienna's Music University. He and his colleagues have inspired young musicians who can be found performing in the city's many jazz clubs.

**Jazzland.** In a cellar under St. Ruprecht's church, this is the granddaddy of Vienna's jazz clubs. Thanks to the pioneering work of the club's founder, Axel Melhardt, Austrian jazz musicians have grooved with the best American stars. The club also serves excellent, inexpensive, and authentic cuisine. ⊠ *Franz-Josefs-Kai 29, 1st District* ☎ *01/533–2575* ⊕ *www.jazzland.at.*

**Porgy & Bess.** In the heart of the Innere Stadt, Porgy & Bess has become a fixed point in the national and international jazz scene. ⊠ *Riemergasse 11, 1st District* ☎ *01/512–8811* ⊕ *www.porgy.at.*

# PERFORMING ARTS

Vienna learned long ago that a thriving arts scene is a boon to tourism, so it lends its support to everything from grand opera to intimate cabaret performances. As a result, artists from around the world have also settled in the city. That's why in addition to waltzes you can enjoy such varied fare as Greek *rembetiko* and Turkish Sufi music. Anyone who knows a bit of German should attend a performance at such major theaters as the Burgtheater and the Theater in der Josefstadt. Ever since Tanzquartier took up residence in the MuseumsQuartier, aficionados of contemporary dance have been able to enjoy avant-garde performances.

## DANCE

As they live in the city of waltzes, the Viennese hold both ballet and contemporary dance especially dear. When the MuseumsQuartier was opened in 2001, the powers that be made sure to include space for dance performances, rehearsals, and classes.

Dance performances at the Staatsoper and Volksoper feature both classic and contemporary choreography. Dancers from both houses belong to the Vienna State Ballet under the direction of Manuel Legris, former star of the Paris Ballet.

Fodor'sChoice
★ **ImPulsTanz** (*Vienna International Dance Festival*). Europe's largest contemporary dance festival takes place in venues large and small all over the city between mid-July and mid-August. In 2017, the festival venues were at nearly 100% capacity, with a record-breaking number of

visitors; nearly 130,000 people packed into the halls, museums, and theaters to see some of the world's leading companies take the stage. Recent years have brought stars such as Alaine Platel, Jerome Bel, Mathilde Monnier, Anne Teresa De Keersmaker, and Marie Chouinard. ⊠ *Vienna* ☎ *01/523–5558* ⊕ *www.impulstanz.com.*

**Tanzquartier Wien** (*DanceQuarter Vienna*). Austria's foremost center for contemporary dance performances is Tanzquartier Wien. The season runs from September to June, and is followed by the so-called Factory Season, when the center concentrates solely on the projects presented in its dance studios. ⊠ *Museumsplatz 1, 7th District/Neubau* ☎ *01/581– 3591* ⊕ *www.tqw.at.*

## FILM

Vienna has a thriving film culture, with many viewers seeking original rather than German-dubbed versions of English-language films. If you're here in late October, make sure to check out Europe's oldest Viennale Film Festival ⊕ *www.viennale.at/en*, which draws crowds of nearly 100,000 to the city's historic movie palaces and showcases films by national and international directors.

**Artis International.** Around the corner from Tuchlauben, the Artis has six screens showing the latest blockbusters (all in English) three to four times a day. ⊠ *Shultergasse 5, 1st District* ☎ *01/535–6570.*

**Burg Kino.** Carol Reed's Vienna-based classic *The Third Man,* with Orson Welles and Joseph Cotton, is screened every day except Wednesday. Hollywood's latest releases are usually shown here in the original English version. ⊠ *Opernring 19, 1st District* ☎ *01/587–8406* ⊕ *www.burgkino.at.*

**Filmmuseum.** Located in the Albertina, the Filmmuseum has one of the most ambitious and sophisticated schedules around, with a heavy focus on English-language films. A stylish bar serving drinks and snacks spills out onto the street. It's open until well past midnight and often hosts lectures and retrospectives, but note that it is closed from July to September. ⊠ *Augustinerstrasse 1, 1st District* ☎ *01/533–7054* ⊕ *www. filmmuseum.at.*

**Haydn.** One of the city's original movie theaters, this family-run place shows blockbuster movies (some in 3-D) on four screens. ⊠ *Mariahilferstrasse 57, 6th District/Mariahilf* ☎ *01/587–2262* ⊕ *www. haydnkino.at.*

**Votiv Kino.** This artsy theater usually features more alternative options, with most movies shown in their original language with German subtitles. From October to June the Votiv Kino offers a leisurely Sunday brunch–feature film package, *Filmfrühstück,* for €14.90. There are also special children's performances on the weekends. ⊠ *Währingerstrasse 12, 9th District/Alsergrund* ☎ *01/317–3571* ⊕ *www.votivkino.at.*

5

## GALLERIES

Contemporary art museums are springing up in cities all across Austria, with Vienna at the center of the trend. You can find cutting-edge art and design in and around the MuseumsQuartier complex. The Freihaus-Quartier, in the 4th District, is where some of the most exciting contemporary galleries in town have set up shop, appropriately within range of the Secession Pavilion. The more traditional art galleries are still grouped around the Dorotheum auction house in the city center.

**Bäckerstrasse4.** Owner Gabriele Schober has successfully established a way for young artists to display their works at this multigenre gallery, showcasing both Austrian and international talents. Student works are submitted to an international jury four times a year. ⊠ *Bäckerstrasse 4, 1st District* ☎ *0676/555–1777* ⊕ *www.baeckerstrasse4.at.*

**Brotfabrik** (*Bread Factory*). A former bread factory once slated for demolition is now the site of Vienna's most celebrated contemporary art venue. Ateliers, galleries, showrooms, and studios for artists-in-residence are set up inside, making it akin to an urban artists' colony. It showcases some of the country's premier artists, as well as many up-and-comers. ⊠ *Absberggasse 27, 10th District/Favoriten* ☎ *01/982–3939* ⊕ *www.brotfabrik.wien.*

**Gallery Georg Kargl.** The Schleifmühlgasse has recently emerged as one of Vienna's most renowned gallery districts. Among the top contemporary galleries here is this one, located inside a former print shop. ⊠ *Schleifmühlgasse 5, 4th District/Wieden* ☎ *01/585–4199* ⊕ *georgkargl.com.*

**Lukas Feichtner Gallery.** Opposite Vienna's House of Music, Lucas Feichtner's two-story gallery is abundant with natural light, which helps showcase the array of bold works ranging from photography to collage. National and international artists, such as Petar Mirkovic and Stylianio Schico, are represented here. ⊠ *Seilerstätte 19, 1st District* ☎ *0676/338–7145* ⊕ *www.feichtnergallery.com.*

**TB A-21.** While her father, Baron H. H. Thyssen-Bornemisza, amassed one of the greatest collections of Old Master paintings, Francesca von Habsburg has chosen to spearhead Austria's avant-garde scene at her TB A-21. New media installations, puppet rock operas, and exhibits by hot new international artists keep people talking. ⊠ *Himmelpfortgasse 13, 1st District* ☎ *01/513–9856* ⊕ *tba21.org.*

## MUSIC

Vienna is one of the world's foremost music centers. Contemporary music gets its due, but it's the classics—the works of Beethoven, Brahms, Haydn, Mozart, Strauss, and Schubert—that draw the Viennese public and make tickets to the Wiener Philharmoniker the hottest of commodities. Vienna is home to four full symphony orchestras: the great Wiener Philharmoniker (Vienna Philharmonic), the outstanding Wiener Symphoniker (Vienna Symphony), the broadcasting service's ORF Symphony Orchestra, and the Niederösterreichische Tonkünstler. There are also hundreds of smaller groups, from world-renowned trios to chamber orchestras.

Although the well-known mid-May to mid-June Wiener Festwochen (Vienna Festival) signals the official end of the concert season, the rest of the summer brims with musical performances, particularly in the Theater an der Wien.

**Fodor's Choice**
★

**Deutschordenskloster.** The most enchanting place to hear Mozart in Vienna (or anywhere, for that matter) is the exquisite 18th-century Sala Terrena of the Deutschordenskloster. In this intimate room (it seats a maximum of 80 people), a chamber group in historic costumes offers concerts in a jewel box overrun with Rococo frescoes in the Venetian style. The concerts are held Thursday, Friday, and Sunday at 7:30 and Saturday at 6. Tickets are priced at €49 and €59. Said to be the oldest concert hall in Vienna, the Sala Terrena is part of the German Monastery, where, in 1781, Mozart lived and worked for his despised employer, Archbishop Colloredo of Salzburg. ✉ *Singerstrasse 7, 1st District* ☎ *01/911–9077* ⊕ *www. musicofvienna.com.*

**Hofburg Palace Concert Halls.** Much of the Imperial Palace is used today for orchestral concerts. The Festsaal, the largest hall of the Hofburg and originally conceived as a throne room, hosts frequent Strauss and Mozart concerts. If dripping opulence is a must, the Zeremoniensaal, considered the most magnificent hall of the palace, is an unparalleled venue for experiencing Vienna's classical soul. ✉ *Hofburg Palace, Heldenplatz, 1st District* ☎ *01/587-2552* ⊕ *www. hofburgorchester.at.*

**Konzerthaus.** A three-minute walk from the Musikverein is the Konzerthaus, home to three performance halls. The Grosser Konzerthaussaal, Mozartsaal, and Schubertsaal are all esteemed venues for a range of musical genres, including classical, cabaret, pop, and jazz. The lineup has included greats like Mnozil Brass, Dianne Reeves, Goran Begovic, and the Herbert Pixner Project. ✉ *Lothringerstrasse 20, 1st District* ☎ *01/242-002* ⊕ *www.konzerthaus.at.*

**Fodor's Choice**
★

**Musikverein.** The city's most important concert halls are in the 1869 Gesellschaft der Musikfreunde, better known as the Musikverein. This magnificent theater holds six performance spaces, but the one that everyone knows is the venue for the annual New Year's Day Concert— the Goldene Saal. Possibly the world's most beautiful music hall, it was designed by the Danish 19th-century architect Theophil Hansen, a passionate admirer of ancient Greece who festooned it with an army of gilded caryatids. Surprisingly, the smaller Brahms Saal is even more sumptuous—a veritable Greek temple with more caryatids and lots of gilding and green malachite. What Hansen would have made of the four subsidiary halls added in 2004 and set below the main theater will forever remain a mystery, but the avant-garde Gläserne, Hölzerne, Metallene, and Steinerne Säle (Glass, Wooden, Metal, and Stone Halls) make fitting showcases for contemporary music. In addition to being the main venue for the Wiener Philharmoniker and the Wiener Symphoniker, the Musikverein hosts many of the world's finest orchestras. ✉ *Bösendorferstrasse 12A, 1st District* ☎ *01/505-8190* ⊕ *www.musikverein.at.*

5

**MuTh.** A play on the words music and theater, MuTh is the concert hall and permanent home of the world-famous Vienna Boys' Choir (Wiener Sängerknaben). Since it opened in 2012, the 400-seat theater has become the official music center inside the Augarten, the oldest Baroque garden in Vienna. Here the legendary Vienna Boys' Choir performs music that ranges from classical to world music to pop. The vast stage has some of the finest acoustics in Vienna and is equipped with an orchestra pit, specially designed seating, and distinctive acoustic panels. The building itself combines a unique mix of Baroque and modern architecture and includes a café, shop, and seminar room where musical education and other performances take place. ⊠ *Am Augartenspitz 1* ⊕ *www.muth.at.*

**Schlosstheater Schönbrunn.** For nearly 80 years, the theater has been associated with the University of Music and Performing Arts. Here visitors can watch student performances of both opera and dramatic arts. ⊠ *Schönbrunner Schloss, Schönbrunner Schlossstrasse 47, 13th District/Hietzing* ☎ *0664–1111–600* ⊕ *www.musik-theater-schoenbrunn.at.*

**Wiener Kursalon.** If the whirling waltzes of Strauss are your thing, head to the Johann Strauss concerts at the Wiener Kursalon, a majestic palacelike structure built in the Italian Renaissance Revival style in 1865 and set in Vienna's sylvan Stadtpark. Here, in gold-and-white salons, the Salonorchester Alt Wien performs concerts of the works of "Waltz King" Johann Strauss and his contemporaries. You'll hear waltzes, polkas, and operetta melodies, replete with singers, dancers, and your own glass of champagne (no dancing by the audience allowed). ⊠ *Johannesgasse 33, 1st District* ☎ *01/512–5790* ⊕ *www.kursalonwien.at.*

**Fodor's Choice** ★ **Wiener Sängerknaben** (*Vienna Boys' Choir*). The beloved Vienna Boys' Choir, known here as the Wiener Sängerknaben, isn't just a set of living dolls out of a Walt Disney film (like the 1962 movie *Almost Angels*); its pedigree is royal, and its professionalism such that the choir regularly appears with the best orchestras in the world. The troupe was founded by Emperor Maximilian I in 1498, but with the demise of the Habsburg Empire in 1918, it became its own entity and began giving public performances in the 1920s to keep afloat.

From mid-September to late June, the apple-cheeked lads sing mass at 9:15 Sunday mornings in the Hofburgkapelle. Written requests for seats should be made at least six weeks in advance. Tickets are also sold at ticket agencies and at the box office (open Friday 11–1 and 3–5). Expect to pay a top price of €37 for a seat near the nave, and note that only the 10 side-balcony seats allow a view of the choir. On Sunday at 8:45 am, any unclaimed tickets are sold. If you miss hearing the choir at a Sunday mass, you may be able to catch it in a more popular program in the Musikverein. ⊠ *Hofmusikkapelle, Hofburg-Schweizerhof, 1st District* ☎ *01/216–3942* ⊕ *www.wsk.at.*

## OPERA AND OPERETTA

Austria's handling of political scandals has led some to call it an "operetta state." It's small wonder that this antiquated art form is still cherished in musical theaters such as the Volksoper, albeit in a tongue-in-cheek manner. Although the Viennese officially boast of opera productions at the Staatsoper, many secretly prefer light-hearted operettas. Expect grand opera with all the attendant pomp and circumstance at the Staatsoper. In addition to offering operas that are just as satisfying as those at the Staatsoper, the Volksoper strikes just the right balance between operetta, musicals, and dance performances.

**Kammeroper.** The management of this Vienna institution was taken over by Theater an der Wien in 2012. Since then, the operas and operettas are performed here under the artistic direction of Sebastian F. Schwarz to sold-out crowds. ⊠ *Fleischmarkt 24, 1st District* ☎ *01/588–30–1010* ⊕ *www.theater-wien.at.*

**Fodor's Choice**

★

**Letztes Erfreuliches Openntheater.** What would *La Traviata* be like with two soloists and a piano? Or how about a *Tosca* where you can join in the chorus? Stefan Fleischhacker's Letztes Erfreuliches Operntheater (otherwise known as the Last Enjoyable Opera Theater, or L.E.O. for short) offers marvelously funny and entertaining performances of grand operas that are appropriate for audiences of all ages (and much shorter than their originals). For a small donation, bread and wine are also available. ⊠ *Ungargasse 18, 3rd District/Landstrasse* ☎ *01/712–1427* ⊕ *www.theaterleo.at.*

**Staatsoper** (*State Opera House*). One of the world's great opera houses, the Staatsoper has been the scene of countless musical triumphs and a center of unending controversy over how it should be run and by whom. The Culture Ministry has slated Sony manager Bogdan Roscic to take over by 2020; the appointment is intended to settle storms whipped up during the tumultuous tenure of Dominic Meyer. A performance takes place virtually every night from September to June, drawing on the vast repertoire of the house, with emphasis on Mozart, Verdi, and Wagner. Guided tours are given year-round. ⊠ *Opernring 2, 1st District* ☎ *01/514–440* ⊕ *www.wiener-staatsoper.at.*

**Theater an der Wien.** This beautiful Rococo-style historic theater located in Mariahilf is more than 200 years old. It was used and abused for decades as a contemporary musical venue, but now the building—which is closely linked to Beethoven, who lived here—has renewed its role as an opera house, attracting an international crowd. It's open year-round, and hosts a premiere nearly every month. The selection of works performed here is tremendous, including Janáček, Prokofiev, Britten, Handel, Monteverdi, Rossini, and Bach. ⊠ *Linke Wienszeile 6, 6th District/Mariahilf* ☎ *01/58885, 01/588–301010* ⊕ *www.theater-wien.at.*

**Volksoper.** Opera, operetta, and ballet are performed at the Volksoper, just on the outer edge of the Innere Stadt at Währingerstrasse and Währinger Gürtel. Prices here are significantly lower than at the Staatsoper, and performances can be every bit as rewarding. This theater has a packed calendar, with offerings ranging from the grandest opera, such as Mozart's *Don Giovanni,* to an array of Viennese operettas, including Johann Strauss's *Die Fledermaus,* to Broadway musicals. Most operas and musicals are sung in German. The opera house is at the third stop on streetcar Nos. 41, 42, or 43, which run from Schottentor, U2, on the Ring. ⊠ *Währingerstrasse 78, 9th District/Alsergrund* ☎ *01/513–1513* ⊕ *www.volksoper.at.*

## THEATER

Opera and classical music get all the attention, but theater is also very popular among the Viennese. Tickets to the Burgtheater, one of the world's top German-language theaters, can be hard to come by.

**Burgtheater.** The Austrian National Theater is among the leading German-language theaters of the world. The Burgtheater's repertoire frequently mixes German classics with more modern and controversial pieces. The Burg also emphasizes works by Austrian playwrights, incluing Elfriede Jelinek, who won the 2004 Nobel Prize for Literature.

The Burg's smaller house, the Akademietheater, draws on much the same group of actors for classical and modern plays, but performances are in a more relaxing setting.

✉ *Dr.-Karl-Lueger-Ring 2, 1st District* ☎ *01/514–444–4140* ⊕ *www. burgtheater.at.*

**Kammerspiele der Josefstadt.** The recently renovated theater offers a season of modern dramas and comedies. ✉ *Rotenturmstrasse 20, 1st District* ☎ *01/42–700–359* ⊕ *www.josefstadt.org.*

FAMILY   **Marionettentheater Schloss Schönbrunner.** Historical recordings of Mozart's *Magic Flute* and other favorites are on the program at this magnificent puppet theater in Schönbrunn Palace. These outstanding performances fill a whole evening, with programs designed for adults as well as for children. ✉ *Schönbrunn Palace, Schönbrunner Schloss-Strasse 47, 13th District/Hietzing* ☎ *01/817–3247* ⊕ *www.marionettentheater.at.*

**Raimund Theater.** Originally built as a theater for the people, the Raimund staged popular folk plays in its early days. It then moved on to opera for a spell before becoming a leading venue for long-running musicals. Here, lovers of the genre can catch enjoy such hits as *Hair* and *Mamma Mia!* ✉ *Wallgasse 18, 6th District/Mariahilf* ☎ *01/58885, 01/588–301010* ⊕ *www.musicalvienna.at.*

**Ronacher Theater.** Extensively restored in recent years, the Ronacher presents the latest musical smash hits from Broadway. ✉ *Seilerstätte 9, 1st District* ☎ *01/58885* ⊕ *www.musicalvienna.at.*

**Theater in der Josefstadt.** The Theater in der Josefstadt stages classical and modern works year-round in a space once run by the great producer and teacher Max Reinhardt. The theater had, of late, been seeming to gather layers of dust, but happily director Herbert Föttinger has restored its reputation for more avant-garde and daring productions. ✉ *Josefstädterstrasse 26, 8th District/Josefstadt* ☎ *01/42–700–300* ⊕ *www.josefstadt.org.*

**Vienna's English Theater.** For English-language theater—mainly classic comedies and dramas—head for this cozy and charming venue. The season runs early September to early July. ✉ *Josefsgasse 12, 8th District/Josefstadt* ☎ *01/402–1260* ⊕ *www.englishtheatre.at.*

**Volkstheater.** Dramas and comedies are presented here. ✉ *Neustiftgasse 1, 7th District/Neubau* ☎ *01/523–3501–0* ⊕ *www.volkstheater.at.*

# SHOPPING

Updated by
Jacy Meyer

As upscale as ever, Vienna remains an exclusive and high-end place to shop, even as young designers are raising their profiles and creating new ways to shop throughout the city. The Goldenes Quartier, or Golden Quarter, in the heart of the Innere Stadt, remains the most exclusive shopping area, located on the extension of the Kohlmarkt, between Tuchlauben, Bognergasse, and Am Hof. Flagship stores such as Prada, Saint Laurent, Bottega Veneta, and Louis Vuitton are just a few among the many that will entice all manner of serious shoppers. Visitors can also stroll easily along, as the area has been turned into a pedestrian zone.

In the pedestrian-only streets of Kärntner Strasse, Graben, and Kohlmarkt, shopaholics can readily give into their passion. Sleekly cut dresses and intricately crafted jewelry beckon from the windows of shops formerly occupied by purveyors to His Imperial Majesty. Even the Swedish clothing store H&M presents itself in exclusive garb; on Graben near St. Stephen's Cathedral, it has found a home in the mahogany-clad building that was once home of the department store of Braun & Co. Where baronesses once bought fur muffs, tattooed teens now rummage for cheap T-shirts. Luxury brands such as Hermès, Burberry, and Cartier have set up shop on or around Kohlmarkt, the street leading up to the Hofburg.

As you walk along Michaelerplatz, in front of the imperial palace, be sure to explore the little passageway next to the Michaeler Church. You'll find a few wonderful shops selling precious stones and silverware. If you want to venture farther afield, explore Mariahilferstrasse, Vienna's best-known shopping mile outside the city center. Much of this area has been turned into a "shared space zone"—part of it now pedestrian-only—making it very friendly to shoppers. Running from MuseumsQuartier to the BahnhofCity Wien shopping mall, it's peppered with department stores like Peek & Cloppenburg, Gerngross, and s.Oliver. Neubaugasse, which runs into Mariahilferstrasse about halfway up, is bustling with young designers who sell their wares in little boutique shops. The creativity continues on nearby Lindengasse, Kirchengasse, and Burggasse.

## PLANNER

### HOURS

Outside the city center, shops are generally open weekdays from 9 am to 6 pm and on Saturday from 9 am to noon. On the busy shopping thoroughfares, most shops stay open until 8 pm during the week and 5 or 6 pm on Saturday. Stores are closed on Sunday and public holidays. In the 7th District of Neubau, the boutiques often don't open until 11 am.

## TAXES

Visitors from non-EU countries may claim a refund of Austria's value-added tax for goods costing more than €75. Ask your sales clerk to fill out a Global Blue tax-free form and to staple the original receipt to it. When you're leaving the country, bring your purchase and tax-free form to the customs counter. The officer will stamp your slip and you can obtain the refund from one of the airport banks.

Alternately, you can receive your refund at more than 700 refund points around the world or send the form to Global Blue and have the money transferred to your bank account. If you want to use this method, ask the sales clerk for a Global Blue envelope.

## SALES

You should definitely haggle over prices at the flea markets. The biggest sale day of the year is Boxing Day (December 26), the first business day after Christmas, when nearly everything in the city is half price. Look for signs reading *ausverkauf* (sale), *aktion* (action), or *angebote* (special offer) in shop windows. Deep-discount sales also occur in January and July.

## SHOPPING DISTRICTS

The Kärntner Strasse, Graben, and Kohlmarkt—the latter is home to the so-called Goldenes Quartier (Golden Quarter)—are pedestrian areas in the Inner City that claim to have the best shops in Vienna. For some items, such as jewelry, they're probably some of the best anywhere. The side streets in this area have shops selling antiques, art, clocks, jewelry, and period furniture. A collection of attractive small boutiques can also be found in the Palais Ferstel passage at Freyung 2 in the 1st District.

Gumpendorferstrasse, in the 6th District, and the nearby 7th District, Neubau, are two of the hippest shopping destinations in town, with small boutiques, trendy hairstylists, and great eateries. On Neubaugasse, Kirchengasse, Lindengasse, and the quaint Mondscheingasse, fashionistas find unique clothing, jewelry, and footwear in lovely little boutiques. Also in the 7th District, on Spittelberggasse between Burggasse and Siebensterngasse, are small galleries and handicraft shops. In competition for the top neighborhood of them all is Praterstrasse in the 2nd District. From the city center towards the Praterstern U station, great boutiques, cafés, and restaurants have popped up.

Vienna's Naschmarkt (between Linke and Rechte Wienzeile, starting at Getreidemarkt) is one of Europe's great and most colorful food and produce markets. Stalls open at 6 am, and the pace is lively until about 6 pm. Saturday is the big day, though, when farmers come into the city to sell at the back end of the market. Also on Saturday is a huge flea market at the Kettenbrückengasse end. The Naschmarkt is closed Sunday. Christmas is the time for the tinselly Christkindlmarkt (Rathausplatz in front of City Hall). In protest of its commercialization, smaller markets specializing in handicrafts have sprung up on such traditional spots as Am Hof, the Freyung, and in front of the Schönbrunn and Belvedere palaces.

## TOP SHOPPING EXPERIENCES

**Hit up the food shops.** Fill your bags with some edible delicacies, such as artisanal chocolates from Meinl am Graben (try some with poppy seeds and apricot brandy), small chocolate-rum-punch cubes from the shop at Hotel Sacher (even tastier than the classic torte), the famed Sisi Cake from Gerstner K. u. K. Hofzuckerbäcker, miniature chocolates from Altmann & Kühne on Graben, and a bottle of Styrian pumpkinseed oil or Zweigelt wine from supermarkets like Billa or Merkur.

**Serve in style.** Once back home, you'll want to share your food souvenirs. Check out delicate Augarten china in Spiegelgasse near Graben or pieces painted with real gold from Das Goldene Wiener Herz in the 7th District.

**Dress like an Austrian.** Treat yourself to an Austrian dirndl at Gexi Tostmann's shop on Schottengasse or a trachten jacket at Loden Plankl on Michaelerplatz. If you consider wearing these garments a bit silly, think again; even Klimt model Emilie Flöge wore them when she vacationed in the Alps. Complement your look with a unique piece of jewelry from Austrian designer Susanne Kitz.

**Explore the flea markets.** The best deals on the Naschmarkt flea market can be found at 6 am on Saturday. Avoid the elaborate stalls of the antiques dealers and check out what regular folks have scattered about on the pavement next to the metro. Who knows, maybe you'll discover Emilie Flöge's long-lost necklace or sugar tray.

# VIENNA SHOPPING REVIEWS

*Shopping listings are organized by neighborhood.*

## THE EASTERN CITY CENTER: STEPHANSDOM AND MEDIEVAL VIENNA

### ANTIQUES

**Gallery Dr. Sternat.** Just around the corner from the Opera House, this is one of the more traditional art galleries in the city. Austrian paintings, Viennese bronzes, Thonet furniture, and beautiful Biedermeier pieces crowd the small space. ⊠ *Lobkowitzplatz 1, 1st District* ☎ *01/512–2063* ⊕ *www.sternat.com.*

### BOOKS

**Frick.** Four floors of books, including an English-language section, can be found at the largest Frick location in the city. Art history and guidebooks on Vienna and Austria are here, but you can also find small gift items like calendars and cards. The staff is helpful, and bargains can often be found in the trays by the door. ⊠ *Graben 27, 1st District* ☎ *01/533–9914* ⊕ *www.buchhandlung-frick.at.*

**Morawa.** This could be the best-stocked bookstore in Vienna, with titles on everything under the sun. Thankfully, help is always at hand if you can't find that specific one you're looking for. The magazine and newspaper section is particularly impressive. ⊠ *Wollzeile 11, 1st District* ☎ *01/51–37–51–34–50* ⊕ *www.morawa-buch.at.*

## CERAMICS, GLASS, AND PORCELAIN

**Albin Denk.** If you want to enter an old-fashioned interior that has changed little from the time when Empress Sisi shopped here, Albin Denk is the place. The shop entrance is lined with glass cases and filled with a wonderful, if kitschy, army of welcoming porcelain figurines. ⊠ *Graben 13, 1st District* ☎ *01/512–4439* ⊕ *www.albindenk.at.*

**Berger.** Crafting made-to-order ceramics for his customers for 40 years, Herr Berger has now been joined in the business by his daughter Lisa. Here you might find a handcrafted ceramic stove made to measure for your Alpine chalet, or a decorative wall plate blooming with a hand-painted flowering gentian. ⊠ *Weihburggasse 17, 1st District* ☎ *01/512–1434* ⊕ *www.valcoholic.at/val04/keramikberger.*

**Lobmeyr.** Nearly 200 years old, this shop is world renowned for its exquisite glassware. One of its collections is housed in the Metropolitan Museum of Art (MOMA) in New York and its chandeliers have graced opera houses (including New York's Metropolitan Opera) and private homes for centuries. This is one of the only stores left in Vienna that retains its interior of imperial glory, yet allows the cutting edge of design to enter its realm. (See the breathtakingly beautiful black Rococo mirrors by Austrian designer Florian Ladstätter). Even if you're not buying, head upstairs to the glass museum. ⊠ *Kärntner Strasse 26, 1st District* ☎ *01/512–5088* ⊕ *www.lobmeyr.at.*

**Swarovski.** Ireland has its Waterford, France its Baccarat, and Austria has Swarovski, purveyors of some of the finest cut crystal in the world. You'll find your typical collector items and gifts here, but also high-style fashion accessories (Paris couturiers now festoon their gowns with Swarovski crystals the way they used to with ostrich feathers), crystal figurines, and home accessories. This flagship store is a cave of coruscating crystals that gleam and glitter. Breathtakingly beautiful window displays change monthly. ⊠ *Kärntner Strasse 24, 1st District* ☎ *01/324–0000* ⊕ *www.swarovski.com.*

## CLOTHING: AUSTRIAN

**Giesswein.** Dirndls and *trachten* (the typical Austrian costume with white blouse, print dress, and apron) for toddlers to ladies, and cute hand-embroidered cardigans for the kids, are all found here, with some of the best traditional clothing in town. ⊠ *Kärntnerring 5–7, 1st District* ☎ *01/512–4597* ⊕ *www.giesswein.com.*

## CLOTHING: MEN'S

**Grandits.** This men's shop has a great selection of both business and casual wear from a variety of labels, including Armani, Boss, Ralph Lauren, and Versace, all displayed quite stylishly. ⊠ *Rotenturmstrasse 10, 1st District* ☎ *01/512–6389* ⊕ *www.grandits.at.*

**Sir Anthony.** For a classic suit-and-tie look, this is the place to shop. But Sir Anthony may also surprise those interested in nontraditional clothing. A second location is nearby at the Ringstrassen Gallerien. ⊠ *Kärntner Strasse 21–23, 1st District* ☎ *01/512–6835* ⊕ *www.sir-anthony.com.*

6

**Sturm am Parkring.** Come here for dapper suits for well-dressed men. ⊠ *Parkring 2, 1st District* ☎ *01/706–4600* ⊕ *www.sturm-parkring.at.*

## CLOTHING: WOMEN'S

**Callisti.** Chic and avant-garde, the designs here have a definite biker's edginess. There are options for both men and women by Austrian designer Martina Mueller Callisti. ⊠ *Weihburggasse 20, 1st District* ☎ *676/301–301–0* ⊕ *www.callisti.at.*

**Sisi.** Traditional Austrian attire goes gorgeously modern at this boutique from Sissy Schranz. A charming take on the nostalgic styles donned in the days of beloved Empress Sisi, these creations are elegant yet versatile. A range of clothing from Austria's best designers are showcased here, as well as accessories, jewelry, and hats. ⊠ *Annagasse 11, 1st District* ☎ *01/513–0518* ⊕ *www.sisi-vienna.at.*

> **CHRISTKINDLMÄRKTE**
>
> Vienna keeps the Christmas flame burning perhaps more brightly than any other metropolis in the world. Here, during the holiday season, no fewer than nine major *Christkindlmärkte* (Christmas Markets) proffer their wares, with stands selling enough wood-carved Austrian toys, crèche figures, and Tannenbaum ornaments to tickle anybody's mistletoes. Many of the markets have food vendors selling *Glühwein* (mulled wine) and *Kartoffelpuffer* (potato patties).

## DEPARTMENT STORES

**Peek & Cloppenburg.** British star architect Sir David Chipperfield designed the six-story P & C store. With the longest facade on the Kärntner Strasse, huge windows, and almost a complete lack of ornamentation, it can't be missed. Find the best-known fashion labels, as well as inexpensive off-the-rack garb. ⊠ *Kärntner Strasse 29, 1st District* ☎ *0800/20–28–04* ⊕ *www.peek-cloppenburg.at.*

**Steffl.** One of Vienna's most prominent department stores, Steffl stocks just about everything. It's moderately upscale without being overly expensive. Celebrate your shopping finds with a drink in the top-floor Sky Bar. ⊠ *Kärntner Strasse 19, 1st District* ☎ *01/93–05–66–10* ⊕ *www.steffl-vienna.at.*

## GALLERIES

**Bel Etage.** This gallery specializes in Viennese Jugendstil with furniture and accessories, but also has an impressive selection of paintings by Austrian artists. ⊠ *Mahlerstrasse 15, 1st District* ☎ *01/512–2379* ⊕ *www.beletage.com.*

## GIFTS AND SOUVENIRS

**Alt-Österreich.** Are you looking for a vintage postcard, a hand-carved walking stick, a classic record, or even an old photograph of the Opera House from before the war? Head to Alt-Österreich—its name translates as "Old Austria"—and you'll find that this treasure trove has just about everything dealing with that time-burnished subject. ⊠ *Himmelpfortgasse 7, 1st District* ☎ *01/512–1296.*

**Fodor's Choice**  **Herzilein Papeterie.** This gorgeous paper shop is a joy to wander around.
★  There is a lovely selection of paper products, but also cards, wrapping paper, small gifts, and leather goods. ✉ *Wollzeile 18, 1st District* ☎ *67–64/20–54–52* ⊕ *www.herzilein-papeterie.at.*

**Österreichische Werkstätten.** Austria's one-and-only cooperative for arts and crafts stocks Austrian handicrafts of the finest quality. It has everything from brass or pewter candlesticks to linen tablecloths to embroidered brooches. ✉ *Kärntner Strasse 6, 1st District* ☎ *01/512–2418* ⊕ *www.austrianarts.com.*

**Petit Point Kovacec.** For that Alt Wien flourish, choose a needlepoint handbag, pill box, or brooch from one of the oldest shops in the city center—family-run for nearly a hundred years. ✉ *Kärntner Strasse 16, 1st District* ☎ *01/512–4886* ⊕ *www.petitpoint.eu.*

### JEWELRY

**A. E. Köchert.** One of Vienna's original purveyors to the Imperial Court, A. E. Köchert has been Vienna's jeweler of choice for nearly two centuries. In the 19th century, Emperor Franz Josef commissioned 27 diamond-studded stars for the Empress Elizabeth's legendary auburn hair. A new European trend was born, and today "Sisi's stars" are again fashionable after Köchert started reissuing them. Plus, if you're ever in need of a crown, Köchert will craft one for you. ✉ *Neuer Markt 15, 1st District* ☎ *01/512–5828* ⊕ *www.koechert.com.*

**Bucherer.** For one of the finest selections of watches head to Bucherer's, where the gold- and diamond-jewelry selections are also top-notch. ✉ *Kärntner Strasse 2, 1st District* ☎ *01/512–6730* ⊕ *www.bucherer.com.*

**Juwelier Heldwein.** This established Vienna jeweler has been creating a range of jewelry, watches, silverware, and gifts since 1902. Now run by the fourth generation of the Heldwein family, the shop sells not only its own designs, but those from the likes of Carrera y Carrera, Georg Jensen, and more. ✉ *Graben 13, 1st District* ☎ *01/512–5781* ⊕ *www.heldwein.at.*

**Reingold.** This small shop might be hard to find (look for the Tissot sign), but once you do, you'll find a large watch selection. Reingold also specializes in jewelry design, especially pearls and diamonds. ✉ *Kärntner Strasse 16, 1st District* ☎ *01/512–7103* ⊕ *www.wiener-juweliere.at/juwelier-reingold.*

**Susanne Kitz.** Austrian designer Susanne Kitz designs both exclusive leather bags and unique jewelry pieces. Her central Vienna shop features items that are at once bold and elegant. ✉ *Weihburggasse 7, 1st District* ☎ *01/512–8648* ⊕ *www.susannekitz.com.*

### MUSIC

**EMI.** Helpful sales assistants are at the ready if you're looking for any special titles at EMI—one of the big mainstays for classical music. The selections run the gamut from ethno to pop. ✉ *Kärntner Strasse 30, 1st District* ☎ *01/512–3675* ⊕ *www.emistore.at.*

6

### PERFUMES

**J.B. Filz Perfumery.** The perfumery to the Imperial Court, J.B. Filz has been creating beautiful scents since 1809. Bring back memories of Vienna with its Wiener Lieblingsduft, or try the Eau de Lavande, a scent made with three different kinds of lavender and suitable for both men and women. ⊠ *Graben 13, 1st District* ☎ *01/512–1745* ⊕ *www. parfumerie-filz.at.*

## THE INNER CITY CENTER

### ANTIQUES

Fodor'sChoice
★

**Dorotheum.** If you're looking for something truly special—an 18th-century oil portrait or a real fur, a Rococo mirror or a fine silk fan, a china figurine or sterling-silver spoon, an old map of the Austrian Empire or even a stuffed parrot—the best place to try and find it is Dorotheum, Vienna's fabled auction house. Have you ever wanted to see how the Austrian aristocracy once lived, how their sumptuous homes were once furnished? Well, don't bother with a museum—you can inspect their antique furnishings, displayed as if in use, for free, and without the eagle eyes of sales personnel following your every move. This was the first imperial auction house, established in 1707 by Emperor Josef I as a pawnshop. Occupying the former site of the Dorothy Convent (hence the name), the Dorotheum has built up a grand reputation.

The neo-Baroque building was completed in 1901 and deserves a walk-through (you can enter from Spiegelgasse and exit on Doro-theergasse) just to have a look, even if you only admire the gorgeous stuccoed walls and palatial interiors, or peek into the glass-roofed patio stocked with early-20th-century glass, furniture, and art. With more than 600 auctions a year, this has become one of the busiest auction houses in Europe. There are auctions held frequently throughout the week, though not Saturday, and it's closed entirely Sunday. And if you don't fancy bidding for something, there are sale areas on the ground and second floors where loads of stuff can simply be bought off the floor. ⊠ *Dorotheergasse 17, 1st District* ☎ *01/515–600* ⊕ *www. dorotheum.com/en.html.*

**Kulcsar Antiques.** This is your best bet for some of the finer collectibles in the city. Peter Kulcsar's special focus is on silverware, watercolors, and objets d'art. ⊠ *Spiegelgasse 19, 1st District* ☎ *01/512–7267* ⊕ *www.kulcsar.at.*

### BOOKS

**Freytag & Berndt.** If you're planning a hiking holiday in Austria, stock up on the necessary maps at Freytag & Berndt, the best place for maps and travel books in Vienna. ⊠ *Wallnerstrasse 3, 1st District* ☎ *01/533–8685* ⊕ *www.freytagberndt.com.*

**Wolfrum.** Art-book lovers will adore Wolfrum. If you have money to burn, you can also spring for a Schiele print or special art edition to take home. ⊠ *Augustinerstrasse 10, 1st District* ☎ *01/512–5398.*

## CERAMICS, GLASS, AND PORCELAIN

**Augarten.** The best china in town can be found at this flagship store, designed by Philipp Bruni, which has a sleek, modern design that shines a contemporary light on the traditional side of historic porcelain products. ✉ *Spiegelgasse 3, 1st District* ☎ *01/512–1494* ⊕ *www.augarten.com.*

## CLOTHING: AUSTRIAN

**Loden-Plankl.** The Austrians take special pride in their traditional clothing (called trachten) and think naught of the kitschy von Trapp clan when doing so. Lederhosen and dirndls are worn at festivals and special occasions, and men's and women's *trachtenjacken* are worn in daily attire. Perhaps the best place to purchase traditional clothing is at Loden-Plankl, which stocks hand-embroidered jackets and lederhosen for kids. The building, opposite the Hofburg, is a centuries-old treasure. ✉ *Michaelerplatz 6, 1st District* ☎ *01/533–8032* ⊕ *www.loden-plankl.at.*

## CLOTHING: WOMEN'S

**Lena Hoschek.** One of the shooting stars of Austria's fashion industry, Lena Hoschek finds inspiration in traditional styles. She uses floral fabrics to create petticoat dresses, blouses, and outfits worn by pop stars and celebrities. Singer Katy Perry is just one of many who love her figure-hugging fashions. ✉ *Goldschmiedgasse 7A, 1st District* ☎ *01/50–30–92–00* ⊕ *www.lenahoschek.com.*

**Mühlbauer Headwear.** This shop has been making hats in Vienna since 1903 and today its headwear has gained fame from the patronage of customers like Brad Pitt and Meryl Streep. The designs are timeless and the selection is broad enough to include elegant designs as well as hats for everyday wear. ✉ *Seilergasse 10, 1st District* ☎ *01/512–2241* ⊕ *www.muehlbauer.at.*

**Schella Kann.** Fashionistas make a beeline for the flagship store of this Austrian designer and national treasure. Extravagant and trendy, these are clothes you never want to take off. ✉ *Spiegelgasse 15, 1st District* ☎ *01/997–2755* ⊕ *www.schellakann.com.*

## FLEA MARKETS

**Am Hof.** On Friday and Saturday from March to early November, a small outdoor market with arts, crafts, and collectibles takes place on Am Hof. It's open 10 am to 6 pm. ✉ *Am Hof, 1st District.*

## FOOD AND CANDY

**Gerstner K. u. K. Hofzuckerbäcker.** At Gerstner K. u. K. Hofzuckerbäcker, which is spread out over three floors, you can pick up a true taste of Vienna to bring home. The famed "Sisi" cake (a layer cake with chocolate, buttercream, and whipped cream) as well as handmade cakes, truffles, and pralines are ready for purchase from this traditional confectioner for the Imperial and Royal Court. On the second floor is a café where you can enjoy a coffee and cake with a view of the State Opera. The third floor holds a restaurant. ✉ *Kärntner Strasse 51, 1st District* ☎ *01/526–1361* ⊕ *www.gerstner-konditorei.at.*

6

### JEWELRY

**Artup.** This shop features one-off and limited-edition items ranging from fashion and accessories to home products from Austrian designers. ⊠ *Bauernmarkt 8, 1st District* ☎ *01/535–5097* ⊕ *www.artup.at.*

**Pomellato Boutique.** In Vienna's prestigious "Golden Quarter," this fine jewelry store offers a unique collection of precious stones and silver. ⊠ *Tuchlaubenhof 7A, 1st District* ☎ *1/905–2324* ⊕ *www.pomellato.com.*

### MUSIC

**Arcardia.** In case you bump into Placido Domingo or Anna Netrebko, you can buy a picture here so you can have it autographed. Arcardia, in the Opera House, stocks a grand selection of the latest releases from the operatic world, and quite a few classic rarities, too. ⊠ *Staatsoper, Opernring 2, 1st District* ☎ *01/513–9568.*

## ACROSS THE DANUBE: THE 2ND DISTRICT

### CLOTHING

**Bocca Lupo.** This luxury boutique features vintage fashion by well-known designers. See if you can track down a classic Hermès scarf, Louis Vuitton purse, or a fabulous, new-to-you cocktail dress. ⊠ *Praterstrasse 14, 2nd District/Leopoldstadt* ☎ *01/904–3776* ⊕ *www.boccalupo.at.*

**Song.** This former fur factory in Vienna's 2nd District has been transformed into a fashion temple. The stylish interior design is by architect Gregor Eichinger. A lover of the avant-garde styles, Song combines the finest luxury labels with its own fashion designs, plus contemporary styles from young, up-and-coming designers. Shop for fashion, bags, shoes, and furniture here. The website is regularly updated with a variety of events. ⊠ *Praterstrasse 11–13, 2nd District/Leopoldstadt* ☎ *01/532–2858* ⊕ *www.song.at.*

### FOOD

**Kaas am Markt.** Local cheeses, meats, and breads, fresh farm produce, and handmade specialty items look and taste delicious here. Stop by for a good hearty snack or a three-course meal at lunch, but try to get here on the early side in order to nab a table. ⊠ *Karmelitermarkt 33–36, 2nd District/Leopoldstadt* ☎ *69/91–81–40–60–1* ⊕ *www.kaasammarkt.at* ⊘ Closed Mon.

## THE WESTERN CITY CENTER: BURGTHEATER AND BEYOND

### CHRISTKINDLMÄRKTE

**Altwiener Christkindlmarkt.** This festive seasonal market is held on one of Vienna's cozier squares. ⊠ *Freyung, 1st District.*

### CLOTHING: AUSTRIAN

**Tostmann.** Fancy having your very own tailor-made Austrian dirndl? Tostmann will create a bespoke one just for you, or you can browse the ready-made selection. There is also a nice selection of men's sweaters. ⊠ *Schottengasse 3A, 1st District* ☎ *01/533–5331* ⊕ *www.tostmann.at.*

### GIFTS AND SOUVENIRS

**Viennastore.** For a taste of Vienna without the kitsch, the Viennastore has an upscale selection of design items including glass and porcelain from Lobmeyr and Augarten as well as fun items like a cookie cutter shaped like the Prater Ferris wheel. A few doors down at Herrengasse 1, the Vienna1900store specializes in objects from the turn of the 20th century. ✉ *Herrengasse 5, 1st District* ☎ *01/535–0565* ⊕ *www.theviennastore.at.*

## EAST OF THE RINGSTRASSE: STADTPARK AND KARLSPLATZ

### CHRISTKINDLMÄRKTE

**Karlsplatz Christkindlmärkte.** The Christmas market at Karlsplatz has some of the more refined stands in town, selling homemade wares. ✉ *Karlsplatz, 4th District/Wieden.*

### CLOTHING: MEN'S

**Collins Hüte.** This is one of the best sources for such accessories as scarves, gloves, and especially hats, including a wide-brimmed sombrero (for that glaring summer sun on the slopes at Lech). ✉ *Opernpassage, 1st District* ☎ *01/587–1305* ⊕ *www.collins-hats.at.*

## SOUTH OF THE RINGSTRASSE: THE MUSEUMSQUARTIER

### BOOKS AND STATIONERY

**Sous-Bois.** Lovely cards, notepads, planners, pens, and even art books can be found in this crafty 7th District shop. Items are carefully chosen from a global selection of artists and designs. ✉ *Neustiftgasse 33, 7th District/Neubau* ☎ *699/13–06–68–78.*

### CHRISTKINDLMÄRKTE

**Spittelberg Christkindlmärkte.** The city's most fashionable love this artsy market, held in Spittelberg's enchanting Biedermeier quarter. ✉ *Burggasse and Siebensterngasse, 7th District/Neubau.*

### CLOTHING: WOMEN'S

**Anukoo.** Fair-trade fashion is the philosophy behind Anukoo. The designs here are fresh, and only organic material is used in the relaxed dresses, T-shirts, trousers, and more. ✉ *Gumpendorfer Strasse 28, 6th District/Mariahilf* ☎ *01/581–1343* ⊕ *www.anukoo.com.*

**Arnold's.** This appealing boutique stocks a wide range of sought-after international brands and labels for urban fashionistas, like Wood Wood, Scarti Lab, and Edwin. A large selection of menswear and shoes include Arnold's own signature T-shirts. ✉ *Siebensterngasse 52, 7th District/Neubau* ☎ *01/923–1316* ⊕ *www.arnolds.at.*

**Art Point.** Russian designer Lena Kvadrat treats Viennese hipsters to cutting-edge fashion, unveiling two collections each year. ✉ *Neubaugasse 35, 7th District/Neubau* ☎ *01/522–0425* ⊕ *www.artpoint.eu.*

**Bisovsky.** Haute couture and prêt-à-porter are by appointment only in Susanne Bisovsky's Neubau district studio. Email or phone ahead for an appointment. ✉ *Seidengasse 13/6, 7th District/Neubau* ☎ *699/11–17–67–55* ⊕ *www.bisovsky.com.*

6

**EbenBERG.** Billing itself as an ethical concept store, EbenBERG combines the designs of Laura Ebenberg with a carefully crafted lineup of other sleek designers who share her vision of using organic and fair-trade materials. ⊠ *Neubaugasse 4, 7th District/Neubau* ☎ *699/15–28–72–26.*

**Ferrari Zöchling.** For those with a love of creative prints, Romana Zöchling's label Ferrari Zöchling designs very eye-catching clothing. Sometimes bold, sometimes mellow, but always artistic, Romana takes inspiration from the art and photography that she often uses in her prints. ⊠ *Kirchengasse 27, 7th District/Neubau* ☎ *66/41–21–11–27* ⊕ *www.ferrarizoechling.com* ☾ *Closed Mon. and Tues.*

**Ina Kent.** This store showcases exquisite, exclusive handbags that can be worn in a variety of ways thanks to their versatile design. A second location is at Siebensternstrasse 50, also in the 7th District. ⊠ *Neubaugasse 34, 7th District/Neubau* ☎ *699/19–54–10–90* ⊕ *www.inakent.com.*

**Lila.** Informal women's fashion from designer Lisi Lang is found at this store. Her label offers lovely pieces that will go perfectly in many wardrobes. ⊠ *Kirchengasse 7, 7th District/Neubau* ⊕ *www.lila.cx.*

**Maronski.** Austrian fashion label Maronski's designs for women are well cut in beautiful colors and very mix-and-matchable. Organic cotton and bamboo material is used for a fresh and comfortable feel. ⊠ *Neubaugasse 7, 7th District/Neubau* ☎ *699/11–34–74–54* ⊕ *www.maronski.at.*

**Nachbarin.** European avant-garde fashion can be found here, where select labels include Veronique Leroy, Amber & Louise, and Elena Ghisellini. ⊠ *Gumpendorfer Strasse 17, 6th District/Mariahilf* ☎ *01/587–2169* ⊕ *www.nachbarin.co.at.*

**Nfive.** Neutral, unadorned walls are as minimalistic as the fashion on sale here at Nfive. American Vintage, Tiger of Sweden, Filippa K, Vanessa Bruno, and many more labels are on offer. A men's clothing department is also on-site. ⊠ *Neubaugasse 5, 7th District/Neubau* ☎ *01/523–8313* ⊕ *www.nfive.at.*

**Ulliko.** Ullrike Kogelmüller, known as Ulliko, creates two lines every year of pure yet modern designs and has them manufactured locally. Her aesthetic is geometrical shapes of red, black, and white. ⊠ *Kirchengasse 7, 7th District/Neubau* ☎ *699/12–84–39–22* ⊕ *www.ulliko.com.*

**Wabisabi.** Local designer Stefanie Wippel creates breezy, easy-to-wear pieces that flatter any figure. ⊠ *Lindengasse 20, 7th District/Neubau* ☎ *644/54–51–280* ⊕ *www.alle-tragen-wabi-sabi.at.*

**Wall.** At this eclectic boutique in the Neubau district, shoppers will find a mix of books, accessories, and clothes for both men and women. Designers include Barbara i Gongini, Esther Perbandt, and Trippen, to just name a few. ⊠ *Westbahnstrasse 5A, 7th District/Neubau* ☎ *01/524–4728* ⊕ *www.kaufhauswall.com.*

## DEPARTMENT STORES

**Grüne Erde.** Beautiful scents greet you upon entering Grüne Erde, a shop specializing in organic household goods, ecologically sound furniture and tableware, natural cosmetics, and "fashion with responsibility." The name literally translates to "green earth," and products are created using natural materials and with sustainability in mind. ⊠ *Mariahilferstrasse 11, 6th District/Mariahilf* ☎ *01/520–3410* ⊕ *www.grueneerde.com.*

### FLEA MARKETS

**Flohmarkt am Naschmarkt.** In back of the Naschmarkt, stretching along the Linke Wienzeile from the Kettenbrückengasse U4 subway station, you'll find the city's most celebrated flea market. It offers a staggering collection of items, ranging from serious antiques to plain junk. It's held every Saturday, rain or shine, from 6:30 am to 6 pm. ⊠ *6th District/Mariahilf.*

### GIFTS AND SOUVENIRS

Fodor's Choice
★

**Das Goldene Wiener Herz.** A bit off the beaten path of the shopping streets of the 7th District, Das Goldene Wiener Herz produces some truly unique items. It's best known for mugs and glasses decorated with real gold. The store's name translates to the "golden Viennese heart," and classic Viennese traditions from Art Nouveau artwork to the famous wine *heurigers* are reflected in the motifs throughout the shop. ⊠ *Kirchberggasse 17, 7th District/Neubau* ☎ *68/03–23–26–66* ⊕ *www.dgwh.at.*

### HOUSEHOLD ITEMS AND FURNITURE

**Die Werkbank.** This small shop has a bold concept: absolutely everything at Die Werkbank is completely handcrafted. From contemporary furniture to jewelry and ceramics, something truly memorable will be discovered by any shopper who stops by to browse. ⊠ *Breite Gasse 1, 7th District/Neubau* ☎ *65/05–24–81–36* ⊕ *www.werkbank.cc.*

### SHOES AND LEATHER GOODS

**Freitag Bags.** This is the Vienna location of the Swiss brand Freitag, known for its selection of one-of-a-kind bags, backpacks, purses, and other accessories made from old truck tarpaulins. ⊠ *Neubaugasse 26, 7th District/Neubau* ☎ *01/523–3136* ⊕ *www.freitag.ch.*

### SHOPPING MALLS

**BahnhofCity Wien West.** Located in the Westbahnhof train station at one end of the busy Mariahilferstrasse shopping zone, BahnhofCity has about 80 shops selling clothing, electronics, shoes, sporting goods, and more. There's also a food court, plus a small grocery store that's open Sunday. ⊠ *Mariahilferstrasse, 6th District/Mariahilf* ⊕ *www.bahnhofcitywienwest.at.*

---

## WEST OF THE RINGSTRASSE: PARLIAMENT AND CITY HALL

### BOOKS

**Babette's.** More than 2,000 cookbooks from every corner of the world are piled on every conceivable space in Bernadette Wörndl's shop. Exotic aromas linger in the air; Wörndl is skilled at creating superb dishes, which she serves herself at the counter. Spices are also for sale, and cooking classes are held regularly. ⊠ *Schleifmühlgasse 17, at Mühlgasse, 4th District/Wieden* ☎ *01/585–5165* ⊕ *www.babettes.at.*

## CHRISTKINDLMÄRKTE

**Rathausplatz Christkindlmärkte.** The biggest holiday market is the one on Rathausplatz, in front of the Gothic fantasy that is Vienna's city hall. An ice rink is set up around it and remains for ice-skaters to enjoy into the New Year. ⊠ *Rathausplatz 1, 1st District.*

## CLOTHING

**Flo Vintage.** For preworn fashions, enter this vintage world extraordinaire. Here you'll find pieces from 1880 through 1980, which might include that pearl-embroidered Charleston dress you always wanted, or a fabulous antique kimono. Besides bags, shoes, and jewelry, there are also hats and even sheer silk stockings. ⊠ *Schleifmühlgasse 15A, 4th District/Wieden* ☎ *01/586–0773* ⊕ *www.flovintage.com.*

**Pregenzer.** The timeless fashions, shoes, and accessories here are either created by or selected by Jutta Pregenzer. Brands include those from Austrian, German, and Italian designers. ⊠ *Schleifmühlgasse 4, 4th District/Wieden* ☎ *01/586–5758* ⊕ *www.pregenzer.com.*

## GIFTS AND SOUVENIRS

Fodor's Choice ★ **Gabarage.** Old skis become coat stands, bowling pins turn into vases, traffic signs are transformed into lamps, and garbage bins find new lives as chairs here at the fabulously offbeat Gabarage. ⊠ *Schleifmühlgasse 6, 4th District/Wieden* ☎ *01/585–7632* ⊕ *www.gabarage.at.*

# SCHÖNBRUNN PALACE, PARK, AND ZOO

## CHRISTKINDLMÄRKTE

**Schönbrunn Christkindlmärkte.** All the glitter and gilt of the season frames the market held at the Habsburgs' Schönbrunn. The Schönbrunn market offers the best selection of works by Austrian and Viennese designers of all the city's Christmas markets. ⊠ *Schönbrunn Palace, Schönbrunner-Schloss-Strasse, 13th District/Hietzing.*

# VIENNA WOODS, LAKE NEUSIEDL, AND THE DANUBE RIVER

Updated
by Patti
McCracken

The area along the Danube and around Vienna is drenched in history. Composers like Johann Strauss were inspired by the woodlands and river, and Joseph Haydn and Anton Bruckner both lived in the region and left their traces. A trip here unfolds like a treasured picture book, with Roman ruins, medieval castles, and Baroque monasteries perching precariously above the river. This is where the Nibelungs—later immortalized by Wagner—caroused operatically, and where Richard the Lionheart was locked in a dungeon and held to (a substantial) ransom for nearly two years.

Passenger boats can take you along the Danube on pleasure cruises that stop at quaint villages. Aside from the Danube, water sports are on offer in the Neusiedl Lake area, where Viennese go to escape the city. Biking both in the lake area and along the Danube is becoming increasingly popular, and the nearby town of Baden, a favorite haunt of Beethoven, offers superb postpedaling spa relaxation.

In the towns and hamlets throughout the region, time seems to be on pause. Colorful 17th- and 18th-century buildings now serve as hotels and inns, with old-fashioned charm and well-made traditional food that invites you to sit outdoors and savor the countryside. No one is in a hurry here. But not everything is old-fashioned. A little exploring, especially in the vineyards around Neusiedl Lake, will turn up eateries pushing the envelope with modern cuisine, matched with top-notch local wines. Time suddenly leaps forward in Linz, which has more and more modern buildings punctuating the skyline along with its churches and castles, helping the city to become a unique melange of past and future.

# ORIENTATION AND PLANNING

## GETTING ORIENTED

The northeastern part of Austria has quite a diverse geography, with the practically untouched Vienna Woods to the southwest of the capital and the Weinviertel (Wine District) stretching northeast to the border. Along with hearty food, the region produces some remarkable wines, many of which inexplicably never travel beyond the borders. The diverse area has wooded hills as well as one of Europe's largest lakes. The lifeblood of the region is the Danube, which originates in Germany's Black Forest and empties into the Black Sea. The Romans used to say, "Whoever controls the Danube controls all of Europe." That may no longer be true, but the scenery is still something to behold.

## TOP REASONS TO GO

**Baden:** Spend an afternoon discovering the attractive spa and casino town of Baden.

**Leisurely bike rides:** Pedal across the plains surrounding Neusiedl Lake, stopping to explore scenic hamlets and dine on fresh fish from the lake.

**The Melk Abbey:** Magnificent Benedictine Baroque splendor leaves you breathless. The enormous edifice, stately royal rooms, lovely library, and golden, glittering church are incomparable.

**Linz:** As the saying goes, "It begins in Linz." Noted internationally for its bold, daring architecture, the capital of the province of Upper Austria has awakened to a new future, taking a leading role in contemporary art, style, and design.

**Wachau Valley:** Travel in tranquility by boat or bike between the historic towns of Krems and Melk to experience the Danube Valley's most picturesque and verdant vistas.

**Vienna Woods.** Taking a trip to the spa town of Baden means following the Vienna Woods' southern trail past ancient monasteries, fertile plains, and bucolic vineyards. Unlike other major metropolitan areas, Vienna knows nothing of suburban sprawl, so the countryside is right outside its door.

**The Weinviertel.** North of Vienna, the rolling hills, vineyards, and pleasant rural vistas invite visitors to experience a slow-moving, almost dreamy kind of lifestyle, much different from any Austriam clichés; this is the region that was for years the least developed, least modern part of the country.

**Neusiedl Lake Area.** The natural preserve at this lake is where storks come in the thousands to feed. Music lovers will want to make the pilgrimage to Eisenstadt, where the great composer Joseph Haydn (1732–1809) was in the employ of Prince Esterházy.

**Along the Danube River.** Dürnstein, Krems, and many other small medieval towns offer a peaceful respite to the wandering traveler. Wine taverns abound, and good home cooking in quaint restaurants is a perfect way to end the day. Travel through picturesque vineyards and orchards to the mighty Melk Abbey. Pass by ruins of old castles, or stop and hike through the woods for a closer look at the remnants. The views across the Danube will reward you for your toil.

**Linz.** Austria's third-largest city basks in amazing cutting-edge design. You can experience exciting insights into the latest technology at one of its incredible museums.

## PLANNING

### WHEN TO GO

Most of the regions around Vienna and along the Danube are best seen in the temperate months between mid-March and mid-November; not much is offered for winter sports and a number of hotels as well as sights close in the winter. The glorious riverside landscape takes on a fairy-tale quality when apricot and apple trees burst into blossom late April to mid-June. Others might prefer the early to mid-autumn days, when the vineyards on the terraced hills turn reddish-blue and a bracing chill settles on the Danube. From mid-September until the beginning of October, the Bruckner Festival in Linz joins forces with Ars Electronica, combining the classic with the contemporary. No matter the season, crowds jam the celebrated abbey at Melk; you're best off going first thing in the morning before the tour buses arrive, or at midday, when the throngs have receded.

## GETTING HERE AND AROUND

To get to the area between Linz and Weinviertel you can fly into the airport in Vienna or take a EuroCity train to Vienna or Linz. Once here, driving is the most convenient and scenic way to explore the region, especially if you're visiting the smaller towns and villages. If you don't want to drive, opt for the train—rather than a bus—for the main routes and longer distances. Local trains that stop at every station take a long time to get anywhere, but if you have time to spare, train rides can be fun and there are great views of the countryside from the broad windows.

### AIR TRAVEL

The northern part of eastern Austria is served by Vienna's international airport at Schwechat, 19 km (12 miles) southeast of the city center.

The Blue Danube Airport Linz is a good alternative to Vienna's Schwechat Airport if you want to start your journey in calmer surroundings. Located just 15 minutes from the city center by car or train, the airport is serviced regularly by Lufthansa, Austrian Airlines, and several low-cost airlines.

### BIKE TRAVEL

Bicycling is enormously popular in the flatlands around Neusiedl Lake. There are places that rent bikes in Neusiedl am See and Rust. Many hotels in the area also offer rentals, though some offer this only to their guests.

### BOAT TRAVEL

You can take a day trip by boat from Vienna or Krems and explore one of the stops, such as Dürnstein or Melk. Boats run from May to late September. There are two boat companies that ply the Danube. *For full information on cruises offered by the Blue Danube Schifffahrt/ DDSG (Vienna to Dürnstein) and Brandner Schifffahrt (Krems to Melk), see Danube River Cruises box.* Along this stretch of the river, bridges are few and far between. Old-fashioned tow ferries, attached to cables stretched across the river, allow a speedy crossing for people, cars, and bikes for a small fee.

### BUS TRAVEL

Frequent scheduled bus service runs between Vienna and Baden, departing across from the Opera House in Vienna to the center of Baden. Connections are available to other towns in the area. Blaguss Reisen connects Vienna to towns in eastern Austria. Buses run by the

Austrian railroad system and those run by the Austrian postal service cover the area thoroughly for short distances, although services are sometimes infrequent in the less populated areas. If you link them together, bus routes will get you to the main points in this region, assuming you have the time. You can book bus tours in Vienna or Linz by calling central bus information.

**Bus Information** Blaguss Reisen. ☎ *01/610 90–0* ⊕ *www.blaguss.at.* **Central bus information.** ☎ *01/71101.*

### CAR TRAVEL

To reach Baden and the surrounding villages by car, take the A2 autobahn south in the direction of Graz, getting off in Baden and taking Route 210 west.

The Weinviertel is accessed by major highways but not by autobahns. Follow signs to Prague, taking Route E461 toward Mistelbach and Poysdorf if you want to go northeast.

The A4 autobahn is a quick way to reach the Carnuntum region. If you're going east to Carnuntum, follow signs to the A23 and the airport (Schwechat). From the highway, take Route 9.

The A3 goes from Vienna and Eisenstadt. Route 10 from Vienna to Neusiedl Lake in Burgenland is the preferred scenic alternative to the A4 autobahn.

The main route along the north bank of the Danube is Route 3; along the south bank, there's a choice between the autobahn Route A1 and a collection of lesser roads. Roads are good and well marked, and you can switch over to the A1 autobahn, which parallels the general east–west course of the Danube Valley route. Car rental is best in Vienna or Linz.

### TRAIN TRAVEL

The train system is excellent, and reliable trains run frequently from Vienna's Schnellbahn stations to most of the destinations around Vienna. The main east–west train line cuts through the Vienna Woods; the main north–south line out of Vienna traverses the eastern edge of the Vienna Woods. Trains leave Vienna Central Station regularly for Baden.

You can get from Wien-Nord/Praterstern to the Weinviertel, where you can connect to buses running between the small villages.

The Schnellbahn No. 7 running from Wien-Mitte (Landstrasser Hauptstrasse) stops at Petronell, with service about once an hour. Carnuntum is about a 10-minute walk from the Petronell station. Trains go on to Hainburg, stopping at Bad Deutsch-Altenburg.

Trains depart from Vienna Central Station frequently for the one-hour ride to Neusiedl am See.

Regional rail tracks run parallel to the north and south banks of the Danube, and while trains reach all the larger towns and cities in the region, they miss the smaller towns of the Wachau Valley along the Danube's south bank. You can combine rail and boat transportation along this route, taking the train upstream and crisscrossing your way back on the river.

**Train Information** ÖBB—National Train Information. ☎ *05/1717* ⊕ *www. oebb.at.*

## TOURS

The Vienna Woods is one of the standard routes offered by the sightseeing-bus tour operators in Vienna. These short tours give only a quick taste of the region; if you have more time, investigate further.

One-day tours to Neusiedl Lake usually include a boat ride. Tours from Vienna also take you to Melk and back by bus and boat. These tours usually run about eight hours, with a stop at Dürnstein. Bus tours operate year-round except as noted, but the boat runs only April to October. For details, check with your hotel or with Vienna Sightseeing Tours.

**Vienna Sightseeing.** In addition to its city tours, this company offers the Danube-Panorama tour, which heads out into the Vienna Woods and brings you back into the city by boat. The duration of the tour is four hours and it is offered from mid-April to mid-October. A four-hour trip out into the Vienna Woods includes the Helenental Valley, Mayerling, Heiligenkreuz Abbey, and the Seegrotte, where you take a boat ride on the huge subterranean lake. Those tours run year-round. Pickup for all tours is from select hotels. ⊠ *Opernpassage Top 3, Vienna* ☎ *01/504–7500* ⊕ *www.viennasightseeing.at* ⊠ *€44.*

## VISITOR INFORMATION

For information on Lower Austria, call the Niederösterreich Tourismus in Vienna. Local tourist offices in the Vienna Woods, including those in Baden, are generally open weekdays. The Weinviertel region also has several tourist centers. The regional tourist information office for Burgenland province is the Burgenland Tourismus. There are helpful local *Fremdenverkehrsämter* (tourist offices), listed in the individual towns. If you plan on seeing many museums, galleries, and castles in Lower Austria—including in Vienna, the Vienna Woods, Melk, Krems, and the Weinviertel—consider getting the Niederösterreich-Card (Lower Austria Card) for €54, which allows free entry to more than 300 sites and offers a host of discounts on concerts, rail travel, and accommodations. It's available at tourist information offices, Raiffeisen banks, tobacco shops, and online at ⊕ *www.niederoesterreich-card.at.*

**Tourist Information Burgenland Tourismus.** ⊠ *Johann Permayer-Strasse 13, Eisenstadt* ☎ *02682/63384–0* ⊕ *www.burgenland.info.* **Lower Austria.** ☎ *02742/9000–9000* ⊕ *www.niederoesterreich.at.* **Steiermark Tourism.** ⊠ *St. Peter–Hauptstrasse 243, Graz* ☎ *0316/4003–0* ⊕ *www.steiermark.com.* **Upper Austria.** ⊠ *Freistaedter Strasse 119, Linz* ☎ *0732/221022* ⊕ *www.oberoesterreich.at.*

## RESTAURANTS

With only a few exceptions, food in this region is on the simple side. The basics are available in abundance: roast meats, customary schnitzel variations, game (in season), fresh vegtables, and standard desserts such as *Palatschinken* (crepes filled with jam or nuts, topped with chocolate sauce) and *Apfelstrüdel.* However, imaginative cooking is beginning to spread, and most places have fresh fish and other lighter fare. Look for at least one vegetarian course on most menus.

Around Neusiedl Lake, the local Pannonian cooking, strongly influenced by neighboring Hungary, showcases such spicy dishes as *gulyas* (goulash) flavored with paprika. You'll also find fresh fish, goose,

game, and an abundance of fresh local vegetables. Along the Danube, restaurants make the most of the river views. Simple *Gasthäuser* are everywhere, but better dining is more often found in country inns. Restaurants, whether sophisticated and stylish or plain and homey, are often rated as much by their wine as by their cuisine.

Dining in the countryside is a casual affair. Meal times are usually from noon to 2 pm for lunch and from 6 to 10 for dinner. It's rare to find a restaurant that serves all afternoon, so plan ahead. It's a good idea to reserve a table, especially for Sunday lunch, which is a popular time for families to get together. As in Vienna, tipping is usually rounded to the nearest euro. When in doubt, tip 5%. *Restaurants reviews have been shortened. For full information, visit Fodors.com.*

## HOTELS

Although there are some luxury hotels in Linz and a few castle-hotels along the Danube, in general accommodations in the countryside are no frills. That said, the region has become much more heavily traveled than it was a generation ago, and many lodgings have been upgraded and restyled to attract the growing number of guests. Establishments are family-run, and there is usually somebody on staff who speaks English. You'll probably have to carry your own bags, and sometimes climb stairs in older buildings. Booking ahead is a good idea, as most places have relatively few rooms, particularly rooms with private baths. The standard country pillows and bed coverings are down-filled, so if you're allergic to feathers, ask for other blankets. Accommodations in private homes are cheaper still, and these bargains are usually identified by signs reading *"zimmer frei"* (room available) or *"früstückspension"* (bed-and-breakfast).

Some hotels offer half-board, with dinner in addition to buffet breakfast. The half-board rate is usually an extra €15–€30 per person. Occasionally, quoted room rates for hotels already include half-board accomodations, though a discounted rate is generally offered if you prefer not to take the evening meal; inquire when booking. Rooms rates include taxes and service, and usually breakfast—although this is likely little more than bread or rolls with slices of ham and cheese. In summer, nights are generally cool, but days can get uncomfortably hot. Most older hotels don't have air-conditioning, and rooms can get stuffy; whenever possible, see the rooms before checking in. *Hotel reviews have been shortened. For full information, visit Fodors.com.*

| WHAT IT COSTS IN EUROS | | | | |
|---|---|---|---|---|
| | $ | $$ | $$$ | $$$$ |
| RESTAURANTS | under €12 | €12–€17 | €18–€22 | over €22 |
| HOTELS | under €100 | €100–€135 | €136–€175 | over €175 |

Prices in the restaurant reviews are the average cost for a main course at dinner or, if dinner is not served, at lunch. Prices in the hotel reviews are the lowest cost of a standard double room in high season.

# VIENNA WOODS

Pass through the legendary Vienna Woods bordering Vienna on the west. The hills are skirted by vineyards forming a "wine belt," which also follows the valleys south of Vienna. You can tour this area easily in a day, either by car or by public transportation, or you can spend the night in Baden to allow for a more leisurely exploration of other towns and villages along the way.

## BADEN

*38 km (24 miles) southwest of Vienna.*

The Weinstrasse brings you to the serenely elegant spa town of Baden. Since antiquity, Baden's sulfuric thermal baths have attracted both the ailing and the fashionable from all over the world. When the Romans came across the springs, they dubbed the town Aquae; the Babenbergs revived it in the 10th century; and with the visit of the Russian czar Peter the Great in 1698, Baden's golden age began. Austria's Emperor Franz II spent 31 successive summers here. Later in the century, Emperor Franz Josef was a regular visitor, his presence inspiring many of the regal trappings the city still displays. It was in Baden that Mozart composed his "Ave Verum"; Beethoven spent 15 summers here and wrote large sections of his Ninth Symphony and *Missa Solemnis* when he lived at Frauengasse 10; Franz Grillparzer wrote his historical dramas here; and Josef Lanner, both Johann Strausses (father and son), Carl Michael Ziehrer, and Karl Millöcker composed and directed many of their waltzes, marches, and operettas here.

### GETTING HERE AND AROUND

A streetcar was built in the 19th century for the sole purpose of ferrying the rich Viennese from their summer homes in Baden to the opera in Vienna—the last stop is directly in front of the opera house. Today, the modern streetcar still winds its way through Vienna's suburbs on its 50-minute journey to Baden, though things only start to get scenic about 25 minutes before Baden, when the car passes through the wine villages. A faster option is to take the train. It's about a half hour from Westbahnhof, and most trains are double-deckers (so you can sit up top and have a great view of the countryside).

### ESSENTIALS

**Tourist Information Baden.** ⊠ *Brusattiplatz 3* ☎ *02252/22600–600* ⊕ *www. tourismus.baden.at.*

### EXPLORING

**Arnulf Rainer Museum.** A former 19th-century bathhouse—one which Emperors Franz Josef frequented on his visits to Baden—was converted in 2009 to a museum highlighting Austria's internationally renowned abstract artist Arnulf Rainer. Exhibits also include other contemporary greats, including Damien Hirst. Rainer's work has been displayed in the Museum of Modern Art in New York and other noteworthy museums. ⊠ *Josefsplatz 5* ☎ *02252/209–19–611* ⊕ *www. arnulf-rainer-museum.at* 🎫 *€6.*

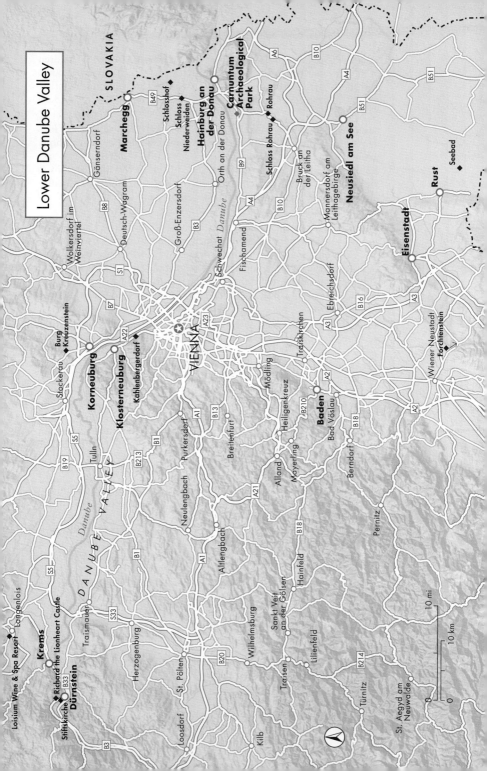

**Badener Puppen und Spielzeugmuseum** (*Doll and Toy Museum*). Children of all ages will enjoy this enchanting museum, which has four rooms with dolls dating from the late 1700s to the 1950s, alongside other exhibits. ⊠ *Erzherzog Rainer-Ring 23* ☎ *02252/86800–578* ⓔ *€3.80* ⊙ *Closed Mon.*

**Beethoven Haus.** Known locally and affectionately as Beethoven's *Haus der Neunten,*or Ninth House, since he composed his Ninth Symphony while living at this address, the house was fully restored after workers discovered artwork within that dated back to the time Beethoven lived there. The art, which hung on the walls of Beethoven's summer apartment, has been fully restored as well. ⊠ *Rathausgasse 10* ☎ *02252/86800–231* ⓔ *€6* ⊙ *Closed Mon.*

**Casino.** The ornate Casino—with a bar, restaurant, and gambling rooms—still includes traces of its original 19th-century touches, but has been enlarged and, in the process, overlaid with glitz rivaling that of Las Vegas. Evening attire is expected, and jackets are available on loan at the coat check. Casual dress is only acceptable in the Jackpot Casino. ⊠ *Kaiserallee 1* ☎ *7221/30–24–0* ⊕ *www.casino-baden-baden.de/en.*

**Kurpark.** One of the biggest draws to Baden, outside of the spa, is the vast, lovely, sloping Kurpark almost smack in the middle of town. It was created back in 1792 for Austria's beloved Empress Maria Theresa. But as her highness only occasionally made her way to this Vienna outpost, the locals were free to enjoy it themselves, and they've been doing so ever since. In summer the park is in full flush: concerts are held each weekend afternoon under the hundred-year-old music pavilion, and operettas are performed at the arena (it's fitted with a glass dome, which comes out when it rains.) ▪TIP➔ **The Grand Casino and Kurtheater are located in the park—enticing indoor venues during wintry or bad weather.** ⊠ *Kaiser Franz-Ring.*

## WHERE TO EAT AND STAY

$$
AUSTRIAN
✕ **Rudolfshof.** Enjoy a walk through the Kurpark, where you'll find this 19th-century hunting lodge. The fine restaurant serves traditional dishes from the region, including Wiener and chicken schnitzel, pork fillet, and venison stew. **Known for:** traditional and hearty Austrian fare; excellent local wine; beautiful views from the terrace. ⓢ *Average main: €16* ⊠ *Am Gamingerberg 5* ☎ *02252/209–2030* ⊕ *www.rudolfshof.at* ⊙ *Closed Mon., Tues., and early Jan.–early Mar.*

$$
HOTEL
🛏 **Krainerhütte.** About 5 km (3 miles) from Baden, this typical Alpine house (think lots of balconies and natural wood) has an almost Scandinavian feel thanks to its sleek, modern rooms. **Pros:** beautiful location; great for hiking or outdoor seminars; nice restaurant with vegan options. **Cons:** often gets booked up; some noise from nearby highway; restaurant doesn't serve after 9 pm. ⓢ *Rooms from: €105* ⊠ *Helenental 41, Heiligenkreuz* ☎ *02252/445–110* ⊕ *www.krainer-huette.at* ➳ *62 rooms* ⓞ| *Breakfast.*

$$$
HOTEL
🛏 **Schloss Weikersdorf.** On beautiful grounds, this restored Imperial castle is minutes from the town center, on the edge of a vast public park. **Pros:** helpful staff; beautiful surroundings; sometimes offers special

last-minute rates. **Cons:** rooms vary greatly in size; can feel crowded; air-conditoning available only in the Residenz wing. $ *Rooms from:* €*169* ✉ *Schlossgasse 9–11* ☎ *02252/48301* ⊕ *www.hotelschlossweikersdorf.at* ⟿ *100 rooms* ⦿ *Breakfast.*

# THE WEINVIERTEL

Luckily, Austria's Weinviertel (Wine District) has been largely neglected by the "experts," and its deliciously fresh wines reward those who enjoy partaking of the grape without the all-too-frequent nonsense that goes with it. The Weinviertel is bounded by the Danube on the south, the Thaya River and the Czech border on the north, and the March River and Slovakia to the east. No well-defined line separates the Weinviertel from the Waldviertel to the west; the Kamp River valley, officially part of the Waldviertel, is an important wine region. A tour by car, just for the scenery, can be made in a day. You may want two or three days to savor the region and its wines, which are generally on the medium-dry side. Don't expect to find here the elegant facilities found elsewhere in Austria; prices are low by any standard, and village restaurants and accommodations are mainly *Gasthäuser* that meet local needs. This means that you'll be rubbing shoulders with the country folk over your glass of Blaufrankisch.

## MARCHEGG

7

*43 km (27 miles) northeast of Vienna.*

This tiny corner of the lower Weinviertel is known as the Marchfeld, for the fields stretching east to the March River that form the border with Slovakia. In this region—known as the granary of Austria—two elegant Baroque castles are worth a visit; while totally renovated, these country estates have lost none of their gracious charm over the centuries.

### GETTING HERE AND AROUND

From Vienna, take the E58 motorway to Petronell and change to B49, which goes directly to Marchegg. Trains go from Vienna Central Station several times daily.

### EXPLORING

FAMILY
Fodor'sChoice
★

**Schlosshof.** A true Baroque gem, this castle is shining even more brilliantly since the completion of extensive restorations. The product of that master designer and architect Johann Lukas von Hildebrandt, who in 1732 reconstructed the square castle into an elegant U-shape building, the Schloss opens up on the eastern side to a marvelous Baroque formal garden that gives way toward the river. The famed landscape painter Bernardo Bellotto, noted for his Canaletto-like vistas of scenic landmarks, captured the view before the reconstruction. His three paintings were used as a guide for restoring the gardens to their Baroque appearance. The castle was once owned by Empress Maria Theresa, mother of Marie Antoinette. You can visit the suite the empress used during her royal visits, faithfully re-created down to the tiniest details, as well as the two-story chapel in which she prayed.

In 2016, the Schlosshof added some highly popular adventure paths to the interactive visitor experience. Children can play the roles of stable boys and maidens, performing various chores and encountering blacksmiths, falconers, or bakers along the path. You might stumble upon a large estate farm that is home to horses, goats, donkeys, and several other animals. The complex also includes a restaurant and pâtisserie, both with indoor and outdoor seating. Guided tours and audio tours of the castle and garden are available in English, but it's also possible to wander around the buildings and grounds on your own. The castle is about 8 km (5 miles) south of Mar-

> ## WEINSTRASSE CYCLING
>
> A great way to see Carnuntum and the towns along the Danube is by bicycle. Bike routes are well marked, extensive, and in excellent condition. Many shops in Vienna rent bikes, and some hotels have bikes available to their guests. For the most part, you can take a bike free of charge on the local and regional trains, which makes it easy to explore a larger area. And you'll be in good company: weekend cycle tours along the Danube are popular with the Viennese and neighboring Slovaks.

chegg. Be sure to enjoy the panoramic view (you can even see Bratislava from here). If you come in winter, you can enjoy the charming Adventmarkt set up on the sprawling grounds. ⊠ *Schlosshof* ☎ *02285/200–000* ⊕ *www.schlosshof.at* 🎫 *€13.*

**Schloss Niederweiden.** Three kilometers (nearly 2 miles) southwest of Schlosshof is Schloss Niederweiden, on the outskirts of the village of Engelhartstetten. Designed as a hunting lodge in 1694 by Fischer von Erlach, this jewel was subsequently owned in turn by Prince Eugene and Empress Maria Theresa, who added a second floor and the mansard roof. The castle fell into disrepair after World War II, but was completely renovated in the 1980s and contains a photo exhibit of the region's castles and the Imperials who lived in them. ⚠ **Be aware that the space is often rented out for private celebrations and polo matches.** Tours are only in German. ⊠ *Engelhartstetten* ☎ *02285/20000* ⊕ *www.schlosshof.at* 🎫 *€3; free with Schlosshof admission.*

## CARNUNTUM AND HAINBURG AN DER DONAU

*32 km (20 miles) southeast of Vienna.*

Until a few years ago, the village of Carnuntum was a yawning backwater on the Austrian plain and, along with its slightly larger neighbor, Hainburg, was the last stop before the Iron Curtain. But the fall of the wall turned the main road into a major throughway connecting East to West. The development of the Carnuntum archaeological complex and the rise of the Donau-Auen National Park (the last remaining intact wetlands in Central Europe) turned this once-forgotten region into a significant destination for travelers.

### GETTING HERE AND AROUND

From Vienna, take the E58 motorway east directly to Petronell-Carnuntum. By train, take the S7, a local service that departs from Wien-Mitte/ Landstrasse or Wien-Nord/Praterstern; it stops at both Petronell and

Bad Deutsch-Altenburg. The tiny village of Rohrau, Joseph Haydn's birthplace, is 5 km (3 miles) south of Petronell, on Route 211.

## EXPLORING

FAMILY
Fodor's Choice
★

**Carnuntum.** The remains of the important Roman legionary fortress and civil town of Carnuntum, which once numbered 55,000 inhabitants, extend about 5 km (3 miles) along the Danube from the tiny village of Petronell to the next town of Bad Deutsch-Altenburg. The recent discovery here of an ancient school of gladiators delighted archaeologists and significantly raised Carnuntum's stature, and rightfully so. Visitors can tour the grounds, which include two amphitheaters (the first one seating 8,000) and the foundations of former residences, reconstructed baths, and trading centers—some with mosaic floors. The ruins are quite spread out, with the impressive remains of a Roman arch, the **Heidentor** (Pagans' Gate), a 15-minute pleasant walk from the main excavations in Petronell. You can experience what Roman life was like circa AD 380 in the elegantly furnished Villa Urbana. Many of the excavated finds are housed at the Museum Carnuntinum at Bad Deutsch-Altenburg. The star of the collection is a carving of Mithras killing a bull. Guided tours in English are available in July and August at noon; otherwise they are in German only. ⊠ *Hauptstrasse, Petronell* ☎ *02163/33770* ⊕ *www. carnuntum.co.at* 🎫 *€11* ⊙ *Closed mid-Nov.–mid-Mar.*

**Kulturfabrik.** A hundred years after the 1683 Turkish invasion that wiped out the town, the construction of the Imperial Royal Tobacco Factory brought Hainburg back to life. Today, Kulturfabrik is part of the Petronell-Carnuntum Archaeological complex. Mostly used for conventions and seminars, it houses a small exhibit of Roman ruins, as well as a gift store. The spectacular panoramic views of the Danube from the second-floor café are a real treat. ⊠ *Kulturplatz 1, Hainburg an der Donau* ☎ *01263/3377–799* ⊕ *www.carnuntum.co.at* ⊙ *Closed Sun.*

**Rohrau.** Just 5 km (3 miles) south of Petronell, this tiny village was the birthplace of Joseph Haydn, and the quaint, reed-thatched cottage where the composer, son of the local blacksmith, was born in 1732 is now a small museum. You'll see a pianoforte he is supposed to have played, as well as letters and other memorabilia. The furnishings are homey, if a bit spartan. After Haydn had gained worldwide renown, he is said to have returned to his native Rohrau and knelt to kiss the steps of his humble home. Concerts are occasionally held on the grounds. ⊠ *Obere Hauptstrasse 25, Rohrau* ☎ *02164/2268* ⊕ *www.haydnge-burtshaus.at* 🎫 *€5* ⊙ *Closed Mon. and early Nov.–Feb.*

**Schloss Rohrau.** This palace is where Haydn's mother worked as a cook for Count Harrach. The palace has one of the best private art collections in Austria, with an emphasis on 17th- and 18th-century Spanish and Italian painting. The upper level has been renovated and turned into private apartments; there is now also a good restaurant on the grounds serving Austrian fare. Be mindful of the peacocks that wander the grounds, and sometimes beyond. ⊠ *Rohrau* ☎ *02164/225318* ⊕ *www.schloss-rohrau.at* 🎫 *€12* ⊙ *Closed Nov.–Easter.*

**Schlossberg Castle Ruins.** These castle ruins are easily approached on foot, and the views from the top are lovely, but the place is equally appealing

7

for the castle's long and illustrious history. During the 11th century, Hainburg was a fortified town on the far eastern front of the Holy Roman Empire, and in 1252, Przemsyl Ottaker, the king of Bohemia, married Duchess Margarethe of Austria here, a union designed to considerably expand his kingdom. The castle had been built shortly before that with part of the ransom received from the capture of King Richard the Lionheart in Dürnstein. The Schloss was attacked many times, most severely by the 1683 Turkish invasion, which also took the lives of 8,000 residents, nearly the entire community. Each summer the town hosts "Burgspiele Hainburg," where open-air plays (often Shakespeare) are performed in German on the castle grounds. ⊠ *Schlossbergstrasse, Hainburg an der Donau* ☎ 🖾 *Free.*

**Stadtmuseum Wienertor.** The imposing "Vienna Gate" still represents the entrance to the medieval town of Hainburg on the Danube, and buses, tractors, and a steady stream of cars still squeeze through its passage daily. The town is encircled by remarkably well-preserved 13th-century walls with 12 gates and towers, including the Wienertor, which is the largest extant medieval gate in Europe. In 1683, the Turks devastated the town, leaving only a handful of survivors, including composer Josef Haydn's grandfather, who as a small boy scrambled up a chimney and hid from the marauders. Climb up inside the Wienertor, now a museum, and see an impressive supply of weaponry left behind by the invaders—clearly in a hurry to get to Vienna—as well as a stockpile from other ancient wars. A view out the narrow window offers a charming look down at the winding main street and the church steeple. While you can always stop by and view the exterior of the tower, inside access is only available Sunday and holidays. ⊠ *Wienerstrasse 1, Hainburg an der Donau* ☎ *02165/62111* ⊕ *www.wienertor.at* 🖾 *€4* ⊙ *Closed Mon.–Sat.*

### WHERE TO STAY

$$    🖭 **Hotel Altes Kloster.** Adjacent to the Kulturfabrik and just around the
HOTEL    corner from where little Joseph Haydn used to have his music lessons, this 17th-century monastery retains all its historic serenity in the sleepy, romantic town of Hainburg. **Pros:** live piano music in the restaurant-café adds to the atmosphere; very quiet, peaceful setting; five-minute walk to town center. **Cons:** carpeting in rooms may aggravate allergies; not all staff speaks English; no air-conditioning. ⓢ *Rooms from: €110* ⊠ *Fabrikplatz 1a, Hainburg an der Donau* ☎ *02165/64020* ⊕ *www. alteskloster.at* ⇗ *52 rooms* ⫶⊙⫶ *Breakfast.*

# NEUSIEDL LAKE AREA

In the north part of the Burgenland region, Neusiedl Lake occupies a strange world. One of the largest lakes in Europe, it is the Continent's only true steppe lake—a bizarre body of warm, brackish water. Underground springs feed it, but when they fail it dries up, which last happened in the 1860s. Currently the water is not more than about 7 feet deep at any spot; its many shallower sections make it possible (but still hazardous) to wade across the lake. Its depth has varied dramatically, however, at times nearly engulfing the villages on its banks. Most of its 318-square-km (124-square-mile) surface area is in Austria, but the southern reaches extend into Hungary.

What really sets Neusiedl Lake apart is the thick belt of tall reeds—in some places more than a mile wide—that almost completely encircles it. This is the habitat of more than 250 species of large and varied flocks of birds, which nest near the water's edge. The lake is also a magnet for anglers, boaters, and windsurfers; other activities include swimming and bicycling along its scenic banks.

Through a partnership deal, many hotels in the area offer the Neusiedler See Card ("*see*" means lake) for free, valid for the duration of your stay. From April through October it provides free or reduced admissions to main attractions and tours as well as free parking and use of public transportation.

> ## BICYCLING AROUND NEUSIEDL
>
> The plains around Neusiedl Lake, upon which sit tiny, undisturbed hamlets amid unspoiled scenery, are perfect for leisurely bicycling. Practically every village has a bike-rental shop (*Fahrradverleih* or *Radverleih*), but on weekends demand is so great that it's a good idea to reserve in advance. A bike route encircles the lake, passing through Hungary (you can shorten the route by taking the ferry between Illmitz beach and Mörbisch). Bike route maps are available at tourist offices.

The beach in Neusiedl am See makes the town a big draw in the summer. The town also has some ruins and a Trinity Column to check out, but history buffs will be more satisfied elsewhere in the area. The Burgenland state capital, Eisenstadt, due to its long association with the noble Esterházy family, offers the most in terms of historical sightseeing—a castle, opulent churches, museums, a Jewish quarter, and a cemetery. If you want to get away from the crowds, try the town of Rust. With just 1,700 inhabitants, it is Austria's smallest administrative district and prides itself on its wine-making tradition, the keystone of the local economy, as well as its population of storks. The small size of the town makes it a snap to get into the countryside on marked paths for Nordic walking.

## NEUSIEDL AM SEE

*51 km (32 miles) southeast of Vienna.*

At the north end of the lake for which it is named is a pleasant resort town with good facilities. Direct hourly commuter trains from Vienna have made it very popular, so you won't be alone here. To reach the lake, where you can rent small boats, swim, or just relax on the beach, follow the main street for three blocks east of the Hauptplatz and turn right on Seestrasse. In the town itself, visit the ruins of the 13th-century hill fortress, Ruine Tabor, and the 15th-century parish church near the town hall.

### GETTING HERE AND AROUND
Trains leave from Vienna Central Station frequently every day. By car, take the A4 motorway east to the A50 and then B51, following the signs for Neusiedl am See.

### ESSENTIALS

**Tourist Information** Neusiedl am See Tourismusbüro. ✉ *Untere Hauptstrasse 7* ☎ *02167/2229* 🌐 *www.neusiedlamsee.at.*

### WHERE TO EAT AND STAY

$$$ MEDITERRANEAN 🍴 **Gasthaus Nyikospark.** On the main street of Neusiedl, this well-regarded upscale eatery is ill-marked, but worth the search (it's on the left side about halfway down as you're driving through town from north to south). Begin with a starter of organic sheep cheese and watercress puree, and continue with big, tender roasted duck or glazed calf's liver. **Known for:** canvas-covered terrace among chestnut trees; upscale Vienna cuisine; friendly owner. [$] *Average main: €18* ✉ *Untere Hauptstrasse 59* ☎ *02167/40222* 🌐 *www.nyikospark.at* 🕒 *Closed Wed. and Thurs.*

$$$$ HOTEL 🏨 **Hotel Wende.** This sprawling three-story hotel complex is close to the lake and has more than standard amenities, whether you want to get a massage or rent bicycles and set off on the path that begins at its doorstep. **Pros:** friendly and knowledgeable staff; spacious lobby; very good location. **Cons:** little charm; outdated televisions; no a/c. [$] *Rooms from: €189* ✉ *Seestrasse 40* ☎ *02167/8111* 🌐 *www.hotel-wende.at* 🕒 *Closed Christmas wk and the 1st 2 wks in Feb.* 🛏 *104 rooms* 🍽 *Breakfast.*

## EISENSTADT

*22 km (14 miles) northwest of Mörbisch, 48 km (30 miles) south of Vienna, 26 km (16¼ miles) southwest of Wiener Neustadt.*

Burgenland's provincial capital, Eisenstadt, is a really small town. Nevertheless, it has an illustrious history and enough sights to keep you busy for a half day, if not quite a full one. Although the town has existed since at least the 12th century, it only rose to significance in the 17th century when it became the seat of the Esterházys, a princely Hungarian family that traces its roots to Attila the Hun. The original Esterházy made his fortune by marrying a succession of wealthy landowning widows. Esterházy's support was largely responsible for the Habsburg reign in Hungary under the Dual Monarchy. At one time the family controlled a far-flung agro-industrial empire, and it still owns vast forest resources. The composer Joseph Haydn lived in Eisenstadt for some 30 years while in the service of the Esterházy family. When Hungary ceded Burgenland to Austria after World War I, its major city, Sopron, elected to remain a part of Hungary, so in 1925 tiny Eisenstadt was made the capital of the new Austrian province.

Eisenstadt's main draw is the former palace, Schloss Esterházy, and the tourist office can tell you about its other attractions, including the Museum of Austrian Culture, the Diocesan Museum, the Fire Fighters Museum, Haydn's little garden house, and an assortment of churches.

### GETTING HERE AND AROUND

Eisenstadt is connected to Vienna and Neusiedl am See by train and to places throughout Burgenland by bus. By car from Rust, take Route B52 west past St. Margarethen and Trausdorf to the capital.

## ESSENTIALS

**Contacts Eisenstadt Tourismus.** ✉ *Glorietteallee 1* ☎ *02682/67390* ⊕ *www. eisenstadt-tourismus.at.*

## EXPLORING

**Bergkirche.** At the crest of Esterházystrasse perches the Bergkirche, an ornate Baroque church that includes the strange *Kalvarienberg,* an indoor Calvary Hill representing the Way of the Cross with life-size figures placed in small grottoes along an elaborate path. At its highest point, the trail reaches the platform of the belfry, offering a view over the town and this section of Burgenland. The magnificent wooden figures were carved and painted by Franciscan monks more than 250 years ago. The main part of the church contains the tomb of Joseph Haydn, who died in 1809 in Vienna. Restoration work will be ongoing until 2020, but both the church and Haydn's mausoleum will stay open to visitors. ✉ *Josef Haydn Platz 1* ☎ *02682/62638* ⊕ *www.haydnkirche. at* 🎟 *€3* ⊘ *Closed Nov.–Mar.*

**Haydn Museum.** The composer lived in the simple house on a street that now bears his name—Joseph Haydn-Gasse—from 1766 until 1778. Now the Haydn Museum, it contains several first editions of his music and other memorabilia. The house itself, and especially its flower-filled courtyard with the small back rooms, is quite delightful. A guided costumed tour involves tales about love and music in the real Haydn's life. ✉ *Joseph-Haydn-Gasse 19–21* ☎ *02682/719–3900* ⊕ *www.haydnhaus. at* 🎟 *€4.50* ⊘ *Closed Nov.–Mar. and Mon. in Apr. and May.*

**Landesmuseum Burgenland** (*Burgenland Provincial Museum*). This museum brings the history of the region to life with displays on such diverse subjects as Roman culture and the area's wildlife. There's a section on the rich musical heritage of the area, including a memorial room to the composer Franz Liszt, along with more relics of the town's former Jewish community. ✉ *Museumgasse 1–5* ☎ *02682/719–4000* ⊕ *landesmuseum-burgenland.at* 🎟 *€6* ⊘ *Closed Sun. in June–mid-Nov. and weekends in mid-Nov.–mid-Dec.*

**Österreichisches Jüdisches Museum** (*Austrian Jewish Museum*). Wertheimergasse and Unterbergstrasse were boundaries of the Jewish ghetto from 1671 until 1938. During that time Eisenstadt had a considerable Jewish population; today the Österreichisches Jüdisches Museum recalls the experience of Austrian Jews throughout history. A fascinating private synagogue in the complex survived the 1938 terror and is incorporated into the museum. ✉ *Unterbergstrasse 6* ☎ *02682/65145* ⊕ *www.ojm.at* 🎟 *€5* ⊘ *Closed Nov.–Apr. and Mon.*

**Fodor's Choice** ★ **Schloss Esterházy.** The former palace of the ruling princes reigns over the town. Built in the Baroque style between 1663 and 1672 on the foundations of a medieval castle and later modified, it is still owned by the Esterházy family, who lease it to the provincial government for use mostly as offices. The Esterházy family rooms are worth viewing, and the lavishly decorated Haydn Room, an impressive concert hall where the composer conducted his own works from 1761 until 1790, is still used for presentations of Haydn's works, with musicians often dressed in period garb. The hall is one of several rooms on a guided tour (in

7

English on request if there are at least 10 people) that lasts about 30 minutes. The cellar has the largest wine museum in Austria with 700 objects including a massive wine barrel and historical grape press. A tour of the princess's apartment includes objects relating to three royal women. The park behind the Schloss is pleasant for a stroll or a picnic, and in late August it's a venue for the Burgenland wine week—Eisenstadt hosts the "Festival of 1,000 Wines"—and there's a two-hour tour on wine and culture at the palace, ending with a tasting. ✉ *Esterházy Platz* ☎ *02682/719–63004* 🌐 *www.schloss-esterhazy.at* 🎫 *€11; €36 for combined ticked to all exhibitions and wine museum* 🕑 *Closed weekdays in mid-Nov.–Mar.*

**HAYDN FULLY AT REST**

Composer Joseph Haydn's body was returned to Eisenstadt for burial at the request of Prince Esterházy in 1821. The head, however, had been stolen by phrenologists and eventually became the property of the Gesellschaft der Musikfreunde, a Viennese musical society. A new marble tomb was built for Haydn in 1932 at Eisenstadt's Bergkirche, but the head was not returned until 1954. In the meantime a substitute head had been placed with the remains. Both skulls are now in the marble tomb.

### WHERE TO EAT AND STAY

$$$$ ECLECTIC Fodor's Choice ★

🍴 **Taubenkobel.** Consistently ranked as one of the top restaurants in Austria, the "Dovecote" is a rambling, elegantly restored 19th-century farmhouse 5 km (3 miles) from Eisenstadt in the village of Schützen. The seasonally changing menu has featured dishes such as saddle of lamb with mangold blossoms and asparagus in saffron sauce. **Known for:** fresh herbs taken from nearby meadows; menu that changes seasonally; packages that include wine pairings and hotel stays. [$] *Average main: €98* ✉ *Hauptstrasse 33, Schützen am Gebirge* ☎ *02684/2297* 🌐 *www.taubenkobel.com* 🕑 *Closed Mon., Tues., and Jan.–Feb. 15.*

$$ HOTEL

🏨 **Gasthof Ohr.** Personal service is the hallmark of this family-run hotel and restaurant, an easy 10-minute walk from the town center. **Pros:** spacious rooms; good food. **Cons:** no real lobby; a/c in only some of the rooms. [$] *Rooms from: €130* ✉ *Rusterstrasse 51* ☎ *02682/62460* 🌐 *www.hotelohr.at* 🛏 *39 rooms* 🍽 *Breakfast.*

$$$ HOTEL

🏨 **Hotel Burgenland.** This sprawling hotel in the town center has everything you'd expect in a first-class establishment, and the friendly staff goes out of its way to assist guests. **Pros:** well-equipped, modern hotel; sauna available to guests. **Cons:** business-hotel atmosphere; outdated furniture. [$] *Rooms from: €170* ✉ *Franz Schubertplatz 1* ☎ *02682/6960* 🌐 *www.hotelburgenland.at* 🛏 *88 rooms* 🍽 *Breakfast.*

### NIGHTLIFE AND PERFORMING ARTS

**Haydn Festival.** Eisenstadt devotes much cultural energy to one of its favorite sons. In the first half of September it plays host to the annual Haydn Festival in the Esterházy Palace and several other venues in Burgenland and Lower Austria. Many of the concerts are by renowned performers, and admission prices vary with the event. Other concerts featuring the works of Joseph Haydn run from mid-May to early

October. Contact the Haydnfestspiele office in Schloss Esterházy or the local tourist office. ⊠ *Eisenstadt* ☎ *02682/61866* ⊕ *www.haydn-festival.at.*

**EN ROUTE**

Heading southwest from Eisenstadt brings you to the waist of Burgenland, the narrow region squeezed between Lower Austria and Hungary. The leading attraction here is Forchtenstein; take Route S31 for 20 km (12½ miles) to Mattersburg, then a local road 3 km (2 miles) west.

## RUST

*14 km (9 miles) south of Purbach, 28 km (17½ miles) southwest of Neusiedl am See.*

**Fodor's Choice**
★

Picturesque Rust, a UNESCO World Cultural Heritage site, is easily the most popular village on the lake for the colorful pastel facades of its houses and for lake sports. Tourists flock here in summer to see storks nesting atop the Renaissance and Baroque houses in the well-preserved historic center. ■ TIP→ **Be sure to look for Steckerl, a delicious local fish caught from Neusiedl Lake and grilled barbecue-style with spices. It's available in most restaurants, but only in the hot months of summer.**

**GETTING HERE AND AROUND**
By car from Eisenstadt, take Route B52 east about 12 km (7½ miles). Bus service is also available from Eisenstadt.

**ESSENTIALS**
**Tourist Information** Tourismusbüro Rust. ⊠ *Conradplatz 1* ☎ *02685/502* ⊕ *www.rust.at.*

**EXPLORING**
**Fischerkirche** (*Fishermen's Church*). The restored Gothic Fischerkirche is off the west end of the Rathausplatz. Built between the 12th and 16th centuries, it is surrounded by a defensive wall and is noted for its 15th-century frescoes and an organ from 1705. The church sometimes has classical concerts. Tours are available but must be arranged in advance. ⊠ *Conradplatz 1* ☎ *02685/295, 0676/970–3316* ☞ *€2, €4 with tour.*

**Kremayr Haus.** Three decades ago, local arts patron Rudolf Kremayr bestowed to Rust one of the most stunning buildings on the town's main square. The interior is rather lavishly decorated and holds some of the town's historical archives. The chimney room, an outbuilding off the courtyard, is where local exhibitions and small concerts are held. ⊠ *Conradplatz 2* ☎ *676/8416–0623* ☞ *Free.*

**Seebad.** A causeway leads through nearly a mile of reeds to the Seebad beach and boat landing, where you can take a sightseeing boat either round-trip or to another point on the lake. You can also rent a boat, swim, or enjoy a waterside drink or snack at an outdoor table.

**Weingut Feiler-Artinger.** Like many family-run wineries in Rust (most in Austria are family businesses), this one produces white and red sweet wine from the vineyards around Rust. Many are for sale, including a selection of organic wines. ⊠ *Hauptstrasse 3* ☎ *02685/237.*

7

### WHERE TO EAT AND STAY

$$$ AUSTRIAN
🍴 **Rusterhof.** A lovingly renovated burgher's house—the town's oldest—at the top of the main square houses an excellent and imaginative restaurant. The menu depends on what's fresh, and might include grilled fish or Wiener schnitzel made with organic veal. **Known for:** terrace view over main street; fresh and organic menu; wine from Rust and surrounding locale. [$] *Average main: €21* ✉ *Rathausplatz 18* ☎ *02685/6162* 🌐 *www.hotelbuergerhaus-rust.at* 🕒 *Closed Mon.*

$$ AUSTRIAN
🍴 **Schandl.** The Schandl family of Rust is one of the best-known wine growers of the Neusiedl Lake area; their devotees come for wine tastings and stay for dinner. For good, simple food to go along with their excellent wine, join the locals at this popular *Heurige* (wine tavern). **Known for:** generous buffet with sausages and salads; large courtyard for outdoor summer dining; family wine for sale at adjacent shop. [$] *Average main: €13* ✉ *Hauptstrasse 20* ☎ *02685/265* 🌐 *www.schandlwein.com* 🕒 *Closed Tues. and mid-Nov.–mid-Mar. No lunch weekdays.*

$$$ HOTEL FAMILY
🏨 **Sifkovits.** This charming hotel run by the Hallwirth family has lovely and tastefully redecorated rooms in a prime location, close to the lake and a block away from Rust's bustling center. **Pros:** spacious and welcoming lobby; quiet rooms; large park behind the hotel. **Cons:** rooms facing street are sometimes noisy; room decor might not be for everyone; books up quickly. [$] *Rooms from: €146* ✉ *Am Seekanal 8* ☎ *02685/276* 🌐 *www.sifkovits.at* 🕒 *Closed Dec.–mid-Mar.* 🛏 *20 rooms* 🍽 *Breakfast.*

### NIGHTLIFE AND PERFORMING ARTS

**Römersteinbruch.** Between Rust and Eisenstadt, outside the tiny village of St. Margarethen, is Römersteinbruch, a delightful rock quarry used for outdoor opera performances for six or seven weeks in July and August. It's one of the three largest outdoor opera venues in Europe, seating 7,000 nightly. The opera changes annually—usually a work by Verdi or Bizet's *Carmen,* with a Passion play running every fifth year. Performances also include a dazzling fireworks display. Ticket prices range from €43 to €90. It's a good idea to bring a seat cushion, if possible, to soften the metal chairs. Bus trips from Vienna and back to see performances can be arranged through several tour agencies. Daytime tours of the quarry (in German) are possible from April to October. ☎ *02680/42042* 🌐 *www.roemersteinbruch.at.*

## ALONG THE DANUBE RIVER

The loveliest stretches of the Danube's Austrian course run from the outskirts of Vienna through the narrow defiles of the Wachau to the Nibelungengau—the region where the mystical race of dwarfs, the Nibelungs, are supposed to have settled, at least for a while.

The gentle countryside south of the Danube and east of Linz is crossed by rivers that rise in the Alps and eventually feed the Danube. In this prosperous country of light industry and agriculture, there's little remaining evidence that the area was heavily fought over in the final days of World War II. From 1945 to 1955, the River Enns marked the border between the western (U.S., British, and French) and eastern

(Russian) occupation zones. The great attraction here is a string of Baroque-era abbeys, including the incomparable Stift Melk, set above the Danube.

## KLOSTERNEUBURG

*13 km (8 miles) northwest of Vienna.*

This moderate-size town, with forest mixed in between the houses, seems much farther from the big city than just a few miles. In antiquity the area was a Roman fort, and its modern habitation began in the 11th century.

### GETTING HERE AND AROUND

Commuter trains from Vienna's Franz-Josefs-Bahnhof and buses from the Heiligenstadt station leave frequently for the short trip to Klosterneuburg. By car, follow Route B14.

### ESSENTIALS

**Tourist Information Klosterneuburg Tourismus.** ⊠ *Niedermarkt 4* ☎ *02243/32038* ⊕ *www.klosterneuburg.net.*

### EXPLORING

**OFF THE BEATEN PATH**

**Kahlenbergerdorf.** Near Klosterneuburg and just off the road tucked under the Leopoldsberg promontory is this charming little vintners' village, an excellent spot to stop and sample the local wines. You're just outside the Vienna city limits here, which accounts for the crowds (of Viennese, not international visitors) on weekends.

**Fodor'sChoice**
★

**Stift Klosterneuburg.** The great Augustinian abbey Stift Klosterneuburg dominates the town. The structure has undergone many changes since the abbey was established in 1114, most recently in 1892, when Friedrich Schmidt, architect of Vienna's City Hall, added neo-Gothic embellishments to its two identifying towers. Klosterneuburg was unusual in that until 1568 it housed both men's and women's religious orders. In the abbey church look for the carved-wood choir loft and oratory and the large 17th-century organ. Among Klosterneuburg's treasures are the beautifully enameled 1181 Verdun Altar in the Leopold Chapel, stained-glass windows from the 14th and 15th centuries, Romanesque candelabra from the 12th century, and gorgeous ceiling frescoes in the great marble hall. In an adjacent outbuilding there's a huge wine cask over which people slide; the exercise, called *Fasslrutsch'n*, takes place during the Leopoldiweinkost, the wine tasting around St. Leopold's Day, November 15. The Stiftskeller, with its atmospheric underground rooms, serves standard Austrian fare and wine bearing the Klosterneuberg label. There are several different tours available covering religious artifacts, imperial rooms and treasures, wine making, and the garden. Guided tours are in German; audio guides are available for some of the tours. ⊠ *Stiftsplatz 1* ☎ *02243/411–0* ⊕ *www.stift-klosterneuburg.at* ⊠ *€17.*

7

## KORNEUBURG

*18 km (11 miles) northwest of Vienna.*

Aside from Burg Kreuzenstein, a castle a short distance outside the town, Korneuburg has a few attractions, including sections of a town wall, a Trinity column, and a Pied Piper well, to justify a brief stopover or drive-through on the way to Krems. Until recently, the town was the center of Austrian shipbuilding, where river passenger ships, barges, and transfer cranes were built to order for Russia, among other customers. Stop for a look at the imposing neo-Gothic city hall (1864), which dominates the central square and towers over the town.

### GETTING HERE AND AROUND

Commuter trains go frequently from Vienna's Praterstern station from here. To see the castle, go to the Leobendorf-Burg Kreuzenstein stop. By car from Vienna, take the A22 to Exit 16, and then follow Route B3.

### EXPLORING

Fodor'sChoice   **Burg Kreuzenstein.** Seemingly lifted from the pages of a German fairy
★   tale, Burg Kreuzenstein bristles with storybook turrets and towers. Sitting atop a hillside 3 km (2 miles) beyond Korneuburg along Route 3, "Castle Cross-stone" is, in fact, a 19th-century architectural fantasy built to conjure up "the last of the knights"—Emperor Maximilian I himself. Occupying the site of a previously destroyed fort, the enormous structure was built by Count Nepomuk Wilczek between 1879 and 1908 to house his collection of late-Gothic art objects and armor, including the "Brixner Cabinet" dating from 15th-century Salzburg. Using old elements and Gothic and Romanesque bits and pieces, the castle was carefully laid out according to the rules of yore, complete with a towering Burgtor, "kennel" corridor (where attackers would have been cornered), Gothic arcades, and tracery parapet walls. The Burghof courtyard, with its half-timbered facade and Baltic loggia, could be a stand-in for a stage set for Wagner's *Tannhäuser*. Inside, the medieval thrills continue with rooms full of armaments, a festival and banquet hall, a library, a stained-glass chapel, vassal kitchens, and the Narwalzahn, a room devoted to hunting trophies (if you've ever wanted to see a "unicorn horn," here's your chance). Guided tours are available on the hour.

A group of falconers keeps peregrine falcons and other birds of prey near the castle grounds. Eagles and falcons take flight, hunt, and return to their trainer's arm with the catch at least twice a day, taking part in a sport that goes back nearly 4,000 years. Shows, which run from April through October, are scheduled every day (except Monday) at 11 am and 3 pm and on Sunday at 11 am and 2 and 4 pm. Tickets cost €7.50 each.

It is possible to reach Kreuzenstein from Vienna via the suburban train (S-Bahn) to Leobendorf, followed by a ¾-hour hike up to the castle. ⊠ *Leobendorf bei Korneuburg* ☎ *0664/422–53–63, 01/283–0308 falconer* ⊕ *www.kreuzenstein.com* ✉ *€10.*

# KREMS

*10 km (6 miles) west of Haitzendorf, 80 km (50 miles) northwest of Vienna.*

Krems marks the beginning (when traveling upstream) of the Wachau section of the Danube. The town is closely tied to Austrian history; here the ruling Babenbergs set up a dukedom in 1120, and the earliest Austrian coin was struck in 1130. In the Middle Ages, Krems looked after the iron trade, while neighboring Stein traded in salt and wine. Now, according to Austrian law, any town that houses a jail must receive massive funding for the arts. Thus, charming Krems is fat with culture, starting with its Arts Mile. Besides a number of galleries and eateries, it includes the Karikaturmuseum, the Kunsthalle Krems, the Frohner Museum (dedicated to the late Austrian graphic artist and painter), and the Lower Austria literature center.

The area is also at the center of a thriving wine-producing area, but Krems is most famed for the cobbled streets of its Altstadt (Old Town), which is virtually unchanged since the 18th century. The lower Old Town is an attractive pedestrian zone, while up a steep hill (a car can be handy) you'll find the upper Old Town, with its Renaissance Rathaus and a parish church that is one of the oldest in Lower Austria.

**GETTING HERE AND AROUND**

By car from Vienna, take the A22 to the Knoten Floridsorf exit, then following the S5 to Krems. Trains from Vienna's Franz-Josefs-Bahnhof to Krems take a little over an hour.

**ESSENTIALS**

**Tourist Information** Krems/Stein. ⊠ *Utzstrasse 1* ☏ *02732/82676* ⊕ *www. krems.info.*

**EXPLORING**

**Karikaturmuseum** (*Caricature Museum*). In 2016, Austrians grieved the death of Manfred Deix, whose world-famous works are housed here ("Deixfiguren" became so popular that the word was added to the German dictionary). More than 250 works from the 20th century to the present can also be viewed here, including a large collection of English-language political satire and caricature. ⊠ *Steiner Landstrasse 3a* ☏ *02732/908020* ⊕ *www.karikaturmuseum.at* 🎟️ *€10.*

**Kunsthalle Krems.** An old tobacco factory is now a showcase for art by both known and unknown artists from the 19th to 21st centuries. Notable examples include Martha Jungwirth and Gregor Schmoll. The town's Dominican church (formerly Weinstadt Museum Krems) was recently added as a venue for Kunsthalle's exhibitions, thus extending the Kunsthalle Mile, as it's known. ⊠ *Franz-Zeller-Platz 3* ☏ *02732/908010* ⊕ *www.kunsthalle.at* 🎟️ *€10* ⊙ *Closed Mon.*

**Loisium Wine & Spa Resort.** About 10 km (6 miles) north of Krems, Langenlois is home to the Loisium, a hotel and wellness spa inside a sleek, ultramodern complex. Here you'll find a comprehensive selection of wines, sparkling wines, and other delectables from the area. The labyrinthian wine cellar takes more than an hour to tour and has 15 stops. The hotel also has a restaurant featuring international cuisine, and the

## Wachau Wines

The epitome of Austrian viticulture is found in the Wachau, those few precious kilometers of terraced vineyards along the north bank of the Danube River. There are few nicer ways to spend an afternoon than to travel to the fabled wineries of the valley and sample the golden nectar coaxed from the vines. It's usually possible to stop in and meet the winemaker, who will be happy to pour you a taste from the latest vintage and share some of the secrets of the trade. A late-spring drive through enchanting villages like Dürnstein, when the apricots are in blossom, is an experience not easily forgotten.

Here you can discover some of the finest white wines in Europe. The elegant, long-lived Rieslings are world-renowned, but the special glory of Austria is the Grüner Veltliner, an indigenous grape that can produce anything from simple *Heurigen* thirst-quenchers to wines of a nobility that rival the best of Burgundy.

The area has its own unique three-tiered classification system, ranging from the young, fresh Steinfeder and medium-bodied Federspiel to the rich, ripe Smaragd. Some of the already legendary vintners include Toni Zöhrer, F.X. Pichler, Prager, Knoll, and Hirtzberger, as well as the exemplary cooperative of the Freie Weingärtner Wachau.

Straddling both sides of the Danube is the Kremstal, centering on the medieval town of Krems, the hub of the area's wine trade. The range of grape varieties expands here to include intensely fragrant Traminer, Grauburgunder (more familiar as Pinot Gris), and even some full-bodied reds from Cabernet Sauvignon and Pinot Noir. To sample some of these wines, you may be tempted to make an excursion to one of the nearby wineries like Nigl, Salomon, Malat, or Zöhrer. Toni Zöhrer runs vineyard tours—his wines have been among the most successful in recent challenges.

Venturing farther from the Danube takes you through lush, rolling hills to the Kamptal, the valley that follows the winding course of the gentle Kamp River. Here is another premium wine region, this one dominated by Langenlois, the country's largest wine-producing town.

After you've had your fill of wine tasting, you might want to relax over a good meal at one of these distinguished wineries. Several have very nice restaurants on-site, including Jamek, near Dürnstein.

For more information on Wachau wineries, visit ⊕ *www.vinea-wachau.at*.

---

spa offers a variety of indulgent treatments and massages. ⊠ *Kornplatz, Langenlois* ☎ *2734/77100* ⊕ *www.loisium.at.*

### WHERE TO EAT AND STAY

**$$**

**AUSTRIAN**

✕ **Jell.** In the heart of the medieval Altstadt is this storybook stone cottage run by Ulli Amon-Jell (pronounced "Yell"), who serves the tried-and-true recipes of her grandmother and great-grandmother, with a bit of her own modern flair added to the mix. Wild-mushroom omelets, pasta with forest fruits, cabbage lasagna, and cucumber soup with goat cheese are popular items on the menu. **Known for:** preserves, sauces, and other jarred delicacies for sale; huge portions; small, secluded terrace covered by grape arbor. [$] *Average main: €17* ✉ *Hoher Markt 8–9* ☎ *02732/82345* ⊕ *www.amon-jell.at* ⊘ *Closed Mon. and 1st 2 wks in July. No dinner weekends.*

**$$$**
AUSTRIAN

✕ **Zum Kaiser von Österreich.** At this landmark in Krems's Old City district, you'll find excellent regional cuisine along with an outstanding wine selection (some of these vintages come from the backyard). Owner-chef Haidinger learned his skills at Bacher, across the Danube in Mautern, so look for refined fish dishes along with specialties such as potato soup and roast shoulder of lamb with scalloped potatoes. **Known for:** fresh fish from the Danube and locally hunted pork and venison; selection of gluten-free foods; need to make reservations at least a day ahead. [$] *Average main: €36* ✉ *Körnermarkt 9* ☎ *0800/400–171–052* ⊕ *www.kaiser-von-oesterreich.at* ⊘ *Closed Sun., Mon., last 2 wks in July, and 1st wk in Aug. No lunch.*

**$**
B&B/INN

🛏 **Alte Post.** The oldest inn in Krems, which for almost 140 years was a mail-route post house, is centered on an adorable Renaissance-style courtyard topped with a flower-bedecked arcaded balcony and storybook mansard roof. **Pros:** excellent restaurant with large portions; cool historical vibe; friendly staff. **Cons:** old-fashioned; most rooms have shared shower and toilet facilities. [$] *Rooms from: €85* ✉ *Obere Landstrasse 32* ☎ *02732/822–76* ⊕ *www.altepost-krems.at* ⊘ *Closed Dec.–Mar.* ⌑ *23 rooms* ⏀ *Breakfast.*

**$$**
HOTEL
FAMILY
Fodor'sChoice
★

🛏 **Gasthaus Prankl.** Located about 16 km (10 miles) outside Krems in the charming town of Spitz, the Gasthaus Prankl is located in the old shipmaster's house, which dates back to 1680, and is a Danube gem. **Pros:** romantic ambience; great views; huge rooms. **Cons:** only one room is wheelchair accessible; menu is limited; restaurant closes at 8:30 pm. [$] *Rooms from: €130* ✉ *Hinterhaus 16, Spitz* ☎ *2713/2323* ⊕ *www.gasthaus-prankl.at* ⌑ *8 rooms.*

# DÜRNSTEIN

*4 km (2½ miles) west of Stein, 90 km (56 miles) northwest of Vienna, 34 km (21¼ miles) northeast of Melk.*

If a beauty contest were held among the towns along the Wachau Danube, chances are Dürnstein would be the winner—as you'll see when you arrive along with droves of tourists. The town is small; leave the car at one end and walk the narrow streets. The main street, Hauptstrasse, is lined with picturesque 16th-century residences.

■ **TIP→ The trick is to overnight here—when the day-trippers depart, the storybook spell of the town returns.** The top night to be here is the summer solstice, when hundreds of boats bearing torches and candles sail down the river at twilight to honor the longest day of the year—a breathtaking sight best enjoyed from the town and hotel terraces over the Danube. In October or November the grapes from the surrounding hills are harvested by volunteers from villages throughout the valley— locals garnish their front doors with straw wreaths if they can offer tastes of the new wine, as members of the local wine cooperative, the Winzergenossenschaft Wachau.

#### GETTING HERE AND AROUND

Dürnstein is 8 km (5 miles) west of Krems on Route B3. Buses go from Krems/Donau Bahnhof at least once an hour in the daytime.

#### ESSENTIALS

**Tourist Information** **Dürnstein.** ✉ *Dürnstein No. 132* ☎ *02711/200* 🌐 *www.duernstein.at.*

### EXPLORING

**Richard the Lionheart Castle.** After taking in the Stiftskirche, head up the hill, climbing 500 feet above the town, to the ruins of the famous Richard the Lionheart Castle—known locally as Ruine Dürnstein—where Leopold V held Richard the Lionheart of England captive, captured on his way back home from the Crusades. Leopold had been insulted, so the story goes, by Richard while they were in the Holy Land and when the English nobleman was shipwrecked and had to head back home through Austria, word got out—even though Richard was disguised as a peasant—and Leopold pounced. In the tower of this castle, the Lionheart was imprisoned (1192–93) until he was located by Blondel, the faithful Minnesänger (troubadour). It's said that Blondel was able to locate his imprisoned king when he heard his master's voice completing the verse of a song Blondel was singing aloud—a bit recycled in Sir Walter Scott's *Ivanhoe*. Leopold turned his prisoner over to the emperor, Henry VI, who held him for months longer until ransom was paid by Richard's mother, Eleanor of Aquitaine. The rather steep 30-minute climb to the ruins will earn you a breathtaking view up and down the Danube Valley and over the hills to the south. ✉ *Dürnstein.*

**Stiftskirche.** Set among terraced vineyards, the town is landmarked by its gloriously Baroque Stiftskirche, dating from the early 1700s, which sits on a cliff overlooking the river. This cloister church's combination of luminous blue facade and stylish Baroque tower is considered the most beautiful of its kind in Austria. ✉ *Grübelgasse.*

### WHERE TO EAT AND STAY

**$$$$** AUSTRIAN 🍴 **Loibnerhof.** It's hard to imagine a more idyllic setting for a memorable meal, especially if the weather is nice and tables are set out in the fragrant apple orchard. One of the oldest restaurants in the area, its kitchen offers inventive variations on regional themes, like Wachau fish soup, crispy roast duck, and foie gras parfait. **Known for:** its unique Butterschnitzel (panfried veal with pork); outdoor dining at apple orchard; historic atmosphere. [$] *Average main: €30* ✉ *Unterloiben 7* ☎ *02732/82890–0* 🌐 *www.loibnerhof.at* 🕒 *Closed Mon., Tues., and early Jan.–mid-Feb.*

**$$$$** B&B/INN 🏨 **Richard Löwenherz.** Built up around the former church of a vast 700-year-old convent, this noted inn overlooks the Danube. **Pros:** river view; überromantic; beautiful pool. **Cons:** rooms can get hot in summer; no elevator; bathrooms are bland. [$] *Rooms from: €214* ✉ *Dürnstein 8* ☎ *02711/222* 🌐 *www.richardloewenherz.at* 🕒 *Closed Nov.–Easter or mid–Apr.* 🛏 *37 rooms* 🍽 *Breakfast.*

**$$** ▣ **Sänger Blondel.** Nearly under the shadow of the Baroque spire of
**B&B/INN** Dürnstein's parish church, this Gasthof-pension welcomes you with
a lovely, sunny-yellow, flower-bedecked facade. **Pros:** great value for
money; beautiful garden; quiet area. **Cons:** no elevator; outdated
room style. $ *Rooms from: €119* ✉ *Dürnstein 64* ☎ *02711/253–0*
⊕ *www.saengerblondel.at* ⊘ *Closed mid-Nov.–mid-Mar.* ↩ *16
rooms* ❘◯❘ *Breakfast.*

**$$$$** ▣ **Schloss Dürnstein.** Once the preserve of the princes of Starhemberg,
**HOTEL** this 17th-century early-Baroque castle on a rocky terrace with exquisite
**Fodor's** Choice views over the Danube is one of the most famous hotels in Austria. **Pros:**
★ great indoor and outdoor pools; exquisite views from the terrace. **Cons:**
no air-conditioning. $ *Rooms from: €259* ✉ *Dürnstein 2* ☎ *02711/212*
⊕ *www.schloss.at* ⊘ *Closed Nov.–Mar.* ↩ *47 rooms* ❘◯❘ *Breakfast.*

---

# MELK

*22 km (13 miles) east of Ybbs an der Donau, 33 km (21 miles) south-
west of Krems.*

One of the most impressive sights in all of Austria, the abbey of Melk is
best approached in mid- to late afternoon, when the setting sun ignites
the abbey's ornate Baroque yellow facade. As you head eastward paral-
leling the Danube, the abbey, shining on its promontory above the river,
comes into view. It easily overshadows the town, but remember that the
riverside village of Melk itself is worth exploring. A self-guided tour (in
English, from the tourist office) will point you toward the highlights
and the best spots from which to photograph the abbey.

**GETTING HERE AND AROUND**

By car from Krems, follow the signs on Route B3 to the Melk exit. A
bus goes from Krems/Donau Bahnhof to the center of Melk. Train travel
from Linz is possible with a change at St. Pölten.

**ESSENTIALS**

**Tourist Information Melk.** ✉ *Babenbergerstrasse 1* ☎ *02752/52307–410.*

**EXPLORING**

**Fodor's**Choice **Stift Melk** (*Melk Abbey*). Part palace, part monastery, part opera
★ set, this masterpiece is a magnificent vision thanks greatly to the
upward-reaching twin towers capped with Baroque helmets and
cradling a 208-foot-high dome, and a roof bristling with Baroque
statuary. Symmetry here beyond the towers and dome would be mis-
placed, and much of the abbey's charm is due to the way the early
architects were forced to fit the building to the rocky outcrop that
forms its base. Erected on the site of an ancient Roman fort, used
by Napoléon as his Upper Austrian redoubt, exploited as the setting
for part of Umberto Eco's *Name of the Rose,* and still a working
monastery, the Benedictine abbey has a history that extends back
to its establishment in 1089. The glorious building you see today is
architect Jakob Prandtauer's reconstruction, completed in 1736, in
which some earlier elements are incorporated. A tour of the building
includes the main public rooms: a magnificent library, with more
than 100,000 books, nearly 2,000 manuscripts, and a superb ceiling

7

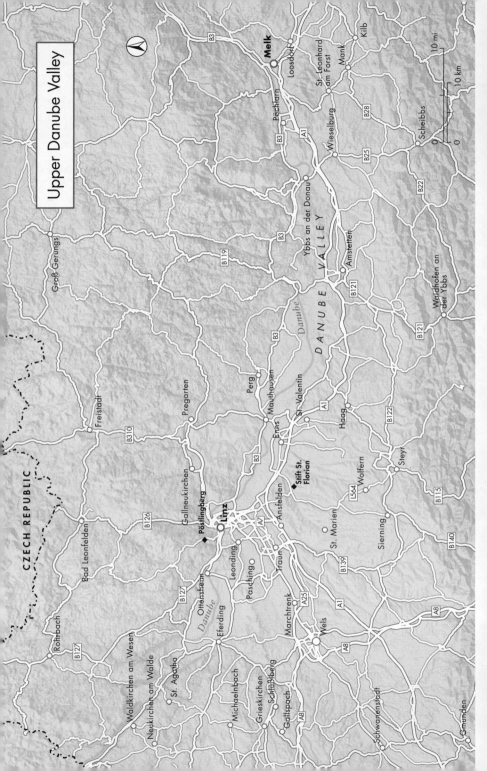

# Upper Danube Valley

CZECH REPUBLIC

Groß Gerungs

Freistadt

B310

Pregarten

Perg

Mauthausen

Enns

St. Valentin

Ybbs an der Donau

DANUBE VALLEY

Amstetten

B121

Waidhofen an der Ybbs

B121

Danube

B3

Melk

Loosdorf

Pöchlarn

B3

A1

Wieselburg

St. Leonhard am Forst

Mank

Kilb

Scheibbs

B28

B25

B22

Rohrbach

B127

Bad Leonfelden

B126

Gallneukirchen

Pöstlingberg

Linz

Danube

B119

B3

Waldkirchen am Wesen

Neukirchen am Walde

B127

Ottensheim

Eferding

St. Agatha

Michaelnbach

Grieskirchen

Schlüßlberg

Gallspach

A8

Leonding

Pasching

Traun

Marchtrenk

Wels

A25

A8

A8

Schwanenstadt

Gmunden

Ansfelden

A7

Stift St. Florian

St. Marien

Sierning

L564

Wolfern

Steyr

B115

B139

A1

Haag

St. Valentin

B122

B140

10 mi

10 km

## DANUBE RIVER CRUISES

A cruise up the Danube to the Wachau Valley is a tonic in any season. A parade of storybook-worthy sights—fairy-tale castles-in-air, medieval villages, and Baroque abbeys crowned with "candle-snuffer" cupolas—unfolds before your eyes. Remember that it takes longer to travel north: the trip upstream to Krems, Dürnstein, and Melk will be longer than the return back to Vienna, which is why many travelers opt to return to the city by train, not boat. Keep your fingers crossed: rumor has it that on some summer days the river takes on an authentic shade of Johann Strauss blue.

**Blue Danube Schifffahrt/DDSG.** The main company offering sightseeing cruises is based in Vienna. Boats depart from the company's piers at Handelskai 265 (by the Reichsbrücke bridge). There are thematic and brunch cruises as well, and you can also get trips from Krems to Melk. The ticket office is at the Vienna piers (take the U-Bahn line U1 to Vorgartenstrasse). For €12, you can steer the ship for 15 minutes while the captain observes closeby. ✉ *Handelskai 265, Vienna* ☎ *01/588–800* 🌐 *www.ddsg-blue-danube.at* 🎫 *€19.90 one way, €26 round-trip, with a possible €1 surcharge for rising fuel prices.*

**Brandner Schifffahrt.** Another way to cruise the Danube is to leapfrog ahead by train from Vienna to Krems. A short walk takes you to the Schiffstation Krems piers, where river cruises run by Brandner Schifffahrt from April through October depart at 10:05 am for a ride to glorious Melk Abbey and Dürnstein. Other options include special day and evening cruises with oompah band concerts, wine cruises, and the like. There is an occasional "crime cruise" (in German) with a murder mystery to be solved. ✉ *Ufer 50, Wallsee* ☎ *07433/2590–21* 🌐 *www.brandner.at* 🎫 *€25.*

fresco by the master Paul Troger; the Marmorsaal, whose windows on both sides enhance the ceiling frescoes; and the glorious *Stiftskirche* (abbey church) of Saints Peter and Paul, an exquisite example of the Baroque style. The Stiftsrestaurant (closed Jan.–mid-Mar.) offers standard fare, but the abbey's excellent wines elevate a simple meal to a lofty experience—particularly on a sunny day on the terrace. There is also a café in the garden pavilion. From April through October, you're free to wander on your own, but from November through March, visitors must book a tour ahead of time in order to see the abbey. ✉ *Abt Berthold Dietmayr-Strasse 1* ☎ *02752/555–232* 🌐 *www.stiftmelk.at* 🎫 *€13.*

### WHERE TO STAY

$$ HOTEL 🏨 **Hotel zur Post.** Here in the center of town you're in a typical village hotel with the traditional friendliness of family management. **Pros:** close to the abbey; friendly and accommodating; in-house sauna. **Cons:** parking area behind the hotel is small; noise from the abbey's bells can be intrusive. [$] *Rooms from: €117* ✉ *Linzer Strasse 1* ☎ *02752/52345* 🌐 *www.post-melk.at* 🕒 *Closed Jan.–mid-Feb.* 🔑 *27 rooms* 🍴 *Breakfast.*

# LINZ

*48 km (22 miles) northwest of Baumgartenberg, 130 km (81 miles) northeast of Salzburg, 185 km (115 miles) west of Vienna.*

The capital of Upper Austria—set where the Traun River flows into the Danube—has a fascinating Old City core and an active cultural life. Once known as the "Rich Town of the River Markets" because of its importance as a medieval trading post, it is today the center of Austrian steel and chemical production, both started by the Germans in 1938. Linz is also a leader in computer technology; every September the city hosts the internationally renowned Ars Electronica Festival, designed to promote artists, scientists, and the latest technical gadgets. A city where past and present collide, Linz has Austria's largest medieval square and one of the country's most modern multipurpose halls, the Brucknerhaus, which is used for concerts and conventions. Its newest addition, the Landestheater, is now one of the most modern theaters in Europe.

Linz can cast a spell, thanks to the beautiful old houses on the Hauptplatz; a Baroque cathedral with twin towers and a fine organ over which composer Anton Bruckner once presided; and its "city mountain," the Pöstlingberg, with a unique railroad track to the top. Mozart often stayed here as his family relentlessly traveled up and down Europe, most notably in November 1783, when he was a guest of Count Johann Thun-Hohenstein at Thun Palace. Today extensive redevelopment, ongoing restoration, and the creation of traffic-free zones and bicycle paths through the city continue to transform Linz. ■ **TIP→ If you will be in Linz for a day or more, consider purchasing the Linz Card, available at the Tourist Office at Hauptplatz 1, some museums, and in most hotels.** Valid for public transportation and free entry into several museums, including the Ars Electronica Center, the card also provides discounts on entry to the zoo, botanical gardens, St. Florian's Abbey, and other venues. It includes deals on Segway tours, casino chips, and a river cruise. The card comes in one-day (€15) and three-day (€25) versions. The three-day card also includes a round-trip on the Pöstlingberg Railway.

## GETTING HERE AND AROUND

Linz is served by Austrian Airlines, Lufthansa, and Ryanair. Regular flights connect with Vienna, Berlin, Düsseldorf, Frankfurt, Stuttgart, and London-Stansted. The Linz airport is in Hörsching, about 12 km (7½ miles) southwest of the city. Buses run between the airport and the main train station according to flight schedules. High speed trains connect German cities via Passau with Linz

The city center is easy to manage on foot. The heart of the city—the Altstadt (Old City)—has been turned into a pedestrian zone; either leave your car at your hotel or use the huge parking garage under the main square in the center of town. Distances are not great, and you can take in the highlights of the city in two or three hours.

Easy-to-use trams take visitors to sites of interest not directly in the city center. If in doubt, grab a cab; there are many taxi stands in Linz. From Linz, you can also take the delightful LILO (Lizner Lokalbahn)

interurban line, which makes the run up to Eferding. A charming narrow-gauge line meanders south to Waidhofen an der Ybbs.

**Airport Information LILO (Linzer Lokalbahn).** ☎ *7272/2232–0, 7612/795–201* ⊕ *www.linzer-lokalbahn.at.* **Linz Blue Danube Airport.** ☎ *07221/600–0* ⊕ *www.flughafen-linz.at.* **ÖBB—Österreichisches Bundesbahn.** ☎ *05/1717* ⊕ *www.oebb.at.*

### ESSENTIALS

**Tourist Information Linz Card.** ⊕ *www.linz.at.* **Linz Tourism.** ✉ *Hauptplatz 1* ☎ *0732/7070–2009* ⊕ *www.linz.at.*

# EXPLORING

## TOP ATTRACTIONS

FAMILY
Fodor's Choice
★

**Ars Electronica Center.** Just across the Nibelungen Bridge from the Hauptplatz, this highly acclaimed center pays tribute to the confluence of art, technology, and society. It hosts annual festivals, with a different theme each year. Permanent features at the museum include the 3-D cinema room, which allows you to fly over Renaissance cathedrals or explore ancient civilizations. Other exhibits delve into the latest developments in robotics and the origins of the universe. Explanations for all the exhibits are in English. Allow at least a whole morning or afternoon to experience all the cybersites. When you need a break, visit the Cubus Café Restaurant Bar on the third floor for refreshments and a spectacular view overlooking the Danube and Lentos Museum. ✉ *Hauptstrasse 2* ☎ *0732/72720* ⊕ *www.aec.at* 🎫 *€9.50* ☾ *Closed Mon.*

**Lentos.** Taking its name from the ancient Celtic settlement that was the origin of the city of Linz, this contemporary art museum hugs the banks of the Danube on the Altstadt side of the river. Designed by Zurich architects Weber and Hofer, its long, low-slung "shoe-box" gray-glass structure picks up the reflection of the water and, at night, lit in shimmering blue or red, really stands out. The collection contains an impressive number of paintings by Austrian Secession artists Klimt, Schiele, and Kokoschka, along with works by other artists, including sculptures by Alfred Hrdlicka and one of the famous silkscreen portraits of Marilyn Monroe by Andy Warhol. All in all, the museum has about 1,500 artworks, more than 10,000 sketches, and nearly 1,000 photographs, but it's worth a visit for the magnificence of the building alone. The excellent restaurant has an outdoor terrace with beautiful views of the river. ✉ *Ernst-Koref-Promenade 1* ☎ *070/7070–3600–0* ⊕ *www.lentos.at* 🎫 *€8* ☾ *Closed Mon.*

**Neuer Dom** (*New Cathedral*). In 1862, the bishop of Linz engaged one of the architects of Cologne cathedral to develop a design for a grand cathedral in the French neo-Gothic style to accommodate 20,000 worshipers, at that time one-third of the population of Linz. According to legend, the tower was not to be higher than that of St. Stephen's in Vienna. The result was the massive 400-foot tower, shorter than St. Stephen's by a scant 6½ feet, but nevertheless, the "New Cathedral" was and remains the largest cathedral in the country. It contains gorgeous stained-glass windows and offers organ recitals. ✉ *Herrenstrasse 26* ☎ *0732/946100.*

7

**Pillar to the Holy Trinity.** One of the symbols of Linz is the 65-foot Baroque column in the center of the Hauptplatz. Made in 1723 from white Salzburg marble, the memorial offers thanks from an earthly trinity—the provincial estates, city council, and local citizenry—for deliverance from the threats of war (1704), fire (1712), and plague (1713). ■ **TIP➜ From March through October there's a large flea market here with more than 100 vendors each Saturday (except holidays), from 7 to 2, and a farmers' market each Tuesday and Friday from 9 to 2.** ✉ *Hauptplatz.*

FAMILY  **Pöstlingberg.** When you want to escape the hustle and bustle of Linz, just hop on the electric railway Pöstlingbergbahn for a scenic ride up to the famous mountain belvedere, the Pöstlingberg. The narrow-gauge marvel has been making the 16-minute journey since 1898, and today the line extends to Hauptplatz. Europe's steepest non-cog mountain railway gains 750 feet in elevation in a journey of roughly 4 km (2½ miles), with neither pulleys nor cables to prevent it from slipping. In summer the old open-bench cars are used. On a clear day the view from the top of the Pöstlingberg is superb, with the city and the wide sweep of the Danube filling the foreground and the snowcapped Alps on the horizon. With a glass of chilled white wine in hand, drink in the grand vista over Linz and the Danube from the terrace of the Pöstlingberg-Schlössl restaurant, at the top of Linz's city mountain. There are also cafés and beer gardens at the summit, along with the Church of the Seven Sorrows of the Virgin (Sieben Schmerzen Mariens), an immense and opulent twin-towered Baroque pilgrimage church (1748) visible for miles as a Linz landmark. A museum with an original carriage from the Pöstlingbergbahn and an interactive mock-up of the driving controls is at the former ticket office in Landgutstrasse 19. Halfway up is the Linz Zoological Garden and a children's petting zoo. ✉ *Linz* ☎ *0732/7801–7002* ⊕ *www.linzag.at* 🎫 *€3.80 one way, €6.20 round-trip.*

**Schlossmuseum Linz** (*Linz Castle*). The massive four-story building on Tummelplatz was rebuilt by Friedrich III around 1477, literally on top of a castle that dated from 799. Note the **Friedrichstor** (the Frederick Gate), with the *A.E.I.O.U.* monogram (some believe it stands for the Latin sentence meaning "All Earth pays tribute to Austria") and two interior courtyards. This is widely known as one of the best provincial museums in the country. The interior of the castle is well worth a visit, with a 17th-century inlaid walnut portal from Schloss Hartheim, historical musical instruments (including Beethoven's Hammerklavier), re-creations of rooms from 19th-century Austrian homes, fine 19th-century portraits, and landscapes by Dutch and Austrian artists, as well as weaponry, coins, and ceramics. ✉ *Tummelplatz 10* ☎ *0732/774–419* ⊕ *www.landesmuseum.at* 🎫 *€6.50* ☾ *Closed Mon.*

■ OFF THE
BEATEN
PATH
**Stift St. Florian** (*St. Florian Abbey*). Built to honor the spot on the River Enns where St. Florian was drowned by pagans in 304 (he is still considered the protector against fire and flood by many Austrians), the Stift St. Florian over the centuries came to comprise one of the most spectacular Baroque showpieces in Austria, landmarked by three gigantic "candle-snuffer" cupolas. In 1686, the Augustinian abbey was built by the Italian architect Carolo Carlone, then finished by Jakob Prandtauer. More a palace than anything else, it is centered on a mammoth

**Marmorsaal** (Marble Hall)—covered with frescoes honoring Prince Eugene of Savoy's defeat of the Turks—and a sumptuous library filled with 140,000 volumes. In this setting of gilt and marble, topped with ceiling frescoes by Bartolomeo Altomonte, an entire school of Austrian historiographers was born in the 19th century. Guided tours of the abbey begin with the magnificent figural gateway, which rises up three stories and is covered with symbolic statues. The Stiegenhaus, or Grand Staircase, leads to the upper floors, which include the **Kaiserzimmer,** a suite of 13 opulent salons (where you can see the "terrifying bed" of Prince Eugene, fantastically adorned with wood-carved figures of captives). The tour includes one of the great masterworks of the Austrian Baroque, Jakob Prandtauer's **Eagle Fountain Courtyard,** with its richly sculpted figures. In the over-the-top **abbey church,** where the ornate surroundings are somewhat in contrast to Bruckner's music, the Krismann organ (1770–74) is one of the largest and best of its period, and Bruckner used it to become a master organist and composer. ■TIP→ **From mid-May through mid-October, you can attend a 20-minute organ concert, held on Sunday, Monday, and Wednesday–Friday at 2:30.** Another highlight is the **Altdorfer Gallery,** which contains several masterworks by Albrecht Altdorfer, the leading master of the 16th-century Danube School and ranked with Dürer and Grunewald as one of the greatest northern painters. There are also rooms where you can spend the night on the grounds of the abbey, which run about €90 per night and come with breakfast. ⊠ *Stiftstrasse 1, St. Florian* ☎ *07224/8902–0* ⊕ *www.stift-st-florian.at* ⊠ *€9.50 for tour; €5.50 for concert.*

## WORTH NOTING

**Alter Dom** (*Old Cathedral*). Hidden away off the Graben, a narrow side street off the Taubenmarkt above the Hauptplatz, is this Baroque gem (1669–78), where the striking feature is its single nave with side altars. Anton Bruckner was the organist here from 1856 to 1868. ⊠ *Domgasse 3* ⊕ *www.dioezese-linz.at.*

**Altes Rathaus** (*Old City Hall*). At the lower end of the main square, the original 1513 building was mostly destroyed by fire and replaced in 1658–59. Its octagonal corner turret and lunar clock, and some vaulted rooms, remain, and you can detect traces of the original Renaissance structure on the Rathausgasse facade. The present exterior dates from 1824. The approach from Rathausgasse 5, opposite the Kepler Haus, leads through a fine, arcaded courtyard. On the facade here you'll spot portraits of Emperor Friedrich III, the mayors Hoffmandl and Prunner, the astronomer Johannes Kepler, and the composer Anton Bruckner. The building houses a museum dedicated to the history of Linz and a rather odd museum of dentistry. ⊠ *Hauptplatz.*

**Bischofshof** (*Bishop's Residence*). This impressive mansion, which dates from 1721, was the residence of Mozart's friend Count Herberstein, who was later appointed Bishop of Linz, and is one of the the city's most impressive Baroque buildings. It was designed by Jakob Prandtauer, the architectural genius responsible for the glorious Melk and St. Florian abbeys. The building still serves as the bishop's residence and ecclesiatical offices. ⊠ *Herrenstrasse and Bischofstrasse.*

**Karmelitenkonvent.** This magnificent Baroque church on Landstrasse was modeled after St. Joseph's in Prague. ⊠ *Landstrasse 33* ☎ *0732/770217.*

**Linzer Landhaus.** The early Renaissance monastery adjoining the Minoritenkirche is now the Landhaus, which serves as the seat of the Upper Austria government. Look inside to see the arcaded courtyard with the Planet Fountain (honoring Johannes Kepler, the astronomer who taught here when it was the city's college) and the Hall of Stone on the first floor, above the barrel-vaulted hall on the ground floor. This hall, the Steinerner Saal, was probably the setting for a noted concert given by the Mozart children in October 1762 (from which Count Pálffy hurried back to Vienna to spread the word about the musical prodigies). For a more extensive look at the interior, inquire at the local tourist office about its scheduled guided tours. The beautiful Renaissance doorway (1570) is of red marble. ⊠ *Klosterstrasse 7.*

**Minoritenkirche.** This Church of the Minor Friars was once part of a monastery and dates back to the 13th century. The present building dates from 1758 and has a delightful Rococo interior with side-altar paintings by Kremser Schmidt and a main altar by Bartolomeo Altomonte. Mozart probably worshipped here when he stayed at the Thun Palace across the way. ⊠ *Klosterstrasse 7* ☎ *0732/7720–11364.*

**Mozart Haus.** This three-story Renaissance town house, actually the Thun Palace, has a later Baroque facade and portal. Mozart arrived here with his wife in 1783 to meet an especially impatient patron (Mozart was late by 14 days). As the composer forgot to bring any symphonies along with him, he set about writing one and completed the sublime Linz Symphony in the space of three days. The palace now houses private apartments, but the courtyard, which can be entered from Altstadt 17 around the corner, has a café. ⊠ *Klostergasse 20.*

**Nordico.** At the corner of Dametzstrasse and Bethlehemstrasse you'll find the city museum, dating from 1610. Its collection follows local history from pre-Roman times to the mid-1880s. ⊠ *Dametzstrasse 23* ☎ *0732/7070–1912* ⊕ *www.nordico.at* ⊠ *€6.50* ⊙ *Closed Mon.*

**Seminarkirche** (*Seminary Church*). Dating from 1725, this yellow-and-white Baroque treasure has an elliptical dome designed by Johann Lukas von Hildebrandt, who also designed its high altar. It was commissioned by the Order of the German Knights. ⊠ *Harrachstrasse 7* ☎ *0732/771205.*

**Stadtpfarrkirche.** This city parish church dates from 1286 and was rebuilt in Baroque style in 1648. The tomb in the right wall of the chancel contains Frederick III's heart and entrails (the corpse is in Vienna's St. Stephen's Cathedral). The ceiling frescoes are by Altomonte, and the figure of Johann Nepomuk (a local saint) in the chancel is by Georg Raphael Donner, with grand decoration supplied by the master designer Hildebrandt. ⊠ *Pfarrplatz 4* ☎ *0732/7761–200.*

**Ursulinenkirche.** The towers at this Baroque church are one of the identifying symbols of Linz. Inside is a blaze of gold and crystal ornamentation. Note the Madonna figure wearing a hooded Carmelite cloak with huge pockets, used to collect alms for the poor. ✉ *Landstrasse 31* ☎ *0732/7610–3151.*

## WHERE TO EAT

**$$$$** EUROPEAN Fodor's Choice ★ 🍴 **Herberstein.** Tucked in the historic Kremsmünsterhaus, you'll find an elegant and popular restaurant with a mod-retro look, defined by cozy tables, muted lighting, and attractive stonework. The cuisine is Austrian with a touch of Asia, as evidenced by the selection of wok dishes and an excellent sushi bar. **Known for:** sushi menu on Monday; excellent rib-eye steak; courtyard seating. [$] *Average main: €35* ✉ *Altstadt 10* ☎ *0732/786161* 🌐 *www.herberstein-linz.at* 🕒 *Closed Sun. No lunch.*

**$$$** AUSTRIAN 🍴 **Promenadenhof.** The atmosphere here is that of a spacious, contemporary Gasthaus, with a fabulous roofed garden filled with flowers. The varied menu of regional cuisine is reasonably priced and has a touch of the Mediterranean, with plenty of vegetarian options available. **Known for:** great Tafelspitz (boiled beef); excellent service; wine from the cellar available by the glass. [$] *Average main: €20* ✉ *Promenade 39* ☎ *0732/777661* 🌐 *www.promenadenhof.at* 🕒 *Closed Sun.*

**$** EUROPEAN 🍴 **Schloss Café.** A more pleasant spot for casual dining in Linz can hardly be imagined, tucked to the side of the town's landmark castle and affording lordly views of the Danube and the opposite bank. The menu offers reasonably priced lunch specials as well as typical café fare. **Known for:** great views of the Danube; outdoor seating; nice wine and beer list. [$] *Average main: €12* ✉ *Tummelplatz 10* ☎ *6641/303–705.*

**$** CAFÉ 🍴 **Traxlmayr Cafe.** One of Austria's grand old coffeehouses, this is the only one of its kind in Upper Austria. It's the perfect place to savor a cup of coffee, read the newspapers, and enjoy a light meal. **Known for:** house specialty, the Linzertorte; outside terrace; grand coffeehouse atmosphere. [$] *Average main: €5* ✉ *Promenade 16* ☎ *0732/773353* 🌐 *www.cafe-traxlmayr.at.*

**$$$** AUSTRIAN 🍴 **Verdi Einkehr.** This trendy bistro is a more affordable alternative to other Linz restaurants, including Verdi, which shares the same house and kitchen. The standard Austrian fare is served in a modern retro setting, with a blend of warm woods and natural light. **Known for:** traditional Tafelspitz and Wiener schnitzel; two restaurants in one location; terrace seating in summer. [$] *Average main: €18* ✉ *Pachmayrstrasse 137* ☎ *0732/733005* 🕒 *Closed Sun., Mon., and 2 wks in Sept.*

## WHERE TO STAY

**$** HOTEL 🏨 **Arcotel Nike.** Right next door to the Brucknerhaus concert hall and a good 10-minute walk from the Altstadt, this modern, relatively uninspiring high-rise on the banks of the Danube is a practical option for concertgoers. **Pros:** modern rooms, some with a view; spacious spa area; convenient location for shows. **Cons:** lacks charm; fee for Wi-Fi; breakfast not included in rate. [$] *Rooms from: €95* ✉ *Untere Donaulände 9* ☎ *0732/76260* 🌐 *www.arcotelhotels.com* 🛏 *174 rooms.*

7

$$   🏨 **Wolfinger.** A 500-year-old former nunnery, the centrally located Wolfin-
HOTEL   ger has been a hostelry since the late 1700s, and that gives the interior some
real charm. **Pros:** great location for museums and restaurants; charming
rooms; very helpful and friendly staff. **Cons:** old fittings in some rooms;
a few rooms share bathrooms. $ *Rooms from: €126* ✉ *Hauptplatz 19*
☎ *0732/773291–0* ⊕ *www.hotelwolfinger.at* ⤷ *50 rooms* ⦿ *Breakfast.*

$$$   🏨 **Zum Schwarzen Bären.** The birthplace of the renowned Mozart tenor
HOTEL   Richard Tauber (1891–1948), the "Black Bear" is a traditional house
filled with memorabilia on a quiet side street in the center of the Old
City, a block from the pedestrian zone. **Pros:** quiet location; on-site
underground parking; nice rooftop bar. **Cons:** variance in room size.
$ *Rooms from: €140* ✉ *Herrenstrasse 9–11* ☎ *0732/772477–0* ⊕ *www.
linz-hotel.at* ⤷ *50 rooms* ⦿ *Breakfast.*

---

# NIGHTLIFE AND PERFORMING ARTS

Linz is far livelier than even most Austrians realize. The local population is friendlier than that of either Vienna or Salzburg, and much
less cliquish. And Linz hasn't lagged behind other Austrian cities in
developing its own fashionable neighborhood, known as the Bermuda
Triangle. Around the narrow streets of the Old City (Klosterstrasse,
Altstadt, Hofgasse) are dozens of fascinating small bars and lounges;
as you explore, you'll probably meet some Linzers who can direct you
to the current "in" location.

## NIGHTLIFE

**Easy.** This cocktail bar has been a mainstay of the bar scene for
about three decades and is still going strong. ✉ *Baumbachstrasse 14*
☎ *732/770090* ⊕ *www.cocktailbareasy.at.*

**Josef.** This hopping establishment has its own home-brewed beer on tap,
light snacks, and hearty regional dishes, and is open every day from 11
am until quite late. ✉ *Landstrasse 49* ☎ *0732/773165* ⊕ *www.josef.eu.*

**Linz Casino.** Located in the Hotel Schillerpark, the casino has roulette,
blackjack, poker, and slot machines (and a formal dress code). The less
formal Jackpot Casino does not require a jacket and tie. Note that a
passport is required for entry. The Jackpot Café, located on the ground
floor, is open until midnight. ✉ *Rainerstrasse 2–4* ☎ *0732/654–4870*
⊕ *www.casinos.at.*

## PERFORMING ARTS

**Brucknerhaus.** A vast array of concerts and recitals are presented in the
noted Brucknerhaus, the modern hall on the south bank of the Danube.
From early to late September it's home to the International Bruckner
Festival. The venue also hosts some events for Ars Electronica, a festival that explores art, science, and society. ✉ *Untere Donaulände 7*
☎ *0732/775230* ⊕ *www.brucknerhaus.at.*

Fodor's Choice   **Landestheater Linz.** After 40 years of political badminton, the Landes-
★   theater, also known as the Musiktheater am Volksgarten, finally made
its grand debut in 2013. Designed by British architect Terry Pawson
and considered Europe's most state-of-the-art opera house, it's now the
stage for hit musicals and orchestra and choir performances, along with

hosting a youth theater. The Main Hall seats 1,200 with several smaller halls seating up to 270 each. The remarkable Sound Foyer was created in cooperation with Ars Electronica Future Lab. Visitors to the theater, whether they see a show or not, are welcome to stop in and experience the technological wonder of the so-called sound path. ⌂ *Promenade 39* ⊕ *www.landestheater-linz.at.*

**Fodor's**Choice
★
**Posthof.** Located at the docks, the Posthof has been a popular arts arena for more than 30 years. It's considered to be the largest venue for contemporary arts not only in Austria, but in all of Europe. It's also a multidisciplinary arts center, offering everything under the arts umbrella, making it a place for music (of all genres, from reggae to techno), cabaret, dance, theater, and literature. Some 220 events are hosted each year throughout the September through June season. ⌂ *Posthofstrasse 43* ☎ *732/77–05–48* ⊕ *www.posthof.at.*

# SHOPPING

Linz is a good place to shop; prices are generally lower than those in resorts and the larger cities, and selections are varied. The major shops are found in the main square and the adjoining side streets, in the old quarter to the west of the main square, in the pedestrian zone of the Landstrasse and its side streets, and in the Hauptstrasse of Urfahr, over the Nibelungen Bridge across the Danube.

### GIFTS AND SOUVENIRS

**O. Ö. Heimatwerk.** This is a good option if you're looking for local handmade goods and good-quality souvenirs. You'll find silver, pewter, ceramics, fabrics, and some clothing. In the summer, be on the lookout for good discounts. ⌂ *Landstrasse 31* ☎ *0732/773–3770* ⊕ *ooe.heimatwerk.at* ☉ *Closed Sun.*

### JEWELRY

There are two superior places in the city center to shop for elegant jewelry at reasonable prices.

**Atelier Almesberger.** Also known as Donau Stein Designs (Danube Stone Designs), this shop creates little works of art from stones found along the river's shore. ⌂ *Hofgasse 7* ☎ *0732/790561* ⊕ *www.donausteindesign.com.*

**Göttin des Glücks.** Fair-trade items and sustainable clothing make this shop stand out. ⌂ *Herrenstrasse 2* ☎ *676/6093040* ⊕ *www.goettindesgluecks.com.*

**In the Attic.** At this delightful shop filled with hand-picked treasures, the home accessories and furniture are laid out in what feels like a living room. Be sure to flip through the old vinyl records for sale in the corner. ⌂ *Rosenauerstrasse 4* ☎ *650/852–2694* ⊕ *www.intheattic.at.*

**Vega Nova.** Shop here for charming (even gorgeous) shoes for women, men, and children. ⌂ *Pfarrplatz 1* ☎ *732/773015* ⊕ *www.veganova.at/standorte/linz.*

7

### MARKETS

**Flea Market.** Everything from clothing to china is sold at the Flea Market, open every Saturday from 7 to 2 on the Hauptplatz (main square) from March through early November. In the winter, it moves to the square in front of the Neues Rathaus (New Town Hall) on Hauptstrasse. Check with the tourist office about other flea markets. ⊠ *Linz.*

## SPORTS AND THE OUTDOORS

### BICYCLING

Cyclists appreciate the relatively level terrain around Linz, and within the city there are 200 km (125 miles) of marked cycle routes. Cycling at slow speeds is also allowed in the city's pedestrian zones. The international Donauradweg, or Danube Cycling Path, runs from Germany through Linz and to the Black Sea. Get bike maps from the tourist office.

**Donau Reisen.** Rent bikes here, or book a guided cycling tour along the Danube River. Bikes rented in Linz can be returned at several points along the Danube Cycling Path. ⊠ *Lederergasse 4–12* ☎ *0732/2080* ⊕ *www.donaureisen.at.*

# SALZBURG

Updated by
Jacy Meyer

Art lovers call it the Golden City of High Baroque; historians refer to it as the Florence of the North or the German Rome; and music lovers know it as the birthplace of one of the world's most beloved composers, Wolfgang Amadeus Mozart (1756–91). While the city might not have given Mozart much love when he was alive, Salzburg is now fiercely proud of its role as one of Austria's top cultural draws. Since 1920 the world-famous Salzburger Festspiele (Salzburg Festival), the third-oldest on the continent, has honored "Wolferl" with performances of his works by the world's greatest musicians.

Ironically, many who come to this golden city of High Baroque may first hear the instantly recognizable strains of music from the film that made Salzburg a household name: from the Mönchsberg to Nonnberg Convent, it's hard to go exploring without hearing someone humming "How Do You Solve a Problem Like Maria?" A popular tourist exercise is to make the town's acquaintance by visiting all the sights featured in that beloved Hollywood extravaganza, *The Sound of Music,* filmed here in 1964. Just like Mozart, the von Trapp family—who escaped the Third Reich by fleeing their beloved country—were little appreciated at home; Austria was the only place on the planet where the film failed, closing after a single week's showing in Vienna and Salzburg. It's said that the Austrian populace at large didn't cotton to a prominent family up and running in the face of the Nazis.

## ORIENTATION AND PLANNING

### GETTING ORIENTED

Salzburg lies on both banks of the Salzach River, at the point where it's pinched between two mountains, the Kapuzinerberg on one side, the Mönchsberg on the other. In broader view are many beautiful Alpine peaks.

Salzburg's rulers pursued construction on a grand scale ever since Wolf-Dietrich von Raitenau began his regime in the latter part of the 16th century. At the age of only 28, Wolf-Dietrich envisioned "his" Salzburg to be the Rome of the Alps, with a town cathedral grander than St. Peter's, a Residenz as splendid as a Roman palace, and his private Mirabell Gardens flaunting the most fashionable styles of Italianate horticulture. After he was deposed by the rulers of Bavaria, other cultured prince-archbishops took over. Johann Ernst von Thun and Franz Anton von Harrach commanded the masters of Viennese Baroque, Fischer von

Erlach and Lukas von Hildebrandt, to complete Wolf-Dietrich's vision. The result is that Salzburg's many fine buildings blend into a harmonious whole. Perhaps nowhere else in the world is there so cohesive a flowering of Baroque architecture.

But times change and the Salzburgians with them. It is not surprising to learn that Salzburg is now home to one of the most striking museums: the Museum der Moderne. The avant-garde showcase stands on the very spot where Julie Andrews "do-re-mi"-ed with the von Trapp brood; where once the fusty Café Winkler stood atop the Mönchsberg mount, a modern, cubical museum of cutting-edge art now commands one of the grandest views of the city.

**The Altstadt.** Salzburg is the only city in the world with 1,300 years of continuous music history, which you can experience in concert halls, churches, restaurants and bars, and even outdoors in city squares.

**Around Fortress Hohensalzburg.** The showstopping medieval fortress is an attraction on its own, but it also offers sweeping Salzburg views.

**North of the River Salzach.** Here you can simultaneously enjoy outstanding old and new architecture and beautiful nature, from gardens to the hills.

# PLANNING

## GETTING HERE AND AROUND
### AIR TRAVEL
Salzburg Airport, 4 km (2½ miles) west of the city center, is Austria's second-largest international airport. There are direct flights from London and other European cities to Salzburg, but not from the United States. From the United States you can fly to Munich and take the 90-minute train ride to Salzburg, or you can take a bus run by Salzburger Mietwagenservice. Taxis are the easiest way to get downtown from the Salzburg airport; the ride costs around €14–€15 and takes about 20 minutes. City Bus No. 2, which makes a stop by the airport every 15 minutes, runs down to Salzburg's train station (about 20 minutes). Bus No. 8 runs directly to the city center.

**Airport Contacts Flughafen München (MUC).** ☎ 089/975–00 ⊕ www. munich-airport.de. **Salzburg Airport (SZG).** ✉ Innsbrucker Bundesstrasse 95 ☎ 0662/8580-0 ⊕ www.salzburg-airport.com. **Salzburger Mietwagenservice (SMS).** ✉ Wasserfeldstrasse 24A ☎ 0622/8161-0 ⊕ www.flughafentransfer.at/index_e.php.

### BUS TRAVEL
A tourist map (available from tourist offices in Mozartplatz and the train station) shows all bus routes and stops; there's also a color-coded map of the public transport network, so you should have no problem getting around. Virtually all buses and trolleybuses (O-Bus) run via Mirabellplatz and/or Hanuschplatz. Single bus tickets bought from the driver cost €2.60.

**Contacts Salzburger Verkehrsverbund** (Main ticket office). ✉ Schallmooser Hauptstrasse 10 ☎ 0662/632900 ⊕ www.salzburg-verkehr.at.

8

### CAR TRAVEL

If driving, the fastest routes into Salzburg are the autobahns. From Vienna (320 km [198 miles]), take A1; from Munich (150 km [93 miles]), A8 (in Germany it's also E11); from Italy, A10. The only advantage to having a car in Salzburg itself is that you can get out of the city for short excursions. The Old City on both sides of the river is a pedestrian zone, and the rest of the city, with its narrow, one-way streets, is a driver's nightmare.

**Taxis 81-11.** ☎ *0662/8111* ⊕ *www.taxi.at.*

### TRAIN TRAVEL

You can get to Salzburg by rail from most European cities. Salzburg Hauptbahnhof is a 20-minute walk from the center of town in the direction of Mirabellplatz. The bus station and the suburban railroad station are at the square in front. A taxi to the center of town should take about 10 minutes and cost €10.

**Train Information ÖBB (Österreichische Bundesbahnen).** ☎ *05/1717* ⊕ *www.oebb.at.* **Salzburg Hauptbahnhof.** ⊠ *Südtirolerplatz 1* ☎ *435/1717* ⊕ *www.oebb.at.*

### TOURS

The Old City, composed of several interconnecting squares and narrow streets, is best seen on foot. Salzburg's official licensed guides offer a one-hour walking tour (€10) through the Old City every day at 12:15, and a more in-depth art and architecture 1½-hour tour (€11) Monday through Saturday at 2, which start in front of the Information Center at Mozartplatz 5. A Salzburg Card reduces the fee.

Several local companies conduct 1½- to 2-hour city tours. The tours are by minibus, since large buses can't enter the Old City, and briefly cover the major sights, including Mozart's birthplace, the festival halls, major squares, churches, and the palaces at Hellbrunn and Leopoldskron. Bob's Special Tours is well-known to American visitors—the company offers a discount to Fodor's readers who book directly with it, show their Fodor's book, and pay cash. Salzburg Panorama Tours and Salzburg Sightseeing Tours offer similar tours.

To reach spots buses can't, ride along with one of Fraulein Maria's daily 3½-hour bicycle tours (€30).

**Bob's Special Tours.** Bob's small vans allow access to the narrow streets of Salzburg that lumbering buses can't maneuver. Explore the city, nearby mountain regions, or *The Sound of Music* filming highlights on daily and seasonal tours. Experienced multilingual guides are available. ⊠ *Rudolfskai 38* ☎ *0662/849511* ⊕ *www.bobstours.com* ✉ *From €48.*

FAMILY **Fräulein Maria's Bicycle Tours.** Ride through the streets of Salzburg singing the soundtrack favorites and learn a surprising amount of the city's history with fellow movie and musical fans on these *Sound of Music*–themed small group bicycle tours. Guides share the von Trapp family cheer rain or shine with riders of all ages and abilities—inclement weather gear, tandem bikes, children's bikes, trailers, and baby seats are offered at no additional cost. ⊠ *Mirabellplatz 4* ☎ *0650/3426297* ⊕ *www.mariasbicycletours.com* ✉ *Sound of Music Tour €30.*

## TOP REASONS TO GO

**Fortress Hohensalzburg:** Ascend to the fortress on the peak and see what romantic visitors in the 19th century enjoyed so much—the soul-stirring combination of gorgeous architecture in a stunning natural location.

**Baroque churches:** See the magnificent Baroque churches built not only to honor God but also to document the importance of the ruling prince-archbishops during the 17th century.

**Concerts, operas, and more:** Feel the spirit of 1,300 years of musical history as you listen to the music of Wolfgang Amadeus Mozart, arguably the greatest Western composer who ever lived, in the Marble Hall of Mirabell Palace. World-class talent in a wide array of genres populates Salzburg's numerous music festivals, handcrafted marionettes perform well-known operas, and stunning, reverberant choral music accompanies a Mass or concert at many of the gorgeous churches. You'll run out of time, not options, in Salzburg.

**Steingasse:** After exploring the Altstadt's grand churches and squares, cross the River Salzach to take in the completely different atmosphere of the narrow, 16th-century Steingasse, where working people once lived, and shops, galleries, and clubs now beckon.

**Schloss Hellbrunn:** Drive, bike, walk, or take the boat out to Schloss Hellbrunn, a Renaissance-inspired pleasure palace with trick fountains, a lush, green lawn perfect for picnics, and the gazebo that witnessed so much wooing in *The Sound of Music.*

**Salzburg Panorama Tours.** One of the most reliable, respected tour companies in the area offers a variety of themes and ways to become acquainted with Salzburg and the surrounding areas, either by bus, on foot, or in a luxurious private car. The "Original Sound of Music Tour" hits the movie location highlights and includes much about the city itself. The "Walking City Tour" is the perfect introduction to Salzburg's architectural history, churches and cathedrals, and Mozart. Bus pick-up is available at several local hotels. ⊠ *Schrannengasse 2/2* ☎ *0662/883211* ⊕ *www.panoramatours.com* ✉ *From €18.*

**Salzburg Sightseeing Tours.** One of the oldest tour companies in the city, Salzburg Sightseeing Tours offers prepackaged programs including the best of the city, *Sound of Music* locations, and nearby Alpine highlights, or custom tours. The yellow hop-on, hop-off buses stop at the most famous Salzburg landmarks, with informative recorded audio guides between stops. The complete circuit (without getting off) takes an hour. All tickets include free access to all local Salzburg buses, as well as the Gaisberg bus (No. 151). ⊠ *Mirabellplatz 2* ☎ *0662/881616* ⊕ *www.salzburg-sightseeingtours.at* ✉ *From €18.*

### VISITOR INFORMATION
**Visitor Information Tourist Information at Train Station.** ⊠ *Salzburg Hauptbahnhof, Südtirolerplatz 1* ☎ *0662/88987–340* ⊕ *www.salzburg.info/en/.* **Salzburg City Tourist Office.** ⊠ *Mozartplatz 5* ☎ *0662/88987–330* ⊕ *www.salzburginfo.at.*

## FESTIVALS

**Salzburger Festspiele.** The biggest event on the calendar since it was first organized in 1920 is the world-famous Salzburger Festspiele, usually held late July through late August. The festival also presents the Whitsun Festival (mid-May). The most star-studded events feature top opera stars and conductors and are very expensive, but other performances can be more reasonably priced, and events outside the main festival halls, the **Grosses Festspielhaus** (Great Festival Hall) and the **Haus für Mozart** (House for Mozart), located on the grand promenade of Hofstallgasse, are even cheaper. This street is especially dazzling at night, thanks to the floodlighted Fortress Hohensalzburg. There are also concerts and operas at other theaters in the city, including the the Summer Riding School (Felsenreitschule), Kollegienkirche, and the Mozarteum. ■ TIP→ **Order your tickets early; major performances sell out several months in advance.** ✉ *Hofstallgasse 1* ☎ *0662/8045–500* ⊕ *www.salzburgfestival.at.*

# EXPLORING SALZBURG

Getting to know Salzburg is not too difficult, because most of its sights are within a comparatively small area. The Altstadt (Old City) is a compact area between the jutting outcrop of the Mönchsberg and the Salzach River. The cathedral and interconnecting squares surrounding it form what used to be the religious center, around which the major churches and the old archbishops' residence are arranged (note that entrance into all Salzburg churches is free). The Mönchsberg cliffs emerge unexpectedly behind the Old City, crowned to the east by the Hohensalzburg Fortress. Across the river, in the small area between the cliffs of the Kapuzinerberg and the riverbank, is the Steingasse, a narrow medieval street where laborers, craftsmen, and traders served the salt-mining industry and travelers coming in and out of the region's important mercantile hub. Northwest of the Kapuzinerberg lies Mirabell Palace and its manicured gardens.

It's best to begin by exploring the architectural and cultural riches of the Old City, then go on to the fortress. Afterward, cross the river to inspect the other bank. Ideally, you need two days to do it all. An alternative, if you enjoy exploring churches and castles, is to go directly up to the fortress, either on foot or by returning through the cemetery to the funicular railway.

## THE ALTSTADT

Intent on becoming a patron of the arts, the prince-archbishop Wolf-Dietrich lavished much of his wealth on rebuilding Salzburg into a beautiful and Baroque city in the late 16th and early 17th centuries. In turn, his grand townscape came to inspire the young Joannes Chrysostomus Wolfgangus Amadeus (Theophilus) Mozart. In fact, by growing up in the center of the city and composing already at five years of age, Mozart set lovely Salzburg itself to music. He was perhaps the most purely Austrian of all composers, a singer of the smiling Salzburgian countryside and of the city's Baroque architecture. So even if you're not lucky enough to snag a ticket to a performance of *The Marriage of Figaro* or *Don Giovanni* in the Haus für Mozart, you can still appreciate what inspired his melodies just by strolling through these streets.

Ever since the 1984 Best Film Oscar-winner *Amadeus,* the composer has been the 18th-century equivalent to a rock star. Born in Salzburg on January 27, 1756, he crammed a prodigious number of compositions into the 35 short years of his life, many of which he spent in Salzburg (he moved to Vienna in 1781). Indeed, the Altstadt revels in a bevy of important sights, ranging from his birthplace on the Getreidegasse to the abbey of St. Peter's, where the composer's *Great Mass in C Minor* was first performed.

## TOP ATTRACTIONS

**Alter Markt** (*Old Market*). Right in the heart of the Old City is the Alter Markt, the old marketplace and former center of secular life in the city. The square is lined with 17th-century middle-class houses, colorfully hued in shades of pink, pale blue, and yellow ocher. Look in at the old royal pharmacy, the **Hofapotheke,** whose ornate black-and-gold Rococo interior was built in 1760. Inside, you'll sense a curious apothecarial smell, traced to the shelves lined with old pots and jars (labeled in Latin). These are not just for show: this pharmacy is still operating today. You can even have your blood pressure taken—but preferably not after drinking a *Doppelter Einspänner* (black coffee with whipped cream, served in a glass) in the famous Café Tomaselli just opposite. In warm weather the café's terrace provides a wonderful spot for watching the world go by as you sip a *Melange* (another coffee specialty, served with frothy milk), or, during the summer months, rest your feet under the shade of the chestnut trees in the Tomaselli garden at the top end of the square.

Next to the coffeehouse you'll find the smallest house in Salzburg; note the slanting roof decorated with a dragon gargoyle. In the center of the square, surrounded by flower stalls, is the marble St. Florian's Fountain, dedicated in 1734 to the patron saint of firefighters. ⊠ *Salzburg.*

**Fodor'sChoice**
★

**Dom** (*Cathedral*). One of Salzburg's most beautiful urban set pieces, the Domplatz contains the Virgin's Column in its center, and at one side is the gorgeous cathedral, considered to be the first early-Italian Baroque building north of the Alps. Its facade is of marble, its towers reach 250 feet into the air, and it holds 10,000 people. There has been a cathedral on this spot since the 8th century, but the present structure dates from the 17th century. The cathedral honors the patron saint of Salzburg, St. Rupert, who founded Nonnberg Abbey around 700, and also the Irish St. Virgil, the founder of the first cathedral, consecrated in 774, whose relics lie buried beneath the altar. Archbishop Wolf-Dietrich took advantage of the old Romanesque-Gothic cathedral's destruction by fire in 1598 to demolish the remains and make plans for a huge new structure facing onto the Residenzplatz to reaffirm Salzburg's commitment to the Catholic cause. His successor, Markus Sittikus, and the new court architect, Santino Solari, started the present cathedral in 1614; it was consecrated with great ceremony in 1628 during the Thirty Years' War. The church's simple sepia-and-white interior, a peaceful counterpoint

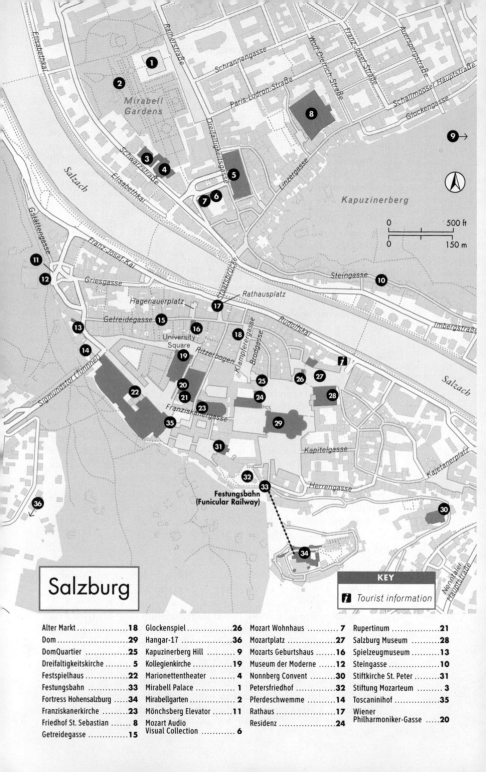

# Salzburg

## KEY

**i** *Tourist information*

to the usual Baroque splendor, dates from a later renovation. To see remains of the old cathedral, go down the steps from the left-side aisle into the crypt where the archbishops from 1600 on are buried. Mozart's parents, Leopold and Anna-Maria, were married here in 1747. Mozart was christened, the day after he was born, at the 14th-century font here, and he later served as organist from 1779 to 1781. Some of his compositions, such as the *Coronation Mass,* were written for the cathedral. ■TIP→ **On Sunday and all Catholic holidays, mass is sung at 10 am—the most glorious time to experience the cathedral's full splendor.** This is the only house of worship in the world with five independent fixed organs, which are sometimes played together during special church-music concerts. Many of the church's treasures are in a special museum on the premises, entry to which now offers visitors access to the corridors that once only the archbishops walked, linking the five historic landmarks overlooking the Domplatz. ⊠ *Domplatz 1a* ☎ *0662/8047–1860* ⊕ *www. kirchen.net/dommuseum* ⊠*€12, includes access to all five museums in the DomQuartier* ☉ *Closed Tues. in Sept.–June.*

**Fodor's**Choice **DomQuartier.** For the first time since the early 1800s, you can look down
★ on the original heart of Salzburg as once only the powerful archbishops could, as you walk the top-floor corridors surrounding the Domplatz that connect the Residenz (palace), Dom (cathedral), and St. Peter's Abbey. Admission grants access to resplendent museums in each location. Sunny weather offers expansive views of the city, and the interior walkways make it an appealing option for one of Salzburg's frequent rainy days. ⊠ *Residenzplatz 1/Domplatz 1a* ☎ *0662/80–42–21–09* ⊕ *www.domquartier.at* ⊠*€12, includes access to all five museums in the DomQuartier* ☉ *Closed Tues. in Sept.–June.*

**Getreidegasse.** For centuries, this has been the main shopping street in the Old City center. Today you'll find elegant international fashion houses, traditional Austrian clothiers, familiar international brands, and a delicious ice-cream shop, all with intricate wrought-iron signs conforming with Salzburg's strict Old City conservation laws. Besides coming to shop, crowds flock to this street because at No. 9 is Mozart's birthplace, the **Mozarts Geburtshaus.** In summer, the street is densely packed with people. You can always escape for a while through one of the many arcades—mostly flower bedecked and opening into delightful little courtyards—that link the Getreidegasse to the river and the Universitätsplatz. At No. 37 you'll find the glamorous Goldener Hirsch hotel—just look for its filigree-iron sign showing a leaping stag with gilded antlers. The Goldener Hirsch's interiors are marvels of Salzburgian *gemütlichkeit,* so, if you're appropriately attired, you may wish to view the lobby and enjoy an aperitif in its gorgeous bar. The southern end of Getreidegasse becomes Judengasse, once the heart of the city's medieval Jewish community, which is also packed with shops and galleries festooned with more of Salzburg's famous wrought-iron signs. ⊠ *Salzburg.*

**Glockenspiel.** The famous carillon bell tower is perched on top of the **Neue Residenz** (New Residence), Prince-Archbishop Wolf-Dietrich's government palace. The carillon is a later addition, brought from today's Belgium in 1695 and finally put in working order in 1704. The 35 bells play classical tunes (usually by Mozart or Haydn) with charm

**8**

and ingenuity at 7 am, 11 am, and 6 pm. On Sunday at 11:45 am, musicians perform in the "Trumpeter Tower" at Hohensalzburg Fortress, and their Baroque fanfares can be heard across the Old Town. Details about the music selections are listed on a notice board across the square on the corner of the Residenz building. ✉ *Mozartplatz 1* ⊕ *www.salzburgmuseum.at.*

**Mönchsberg Elevator.** Just around the corner from the Pferdeschwemme horse fountain, at Anton-Neumayr Platz, you'll find the Mönchsberg elevator, which carries you up through solid rock not only to the **Museum der Moderne** but also to wooded paths that are great for walking and gasping—there are spectacular vistas of Salzburg. In summer this can be a marvelous—and quick—way to escape the tiny, crowded streets of the Old City. ✉ *Gstättengasse 13* ▨ *Round-trip €3.60, one way €2.30.*

**Fodor'sChoice**
★
**Mozarts Geburtshaus** (*Mozart's Birthplace*). This homage to Salzburg's prodigal son offers fascinating insights into the life and works of Wolfgang Amadeus Mozart, with carefully curated relics of his youth, listening rooms, and models of famous productions of his operas. As an adult, the great composer preferred Vienna to Salzburg, complaining that audiences in his native city were no more responsive than tables and chairs. Still, home is home, and this was Mozart's—when not on one of his frequent trips abroad—until the age of 17. Mozart was born on the third (in American parlance, the fourth) floor of this tall house on January 27, 1756, and his family lived here in the front apartment, when they were not on tour, from 1747 to 1773. As the child prodigy composed many of his first compositions in these rooms, it is fitting and touching to find Mozart's tiny first violin on display. ✉ *Getreidegasse 9* ☎ *0662/844–313* ⊕ *www.mozarteum.at* ▨ *€11; combined ticket for Mozart Residence and Birthplace €18.*

**Museum der Moderne.** Enjoying one of Salzburg's most famous scenic spots, the dramatic museum of modern and contemporary art reposes atop the sheer cliff face of the Mönchsberg. Clad in minimalist white marble, the museum was designed by Friedrich Hoff Zwink of Munich. It has three exhibition levels, which bracket a restaurant with a large terrace—now, as always, the place to enjoy the most spectacular view over the city while sipping a coffee. Collection highlights include graphics and paintings by Austrian and international artists, including Oskar Kokoschka and Erwin Wurm, with a focus on large-scale installations and sculptural works. Visit in the evening to see the city illuminated. ✉ *Mönchsberg 32* ☎ *0662/84–22–20–403* ⊕ *www.museumdermoderne.at* ▨ *€8; combined ticket to Mönchsberg and Rupertinum, €12* ⊘ *Closed Mon.*

**Residenz.** At the very heart of Baroque Salzburg, the Residenz overlooks the spacious Residenzplatz and its famous fountain. The palace in its present form was built between 1600 and 1619 as the home of Wolf-Dietrich, the most powerful of Salzburg's prince-archbishops. The Kaisersaal (Imperial Hall) and the Rittersaal (Knight's Hall), one of the city's most regal concert halls, can be seen along with the rest of the magnificent **State Rooms** on a self-guided tour as part of the **Dom-Quartier** collaboration. Of particular note are the frescoes by Johann

Michael Rottmayr and Martino Altomonte depicting the history of Alexander the Great. Upstairs on the third floor is the **Residenzgalerie,** a princely art collection specializing in 17th-century Dutch and Flemish art and 19th-century paintings of Salzburg. On the State Rooms floor, Mozart's opera *La Finta Semplice* premiered in 1769 in the Guard Room. Mozart often did duty here, as, at age 14, he became the first violinist of the court orchestra. Today the reception rooms of the Residenz are often used for official functions, banquets, and concerts, and might not always be open for visitors. The palace courtyard has been the lovely setting for Salzburg Festival opera productions since 1956—mostly the lesser-known treasures of Mozart. ⊠ *Residenzplatz 1* ☎ *0662/840451–0* ⊕ *www.residenzgalerie.at* ☒ *€12* ⊙ *Closed Tues.*

**Fodor's Choice**
★
**Salzburg Museum** (*Neue Residenz*). Encompassing six different buildings, the Salzburg Museum's largest location is the 17th-century Neue Residenz (New Residence). This building was Prince-Archbishop Wolf-Dietrich's "overflow" palace (he couldn't fit his entire archiepiscopal court into the main Residenz across the plaza), and as such, it features 10 state reception rooms that were among the first attempts at Renaissance-style design in the North. The permanent exhibition focuses on the city's artistic, cultural, and historical development. The Mirror Hall contains an archaeological collection including Hallstatt Age relics, remains of the town's ancient Roman ruins, and the famous Celtic bronze flagon found earlier this century on the Dürrnberg near Hallein, 15 km (10 miles) south of Salzburg. The Panorama Passage is lined with archaeological excavations from the New Residence and leads to the Panorama Museum, home to the spectacular Sattler Panorama. One of the few remaining 360-degree paintings in the world, it shows the city of Salzburg in the early 19th century. Also here is the original composition of "Silent Night," composed by Franz Gruber in nearby Oberndorf in 1818. The Art Hall hosts three major exhibitions a year. ⊠ *Mozartplatz 1* ☎ *0662/620808–700* ⊕ *www.salzburgmuseum.at* ☒ *€8.50; combined with entrance to the Panorama Museum, €10* ⊙ *Closed Mon.*

**Stiftkirche St. Peter** (*St. Peter's Abbey*). The most sumptuous church in Salzburg, St. Peter's is where Mozart's famed *Great Mass in C Minor* premiered in 1783, with his wife, Constanze, singing the lead soprano role. Wolfgang directed the orchestra and choir and also played the organ. During every season of the city's summer music festival in August, the work is performed here during a special church-music concert. The porch has beautiful Romanesque vaulted arches from the original structure built in the 12th century; the interior was decorated in the voluptuous late-Baroque style when additions were made in the 1770s. Note the side chapel by the entrance, with the unusual crèche portraying the Flight into Egypt and the Massacre of the Innocents. Behind the Rupert Altar is the "Felsengrab," a rock-face tomb where—according to a legend—St. Rupert himself was originally buried. To go from the sacred to the profane, head for the abbey's legendary St. Peter Stiftskeller restaurant, adjacent to the church. ⊠ *St. Peter Bezirk* ☎ *0662/844576–0* ☒ *Free* ⊙ *Closed during Mass.*

8

## WORTH NOTING

**Festspielhaus** (*Festival Hall Complex*). With the world-famous Salzburg Festival as their objective, music lovers head for the Hofstallgasse, the street where the three festival theaters are located in the complex known as Festspielhaus. Arrow-straight and framing a grand view of the Fortress Hohensalzburg, the street takes its name from the court stables once located

here. Now, in place of the prancing horses, festivalgoers promenade along Hofstallgasse during the intervals of summer performances, showing off their suntans and elegant attire. ■TIP➔ If you want to see the inside of the halls, it's best to go to a performance, but guided tours are given and group tours can be booked on request.

The first theater is the **Haus für Mozart** (House for Mozart), formerly the Kleines Festspielhaus, or Small Festival Hall. The massive lobby frescoes by Salzburg painter Anton Faistauer welcome 1,600 patrons to world-class Lied (song) recitals and smaller-scale operas. The center ring is occupied by the famous **Grosses Festspielhaus** (Great Festival Hall), leaning against the solid rock of the Mönchsberg. Opened in 1960, it seats more than 2,150. In recent times the Grosses Festspielhaus, nicknamed the Wagner Stage because of headline-making productions of the *Ring of the Nibelungs*, has been the venue for spectacular operas and concerts by the world's top symphony orchestras and soloists. Stage directors are faced with the greatest challenge in the third theater, the **Felsenreitschule** (the Rocky Riding School), the former Summer Riding School, which—hewn out of the rock of the Mönchsberg during the 17th century by architect Fischer von Erlach—offers a setting that is itself more dramatic than anything presented on stage. With its retractable roof it gives the impression of an open-air theater; the three tiers of arcades cut into the rock of the Mönchsberg linger in the mind of fans of *The Sound of Music* film, for the von Trapps were portrayed singing "Edelweiss" here in their last Austrian concert. (In reality, the 1950 Festival farewell by the Trapp Family Singers, conducted by Franz Wasner, was given in the Mozarteum and at the cathedral square.) The theaters are linked by tunnels (partially in marble and with carpeted floors) to a spacious underground garage in the Mönchsberg. ✉ *Hofstallgasse 1* ☎ *0662/849097* ⊕ *www.salzburgfestival.at* ✍ *Guided tours €7.*

**Franziskanerkirche** (*Franciscan Church*). The graceful, tall spire of the Franciscan Church stands out from all other towers in Salzburg; the church itself encompasses the greatest diversity of architectural styles. There was a church on this spot as early as the 8th century, but it was destroyed by fire. The Romanesque nave of its replacement is still visible, as are other Romanesque features, such as a stone lion set into the steps leading to the pulpit. In the 15th century the choir was built in Gothic style, then crowned in the 18th century by an ornate red-marble-and-gilt altar designed by Austria's most famous Baroque architect, Johann Bernhard Fischer von Erlach. Mass—frequently featuring one of Mozart's compositions—is celebrated here on Sunday at 9 am. ⊠ *Franziskanergasse 5* ☎ *0662/843629* ☜ *Free.*

**Kollegienkirche** (*Collegiate Church*). Completed by Fischer von Erlach in 1707, this church, sometimes called the Universitätskirche, is one of the purest examples of Baroque architecture in Austria. Unencumbered by Rococo decorations, the modified Greek cross plan has a majestic dignity worthy of Palladio. ⊠ *Universitätsplatz* ☎ *0662/841–327.*

**Mozartplatz** (*Mozart Square*). In the center of the square stands the statue of Wolfgang Amadeus Mozart, a work by sculptor Ludwig Schwanthaler unveiled in 1842 in the presence of the composer's two surviving sons. It was the first sign of public recognition the great composer had received from his hometown since his death in Vienna in 1791. The statue, the first for a non-noble person in old Austria, shows a 19th-century stylized view of Mozart, draped in a mantle, holding a page of music and a copybook. A more appropriate bust of the composer, modeled by Viennese sculptor Edmund Heller, is found on the Kapuzinerberg. ⊠ *Salzburg.*

**Petersfriedhof** (*St. Peter's Cemetery*). Eerie but intimate, this is the oldest Christian graveyard in Austria, dating back to 1627. Enclosed on three sides by elegant wrought-iron grilles, Baroque arcades contain chapels belonging to Salzburg's old patrician families. The graveyard is far from mournful: the individual graves are tended with loving care, decorated with candles, fir branches, and flowers—especially pansies (because the name means "thoughts"). In Crypt XXXI is the grave of Santino Solari, architect of the cathedral; in XXXIX that of Sigmund Haffner, a patron for whom Mozart composed a symphony and named a serenade. The final communal Crypt LIV (by the so-called catacombs) contains the body of Mozart's sister Nannerl and the torso of Joseph Haydn's younger brother Michael (his head is in St. Peter's church). The cemetery is in the shadow of the Mönchsberg mount; note the early-Christian tombs carved in the rock face. ⊠ *3 Sankt-Peter-Bezirk* ☎ *0662/844576–0.*

**Pferdeschwemme** (*Horse Pond*). If Rome had fountains, so, too, would Wolf-Dietrich's Salzburg. The city is studded with them, and none is so odd as this monument to all things equine. You'll find it if you head to the western end of the Hofstallgasse to Herbert-von-Karajan-Platz, named after Salzburg's second-greatest musical son, the legendary conductor who was the music director of the Salzburg Festival for many decades. On the Mönchsberg side of the square is the Pferdeschwemme—a royal trough, constructed in 1695, where prize horses used to be cleaned and watered; as they underwent this ordeal they could delight in the frescoes of their pin-up fillies on the rear wall. The Baroque monument in the middle represents the antique legend of the taming of a horse, Bellerophon and his mount, Pegasus. ⊠ *Herbert-von-Karajan-Platz.*

**Rathaus** (*Town Hall*). Where Sigmund-Haffner-Gasse meets the Getreidegasse you will find the Rathaus, an insignificant building in the Salzburg skyline—no doubt reflecting the historical weakness of the burghers vis-à-vis the Church, whose opulent monuments are evident

8

# Mozart: Marvel and Mystery

"Mozart is sunshine." So proclaimed Antonín Dvořák—and how better to sum up the prodigious genius of Wolfgang Amadeus Mozart (January 27, 1756 to December 5, 1791)? Listening to his Rococo orchestrations, his rose-strewn melodies, and his insouciant harmonies, many listeners seem to experience nothing short of giddiness. Scientists have found Mozart's music can cause the heart to pound, bring color to the cheeks, and provide the expansive feeling of being thrillingly alive. Yet, Mozart must have sensed how hard it is to recognize happiness, which is often something vaguely desired and not detected until gone. It is this melancholy undercurrent that makes Mozart modern—so modern that he is now the most popular classical composer, having banished Beethoven to second place. Shortly after *Amadeus* won the 1984 Oscar for best film—with its portrayal of Mozart as a giggling, foul-mouthed genius—*Don Giovanni* began to rack up more performances than *La Bohème*. The bewigged face graces countless "Mozartkugeln" chocolates, and Mostly Mozart festivals pay him homage. But a look behind the glare of the spotlights reveals that this blond, slightly built tuning fork of a fellow was a quicksilver enigma.

Already a skilled pianist at age three, the musical prodigy was dragged across Europe by his father, Leopold, to perform for empresses and kings. In a life that lasted a mere 35 years, he spent 10 on the road—a burden that contributed to making him the first truly European composer. Growing up in Salzburg, the *Wunderkind* became less of a *Wunder* as time went by. Prince-Archbishop Hieronymus von Colloredo enjoyed dissing his resident composer by commanding him to produce "table music" with the same disdainful tone he commanded his chef's dinner orders. Being literally forced to sit with those cooks, Mozart finally rebelled. In March 1781 he married Constanze Weber and set out to conquer Vienna.

Hated by Mozart's father, Constanze is adored today, since we now know she was Mozart's greatest ally. She no doubt heartily enjoyed the fruits of his first operatic triumph, the naughty *Abduction from the Seraglio* (1782). His next opera, *The Marriage of Figaro* (1786), to no one's surprise, bombed. Always eager to thumb his nose at authority, Mozart had adapted a Beaumarchais play so inflammatory in its depiction of aristos as pawns of their own servants, it soon helped ignite the French Revolution. In revenge, wealthy Viennese gave a cold shoulder to his magisterial *Don Giovanni* (1787). Mozart was relegated to composing, for a lowly vaudeville house, the now immortal *Magic Flute* (1790), and to ghosting a *Requiem* for a wealthy count. Sadly, his star only began to soar after a tragic, early death in 1791.

throughout the city. On the other hand, this structure is a prime example of the Italian influence in Salzburg's architecture. Originally this was a family tower (and the only one still remaining here), but it was sold to the city in 1407. ⊠ *Rathausplatz and Kranzlmarkt.*

**Rupertinum.** For a refreshing break from churches and gilded treasures of yore, don't miss the chance to see changing exhibitions of modern graphic art and interactive special exhibits on display in this lovely early-Baroque-era building, part of Salzburg's **Museum der Moderne.** Stop for a delicious slice of *Topfentorte* (an airy, fresh cheesecake) or *Apfelstrudel mit Obers* (apple strudel with whipped cream) in the street-level **Café Sarastro.** ✉ *Wiener-Philharmoniker-Gasse 9* ☎ *0662/842220–451* ⊕ *www.museumdermoderne.at* 🖿 *€6; combined ticket with Mönchsberg, €12* ⊘ *Closed Mon.*

FAMILY   **Spielzeugmuseum** (*Toy Museum*). On a rainy day this is a delightful diversion for both young and old, with an interactive collection of dolls, teddy bears, model trains, and wooden sailing ships. Special Punch and Judy–style *Kasperltheater* puppet shows leave everyone laughing. Performances are held every Wednesday at 3 pm. ✉ *Bürgerspitalplatz 2* ☎ *0662/620808–300* ⊕ *www.spielzeugmuseum.at* 🖿 *€4.50; theater performances €5.50* ⊘ *Closed Mon.*

**Toscaninihof** (*Arturo Toscanini Courtyard*). The famous Italian maestro Arturo Toscanini conducted some of the Salzburg Festival's most legendary performances during the 1930s. Throughout the summer months the courtyard of his former festival residence is a hive of activity, with sets for the stage of the "House for Mozart" being brought in through the massive iron folding gates. ✉ *Salzburg.*

**Wiener Philharmoniker-Gasse.** Leading into Max-Reinhardt-Platz at the head of the grand Hofstallgasse, this street was named after the world-famous Vienna Philharmonic Orchestra in recognition of the unique contribution it has made annually to the Salzburg Festival, playing for most opera productions and for the majority of orchestral concerts. ■**TIP**→ **The street blossoms with an open-air food market every Saturday morning; there is also a fruit-and-vegetable market on Universitätsplatz every day except Sunday and holidays.** ✉ *Salzburg.*

8

# AROUND FORTRESS HOHENSALZBURG

According to a popular saying in Salzburg, "If you can see the fortress, it's just about to rain; if you can't see it, it's already raining." Fortunately, there are plenty of days when spectacular views can be had of Salzburg and the surrounding countryside from the top of this castle.

## TOP ATTRACTIONS

**Festungsbahn** (*funicular railway*). More than 110 years old, the Festungsbahn (funicular railway), behind St. Peter's Cemetery, is the easy way up to the Fortress Hohensalzburg (advisable with young children). ✉ *Festungsgasse 4* ☎ *0662/8884–9750* ⊕ *www.festungsbahn.at* 🖿 *€12 round-trip (includes all museums); €6.80 one-way ride down.*

FAMILY   **Fortress Hohensalzburg.** Founded in 1077, the Hohensalzburg is Salz-
Fodor'sChoice   burg's acropolis and the largest preserved medieval fortress in Central
★   Europe. Brooding over the city from atop the Festungsberg, it was originally founded by Salzburg's Archbishop Gebhard, who had supported the pope in the investiture controversy against the Holy Roman Emperor. Over the centuries the archbishops gradually enlarged the castle, originally using it only sometimes as a residence, then as a siege-proof haven against invaders and their own rebellious subjects. The exterior may look grim, but inside there are lavish state rooms, such

as the glittering **Golden Room,** the **Castle Museum** (dedicated to life in the fortress over the centuries), and the **Rainer's Museum,** with its collections honoring Salzburg's former home regiment. There's also a torture chamber not far from the exquisite late-Gothic **St. George's Chapel** (although the implements on view came from another castle and were not used here). The 200-pipe organ from the beginning of the 16th century, played three times daily, is best heard from a respectful distance (it's called "the Bull" for a reason). ■TIP→ **Climb up the 100 tiny steps to the Recturm, a grand outpost with a sweeping view of Salzburg and the mountains.** Children will enjoy the Puppet Museum filled with marionette fun from the Salzburg Puppet Theater and the chance to try their hands at being a puppeteer.

To reach the fortress, walk up the zigzag path that begins just beyond the Stieglkeller on the Festungsgasse. You don't need a ticket to walk the footpath, but sturdy shoes are recommended. Visitor lines to the fortress can be long, so try to come early. The standard ticket includes a round-trip funicular ride, entrance to the fortress, and an audio guide. ⊠ *Mönchsberg 34* ☎ *0662/842430–11* ⊕ *www.salzburg-burgen.at* ☞ *€15.20.*

FAMILY
Fodor'sChoice
★

**Hangar-7.** Red Bull founder Dietrich Mateschitz opens his fantasy toy chest for all to admire: vintage airplanes, helicopters, motorbikes, and Formula One racing cars gleam under the glass and steel of this modern multipurpose dome. The Flying Bulls, Red Bull's aerobatics experts, and their pristine fleet call this home when not circling the world on their frequent air-show tours. Watch daytime takeoffs and landings from under the shadow of a massive, silver World War II bomber at the Carpe Diem Lounge-Café or in the sunny Outdoor Lounge. The Mayday Bar is an affordable way to experience the evening atmosphere if you can't get a table at the popular Ikarus Restaurant, where each month a new international guest top chef takes over the kitchen and transforms the menu. Reservations are hard to come by; book early. If you're lucky, you can snag the chef's table in the kitchen for an unforgettable evening. ⊠ *Salzburg Airport, Wilhelm-Spazier-Strasse 7A* ☎ *0662/2197* ⊕ *www.hangar-7.com* ☞ *Free.*

**Nonnberg Convent.** Just below the south side of the Fortress Hohensalzburg—and best visited in tandem with it—the Stift Nonnberg was founded right after 700 by St. Rupert, and his niece St. Erentrudis was the first abbess (in the archway a late-Gothic statue of Erentrudis welcomes visitora). ■TIP→ **To see the frescoes located below the Nuns' Gallery as well as the altar in St. John's Chapel, ask at the convent entrance for the key.** The church is more famous these days as "Maria's convent"—both the one in *The Sound of Music* and that of the real Maria on which the move was based. She returned to marry her Captain von Trapp here in the Gothic church (as it turns out, no filming was done here—"Nonnberg" was re-created in the film studios of Salzburg-Parsch). Each evening in May at 7 the nuns sing a 15-minute service called Maiandacht in the old Gregorian chant. Their beautiful voices can be heard also at the 11 pm mass on December 24. Parts of the private quarters for the nuns, which include some lovely, intricate wood carvings, can be seen by prior arrangement. ⊠ *Nonnberggasse 2* ☎ *0662/841607.*

## NORTH OF THE RIVER SALZACH

Across the River Salzach is the Neustadt (New Town) area of historic Salzburg, where you'll find Mirabell Palace and Gardens, the Landestheater, the Mozart Residence, and the Mozarteum. The Church of the Holy Trinity and the Kapuzinerkloster perched atop the Kapuzinerberg are also worth a visit, as is the celebrated Salzburg Marionette Theater. If you want to see the most delightful Mozart landmark in this section of town, the Zauberflötenhäuschen—the mouthful used to describe the little summerhouse where he finished composing *The Magic Flute*—can be viewed when concerts are scheduled in the adjacent Mozarteum.

### TOP ATTRACTIONS

**Friedhof St. Sebastian** (*St. Sebastian's Cemetery*). This final resting place for many members of the Mozart family, in the shadows of St. Sebastian's Church, is one of the most peaceful spots in Salzburg. Prince-Archbishop Wolf-Dietrich commissioned the cemetery in 1600 to replace the old cathedral graveyard, which he planned to demolish. It was built in the style of an Italian *campo santo* (sacred field), with arcades on four sides, and in the center of the square he had the Gabriel Chapel, an unusual, brightly tiled Mannerist mausoleum, built for himself; he was interred here in 1617 (the site is now closed to visitors). Several famous people are buried in this cemetery, including the medical doctor and philosopher Theophrastus Paracelsus, who settled in Salzburg in the early 16th century (his grave is by the church door). Around the chapel is the grave of Mozart's widow, Constanze, her second husband, Georg Nikolaus Nissen, and probably also the one of Genoveva Weber, the aunt of Constanze and the mother of Carl Maria von Weber (by the central path leading to the mausoleum). According to the latest research, Mozart's father, Leopold, came to rest in the unmarked community grave here, too. If the gate is closed, enter through the back entrance around the corner in the courtyard. ✉ *Linzer Gasse 41.*

**Kapuzinerberg Hill.** Directly opposite the Mönchsberg on the other side of the river, Kapuzinerberg Hill is crowned by several interesting sights. By ascending a stone staircase near Steingasse 9 you can start your climb up the peak. At the top of the first flight of steps is a tiny chapel, **St. Johann am Imberg**, built in 1681. Farther on are a signpost and gate to the **Hettwer Bastion**, part of the old city walls and one of the most spectacular viewpoints in Salzburg. At the summit is the gold-beige **Kapuzinerkloster** (Capuchin Monastery), originally a fortification built to protect the one bridge crossing the river. It is still an active monastery and thus cannot be visited, except for the church. The road down—note the Stations of the Cross along the path—is called Stefan Zweig Weg, after the great Austrian writer who rented the **Paschingerschlössl** house (on the Kapuzinerberg to the left of the monastery) until 1934, when he left Austria after the Nazis had murdered Chancellor Dollfuss. As he was one of Austria's leading critics and esthetes, his residence became one of the cultural centers of Europe. Continue along to the northeast end of the Kapuzinerberg road for a well-earned meal with a stunning 180-degree view from the garden of the **Franziskischlössl Wirtzhaus**. ✉ *Salzburg.*

# The Sound of Music in Salzburg

Few Salzburgers would publicly admit it, but *The Sound of Music,* Hollywood's interpretation of the trials and joys of the local von Trapp family, has become their city's most eminent emissary when it comes to international promotion. The year after the movie's release, international tourism to Salzburg jumped 20%, and soon *The Sound of Music* was a Salzburg attraction. Nowadays, the Salzburg Marionette Theater shows its own fairy-tale version, and the Landestheater has produced the musical.

Perhaps the most important *Sound* spin-offs are the tours offered. Besides showing you some of the film's locations (usually very briefly), these four-hour rides have the advantage of giving a very concise tour of the city. The buses generally leave from Mirabellplatz; lumber by the "Do-Re-Mi" staircase at the edge of the beautifully manicured Mirabell Gardens; pass by the hardly visible Aigen train station, where in reality the Trapps caught the escape train; and then head south to Schloss Anif. This 16th-century water castle, which had a cameo appearance in the opening scenes of the film, is now in private hands and not open to the public.

The first official stop for a leg stretch is at the gazebo in the manicured park of Schloss Hellbrunn at the southern end of the city. Originally built in the gardens of Leopoldskron Palace, it was brought out here for photo ops.

This is where Liesl von Trapp sings "I Am Sixteen Going on Seventeen" and where Maria and the Baron woo and coo "Something Good." The simple little structure is the most coveted prize of photographers. The bus then drives by other private palaces with limited visiting rights: Schloss Frohnburg; and Schloss Leopoldskron, with its magical water-gate terrace, adorned with rearing horse sculptures and site of so many memorable scenes in the movie. The bus continues on to Nonnberg Convent at the foot of the daunting Hohensalzburg fortress, then leaves the city limits for the luscious landscape of the Salzkammergut. You get a chance for a meditative walk along the shore of the Wolfgangsee in St. Gilgen before the bus heads for the pretty town of Mondsee, where, in the movie, Maria and Georg von Trapp were married at the twin-turreted Michaelerkirche.

**Sound of Salzburg Dinner Show.**
If you don't mind a healthy dose of cheese with your dinner theater, you can hum along to those unforgettable songs from the *Sound of Music,* traditional Salzburg folk songs, and a medley of Austrian operettas between courses of your traditional Austrian meal. Performances occur May through October and in December. The cost of the full dinner show is €57–€78; without dinner it's €36. ⊠ *Sternbräu, Griesgasse 23* ☎ *0662/2310–5800* ⊕ *www.soundofsalzburg.info* ⏲ *No performances Mon.*

---

**FAMILY**
**Fodor's Choice**
★

**Marionettentheater** (*Marionette Theater*). The Salzburger Marionetten-theater is both the world's greatest marionette theater and a surprisingly sublime theatrical experience. Many critics have noted that viewers quickly forget the strings controlling the puppets, which assume lifelike dimensions and provide a very real dramatic experience. The Marionettentheater is identified above all with Mozart's operas, which seem particularly suited to the skilled puppetry. Their repertoire extends to Rossini (*The Barber of Seville*) and Strauss (*The Bat*), among others, as well as numerous fairy tales. *The Sound of Music* has also been performed here since 2007. For children, the theater recommends its one-hour afternoon performances. All productions are accompanied by historic recordings and are subtitled in several languages. The theater itself is a Rococo concoction. The company is famous for its world tours, but is usually in Salzburg during the summer and around major holidays. ⊠ *Schwarzstrasse 24* ☏ *0662/872406* ⊕ *www.marionetten.at* ☞ *€18–€35.*

**Mirabell Palace.** The "Taj Mahal of Salzburg," Schloss Mirabell was built in 1606 by the immensely wealthy and powerful Prince-Archbishop Wolf-Dietrich for his mistress, Salomé Alt, and their 15 children. It was originally called Altenau in her honor. Such was the palace's beauty that it was taken over by succeeding prince-archbishops, including Markus Sittikus (who renamed the estate), Paris Lodron, and finally, Franz Anton von Harrach, who brought in Lukas von Hildebrandt to give the place a Baroque face-lift in 1727. A disastrous fire hit in 1818, but happily, three of the most spectacular set pieces of the palace—the Chapel, the Marble Hall, and the Angel Staircase—survived. The Marble Hall is now used for civil wedding ceremonies, and is regarded as the most beautiful registry office in the world. Its marble floor in strongly contrasting colors and its walls of stucco and marble ornamented with elegant gilt scrollwork are splendid. The young Mozart and his sister gave concerts here, and he also composed *Tafelmusik* (Table Music) to accompany the prince's meals. ■**TIP→ Candlelight chamber music concerts in the Marble Hall provide an ideal combination of performance and atmosphere.** The magnificent marble Angel Staircase was laid out by von Hildebrandt and has sculptures by Georg Rafael Donner. The staircase is romantically draped with white marble putti, whose faces and gestures reflect a multitude of emotions, from questioning innocence to jeering mockery. The very first putto genuflects in an old Turkish greeting (a reminder of the Siege of Vienna in 1683). ⊠ *Mirabellplatz 4* ☏ *0662/8072* ☞ *Free.*

FAMILY

Fodor's Choice

★

**Mirabellgarten** (*Mirabell Gardens*). While there's a choice of entrances to the Mirabell Gardens—from the Makartplatz (framed by the statues of Roman gods), the Schwarzstrasse, and Mirabell Square—you'll want to enter from the Rainerstrasse and head for the Rosenhügel (Rosebush Hill); you'll arrive at the top of the steps where Julie Andrews and her seven charges showed off their singing ability in *The Sound of Music*. This is also an ideal vantage point from which to admire the formal gardens and one of the best views of Salzburg, as it shows how harmoniously architects of the Baroque period laid out the city. The center of the gardens—one of Europe's most beautiful parks, partly designed by Fischer von Erlach as the grand frame for the Mirabell Palace—is dominated by four large groups of statues representing the elements water, fire, air, and earth, and designed by Ottavio Mosto, who came to live in Salzburg from Padua. A bronze version of the winged horse Pegasus stands in front of the south facade of the palace in the center of a circular water basin. The most famous part of the Mirabell Gardens

8

## CYCLING IN SALZBURG

As most Salzburgers know, one of the best and most pleasurable ways of getting around the city and the surrounding countryside is by bicycle. Find bike and e-bike rental points along the Salzach, and visit local bookstores for maps of the extensive network of cycle paths. Check out the interactive map at ⊕ *www.radlkarte.info* to plan your trip. The most delightful ride in Salzburg? The **Hellbrunner Allee** from Freisaal to Hellbrunn Palace is an enjoyable run, taking you past Frohnburg Palace and a number of elegant mansions on either side of the tree-lined avenue. The more adventurous can go farther afield, taking the **Salzach cycle path** north to the village of Oberndorf, or south to Golling and Hallein.

is the **Zwerglgarten** (Dwarfs' Garden), which can be found opposite the Pegasus fountain. Here you'll find 12 statues of "Danubian" dwarves sculpted in marble—the real-life models for which were presented to the bishop by the Landgrave of Göttweig. Prince-Archbishop Franz Anton von Harrach had the figures made for a kind of stone theater below. The **Heckentheater** (Hedge Theater) is an enchanting natural stage setting that dates from 1700. ⊠ *Mirabellplatz 4.*

FAMILY
Fodor's Choice
★
**Mozart Wohnhaus** (*Mozart Residence*). The Mozart family moved from its cramped quarters in Getreidegasse to this house on the Hannibal Platz, as it was then known, in 1773. Wolfgang Amadeus Mozart lived here until 1780, his sister Nannerl stayed here until she married in 1784, and their father Leopold lived here until his death in 1787. The house is accordingly referred to as the Mozart Residence, signifying that it was not only Wolfgang who lived here. During the first Allied bomb attack on Salzburg in October 1944, the house was partially destroyed, but was reconstructed in 1996. Mozart composed the "Salzburg Symphonies" here, as well as all five violin concertos, church music and some sonatas, and parts of his early operatic masterpieces, including *Idomeneo.* Take the informative audio tour for an introduction to the museum's interesting collection of musical instruments (for example, his own pianoforte) in the Dance Master Hall that are still played during frequent chamber concerts, as well as books from Leopold Mozart's library, family letters, and portraits. One room offers an informative multimedia show and wall-size map with more personal details about Mozart, like his numerous travels across Europe. Bring along your camera to capture a fun, virtual step into a family portrait at the end of the tour. ⊠ *Makartplatz 8* ☎ *0662/874227–40* ⊕ *www.mozarteum. at* 🎫 *€11; combined ticket with Mozart's Birthplace €18.*

**Steingasse.** This narrow medieval street, walled in on one side by the bare cliffs of the Kapuzinerberg, was originally the ancient Roman entrance into the city from the south. The houses stood along the riverfront before the Salzach was regulated. Nowadays it's a fascinating mixture of shops and nightclubs, but with its tall houses the street still manages to convey an idea of how life used to be in the Middle Ages. The **Steintor** marks the entrance to the oldest section of the street; here on summer afternoons the light can be particularly striking. House No. 23 on the right still has deep, slanted peep-windows for guarding the gate. House No. 31 is the birthplace of Josef Mohr, the poet of "Silent Night, Holy Night" fame (not No. 9, as is incorrectly noted on the wall). ⊠ *Salzburg.*

### WORTH NOTING

**Dreifaltigkeitskirche** (*Church of the Holy Trinity*). The Makartplatz—named after Hans Makart, the most famous Austrian painter of the mid-19th century—is dominated at the top (east) end by Fischer von Erlach's first architectural work in Salzburg, built 1694–1702. It was modeled on a church by Borromini in Rome and prefigures von Erlach's Karlskirche in Vienna. Dominated by a lofty, oval-shape dome—which showcases a painting by Johann Michael Rottmayr—this church was the result of the archbishop's concern that Salzburg's new town was developing in an overly haphazard manner. The church interior is small but perfectly proportioned, surmounted by its dome, whose trompel'oeil fresco seems to open up the church to the sky above. ⊠ *Dreifaltigkeitsgasse 14* ☎ *0662/877495.*

**Mozart Audio Visual Collection.** In the same building as the Mozart Wohnhaus (Residence), this is an archive of thousands of Mozart recordings as well as films and video productions, all of which can be listened to or viewed on request. ⊠ *Makartplatz 8* ☎ *0662/883454* ⊕ *www.mozarteum.at* 🛒 *Free* ☉ *Closed weekends.*

**Stiftung Mozarteum.** Organizer of the important Mozart Week held every January and the forward-looking Dialogue Festival held during the first week of December, the Stiftung Mozarteum is the center for scholarly research and continued support of Mozart's life and works. The libraries, containing rare editions and significant publications, are open to the public. Thousands flock here for its packed calendar of concerts. ⊠ *Schwarzstrasse 26* ☎ *0662/88940–13* ⊕ *www.mozarteum.at.*

8

# WHERE TO EAT

Salzburg has some of the best—and most expensive—restaurants in Austria, so if you happen to walk into one of the Altstadt posh establishments without a reservation, you may get a sneer worthy of Captain von Trapp. Happily, the city is plentifully supplied with pleasant eateries, offering not only good, solid Austrian food (not for anyone on a diet), but also exceptional Italian dishes and *neue Küche* (nouvelle cuisine) delights. There are certain dining experiences that are quintessentially Salzburgian, including restaurants perched on the town's peaks that offer "food with a view" or rustic inns that offer "Alpine evenings" with entertainment. Some of the most distinctive places in town are the fabled hotel restaurants, such as those of the Goldener Hirsch or the "S'Nockerl," the cellar of the Hotel Elefant.

For fast food, Salzburgers love their broiled-sausages street stands. Some say the most delicious fare is found at the Balkan Grill at Getreidegasse 33 (its recipe for spicy Bosna sausage has always been a secret).

■TIP➔ **For a quick lunch on weekdays, visit the market in front of the Kollegienkirche—a lot of stands offer a large variety of boiled sausages for any taste, ranging from mild to spiced.**

In the more expensive restaurants the set menus give you an opportunity to sample the chef's best; in less expensive ones they help keep costs down. Note, however, that some restaurants limit the hours during which the set menu is available. Many restaurants are open all day; otherwise, lunch is served from approximately 11 to 2 and dinner from 6 to 10. In more expensive restaurants it's always best to make a reservation. At festival time most restaurants are open seven days a week, and have generally more flexible late dining hours. *Restaurant reviews have been shortened. For full information, visit Fodors.com.*

| WHAT IT COSTS IN EUROS | | | | |
|---|---|---|---|---|
| | $ | $$ | $$$ | $$$$ |
| AT DINNER | under €12 | €12–€17 | €18–€22 | over €22 |

Restaurant prices are the average cost of a main course at dinner, or if dinner is not served, at lunch.

## THE ALTSTADT

$ ✗**Augustinerbräu.** One of the largest beer cellars in Europe, the cel-
AUSTRIAN ebrated Augustinerbräu is at the north end of the Mönchsberg. Shops in the huge monastery complex sell a vast array of salads, breads, and pastries, as well as sausage and spit-roasted chicken. **Known for:** sprawling and impressive beer garden; food stalls with various Austrian specialties; some of the best brews in Austria. Ⓢ *Average main: €10* ⊠ *Lindhofstrasse 7* ☎ *0662/431246* ⊕ *www.augustinerbier.at* ⊟ *No credit cards.*

$ ✗**Balkan Grill.** Known simply as "The Bosna Grill," this tiny sausage
HOT DOG stand has become a cult destination for locals and international travel-
Fodor'sChoice ers. Find the long line of hungry people in the tiny passageway between
★ the busy Getreidegasse and the Universitätsplatz to try this Bulgarian-inspired, Salzburg-born specialty: two thin, grilled bratwurst sausages in a toasted white bread bun, topped with chopped onions, fresh parsley, and a curry-based seasoning mixture that's been a secret since the owner, Zanko Todoroff, created it more than 50 years ago. **Known for:** phenomenal curry sausage; long lines; cash-only policy. Ⓢ *Average main: €4* ⊠ *Getreidegasse 33* ☎ *0662/841483* ⊟ *No credit cards* ⊘ *Closed Sun.*

$$ ✗**Bärenwirt.** Regionally sourced, top-quality ingredients elevate tradi-
AUSTRIAN tional Austrian dishes in this inviting Wirtshaus. Since 1663, locals have shared mugs of beer from the neighboring Augustiner Kloster Mülln brewery in these warmly lighted, wood-paneled rooms, adorned with traditional Salzburg-style heating ovens and cushioned benches. **Known for:** cozy atmopshere; juicy Backhendl (breaded, fried chicken); house-made schnapps. Ⓢ *Average main: €15* ⊠ *Müllner Hauptstrasse 8* ☎ *0662/422404* ⊕ *www.baerenwirt-salzburg.at.*

$$$ ✗**Blaue Gans.** In a 500-year-old building with vaulted ceilings and win-
AUSTRIAN dows looking out onto the bustling Getreidegasse, the restaurant of the

Blaue Gans Hotel offers innovative, modern interpretations of traditional Austrian cooking. The fresh flavors are evident in dishes like the house-smoked *Lachsforelle* (salmon trout) and perfectly prepared beef carpaccio. **Known for:** great service; historic building; excellent Austrian and German wine list. $ *Average main: €21* ⊠ *Blaue Gans Hotel, Getreidegasse 41–43* ☎ *0662/842491–0* ⊕ *www.blauegans.at* ☯ *Closed Sun.*

$

AUSTRIAN

**Fodor's** Choice

★

✕ **Café Tomaselli.** This inn opened its doors in 1705 as an example of that newfangled thing, a Wiener Kaffeehaus (Vienna coffeehouse), and was an immediate hit. Enjoying its 11 types of coffee was none other than Mozart's beloved, Constanze, who often dropped in, as her house was just next door. **Known for:** great selection of pastries, including the Erdbeerschüsserl (cream cake with strawberries); gorgeous upstairs terrace dining; historic Vienna coffeehouse experience. $ *Average main: €10* ⊠ *Alter Markt 9* ☎ *0662/844488–0* ⊕ *www.tomaselli.at* ⊟ *No credit cards.*

$$

EUROPEAN

✕ **Café 220°.** Whether you're craving a stellar late breakfast (served until 2 pm) or you're on the hunt for a carefully crafted espresso, you'll want to put this lively café on your daytime itinerary. The husband-and-wife team infuses care and quality into each step, from farm to cup, which takes them around the world to meet growers. **Known for:** great breakfasts and brunches; constantly changing menu with seasonal specialties; amazing coffee roasted by the owners themselves. $ *Average main: €14* ⊠ *Chiemseegasse 5* ☎ *0662/827881* ⊕ *www.220grad.com* ☯ *Closed Sun. and Mon. No dinner.*

$$$

AUSTRIAN

✕ **Carpe Diem.** Dietrich Mateschitz (who also invented the Red Bull energy drink) together with Jörg Wörther put their heads together to create something unique: small dishes—both savory and sweet—served in "cones." Pickled perch with artichokes and asparagus tips arrives in a polenta cone, while a potato cone bursts with prime beef with creamed spinach and horseradish. Mix and match to create a delicious meal; be prepared to have your bill add up quickly. **Known for:** unique, mix-and-match "cone" food; open terrace dining in summer; more traditional menu upstairs. $ *Average main: €21* ⊠ *Getreidegasse 50* ☎ *0662/848800* ⊕ *www.carpediemfinestfingerfood.com* ☯ *Closed Sun.*

8

$

AUSTRIAN

✕ **Fabrizi Espresso.** Named after the former Italian owner of this historic house (note the beautiful small archway passage), this is a top spot for tasting Marzemino, the red wine Don Giovanni drinks in Mozart's opera. But there are plenty of other goodies here: some of the best Italian coffees in the city; outstanding Austrian *Apfel-oder Topfenstrudel* (apple or cheese pie) and the best Salzburger *Nockerl*; excellent prosecco; various salads; and a fine Wiener schnitzel. **Known for:** menu of Marzemino wine and prosecco; traditional Austrian desserts; fantastic Italian coffee. $ *Average main: €9* ⊠ *Getreidegasse 21* ☎ *0662/845914* ⊕ *www.espresso-fabrizi.com* ⊟ *No credit cards* ☯ *No dinner.*

$$

AUSTRIAN

✕ **Gasthaus Wilder Mann.** Here you'll find a true time-tinged feel of an old Salzburg *Gasthaus,* right down to a huge ceramic stove next to wooden chairs that welcomed generations of locals as they tucked into enormous plates of *Bauernschmaus* (Farmer's Feast): roast pork, ham, sausage, sauerkraut, and a massive dumpling. Pair it with a frothy-headed mug of the hometown "liquid bread"—Stiegl beer—from the oldest private brewery in Austria. **Known for:** huge, meat-filled plates; local,

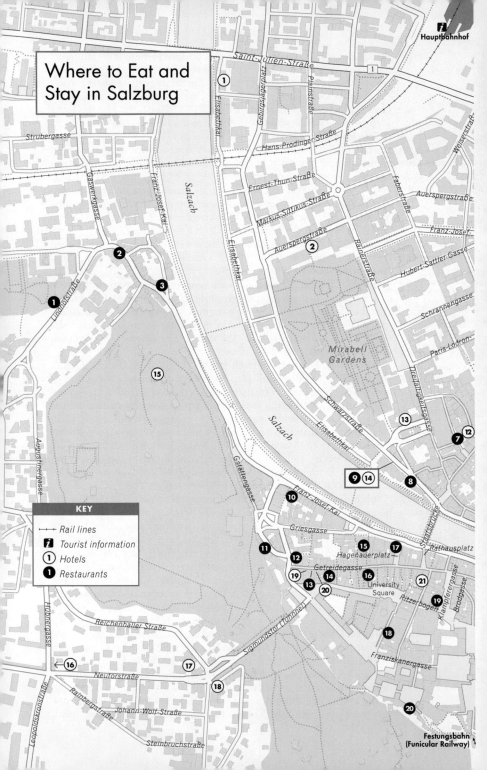

# Where to Eat and Stay in Salzburg

## Restaurants ▼

## Hotels ▼

traditional vibe; beer from Austria's oldest private brewery. [$] *Average main: €12* ✉ *Getreidegasse 20* ☎ *0662/841787* 🌐 *www.wildermann.co.at* 💳 *No credit cards* 🕓 *Closed Sun.*

$$ MODERN EUROPEAN 🍴 **Glüxfall.** A personalized, choose-your-own-breakfast-adventure menu (served until 2 pm) lets you savor several beautifully prepared, whimsically presented small dishes without encroaching on your date's plate. Mix and match two, four, or six sweet and savory choices: venison carpaccio with lingonberry chutney; heart-shape waffle with sour-cherry sauce; or nonalcoholic Bloody Mary shooter with a salmon canapé. **Known for:** well-crafted cocktails; creative brunch and breakfast dishes; peaceful courtyard. [$] *Average main: €13* ✉ *Franz-Josef-Kai 11* ☎ *0662/265017* 🌐 *www.gluexfall.at* 🕓 *Closed Mon. and Tues. No dinner Sun.*

$$$ AUSTRIAN 🍴 **K&K am Waagplatz.** With white-linen tablecloths, candles, flowers, and windows opening onto the street, this is one of Salzburg's most pleasant restaurants. Menu selections consist of local fish, mouthwatering steaks, traditional Austrian dishes, and game in season. **Known for:** Austrian classics; lovely outdoor seating in summer; notable business lunch. [$] *Average main: €21* ✉ *Waagplatz 2* ☎ *0662/842156* 🌐 *www.kollerkoller.com.*

$$ AUSTRIAN 🍴 **Krimpelstätter.** About a 15-minute walk downriver from the Altstadt in the Mülln neighborhood, you'll discover traditional Salzburg cooking. You can choose from the delicious *Schott* (cheese) soup, the potato goulash with chunks of country ham, spinach dumplings in brown butter, or original Wiener schnitzel, and freshly tapped beer from the neighboring Augustinerbräu. **Known for:** historical ambience; freshly tapped beer; garden dining in summer with nice views. [$] *Average main: €15* ✉ *Müllner Hauptstrasse 31* ☎ *0662/432274* 🌐 *www.krimpelstaetter.at* 🕓 *Closed Sun. and Mon.*

$$$$ ITALIAN 🍴 **Pan e Vin.** This tiny trattoria has only a handful of tables but it offers some lovely Italian specialties. Feel the spirit of the city called the "Rome of the North" here: burnt-sienna walls are lined with wine bottles, colorful ceramic plates, and Italian dry stuffs, and the chef cooks in full view. **Known for:** excellent Italian dishes; extensive wine list. [$] *Average main: €24* ✉ *Gstättengasse 1* ☎ *0662/844666–14* 🌐 *www.panevin.at* 🕓 *Closed Mon.*

$$$$ AUSTRIAN 🍴 **St. Peter Stiftskulinarium.** Legends swirl about the famous St. Peter's Beer Cellar: locals claim that Mephistopheles met Faust here, others say Charlemagne dined here, and some believe Columbus enjoyed a glass of its famous Salzburg Stiegl beer just before he set sail for America in 1492. But there is no debating the fact that this place—first mentioned in a document dating back to 803—is Austria's oldest restaurant. **Known for:** country's oldest restaurant; historical dining spaces; sophisticated Austrian classics. [$] *Average main: €26* ✉ *St. Peter Bezirk 4* ☎ *0662/841268–0* 🌐 *www.stpeter.at.*

$$ AUSTRIAN 🍴 **Triangel.** See and be seen among the Salzburg Festival glitteratti in Triangel's large outdoor seating area or cozy up in the intimate dining room of this organic-farming-focused Austrian restaurant. You can't go wrong with "absolutely Styrian" *Oma's Schweinsbraten* (owner Franzi's grandmother's roast pork belly recipe), and that pounding coming from the back room tells you that the Wiener schnitzel is a properly prepared choice. **Known for:** crowd of Salzburg Festival artists; organic

ingredients; old-school roast pork belly recipe. [$] *Average main: €16* ✉ *Wiener Philharmonikergasse 7* ☎ *0662/842–229* 🌐 *www.triangel-salzburg.co.at* 🕓 *Closed Sun. and Mon.*

$$ AUSTRIAN
🍴 **Zum Eulenspiegel.** This spot allures with rustic wooden furniture, old folio volumes, antique weapons, and open fireplaces. Tables gleaming with white linen are set in wonderful nooks and crannies reached by odd staircases and charming salons. **Known for:** ingredients sourced from bio-farm; rustic and charming ambience; central location near Mozart's birthplace. [$] *Average main: €16* ✉ *Hagenauerplatz 2* ☎ *0662/843180–0* 🌐 *www.zum-eulenspiegel.at.*

## NORTH OF THE RIVER SALZACH

$ CAFÉ
🍴 **Café Bazar.** Sip a Melange under the shade of the leafy trees at this people-watching coffeehouse institution on the Salzach River. Salads, soups, and toasted ham-and-cheese sandwiches served with ketchup satisfy savory cravings; homemade Topfen- and Apfelstrudel beckon from the glass case of house-made tortes. **Known for:** homemade cakes; sumptuous traditional coffeehouse atmosphere; beautiful river views from the terrace. [$] *Average main: €7* ✉ *Schwarzstrasse 3* ☎ *0662/874278* 🌐 *www.cafe-bazar.at.*

$$ AUSTRIAN
🍴 **Café Sacher.** Red-velvet banquettes, sparkling chandeliers, and lots of gilt mark this famous gathering place, a favorite of well-heeled Salzburgers and an outpost of the celebrated Vienna landmark. It's a perfect choice for a leisurely afternoon pastry. **Known for:** elegant Salzburg decor; famous homemade chocolate Sachertorte; top-rate coffee. [$] *Average main: €12* ✉ *Schwarzstrasse 5–7* ☎ *0662/889770* 🌐 *www.sacher.com.*

$$ AUSTRIAN
🍴 **Daxlueg.** If you really want to enjoy food with a view, drive 3 km (2 miles) north along the B1 Linzer Bundesstrasse to Mayrwies and turn right up through the woods. Here you can take in a view of Salzburg from the mountainside perch of this former Rupertialm (St Rupert's Pasture), a famous scenic lookout even in Mozart's time. **Known for:** panoramic views; Alpine chalet charm; seasonal dishes and garnishes. [$] *Average main: €15* ✉ *Daxluegstrasse 5, Hallwang bei Salzburg* ☎ *0662/665800* 🌐 *www.daxlueg.at* 🕓 *Closed Mon. and Tues.*

$$ AUSTRIAN
🍴 **Die Weisse.** This *Weissbierbrauerei* combines the original charm of one of Salzburg's most historic breweries and adds a high-ceilinged, wood-paneled modern bar to satisfy the many locals who consider it to be the ultimate private retreat (so much so that from Wednesday through Saturday it's best to make a reservation). The beer garden really hits the spot on a hot summer day, but all year long you can savor traditional Bavarian style *Weisswurst* (veal sausages with sweet mustard) as well as the usual array of tempting Salzburg delights. **Known for:** original beers brewed on-site; local neighborhood vibe; Bavarian-style sausages. [$] *Average main: €17* ✉ *Rupertgasse 10* ☎ *0662/872246* 🕓 *Closed Sun.*

$$$$ ECLECTIC
**Fodor's Choice** ★
🍴 **Pfefferschiff.** The Pepper Ship is one of the most acclaimed restaurants in Salzburg—though it's 3 km (2 miles) northeast of the center. It's in a pretty, renovated rectory, dated 1640 and adjacent to a pink-and-cream chapel. **Known for:** beautifully composed set menus that change with the seasons; impressive Austrian wine list; country-chic atmosphere.

8

[$] *Average main: €30* ✉ *Söllheim 3* ☎ *0662/661242* 🌐 *www.pfeffer-schiff.at* 🕒 *Closed Sun.*

$$ AUSTRIAN 🍴 **Zum Fidelen Affen.** The name means "At the Faithful Ape," which explains the monkey motifs in this popular Gasthaus dominated by a round, copper-plated bar and stone pillars under a vaulted ceiling. Besides the beer on tap, the kitchen offers tasty Austrian dishes, such as *Schlutzkrapfen,* handmade cheese ravioli with a light topping of chopped fresh tomatoes, or a big salad with jucy *Backhendl* (breaded, fried chicken). **Known for:** large portions of traditional Austrian dishes; fun party vibe; big crowds. [$] *Average main: €12* ✉ *Priesterhausgasse 8* ☎ *0662/877361* 🌐 *www.fideleraffe.at* 🕒 *Closed Sun. No lunch.*

# WHERE TO STAY

It's difficult for a Salzburg hotel not to have a good location—you can find a room with a stunning view over the Kapuzinerberg or Gaisberg or one that simply overlooks a lovely Old City street—but it's possible. Salzburg is not a tiny town, and location is important. It's best to be near the historic city center; it's about a mile from the railway station to historic Zentrum (center), right around the main bridge of the Staatsbrücke. The Old City has a wide assortment of hotels and pensions, but there are few bargains. Also note that many hotels in this area have to be accessed on foot, as cars are not permitted on many streets. If you have a car, you may opt for a hotel or converted castle on the outskirts of the city. Many hostelries are charmingly decorated in *Bauernstil*—the rustic look of Old Austria; the ultimate in peasant-luxe is found at the world-famous Hotel Goldener Hirsch.

If you're looking for something really cheap (less than €60 for a double), clean, and comfortable, stay in a private home, though the good ones are all a little way from downtown.

The tourist information office can assist with booking B&Bs, farmhouses, and religious institutions, as well as hotels and apartments.

If you're planning to come at festival time (July and August), you must book as early as possible; try to reserve at least two months in advance. Prices soar over the already high levels—so much so that during the high season a hotel may edge into the next-higher price category.

Room rates include taxes and service charges. Many hotels include a breakfast in the room rate—check when booking—but the more expensive hostelries often do not. A property that provides breakfast and dinner daily is known as *halb pension,* and one that serves three meals a day is *voll pension.* If you don't have a reservation, go to one of the tourist information offices, either in the center or the railway station. *Hotel reviews have been shortened. For full information, visit Fodors.com.*

| WHAT IT COSTS IN EUROS | | | | |
|---|---|---|---|---|
| | **$** | **$$** | **$$$** | **$$$$** |
| FOR TWO PEOPLE | under €120 | €120–€170 | €171–€270 | over €270 |
| | Prices are for a standard double room in high season, including taxes and service. | | | |

## THE ALTSTADT

$$$$ HOTEL **Altstadt Radisson Blu Salzburg.** This venerable 1372 building, one of the city's oldest inns, is an impressive riverside landmark with its buff pink facade and iron lanterns. **Pros:** central location; expansive river views; generous breakfast buffet. **Cons:** inconvenient location if you have a car; chain-hotel feel; can be noisy. [$] *Rooms from: €350* ✉ *Judengasse 15/Rudolfskai 28* ☎ *0662/84–85–71–0* 🌐 *www.austria-trend.at/ass* 🛏 *62 rooms.*

$$$$ HOTEL **Arthotel Blaue Gans.** The sleek, contemporary style of the Blue Goose boutique art hotel counters the building's 400-year-old pedigree and offers guests a stellar location at the top of the main shopping street and steps away from the Grosses Festspielhaus. **Pros:** wonderful art throughout; near the city's major sights; close to shopping. **Cons:** on a noisy street; its popularity makes getting a reservation difficult; front-desk staff can sometimes seem scattered. [$] *Rooms from: €300* ✉ *Getreidegasse 43* ☎ *0662/842–491* 🌐 *www.blaue-gans.com* 🛏 *35 rooms.*

$$$$ HOTEL Fodor's Choice ★ **Goldener Hirsch.** Celebrities from Picasso to Pavarotti have favored the Golden Stag for its legendary gemütlichkeit, patrician pampering, and adorable interiors. **Pros:** unbeatable location; top-notch dining; incredibly charming. **Cons:** rooms are on the small side; parking and other extras expensive; no coffee/tea in rooms. [$] *Rooms from: €585* ✉ *Getreidegasse 37/Herbert-von-Karajan-Platz 5* ☎ *0662/80840* 🌐 *www.goldenerhirsch.com* 🛏 *70 rooms.*

$$ HOTEL **Hotel am Dom.** Tucked away on a tiny street near Residenzplatz, this small boutique hotel in a 14th-century building offers stylish, comfortable rooms, some with oak-beam ceilings. **Pros:** rustic atmosphere; well-kept rooms; air-conditioning throughout. **Cons:** few amenities; no on-site parking; elevator doesn't reach the top-floor rooms. [$] *Rooms from: €160* ✉ *Goldgasse 17* ☎ *0662/842–765* 🌐 *www.hotelamdom.at* 🛏 *14 rooms.*

$$$$ HOTEL **Hotel Elefant.** An old, historic favorite, Hotel Elefant offers great stories, cozy rooms, modern touches, a fantastic central location, and delicious traditional Austrian meals at the on-site restaurant and bar. **Pros:** lots of history; excellent location; quiet yet centrally located street. **Cons:** some rooms are cramped; difficult to access with a car; room temperature can vary widely. [$] *Rooms from: €278* ✉ *Sigmund-Haffner-Gasse 4* ☎ *0662/843–397* 🌐 *www.hotelelefant.at* 🛏 *31 rooms* 🍴 *Breakfast.*

$$ HOTEL **Hotel Neutor.** A two-minute walk from the Old City, next to the historic tunnel that plows through the Mönchsberg, and directly in front of a stop on several bus lines, this basic hotel has location and

8

transportation covered. **Pros:** excellent location; easy access to public transportation; parking available. **Cons:** on a busy street; very dated interior; staff could use some hospitality training. $\boxed{\$}$ *Rooms from: €165* ⊠ *Neutorstrasse 8* ☎ *0662/844–1540* ⊕ *www.neutor.com* ☞ *90 rooms.*

**\$\$**
B&B/INN

▢ **Hotel Wolf.** The embodiment of Austrian gemütlichkeit, just off Mozartplatz, the small, family-owned, in-the-center-of-everything Wolf offers spotlessly clean and cozy rooms in a rustic building from the year 1429. **Pros:** plenty of atmosphere; in a historic house; lovely breakfast. **Cons:** parking is a problem; no air-conditioning or fans; staff can sometimes be unhelpful. $\boxed{\$}$ *Rooms from: €150* ⊠ *Kaigasse 7* ☎ *0662/843–4530* ⊕ *www.hotelwolf.at* ☉ *Closed early Feb.–early Mar.* ☞ *14 rooms* ⅠⓄⅠ *Breakfast.*

**\$\$\$\$**
HOTEL

▢ **Schloss Mönchstein.** With gorgeous gardens and hiking trails, it's little wonder the 19th-century naturalist Alexander von Humboldt called this retreat outside the city center a "small piece of paradise." Catherine of Russia and the Duchess of Liechtenstein are among the notables who have stayed in the gable-roofed, tower-studded mansion. **Pros:** luxurious rooms; lovely views; extensive and exclusive spa. **Cons:** outside of city center; need a car to get around; a/c and pipes are a bit noisy. $\boxed{\$}$ *Rooms from: €450* ⊠ *Mönchsberg Park 26* ☎ *0662/848–5550* ⊕ *www.monchstein.at/en* ☉ *Closed Feb.* ☞ *24 rooms* ⅠⓄⅠ *Breakfast.*

# NORTH OF THE RIVER SALZACH

**\$\$**
HOTEL

▢ **Bergland.** A 10-minute walk from the train station, this cheerful, pleasant, fourth-generation family-owned pension offers modern, comfortable rooms. **Pros:** quiet location; 12 free parking spots; very good value. **Cons:** long walk to the center; basic accommodations; residential street may not appeal to everyone. $\boxed{\$}$ *Rooms from: €130* ⊠ *Rupertgasse 15* ☎ *0662/872–318* ⊕ *www.berglandhotel.at* ☉ *Closed end Oct.–Nov.* ☞ *18 rooms.*

**\$\$**
HOTEL
FAMILY

▢ **Gersberg Alm.** A picture-perfect Alpine chalet on the lofty perch of the Gersberg, high above Salzburg, this hotel is less than 15 minutes by car from the center of the city. **Pros:** beautiful location; pleasant rooms; great restaurant. **Cons:** outside the city; car is required; balconies are shared. $\boxed{\$}$ *Rooms from: €142* ⊠ *Gersberg 37* ☎ *0662/641–257* ⊕ *www.gersbergalm.at* ☞ *44 rooms* ⅠⓄⅠ *Breakfast.*

**\$\$**
HOTEL

▢ **Goldenes Theater.** Close enough to the top of the Linzergasse shopping district and the theaters in the Neustadt but far enough to offer a respite from the summer crowds, this simple hotel is a decent value choice. **Pros:** close to Linzergasse shops; quiet terrace; helpful staff. **Cons:** on a busy street; some rooms are quite dated; garage parking extra. $\boxed{\$}$ *Rooms from: €159* ⊠ *Schallmooser Hauptstrasse 13* ☎ *0662/881–681* ⊕ *www.gt-hotel-salzburg.com* ☞ *58 rooms* ⅠⓄⅠ *Breakfast.*

**\$\$\$**
HOTEL

▢ **Hotel Amadeus.** If you're wondering why the hotel has Mozart's middle name, this 500-year-old, rather ramshackle yet charming house is not far from the St. Sebastian church and cemetery where many members of his family are booked for an eternal stay. **Pros:** charming decor; historic house; good restaurants nearby. **Cons:** church bell next door goes off every quarter hour from 6 am to 11 pm; no air-conditioning;

reception desk is not open 24 hours. $ *Rooms from: €220 ⊠ Linzergasse 43–45 ☎ 0662/871–401 ⊕ www.hotelamadeus.at ↪ 20 rooms.*

$$$
HOTEL
FAMILY
Fodor's Choice
★

**⊡ Hotel Auersperg.** A lush, green oasis is tucked between the two buildings that comprise the Auersperg: the hotel, built in 1892 by the noted Italian architect Ceconi, and its neighboring villa. **Pros:** family-friendly; great breakfast; hidden urban oasis. **Cons:** on a busy intersection; not in the city center; "villa" building not as convenient. $ *Rooms from: €205 ⊠ Auerspergstrasse 61 ☎ 0662/88944 ⊕ www.auersperg.at ↪ 55 rooms ⊙ Breakfast.*

$$$$
HOTEL

**⊡ Hotel Bristol.** There is little wonder that this pale-yellow palace, just across the river from the Altstadt and with stunning historic detail and fine artwork, has attracted an impressive roster of royal and celebrity guests. **Pros:** some fantastic views; charming accommodations; elegant restaurant. **Cons:** not in the old city; lower-floor rear rooms lack views; non-suite rooms can be cramped. $ *Rooms from: €400 ⊠ Makartplatz 4 ☎ 0662/873–557 ⊕ www.bristol-salzburg.at ☽ Closed Feb. and Mar. ↪ 60 rooms ⊙ Breakfast.*

$
HOTEL

**⊡ Motel One Salzburg Mirabell.** This simple, no-frills, freshly modern hotel is a 15-minute walk from all that the historic city has to offer. **Pros:** riverfront location; close to city and train station; budget friendly. **Cons:** few extras; no room safe; small bathrooms. $ *Rooms from: €86 ⊠ Elisabethkai 58 ☎ 0662/885200 ⊕ www.motel-one.com/en/hotels/salzburg ↪ 119 rooms.*

$$$
HOTEL

**⊡ NH Salzburg.** Part of a Spanish hotel chain, this pretty building is in a nice location, around the corner from Linzergasse (the shopping street leading to the Salzach River) and five minutes away from the beautiful Mirabell Gardens. **Pros:** in a historic setting; tasty breakfast; underground parking on-site. **Cons:** noisy common areas; popular hotel for groups so can get crowded; rooms could use a little freshening up. $ *Rooms from: €190 ⊠ Franz-Josef-Strasse 26 ☎ 0662/882–0410 ⊕ www.nh-hotels.com ↪ 140 rooms ⊙ Breakfast.*

$$
HOTEL

**⊡ Rosenvilla.** A haven of peace and tranquility, this family-owned, upscale bed-and-breakfast is across the Salzach River from the Altstadt. **Pros:** quiet location; tasteful rooms; lovely garden. **Cons:** long walk to downtown; no restaurants or cafés nearby; no air-conditioning. $ *Rooms from: €165 ⊠ Höfelgasse 4 ☎ 0662/621–765 ⊕ www.rosenvilla.com ↪ 13 rooms.*

$$$$
HOTEL
FAMILY
Fodor's Choice
★

**⊡ Sacher Salzburg.** On the Salzach River, this mammoth hotel has attracted guests from the Beatles and the Rolling Stones to Hillary and Chelsea Clinton, but the owners, the Gürtler family, will ensure that even if you don't have a Vuitton steamer trunk you'll feel welcome. **Pros:** great views; good riverside location; plenty of dining options. **Cons:** gets overcrowded during festival time; some rooms need renovating; service can be slow. $ *Rooms from: €403 ⊠ Schwarzstrasse 5–7 ☎ 0662/889770 ⊕ www.sacher.com ↪ 113 rooms.*

$$$
HOTEL
Fodor's Choice
★

**⊡ Schloss Leopoldskron.** Expansive grounds surround this historic palace immortalized in *The Sound of Music,* and the smart rooms are surprisingly modest in price. **Pros:** idyllic, peaceful location; free parking; a few free bicycles available from reception. **Cons:** the closest bus stop is a 12-minute walk; no on-site restaurant; no air-conditioning. $ *Rooms*

**8**

*from: €200* ✉ *Leopoldskronstrasse 56–58* ☎ *0662/839–830* 🌐 *www.schloss-leopoldskron.com* 🛏 *69 rooms* 🍴 *Breakfast.*

$ HOTEL 🏨 **Schwarzes Rössl.** Once a favorite with Salzburg regulars, this traditional gasthof now serves as student quarters for most of the year, but is well worth booking when available. **Pros:** near city center; lots of bars and restaurants nearby; budget friendly. **Cons:** few amenities; rooms can feel spartan; some rooms have shared bathrooms. [$] *Rooms from: €100* ✉ *Priesterhausgasse 6* ☎ *0662/874–426* 🌐 *www.academiahotels.at* 🕓 *Closed Oct.–June* 🛏 *50 rooms.*

$$$$ HOTEL 🏨 **Sheraton Grand Salzburg.** With the lovely Mirabell Park and Gardens virtually at its back door, this modern hotel tastefully blends in with the belle-epoque buildings that surround it. **Pros:** spacious rooms; good on-site meal options; friendly staff. **Cons:** often filled with conferences; chain-hotel feel; in-room Wi-Fi is only free to hotel club members. [$] *Rooms from: €350* ✉ *Auerspergstrasse 4* ☎ *0662/889–990* 🌐 *www.starwoodhotels.com/sheraton* 🛏 *166 rooms.*

$$$$ HOTEL 🏨 **Stadtkrug.** Snuggled under the monument-studded Kapuzinerberg and a two-minute walk from the bridge leading to the center of the Altstadt, the Stadtkrug (dated 1353) hits an idyllic, romantic, and quiet vibe, thanks to its mountainside setting. **Pros:** good location; lots of charm; helpful staff. **Cons:** parking off-site; the hotel's four levels mean some stairs to climb; no air-conditioning. [$] *Rooms from: €350* ✉ *Linzergasse 20* ☎ *0662/873–5450* 🌐 *www.stadtkrug.at* 🛏 *35 rooms* 🍴 *Breakfast.*

$$ HOTEL 🏨 **Star Inn Zentrum.** Behind the Mönchsberg, this no-frills hotel stands close to the center of the historic section, and if you want to fit in a quiet morning stroll through the area, this is a decently priced option. **Pros:** excellent location; close to public transportation; friendly staff. **Cons:** front rooms on a busy street; spartan, outdated rooms; the standard rooms are small. [$] *Rooms from: €160* ✉ *Hildmannplatz 5* ☎ *0662/846–846* 🌐 *www.starinnhotels.com* 🛏 *86 rooms* 🍴 *No meals.*

$ HOTEL FAMILY 🏨 **Turnerwirt.** In the former farmer's village of Gnigl, now on Salzburg's outskirts, this is a quaint complex of three buildings. **Pros:** family-run friendliness; lots of charm; bus stop to city center in front of the building. **Cons:** outside city center; no elevator; dated. [$] *Rooms from: €95* ✉ *Linzer Bundesstrasse 54* ☎ *0662/640–630* 🌐 *www.turnerwirt.at* 🛏 *70 rooms.*

$$ HOTEL Fodor's Choice ★ 🏨 **Villa Trapp.** Stay at the home of the real von Trapp family in the southern suburb of Aigen, where each of the comfortable rooms is individually decorated. **Pros:** quiet location; a must-stay for Sound of Music fans; gorgeous views. **Cons:** far outside the city center; no 24-hour reception; no air-conditioning. [$] *Rooms from: €170* ✉ *Traunstrasse 34* ☎ *0662/630–860* 🌐 *www.villa-trapp.com* 🛏 *14 rooms.*

$$$ HOTEL 🏨 **Wolf-Dietrich.** This small, family-owned hotel across the river from the Altstadt is an inviting choice. **Pros:** elegantly decorated rooms; nice views; great location. **Cons:** nearby church bells ring constantly; rooms vary wildly; not all rooms have air-conditioning. [$] *Rooms from: €230* ✉ *Wolf-Dietrich-Strasse 7* ☎ *0662/871–275* 🌐 *www.salzburg-hotel.at* 🛏 *29 rooms* 🍴 *Breakfast.*

# NIGHTLIFE AND PERFORMING ARTS

## NIGHTLIFE

Music in Salzburg is not just Mozart's greatest hits; the city's nightlife is actually much livelier than it is reputed to be. The "in" areas include the "Bermuda Triangle" (Steingasse and Imbergstrasse) and Kaigasse, while young people tend to populate the bars and discos around Gstättengasse and Rudolfskai.

Salzburg loves beer, and has some of the most picturesque beer gardens in Austria. The Augustinerbräu is a legendary Munich-style beer hall.

**Fodor's Choice** **Augustinerbräu.** One of the largest beer cellars in Europe and the only one ★ of its kind in Austria, the celebrated Augustinerbräu serves its 10-week aged Märzen—using the same recipe since 1621—directly from wooden kegs into your overflowing stoneware mug at this sprawling, historic landmark at the north end of the Mönchsberg. With communal, dark-wood tables and beautifully restored chandeliers, the halls overflow with cheerful locals, and outside, where massive chestnut trees shade the sprawling garden, you'll find a complete cross section of Salzburg society. Advent and Lent offer special beers, because the Catholic church decreed that "drinking does not interrupt fasting." You can tour the brewery by appointment on weekday afternoons (€14.90 per person); call or register online. ⊠ *Lindhofstrasse 7* ☎ *0662/431246* ⊕ *www. augustinerbier.at.*

**Fridrich.** This cozy little bar on the narrow Steingasse serves well-crafted drinks, an extensive selection of Austrian wines, antipasti, cold smoked locally caught fish, and small portions of savory Austrian favorites like *Faschierte Laibchen* (finely minced meatballs with bread and pickles) and *Krautfleckerl* (square pasta with caramelized onions, shredded white cabbage, sweet wine, and cumin). Eclectic music runs the gamut from Tarantino soundtracks to Italian music to jazz. ⊠ *Steingasse 15* ☎ *0662/87–62–18* ⊕ *www.gastlokal-fridrich.at.*

**Glüxfall.** Venture through the unassuming riverfront exterior and find a sophisticated alternative to the nearby raucous bar and club scene at Glüxfall's. The late-night cocktail and wine bar comes with a deliciously tempting menu and an illuminated inner courtyard. Cocktail Thursdays draw a lively crowd. ⊠ *Franz-Josef-Kai 11* ☎ *0662/265017* ⊕ *www.gluexfall.at.*

**Stieglkeller.** Sample the selections of this hometown-pride brew under the shade of chestnut trees as you watch the sun set over the rooftops and steeples of the Old City. The noted local architect Ceconi devised this sprawling place around 1901. The Keller is partly inside the Mönchsberg hill, so its cellars guarantee the quality and right temperature of the drinks. It's a great place to stop for lunch, an afternoon *Jause* (snack), or an evening *Prost* with friends, though beware: climbing up the relatively steep incline is easier than stumbling down after a few *Grosses* (large beers). ⊠ *Festungsgasse 10* ☎ *0662/842681* ⊕ *www.restaurant-stieglkeller.at* ☉ *Closed Feb.*

8

# PERFORMING ARTS

Before you arrive in Salzburg, do some advance research to determine the city's music schedule for the time you will be there, and make reservations; if you'll be attending the summer Salzburg Festival, this is a must. After you arrive in the city, any office of the Salzburg Tourist Office and most hotel concierge desks can provide you with schedules for all the arts performances held year-round in Salzburg, and you can find listings in the daily newspaper, *Salzburger Nachrichten*.

The Advent season transforms this picture-perfect city into an even more magical wonderland. Music fills the streets of the Old City during the Christmas markets. Warm up with a cup of *Glühwein* (mulled wine) from one of the numerous wooden stands and find the nearest festively attired brass ensemble for a lovely free concert.

To experience a true local tradition, get tickets to one of several Adventsingen performances. Folk singers, choral ensembles, children's choirs, traditional instrument ensembles, and actors weave music and theater into the Advent season. The stories and songs are typically in local dialect, which can be difficult for even High German speakers to understand, but the atmosphere and experience are worth it.

The spiritual surroundings of the St. Andrew's Church on Mirabell Square offer the perfect atmosphere for the performances by Salzburger Advent (⊕ *www.salzburgeradvent.at*). Salzburg Advent Singing (⊕ *www.salzburgeradventsingen.at*) in the Great Festival Hall is the largest event of the season.

**Salzburg Ticket Service.** This service provides tickets for a wide array of Salzburg area concerts, theater performances, and sightseeing tours. ⊠ *Mozartplatz 5* ☎ *0662/840310* ⊕ *www.salzburgticket.com*.

**Salzburg Ticket Shop.** Book ahead for tickets to a variety of entertainment options including the Salzburg Festival, Fortress concerts, and Advent performances. You can also prearrange sightseeing tours and river cruises. ⊠ *Getreidegasse 5* ☎ *662/825–769–16* ⊕ *www.salzburg-ticketshop.at*.

## MUSIC FESTIVALS

**Salzburger Festspiele.** The biggest event on the Salzburg social calendar—as it has been since it was first organized by composer Richard Strauss, producer Max Reinhardt, and playwright Hugo von Hofmannsthal in 1920—is the world-famous Salzburger Festspiele. The main summer festival is usually scheduled for the middle of July through the end of August. The festival also presents the annual Whitsun Festival in May.

The most star-studded events—featuring the top opera stars and conductors—have tickets ranging from €55 to €450; for these glamorous events, first-nighters still pull out all the stops—summer furs, Dior dresses, and white ties stud the more expensive sections of the theaters. Other performances run from €10 to €115, with lesser prices for events outside the main festival halls, the **Grosses Festspielhaus** (Great Festival Hall) and the **Haus für Mozart** (House for Mozart), located shoulder to shoulder on the grand promenade of Hofstallgasse. This street, one of the most festive settings for a

## EVENING MUSIC ABOUNDS

Salzburg is most renowned for the Salzburger Festspiele. But much of Salzburg's special charm can be best discovered and enjoyed off-season. Music lovers face loads of riches, including chamber concerts held in Mirabell Palace and the Fortress, as well as bountiful sacred music choices at the cathedral or any of the other churches offering impressive backdrops. Salzburg concerts by the Mozarteum Orchestra and the Camerata are now just as popular as the Vienna Philharmonic's program in the Musikverein in Vienna. The Landestheater season runs from September to June. And no one should miss the chance to be enchanted and amazed by the skill and artistry of the Salzburg Marionetten Theater.

music festival, is especially dazzling at night, thanks to the floodlighted Fortress Hohensalzburg, which hovers on its hilltop above the theater promenade. Behind the court stables first constructed by Wolf-Dietrich in 1607, the Festspielhäser (festival halls) are modern constructions—the Grosses Haus was built in 1960 with 2,200 seats—but are actually "prehistoric," being dug out of the bedrock of the Mönchsberg mountain. There are glittering concerts and operas performed at many other theaters in the city. You can catch Mozart concertos in the 18th-century splendor of two magnificent state rooms in which the composer himself once conducted: the Rittersaal of the Residenz and the Marble Hall of the Mirabell Palace. Delightful Mozart productions are offered by the Salzburger Marionetten Theater. In addition, many important concerts are offered in the two auditoriums of the Mozarteum.

■ TIP→ **Since you must order your tickets as early as possible, make your decisions as soon as the program comes out (usually in the middle of November).** Many major performances are sold out two or three months in advance, as hordes descend on the city to enjoy staged opera spectacles, symphony concerts by the Vienna Philharmonic and other great orchestras, recitals, church oratorios, and special evenings at the Mozarteum year after year.

Tickets to the Summer and Whitsun Festivals can be purchased directly at the box office (across the street from the Great Festival Hall against the Mönchsberg), at some hotels, or, most conveniently, on the festival's website. ✉ *Hofstallgasse 1* ☎ *0662/8045–500* ⊕ *www.salzburgfestival.at.*

### MUSIC

There is no shortage of concerts in this most musical of cities. Customarily, the Salzburg Festival hosts the Vienna Philharmonic, and the Staatskapelle Dresden is in residence during the Easter Festival, but other orchestras can be expected to take leading roles as well. The Kulturvereinigung fills the Festival Hall during the fall and winter with more top-notch concerts and operas. In addition, there are Mozart Week (late January), Salzburg Cultural Days (October), and the Dialogues Festival

(December). Mozart Week offers many musical gems; in recent seasons Daniel Barenboim, Pierre Boulez, and Nikolaus Harnoncourt have conducted the Vienna Philharmonic, while Sir John Eliot Gardiner, Rene Jacobs, and Marc Minkowski led other world-renowned orchestras. The Palace Concerts and the Fortress Concerts are year-round solo and chamber music mainstays. Find experimental works in the black box theater at the ArgeKultur.

Fodor's Choice ★ **Mozarteum.** Two institutions share the address in this building finished just before World War I—the International Foundation Mozarteum, set up in 1870, and the University of Music and Performing Arts, founded in 1880. Scholars come here to research in the **Bibliotheca Mozartiana,** the world's largest Mozart library (for research only; public access allowed with advance registration). The Mozarteum also organizes the annual Mozart Week festival in January and the forward-looking Dialogues festival in December, selecting two composers each year, one contemporary and another historic, to intermingle with Mozart works, aiming to spark conversation and bring fresh perspectives to the pieces. Many important concerts are offered from October to June in its two recital halls, the Grosser Saal (Great Hall) and the Wiener Saal (Vienna Hall).

Behind the Mozarteum, sheltered by the trees of the Bastiongarten, is the famous **Zauberflötenhäuschen**—the little summerhouse rumored to be the place where Mozart composed parts of *The Magic Flute,* with the encouragement of his frantic librettist, Emanuel Schikaneder, who finally wound up locking the composer inside to force him to complete his work. The house has more former addresses than most Salzburgers, having been moved numerous times around Salzburg after being donated to the Mozarteum by Vienna's Prince Starhemberg. It is much restored: back in the 19th century, the faithful used to visit it and snatch shingles off its roof, and later it was damaged during World War II bombings. The house isn't currently open to the public. ⊠ *Schwarzstrasse 26* ☎ *0662/88940–0* ⊕ *www.mozarteum.at.*

**Salzburger Festungskonzerte.** The concerts performed by the Salzburg Mozart Ensemble and the Mozart Chamber Orchestra are presented in the grand Golden Hall at Festung Hohensalzburg and often include works by Mozart. A special candlelight dinner and concert-ticket combo is offered. ⊠ *Festung Hohensalzburg, Mönchsberg 34* ☎ *0662/825858* ⊕ *www.salzburghighlights.at* ᠊ *€36–€44.*

**Salzburger Kulturvereinigung.** World-class guest orchestras and Salzburg's own Mozarteum Orchestra appear in the Grosses Festspielhaus and the Great Hall of the Mozarteum during the fall and winter under the auspices of the Salzburg Cultural Association. If you visit over *Sylvester* (New Year's Eve), you can experience the Austrian tradition of the brass-and-wind-powered New Year's Concert. It also created Salzburg Cultural Days, filling the autumn off-season with top talent and exciting performances. ⊠ *Waagplatz 1A* ☎ *0662/845346* ⊕ *www. kulturvereinigung.com.*

**Fodor's**Choice ★ **Schlosskonzerte Mirabell.** Classical soloists and chamber ensembles perform in more than 230 concerts each year in the legendary Marmorsaal (Marble Hall) at **Mirabell Palace,** where Mozart performed. Concerts begin at 8 pm and last 1½ hours. ✉ *Mirabell Palace, Mirabelplatz* 🕾 *0662/828695* ⊕ *www.salzburg-palace-concerts.com* 🎫 *€32–€38.*

## OPERA

**Landestheater.** This neo-Baroque gem has nearly 1,000 seats and presents roughly 25 productions a year, including opera, theater, and ballet. Mozart is always in the repertoire, and it is continuing to expand into daring new works. The Mozarteum Orchester Salzburg is its regular orchestra and the theater has its own opera, theater, and dance ensembles. You can purchase tickets from the theater's box office. ✉ *Schwarzstrasse 22* 🕾 *0662/87-15-12-222* ⊕ *www.salzburger-landestheater.at.*

**Salzburger Festspiele.** Eyes from all corners of the world are on this city during the Salzburger Festspiele, which mounts a full calendar of magnificently produced operas every summer, and even more during the Whitsun Festival in May. These performances are held in the Grosses Festspielhaus (Great Festival Hall), the Haus für Mozart (House for Mozart), the Landestheater, the Felsenreitschule, the Mozarteum, and numerous other smaller venues, where lieder recitals and chamber works dominate. ✉ *Hofstallgasse 1* ⊕ *www.salzburgerfestspiele. at* 🎫 *€25–€450.*

FAMILY Fodor's Choice ★ **Salzburger Marionettentheater.** This delightful, acclaimed cultural institution is devoted to opera, with a particularly renowned production of *Così fan tutte* to its credit. The Marionettentheater not only performs operas by Mozart, but also goodies by Rossini, the younger Strauss, Offenbach, Humperdinck, Mendelssohn (who wrote the music for the troupe's delightful show devoted to William Shakespeare's *A Midsummer Night's Dream*), and a fairy-tale version of *The Sound of Music,* all accompanied by historic recordings. Performances are staged during the first week of January, during Mozart Week (late January), from May through October, and in December. ✉ *Schwarzstrasse 24* 🕾 *0662/872406* ⊕ *www.marionetten.at* 🎫 *€18–€35.*

## THEATER

**ARGEkultur.** The heart of Salzburg's contemporary art and culture scene beats at this modern, multipurpose performance venue. Its two performance spaces host envelope-pushing experimental music concerts, modern dance and theater performances, Austrian cabaret evenings, and poetry slams. The Open Mind Festival in November is the big annual event, featuring productions created especially for the festival. ✉ *Ulrike-Gschwandtner-Strasse 5* 🕾 *0662/848784* ⊕ *www. argekultur.at.*

**Jedermann (Everyman).** This morality play, by Hugo von Hofmannsthal, is famously performed annually (in German) in the front courtyard of the cathedral. It begins with a rousing medieval parade of performers through the streets of the Altstadt, spilling onto the stage for a colorful, intense, and moving presentation of the allegorical story of wealthy, selfish Jedermann's final journey before death. Few of the thousands

8

packing the plaza are unmoved when, at the height of the banquet, church bells around the city ring out and the voice of Death is heard calling "Jedermann—Jedermann—Jed-er- *mann*" from the Franziskanerkirche tower, followed by echoes of voices from other steeples and from atop the Fortress Hohensalzburg. ✉ *Domplatz.*

# SHOPPING

For a small city, Salzburg has a wide spectrum of stores. The specialties are traditional clothing, like lederhosen and loden coats, jewelry, glassware, handicrafts, confectionary, dolls in native costume, Christmas decorations, sports equipment, and silk flowers. A *Gewürzsträussl* is a bundle of whole spices bunched and arranged to look like a bouquet of flowers (try the markets on Universitätsplatz). This old tradition goes back to the time when only a few rooms could be heated, and people and their farm animals would often cohabitate on the coldest days. You can imagine how lovely the aromas must have been—so this spicy room freshener was invented.

> ### SHOPPING STREETS
>
> The most fashionable specialty stores and gift shops are found along Getreidegasse and Judengasse and around Residenzplatz. Linzergasse, across the river, is less crowded and good for more practical items. There are also interesting antiques shops in the medieval buildings along Steingasse and on Goldgasse.

At Christmas there is a special **Advent market** on the Domplatz and the Residenzplatz, offering regional decorations, from the week before the first Advent Sunday until December 26, daily 9–8. Stores are generally open weekdays 10–6, and many on Saturday 10–5. Some supermarkets stay open until 7:30 on Thursday or Friday. Only shops in the railway station, the airport, and near the general hospital are open on Sunday.

## THE ALTSTADT

### ANTIQUES

**A.E. Köchert.** As the Imperial Court Jeweler and Personal Jeweler to Emperor Franz Josef I, the Köchert goldsmiths have crafted such world-renowned treasures as the Austrian imperial crown and the diamond stars adorning Empress Sisi's hair in her famous portrait. Today's sixth-generation jeweler creates modern pieces using traditional techniques, replicas of the "Sisi Stars," and offers stunning antique jewelry in the firm's small Salzburg outpost. ✉ *Alter Markt 15* ☎ *0662/843398* ⊕ *www.koechert.com.*

**Beate Hillinger Antiquitäten Kunst & Design.** Tucked behind the Gstättentor archway, this family-run antiques shop offers myriad objects ranging from the 15th century to modern times, including jewelry, ceramics, porcelain, and Art Nouveau pieces. ✉ *Gstättengasse 2* ☎ *0664/2002004.*

**Internationale Messe für Kunst und Antiquitäten.** The annual art and antiques fair takes place from Palm Sunday to Easter Monday in the state rooms of Salzburg's Residenz. ⊠ *Residenz-platz 1* ☎ *01/587–12–93* ⊕ *www. artantique-residenz.at* ⊠ *€13*.

**Madero CollectorsRoom.** It's worth a short trip around the southeast tip of the Mönchsberg into Nonntal to discover the impressive collection of mid-20th-century furniture, contemporary design pieces, and delicate porcelain and glassware; all celebrating the tradition of European craftsmanship and offered at a variety of price levels. ⊠ *Nonntaler Hauptstr. 10/1* ☎ *0662/844–008* ⊕ *www.madero.at*.

## CONFECTIONARY AND SCHNAPPS

**Konditorei Fürst.** If you're looking for the kind of *Mozartkugeln* (chocolate marzipan confections) you can't buy at home, try the store that claims to have invented them in 1890. It still produces the candy by hand according to the original, secret family recipe. Stock up on the *Bach Würfel* (coffee, nut, and chocolate truffle) and other delicacies at one of its four locations while you're in town—Konditoriei Fürst does not offer overseas shipping. ⊠ *Brodgasse 13* ☎ *0662/843759–0* ⊕ *www.original-mozartkugel.com*.

**Konditorei Schatz.** Salzburg locals have relied on this small family-owned bakery since 1877 to satisfy their cravings for *Cremeschnitte* (vanilla custard cream between puff-pastry layers), *Rigo-Jancsi* (Hungarian chocolate sponge cake, chocolate mousse, and chocolate glaze), *Himbeer-Obers-Souffle* (strawberry-cream souffle), apple strudel, and other mouthwatering selections from the 30 to 50 daily cakes and pastries. ⊠ *Schatz passageway, Getreidegasse 3* ☎ *0662/842792* ⊕ *www.schatz-konditorei.at*.

**Sporer.** Leave room in your suitcase for a few bottles from the excellent selection of house brands and locally produced distilled Austrian schnapps, liqueurs, brandies, festive punch, spirits, and wines at this fourth-generation family-owned shop and tavern. Locals look forward to the Christmas markets so they can warm up from the inside with their annual fix of orange-flavored Sporer Punsch, which you can purchase year-round in the store. Chat with the friendly owners and regular customers at the small bar while you sample the wares. ⊠ *Getreidegasse 39* ☎ *0662/845431* ⊕ *www.sporer.at* ☾ *Closed Sun. and holidays*.

## CRAFTS

**Christmas in Salzburg.** Rooms of gorgeous Christmas-tree decorations, notably an abundance of hand-painted blown egg ornaments for all holidays, fill this charming year-round shop. ⊠ *Judengasse 11* ☎ *0662/846784*.

---

**SOUVENIR SWEETS**

*Mozartkugeln,* candy balls of pistachio marzipan rolled in nougat cream and dipped in dark chocolate, which bear a miniportrait of Mozart on the wrapper, are omnipresent in Salzburg. Those handmade by Konditorei Fürst cost more but can be purchased individually. In hot summer months, ask for a thermos bag to prevent melting. You can find mass-produced products like those from Mirabell—500,000 pieces every day—or from the German competitor Reber almost everywhere. Discounts are easy to find in supermarkets or duty-free shops at the airport.

8

**Fritz Kreis.** Explore the finely crafted, hand-etched, traditionally blown glass pieces in this specialty shop. ⊠ *Sigmund-Haffner-Gasse 14* ☎ *0662/841–323* ⊕ *www.glaskunstkreis.com.*

**Gehmacher.** Find chic European traditional to modern-style home design and accessories at this centrally located shop. ⊠ *Alter Markt 2* ☎ *0662/845506* ⊕ *www.gehmacher.at.*

**Salzburger Heimatwerk.** Salzburg ladies choose fabrics for their custom made *Dirndln* from the store's floor-to-ceiling wall of colorful linen, silk, and cotton. They can also outfit their homes with locally produced ceramics, hand-stenciled linens, and regional cookbooks at good prices. ⊠ *Residenzplatz 9* ☎ *0662/844110* ⊕ *www.salzburgerheimatwerk.at.*

### TRADITIONAL CLOTHING

**Dschulnigg.** This is a favorite among elegant Salzburgers for *Trachten,* the traditional Austrian costume including lederhosen and dirndl (region-specific dresses with white blouse, printed skirts, and apron). You can also get high-quality field and hunting gear, and unique home decorations. ⊠ *Griesgasse 8, corner of Münzgasse* ☎ *0662/842376–0* ⊕ *www.jagd-dschulnigg.at.*

**Jahn-Markl.** Admire the traditional craftsmanship of the leather clothing and other goods here, some made to order. ⊠ *Residenzplatz 3* ☎ *0662/842610* ⊕ *www.jahn-markl.at.*

**Madl am Grünmarkt.** Flair and elegance distinguish the traditional Austrian designs here. ⊠ *Universitätsplatz 12* ☎ *0662/845457* ⊕ *www. madlsalzburg.at.*

## NORTH OF THE RIVER SALZACH

### TRADITIONAL CLOTHING

**Lanz.** A good selection of loden coats and Dirndln in the signature "Lanz cut" can be found at this famous Salzburg Trachten maker, known for leading the modern revival of traditional Austrian clothing. ⊠ *Schwarzstrasse 4* ☎ *0662/874272* ⊕ *www.lanztrachten.at.*

# EXCURSIONS FROM SALZBURG

**Gaisberg and Untersberg.** Salzburg's "house mountains" are so called because of their proximity to the city settlements. You can take the bus from Mirabellplatz to the summit of the Gaisberg, where you'll be rewarded with a spectacular panoramic view of the Alps and the Alpine foreland. The Untersberg is the mountain Captain von Trapp and Maria climbed as they escaped the Nazis in *The Sound of Music*. In the film they were supposedly fleeing to Switzerland; in reality, the climb up the Untersberg would have brought them almost to the doorstep of Hitler's retreat at the Eagle's Nest above Berchtesgaden. A cable car from St. Leonhard, about 13 km (8 miles) south of Salzburg, takes you 6,020 feet up to the top of the Untersberg for a breathtaking view. In winter you can ski down (you arrive in the village of Fürstenbrunn and taxis or buses take you back to St. Leonhard); in summer there are a number of hiking routes from the summit. To get here, the Albus "Gaisberg Bus" No. 151 leaves four times a day weekdays and six times a day weekends from Mirabellplatz; the journey takes about a half hour. ⊠ *Doktor-Friedrich-Oedl-Weg 2, St. Leonhard* ☎ *06246/72477* ⊕ *www.untersbergbahn.at* 🖾 *Round-trip €23.50.*

**Hallein.** The second-largest town of the region, 15 km (10 miles) south of Salzburg, Hallein was once famed for its caves of "white gold"—aka salt. "Hall" is the old Celtic word for salt, and this treasure was mined in the neighboring Dürrnberg mountain. You can get to Hallein by regular bus, by car, or by bicycle alongside the River Salzach. Once in Hallein, take a ride on a mine train through the oldest salt mine in the world at the **Salzwelten.** You can also visit the Silent Night Museum, which features autographs and documents about the famous Christmas carol as well as some of composer Franz Gruber's original furnishings. ⊠ *Hallein-Taxach.*

**Keltenmuseum** (*Museum of the Celts*). At one of the largest Celtic art and history museums in Europe, you'll not only learn all about the town of Hallein, but also discover Ice Age burial grounds and settlements. In the three state rooms, more than 70 oil paintings show the working conditions of the area's salt mines. ⊠ *Pflegerplatz 5, Hallein-Taxach* ☎ *06245/80783* ⊕ *www.keltenmuseum.at* 🖾 *€7.50.*

**Oberndorf.** This little village 21 km (13 miles) north of Salzburg has just one claim to fame: it was here on Christmas Eve, 1818, that the world-famous Christmas carol "Silent Night," composed by the organist and schoolteacher Franz Gruber to a lyric by the local priest, Josef Mohr, was sung for the first time. The church was demolished and replaced in 1937 by a tiny commemorative chapel containing a copy of the original composition (the original is in the Salzburg Museum), stained-glass windows depicting Gruber and Mohr, and a Nativity scene. ■TIP→ **Every December 24 at 5 pm, a traditional performance of the carol—two male voices plus guitar and choir—in front of the chapel is the introduction to Christmas.** You can get to Oberndorf by the local train (opposite the main train station), by car along the B156 Lamprechtshausener Bundesstrasse, or by bicycle along the River Salzach.

**Heimatmuseum.** About a 10-minute walk from the village center along the riverbank, the local Heimatmuseum, opposite the chapel, documents the history of the classic Christmas carol, "Silent Night." ⊠ *Stille-Nacht-Platz 7* ☎ *06272/4422–0* ⊕ *www.stillenacht-oberndorf.com* 🖾 *€4.50* ⊙ *Closed Mon.–Wed. in Sept.–June (except during Advent).*

FAMILY

Fodor's Choice

★

**Schloss Hellbrunn** (*Hellbrunn Palace*). Just 6½ km (4 miles) south of Salzburg, the Lustschloss Hellbrunn was the prince-archbishops' pleasure palace. It was built early in the 17th century by Santino Solari for Markus Sittikus, after the latter had imprisoned his uncle, Wolf-Dietrich, in the fortress. The castle has some fascinating rooms, including an octagonal music room and a banquet hall with a trompe-l'oeil ceiling. Hellbrunn Park became famous far and wide because of its **Wasserspiele,** or trick fountains. In the formal gardens (a beautiful example of the Mannerist style) owners added an outstanding mechanical theater that includes exotic and humorous fountains spurting water from

8

strange places at unexpected times. You will probably get doused (bring a raincoat). A visit to the gardens is highly recommended: nowhere else can you experience so completely the realm of fantasy in which the grand Salzburg archbishops indulged. The **Monatsschlösschen,** the old hunting lodge (built in one month), contains an excellent folklore museum. Following the path over the hill you find the **Steintheater** (Stone Theater), an old quarry made into the earliest open-air opera stage north of the Alps. The former palace deer park has become a **zoo** featuring free-flying vultures and Alpine animals that largely roam unhindered. You can get to Hellbrunn by Bus 25, by car via B150, or by bike or on foot along the beautiful Hellbrunner Allee past several 17th-century mansions. On the estate grounds is the little gazebo filmed in *The Sound of Music* ("I am 16, going on 17")—though the doors are now locked. ⊠ *Fürstenweg 37, Hellbrunn* ☎ *0662/82–03–72–0* ⊕ *www. hellbrunn.at* 🎫 *€12.50* ⊗ *Closed Nov.–Mar.*

# EASTERN ALPS

Updated by
Rob Freeman

The entire Eastern Alps region is a feast of dramatic countryside, with breathtaking scenery and mountainous terrain that offers great winter sports opportunities. Here, majestic peaks, many well over 9,750 feet, soar above glaciers that give way to sweeping Alpine meadows ablaze with flowers in spring and summer. Long, broad valleys (many names have the suffix -au, meaning "water-meadow") are basins of rivers that cross the region between mountain ranges, sometimes meandering, sometimes plunging.

The land is full of ice caves and salt mines, deep gorges and hot springs. Tourism thrives through the towns and villages, with resorts such as Heiligenblut, in the shadow of the Grossglockner, Austria's highest mountain, a major draw for hikers and climbers. Wherever you go, you'll find a range of good lodging, solid local food, and friendly folk. Western Carinthia and Salzburg province are dotted with quaint villages that have charming churches, lovely mountain scenery, and access to plenty of outdoor action—from hiking and fishing in summer to skiing in winter.

# ORIENTATION AND PLANNING

## GETTING ORIENTED

Austria's Eastern Alps straddle four provinces: Carinthia, East Tyrol, Salzburgerland, and Styria. Imposing mountain ranges ripple through the region, isolating Alpine villages whose picture-postcard perfection has remained unspoiled through the centuries. The mountainous terrain makes some backtracking necessary if you're interested in visiting the entire area, but driving through the spectacular scenery is part of the appeal of touring the region.

**Across the Grossglockner Pass.** There's a thrill every hundred yards along this scenic route, but your first will be sighting Heiligenblut, one of Austria's most captivating towns, at the foot of the Grossglockner.

**Salzburgerland.** Mountain magic and healing waters abound in this traditional and historic area.

## PLANNING

### WHEN TO GO

Snowy conditions can make driving a white-knuckle experience, but winter also brings extensive, superb skiing throughout the region—and it's somewhat cheaper here than at the better-known resorts in Tyrol. In summer the craggy mountain peaks and lush meadows provide challenge and joy to hikers, while spelunkers head into the bowels of

## TOP REASONS TO GO

**Drive the Grossglockner Highway:** As long as weather conditions permit, this panoramic road is one of Austria's most spectacular mountain passes and an absolute must.

**Take pictures at Heiligenblut:** Of all the picture-book images in the country, this jewel of a photo-op town has to be the winner, with its slender church steeple and gorgeous mountain backdrop.

**Head to the lake at Velden:** There is a decidedly Mediterranean feel to this upscale lakeside town, where heavily wooded hills slope gently down to the Worthersee. The lakeshore is lined with hotels and the fabulous villas of Austria's rich and famous—not to mention the casino.

**Ski at Bad Kleinkirchheim:** The province of Carinthia's best-known and most fashionable ski resort is home to the greatest downhill racer of all time, Franz Klammer. Join him—or follow in his tracks—on the slopes.

**Explore Eisriesenwelt:** This wonder of nature (the name translates to "the giant ice world") is one of the biggest ice caves in the world—don't miss this unforgettable experience.

**"Take the cure" at Bad Gastein:** This is, perhaps, the most famous of all Alpine mountain spas.

the behemoths. Placid lakes and meandering mountain streams attract anglers for some of the best fishing to be found in the country.

### GETTING HERE AND AROUND

Driving is by far the preferred means of seeing this area; the roads are good and you can stop to picnic or just to marvel at the scenery. There is a cost to driving these roads, though, as tunnels, passes, and panoramic roads often have tolls. Bus travel is also a relatively hassle-free option.

### AIR TRAVEL

The busiest airport in the Eastern Alps region is the Mozart airport in Salzburg, larger and with more connections than the one in Carinthia at Klagenfurt. Both have frequent connections to other Austrian cities and points in Europe, but neither has scheduled overseas direct flights, except to the United Kingdom.

### BUS TRAVEL

As is typical throughout Austria, where trains don't go the buses do, though some side routes are less frequently covered. Coordinating your schedule with that of the buses is not as difficult as it sounds. Austrian travel offices are helpful in this regard, or bus information is available in Klagenfurt and Salzburg. The Postbus network is extensive throughout Austria, with services remaining reliable even through adverse weather, including heavy snow. You can take Postbus 650/651 from the Zell am See train station up and over the mountains to the Grossglockner glacier at Kaiser-Franz-Josefs-Höhe, a 2½-hour trip. The bus runs twice a day from late June to the end of September. There's also a connecting bus from the glacier to Heiligenblut twice a day, so you can start the route from there, too.

**Bus Information Postbus.** ☎ *43/051717* ⊕ *www.postbus.at.*

## CAR TRAVEL

If you're coming from northern Italy, you can get to the Eastern Alps from Villach on the E55/A13 in Italy, which becomes the A2 and then the A10; from Klagenfurt, farther east in Carinthia, taking the A2 autobahn is quickest. The fastest route from Salzburg is the A10 autobahn, but you'll have to take two tunnels into account at a total cost of €11.50 (Tauern- and Katschbergtunnel). In summer on certain weekends (especially during Germany's official holidays), the A10 southbound can become one very long parking lot, with hour-long waits before the tunnels. Taking the normal road over the passes, although long, is a very attractive option, but you won't be the only person who thought of it. A good alternative to the busy Tauern Highway is the Tauern Motorail link, connecting Bad Gastein with Carinthia (Mallnitz) through an 8-km (5-mile) tunnel. It's a 20-minute ride and cars are transported from one side to the other by train while passengers ride in a proper carriage. One way costs €17, round-trip €30. Prices are per car, including all passengers. If coming from abroad, don't forget to buy the autobahn vignette (sticker) for Austria; it's €8.90 for 10 days.

Be aware that the Grossglockner High Alpine Highway is closed from the first heavy snow (mid-November or possibly earlier) to mid-May or early June. Though many of the other high mountain roads are kept open in winter, driving them is nevertheless tricky and you may even need wheel chains.

## TRAIN TRAVEL

Salzburg is the main hub for visiting the Eastern Alps, with frequent rail service from Vienna. Bad Gastein is also connected to Vienna, but with fewer direct trains; to get to Zell am See you must change trains in Salzburg. Most of the towns in the Eastern Alps are reachable by train, but the Grossglockner is reachable in a practical sense only by road.

If your onward travel plans from the Eastern Alps point you in the direction of Vienna, or you plan to travel to Carinthia after flying into Vienna, keep in mind the route via the **Semmering Railway.** It is now a section of rail travel that is part of the Austrian network, but the 41 km (25 miles) that is still called the Semmering is probably the most spectacular regular-gauge train journey you will ever take—and it has been in constant use for more than 160 years. Built between 1848 and 1854, it traverses high mountain terrain between Gloggnitz, southwest of Vienna, to Murzzuschlag over the Semmering Pass. It's commonly referred to as the world's first true mountain railway and is a marvel of civil engineering. It features 14 tunnels, 16 viaducts (some of them two stories), and more than 100 curved stone bridges and 11 small iron ones. It's possible to incorporate traveling this wonder on your way to or from Vienna and Klagenfurt, Heiligenblut, or Zell am See. Get information about tickets and timetable from ÖBB (Austrian Railways).

**Train Information Österreichisches Bundesbahn.** ☎ 05/1717 ⊕ www.oebb.at

## VISITOR INFORMATION

For information about Carinthia, contact Kärntner Tourismus. The central tourist board for East Tyrol is Osttirol Information. For information about Salzburg Province, contact Salzburger Land Tourismus. The main tourist bureau for Styria is Steiermark Information.

Many individual towns have their own *Fremdenverkehrsamt* (tourist office); these are listed under the specific towns.

**Tourist Information Kärntner Tourismus.** ⊠ *Völkermarkter Ring 21–23, Klagenfurt* ☎ *0463/3000* ⊕ *www.carinthia.at.* **Osttirol Information.** ⊠ *Mühlgasse 11, Innsbruck* ☎ *050/212-212* ⊕ *www.osttirol.com.* **Salzburgerland Tourismus.** ⊠ *Wiener Bundesstrasse 23, Postfach 1, Hallwang bei Salzburg* ☎ *0662/6688-44* ⊕ *www.salzburgerland.com.* **Steiermark Information.** ⊠ *St. Peter-Hauptstrasse 243, Graz* ☎ *0316/4003-0* ⊕ *www.steiermark.com/en.*

## RESTAURANTS

Although this region contains fine restaurants—in fact, two of the country's top dozen dining establishments are here—most of the dining in the small towns of the Eastern Alps will take place in *Gasthöfs* or *Gasthäuses*—chalet-style country hotels and inns with flower-decked balconies and overhanging eaves. Note that in many cases such inns are closed in the off-season, particularly November and possibly April or May. *Restaurant reviews have been shortened. For full information, visit Fodors.com.*

## HOTELS

This part of Austria is relatively inexpensive, except for the top resort towns of Bad Gastein and Zell am See. Even there, budget accommodations are available outside the center of town or in pensions. Note that room rates include taxes and service and almost always breakfast (except in the most expensive hotels) and one other meal, which is usually dinner. *Halb pension* (half-board), as this plan is called, is de rigueur in most lodgings. However, most will offer a breakfast-buffet-only rate if requested. Most hotels provide in-room phones and TVs. A few of the smaller hotels still take no credit cards. In the prominent resorts summer prices are often as much as 50% lower than during ski season. *Hotel reviews have been shortened. For full information, visit Fodors.com.*

| WHAT IT COSTS IN EUROS | | | | |
|---|---|---|---|---|
| | **$** | **$$** | **$$$** | **$$$$** |
| RESTAURANTS | under €14 | €14–€18 | €19–€26 | over €26 |
| HOTELS | under €120 | €120–€150 | €151–€200 | over €200 |

Restaurant prices are per person for a main course at dinner. Hotel prices are for a standard double room in high season, including taxes and service.

9

# ACROSS THE GROSSGLOCKNER PASS

This is the excursion over one of the longest and most spectacular highways through the Alps, the Grossglockner High Alpine Highway, which is a true engineering marvel. To explore this region from Salzburg, head south on the A10 highway and take Route 311 to enter the valley to Zell am See. Go south over the Grossglockner Highway to Heiligenblut. (The trip can be done by car or bus.) If the Grossglockner road is closed due to weather conditions, you must drive west of Zell am See to Mittersill toward Lienz via the 5-km (3-mile) Felbertauern toll tunnel (€11 one way) under the Tauern mountains. Exiting the tunnel, continue on Route 107 to Heiligenblut.

## ZELL AM SEE

*108 km (67 miles) southwest of Salzburg.*

This lovely lakeside town got its name from the monks' cells of a monastery founded here in about 790. It has excellent skiing and is busy throughout the winter. But it is now also one of Austria's most popular summer destinations, with an idyllic setting that's hard to beat, and the town can get very crowded in the peak season of July and August. If you want to stay in the town center, booking well ahead of time is strongly advised.

Interestingly, Zell am See has also become one of Europe's top vacation destinations for people from the Middle East, and some Middle Eastern airlines have heavily increased their services into Vienna to meet this demand. The town faced considerable controversy after a booklet was issued by the city authorities in early summer 2014 offering "cultural advice" to visitors—it pointed out that Austrian shopkeepers don't expect customers to haggle over prices, and that eating on the floor in hotel rooms is very much a no-no. Visitors were advised not to wear burkas and to "adopt the Austrian mentality." It added: "Here the colour black symbolises mourning, and is rarely worn in daily life. In our culture, we are accustomed to look into the smiling face of the person opposite us in order to gain a first impression and establish mutual trust." The town's mayor claimed that the number of women wearing a full burka has been causing friction with locals. Some hotels criticize the booklet, saying it unfairly stigmatizes Arab visitors, while many see the matter as a fascinating example of how the spread of global tourism can bring interesting cultural interaction.

### GETTING HERE AND AROUND

Enter the Pongau valley from the A10 highway from Salzburg by taking Exit 47 Pongau/Bischofshofen to merge onto Route B311, Bruckner Bundesstrasse.

### ESSENTIALS

**Tourist Information Zell am See.** ⊠ *Brucker Bundesstrasse 1A* ☎ *06542/770* ⊕ *www.zellamsee-kaprun.com.*

### EXPLORING

**Pinzgauer Railroad.** This romantic narrow-gauge train winds its way under steam power on a two-hour trip through the Pinzgau, following the Salzach River valley westward 54 km (34 miles) to Krimml. Nearby are the famous Krimml waterfalls, with a 1,300-foot drop, which you can see from an observation platform or explore close at hand if you don't mind a steep hike. Be sure to take a raincoat and sneakers. A one-day ticket is included with a SalzburgerLand Card. ☎ *06542/40600* ⊕ *www.pinzgauer-lokalbahn.info* ✉ *Zell am See to Krimml €10.60, round-trip €18.20.*

**Schloss Rosenberg.** In the town center, visit the very handsome 16th-century Schloss Rosenberg, which now houses the Rathaus (town hall). ✉ *Brucker Bundestrasse 2.*

**Schmittenhöhe.** A cable car will take you virtually from the center of Zell am See up to the Schmittenhöhe, at 6,453 feet, for a far-reaching panorama that takes in the peaks of the Glockner and Tauern granite ranges to the south and west and the very different limestone ranges to the north. You can have lunch at the Berghotel at the top. Four other cable-car trips are available up this mountain, part of the ski-lift system in the winter, but open in the summer for walkers and mountain bikers. 🌐 *www.schmitten.at/en.*

**St. Hippolyt Pfarrkirche** (*parish church*). Unusually fine statues of St. George and St. Florian can be found on the west wall of the splendid Romanesque St. Hippolyt Pfarrkirche, built in 1217. The tower was added about two centuries later, and the church itself was beautifully renovated in 1975. ✉ *Stadtplatz.*

**Thumersbach.** Several locations offer up stunning vistas of the town and its environs. On ground level, take a boat ride to the village of Thumersbach, on the opposite shore, for a wonderful reflected view of Zell am See.

**Votter's Vehicle Museum** (*Votter's Vehicle Museum*). Beautiful (and not so beautiful) cars and motorcycles from the 1950s, 1960s, and 1970s are on display here, including the remarkable one-person Messerschmitt Bubble Car and other, dare we say more appealing, automobiles. Altogether, the museum has more than 170 exhibits. ✉ *Schlossstrasse 32, Kaprun* ☎ *0699/1717–1342* 🌐 *www.oldtimer-museum.at* 🎟 *€9.90.*

## WHERE TO EAT

$$$ AUSTRIAN

🍴 **Restaurant Zum Hirschen.** In the hotel of the same name, the restaurant is in a charming, typically Austrian stube—all wood paneled and cozy—and serves regional specialties and international cuisine. Its popularity extends to locals and visitors alike, which makes for a good atmosphere. **Known for:** traditional wood-paneled ambience, both elegant and cozy; popularity with locals and visitors alike; excellent-value set lunch. [$] *Average main: €24* ✉ *Dreifaltigkeitsstrasse 1* ☎ *06542/774–0* 🌐 *www.hotel-zum-hirschen.at.*

$$$ AUSTRIAN

🍴 **Steinerwirt1493.** As the name suggests, the Steinerwirt dates back almost as far as Columbus's discovery of the New World. It is family run, and its newest generation of owners and staff have brought modernity to the cuisine while maintaining the original Alpine flair. **Known for:** amazing history of more than 500 years; high-end interpretation of Austrian favorites; combination of tradition and modern flair. [$] *Average main: €20* ✉ *Dreifaltigkeitsgasse 2* ☎ *06542/72502* 🌐 *www.steinerwirt.com.*

## WHERE TO STAY

$$$$ HOTEL FAMILY

🏨 **Grand Hotel Zell am See.** In the style of the great turn-of-the-twentieth-century resort hotels, this palatial lake house is the best located address in Zell am See, with direct beach access and wonderful lake views. **Pros:** great location; big standard rooms; kids' club for ages 3–10 and other child-friendly services. **Cons:** some rooms face noisy railroad; rooms with a view are more expensive; no air-conditioning, which is

9

GERMANY

Kufstein

A12

B178    St. Johann in Tirol    B311

Wörgl
Hopfgarten
im Brixental    Kitzbühel    B164

Brixlegg

Saalfelde

Saalbach

Hintergle    L111    B311    B164

B161    Zell am See ◆ Thumersbach

Zell am Ziller    Mittersill    B168    Votter's ◆
Vehicle Museum

B165    Krimml Waterfalls ◆

Mayrhofen    B108

Grossglockner
Highway ◆

Hohe Tauern
National Park ◆

Church of    Alten
St. Vincent ◆    ◆ Pocher
Bobojach    Heiligenblut

Matrei    Döllach-
in Osttirol    Grosskirchheim

Zotten    Kienburg    B107
St. Jakob in    B108
Defereggen    Winklern

B106

0        10 mi    Lienz
0    10 km    B100

Sillian    Oberdrauburg
Tassenbach
Leiten    B111

Podlanig

Eastern Alps

ITALY

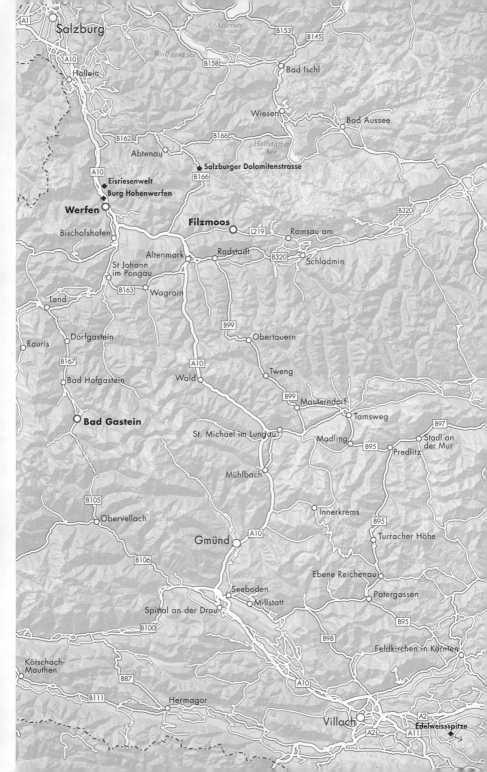

common with most Austrian hotels as the mountain climate is normally mild. $ *Rooms from: €280* ✉ *Esplanade 4–6* ☎ *06542/788* 🌐 *www.grandhotel-zellamsee.at* 🛏 *133 rooms.*

$$$$ HOTEL Fodor's Choice ★ 🏨 **Salzburgerhof.** The well-located five-star hotel, styled like an oversized chalet, stands out with its lovely courtyard garden, a natural swimming pool, and the best spa in the area. **Pros:** the region's best place to stay; top-notch staff; big standard rooms. **Cons:** rooms at rear of building are near railroad tracks; standard rooms do not face garden; no air-conditioning (only a concern on the hottest of days). $ *Rooms from: €400* ✉ *Auerspergstrasse 11* ☎ *06542/7650* 🌐 *www.salzburgerhof.at* ⏲ *Closed Nov.* 🛏 *70 rooms.*

$$$$ B&B/INN 🏨 **Schloss Prielau.** Attentive hosts Anette and Andreas Mayer take extra special care of their guests in this fairy-tale castle, with its turreted towers and striped shutters. **Pros:** eye-popping architecture; very personal feeling; private lake beach is only five minutes' walk. **Cons:** 20-minute walk to town; no elevator; no air-conditioning (common in most Austrian mountain hotels). $ *Rooms from: €286* ✉ *Hofmannsthalstrasse 12* ☎ *06542/729–110* 🌐 *www.schloss-prielau.at* ⏲ *Closed Nov.* 🛏 *9 rooms* 🍴 *Breakfast.*

$$$ HOTEL 🏨 **Steinerwirt1493.** Redesigned by Austrian architects in a minimalistic and modern style that distances itself from the local Alpine kitsch, this centrally located boutique hotel has a lot to offer. **Pros:** has its own art gallery; in the center of Zell am See; known for great cuisine. **Cons:** no swimming pool (there is an outdoor Jacuzzi); some noise from the nearby railroad station; some rooms are quite small. $ *Rooms from: €180* ✉ *Dreifaltigkeitsgasse 2* ☎ *06542/72502* 🌐 *www.steinerwirt.com* ⏲ *Closed mid-Nov.–1st wk in Dec. and last 2 wks of May* 🛏 *28 rooms* 🍴 *Breakfast.*

## NIGHTLIFE

The emphasis in Zell is more on drinking than on dancing, but the scene does change periodically.

**Crazy Daisy.** This restaurant-café and dance pub is in the center of town. It has legendary status among skiers and boarders, and a great summertime scene on the terrace, plus regular live music. ✉ *Salzmannstrasse 8* ☎ *06542/725260* 🌐 *crazy-daisy.at.*

## SPORTS AND THE OUTDOORS

### BICYCLING

The area around Zell am See is ideal for bicycling. From April to October, bike tours run from south of Zell am See up to St. Johann and Salzburg via the Tauern cycle route.

**Adventure Service.** Mountain-bike tours, Segway tours, and other outdoor activities including rafting, canyoning, climbing, and paragliding are available. ✉ *Steinergasse 5–7* ☎ *06542/73525* 🌐 *www.adventureservice.at.*

**Sport Achleitner.** If you left your two wheels at home, you can rent some here for €12 per day for a city bike, €24 for a mountain bike, or €30 for an e-bike. Renting by the week is more economical. In the winter the bikes give way to ski and board rentals. ✉ *Postplatz 2* ☎ *06542/73581* 🌐 *www.sport-achleitner.at.*

**FISHING**

The lake's tranquil waters offer fine fishing, and many hotels in the area have packages for avid anglers.

**SKIING**

**Zell am See-Kaprun.** There's good skiing on the slopes immediately above the town. Most of the runs are intermediate, but there are good areas for beginners, too, and experts will find some steepish, sweeping runs on which to have fun if not be truly tested. Towering over Zell am See, the Schmittenhöhe has tree-lined runs that will feel familiar to Colorado and New England skiers. Kitzsteinhorn mountain, which rises to 10,499 feet above Kaprun, has year-round glacier skiing and was the first glacier ski area in Austria. Together these mountains offer 57 lifts, with 130 km (80 miles) of prepared slopes. In addition, there are more than 200 km (124 miles) of cross-country trails and eight ski schools. ☎ *06542/770 tourist office* ⊕ *www.zellamsee-kaprun.com.*

**WATER SPORTS**

Boating—from paddleboating to sailing—and swimming are excellent on the uncrowded Zeller See.

**Edis Wasserskischule.** Powerboats are restricted on many Austrian lakes, but there is this waterskiing school at Thumersbach. ⊠ *Strandbad, Lindenallee, Thumersbach* ☎ *0664/2068506* ⊕ *www.ediswasserski.com.*

# GROSSGLOCKNER HIGHWAY

*46 km (29 miles) from Bruck to Heiligenblut.*

One of the best-known roads in the Alps, the Hochalpenstrasse—rising to more than 8,000 feet and negotiating 36 hairpin bends, with spectacular views the whole way—leads you deep into the Hohe Tauern National Park. The highway is generally open from early May to early November, but only during daylight hours. There's a toll of €35.50.

**9**

**GETTING HERE AND AROUND**

From Zell am See head south toward Bruck an der Grossglocknerstrasse, and continue on the B107. After the toll station in Ferleitern on the north side of the Grossglockner peak, the highway begins its many hairpin turns and continues to Heiligenblut.

**ESSENTIALS**

**Tourist Information Grossglockner Hochalpenstrasse.** ⊠ *Rainerstrasse 2, Salzburg* ☎ *0662/873673–0* ⊕ *www.grossglockner.at.*

**EXPLORING**

**Grossglockner Hochalpenstrasse** (*Grossglockner High Alpine Highway*). This is the excursion over the longest and most spectacular highway through the Alps. The road was completed in 1935, after five years of labor by 3,200 workers. From Heiligenblut the climb begins up the Carinthian side of the Grossglockner Mountain. The peak itself—at 12,461 feet the highest point in Austria—is to the west. The Grossglocknerstrasse twists and turns as it struggles to the 8,370-foot Hochtor, the highest point on the through road and the border between Carinthia and Salzburg Province.

A side trip on the Edelweiss-Strasse leads to the scenic vantage point at the **Edelweissspitze**. It's an unbelievable view out over East Tyrol, Carinthia, and Salzburg, including 19 glaciers and 37 peaks rising above the 9,600-foot mark. The rare white edelweiss—the von Trapps sang its praises in *The Sound of Music*—grows here. Though the species is protected, don't worry about the plants you get as souvenirs; they are cultivated for this purpose. ■**TIP**➜ **It is strictly forbidden to pick a wild edelweiss (or several other plant species), should you happen to come across one.**

You can get somewhat closer to Grossglockner peak than the main road takes you by following the highly scenic but steep Gletscherstrasse westward up to the Gletscherbahn on the Franz-Josef-Plateau, where you'll be rewarded with absolutely breathtaking views of the Grossglockner peak and surrounding Alps, of the vast glacier in the valley below, and, on a clear day, even into Italy. ☎ *0662/873673 road information* ⊕ *www.grossglockner.at* ✉ *€35.50 per vehicle for a one-day pass, €55 per vehicle for 30-day pass.*

**Hohe Tauern National Park.** This is one of the most varied and unspoiled landscapes on the planet—high Alpine meadows, deep evergreen woods, endless spiraling rock cliffs, and glacial ice fields—and at 1,786 square km (690 square miles) it's the largest national park of central Europe. It touches on three provinces (Salzburg, Carinthia, and Tyrol) and includes the Grossglockner mountain group. The Grossglockner Hochalpenstrasse passes through the park. The hardier traveler may want to spend a few days hiking and lodging at any one of several refuges, where you may occasionally be treated to very rustic, homemade victuals (cheeses and hams). ⊕ *www.hohetauern.at.*

# HEILIGENBLUT

*54 km (34 miles) south of Zell am See.*

**Fodor's** Choice ★  One of the most photographed places in the country, Heiligenblut remains one of Austria's most picturesque Alpine villages. With the majestic Grossglockner—Austria's highest mountain—for a backdrop, the town cradles the pilgrimage church of St. Vincent. Nowhere else does a steeple seem to find such affirmation amid soaring peaks. Some say the best time to experience this little slice of Alpine nirvana is after a leisurely dinner at one of the many Gasthöfs, gazing out at the starry firmament over the Hohe Tauern range. Others relish standing around an early-morning fire used by hikers setting out to conquer the mighty foothills of the Grossglockner peaks. It's the famed mountain-climbing school and climbing and skiing possibilities (there are 40 peaks higher than 10,000 feet here) that draw flocks of all-out active types.

### GETTING HERE AND AROUND
You can get to Heiligenblut from Zell am See via the Grossglockner pass or via Lienz. In winter, Heiligenblut is a ski resort of some repute; buses also run from the village to other nearby ski areas.

### ESSENTIALS
**Tourist Information Heiligenblut.** ✉ *Hof 4* ☎ *04824/2001* ⊕ *www.heiligen-blut.at.*

## EXPLORING

OFF THE BEATEN PATH

**Alten Pocher.** A replica 16th-century gold mining village, Alten Pocher is more than 5,906 feet above sea level. Miners prospected in the Hohe Tauern for gold from the 14th to the end of the 19th century, and it was considered one of the most important gold-mining regions of its day. Today, visitors can rent rubber boots and a panning bowl to try their luck in the Fleissbach. Many caves were created through grueling labor by thousands of miners over this period, under the most arduous conditions (of course, the owners of the mines themselves lived comfortable and rich lives). ✉ *Heiligenblut* 🎫 *Gold panning €8, open-air mining museum free; €4 with guide* 🕓 *Closed Oct.–May.*

**Church of St. Vincent.** According to local legend, St. Briccius, after obtaining a vial of the blood of Jesus, was buried by an avalanche, but when his body was recovered the tiny vial was miraculously found hidden within one of the saint's open wounds. The town gets its name, Heiligenblut (Holy Blood), from this story. Today the relic is housed in the Sakramenthäuschen, the chapel of this small but beautiful Gothic church. Completed in 1490 after more than a century of construction under the toughest conditions, the church is marked by its soaring belfry tower. Sublimely, the sharply pointed spire finds an impressive echo in the conical peak of the Grossglockner. St. Vincent's contains a beautifully carved late-Gothic double altar nearly 36 feet high, and the Coronation of Mary is depicted in the altar wings, richly carved by Wolfgang Hasslinger in 1520. The region's most important altarpiece, it imparts a feeling of quiet power in this spare, high church. The church also has a noble crypt and graveyard, the latter sheltering graves of those lost in climbing the surrounding mountains. ✉ *Heiligenblut* ☎ *04824/2700.*

## WHERE TO STAY

$$$ B&B/INN 🏨 **Chalet-Hotel Senger.** A peaceful location and great views make this farmhouse chalet a great choice. **Pros:** romantic feel; great place for honeymooners; warm welcome from hosts. **Cons:** 10-minute walk to town; very comfortable but doesn't claim to be luxurious; closed part of spring and part of late fall. [$] *Rooms from: €190* ✉ *Hof 23* ☎ *04824/2215* 🌐 *www.romantic.at* 🕓 *Closed 1 wk after Easter–June and Oct.–mid-Dec.* 🛏 *19 rooms.*

$$$$ HOTEL FAMILY 🏨 **Hotel Lärchenhof.** This charming hotel is a true *panoramagasthof*—a guesthouse with spectacular views. **Pros:** a good spa; wonderful country hotel atmosphere; very quiet location. **Cons:** some double rooms are on the small side; uphill walk back from the village; so lovely you won't want to leave. [$] *Rooms from: €208* ✉ *Hof 70* ☎ *04824/2262* 🌐 *www.hotellaerchenhof.at/en* 🛏 *23 rooms* 🍴 *Some meals.*

$$$$ HOTEL FAMILY 🏨 **Hunguest Hotel Heiligenblut.** This family-friendly hotel, a short distance from the town center, runs its own kindergarten on weekdays where you can leave the kids while you hit the slopes. **Pros:** perfect for families; lots of activities; mountain views. **Cons:** not the quietest location in town; sauna is small; views from the rooms vary. [$] *Rooms from: €216* ✉ *Winkl 46* ☎ *04824/4111* 🌐 *www.hotel-heiligenblut.at/* 🕓 *Closed Easter–May and Oct.–Dec.* 🛏 *114 rooms.*

$$$$ HOTEL FAMILY 🏨 **Nationalpark Lodge Grossglockner.** This wooden chalet in the center of the village offers old-fashioned charm and modern amenities. **Pros:** very friendly staff; restaurant focuses on organic local produce; lots of children's activities. **Cons:** some rooms on the small side; bells from neighboring church can be loud; rooms at the front can suffer from road noise. [$] *Rooms from: €226* ✉ *Hof 6* ☎ *04824/2244* 🌐 *www.nationalparklodge.at/en/* 🕒 *Closed May–mid-June, Oct., and Nov.* 🛏 *50 rooms.*

## SPORTS AND THE OUTDOORS

### HIKING AND MOUNTAIN CLIMBING

This is a hiker's El Dorado during summertime, with more than 240 km (150 miles) of marked pathways and trails in all directions. There are relatively easy hikes to the Naturlehrweg Gössnitzfall-Kachlmoor (1½ hours), Wirtsbauer-Alm (two hours), and the Jungfernsprung (one hour), which ends atop a 500-foot cliff above the Mölltal.

**Guided Tours.** Enjoyable group or private guided tours are run by the national park service. These could include walks conducted by a national-park ranger to the foot of the Grossglockner, to see sure-footed ibex in their natural habitat jumping about on seemingly sheer rock walls; a hike to the Pasterze Glacier, the largest in Austria; or a hike to the Mollschlucht gorge, much of it a via ferrata route—not for the fainthearted. ☎ *04824/2700–20 national park programs office* 🌐 *www.hohetauern.at, www.heiligenblut.at* 🎟 *From €10 for short group tour; from €200 per person for private one- to three-day tours.*

**Heiligenblut Climbing Park.** The park has a high-ropes course, climbing wall, zip line, children's playground, and restaurant. The via ferrata has two routes of varying levels of difficulty, which take you along spectacular waterfalls and cliffs. The high-ropes course is at the Gasthof Sonnblick, where the Brandstatter family can give information and make bookings. ✉ *Hof 21* ☎ *04824/21310* 🌐 *www.sonnblick-heiligenblut.at* 🎟 *€20.*

# SALZBURGERLAND

Glaciers, hot springs, luxurious hotels, and tranquil lakes are the enticing combinations this Austrian region serves up superlatively. Gold and silver mined from the mountains were the source of many local fortunes; today glittering gold jewelry finds many buyers in the shops of Bad Gastein's Kaiser Wilhelm Promenade. To set off on this trip, head south from Salzburg on the A10 and take the Bischofshofen exit toward St. Johann im Pongau, which gets you to Route 311 and, 17 km (11 miles) later, the Route 167 junction. From Zell am See, head east on Route 311 to pass Bruck, continue through Taxenbach to Lend, and turn south at the intersection of Route 167.

The SalzburgerLand Card includes admission to thermal baths (including Bad Gastein) and museums, trains and cable-car rides, a 24-hour Salzburg-City card, and more—190 attractions in all. It's definitely worth the money if you plan to do more than a couple of activities in the area. A six-day card costs €66; a 12-day card costs €81. Cards can be purchased from May till October 26. 🌐 *www.salzburgerlandcard.com.*

## BAD GASTEIN

*54 km (34 miles) southeast of Zell am See.*

Though it traces its roots all the way back to the 15th century, this resort, one of Europe's leading spas, gained renown only in the 19th century, when VIPs from emperors to impecunious philosophers flocked to the area to "take the cure." Today Bad Gastein retains much of its allure. The stunning setting—a mountain torrent, the Gasteiner Ache, rushes through the town—adds to the attraction. Much of the town has a solid though timeworn elegance, and some of the aging buildings are in need of a spruce-up. But the old buildings still dominate the townscape, giving it a wonderful feeling of substance and history. The baths themselves, however, are state-of-the-art, as evidenced by the massive **Felsentherme Gastein** and the nearby **Thermalkurhaus.**

A special tradition in Bad Gastein is the old pagan *Perchtenlaufen* processions in January. People wear huge and intimidating masks and make lots of noise to chase the winter away, bringing good blessings for the new year. However, it can be an excuse for excessive drinking by some costume-wearing youths, who often, sadly, cross the line to unruliness.

### GETTING HERE AND AROUND

Bad Gastein is serviced by many rail lines, with many expresses running from Salzburg and Klagenfurt. You can also reach the town by bus from Salzburg.

### ESSENTIALS

**Tourist Information Bad Gastein Tourist Office.** ✉ *Kaiser-Franz-Josef-Strasse 27* ☎ *06432/3393–114* 🌐 *www.gastein.com/en.*

### WHERE TO EAT

$$ AUSTRIAN Fodor's Choice ★ 🍴 **Bellevue Alm.** Idyllically set on the east side of the Stubnerkogel, directly on the ski slope, this Alpine hut is one of the oldest in Europe, remarkably well preserved, with wooden interiors and a huge open fire. Wooden parlors and a big terrace, with a spectacular view over Bad Gastein, invite visitors in for a substantial meal, followed by a couple of drinks after a hike or long skiing day. **Known for:** tempting and substantial Austrian delicacies and desserts; fabulous views; cozy atmosphere. [$] *Average main: €18* ✉ *Bellevue-Alm-Weg 6* ☎ *06434/3881–26* 🌐 *www.bellevuealm.at/en* 💳 *No credit cards* 🕒 *Closed Nov.*

$$ AUSTRIAN 🍴 **Jägerhäusl.** With green wood paneling and a red timber ceiling, the restaurant is strangely stylish. It's also right in the old town center, and has a garden and cozy wooden parlors. **Known for:** warm, family atmosphere; traditional Austrian dishes; good pizzas. [$] *Average main: €15* ✉ *Kaiser-Franz-Josef-Str. 9* ☎ *06434/20254* 🕒 *Closed Nov.*

### WHERE TO STAY

$$ HOTEL 🏨 **Alpenblick.** Perched high above the town, the Alpenblick has a sweeping view of the valley, and is an ideal base for skiers, hikers, and anyone who wants a quiet stay away from the town center. **Pros:** fabulous lofty location with great views; laid-back vibe; family ownership provides a warm welcome. **Cons:** 15-minute walk to town and a bit steep on your way back; poor Wi-Fi service; some rooms are outdated. [$] *Rooms*

*from: €150* ✉ *Kötschachtalerstrasse 17* ☎ *06434/20620* 🌐 *www.alpenblick-gastein.at* 🕓 *Closed Nov.–mid-Dec.* 🛏 *40 rooms.*

$$$$ HOTEL FAMILY Fodor's Choice ★ 🏨 **Haus Hirt Alpine Spa Hotel.** This stylish Alpine lodge, on a hillside about a half mile from the town center, has good amenities for families, spectacular views, and a style that cleverly combines Alpine traditional with contemporary-chic. **Pros:** glorious position with fabulous views; organic breakfast buffet; free transportation. **Cons:** spa and pool are small and can get packed during winter; a 20-minute walk to town; repeat customers mean early reservations are needed. [$] *Rooms from: €340* ✉ *Kaiserhofstrasse 14* ☎ *06434/2797–48* 🌐 *www.haus-hirt.com* 🕓 *Closed Nov.* 🛏 *32 rooms, 9 suites* 🍴 *All meals.*

$$$$ HOTEL 🏨 **Hotel Miramonte.** A somewhat retro-style hotel, with original '50s and '60s elements, is a chic retreat that caters well to the sophisticated traveler, from mostly spacious bedrooms with balconies to high-quality meals. **Pros:** big sundeck; friendly staff; special dietary requirements (vegetarian and vegan) available upon request. **Cons:** no swimming pool; limited parking; 15-minute walk to center of Bad Gastein. [$] *Rooms from: €330* ✉ *Reitlpromenade 3* ☎ *06434/2577* 🌐 *www.hotelmiramonte.com* 🕓 *Closed Nov.* 🛏 *36 rooms.*

## SPORTS AND THE OUTDOORS

Bad Gastein will keep guests entertained with all sorts of events from snowboarding competitions to llama trekking (popular with families). You will not be bored.

### HIKING

**Stubnerkogel Cable Car.** Take the Stubnerkogel gondola lift 2¼ km (1½ miles) above sea level, where spectacular views over the Gastein Valley will take your breath away. A suspension bridge will make you go weak in the knees, and the modern Panorama platform guarantees a view of the Grossglockner. In summer, many hikes are possible from here, while in winter the cable car is used to access the ski slopes. One round-trip is included with the SalzburgerLand Card. ☎ *06434/232–2415* 🎫 *€21 round-trip.*

### SKIING

Although not as well-known to outsiders as other resorts, the Gastein Valley is very popular with Austrians. There are a number of ski areas here, with a free shuttle bus running between them. The main access to the Bad Gastein area is by the Stubnerkogelbahn gondola, and it's possible to link with the Bad Hofgastein sector at Angertal. Sportgastein, quite exposed and with a remote feel, and Graukogel, with some protected wooded runs, are both above Bad Gastein and are not linked with any of the other sectors. Graukogel is delightful and all too often ignored by visitors—it's a great place for family skiing, with super views and a good mountain restaurant. Farther down the valley is the Dorfgastein area, which links with Grossarl on the far side of the Kreuzkogel. All in all, the valley has good and varied skiing for all levels, including a wealth of intermediate runs, but there are also a few challenges to be found. There are 43 ski lifts, and all the sectors have decent rental shops. You can get information on skiing conditions in all the areas from the tourist office.

# FILZMOOS

*74 km (46 miles) northeast of Bad Gastein.*

One of the most romantic villages in Austria, Filzmoos is still something of a well-kept secret. Though skiing in the nearby Dachstein mountains is excellent, the relatively inexpensive winter resort (which is part of the Salzburger Sportwelt ski area) has yet to be fully discovered by foreign tourists. During the summer months meandering mountain streams and myriad lakes attract anglers eager for trout, while hikers come to challenge the craggy peaks.

Filzmoos calls itself a "balloon village," not only for the International Hot Air Balloon Week every January, but because hot-air-balloon trips are a popular attraction for visitors and a great way to see the spectacular region.

## GETTING HERE AND AROUND

Head south on the A10 highway and take Exit 60-Eben onto Filzmooserstrasse-L219.

## ESSENTIALS

**Tourist Information Filzmoos.** ⊠ *Filzmoos 50* ☎ *06453/8235* ⊕ *www.filzmoos.at.*

## WHERE TO EAT AND STAY

**$$$$**
AUSTRIAN
**Fodor'sChoice**
★
✕ **Hubertus.** Every last detail, from romantic furnishings to the doting service, is done to perfection here, making this restaurant the best in the area. Chef Johanna Maier's way with trout is exquisite, but don't overlook the game, roast poultry, or veal sweetbreads. **Known for:** wonderful, tempting presentation of dishes; use of local produce; elegant surroundings. $ *Average main: €32* ⊠ *Am Dorfplatz 1* ☎ *06453/8204* ⊕ *www.johannamaier.at* ⊘ *Closed mid-Apr.–mid-May and mid-Oct.–mid-Dec. No lunch.*

**$$**
HOTEL
FAMILY
⊡ **Alpenkrone.** From the balconies of this hotel above the town center you'll have a great view of the surrounding mountains. **Pros:** great value; friendly staff; wonderful location. **Cons:** steep climb from town; not in the center of the action; hotel not very lively after dinnertime. $ *Rooms from: €150* ⊠ *Filzmoos 133* ☎ *06453/8280–0* ⊕ *www.alpenkrone.com* ⊘ *Closed Easter–mid-May and mid-Oct.–mid-Dec.* ⤴ *58 rooms.*

EN
ROUTE
**Salzburger Dolomitenstrasse** (*Salzburg Dolomites Highway*). From Filzmoos, rejoin Route 99/E14 again at Eben im Pongau. Here you can take the A10 autobahn north to Salzburg if you're in a hurry. But if you have time for more majestic scenery and an interesting detour, continue about 4 km (2½ miles) on Route 99/E14, and turn north on Route 166, the Salzburger Dolomitenstrasse, for a 43-km (27-mile) swing around the Tennen mountains. ■ **TIP→ Be careful, though, to catch the left turn onto Route 162 at Lindenthal; it will be marked to Golling. Head for Abtenau.**

# WERFEN

*30 km (19 miles) west of Filzmoos.*

**Fodor'sChoice**
★
The small size of Werfen, adorned with 16th-century buildings and a lovely Baroque church, belies its importance, for it's the base for exploring three extraordinary attractions: the largest and most fabulous ice

caverns in the world; one of Austria's most spectacular castles; and a four-star culinary delight, Obauer. These riches place Werfen on a par with many larger and more highly touted Austrian cities.

### GETTING HERE AND AROUND

Werfen is close to the A10 highway; take Exit 43 and follow the signs to the town. Many trains from Salzburg stop here.

### ESSENTIALS

**Tourist Information Werfen.** ✉ *Markt 24* ☎ *06468/5388* 🌐 *www.werfen.at.*

## EXPLORING

**Burg Hohenwerfen.** From miles away you can see Burg Hohenwerfen, one of Europe's most formidable fortresses (it was never taken in battle), which dates from 1077. Though fires and renovations have altered its appearance, it maintains historic grandeur. Hewn from the rock on which it stands, the castle was called a "plume of heraldry radiant against the sky" by Maximilian I. It has black-timber-beamed state rooms, an enormous frescoed Knights' Hall, and a torture chamber. Eagles and falcons swoop above, adding to the medieval feel. The fortress has been used as a prison and police training center, but now it harbors Austria's first museum of falconry where the birds are rigorously trained. ■ **TIP→ Shows with music, falconry, and performers in period costume are held at least twice a month; call ahead or check website for dates and times and save money by buying tickets online.** ✉ *Burgstrasse* ☎ *06468/7603* 🌐 *www.salzburg-burgen.at* 🎫 *€15.50 including tour and birds-of-prey performance and funicular; €12 (online price)* ⏲ *Closed Mon.*

OFF THE BEATEN PATH

**Eisriesenwelt** (*Ice Caves*). The "World of the Ice Giants" houses the largest known complex of ice caves, domes, galleries, and halls in Europe. It extends for some 42 km (26 miles) and contains a fantastic collection of frozen waterfalls and natural formations. Drive to the rest house, about halfway up the hill, and be prepared for some seriously scenic vistas. Then walk 15 minutes to the cable car, which takes you to a point about 15 minutes on foot from the cave, where you can take a 1¼-hour guided tour. The entire adventure takes about half a day. And remember, no matter how warm it is outside, it's below freezing inside, so bundle up, and wear appropriate shoes. You must be in reasonable shape, as there are 700 steps, but there's a restaurant with a terrace and a view where you can recover after the tour. You can also take a bus to the cable car from the Werfen train station. Buses run at 8:18 am, 10:18 am, 12:18 pm, and 2:18 pm, or upon request. There are also transfers about every 25 minutes from the bus departure point at Gries, which is about a five-minute walk from the rail station. ✉ *Eisbohenstrasse 30* ☎ *06468/5248* 🌐 *www.eisriesenwelt.at/en* 🎫 *€24, including cable car.*

## WHERE TO EAT

$$$$ CONTEMPORARY Fodor's Choice ★

🍴 **Obauer.** Among Austria's top dining spots, Obauer is presided over by the brothers Karl and Rudolf, who share chef-de-cuisine responsibilities. Thanks to their flair, this has become a culinary shrine, especially for Salzburgers and Germans. **Known for:** alfresco dining in the summer months in its charming garden; a good-value "noon special" of €30 for three courses; a fabulous collection of wines from the extensive cellar. [$] *Average main: €30* ✉ *Markt 46* ☎ *06468/52120* 🌐 *www.obauer.com.*

# SALZKAMMERGUT

Updated by
Jacy Meyer

Remember the exquisite opening scenes of The Sound of Music? Castles reflected in water, mountains veiled by a scattering of downy clouds, flower-strewn valleys dotted with cool blue lakes: a view of Austria as dreamed up by a team of Hollywood's special-effects geniuses—so many thought. But, no, except for the bicycle ride along the Mondsee, those scenes were filmed right here, in Austria's fabled Salzkammergut region.

The Lake District of Upper Austria, centered on the region called the Salzkammergut (literally, "salt estates"), offers stunning sights: soaring mountains and needlelike peaks; a glittering necklace of turquoise lakes; forested valleys populated by the *Rehe* (roe deer) immortalized by Felix Salten in *Bambi*—this is Austria at its most lush and verdant. Some of these lakes, like the Hallstätter See, remain quite unspoiled, partly because the mountains act as a buffer from busier, more accessible sections of the country. Another—historic—reason relates to the presence of the salt mines, which date back to the Celtic era; with salt so common and cheap nowadays, many forget it was once a luxury item mined under strict government monopoly, and the Salzkammergut was closed to the casually curious for centuries, opening up only after Emperor Franz Josef made Bad Ischl—one of the area's leading spa towns (even then, studded with *salt*water swimming pools)—his official summer residence in 1854.

A favorite passion for Austrians is *das Wandern,* or hiking. The Lake District has many miles of marked trails, including the BergeSeen Trail, which stretches 350 km (217 miles) and connects 35 of the region's lakes. The trail can be explored in stages, most of which end in one of the Salzkammergut's lovely towns. Cycling, popular among locals and visitors, offers an athletic way to see miles of landscape at a doable pace. Within this pastoral perfection you can stay in age-old *Schloss*-hotels or modern villas, dine in fine restaurants, and shop for the linens, ceramics, woodcarvings, and painted glass of the region.

# ORIENTATION AND PLANNING

## GETTING ORIENTED

To the west of Bad Ischl are the best known of all the Salzkammergut's 76 lakes—the Wolfgangsee and the Mondsee (*See* is German for "lake"). Not far to the southeast of these lakes lies one of Austria's loveliest spots, Gosau am Dachstein. Here the Gosau lakes are backdropped by a spectacular sight that acts as a landmark for many leagues:

the Dachstein peak. Another scenic wonder is the storybook village of Hallstatt, huddled between mountain and lake.

Whether you start out from Salzburg or set up a base in Bad Ischl—the heart of the Lake District—it's best to take in the beauties of the Salzkammergut in perhaps two separate courses: first around the Fuschlsee, Mondsee, the Wolfgangsee, and Bad Ischl; then southwest to Gosau am Dachstein and back to the Hallstätter See.

**St. Wolfgang and Bad Ischl.** Between its romantic lakes surrounded by Alpine peaks, this region is perfect for both water sports in summer and skiing in winter. The charming Bad Ischl's old-fashioned buildings document the town's importance in the days of the Habsburgs.

**Gosau and Hallstatt.** The sight from atop the Dachstein mountain range gives the impression of being on top of the world. The picturesque towns in this region are full of Austrian folklore and tradition, and have inspired many composers, painters, and poets.

# PLANNING

## WHEN TO GO

Year-round, vacationers flock to the Lake District, but late fall is not the best time to visit the region. It could be rainy and cold, and many sights are closed or operate on a restricted schedule. By far the best months are July and September. August sees the countryside overrun with families on school holidays and music lovers from the nearby Salzburg Music Festival (even so, who can resist a visit to Bad Ischl on August 18, when Emperor Franz Josef's birthday is still celebrated). Others like to visit Hallstatt for its annual procession across the lake, held on Corpus Christi day (weather permitting, around the last weekend in May, or the Sunday after)—a Catholic, and therefore, national holiday all over Austria. December finds several small picturesque markets in the villages around the Wolfgangsee and traditional *Adventsingen* concerts in churches throughout the region.

## GETTING HERE AND AROUND

### AIR TRAVEL

By air, the Lake District is closer to Salzburg than to Linz. The Salzburg airport is about 53 km (33 miles) from Bad Ischl, heart of the Salzkammergut; the Linz airport (Hörsching) is about 75 km (47 miles).

### BUS TRAVEL

**Bus Information ÖBB/Postbus.** ☎ 05/1717 ⊕ www.oebb.at.

### CAR TRAVEL

Driving is by far the easiest and most convenient way to reach the Lake District; traffic is excessive only on weekends (although it can be slow on some narrow lakeside stretches). From Salzburg you can take Route 158 east to Fuschl, St. Gilgen, and Bad Ischl or the A1 autobahn to Mondsee. Coming from Vienna or Linz, the A1 passes through the northern part of the Salzkammergut; get off at the Steyermühl exit or the Regau exit and head south on Route 144/145 to Gmunden, Bad Ischl, and Bad Goisern. But keep in mind that gasoline is expensive in Austria.

10

## TOP REASONS TO GO

**Fairy-tale landscape:** The lakes and mountains resemble the pictures in a children's book.

**Bad Ischl:** This town, where the rich and famous have long come for the healing waters, was Emperor Franz Josef's summer retreat in the 19th century.

**Cradle of culture:** Vienna and Salzburg may get all the credit, but the composers who made those cities cultural capitals also came to this part of Austria to hear the music in the air.

**Sports abound:** Everyone knows about the region's great ski resorts, but there is an endless array of summer sports as well.

### TRAIN TRAVEL

The geography of the area means that rail lines run mainly north–south. Where the trains don't go, buses do, so if you allow enough time you can cover virtually all the area by public transportation. The main bus routes through the region are Bad Ischl to Gosau, Hallstatt, Salzburg, and St. Wolfgang; Mondsee to St. Gilgen and Salzburg; St. Gilgen to Mondsee; Salzburg to Bad Ischl, Mondsee, St. Gilgen, and Strobl.

**Train Information** ÖBB—Österreichisches Bundesbahn. ☎ *05/1717* ⊕ *www.oebb.at.*

### TOURS

Daylong tours of the Salzkammergut, offered by Salzburg Sightseeing Tours and Salzburg Panorama Tours, whisk you all too quickly from Salzburg to St. Gilgen, St. Wolfgang, Fuschl, and Mondsee.

**Salzburg Panorama Tours.** Tours through the Salzkammergut depart from Salzburg and include a four-hour tour (departs daily at 2 pm) or an eight-hour combined tour that includes a visit to the salt mine (departs at 8:45 am). Private guided tours are also available. Bookings are best made online up to 24 hours prior to departure, but you can also go to the meeting place (Mirabellplatz) at least 15 minutes before the tour starts for last-minute tickets. ✉ *Schrannengasse 2/2, Salzburg* ☎ *0662/883211* ⊕ *www.panoramatours.com* 💲 *From €42.*

**Salzburg Sightseeing Tours.** A four-hour tour of the Salzkammergut (with stops in St. Gilgen and St. Wolfgang) leaves from Mirabellplatz in Salzburg daily at 2 pm. The price includes a boat trip on Lake Wolfgang in May through October. A hop-on, hop-off bus is also available for the region. ✉ *Mirabellplatz 2, Salzburg* ☎ *0662/881616* ⊕ *www.salzburgsightseeingtours.at* 💲 *Salzkammergut tour €42.*

### VISITOR INFORMATION

Most towns in the Salzkammergut have their own *Tourismusverband* (tourist office), which is listed in the specific towns. The main tourist offices for the provinces and regions are Salzkammergut and Upper Austria. Upper Austria and the Salzkammergut comprise the backbone of the Dachstein range.

**Visitor Information** **Salzkammergut Tourist Information Office.** ✉ *Salinen-platz 1, Bad Ischl* ☎ *06132/26909* ⊕ *www.salzkammergut.at.* **Upper Austria Tourist Information Center.** ✉ *Freistädterstrasse 119, Linz* ☎ *0732/221022* ⊕ *www.oberoesterreich.at.*

## RESTAURANTS

Culinary shrines are to be found around Mondsee. However, in many of the towns of the Salzkammergut, you'll find country inns with dining rooms but few independent restaurants, other than the occasional simple *Gasthäuser.*

Fresh, local lake fish is on nearly every menu in the area, so take advantage of the bounty. The lakes and streams are home to several types of fish, notably trout, carp, and perch. They are prepared in numerous ways, from plain breaded (*gebacken*), to smoked and served with *Kren* (horseradish), to fried in butter (*gebraten*). Look for *Reinanke,* a mild whitefish straight from the Hallstättersee. Sometimes at country fairs and weekly markets you will find someone charcoaling fresh trout wrapped in aluminum foil with herbs and butter: it's worth every euro. *Knödel*—bread or potato dumplings sometimes filled with either meat or jam—are a tasty specialty. Desserts are doughy as well, though *Salzburger Nockerl,* a sabayon-based soufflé, consists mainly of sugar, beaten egg whites, and air. And finally, keep an eye out for seasonal specialties: spring is *Spargelzeit* (white asparagus time), in summer restaurants often serve chanterelle mushrooms (*Eierschwammerl*) with pasta, and in October it's time for delicious venison and game during the *Wildwochen* (game weeks). *Dining reviews have been shortened. For more information, visit Fodors.com.*

## HOTELS

In the grand old days, the aristocratic families of the region would welcome paying guests at their charming castles. Today most of those castles have been, if you will, degentrified: they are now schools or very fine hotels. But you needn't stay in a castle to enjoy the Salzkammergut—there are also luxurious lakeside resorts, small country inns, even guesthouses without private baths. Although our hotel reviews cover the best in every category, note that nearly every village, however small, also has a *Gasthaus* or village inn; the ubiquitous *Hotel-*or *Gasthof zur Post* is usually a solid choice. Many hotels offer half-board, with dinner in addition to buffet breakfast included in the price (although the most expensive hotels will often charge extra for breakfast). The half-board room rate is usually an extra €15–€30 per person. Occasionally, quoted room rates for hotels already include half-board accommodations, though a "discounted" rate is usually offered if you prefer not to take the evening meal. Inquire when booking. *Hotel reviews have been shortened. For more information, visit Fodors.com.*

**10**

| WHAT IT COSTS IN EUROS | | | |
|---|---|---|---|
| **$** | **$$** | **$$$** | **$$$$** |
| RESTAURANTS under €12 | €12–€17 | €18–€22 | over €22 |
| HOTELS under €100 | €100–€135 | €136–€175 | over €175 |

Prices in the restaurant reviews are the average cost for a main course at dinner or, if dinner is not served, at lunch. Prices in the hotel reviews are the lowest cost of a standard double room in high season.

# ST. WOLFGANG AND BAD ISCHL

The mountains forming Austria's backbone may be less majestic than other Alps at this point, but they are also considerably less stern; glittering blue lakes and villages nestle safely in valleys without being constantly under the threatening eye of an avalanche from the huge peaks. Here you'll find what travelers come to the Lake District for: elegant restaurants, Baroque churches, meadows with green space and privacy, lakeside cabanas, and forests that could tell a tale or two.

## ST. WOLFGANG

*19 km (12 miles) southeast of St. Gilgen, 50 km (31 miles) southeast of Salzburg.*

**Fodor's Choice**
★
The town has everything: swimming and hiking in summer, cross-country skiing in winter, and natural feasts for the eye at every turn. Here you'll find yourself in the Austria of operetta fame. Indeed, St. Wolfgang became known around the world thanks to the inn called the **Weisses Rössl,** which was built right next to the landing stage in 1878. It featured prominently in a late-19th-century play that achieved fame as an operetta by Ralph Benatzky in 1930. Ironically, the two original playwrights, Gustav Kadelburg and Oskar Blumenthal, had another, now destroyed, Weisses Rössl (along the road from Bad Ischl to Hallstatt) in mind. In the years following World War II, the composers Samuel Barber and Gian Carlo Menotti spent summer vacations here, too.

**GETTING HERE AND AROUND**
A lovely way to enter the picture-book town of St. Wolfgang is to leave your car at Strobl, at the southern end of the Wolfgangsee, and take one of the steamers that ply the waters of the lake. Strobl itself is a delightful village, but not as fashionable as St. Wolfgang; if you prefer a quiet vacation base, this may be its attraction for you. Between St. Wolfgang and Strobl, the Wolfgangsee retains its old name of "Abersee." The earliest paddleboat on the lake is still in service, a genuine 1873 steamer called the *Kaiser Franz Josef.* Service is regular from May to mid-October, and on the Advent weekends. The view of the town against the dramatic mountain backdrop is one you'll see again and again on posters and postcards. If you decide to drive all the way to town, be prepared for a crowd. Unless your hotel offers parking, you'll

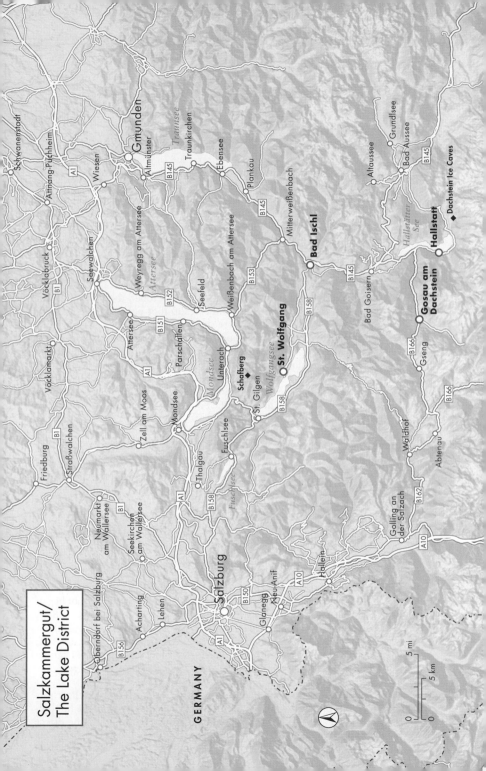

Salzkammergut/
The Lake District

GERMANY

Schwanenstadt
Attnang-Puchheim
A1
Wiesen
Gmunden
Almünster
Traunsee
Traunkirchen
Ebensee
Plankau
B145

Vöcklabruck
B1
Seewalchen
Weyregg am Attersee
Attersee
Seefeld
Weißenbach am Attersee
Mitterweißenbach
Bad Ischl
B145

Vöcklamarkt
B152
Attersee
B151
Parschallen
B153
B145

Friedburg
Zell am Moos
Mondsee
Mondsee
Unterach
Schafberg
St. Gilgen
St. Wolfgang
Wolfgangsee
B158
B158
Bad Goisern
B145

Straßwalchen
B1
Neumarkt am Wallersee
B1
Seekirchen am Wallersee
A1
Thalgau
B158
Fuschlsee
Fuschlsee

Oberndorf bei Salzburg
B56
Acharting
Lehen
Salzburg
B50
Glanegg
Neu Anif
Hallein
A10
Golling an der Salzach
A10
A1
B162

Waldhof
Abtenau
B166
Gseng
B166
Gosau am Dachstein
Dachstein Ice Caves
Hallstatt
Hallstätter See
Grundlsee
Altaussee
Bad Aussee
B145

5 mi
5 km
0
0

N

have to park on the fringes of town and walk a short distance, as the center is a pedestrian-only zone.

**ESSENTIALS**

**Tourist Information Wolfgangsee.** ✉ *Au 140* ☎ *06138/8003* 🌐 *wolfgangsee.salzkammergut.at.*

## EXPLORING

**Wallfahrtskirche St. Wolfgang** (*Pilgrimage Church*). You shouldn't miss seeing Michael Pacher's great altarpiece in the 15th-century Wallfahrtskirche, one of the finest examples of late-Gothic woodcarving to be found anywhere. This 36-foot masterpiece took 10 years (1471–81) to complete. The paintings and carvings on this winged altar were used as an *Armenbibel* (a Bible for the poor)—illustrations for those who couldn't read or write. You're in luck if you're at the church on a sunny day, when sunlight off the nearby lake dances on the ceiling in brilliant reflections through the stained-glass windows. Visit the Wolfgangsee Tourist Office website for a list of frequent concerts in the sanctuary and *Pfarramt* (rectory). ✉ *Markt.*

OFF THE BEATEN PATH

**Schafberg.** From the end of April to mid-October, the historic steam train trip from St. Wolfgang to the 5,800-foot peak of the Schafberg offers a great chance to survey the surrounding countryside from what is acclaimed as the "belvedere of the Salzkammergut lakes." The mountain is also a hiker's paradise—take advantage of one-way train tickets for a less strenuous afternoon. Pause for refreshments at one of two inns on the peak. On a clear day you can almost see forever, or at least as far as the Lattengebirge mountain range west of Salzburg. Crowds waiting for trains are likely, so start out early to get a seat by a window for the best view; call the ticket office to reserve a spot at your preferred departure time. ☎ *06138/2232–0* 🌐 *www.schafbergbahn.at.*

OFF THE BEATEN PATH

**Schafbergbahn.** The steam train itself is a curiosity dating from 1893, and does not run in bad weather. Buy tickets on the train and allow at least a good half day for the outing. ✉ *St. Wolfgang* ☎ *06138/2232–0* 🌐 *www.schafbergbahn.at* 🎫 *€35 round-trip.*

## WHERE TO STAY

$$$ B&B/INN 🏨 **Cortisen am See.** A large chalet-style structure with a glowing yellow facade, "At the Court" has become one of St. Wolfgang's most stylish and comfortable hotels. **Pros:** in the center of the village; a quiet place to relax; unique atmosphere. **Cons:** front rooms face busy street; not family-friendly; no air-conditioning. [$] *Rooms from: €170* ✉ *Pilger Strasse 15* ☎ *06138/2376* 🌐 *www.cortisen.at* 🛏 *32 rooms.*

$ B&B/INN 🏨 **Gasthof Zimmerbräu.** This pleasant, rustic, and central Gasthof began four centuries ago as a brewery and opened its doors to guests in 1895, and though it's not directly on the lake, it does maintain its own bathing cabana on the shore. **Pros:** all rooms have balconies; wonderful staff; pretty views. **Cons:** not on the lake; noisy until evening; Wi-Fi can be spotty. [$] *Rooms from: €84* ✉ *Markt 89* ☎ *06138/2204* 🌐 *www.zimmerbraeu.com* 🕒 *Closed mid-Jan.–Mar.* 🛏 *28 rooms.*

$$$$ HOTEL 🏨 **Landhaus zu Appesbach.** Secluded, quiet, and offering excellent service, this old ivy-covered manor hotel is tucked away from the hubbub of the village and offers sailboats and rowboats to enjoy the direct

lake access. **Pros:** peaceful atmosphere; quiet location; excellent service. **Cons:** need a car to get around; some rooms are more modern than others; 20-minute walk to the town center. [$] *Rooms from: €210* ✉ *Au 18* ☎ *06138/2209* 🌐 *www.appesbach.com* 🕒 *Closed Nov. and Jan.–Easter* 🛏 *20 rooms.*

$$$$ HOTEL 🏨 **Weisses Rössl.** Family-owned since the 1800s, the "White Horse" guest rooms and apartments, in nine connected houses, are full of the country charm, flowered fabrics, and quaint furniture brought to the big screen in the movie version of the idyllic Austrian operetta of the same name. **Pros:** cozy rooms; excellent location; wonderful spa and pools. **Cons:** very touristy; noisy location; not all rooms have a/c. [$] *Rooms from: €254* ✉ *Markt 74* ☎ *06138/2306* 🌐 *www.weissesroessl.at* 🕒 *Closed early Mar.–early Apr.* 🛏 *91 rooms.*

### NIGHTLIFE AND PERFORMING ARTS

Free brass-band concerts are held on the Marktplatz in St. Wolfgang every Saturday evening at 8:30 in May, and on both Wednesday and Saturday at 8:30 pm from June to September. Folk events are usually well publicized with posters (if you're lucky, Benatzky's operetta *Im Weissen Rössl* might be on the schedule). The Wallfahrtskirche also hosts regular concerts, putting its two wonderful organs on proud display. Not far from St. Wolfgang, the town of Strobl holds a Day of Popular Music and Tradition in early July—"popular" meaning brass band, and "tradition" being *Tracht,* the local costume. Check with the regional tourist office for details. Advent is the region's largest event with traditional Christmas markets, nativity scenes, and plenty of special concerts.

## BAD ISCHL

*56 km (35 miles) southeast of Salzburg, 16 km (10 miles) southeast of St. Wolfgang.*

Many travelers used to think of Bad Ischl primarily as the town where Zauner's pastry shop is located, to which connoisseurs drove miles for the sake of a cup of coffee and a slice of *Guglhupf,* a lemon sponge cake studded with raisins and nuts. Pastry continues to be the best-known drawing card of a community that symbolizes, more than any other place except Vienna itself, the Old Austria of resplendent uniforms, balls, waltzes, and operettas.



Although the center is built up, the town is charmingly laid out on a peninsula between the Rivers Traun and Ischl. Bad Ischl was the place where Emperor Franz Josef chose to establish his summer court, and it was here that he met and fell in love with his future empress, the troubled Sisi, though his mother had intended him for Sisi's elder sister. Today you can enjoy the same sort of pastries *mit Schlag* (whipped cream) that the emperor loved. Afterward, you can hasten off to the town's modern spa, one of the best known in Austria.

You'll want to stroll along the shaded **Esplanade,** where the pampered and privileged of the 19th century loved to take their constitutionals, usually after a quick stop at the **Trinkhalle,** a spa pavilion in high 19th-century Austrian style, still in the middle of town on Ferdinand-Auböck-Platz.

## GETTING HERE AND AROUND

Bad Ischl is accessed easily via various routes. From St. Wolfgang, backtrack south to Strobl and head eastward on Route 158. To get to the town directly from Salzburg, take the A1 to Mondsee, then Routes 151 and 158 along the Wolfgangsee and the Mondsee. There are many buses that depart hourly from Salzburg's main train station; you can also travel by train via the junction of Attnang-Puchheim or Stainach-Irdning (several transfers are required)—a longer journey than the bus ride, which is usually 90 minutes. There are also many regular bus and train connections between Gmunden and Bad Ischl.

## ESSENTIALS

**Tourist Information Bad Ischl.** ⊠ *Auböckplatz 5* ☎ *06132/277570* ⊕ *badischl. salzkammergut.at.*

## EXPLORING

**Kaiservilla.** In Bad Ischl the quickest way to travel back in time to the gilded 1880s is to head for the mammoth Kaiservilla, the imperial-yellow (signifying wealth and power) residence, which looks rather like a miniature Schönbrunn: its ground plan forms an "E" to honor the empress Elisabeth. Archduke Markus Salvator von Habsburg-Lothringen, great-grandson of Franz Josef, still lives here, but you can tour parts of the building to see the ornate reception rooms and the surprisingly modest residential quarters (through which sometimes even the archduke guides visitors with what can only be described as a very courtly kind of humor). It was at this villa that the emperor signed the declaration of war against Serbia, which officially marked the start of World War I. The villa is filled with Habsburg and family mementos, none more moving than the cushion, on display in the chapel, on which the head of Empress Elisabeth rested after she was stabbed by an Italian assassin in 1898. ⊠ *Kaiserpark* ☎ *06132/23241* ⊕ *www.kaiservilla.at* 🖭 *€14.50; grounds only €4.60* 🕙 *Closed Nov., Thurs.–Tues. in Jan.–Mar., and weekdays in Dec.*

**Museum der Stadt Bad Ischl.** Fascinating is the only word to describe this museum, which occupies the circa 1880 Hotel Austria—the favored summer address for Archduke Franz Karl and his wife Sophie (from 1834 on). More momentously, the young Franz Josef got engaged to his beloved Elisabeth here in 1853. After taking in the gardens (with their Brahms monument), explore the various exhibits, which deal with the region's salt, royal, and folk histories. Note the display of national folk costumes, which the emperor wore while hunting. From December until the beginning of February, the museum shows off its famous *Kalss Krippe*, an enormous mechanical Christmas crèche. Dating from 1838, it has about 300 figures. The townsfolk of Ischl, in fact, are famous for their Christmas "cribs," and you can see many of them in tours of private houses opened for visits on select dates in January. ⊠ *Esplanade 10* ☎ *06132/25476* ⊕ *www.stadtmuseum.at* 🖭 *€5.40; special exhibits, €3.10; combined ticket to the museum and Lehár Villa, €9.30* 🕙 *Closed Mon., Tues., Nov., and Mon.–Thurs. in Jan.–Mar.*

**Photo Museum.** Don't overlook the small but elegant "marble palace" built near the Kaiservilla for Empress Elisabeth, who used it as a teahouse; this now houses a photography museum. The permanent collection offers an interesting overview of the history of analog photography, with a nice tribute to the empress. The marriage between Franz Josef and Elisabeth was not an especially happy one; a number of houses bearing women's names in Bad Ischl are said to have been quietly given by the emperor to his various lady friends (Villa Schratt was given to Katharina Schratt, the emperor's nearly official mistress). You'll first need to purchase a ticket to the museum or park to visit. ✉ *Kaiserpark* ☎ *06132/24422* 🌐 *www.landesmuseum.at/en* 🎫 *Museum and Kaiserpark €6.70* 🕒 *Closed Nov.–Mar.*

**Stadtpfarrkirche St. Nikolaus.** In the center of town, St. Nikolaus Parish Church graces Ferdinand-Auböck-Platz. It dates back to the Middle Ages, but was enlarged to its present size during Maria Theresa's time in the 1750s. The decoration inside is in the typically gloomy style of Franz Josef's era (note the emperor's family portrayed to the left above the high altar). Anton Bruckner used to play on the old church organ. ✉ *Kirchengasse 2.*

**Villa Lehár.** A steady stream of composers followed the aristocracy and the court to Bad Ischl. Anton Bruckner, Johannes Brahms (who composed his famous *Lullaby* here as well as many of his late works), Johann Strauss the Younger, Carl Michael Ziehrer, Oscar Straus, and Anton Webern all spent summers here, but it was the Hungarian-born Franz Lehár, composer of *The Merry Widow,* who left the most lasting musical impression, the Lehár Festival. Named in his honor, it is Bad Ischl's summer operetta festival, which always includes at least one Lehár work. With the royalties he received from his operettas, he was able to settle into the sumptuous Villa Lehár, where he lived from 1912 until his death in 1948. Now a museum, it contains a number of the composer's fin-de-siècle period salons, which can be viewed only on guided tours. ✉ *Lehárkai 8* ☎ *06132/26992* 🌐 *www.stadtmuseum.at/hg_leharvilla.php* 🎫 *€5.70; combined ticket to Villa and Bad Ischl Museum €9.30* 🕒 *Closed Mon., Tues., and Oct.–Apr.*

## WHERE TO EAT AND STAY

$ CAFÉ Fodor's Choice ★ 🍴 **Café Zauner.** If you haven't been to Zauner, you've missed a true highlight of Bad Ischl. The desserts—particularly the house creation, *Zaunerstollen,* a chocolate-covered confection of sugar, hazelnuts, and nougat—have made this one of Austria's best-known pastry shops. **Known for:** fabulous cakes; gorgeous space; royal history. [$] *Average main: €6* ✉ *Pfarrgasse 7* ☎ *06132/23310–20* 🌐 *www.zauner.at.*

$ HOTEL 🏨 **Goldener Ochs.** The "Golden Ox" is in a superb location in the town center, with the sparkling River Traun a few steps away. **Pros:** great value; close to the major sights; lovely private wellness spa. **Cons:** traffic noise in front rooms; no a/c; need to book ahead for popular times. [$] *Rooms from: €81* ✉ *Grazerstrasse 4* ☎ *06132/23529* 🌐 *www.goldenerochs.at* 🛏 *48 rooms* 🍽 *All meals.*

## NIGHTLIFE AND PERFORMING ARTS

The main musical events of the year in the Salzkammergut are the July and August operetta festivals held in Bad Ischl.

**Kongress- und Theaterhaus.** A number of events grace the imperial interiors of the Kongress- und Theaterhaus each season. Musical performances are held throughout the year, including Advent concerts. The biggest draw is the summer Lehár Festival. Operetta and classic musical theater lovers flock to Bad Ischl during July and August for favorite standards like *The Merry Widow* and *My Fair Lady*. Tickets are sold online, at local tourist offices, and on-site. Pre-sales for the upcoming season begin in October. ⊠ *Kurhausstrasse 8* ☎ *06132/23420* ⊕ *www. leharfestival.at* ☑ *Tickets from €26–€83.*

# GOSAU AND HALLSTATT

It's hard to imagine anything prettier than this region of the Salzkammergut, which takes you into the very heart of the Lake District. The great highlight is Gosau am Dachstein—a beauty spot that even the least impressionable find hard to forget. But there are other notable sights, including Hallstatt and the Dachstein Ice Caves.

## GOSAU AM DACHSTEIN

*67 km (42 miles) southeast of Salzburg, 10 km (6 miles) northwest of the Hallstättersee.*

Fodor's Choice ★ Lovers of scenic beauty should not leave the Hallstatt region without taking in Gosau am Dachstein, considered the most beautiful spot in Austria by 19th-century travelers but often unaccountably overlooked today.

Instead of driving around the area, it's worthwhile to take a serious walk (about 2½ hours, depending on your speed), departing from the tourist information office not far from the crossroads known as the Gosaumühle. Passing by churches, the road follows the valley over the meadows. From Gosauschmied Café on, it's a romantic way through the forest to the first Gosau lake, the Vorderer Gosausee (Front Gosau Lake), which is the crown jewel, some 8 km (5 miles) to the south of the village itself. Beyond a sparkling, almost fjordlike basin of water rises the amazing Dachstein massif, majestically reflected in the lake's mirrorlike surface. Aside from a restaurant and a gamekeeper's hut, the lake is undefiled by man-made structures. At the right hour—well before 2:30 pm, when due to the steepness of the mountain slopes, the sun is already withdrawing—the view is superb. Then you may choose to endure the stiff walk to the other two lakes set behind the first and not as spectacularly located (in fact, the third is used by an electric power station and therefore not always full of water, yet it remains the closest place from which to view the glittering Dachstein glacier). Hiking to the latter two lakes will take about two hours. You can also take a cable car up to the Gablonzer Hütte on the Zwieselalm (you might consider skiing on the Gosau glacier); or tackle the three-hour hike up to the summit of the Grosser Donnerkogel.

At day's end, head back for Gosau village, settle in at one of the many Gasthöfe (reserve ahead) overhung with wild gooseberry and rosebushes (or stay at one of Gosau's charming *Privatzimmer* accommodations). Cap the day off with a dinner of fried *Schwarzrenterl,* a delicious regional lake fish. To get to Gosau, travel north or south on Route 145, turning off at the junction with Route 166, and travel 36 km (20 miles) east through the ravine of the Gosaubach River.

#### GETTING HERE AND AROUND

This lovely spot is 10 km (6 miles) west of the Hallstätter See, just before the Gschütt Pass: you travel either by bus (eight daily from Bad Ischl to Gosau) or car. The village makes a good lunch stop, and, with its many Gasthöfe and pensions, could be a base for your excursions.

#### ESSENTIALS

**Tourist Information Gosau am Dachstein.** ✉ *Gosauseestrasse 5* ☎ *5/95095-20* 🌐 *dachstein.salzkammergut.at.*

### WHERE TO EAT AND STAY

$$$ AUSTRIAN

🍴 **Kirchenwirt.** Adjacent to Gosau's pretty parish church, this inn is evidence of the venerable tradition of placing town restaurants next to houses of worship (on Sunday farmers would attend the service then head for the nearest table and discuss the past week's events). Today, the restaurant is a popular place, with local specialties and lovely views from the terrace. **Known for:** large portions of regional cusine; modern Alpine-style design; friendly hosts. [$] *Average main: €21* ✉ *Wirtsweg 18* ☎ *06136/8196* 🌐 *www.kirchenwirt-peham.at.*

$$$$ HOTEL

🏨 **Hotel Koller.** One of the most charming hotels in Gosau, the peaked gables and weather vanes of this 1850s-era villa give a fairy-tale aura when seen from its pretty park. **Pros:** cheerful interiors; pretty views; friendly staff. **Cons:** no elevator; rooms vary in size; bathrooms are a little outdated. [$] *Rooms from: €200* ✉ *Pass-Gschütt-Strasse 353* ☎ *06136/8841* 🌐 *www.hotel-koller.com* 🕒 *Closed Nov. and 1 month around Easter (dates vary)* 🛏 *22 rooms.*

## HALLSTATT

*89 km (55 miles) southeast of Salzburg, 19 km (12 miles) south of Bad Ischl.*

Fodor's Choice ★

As if rising from Swan Lake itself, the town of Hallstatt is the subject of thousands of travel posters. "The world's prettiest lakeside village" perches precariously on what seems the smallest of toeholds, one that nevertheless prevents it from tumbling into the dark waters of the Hallstättersee. Down from the steep mountainside above it comes the Mühlbach waterfall, a sight that can keep you riveted for hours. Today, the town is a magnet for tourists, and accordingly a bit too modernized, especially considering that Hallstatt is believed to be the oldest community in Austria. More than 1,000 graves of prehistoric men have been found here, and it has been such an important source of relics of the Celtic period that this age is known as the Hallstatt epoch.

#### GETTING HERE AND AROUND

Arriving in Hallstatt is a scenic spectacle if you come by train, with the entire village arrayed on the other side of the lake; from the train station, a boat, the *Stefanie,* takes you across the Hallstättersee to the town, leaving every hour. You can take the train from Bad Ischl or via the Stainach-Irdning junction. To get to Hallstatt from Bad Ischl by car, head south on Route 145 to Bad Goisern (which also has curative mineral springs, but never achieved the cachet of Bad Ischl). Just south of town, watch for signs for the turnoff to the Hallstättersee. Since the lake is squeezed in between two sharply rising mountain ranges, the road parallels the shore, with spectacular views. From Bad Ischl, you can also take a half-hour bus ride to Hallstatt.

**ESSENTIALS**

**Tourist Information Hallstatt.** ✉ *Seestrasse 99* ☎ *5/95095–30* ⊕ *www. hallstatt.net.*

**EXPLORING**

**Archaeological Excavation.** A unexpected peek into the Celtic past is offered at the DachsteinSport Janu shop. A decade ago, its intention to put a new heating system in the cellar unexpectedly turned into a historical excavation when workmen found the remains of a Celtic dwelling, now on view to visitors. ✉ *Seestrasse 50* ☎ *06134/8298* ⊕ *www. dachsteinsport.at/ausgrabungen/ueberblick.php* 🖼 *Free* ⊘ *Closed Sun.*

Fodor's Choice  **Dachstein Ice Caves.** This is one of the most impressive sights of the east-
★  ern Alps—vast ice caverns, many of which are hundreds of years old and aglitter with ice stalactites and stalagmites, illuminated by an eerie light. The most famous sights are the **Rieseneishöhle** (Giant Ice Cave) and the **Mammuthöhle** (Mammoth Cave), but there are other caves and assorted frozen waterfalls in the area. The cave entrance is at about 6,500 feet, accessed via cable car and a hike (or you can hike all the way), but still well below the 9,750-foot Dachstein peak farther south. If you visit in August, you can enjoy the Friday Ice Sounds concert series under the Parsifal Dome of the Dachstein cave. Tickets for these special shows include a cave tour and buffet dinner at the Erlebnisrestaurant Schönbergalm. ■**TIP→ Be sure to wear warm, weatherproof clothing and good shoes; inside the caves it is very cold, and outside the slopes can be swept by chilling winds. Start before 2 pm to see both caves.**
✉ *34 Winkl ✛ From Hallstatt, take the scenic road around the bottom of the lake to Obertraun; then follow the signs to the cable car (Dachsteinseilbahn). From the cable-car landing, a 15-minute hike up takes you to the entrance (follow signs "Dachsteineishöhle")* ☎ *05/0140* ⊕ *www.dachstein-salzkammergut.com/en/* 🖼 *Giant Ice and Mammoth Cave €31.60 each; combined ticket €38.40; cable car €30 round-trip; Ice Sounds concert €75* ⊘ *Closed Nov.–Apr.*

**Michaelerkirche** (*St. Michael's*). The Hallstatt market square, now a pedestrian area, is bordered by colorful 16th-century houses and this 16th-century Gothic church, which is picturesquely situated near the lake. Within, you'll find a beautiful winged altar, which opens to reveal nine 15th-century paintings. The *Karner* (charnel house) beside the church is a rather morbid but regularly visited spot. Because there was little space to bury the dead over the centuries in Hallstatt, the custom developed of digging up the bodies after 12 or 15 years, piling the bones in the sun, and painting the skulls. Ivy and oak-leaf wreaths were used for the men, alpine flowers for the women, and names, dates, and often the cause of death were inscribed. The myriad bones and skulls are now on view in the charnel house, also known as the *"Beinhaus"* (bone house), which has a stunning setting overlooking the lake. Each year at the end of May the summer season kicks off with the Fronleichnahm (Corpus Christi) procession, which concludes with hundreds of boats out on the lake. ✉ *Kirchenweg 40.*

FAMILY **Museum Hallstatt.** Go back 7,000 years and discover the orgins of Hallstatt and its salt mines at this museum. The exhibits include holographic representations, video animations, and a 3-D journey through time. ✉ *Seestrasse 56* ☎ *06134/828015* 🌐 *www.museum-hallstatt.at* 🎫 *€10* ⏲ *Closed Mon. and Tues. in Nov.–Mar.*

**Salzwelten.** Salt has been mined in this area for at least 4,500 years, and the Hallstatt mines of the Salzberg Mountain are the oldest in the world. These "show mines" are in the Salzbergtal valley, accessed either by paths from the village cemetery or, much more conveniently, via a funicular railway that leaves from the southern end of the village. From the railway a 10-minute walk takes you to a small-scale miner's train (tall people, beware), which heads deep into the mountain. Inside, you can famously slide down the wooden chutes once used by the miners all the way down to an artificial subterranean lake, once used to dissolve the rock salt. At the entrance to the mines you'll find an Iron Age cemetery and a restaurant. ■ **TIP→ Buy a "Salzerlebnis" (Salt Adventure) combination ticket from the ÖBB (Austrian Railway) that offers an all-inclusive value fare for travel to and from Hallstatt as well as the salt mine tour.** ✉ *Salzbergstrasse 21* ☎ *06132/200–2400* 🌐 *www.salzwelten.at* 🎫 *Funicular €9 one way, €16 round-trip; mine and tour €22; combination ticket for cable car and salt mines €30* ⏲ *Closed Dec.–Mar.* ☞ *No children under 4 yrs.*

**Schifffahrt Boat Trips.** The same company that ferries train passengers across the lake to Hallstatt also runs three other vessels offering summer boat tours around the lake via Obertraun to the south (50 minutes) or Obersee to the north (80 minutes). You can also link boat trips with hiking along the shore between pick-up points. ✉ *Am Hof 126* ☎ *06134/8228* 🌐 *www.hallstattschifffahrt.at* 🎫 *South lake trip: €7 one way, €10 round-trip; North lake trip: €7–€8 one way, €13 round-trip; full-day unlimited-ride pass, €19; bikes, €5* ⏲ *No south trip early Oct.–May; no north trip early Oct.–mid-July.*

## WHERE TO STAY

$$ B&B/INN **Bräugasthof.** With an idyllic lakeside perch, this former 16th-century brewery (*bräugasthof*) offers distinctive charm. **Pros:** cozy rooms; lakefront setting; fabulous views from balcony rooms. **Cons:** noisy during the day; room furnishings are a bit old; historical building so it's a little creaky. $ *Rooms from: €105* ✉ *Seestrasse 120* ☎ *06134/8221* 🌐 *www.brauhaus-lobisser.com* *8 rooms* 🍴 *Breakfast.*

$$$$ HOTEL **Grüner Baum.** Glowing with a daffodil-yellow facade, sitting directly on the shore of the lake, and at the foot of a picture-perfect square, this traditional inn is one of Hallstatt's most memorable accommodations. **Pros:** great location on the lake; pretty views; lovely sauna. **Cons:** breakfast can be chaotic; parking is outside town; popular with groups. $ *Rooms from: €220* ✉ *Marktplatz 104* ☎ *06134/8263–0* 🌐 *www.gruenerbaum.cc* *20 rooms* 🍴 *Breakfast.*

## SPORTS AND THE OUTDOORS
### ADVENTURE SPORTS

**Outdoor Leadership.** If you're ready for a true Alpine adventure, just name your fear factor—from family-friendly to daredevil—and Heli and Anja Putz's company has you covered, with a full team of skilled outdoor guides ready to take you kayaking, canyoning, climbing, rafting, paragliding, or skiing throughout the Salzkammergut. These experts know the mountains and caves like they're walking through their own backyards, and they personally created many of the half- and full-day routes that they offer. All necessary equipment is meticulously maintained and available for rent. ⊠ *Steinach 4, Bad Goisern* ☎ *6135/6058* ⊕ *www.outdoor-leadership.com.*

### BOATING

**Sport Zopf.** This company organizes two-hour rafting tours on the Hallstättersee, traveling from Steeg to Lauffen. No prior experience is required, and Zopf supplies all the equipment. Trips take place on Wednesday and Saturday afternoons, and must be prebooked by telephone. Private trips can be arranged for groups of six or more. ⊠ *Obere Marktstrasse 6, Bad Goisern* ☎ *06135/8254* ⊕ *www.zopf.co.at/raftingtour* ⊠ *€45.*

### HIKING

There are many great hiking paths around Hallstatt; contact the local tourist office for information about the path along the Echerntal to Waldbachstrub past pleasant waterfalls, or the climb to the Tiergartenhütte, continuing on to the Wiesberghaus and, two hours beyond, the Simony-Hütte, spectacularly poised at the foot of the Dachstein glacier. From here, mountain climbers begin the ascent of the Hoher Dachstein, the tallest peak of the Dachstein massif.

# CARINTHIA AND GRAZ

Updated by
Jacy Meyer

While lesser-known than the mountainous terrain of Tyrol or the culture-rich cities of Vienna and Salzburg, the southern provinces of Carinthia and Styria with its capital Graz— located directly above Italy and Slovenia and 2½ hours by train from Vienna—beckon visitors with spectacular mountain ranges, abundant forests, and glass-clear lakes.

Art lovers gravitate to such architectural landmarks as the Romanesque Gurk Cathedral, a host of Baroque town halls, and the medieval fantasy of the 9th-century castle Hochosterwitz. The provinces' summer season is custom tailored for bicycling, fishing, hiking, and water sports.

The area has a rich history and a distinguished musical past, and the sophistication and beauty of Graz may surprise you.

# ORIENTATION AND PLANNING

## GETTING ORIENTED

Carinthia is protected in the northwest by the vast Hohe Tauern range and the impossibly high and mighty Grossglockner. Along its northern borders are the bulky Nockberge National Park and the massive crests of the Noric mountain range, and to the east are the grassy meadows on the slopes of the Saualpe and Koralpe. Completing the circle in the south and bordering Slovenia and Italy are the steep, craggy Karawanken Mountains and Carnic Alps. Lying serenely in the valleys between these rocky mountains are the long, meandering Drau and Gail rivers and more than 100 lakes, including the best known and largest, the Wörther See, as well as the Ossiacher See and Faaker See.

**Klagenfurt and the Gurktal Region.** On the eastern end of Wörther See, the region's biggest lake, the Carinthian capital Klagenfurt prides itself on its charming city center and mellow lifestyle. The unspoiled Gurktal region attracts both hikers and art lovers. Blessed with verdant forests and Romanesque architecture, the northeastern corner of Carinthia enchants visitors with its pristine landscape.

**Graz.** Austria's second-largest city headlines as one of Europe's best preserved Renaissance town centers, dating to an era when Graz, not Vienna, was the capital. Italian architects, in fact, came to Graz to gain design experience and shaped the city with their exquisite building skills. Located in the Grazer basin and crossed by the Mur River, Graz has now turned into a lively meeting point for art and culture. The surrounding countryside boasts vineyards, thermal spas, and mountains.

---

## TOP REASONS TO GO

**The Wörther See:** In summer, this area turns into Austria's version of the Hamptons. Pleasure-seekers check into mansions-turned-hotels, boat on the crystalline lake, and party until the wee hours.

**Burg Hochosterwitz:** Walt Disney drew the inspiration for Snow White from this magnificent castle on top of a mountain. Not even the Turks were able to pass through its 14 gates.

**Gurk Cathedral:** Supported by 100 marble pillars, the most splendid of all the region's Romanesque churches features the original chair of St. Hemma. When women sit in it, they supposedly have a nice surprise nine months later.

**Graz:** A UNESCO City of Design, this fresh, young, creative city offers an all-year-round cultural program with events for all tastes.

**Museum in a Palace:** Actually, there are four museums—plus the gorgeous Prunkräume (state rooms) in Graz's Schloss Eggenberg, itself a museum piece that sheds light on Austria's past.

**Rogner Bad Blumau:** This natural-spring-water resort, a two-hour train ride northeast of Graz, was designed by artist Friedensreich Hundertwasser.

---

## PLANNING

### WHEN TO GO

Because of the bulwark of mountains that protect it from the cold winds of the north, the Carinthian and Styrian climate is milder than that of the rest of Austria, and it also boasts more sunshine. Consequently, the lakes maintain an average summer temperature of between 75°F and 82°F.

To see the province in its best festive dress of blue and emerald lakes framed by wooded hills and rocky peaks, and also do some swimming, come between mid-May and early October. Early spring, when the colors are purest and the crowds not yet in evidence, and fall, are perhaps the best times for quiet sightseeing. Christmas in Graz and Klagenfurt is a visual spectacle, with whole sections of the cities turned into a Christmas market. Winter in the area is an enigma: the Semmering Mountains mark the eastern tail end of the Alps—north of the divide can be overcast and dreary while the area to the south basks in sunshine.

### FESTIVALS

Lovers of classical music will enjoy Carinthischer Sommer, a festival in July and August with a heavy emphasis on sacred and chamber music. The Musikforum Viktring near Klagenfurt brings together world-renowned classical, electronic, and jazz artists. Through the summer and early fall, villages big and small celebrate their patron saints. These festivals are called Kirtag and feature music, dance, horseback-riding competitions, and lots of wine and beer. The Styriarte Festival in Graz, from June to July, has classical music on the program. The Styrian Autumn Festival, a celebration of contemporary art in October, or the Spring Festival, an electronic-music event, are just two examples of the many events taking place in Graz throughout the year.

## GETTING HERE AND AROUND
### AIR TRAVEL
Klagenfurt–Wörther See airport, just northeast of Klagenfurt, is served by Austrian, and German low-cost carrier Germanwings airlines. Several flights daily connect the provincial capital with Vienna and Köln/ Bonn, Germany. In summer, charter flights will take you from here to several popular Mediterranean tourist destinations.

The northern part of eastern Austria is served by Vienna's international airport at Schwechat, 19 km (12 miles) southeast of the city center.

Graz has its own international airport at Feldkirchen, just south of the city, with flights to and from many major European cities, like London, Paris, and Berlin. Austrian Airlines, Eurowings, and Lufthansa are the most ubiquitous carriers there.

**Airport Information Graz Airport** (*GRZ*). ☎ *0316/2902172* ⊕ *www.flughafen-graz.at.*

### CAR TRAVEL
If you are driving, the most direct route from Vienna is via the Semmering mountain pass through Styria to Graz and on to Klagenfurt. Or take the heavily traveled A2 from Vienna to Graz and farther south. From Salzburg, the A10 autobahn tunnels beneath the Tauern range and the Katschberghöhe to make a dramatic entry into Carinthia, although the parallel Route 99, which runs "over the top," is the more scenic route. A pretty alternative here that leads you straight into the Nock Mountains or Gurk Valley is to leave the A10 at St. Michael after the Tauern Tunnel, head toward Tamsweg, and then take Route 97 through the Mur Valley; at Predlitz the pass road begins its climb over the steep Turracherhöhe into the Nock Mountains. The fork to Flattnitz, the most scenic way into the Gurk Valley, is at Stadl. Several mountain roads cross over from Italy, but the most traveled is Route 83 from Tarvisio.

### TRAIN TRAVEL
As in all of Austria, post-office or railway (*Bundesbahn*) buses go virtually everywhere, but you'll have to allow plenty of time and coordinate schedules carefully so as not to get stranded in some remote location.

The main rail line south from Vienna parallels Route 83, entering Carinthia north of Friesach and continuing on to Klagenfurt and Villach. From Salzburg, a line runs south, tunneling under the Tauern mountains and then tracing the Möll and Drau river valleys to Villach. The main international north–south route connecting Vienna and northeastern Italy runs through Graz and is traversed by EuroCity trains from Munich and Salzburg.

Services on the main routes are fast and frequent. Trains depart hourly from Vienna Hauptbahnhof (Central Station) to Graz for a 2½-hour ride, and from Salzburg five times a day for a two-hour ride.

**Train Information ÖBB—National Train Information.** ☎ *05/1717* ⊕ *www. oebb.at.*

## TOURS

The official tourist office for the province is Kärnten Werbung in Velden. The Kärnten Card costs €42, works between April and October, and includes access to more than 100 museums, attractions, lifts, and other sites of interest in the province. It can be purchased in many hotels, and some offer the card to their guests for free for the duration of their stay.

## ESSENTIALS

**Visitor Information Kärnten Werbung.** ✉ *Völkermarkter Ring 21-23, Klagenfurt* ☎ *463/3000* ⊕ *www.visitcarinthia.at.*

## RESTAURANTS

Through much of Carinthia you'll discover that, other than simple *Gasthäuser* (wine taverns), most dining spots are not independent establishments but belong to country inns. Carinthia's peasant tradition is reflected in its culinary specialties, such as *Kärntner Käsnudeln* (giant ravioli stuffed with a ricotta-like local cheese and a whisper of mint), *Sterz* (polenta served either sweet or salty), and *Hauswürste* (smoked or air-cured hams and sausages, available at butcher shops).

Styria, bordering on Slovenia, has a hearty cuisine with Slavic overtones; a typical dish is *Steirisches Brathuhn* (roast chicken turned on a spit). The intensely nutty *Kürbiskernöl* (pumpkinseed oil) is used in many soup and pasta dishes, as well as in salad dressings, or to top off vanilla ice cream.

Carinthia is full of lakes and rivers that abound with carp, pike, perch, eel, bream, crawfish (in a rather short season), and, best of all, a large variety of trout. The most popular way of serving Austrian brook trout and rainbow trout is *blau* (blue), the whole fish simmered in a court bouillon and served with drawn butter. Or try it *Müllerin*—sautéed in butter until a crisp brown. In summer, try *kalte Räucherforelle* (cold smoked trout) with lemon or horseradish as a delicate hors d'oeuvre. *Dining reviews have been shortened. For full information, visit Fodors.com.*

## HOTELS

Accommodations range from luxurious lakeside resorts to small inns, and even include guesthouses without private baths. Accommodations in private homes are cheaper still. These bargains are usually identified by signs reading "Zimmer frei" (room available) or "Frühstückspension" (bed-and-breakfast). Summers are never too hot, and it cools off delightfully at night, which means that most hotels are not equipped with air-conditioning. Some hotels offer half-board, which includes dinner in addition to buffet breakfast (although most $$$$ hotels will charge extra for breakfast). The half-board room rate is usually an extra €15–€30 per person. Occasionally, quoted room rates for hotels already include half-board accommodations, though a "discounted" rate is usually available if you prefer not to take the evening meal. Inquire when booking. *Hotel reviews have been shortened. For full information, visit Fodors.com.*

| WHAT IT COSTS IN EUROS | | | |
| --- | --- | --- | --- |
| | $ | $$ | $$$ | $$$$ |
| RESTAURANTS | under €12 | €12–€17 | €18–€22 | over €22 |
| HOTELS | under €100 | €100–€135 | €136–€175 | over €175 |

Restaurant prices are the average cost of a main course at dinner, or if dinner is not served, at lunch. Hotel prices are the lowest cost of a standard double room in high season.

# KLAGENFURT TOWARD THE GURKTAL REGION

Heading north from Klagenfurt you enter genuine, rural, Austrian countryside. Small villages, farms, wide pastures, and forests unfold while driving over smooth hills. Burg Hochosterwitz, perched on a steep hill, can be seen from far away. A popular place of pilgrimage is Gurk Cathedral, a Romanesque basilica from the 12th century and an important building full of European religious art. Friesach, a medieval town, and one of the oldest in Carinthia, is another highlight on this route.

## KLAGENFURT

*329 km (192 miles) southwest of Vienna, 209 km (130 miles) southeast of Salzburg.*

Klagenfurt became the provincial capital in 1518, so most of the delightful sites here date from the 16th century or later. However, a group of attention-getting Carinthian architects has also breathed new life into old buildings. The town is an excellent base for excursions to the rest of Carinthia. In the city center you can't miss the *Lindwurm*, Klagenfurt's emblematic dragon with a curled tail, which adorns the fountain on Neuer Platz (New Square). Legend has it that the town was founded on this spot, where the beast was destroyed by resident peasants back in days of yore (but the notion of Klagenfurt's dragon became more intriguing when the fossilized cranium of a prehistoric rhinoceros was found nearby).

### GETTING HERE AND AROUND

If you come from Italy, Klagenfurt can be reached via the southern highway, A2, which continues all the way to Graz and Vienna. Coming from Salzburg take the A10, via Villach. It's well connected by railway from Salzburg and Vienna. Several buses serve the route daily from Graz. A system of public buses connects Klagenfurt and its surroundings. Centrally located Heiligengeistplatz is the major bus hub. Bus tickets can be purchased from the driver (€1.80). Take bus No. 10 or No. 20 to explore the Wörther See (towards Strandbad). Klagenfurt itself is compact and easy to explore on foot. The tourism office rents bicycles from April through October, depending on the weather.

### ESSENTIALS

**Tourist Information Klagenfurt.** ✉ *Neuer Platz 5* ☎ *0463/287–463-0* ⊕ *www.visitklagenfurt.at.*

Carinthia

SLOVENIA

SLOVENIA

ITALY

A9
Piber
Köflach
Voitsberg
A2
Deutschlandsberg
Schwanberg
Knittelfeld
S36
Zeltweg
Spielberg
S36
B77
Bad Sankt Leonhard
im Lavanttal
Wolfsberg
Sankt Andrä
B78
A2
Judenburg
B114
B317
B92
Althofen
Völkermarkt
Bleiburg/Pliberk
B85
Friesach
Hochosterwitz
B317
B92
Klopeinersee
St. Veit
an der Glan
A2
Klagenfurt
Reptilien Zoo
Strassburg
Gurk
B93
Ferlach
B97
B94
Minimundus
Pörtschach
B85
Murau
B95
Maria Wörth
Pyramidenkogel
A2
Egg am Faaker See
Feldkirchen
in Kärnten
Velden am
Wörthersee
Tamsweg
Ossiach
B95
B95
B98
Villach
B99
A10
Seeboden
Millstatt
A10
Warmbad Villach
A10
Gmünd
Bad Bleiberg
B111
Spittal an der Drau
B106
Hermagor
B100
B111

10 mi
10 km

### EXPLORING

**Alter Platz.** The old town square of Klagenfurt, or Alter Platz, is still the center of the city. Brightly colored buildings dating from the 12th century frame this pedestrian meeting area. A Trinity Column representing God, Jesus Christ, and the Holy Spirit, dating from 1680, now stands in the Alter Platz. These columns were built all over Europe as a thanks to God from the people for having survived the plague that killed nearly 25 million Europeans during the Middle Ages. The brightly colored yellow building is the old town hall. ⊠ *Alter Platz.*

**Domkirche** (*Cathedral*). South of Neuer Platz (take Karfreitstrasse) is the Domkirche, completed as a Protestant church in 1581, given over to the Jesuits and reconsecrated in 1604, and finally declared a cathedral in 1787. The 18th-century side-altar painting of St. Ignatius by Paul Troger, the great Viennese Rococo painter and teacher, is a fine example of the qualities of transparency and light he introduced to painting. ⊠ *Domplatz.*

OFF THE
BEATEN
PATH

**Klopeinersee.** With water temperatures averaging 28°C (82°F) from spring to fall, this lake is a popular spot for sunbathing. Surrounded by gentle mountains, it's a little over 1½ km long (1 mile long) and 1 km wide (½ mile wide), and motorboats are not allowed. To reach the Klopeinersee, take the west Völkermarkt/Tainach exit from the A2 autobahn and follow signs to the lake. It's about a 30-minute drive east of Klagenfurt. For information on lakeside hotels and pensions, as well as hiking and biking in the region, contact Klopeinersee Tourismus. ⊠ *Klopein* ⊕ *www.klopeinersee.at.*

**Landhaus** (*District Government Headquarters*). One of the most notable sights of the city is the Landhaus, with its towers and court with arcaded stairways. It was completed in 1590, and at the time formed a corner of the city wall. The only interior on view is the dramatic **Grosser Wappensaal** (Great Hall of Heraldry), which contains 665 coats of arms of Carinthia's landed gentry. On the ceiling is a stirring rendition of the Fürstenstein investiture ceremony portrayed by Fromiller, the most important Carinthian painter of the Baroque period. The Gasthaus im Landhaushof, on the ground floor, is well worth a stop for lunch. ⊠ *Landhaushof 1* ☎ *463/57757–215* ⊕ *www.landesmuseum.ktn.gv.at* ⊠ *€4* ⊙ *Closed weekends in Apr.–Oct. and Sun.–Fri. in Nov.–Mar.*

FAMILY **Minimundus.** From Klagenfurt, bypass the autobahn and instead take Villacher Strasse (Route 83) to the Wörther Lake, Austria's great summer resort area. You'll pass by the entrancing Minimundus, literally "miniature world," with around 150 1:25 scale models. Structures include copies of the White House, the Taj Mahal, the Eiffel Tower, and the Gur-Emir Mausoleum from Uzbekistan, all built when possible from the original materials. Net proceeds support needy children and families in Carinthia. ⊠ *Villacher Strasse 241* ☎ *0463/21194–0* ⊕ *www. minimundus.at* ⊠ *€19* ⊙ *Closed Nov.*

**Museum Moderner Kunst Kärnten.** This museum displays works by modern and contemporary artists. It pays special attention to avant-garde artists with roots in Carinthia. Maria Lassnig, Arnulf Rainer, and Bruno Gironcoli, some of the heavyweights of post–World War II art, hail from the region. The museum also fosters the young art scene by showing works by emerging artists such as Hans Schabus and Heimo Zobernig. ⊠ *Burggasse 8* ☎ *050/53616252* ⊕ *www.mmkk.at* ⊠ *€5* ⊙ *Closed Mon.*

OFF THE BEATEN PATH

**Pyramidenkogel.** On the shore of the Wörthersee, a winding 5-km (3-mile) road ascends to the 2,790-foot observation tower, the Pyramidenkogel; take its elevator (or the climb 441 steps) up to its three platforms and you can see out over half of Carinthia. The quickest way down is via the slide (separate ticket required) which promises to have you at ground level within 18 seconds. ✉ *Linden 62, Keutschach Am See* 🌐 *www.pyramidenkogel.info* 🎫 *€11.*

FAMILY

**Reptilien Zoo.** Adjacent to Minimundus is the Reptilien Zoo, featuring crocodiles, cobras, rattlesnakes, and several kinds of hairy spiders, as well as colorful fish from the nearby Wörther Lake. ✉ *Villacher Strasse 237* ☎ *0463/23425* 🌐 *www.reptilienzoo.at* 🎫 *€14* 🕒 *Closed Nov.*

**Robert Musil Museum.** In the house where Robert Musil—author of the celebrated novel *The Man Without Qualities*—was born in 1880, the Robert Musil Museum displays documents and photographs belonging to him, as well as first editions of his work. Additional permanent exhibition space is given to lyricist Christine Lavant and author Ingeborg Bachmann. Musil's writing focused on the cultural disintegration and spiritual crisis of his day. He fled Nazi-occupied Austria in 1938 and died penniless in Switzerland in 1942. Note the portraits of all three of the museum's subjects, spray painted by French street artist Jef Aérosol, that decorate the building's exterior. ✉ *Bahnhofstrasse 50* ☎ *0463/501–429* 🌐 *www.musilmuseum.at* 🎫 *€2.50* 🕒 *Closed weekends.*

**St. Egyd** (*Stadthauptpfarre St. Egid*). North of Neuer Platz (go along Kramergasse for two blocks, then angle left to the Pfarrplatz) is the parish church of St. Egyd, with its eye-catching totem-pole bronze carving by Austrian avant-garde artist Ernst Fuchs in the second chapel on the right. In the next chapel is the crypt of Julian Green (1900–98), the noted French-born American novelist whose works include *The Closed Garden* and *The Other One*. He perceived the city as a sanctuary of peace in the world and decided he wanted to be buried here. ✉ *Pfarrhofgasse 4/A* 🌐 *www.st-egid-klagenfurt.at.*

## WHERE TO EAT

$$$ CONTEMPORARY

🍴 **Bar-Bistro 151.** Inventive dishes, excellent staff, and an inviting atmosphere sum up a visit to 151. Chef Markus Vidermann cooks up a small but fascinating menu of Austrian and international flavors, including vegan options and multiple-course tasting menus. **Known for:** top service; creative cocktails; beautiful atmosphere. [$] *Average main: €20* ✉ *Höhenweg 151* ☎ *676/615–1151* 🌐 *www.151.at* 🕒 *Closed Sun.*

$ AUSTRIAN

🍴 **Bierhaus zum Augustin.** This rustic brewery is in one of the oldest buildings in Klagenfurt and attracts a mixed and lively clientele. The excellent beer produced here pairs perfectly with the local cuisine. **Known for:** great home-brewed beer menu; large portions of Austrian classics; awesome courtyard. [$] *Average main: €9* ✉ *Pfarrhofgasse 2* ☎ *0463/513–992* 🕒 *Closed Sun.*

$$$$ MEDITERRANEAN

🍴 **Dolce Vita.** Small and exclusive, this tucked-away establishment in the city center offers cutting-edge Mediterranean cuisine. Personalized service is the hallmark here with the chef visiting each table, and creating a culinary experience just for you. **Known for:** locally sourced ingredients;

delicious Mediterranean dishes; affordable lunch tasting menus. [$] *Average main: €25* ✉ *Heuplatz 2* ☎ *0463/55499* ⏲ *Closed weekends.*

$$ AUSTRIAN 🍴 **Kärntner Hamatle.** Like a little family-owned farmhouse in the center of the city, this homey establishment just off the Villacher Ring is the place to go for Kärntner Käsnudeln, a Carinthian specialty resembling large, round ravioli. They're light as a feather and delicately stuffed with your choice of spinach, cheese, or minced beef. **Known for:** cozy atmosphere; Carinthian specialties; affordable lunch menu. [$] *Average main: €15* ✉ *Linsengasse 1* ☎ *0463/555700* 🌐 *www.kaerntnerhamatle.at* ⏲ *Closed Mon.*

$$$ SEAFOOD 🍴 **Maria Loretto.** Gorgeous is the word to describe this spot's perch, which offers a view over the Wörther See and makes a fitting backdrop for some of the area's best seafood. This former villa offers several romantic dining rooms in champagne and red tones, or you can sit outdoors on the wraparound terrace overlooking the glistening water. **Known for:** lake views; beautiful terrace; amazing seafood like trout caviar. [$] *Average main: €19* ✉ *Lorettoweg 54* ☎ *0463/24465* 🌐 *www.restaurant-maria-loretto.at* ⏲ *Closed Tues.*

$$ ITALIAN 🍴 **Ristorante Michelangelo.** Despite Klagenfurt's proximity to Italy, most eateries claiming to serve authentic Italian cuisine don't have it quite right; for the real deal, take the trip out of the town center to Michelangelo. Come for the welcoming environment and stay for a three-course menu or the pasta *alla Norma,* a Sicilian specialty with eggplant and salted ricotta. **Known for:** wood-oven-baked pizzas; sea bass baked in salt crust; family-friendly environment. [$] *Average main: €13* ✉ *St. Veiter Strasse 181* ☎ *0463/481–889* 🌐 *www.ristorante-michelangelo.at* ⏲ *Closed Mon.*

## WHERE TO STAY

$ HOTEL 🏨 **City Hotel zum Domplatz.** Just a few steps from the center's main square, this convenient little hotel is a good choice for leisure or business travelers on a budget. **Pros:** quiet courtyard; good breakfast; complimentary tea and apples. **Cons:** no elevator; no meals other than breakfast; parking is off-site. [$] *Rooms from: €94* ✉ *Karfreitstrasse 20* ☎ *0463/54320* 🌐 *www.cityhotel-klagenfurt.at* 🛏 *12 rooms* 🍽 *Breakfast.*

$$$ HOTEL 🏨 **Sandwirth.** Once *the* watering hole of Klagenfurt society, the Sandwirth now features streamlined furniture and innovative works of art that recast vintage landscape photographs in a new light, while retaining the 19th-century yellow facade. **Pros:** business friendly; good café/restaurant; the hotel maintains a beach hut at the Wörthersee. **Cons:** lobby is used for conference coffee breaks at times; no parking; rooms could use some updating. [$] *Rooms from: €140* ✉ *Pernhartgasse 9* ☎ *0463/56209* 🌐 *www.sandwirth.at* 🛏 *100 rooms.*

$$$ HOTEL 🏨 **Seepark Hotel.** Designed by a group of young Austrian architects, this hotel attracts business and leisure travelers alike, thanks to its position on the shores of the Wörthersee. **Pros:** five-minute walk to Wörthersee lake; modern design; lake views from third floor and higher. **Cons:** street-facing rooms are noisy; breakfast is expensive; out of town. [$] *Rooms from: €150* ✉ *Universitätsstrasse 104* ☎ *0463/204–4990* 🌐 *www.seeparkhotel.at/hotel.html* 🛏 *142 rooms.*

**11**

## NIGHTLIFE AND PERFORMING ARTS

### NIGHTLIFE

For a true after-hours scene in Klagenfurt, head for the Pfarrplatz-Herrengasse area, where you'll find a number of intimate bars and cafés.

### PERFORMING ARTS

**Stadttheater Klagenfurt.** A large variety of operas, operettas, plays, and ballets are performed year-round at the Stadttheater in Klagenfurt, an inviting Art Nouveau building designed by the famous theater architects Helmer and Fellner of Vienna and completed in 1910. The box office is open Monday through Saturday 9–6. ⊠ *Theaterplatz 4* ☎ *0463/54064* ⊕ *www.stadttheater-klagenfurt.at.*

# HOCHOSTERWITZ

*20 km (12 miles) northwest of Klagenfurt.*

Like the impenetrable fortress it is, Burg Hochosterwitz looms over the surrounding countryside. This medieval building sits at 564 feet high, and on a clear day you can see it from nearly 20 miles away. It's a roughly 20-minute drive from Klagenfurt.

### GETTING HERE AND AROUND

From Klagenfurt, head northeast on St. Veiterstrasse and merge onto S37. The castle is well signposted and can be seen from far away.

### EXPLORING

FAMILY

Fodor's Choice

★

**Hochosterwitz.** The dramatic castle of Hochosterwitz crowns the top of a steep, isolated outcropping, looking as if it has just emerged from the pages of a fairy tale. It was in this castle that the forces of "Pocket-Mouthed Meg" (Margarethe Maultasch) were tricked by two slaughtered oxen dropped onto the heads of its soldiers. Those inside the fortress were starving, but the strategy succeeded, and, dispirited by such apparent proof of abundant supplies, the Tyrolese abandoned the siege. The most recent fortifications were added in the late 1500s against invading Turks; each of the 14 towered gates is a small fortress unto itself. Inside, there's an impressive collection of armor and weaponry plus a café-restaurant in the inner courtyard. There's a glass elevator (accommodating wheelchairs) from a point near the parking-lot ticket office. The hike up the rather steep path to Hochosterwitz adds to the drama. Your reward at the summit is spectacular vistas from every vantage point. Get to the castle on the back road from Treibach or via Route 83/E7. ⊠ *Hochosterwitz 1, Launsdorf* ☎ *04213/34597* ⊕ *www. burg-hochosterwitz.com* ⊠ *€13, elevator €9* ⊗ *Closed Oct.–Apr.*

# GURK

*47 km (29 miles) north of Klagenfurt.*

Gurk is located in central Carinthia in the Gurk Valley, surrounded by high mountain meadows and magnificent forests. The actual center of the valley is characterized by the two mighty towers of the cathedral.

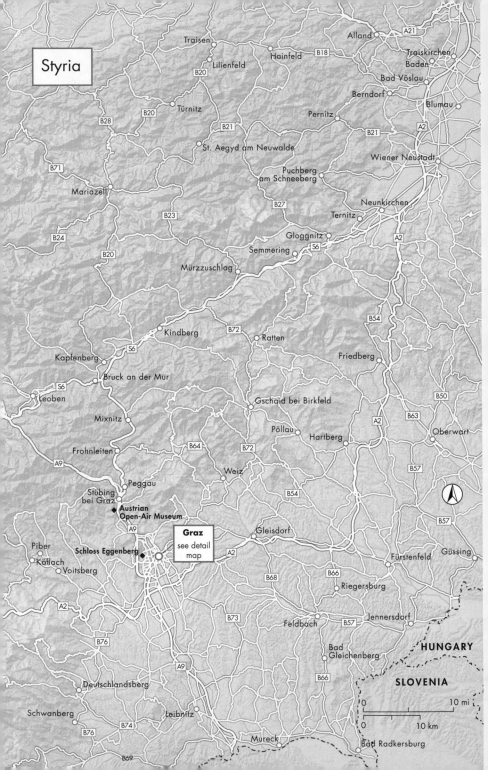

**11**

**GETTING HERE AND AROUND**

Take the Klagenfurter Schnellstrasse S37; at Pöckstein, turn left onto Gurktalstrasse B93.

**EXPLORING**

**Dom** (*Cathedral*). Gurk's claim to fame is its massive Romanesque Dom topped by two onion cupolas and considered the most famous religious landmark in Carinthia. It was founded in the 11th century by Hemma, Countess of Zeltschach, who after losing her two sons and husband decided to turn to religious works. She tied two oxen to a cart and let them walk until they stopped on their own. At that spot, she founded a cloister and gave all her belongings to the church to build a cathedral. Construction on the cathedral began in 1140 and ended in 1200, though Hemma wasn't canonized until 1938. Her tomb is in the crypt, whose ceiling, and hence the cathedral itself, is supported by 100 marble pillars. The Hemma-Stein, a small, green-slate chair from which she personally supervised construction, is also here, and alleged to bring fertility to barren women. In the church itself, the high altar is one of the most important examples of the early Baroque in Austria. Note the *Pietà* by George Rafael Donner, who is sometimes called the Austrian Michelangelo. Be sure to visit the bishop's chapel, which features rare late-Romanesque and Gothic frescoes. At the end of August and in early September, a concert series is held in the cathedral. Tours are restricted by church services, but run daily at 11 and 2:30. ⊠ *Domplatz 11* ☎ *04266/8236–12* ✉ *Tours: church, bishop's chapel, and crypt €9; church and crypt €5.50* ⊗ *Treasury closed Nov.–Apr.*

FAMILY **Zwergenpark.** The Zwergenpark is a vast natural preserve filled with amusing garden statuary, consisting largely of about 1,000 Austrian-German garden gnomes; children can traverse the park via a miniature railway. ⊠ *Dr. Schnerichstrasse* ☎ *0732/39192* ⊕ *www.zwergenpark. com* ✉ *€4* ⊗ *Closed Oct.–Apr.*

# FRIESACH

*22 km (13 miles) northeast of Gurk.*

The oldest settlement in Carinthia, romantic Friesach is great for wandering. The town is peppered with red-roofed buildings encircled by an old stone wall. There is a well-preserved medieval town center and a Romanesque parish church, as well as Petersburg Castle, home to the Friesach City Museum, which features exhibits on the town's history and culture. Friesach has many medieval marvels; be sure to stop in at the tourist office for information on all of them.

**GETTING HERE AND AROUND**

Take the Klagenfurter Schnellstrasse S37 coming from the south.

**ESSENTIALS**

**Tourist Information Friesach Tourism.** ⊠ *Fürstenhofplatz 1* ☎ *04268/221340* ⊕ *www.friesach.at.*

## EXPLORING

**Dominican Monastery.** This Dominican Monastery of St. Nikolaus von Myra is named after St. Nikolaus, the man who eventually became pop culture's Saint Nick and Santa Claus. The monastery is near the town's moat, and was rebuilt in 1673, though the church nearby dates from 1217. Take a moment to notice the stone statue of the Virgin Mary inside the monastery, and the massive crucifix. ✉ *Stadtgrabengasse 5.*

**Hauptplatz.** It's easy to find the Hauptplatz (main square), with its old town hall and gleaming, multicolor, pastel facades. As you stroll you'll discover aspects of the medieval-era town: beautiful stone houses, the double wall, and the towers, gates, and water-filled moat. ✉ *Hauptplatz, off Kirchgasse or Herrengasse.*

**Schloss Petersberg.** From a footpath at the upper end of the Hauptplatz, behind the Raiffeisenbank, take a steep 20-minute climb up 323 steps to the impressive remains of Schloss Petersberg. (An easier path to see the 12th- and 13th-century castle can be found next to the Landhotel Metnitztalerhof.) The **Stadtmuseum** (city museum) displays the history of the oldest city in Carinthia. Additionally, make a stop at the **Petersbergkirche,** a Romanesque church first built in 1130. ✉ *North of Hauptplatz off Kirchgasse* 🕒 *Museum closed Nov.–mid-Apr.*

**Stadtpfarrkirche.** The 12th-century Romanesque Stadtpfarrkirche (parish church) has some excellent stained glass in the choir. ✉ *Friesach.*

## WHERE TO STAY

$ HOTEL 🏨 **Friesacherhof.** Incorporated into a centuries-old building on the main square, this comfortable hotel has rather plain but well-kept rooms. **Pros:** bargain rates; friendly owners; good restaurant. **Cons:** front rooms can be noisy; staff is shared between restaurant and hotel; rooms are a bit dated. [$] *Rooms from: €70* ✉ *Hauptplatz 4* ☎ *04268 2123* 🌐 *www.friesacherhof.at* 🛏 *16 rooms.*

# GRAZ

*200 km (125 miles) southwest of Vienna, 285 km (178 miles) southeast of Salzburg.*

Austria's second-largest city, Graz is graceful, welcoming, and far from the usual tourist routes. Instead of visitors, it's the large university population that keeps the sidewalk cafés, trendy bars, and chic restaurants humming in the vibrant Altstadt. The modern-art museum, the Kunsthaus, has a startling biomorphic blue shape that looms over rooftops like some alien spaceship. Along with this, the annual Styriarte summer music festival has become one of the most prestigious cultural draws in the country, and the city opera theater now attracts top companies like the Bolshoi. Graz is far from the cultural backwater it once was; in fact, it was appointed a UNESCO City of Design in 2011.

With its skyline dominated by the squat 16th-century clock tower, this stylish city has a gorgeous and well-preserved medieval center whose Italian Renaissance overlay gives it, in contrast to other Austrian cities, a Mediterranean feel. The name Graz derives from the Slavic *gradec,* meaning "small castle"; there was probably a fortress atop the

Schlossberg hill as early as the 9th century. By the 12th century a town had developed at the foot of the hill, which in time became an imperial city of the ruling Habsburgs. Graz's glory faded in the 17th century when the court moved to Vienna, but the city continued to prosper as the provincial capital of Styria, especially under the enlightened 19th-century rule of Archduke Johann.

In 1811, the archduke founded the Landesmuseum Joanneum, making it the oldest public museum in Austria. This museum complex, with 17 museums in Graz and Styria, has notable collections of art, archaeology, and armor, as well as fossils and folklife artifacts. A €13, 24-hour ticket allows you entry to all collections and exhibitions.

### GETTING HERE AND AROUND

Streetcars and buses are an excellent way of traveling within the city. Single tickets (€2.30) can be bought from the driver or kiosks, and one-day and multiple-ride tickets are also available. All six streetcar routes converge at Jakominiplatz near the south end of the Old City. One fare may combine streetcars and buses as long as you take a direct route to your destination. Driving in the Graz city center is not advisable, because there are many narrow, one-way, and pedestrian streets and few places to park. In Graz, taxis can be ordered by phone.

If you're pressed for time, choose which part of the Old City you'd rather see: the lower section, with its churches, historical houses, and museums, or the upper town, with its winding wooded paths, famous clock tower, and the Schlossberg, the lookout point of the city. The best time to visit is between April and October, when the weather is at its most inviting.

**Contacts Public Transport Graz.** ⊠ *Jakomin, Graz* ☎ *0316/887–4224* ⊕ *www.holding-graz.at/linien.html.* **Taxis.** ☎ *0316/878, 0316/889, 0316/2801.*

### WALKING TOURS

Guided walking tours of Graz in English and German are conducted daily at 2:30. From November to March, registration is required for tours. The meeting point for these tours is Tourist Information at Herrengasse 16. The cost is €10.50.

### ESSENTIALS

**Tourist Information Grazer Tourismus.** ⊠ *Herrrengasse 16, Graz* ☎ *0316/8075–0* ⊕ *www.graztourismus.at.*

---

# EXPLORING

### TOP ATTRACTIONS

**Burg.** The scanty remains of this former imperial palace now house government offices. Most of this uninspired structure is from the 19th and 20th centuries, but two noteworthy vestiges of the original 15th-century stronghold remain: the **Burgtor** (palace gate), which opens into the sprawling **Stadtpark** (municipal park), and the unusual 49-step, 26-foot carved stone double-spiral **Gothic staircase** from 1494 to 1500, in the hexagonal tower at the far end of the first courtyard. While meandering around take note of the *Spor,* a statue of a seed, which represents the center of Graz. ⊠ *Hofgasse 15, Graz.*

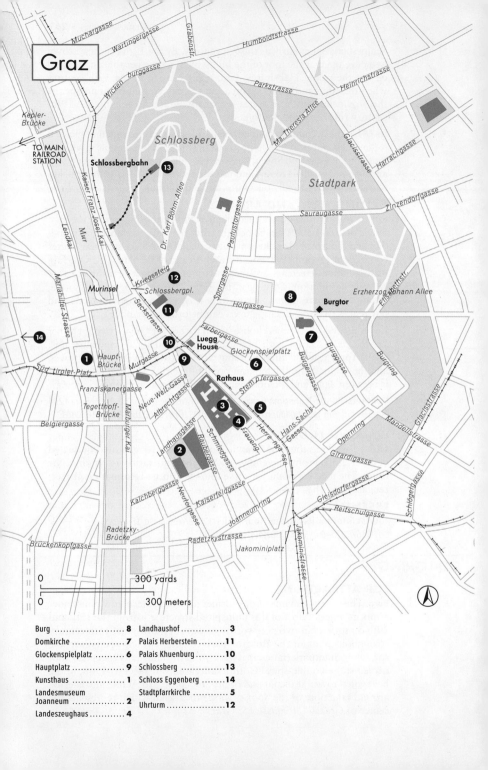

# Graz

TO MAIN RAILROAD STATION

Kepler-Brücke

Muchargasse
Wartingergasse
Grabenstr.
Humboldtstrasse
Wickenburggasse
Parkstrasse
Heinrichstrasse
Ma. Theresia Allee
Glacisstrasse
Harrachgasse
Schlossberg
Stadtpark
Schlossbergbahn
Dr.- Karl Böhm-Allee
Kaiser Franz Josef Kai
Mur
Lendkai
Paulustorgasse
Saueraugasse
Zinzendorfgasse
Erzherzog-Johann Allee
Ehrenfelsstr.
Kriegssteig
Murinsel
Sackstrasse
Sporgasse
Hofgasse
Burgtor
Schlossbergpl.
Färbergasse
Luegg House
Glockenspielplatz
Burggasse
Burgring
Marlahilfer-Strasse
Haupt-Brücke
Murgasse
Süd- tiroler-Platz
Neue-Welt-Gasse
Albrechtgasse
Rathaus
Stempfergasse
Herren gasse
Hans-Sachs-Gasse
Opernring
Glacisstrasse
Mandellstrasse
Franziskanergasse
Landhausgasse
Schmiedgasse
Raubergasse
Fraueng.
Girardigasse
Tegetthoff-Brücke
Belgiergasse
Marburger Kai
Kalchberggasse
Nealtorgasse
Kaiserfeldgasse
Joanneumring
Gleisdorfergasse
Schlögergasse
Radetzky-Brücke
Brückenkopfgasse
Radetzkystrasse
Jakominiplatz
Reitschulgasse
Jakoministrasse

0   300 yards
0   300 meters

**Domkirche.** On the cathedral's south exterior wall is a badly damaged 15th-century fresco called the *Gottesplagenbild,* which graphically depicts contemporary local torments: the plague, locusts, and the Turks. Step inside to see the outstanding high altar made of colored marble, the choir stalls, and Konrad Laib's *Crucifixion* from 1457 (considered one of the top late-Gothic panel paintings of German-speaking Europe). The 15th-century reliquaries on either side of the triumphal arch leading to the choir were originally the bridal chests of Paola Gonzaga, daughter of Ludovico II of Mantua. The Baroque **Mausoleum** of Emperor Ferdinand II, who died in 1637, adjoins the cathedral. Its sumptuous interior is partly a design by native son Fischer von Erlach, and his only work to be seen in Graz. ⊠ *Burggasse 3, Graz* ☎ *0316/821683* ⊕ *www.domgraz.at* 🖂 *Mausoleum €6; Friedrichskapelle and Konrad Laib €3* ☉ *Mausoleum and Friedrichskapelle closed Sat.–Mon., Wed., and Thurs. in Jan.–Apr.*

**Glockenspielplatz.** Every day at 11 am and 3 and 6 pm two mullioned windows open in the mechanical clock high above the square, revealing a life-size wooden couple, the man adorned in lederhosen, a tankard of beer in his upraised fist, accompanied by a dirndl-clad Austrian maiden. An old folk tune plays and they dance on the window ledges before returning to their hidden perch. The musical box was erected in 1905 by the owner of the house. Look into the courtyard at No. 5, which has an impressive 17th-century open staircase. The house at No. 7 has an arcaded Renaissance courtyard. Have a typical Austrian meal right next door at **Glöckl Bräu,** where they brew their own beer. Every time a new barrel is opened, the bells above ring. ⊠ *Glockenspielplatz 4, Graz.*

**Hauptplatz** (*Main Square*). This triangular area was converted from a swampy pastureland to a town square by traveling merchants in 1164; today it's the central meeting spot of Graz. In its center stands the **Erzherzog Johann Brunnen** (Archduke Johann Fountain), dedicated to the popular 19th-century patron whose enlightened policies did much to develop Graz as a cultural and scientific center. The four female figures represent what were Styria's four main rivers; today only the Mur and the Enns are still within the province. The **Luegg House,** at the corner of Sporgasse, is noted for its Baroque stucco facade. On the west side of the square are Gothic and Renaissance houses. The spectacular, late-19th-century **Rathaus** (City Hall) totally dominates the south side. From the Neue-Welt-Gasse and Schmied-gasse you get a superb view of the Hauptplatz. ⊠ *Hauptplatz, Graz.*

**Kunsthaus.** Across the River Mur from the Altstadt is the modern-art museum nicknamed the "Friendly Alien"—and indeed, it does look like an alien ship landed smack in the middle of the town's medieval orange-tile, gabled roofs. Designed by London-based architects Peter Cook and Colin Fournier, with the aim of forging an interaction between the traditional landmarks of Graz and the avant-garde, it resembles a gigantic, blue, beached whale with spiky tentacles—which light up at night. Inside, the vast exhibition rooms are linked by escalators and spiraling walkways, with an open arena at the top offering spectacular views. There is no permanent collection here, only temporary exhibits of renowned modern artists. Check out the gift shop on the ground floor. ⊠ *Lendkai 1, Graz* ☎ *0316/8017–9200* ⊕ *www.kunsthausgraz.at* 🖂 *€9* ☉ *Closed Mon.*

## MURINSEL ISLAND

If you need a break after visiting Graz's many churches and museums, head to Murinsel Island. It's actually not an island but a floating platform, designed by modernist artist Vito Acconci in honor of the city's designation as the European Capital of Culture in 2003. You can access it below the Kunsthaus, where a pedestrian walkway leads from the Haupt-Brucke bridge to the steel structure in the shape of a seashell. Murinsel includes a trendy café, amphitheater, showroom featuring Styrian interior design, and a small gift shop with contemporary Austrian products. It lights up in a rainbow of colors at night.

**Landesmuseum Joanneum.** The oldest public museum in Austria is a vast complex located between Neutorgasse, Kalchberggasse, and Rauber-gasse. The Joanneum Quarter holds the natural history collections, the Neue Galerie Graz, and the Bruseum, dedicated to Styrian artist Günter Brus. The Natural History Museum showcases exhibitions from all of Joanneum Universal Museum's natural sciences departments, including botany, geology, paleontology, mineralogy, and zoology. The Neue Galerie's permanent collection features art from the 19th and 20th centuries. ⊠ *Joanneumsviertel, access Kalchberggasse, Graz* ☎ *0316/8017 9100* ⊕ *www.museum-joanneum.at* ⊠ *Ticket to Natural History Museum or Neue Galerie Graz €9; 24-hour ticket valid for all museums of Landesmuseum €13* ☉ *Closed Mon.*

FAMILY **Landeszeughaus.** With 32,000 items on display, the Styrian Armoury is the largest preserved arsenal in the world, and one of the biggest attractions in Graz. Built between 1642 and 1644 on behalf of the Styrian nobility, the four-story armory still contains the 16th- and 17th-century weapons intended for use by Styrian mercenaries in fighting off the Turks. Empress Maria Theresa closed the armory in 1749, due to extended periods of peace; however, it remained intact to illustrate the history of the area. The collection includes more than 3,000 suits of armor (some of which are beautifully engraved), thousands of halberds, swords, firearms, cannons, and mortars—some hanging off the ceiling, others projecting off the walls, and still more sitting on the floor. The sheer quantity of displays can be daunting, so thankfully the most unusual items are highlighted, sometimes in striking displays. ⊠ *Herrengasse 16, Graz* ☎ *0316/8017–9810* ⊕ *www. museum-joanneum.at* ⊠ *€9, 24-hour ticket valid for all museums of Landesmuseum €13* ☉ *Closed Mon. and Nov.–Mar.*

**Palais Herberstein** (*History Museum*). This 17th-century former city residence of the ruling princes houses the **Cultural History Collection.** In addition to a Baroque interior, the permanent collection of 35,000 items features items related to the political history of Graz and Styria. Palais Herberstein has a special focus on the "status symbols" that defined the time; and as visitors walk down a red carpet they question the equivalent in the world today. ⊠ *Sackstrasse*

*16, Graz* ☎ *0316/8017–9800* ⊕ *www.museum-joanneum.at* ☑ *€9; 24-hour ticket valid for all museums of Landesmuseum €13* ⊙ *Closed Mon. and Tues.*

FAMILY
Fodor'sChoice
★

**Schloss Eggenberg.** This 17th-century palace, a UNESCO World Heritage site on the eastern edge of the city and the largest Baroque palace in Styria, is surrounded by a large park full of peacocks. Enjoy a guided tour of the **Prunkräume** (state rooms); they are noted for their elaborate stucco decorations and frescoes, and contain one of the few depictions of Osaka before 1615. There's also an arcaded courtyard lined with antlers.

The many attractions here include a traditional art gallery, a collection of coins, and an archaeology museum. The Alte Galerie (old gallery) contains a world-famous collection of art from the Middle Ages through the Baroque period. Among its treasures are works by Pieter Brueghel the Younger, Hans and Lucas Cranach, the *Admont Madonna* wood carving from 1400, and a medieval altarpiece depicting the murder of Thomas à Becket. At the Archaelogy Museum, the holdings include a remarkable collection of Styrian archaeological finds, including the small and rather strange Strettweg ritual chariot from the 7th century BC. Stop by the outdoor café for a break, or wander through the park to relax in between visits to the many sights. ☒ *Eggenberger Allee 90, Graz* ☎ *0316/8017–9532* ⊕ *www.museum-joanneum.at* ☑ *€11:50; 24-hour ticket valid for all museums of Landesmuseum €13* ⊙ *State Rooms closed Nov.–Mar., other museums closed Mon. and Tues.*

FAMILY
Fodor'sChoice
★

**Schloßberg** (*Palace Mountain*). The view from the summit of Graz's mid-town mountain takes in the city and much of central Styria. A zigzag-ging stone staircase, beginning at Schlossbergplatz, leads to the top. It's 260 steps, so you may prefer to use the Schlossbergbahn funicular rail-way (Kaiser-Franz-Josef-Kai 38; €2.20) or an elevator carved through the rock face (Schlossbergplatz; €1.40). The Schlossberg, a Romanesque castle with Gothic elements turned Renaissance fortress, constitutes only a portion of this site, and is one of the few places not conquered by Napoléon. A few steps east of the funicular station at the top is the Glockenturm (bell tower), an octagonal structure from 1588 containing Styria's largest bell, the 4-ton Liesl, in the upper belfry. Its 101 chimes resound three times daily, at 7 am, noon, and 7 pm. The Open-Air The-ater, to the north, is built into the old casements of the castle and has a retractable roof. Both opera and theater performances are presented here in summer. There are ruins of the older structure, and many a modern café here, too. ☒ *Am Schlossberg 1, Graz* ☎ *0316/887–405.*

**Uhrturm** (*Clock Tower*). This landmark, dating back to the 16th cen-tury, is the symbol of Graz. The clock has four giant faces that might at first confuse you—until you realize that the *big* hands tell the hour and the *small* hands the minutes. The clock was designed with only hour hands—smaller minute hands were added later. Nearby, notice a statue of a watchdog—he is said to represent a dog who once saved the daughter of an emperor from being kidnapped by a slighted lover. ☒ *Schlossberg 3, Graz.*

## WORTH NOTING

**Landhaushof.** The main wing of the Styrian provincial parliament house was built starting in 1557 by Italian Domenico dell'Allio in the Renaissance Lombard style. Through an archway off Herrengasse, visitors can glimpse a magnificently proportioned three-floor courtyard, surrounding a bronze fountain and copper gargoyles dating from the 16th century. The striking Styrian coat of arms, which depicts a white panther on a green background, is painted as a mural on a nearby wall. In the summer you may discover a small market with sausages, beer, and live music; at Advent, it hosts a Nativity scene made of ice. ✉ *Herrengasse 16, Graz.*

**Palais Khuenburg** (*GrazMuseum*). This was the birthplace in 1863 of Archduke Franz Ferdinand, heir to the throne of the Austro-Hungarian Empire. His assassination at Sarajevo in 1914 led directly to the outbreak of World War I. The palace is now home to the GrazMuseum, whose exhibits trace the history of Graz and includes an old-time pharmacy. ✉ *Sackstrasse 18, Graz* ☎ *0316/872–7600* 🌐 *www.grazmuseum.at* 🎟 *€5* 🕒 *Closed Tues.*

**Stadtpfarrkirche.** You can easily see the city parish church spire from Graz's main street. The church itself was built early in the 16th century from a 15th-century chapel, and later received Baroque touches and an 18th-century spire. Tintoretto's *Assumption of the Virgin* decorates the altar. Badly damaged in World War II, the stained-glass windows were replaced in 1953 by a Salzburg artist, Albert Birkle, who included portrayals of Hitler and Mussolini as malicious spectators at the scourging of Christ (left window behind the high altar, fourth panel from the bottom on the right). ✉ *Herrengasse 23, Graz* ☎ *0316/829–684.*

## WHERE TO EAT

$$$$ INTERNATIONAL

🍴 **Aiola Upstairs.** A tiny bar, café, and restaurant, Aiola is located at the top of the Schlossberg mountain fortress. The restaurant serves traditional Austrian breakfasts with a selection of bread, cheese, and meat, and dinner entrées such as porcini mushroom risotto and the Aiola-style grill plate, which includes beef, lamb, and cheese. **Known for:** gorgeous views; unique architecture; nice wine list. [$] *Average main: €27* ✉ *Schlossberg 2, Graz* ☎ *0316/818797* 🌐 *upstairs.aiola.at.*

$$ AUSTRIAN

🍴 **Altsteirische Schmankerlstub'n.** A good choice to experience authentic Styrian cooking, this old Graz institution is reminiscent of a cozy country cottage. Salads are a must here, prepared with the Styrian specialty, Kürbiskernöl, or pumpkinseed oil. **Known for:** cozy decor (and seating arrangements); local Styrian cuisine; great vegetarian menu. [$] *Average main: €14* ✉ *Sackstrasse 10, Graz* ☎ *0316/833211* 🌐 *www.schmankerlstube.at* 💳 *No credit cards.*

$ CAFÉ

🍴 **Cafe Schwalbennest.** A tiny old house turned coffee shop in the center of the city, Cafe Schwalbennest serves traditional Austrian cakes such as homemade sweet poppy seed and cheese-curd tort. It's also a great breakfast spot with regionally sourced cheese and meat, and has a nice Austrian wine list for later in the day. **Known for:** great breakfasts; homemade cakes; small space that fills up quickly. [$] *Average main: €4* ✉ *Franziskanerplatz 1, Graz* ☎ *0316/818892* 🌐 *cafe-schwalbennest.stadtausstellung.at/home* 💳 *No credit cards* 🕒 *Closed Mon.*

$$ AUSTRIAN Fodor's Choice ★ 🍴 **Die Herzl Weinstube.** Located in Mehlplatz, one of the oldest squares of Graz, Die Herzl restaurant opened in 1934 and is known for both its tavernlike atmosphere and its traditional Austrian cuisine. Seasonal entrées are mixed with typical Austrian dishes such as *Gemischter Salat* (a mix of cucumber, potato, and sauerkraut on lettuce) or the *Gebackener* Camembert (fried Camembert cheese served with tart berry chutney). **Known for:** traditional Austrian cooking; great local wine list; affordable lunch specials. [$] *Average main: €13* ✉ *Prokopigasse 12/Mehlplatz, Graz* ☎ *0316/824 300* 🌐 *www.dieherzl.at.*

$ AUSTRIAN 🍴 **Gasthaus zur Alten Press.** Warm wooden parlors, romantic corners, and authentic Austrian cuisine define this rustic spot. Products are mainly local and seasonal, in keeping with the restaurant's slow-food philosophy. **Known for:** rustic and busy atmosphere; local and seasonal products; pumpkin and pumpkin-seed dishes. [$] *Average main: €11* ✉ *Griesgasse 8, Graz* ☎ *0316/719–770* 🌐 *www.zuraltenpress.at* 🕒 *Closed Sun. No dinner Sat.*

$$$$ AUSTRIAN 🍴 **Landhauskeller.** The magnificent centuries-old Landhaus complex also includes this popular traditional restaurant. Styrian beef is the main event here, but there are lots of other tasty dishes to choose from. **Known for:** beautiful courtyard seating; popular cocktail menu; Styrian beef dishes. [$] *Average main: €23* ✉ *Schmiedgasse 9, Graz* ☎ *0316/830276* 🌐 *www.landhauskeller.at* 🕒 *Closed Sun.*

$ VEGETARIAN FAMILY 🍴 **Mangolds.** This popular vegetarian restaurant offers tasty dishes served cafeteria-style and sold by weight. You can choose between at least five main courses plus salads and desserts (including whole-grain cakes.) Mangolds also serves freshly squeezed juice, wine, and coffee—the *Eiskaffee mit Schlag* (iced coffee with vanilla ice cream and whipped cream) is addictive. **Known for:** vegetarian buffet; fresh juices; reasonable prices. [$] *Average main: €8* ✉ *Griesgasse 11, Graz* ☎ *0316/718002* 🌐 *www.mangolds.com* 💳 *No credit cards* 🕒 *Closed Sun.*

$$$$ ITALIAN 🍴 **Peppino im Hofkeller.** With its vaulted ceiling and dark, gleaming wainscoting, Peppino im Hofkeller offers the most innovative Italian cuisine in the city. The chef serves up a classic Italian menu that includes homemade pasta dressed with seasonal specialties and wonderfully fresh seafood. **Known for:** excellent Italian cooking; Sardinian wine list; good fish selection. [$] *Average main: €25* ✉ *Hofgasse 8, Graz* ☎ *0316/697511* 🌐 *www.peppino-hofkeller.at* 🕒 *Closed Sun.*

$$$ INTERNATIONAL 🍴 **Speisesaal.** The Hotel Wiesler's stylish dining room has become a popular meeting place for guests and nonguests alike. International comfort food from the charcoal grill is served in the shabby-chic space, which combines secondhand furniture with modern art. **Known for:** hip atmosphere; food from the grill; popular Sunday brunch. [$] *Average main: €20* ✉ *Grieskai 4–8, Graz* ☎ *0316/70660* 🌐 *www.speisesaal.at.*

## WHERE TO STAY

$$$ HOTEL [H] **Augarten Art Hotel.** A glass-and-chrome structure in the middle of a residential neighborhood, the Augarten has more than 400 pieces of art, from the 1960s to works by present-day Austrians, spread through every room and common area. **Pros:** extensive art collection; 24-hour pool and fitness area; luxurious guest rooms. **Cons:** a bit cold feeling; not in the city center; no on-site restaurant. [$] *Rooms from: €175* ✉ *Schönaugasse 53, Graz* ☎ *0316/20800* 🌐 *www.augartenhotel.at* 🛏 *57 rooms* 🍴 *Breakfast.*

$$$ HOTEL Fodor's Choice ★ [H] **Erzherzog Johann.** Travelers who prefer a traditionally elegant city hotel will be happy with this historic establishment in a 16th-century building. **Pros:** central location; historical rooms; excellent café. **Cons:** rooms facing main street can be a bit noisy; limited parking in front of hotel; the decor may not be to everyone's tastes. [$] *Rooms from: €149* ✉ *Sackstrasse 3–5, Graz* ☎ *0316/811616* 🌐 *www.erzherzog-johann.com* 🛏 *57 rooms.*

$$ HOTEL [H] **Hotel Daniel.** Located next door the train station, Hotel Daniel's young, fresh concept makes it the go-to budget option in Graz. **Pros:** great design; good value; close to train station. **Cons:** 10-minute walk from the city center; the outside looks a little run-down; no separate space for the shower. [$] *Rooms from: €110* ✉ *Europaplatz 1, Graz* ☎ *0316/711–0800* 🌐 *www.hoteldaniel.com* 🛏 *107 rooms.*

$$$ HOTEL [H] **Hotel Gollner.** A popular hotel since the mid-1800s and family-owned for four generations, the friendly Gollner is close to the Jakominiplatz and about a 10-minute walk from the Old City. **Pros:** family-owned property with personalized service; some rooms face the backyard; bar is open 24/7. **Cons:** breakfast not included; not in the center of town; some rooms are dated. [$] *Rooms from: €150* ✉ *Schlögelgasse 14, Graz* ☎ *0316/822521* 🌐 *www.hotelgollner.at* 🛏 *55 rooms.*

$$ HOTEL [H] **Hotel Mariahilf.** A comfortable hotel in the center of things, the Mariahilf is across the river from the Old City close to the Kunsthaus. **Pros:** quiet central location; modern rooms; good price. **Cons:** no restaurant; some noise from church bells; rooms could use some renovating. [$] *Rooms from: €110* ✉ *Mariahilferstrasse 9, Graz* ☎ *0316/713163* 🌐 *www.hotelmariahilf.at* 🛏 *45 rooms* 🍴 *Breakfast.*

$$ HOTEL [H] **Hotel Pfeifer Kirchenwirt.** An inn has stood on this lofty knoll since 1695, initially providing beds to those who made the pilgrimage to Mariatrost, the magnificent Rococo, daffodil-yellow basilica next door. **Pros:** family-run; quiet surroundings; good restaurant. **Cons:** no elevator; some rooms are outdated; a bit far from the center of town. [$] *Rooms from: €115* ✉ *Kirchplatz 9, Graz* ☎ *0316/391112–0* 🌐 *www.kirchenwirtgraz.com* 🛏 *31 rooms* 🍴 *Breakfast.*

$$ HOTEL [H] **Hotel Wiesler.** Five guesthouses were converted into Hotel Wiesler in 1870 where retro touches delight: Polaroid cameras are available for guests to use throughout their stay; vinyl records are available to rent; and a barbershop caters to male guests while serving up black Turkish coffee. **Pros:** variety of prices for every budget; spacious guest rooms with high ceilings; modern, arty feel. **Cons:** the downstairs restaurant can be too hip at night for everyone's taste; rooms facing the side street can be a bit dark; showers are integrated into the rooms. [$] *Rooms from: €135* ✉ *Grieskai 4–8, Graz* ☎ *0316/70660* 🌐 *www.hotelwiesler.com* 🛏 *97 rooms* 🍴 *No meals.*

$$$ HOTEL Fodor's Choice ★ [H] **Hotel zum Dom.** Occupying the 18th-century Palais Inzaghi, the Dom has whimsically decorated rooms and works to combine the old history of Graz with the new modern style. **Pros:** great location; luxury in a historic building; friendly staff. **Cons:** some baths on the small side; noise from the street on weekends; breakfast not included. [$] *Rooms from: €154* ✉ *Bürgergasse 14, Graz* ☎ *0316/824800* 🌐 *www.domhotel.co.at* 🛏 *29 rooms.*

$$$ HOTEL [H] **Schlossberg Hotel.** Contemporary art meets antiquity and modern convenience at this town house tucked up against the foot of the Schlossberg, which was turned into a hotel in 1982. **Pros:** tastefully furnished rooms; pool with a view; great art. **Cons:** longer walk to city center; expensive breakfast if not included in the rate; some rooms don't have much natural light. [$] *Rooms from: €170* ✉ *Kaiser-Franz-Josef-Kai 30, Graz* ☎ *0316/80700* 🌐 *www.schlossberg-hotel.at* 🛏 *62 rooms.*

## NIGHTLIFE

Graz's after-hours scene is centered on the area around Prokopigasse, Bürgergasse, Mehlplatz, and Glockenspielplatz. Here you'll find activity until the early-morning hours.

**Casino Graz.** At the corner of Landhausgasse and Schmiedgasse in the Old City, Casino Graz offers American roulette, blackjack, poker tables, and more than 100 slot machines. Entry is free, but you are required to buy chips for €30. You must bring a passport and be at least 18. Men are expected to wear a jacket and tie, though it is not required. ✉ *Landhausgasse 10, Graz* ☎ *316/832578* 🌐 *www.casinos.at.*

## PERFORMING ARTS

Graz, a major university town, has a lively, avant-garde theater scene known especially for its experimental productions. Its **Schauspielhaus,** built in 1825, is the leading playhouse, and there are smaller theaters scattered around town. It is also known for its opera, concerts, and jazz. Contact the tourist office for current offerings.

**Opernhaus Graz.** A 19th-century opera house, the Opernhaus Graz, with its resplendent Rococo interior, is a showcase for young talent and experimental productions as well as more conventional works; it stages three to five performances a week during its late September to June season. Tickets are generally available until shortly before the performances; prices start at €11. Call for information or stop by the office. ✉ *Kaiser-Josef-Platz 10, Graz* ☎ *0316/8000* 🌐 *www.oper-graz.com.*

**Springfestival Graz.** This five-day festival during mid-June, the largest of its kind in the country, serves as a showcase for the Austrian and European electronic music and art scene. Concerts take place across Graz in venues ranging from clubs and beaches to empty plots of land. Tickets can be purchased online in advance or during festival week at the various spots where performances take place. ✉ *Graz* 🌐 *www.springfestival.at.*

**Styrian Autumn Festival.** The annual Steirischer Herbst, or Styrian Autumn Festival, a celebration of the avant-garde with the occasional shocking piece in experimental theater, music, opera, dance, jazz, film, video, and other performing arts, is held in Graz from the end of September to the middle of October. ⊠ *Graz* ⊕ *www.steirischerherbst.at.*

**Styriarte.** The Styriarte festival (late June to mid-July) gathers outstanding classical musicians from around the world. Performances take place throughout the city including the Helmut-List-Halle and Schloss Eggenberg. The ticket office is located in the center of the city. ⊠ *Sackstrasse 17, Graz* ☎ *0316/825000* ⊕ *www.styriarte.com.*

## SHOPPING

Graz is a smart, stylish city with great shopping. In the streets surrounding Hauptplatz and Herrengasse you'll find top designer boutiques and specialty shops. Be on the lookout for traditional skirts, trousers, jackets, and coats of gray and dark-green loden wool; dirndls; modern sportswear and ski equipment; handwoven garments; and objects of wrought iron. Take time to wander around the cobblestone streets of the Altstadt near the cathedral, where you'll come across several little specialty shops selling exotic coffees, wine, and cheese.

**Käse-Nussbaumer.** For a wide selection of wine and cheese, as well as hard-to-find Styrian cheese varieties, go to Käse-Nussbaumer, near the Hauptplatz. ⊠ *Paradeisgasse 1, Graz* ⊕ *www.delikatessen-nussbaumer.at.*

**Moser.** This three-story bookstore is at the end of Graz's main street, Herrengasse, near Jakominiplatz. Moser bustles with people buying postcards, CDs, children's books in multiple languages, and quirky gifts (though not from local dealers). There is a large selection of English fiction and nonfiction on the ground floor, as well as cookbooks with Austrian cuisine written in English. There is a basic no-frills coffee shop on the top floor, where shoppers can have a snack and peruse books before purchasing them. ⊠ *Am Eisernen Tor 1, Graz* ☎ *0316/83–01–10.*

Fodor's Choice   **Steirisches Heimatwerk.** The Heimatwerk shop is associated with the local
★   folklore museum and stocks a good variety of regional crafts and luxuries. ⊠ *Sporgasse 23, Graz* ⊕ *www.heimatwerk.steiermark.at/.*

# INNSBRUCK, TYROL, AND VORARLBERG

Updated by
Rob Freeman

The provinces of Tyrol and Vorarlberg make up the western tip of Austria with Innsbruck, the capital of Tyrol, as the natural, historic, and economic center. These two provinces are so different from the rest of Austria that you might think you've crossed a border, and in a way you have. The frontier between Tyrol and the province of Salzburgerland to the east is defined by mountains; four passes routed over them are what make access possible. To the west of Tyrol lies Vorarlberg—"before the Arlberg"—the mountain range straddling the border between the two provinces.

In winter you'll find unrivaled skiing and tobogganing. The famous Arlberg ski resorts are cult destinations for skiers from all over the world. In summer, Bregenz, the historic state capital of Vorarlberg, becomes the "Summer Capital of Austria" when the Bregenz Festival opens with a performance by the Viennese Symphonic Orchestra. Thousands flock to see operas and musicals by Giuseppe Verdi or Leonard Bernstein—to name just two—which take place on a huge floating stage with Lake Constance (the Bodensee) and the Swiss mountains as a backdrop.

Like most mountain peoples, Tyroleans are proud and independent—so much so that for many centuries the natives of one narrow valley fastness had little communication with their "foreign" neighbors in the next valley. Similarly, until a tunnel was cut through the Arlberg range, Vorarlberg was effectively cut off from the rest of the country in winter. The province has much in common with its neighbor, Switzerland. Both peoples are descended from the same ancient Germanic tribes that flourished in the 3rd century BC.

# ORIENTATION AND PLANNING

## GETTING ORIENTED

Innsbruck makes a good starting point for exploring western Austria. It's a city that preserves the charm of ancient times and has lots to offer: culture, stellar restaurants, and trendy nightclubs. But Tyrol's gorgeous geography precludes the convenient loop tour. You must go into the valleys to discover the charming villages and hotels, and a certain amount of backtracking is necessary. It will allow you to discover a cross section of Tyrol's highlights: the old and the new, glossy resorts, medieval castles, and, always, that extraordinary scenery in these breathtaking valleys. On the western side of the Arlberg range, you have the wide-open spaces of Vorarlberg with Bregenz, a city the Romans built up with

## TOP REASONS TO GO

**The Ötz Valley:** Outdoors enthusiasts love hiking through this region because of rich green pastures in summer and glittering expanses of white in winter.

**Highly rated skiing areas:** Known around the world for its extensive and in many cases fashionable ski villages, Tyrol often attracts celebrities and global glitterati to its resorts to experience the high-altitude good life, along with dedicated skiers keen to take on its challenging slopes.

**Tyrolean Stuben:** These warm and cozy wooden parlors, often found today in hotels and restaurants, are traditionally part of old farmhouses in Tyrol.

**Music in Bregenz:** With the sun setting over Lake Constance and the Vienna Philharmonic Orchestra striking up the overture of *West Side Story* on the world's biggest floating stage, this is an unparalleled place to see an opera or a musical.

**See four countries at once:** Take the cable car up Pfänder, the mountain behind Bregenz; the views are incredible: Swiss mountains on your left, German rolling hills on your right, Liechtenstein to your left in the Rhine valley, Austria below your feet, and the glittering expanse of Lake Constance stretching 64 km (40 miles) into the hazy distance.

**Experience top hospitality in a top village:** The Gasthof Post is a bit like Lech itself—full of charming understatement. Teatime in overstuffed armchairs for all houseguests will keep you going until it's time for a delicious dinner. You'll never want to leave.

**12**

a harbor for warships, which today is used for cruise ships zigzagging across Lake Constance to Switzerland and Germany.

Tyrol is famous for the beauty of its valleys, radiating from Innsbruck at the center of it all. To the northeast you find one of Austria's most famous folk-music regions. On the road to Kitzbühel, the sunny valley has plenty of snow in winter and golf in summer. Upscale hotels and a renowned ski area make Kitzbühel the region's number one year-round vacation destination. To the west, in the very heart of Tyrol, the villages of Telfs and Imst are known for tradition and culture. Then there is the Ötz Valley, with its long trekking routes and outdoor facilities. The western part of Tyrol is a winter heaven: steep and challenging slopes along with well-trained instructors made St. Anton famous, whereas high in the mountains, in a valley toward the south, is the renowned ski resort of Ischgl and, a few miles further up the valley, the more homely ski village of Galtür.

And over the Arlberg range (or through it, via road and rail tunnels), you have the province of Vorarlberg, with the mountain villages of Lech and Zürs as havens for highly rated skiing and high-end, expensive hotels. On the other end of the spectrum is the Montafon region, a winter and summer destination for the more cost-conscious—especially families.

**Innsbruck.** A picturesque and lively university city, Innsbruck is set against a backdrop of soaring mountain peaks and has twice been host of the Winter Olympic Games.

**Tyrol.** This Alpine province, a trade hub since Roman times, is full of ancient towns and villages of arresting charm; its numerous side valleys through landscapes of majestic beauty are especially notable.

**Vorarlberg.** Austria's westernmost province is completely mountainous, and borders Germany, Switzerland, and Liechtenstein; it has the nickname of Landle, meaning "tiny province."

# PLANNING

## WHEN TO GO

The physical geography of Tyrol and Vorarlberg makes them perfect for enjoying outdoor life year-round. Ski-crazy travelers descend on the resorts during the winter months; in summer, when the mountains are awash with wildflowers, campers' tents spring up like mushrooms in the valleys as hikers, spelunkers, mountain bikers, and climbers take advantage of the soaring peaks. High season for summer activities is July through August, while the skiing season begins in many resorts in late November or early December and can go on until early May in the higher ski areas. If you're in Vorarlberg in summer be sure to stop in Bregenz, when the city comes to life with the Bregenzer Festspiele (Bregenz Music Festival). Boat excursions to Switzerland and Germany are another must. You can even rent a boat and go out on the lake to do some fishing.

## FESTIVALS

There is more here than just the Bregenz Festival. The annual Tyrolean calendar is packed with special events; a particularly charming festival is the Almabtrieb, when herds of cows come down from the high pastures in the fall, garlanded with flowers and surrounded by bands playing music. In winter, *fasching* is when young men parade through towns and villages wearing wooden masks as part of a ritual to scare away evil spirits, while the famous Hahnenkamm World Cup downhill ski race is held in Kitzbühel. There's also the Gauder Fest at Zell am Ziller, a traditional-costume festival, during the first weekend in May; the castle concerts and music and dance festivals in summer, primarily in Kufstein and Innsbruck; and the many village harvest festivals in the fall throughout Tyrol.

## GETTING HERE AND AROUND
### AIR TRAVEL

All of Tyrol uses the Innsbruck Flughafen, the airport 3 km (2 miles) west of the capital, which is served by a number of international airlines including Austrian Airlines, British Airways, EasyJet, and Lufthansa. But for intercontinental flights the main gateway airports for Tyrol and Vorarlberg are Munich in Germany and Zurich in Switzerland.

Vorarlberg uses the intercontinental airport of Zurich, 120 km (75 miles) from Bregenz. Directly from the airport several Euro City express trains a day make the journey to Bregenz in 1½ hours on their way to Munich.

There are also trains, sometimes direct or with only one change, from the Zurich airport to many stations in Tyrol. Munich is convenient for the eastern part of Tyrol, with rail and coach links available.

**Airport Information** Innsbruck Flughafen Airport (*INN*). ☎ *0512/22525 flight information* ⊕ *www.innsbruck-airport.com.*

**12**

### AIRPORT TRANSFERS

From Innsbruck Flughafen, take the F Line bus into Innsbruck to the main train station (about 20 minutes) or to the city center. Get your ticket (€2.30) from the machine by the bus stop, right outside the arrivals door, or from the bus driver. Taxis into Innsbruck should take no more than 10 minutes, and the fare is about €15.

From Switzerland to Vorarlberg in winter, there are buses from Zurich airport Friday, Saturday, and Sunday several times each day for Zürs and Lech. You can book the transfer through the airline Swiss.

### BUS TRAVEL

Bus lines operated by the railroads and post office connect all the towns and villages not served by train, using vehicles with snow chains when necessary in winter. Even so, some of the highest roads can become impassable for a few hours. And except in the most remote areas, buses are frequent enough that you can get around.

In Innsbruck the deluxe ski buses that depart from the Landestheater on Rennweg, across from the Hofburg, are the most convenient way to reach the six major ski areas outside the city. An Innsbruck Card (€55 for 72 hours) covers most routes on the transport system from the city and surrounding villages to the ski areas, as well as entrance fees to many sights, attractions, cable cars, and ski lifts. Many hotels even provide shuttle service to the ski bus stop.

**Bus Information** Postbus AG. ☎ *01/71101* ⊕ *www.postbus.at.*

### CAR TRAVEL

Driving is the best way to see Tyrol and Vorarlberg, since it allows you to wander off the main routes at your leisure. The autobahns are fastest, but for scenery you're best off on the byways, as you can stop and admire the view. But be aware that roads can be treacherous in winter. Cars are not allowed on some mountain roads in the Arlberg without chains, which you can rent from many service stations. If you are renting a car in the winter specify that you want winter tires. These will be sufficient to deal with fairly heavy snow on the road, although you will often be required to also carry snow chains. Roads with particularly attractive scenery are marked on highway maps with a parallel green line. To drive on Austria's autobahn, you will need a *vignette*, or sticker, available at almost all service stations. A 10-day sticker costs €8.90; for 60 days it's €25.90.

### FERRY TRAVEL

From May to October, passenger ships of the Austrian railroad's Bodensee White Fleet connect Bregenz with Lindau, Friedrichshafen, Meersburg, and Konstanz on the German side of the lake. The Eurailpass and Austrian rail passes are valid on these ships. You must bring your passport.

**Boat Information** Bodensee White Fleet. ☎ *05574/42868* ⊕ *www.vorarlberg-lines.at.*

## TRAIN TRAVEL

Direct trains from Munich serve Innsbruck. From here on, the line follows the Inn Valley to Landeck and St. Anton, where it plunges into an 11-km (7-mile) tunnel under the Arlberg range, emerging at Langen in Vorarlberg, continuing to Bregenz, where you can change to the EuroCityExpress to Zurich (you can also change at Innsbruck for a more direct route to Zurich via Feldkirch) or go back to Munich via Bavaria. A line from Innsbruck to the south goes over the dramatic Brenner Pass (4,465 feet) into Italy.

Some of the most fascinating and memorable side trips can be made by rail. For example, two narrow-gauge lines steam out of Jenbach, one up to the Achensee, the other down to Mayrhofen in the Zillertal. From Innsbruck, the narrow-gauge Stubaitalbahn—which starts off as a regular city tram and morphs into a train as it ascends into the mountains—runs south to Telfes and Fulpmes.

**Train Information Österreichisches Bundesbahn.** ☎ 05/1717 *information and reservations* ⊕ *www.oebb.at.*

## PUBLIC TRANSPORT TRAVEL

As in other areas of Austria, having a car makes travel easy, but you can also use the area trains and buses to get around. In Bregenz a Bodensee-Pass includes the Swiss and German trains, as well as the Austrian lake steamers, all at half price, plus area trains, buses, and cable-car lifts; this pass comes in 7- and 15-day variations. Similar passes exist in Tyrol.

## VISITOR INFORMATION

The headquarters for tourist information about Vorarlberg is in Bregenz. There is a branch office in Vienna. Other regional tourist offices (called either *Tourismusbüro, Verkehrsverein,* or *Fremdenverkehrsamt*) are found throughout the province using the contact information listed under particular towns. They are easily spotted—just look for the large "i" (for information) sign.

**Tourist Information Austrian National Tourist Board.** ☎ 212/944–6880 *in the U.S.,* 00800/400–200–00 ⊕ *www.austria.info.* **Tourist Information Vorarlberg.** ✉ *Postfach 99, Poststrasse 11, Dornbirn* ☎ 05572/377033-0 ⊕ *www. vorarlberg.at* ✉ *Tuchlauben 18, Vienna* ☎ 01/535–7890.

## RESTAURANTS

The gastronomic scene of Austria's westernmost provinces is as varied as its landscape: first-rate gourmet restaurants, traditional inns, rustic local taverns, as well as international chains and ethnic cuisine are all part of the mix. In small towns throughout the region restaurants are often the dining rooms of country inns, and there are plenty of these. Austria used to have a reputation for substantial but stereotypical dishes of meat, dumplings, and sauerkraut, but things have changed considerably. Gourmet meals are available at many wonderful restaurants, often at much more reasonable prices than is typical of Europe's high-class dining scene. That said, in many villages you'll find inns catering largely to local farm workers, where the old favorites are still the order of the day—prepare to be filled rather than thrilled.

# MOUNTAIN SPORTS

## HIKING AND CLIMBING

Tyrol has an abundance of more than 35,000 miles of well-maintained mountain paths that thread the country. Hiking is one of the best ways to experience the truly awesome Alpine scenery, whether you just want to take a leisurely stroll around one of the crystalline lakes mirroring the towering mountains or trek your way to the top of one of the mighty peaks. Mountain climbing is a highly organized activity in Tyrol, a province that contains some of the greatest challenges to devotees of the sport. The instructors at the Alpine School Innsbruck are the best people to contact if you want to make arrangements for a mountain-climbing holiday.

## SKIING

Downhill was practically invented in **Tyrol.** Legendary skiing master Hannes Schneider took the Norwegian art of cross-country skiing and adapted it to downhill running. No matter where your trip takes you, world-class—and often gut-scrambling—skiing is available, from the glamour of Kitzbühel in the east to the imposing peaks of St. Anton am Arlberg in the west.

Close to the Arlberg Pass is **St. Anton,** which proudly claims to have one of the finest ski schools in the world. Although it has some nice piste skiing suitable for intermediates, St. Anton is known for being a challenge in the form of long, tough, and steep mogul runs and spectacular off-piste. The village is a magnet for some of the best skiers from all over the world. It was in the Arlberg in the 1920s that Hannes Schneider started the school that was to become the model for all others.

A short bus ride to the top of the pass brings you to **St. Christoph,** at 5,800 feet. If you care to mingle with royalty and celebrities on the lifts, the upscale ski villages of **Zürs** and **Lech,** on the Vorarlberg side of the pass, are the places for you.

Farther along is the Ötz Valley. From the Ötztal station you can go by bus to **Sölden,** a resort at 4,500 feet that has become almost as well-known for its party scene as for its superb skiing. The up-and-comer of Austrian ski resorts is **Ischgl,** in the Paznaun Valley bordering Switzerland, where good snow and a long ski season are assured on high-altitude slopes with a top station at 9,422 feet. Chic **Kitzbühel** is perhaps most famous for its "Ski Safari," a far-ranging system of ski lifts and trails, some floodlit at night, that allows you to ski for weeks without retracing your steps. **Alpbach** is one of the most popular resorts for families, with many not-too-challenging slopes and a reputation for being one of the most beautiful villages in Austria, full of heavily timbered traditional chalets surrounded by thickly wooded runs. An area east of Innsbruck is collectively known as the **Ski Welt** (Ski World), where the villages of **Soll, Ellmau, Scheffau, Itter, Going, Brixen im Thale, Westendorf, Hopfgarten,** and **Kelchsau** form Austria's largest linked skiing area. It's dotted with cozy, welcoming mountain huts, many of which are family-friendly. Innsbruck itself is at the center of a group of resorts easily reached by bus from the city; the best time to ski Innsbruck's slopes is January through March.

**12**

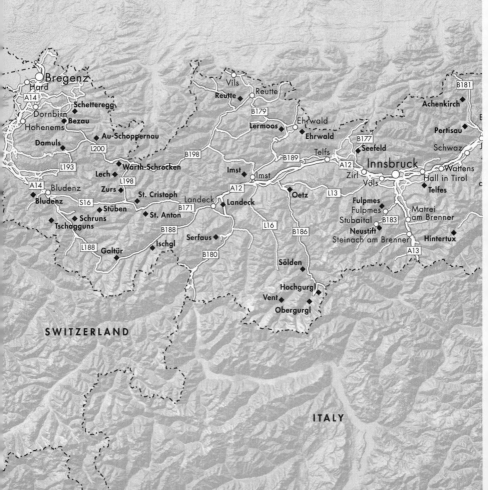

# Ski Areas

GERMANY

SWITZERLAND

ITALY

Bregenz
Hard
A14
Dornbirn
Hohenems
Schetteregg
Bezau
Damuls
Au-Schoppernau
L200
L193
Warth-Schrocken
B198
Lech
L198
Zurs
A14
Bludenz
Bludenz
S16
Stüben
St. Cristoph
Schruns
Tschagguns
St. Anton
Landeck
B171
Landeck
B188
Galtür
L188
Ischgl
Serfaus
B180

Vils
Reutte
Reutte
B179
Lermoos
Ehrwald
Ehrwald
B189
Telfs
Imst
Imst
A12
Oetz
L13
L16
B186
Sölden
Hochgurgl
Vent
Obergurgl

B181
Achenkirch
Pertisau
B177
Seefeld
Schwaz
Innsbruck
Zirl
Völs
Wattens
Hall in Tirol
Telfes
Fulpmes
Fulpmes
Matrei
am Brenner
Stubaital
B183
Neustift
Hintertux
Steinach am Brenner
A13

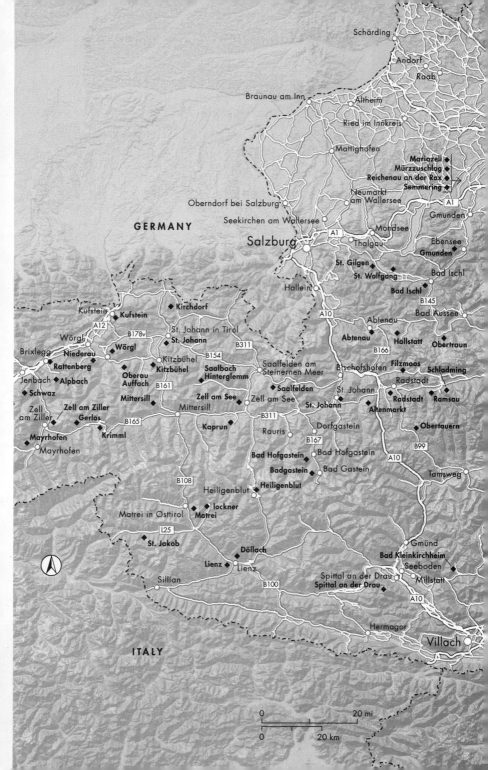

Most hotel restaurants will be closed in the off-season, usually November and April. In ski season breakfast is typically served early enough for you to hit the slopes in good time, and dinner is timed so that exhausted skiers can get an early night in preparation for the next day.

Restaurants range from grand-hotel dining salons to little *Wirtshäuser,* rustic restaurants where you can enjoy hearty local specialties such as *Tyroler Gröstl* (a skillet dish made of ham or pork, potatoes, and onions, with caraway seeds, paprika, and parsley), *Knödel* (dumpling) soup, or *Schweinsbraten* (roast pork with sauerkraut), while sitting on highly polished (and rather hard) wooden seats. Don't forget to enjoy some of the fine Innsbruck coffeehouses, famous for their scrumptious cakes and cappuccino. *Restaurant reviews have been shortened. For full information, visit Fodors.com.*

## HOTELS

In Innsbruck travelers do not seem to stay long, so there is a fast turnover and rooms are almost always available somewhere. Some travelers opt to set up their base not in town but *overlooking* it, on the Hungerburg Plateau to the north perhaps, or in one of the nearby villages perched on the slopes to the south. In any case, the official **Innsbruck Reservation Center,** online at ⊕ *www.innsbruck.info* or ⊕ *www.ski-innsbruck.at,* offers a booking source for Innsbruck and the surrounding villages.

**Innsbruck Reservations Office.** If you arrive in Innsbruck without a hotel room, check with the Innsbruck Reservations Office. The downtown office, in the main tourist office in the Old City, is open weekdays 10–6 and Saturday 8–12:30. The main train station branch is open in summer daily and in winter Monday through Saturday 9–6. ⊠ *Burggraben 3, Innsbruck* 🕾 *0512/562–0000* ⊕ *www.innsbruck.info.*

Book in advance if you're traveling in the region, especially Vorarlberg, in the winter high season and in July and August. Room rates include taxes and service and, almost always, a breakfast buffet. In the resort towns dinner will be included. *Halb pension* (half-board), as plans that include breakfast and dinner are called, is usually the best deal. Hotel rates vary widely by season, the off-peak periods being March–May and September–November. Most hotels take credit cards. Note that at the most expensive hotels in the resort towns of Zürs/Lech, Kitzbühel, St. Anton, and Sölden, rooms can reach as high as €450 a night (or sometimes more). If you're out for savings, it's a good idea to find lodgings in small towns nearby rather than in the bigger towns or in the resorts themselves; local tourist offices can help you get situated, possibly even with accommodations in pensions (simple hotels) or *Bauernhöfe* (farmhouses). It's worth remembering that in Austria, cheap accommodations can still be of a very high standard, with large en suite rooms of sparkling cleanliness. Keep in mind that in hotel saunas and steam baths, nude people of both genders should be expected. Other patrons and management will often take great exception to guests who enter a sauna wearing a swimsuit. Children under certain ages are usually not admitted. *Hotel reviews have been shortened. For full information, visit Fodors.com.*

| WHAT IT COSTS IN EUROS | | | |
|---|---|---|---|
| **$** | **$$** | **$$$** | **$$$$** |
| RESTAURANTS under €12 | €12–€17 | €18–€22 | over €22 |
| HOTELS under €100 | €100–€200 | €201–€300 | over €300 |

Prices in the dining reviews are the average cost of a main course at dinner, or, if dinner is not served, at lunch. Prices in the hotel reviews are the lowest cost of a standard double room in high season.

**12**

# INNSBRUCK

*190 km (118 miles) southwest of Salzburg, 471 km (304 miles) southwest of Vienna, 146 km (91 miles) south of Munich.*

The capital of Tyrol is one of the most beautiful towns of its size anywhere in the world, owing much of its charm and fame to its unique location. To the north, the steep, sheer sides of the Alps rise, literally from the edge of the city, like a shimmering blue-and-white wall—an impressive backdrop for the mellowed green domes and red roofs of the Baroque town tucked below. To the south, the peaks of the Tuxer and Stubai ranges undulate in the hazy purple distance.

Squeezed by the mountains and sharing the valley with the Inn River (Innsbruck means "bridge over the Inn"), the city is compact and very easy to explore on foot. Reminders of three historic figures abound: the local hero Andreas Hofer, whose band of patriots challenged Napoléon in 1809; Emperor Maximilian I (1459–1519); and Empress Maria Theresa (1717–80), the latter two responsible for much of the city's architecture. Maximilian ruled the Holy Roman Empire from Innsbruck, and Maria Theresa, who was particularly fond of the city, spent a substantial amount of time here.

## GETTING HERE AND AROUND

Innsbruck Airport is only minutes from Innsbruck city center and is linked by frequent bus service.

Direct trains serve Innsbruck from Munich, Vienna, Rome, and Zurich, and all arrive at the train station, InnsbruckHauptbahnhof, at SüdTyrolerplatz. The station is outfitted with restaurants, cafés, a supermarket, and even a post office.

Innsbruck is connected by bus to other parts of Tyrol, and the bus terminal is beside the train station. In Innsbruck, most bus and streetcar routes begin or end at Maria-Theresien-Strasse, nearby Boznerplatz, or the main train station. One-way tickets cost €2.30 on the bus or streetcar, and you can transfer to another line with the same ticket as long as you continue in more or less the same direction in a single journey. You can get tickets from machines, or, at a slightly increased cost, from the driver.

If you're driving, remember that the Altstadt (Old City) is a pedestrian zone. Private cars are not allowed on many streets, and parking requires vouchers that you buy from blue coin-operated dispensers found around parking areas. Fees are usually €0.70 per half hour.

In Innsbruck taxis are not much faster than walking, particularly along the one-way streets and in the Old City. Basic fare is €6.20 for the first 1.3 km (0.8 mile) and €1.90 per km after that, so that most rides within the city limits will amount to between €8.10 and €12. Innsbruck Taxi 4 You is a good option if you want to call a cab. There are set fares for longer journeys (to a ski resort from the train station or airport, for example), but if you're prepared to haggle, these are negotiable, particularly on a quiet day when plenty of cabs are waiting in line. Let the driver know that you are aware of the alternatives available, such as train or bus.

Horse-drawn cabs, still a feature of Innsbruck life, can be hired at the stand in front of the Landestheater. Set the price before you head off; a half-hour ride will cost around €30.

Innsbruck's main tourist office is open daily 9–6. Tyrol's provincial tourist bureau, the Tyrol Werbung, is also in Innsbruck. The Österreichischer Alpenverein is the place to go for information on Alpine huts and mountaineering advice. It's open weekdays 8:30–6, Saturday 9–noon.

**Bus Information** Postbus AG. ☎ *0512/390–390–210* ⊕ *www.postbus.at.*

**Taxi Information** City Taxis. ☎ *0512/292915, 0800/201148* ⊕ *www. taxi-292915.at.* **Innsbruck Taxi 4 You.** ☎ *0676/607–8190* ⊕ *www.innsbrucktaxi4you.com.*

**Train Information** Innsbruck Hauptbahnhof. ✉ *Südtiroler Platz* ☎ *0512/930–000.* **ÖBB (Österreichische Bundesbahn).** ☎ *051/1717* ⊕ *www.oebb.at.*

## ESSENTIALS

**Visitor Information** Innsbruck Tourist Office. ✉ *Burggraben 3* ☎ *0512/5356–314* ⊕ *www.innsbruck.info.* **Österreichischer Alpenverein.** ✉ *Wilhelm-Greil-Strasse 15* ☎ *0512/59547* ⊕ *www.alpenverein.at.* **Tirol Werbung.** ✉ *Maria-Theresien-Strasse 55* ☎ *0512/7272* ⊕ *www.tirol.at or www.tirolwerbung.at.*

## TOURS

The red **Sightseer** bus, a service of the Innsbruck Tourist Office, is the best way to see the sights of Innsbruck without walking. It features a recorded commentary in several languages, including English. There are two routes, both beginning from Maria-Theresien-Strasse in the Old City, but you can catch the bus from any of the nine marked stops, and jump off and on the bus whenever you like. The ride is free with your Innsbruck Card, or buy your ticket from the driver or at the tourist office.

Guided walking tours of the Old City run by the tourist office start daily at 11 and 2 from the tourist office and highlight historic personalities and some offbeat features of Innsbruck.

## CLUB INNSBRUCK CARD

Pick up a free Club Innsbruck card at your hotel for no-charge use of ski buses and reduced-charge ski-lift passes. For big savings, buy the **all-inclusive Innsbruck Card,** which gives you free admission to all museums, mountain cable cars, the Alpenzoo, and Schloss Ambras, plus free bus and tram transportation, including bus service to nearby **Hall in Tirol.** The card includes unlimited ride-hopping onboard the big red Sightseer bus, which whisks you in air-conditioned comfort to all of the major sights, and even provides recorded commentary in English and five other languages. Cards are good for 24, 48, and 72 hours at €39, €48, and €55 respectively, with a 50% discount for children ages 6 to 15, and are available at the tourist office, on cable cars, and in larger museums.

**12**

## EXPLORING

### TOP ATTRACTIONS

**Domkirche zu St. Jakob.** Innsbruck's cathedral was built between 1717 and 1724 on the site of a 12th-century Romanesque church. Regarded as possibly the most important Baroque building in Tyrol, its main attraction is the painting of the Madonna by Lucas Cranach the Elder, dating from about 1530 and displayed above the high altar. The tomb of Archduke Maximilian III, Master of the Teutonic Knights, dating from 1620, can be seen in the north aisle. ⊠ *Domplatz 6* ☎ *0512/5839–02* 🖼 *Free.*

**Ferdinandeum** (*Tyrolean State Museum Ferdinandeum*). The Tyrolean state museum houses Austria's largest collection of Gothic art and 19th- and 20th-century paintings, including works by Rembrandt, Brueghel, and Klimt. There are also musical instruments and medieval armory, along with special exhibitions. Here you'll find the original coats of arms from the Goldenes Dachl balcony. Chamber music concerts are offered throughout the year. ⊠ *Museumstrasse 5* ☎ *0512/59489–180* ⊕ *www.tiroler-landesmuseen.at* 🖼 *€11 combined ticket with Zeughaus and Hofkirche* ۞ *Closed Mon.*

**NEED A BREAK**

✕ **Kunstpause.** Within the Ferdinandeum, Kunstpause, the "Art pause," offers breakfast, light meals, and a wine bar in elegant but relaxed surroundings. ⊠ *Museumstrasse 15* ☎ *512/572020* ⊕ *www.kunstpause.at.*

**Fodor's Choice** ★ **Goldenes Dachl** (*Golden Roof*). Any walking tour of Innsbruck should start at the Goldenes Dachl, which made famous the late-Gothic mansion whose balcony it covers. In fact, the roof is capped with 2,657 gilded copper tiles, and its refurbishment is said to have taken nearly 31 pounds of gold. The house was built in 1420 for Frederick IV as the residence of the Tyrolean sovereign. The legend persists that he added the golden look to counter rumors that he was penniless, but the balcony was, in fact, added by Emperor Maximilian I in the late 15th century as a "royal box" for watching various performances in the square below. He had the roof gilded to symbolize the wealth and power of Tyrol, which had recently undergone massive financial reform. The structure was altered and expanded at the beginning of the 18th century, and now only the loggia and the alcove are identifiable as original. Maximilian is pictured in the two central sculpted panels on the balcony. In the one on the left, he is with his first and second wives, Maria of Burgundy and Bianca Maria Sforza of Milan; on the right, he is pictured with an adviser and a court jester. The magnificent coats of arms representing Austria, Hungary, Burgundy, Milan, the Holy Roman Empire, Styria, Tyrol, and royal Germany are copies. You can see the originals (and up close, too) in the Ferdinandeum. The Golden Roof building houses the **Maximilianeum,** a small museum that headlines memorabilia and paintings from the life of Emperor Maximilian I. The short video presentation about Maximilian is worth a look. ⊠ *Herzog-Friedrich-Strasse 15* ☎ *0512/5873–8029* 🎫 *€4.80* ☾ *Closed Nov.*

**NEED A BREAK**

✕ **Kröll.** The small bakery and café, a few steps from the Goldenes Dachl, offers homemade strudel (sweet or savory fillings wrapped in a fine pastry) and Italian coffee specialties. The café opens at 6 am every day of the year, until 11 pm in the summer and 9 pm in the winter. ⊠ *Hofgasse 6* ☎ *0512/574347* ⊕ *www.strudel-cafe.at.*

**Imperial Palace** (*Hofburg*). One of Innsbruck's most historic attractions is the Hofburg, or Imperial Palace, which Maximilian I and Archduke Sigmund the Rich commissioned to be built in late-Gothic style in the 15th century. Center stage is the **Giant's Hall**—designated a marvel of the 18th century as soon as it was topped off with its magnificent trompe-l'oeil ceiling painted by Franz Anton Maulpertsch in 1775. The Rococo decoration and the portraits of Habsburg ancestors in the ornate white-and-gold great reception hall were added in the 18th century by the Empress Maria Theresa; look for the portrait of "Primal" (Primrose)—to use the childhood nickname of the empress's daughter, Marie Antoinette. On the first floor is the Alpine Club Museum, open daily 9 to 5. ⊠ *Rennweg 1* ☎ *0512/587186* ⊕ *www.hofburg-innsbruck.at* 🎫 *€9.*

**Stadtturm.** Down the street from the Goldenes Dachl, the City Tower was built in about 1460. It has a steep climb of 148 steps to the top, where the bulbous cupola was added in the 16th century, and from it there are magnificent views of the city and surrounding mountains. ⊠ *Herzog-Friedrich-Strasse 21* ☎ *0512/5615–00* 🎫 *€3.50.*

## WORTH NOTING

**Annasäule.** St. Anne's Column, erected in 1706, commemorates the withdrawal of Bavarian forces in the war of the Spanish Succession on St. Anne's Day (July 26) in 1703. It and the Triumphal Arch are the two most important sights on Maria-Theresien-Strasse. From here there is a classic view of Innsbruck's Altstadt (Old City), with the glorious Nordkette mountain range in the background. ⊠ *Maria-Theresien-Strasse.*

**Bergisel.** This ski-jumping stadium towers over Innsbruck with a gloriously modern, concrete-and-glass observation deck and restaurant designed by world-celebrated architect Zaha Hadid. It opened in 2003, replacing the old stadium that no longer complied with modern requirements for ski jumping and crowd safety. There's a café at the base area, and if you're lucky you can have a beer while watching ski

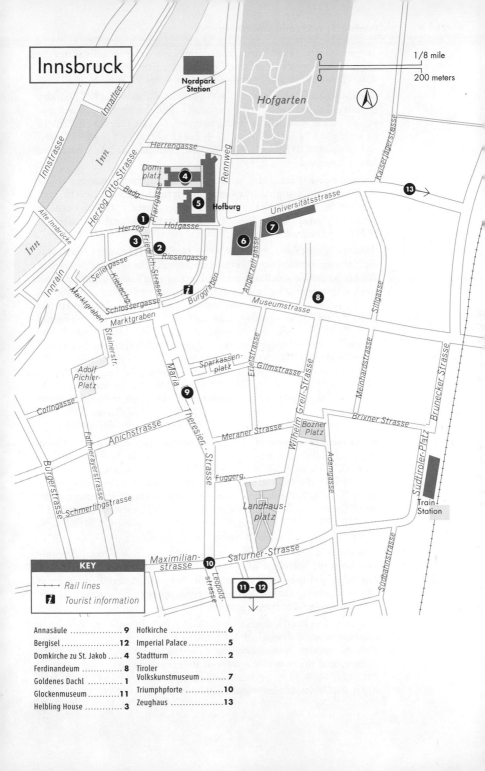

# Innsbruck

Nordpark Station

*Hofgarten*

1/8 mile
200 meters

Herrengasse

Domplatz

**4**

**5** Hofburg

**6** **7**

Universitätsstrasse

**13**

Herzog Otto-Strasse

Badg.

Innstrasse

Innallee

*Inn*

Alte Innbrücke

*Inn*

Herzog

**1**

**3** **2** Hofgasse

Riesengasse

Friedrich-Strasse

Kiebachg.

Seilergasse

Schlossergasse

Marktgraben

Marktgraben

Steinerstr.

Innrain

Adolf Pichler-Platz

Cotingasse

Anichstrasse

Burgerstrasse

Fallmerayerstrasse

Schmerlingstrasse

Schlossergasse

*i*

Burggraben

Rennweg

Angerzellgasse

Museumstrasse

Sparkassen-platz

Gilmstrasse

Erlerstrasse

Wilhelm Greil-Strasse

**8**

Sittgasse

Meinhardtstrasse

Brixner Strasse

Brunecker Strasse

Kaiserjägerstrasse

Maria

Theresien-Strasse

**9**

Meraner Strasse

Fuggerg.

Bozner Platz

Adamgasse

*Landhaus-platz*

Maximilian-strasse

**10**

Saturner-Strasse

Leopold-strasse

Südtiroler-Platz

Train Station

Südbahnstrasse

## KEY

⊢—⊢ *Rail lines*

*i* *Tourist information*

**11** - **12**

jumpers practice, even during the summer when they heavily water the slope (so they can still ski despite the lack of snow). ⊠ *Bergiselweg 3* ☎ *0512/589259* ⊕ *www.bergisel.info* 🖼 *€8.50* ⊙ *Closed Nov.*

**Glockenmuseum.** A visit to the 400-year-old Grassmayr Bell Foundry includes a fascinating little museum and sound chamber, which will give you an idea of how bells are cast and tuned. Guided tours in English can be arranged. ⊠ *Leopoldstrasse 53* ✛ *Take bus J, K, or S south to Grassmayrstrasse* ☎ *0512/59416–37* ⊕ *www.grassmayr.at* 🖼 *€8* ⊙ *Closed Sun. year-round and Sat. in Oct.–Apr.*

**Helbling House.** Facing the Stadtturm is the dramatic blue-and-white Helbling House, originally a Gothic town house dating from the 15th century. In about 1730 the facade was decorated with late-Baroque stuccos by artists of the Wessobrunn school of decorative plasterers. ⊠ *Herzog-Friedrich-Strasse 10.*

**Hofkirche** (*Court Church*). Close by the Hofburg, the Court Church was built as a mausoleum for Maximilian I (although he is actually buried in Wiener Neustadt, south of Vienna). The emperor's ornate black-marble tomb is surrounded by 24 marble reliefs depicting his accomplishments, as well as 28 larger-than-life-size statues of his ancestors (real and imagined), including the legendary King Arthur of England. Freedom fighter Andreas Hofer is also buried here. Don't miss the 16th-century **Silver Chapel,** up the stairs opposite the entrance, with its elaborate altar and silver Madonna. The chapel was built in 1578 to be the tomb of Archduke Ferdinand II and his wife, Philippine Welser, the daughter of a rich and powerful merchant family. ■ TIP➔ **Visit the chapel for picture taking in the morning; the blinding afternoon sun comes in directly behind the altar.** ⊠ *Universitätsstrasse 2* ☎ *0512/59489–511* ⊕ *www.hofkirche. at* 🖼 *€5; €11 combined ticket with Zeughaus and Ferdinandeum.*

**Tiroler Volkskunstmuseum.** In the same complex as the Hofkirche, this is regarded as the most important folk art museum in the Alpine region. Its wood-paneled parlors house furniture, including entire room settings from old farmhouses and inns, decorated in styles from Gothic to Rococo. Other exhibits include costumes, farm implements, carnival masks, and fascinating Christmas cribs. ⊠ *Universitätsstrasse 2* ☎ *0512/594–89–511* ⊕ *www.tiroler-volkskunstmuseum.at* 🖼 *€11 combined ticket with Zeughaus and Ferdinandeum.*

**Triumphpforte.** The Triumphal Arch was built in 1765 to commemorate both the marriage of emperor-to-be Leopold II (then Duke of Tuscany) and the death of Emperor Franz I, husband of Empress Maria Theresa. One side clearly represents celebration, and the other, tragedy. ⊠ *Salurner Strasse.*

**Zeughaus.** The late-Gothic secular building now housing the Zeughaus museum was the arsenal of Maximilian I. Displays include cartography, mineralogy, music, hunting weapons, coins, aspects of Tyrol's culture, and the province's wars of independence. ⊠ *Zeughausgasse* ☎ *0512/59489–11* ⊕ *www.tiroler-landesmuseen.at* 🖼 *€11 combined ticket with Ferdinandeum and Hofkirche* ⊙ *Closed Mon.*

## WHERE TO EAT

**$$$$**
AUSTRIAN
Fodor's Choice
★

✕**Alfred Miller's Schoneck.** With fine views of the city, an atmospheric bar, and veranda and garden for summer dining, this is one of Innsbruck's most exquisite restaurants. Housed in a former imperial hunting lodge across the River Inn from the city center, it has been earning fine-dining accolades since 1899 (including a Michelin star and an impressive 16 Gault Millau points), thanks to a menu that features Austrian staples with a sophisticated twist. **Known for:** excellent-value business lunches; impressive and historic setting; an always-changing menu with fantastic Austrian classics. $ *Average main: €26* ✉ *Weiherburggasse 6* ☎ *0512/272728* ⊕ *www.wirtshaus-schoeneck.com* ☉ *Closed Sun.–Tues.*

**$$**
AUSTRIAN

✕**Cafe Central.** Dark wooden paneling, crystal chandeliers, and the smell of coffee make this Viennese-style café a meeting point for intellectuals, artists, and students. International newspapers and magazines are available, as is a variety of cakes, pastries, and breakfast dishes. **Known for:** film-noir atmosphere; breakfast available all day; live piano music and terrace seating in the summer. $ *Average main: €15* ✉ *Central Hotel, Gilmstrasse 5* ☎ *0512/5920.*

**$$**
ECLECTIC

✕**Cammerlander.** A bright and breezy spot along the Inn River, this place has a distinct Mediterranean feel about it, and that extends to the food. During the summer, take a seat on the open terrace or in the cooler months in the glass-enclosed courtyard. **Known for:** relaxed style; excellent pizza menu; nice vegan options (a rarity in Austria). $ *Average main: €14* ✉ *Innrain 2* ☎ *0512/586–398* ⊕ *www.cammerlander.at.*

**$$$$**
INTERNATIONAL
Fodor's Choice
★

✕**Das Schindler.** Some say this is Innsbruck's current go-to gourmet experience, and its 14 Gault Millau points are a fine endorsement. In the heart of the old town, the restaurant is known for its obsession with using local ingredients as much as possible, with absolutely no artificial additives. **Known for:** attentive service and elegant atmosphere; a true farm-to-table menu; very local ingredients. $ *Average main: €26* ✉ *Maria-Theresien-Strasse 31* ☎ *0512/566969* ⊕ *www.das-schindler.at* ☉ *Closed Sun.*

**$$$**
AUSTRIAN
Fodor's Choice
★

✕**Europastüberl.** Here at the Grand Hotel Europa's acclaimed dining room, you'll find creative cuisine that still draws on traditional recipes. Europastüberl achieves the difficult feat of combining coziness with elegance, with carved wood alcoves—the typical Tyrolean Stüberl—harboring intimate tables dressed with white linens and flickering candles. **Known for:** the epitome of cozy Austrian elegance; excellent local wine menu; signature Dover sole sautéed in butter. $ *Average main: €22* ✉ *Südtirolerplatz 2* ☎ *0512/5931* ⊕ *www.grandhoteleuropa.at.*

**$$$**
AUSTRIAN

✕**Goldener Adler.** This restaurant is as popular with locals as it is with visitors. The kitchen takes a modern approach to traditional dishes, with pork medallions topped with ham and Gorgonzola, and veal steaks ladled with a creamy herb sauce that's as steeped in flavor as the restaurant is steeped in history. **Known for:** the oldest restaurant in Innsbruck (it opened in 1390); alfresco dining in the summer; hearty portions of classical Austrian dishes. $ *Average main: €20* ✉ *Herzog-Friedrich-Strasse 6* ☎ *0512/5711.*

**12**

**$$$$**
ECLECTIC
**Fodor'sChoice**
★

✕ **Lichtblick.** This little restaurant's location on the seventh floor of the chic Rathausgalerie is as lofty as its reputation. The entire restaurant is encased in glass, providing you with sensational views of the Old City, and thanks to the creative menu, it has gained the reputation of one of Innbruck's best hidden gems. **Known for:** impressive location with wonderful views; imaginative and constantly changing menu; fantastic desserts. $ *Average main: €23* ✉ *Rathaus Gallery, Maria-Theresienstrasse 18* ☎ *0512/566550* ☯ *Closed Sun.*

**$**
AUSTRIAN

✕ **Markthalle.** This tidy indoor market offers plenty of farm-fresh produce, including a variety of cheeses, just-picked berries, and a wide choice of mushrooms. You'll also find pastas and other homemade delicacies, with its central location making it a good stop for an inexpensive lunch. **Known for:** relaxed and bustling atmosphere; one of the city's best take-out lunch spots; amazing homemade breads. $ *Average main: €5* ✉ *Herzog-Siegmund-Ufer 1-3, Marktplatz* ☎ *0512/572562* ☰ *No credit cards* ☯ *Closed Sun.*

**$$**
AUSTRIAN

✕ **Ottoburg.** This family-run restaurant offers excellent food, from burgers to Austrian specialties, and an extraordinary location in an ancient landmark. It was originally built in 1180 as a city watchtower, and now retains much of its historical charm. **Known for:** truly historic atmosphere; classic Austrian dishes like Tafelspitz and Pfandl; lovely outdoor seating. $ *Average main: €16* ✉ *Herzog-Friedrich-Strasse 1* ☎ *0512/584338* ⊕ *www.ottoburg.at* ☯ *Closed Mon.*

**$$$$**
ECLECTIC

✕ **Pavillon.** In stark contrast to the surrounding stately buildings (it's between the Hofburg Palace and the National Theatre), this two-story, gleaming glass box houses a café on the ground floor that serves small dishes during the day and a more elaborate dining experience upstairs in the evening. A creative international menu demonstrates a dedication to local and seasonal ingredients. **Known for:** very hip setting; great people-watching; creative cocktail menu. $ *Average main: €28* ✉ *Rennweg 4* ☎ *0512/257–000* ☯ *No dinner Mon. No breakfast Mon.–Sat.*

**$$$**
AUSTRIAN

✕ **Schwarzer Adler.** This intimate, romantic restaurant on the ground floor of the Romantik Hotel Schwarzer Adler Hotel has leaded-glass windows and rustic embellishments offering the perfect backdrop for a memorable meal (in summer, this includes dining on the rooftop terrace). The innovative chefs present a new menu every couple of months based on regional seasonal specialties. **Known for:** charming and intimate interiors; dining room doubles as an art gallery; gorgeous outdoor dining. $ *Average main: €22* ✉ *Kaiserjägerstrasse 2* ☎ *0512/587109* ⊕ *www.deradler.com.*

**$$**
AUSTRIAN
FAMILY

✕ **Seegrube.** Simply put, this restaurant in the Seegrube cableway station is one of the best dinners with a view in the country. At 6,500 feet high, the view of the city lights twinkling below makes a wonderful background for a romantic dinner. **Known for:** sublime views; four-course menu focusing on Tyrolean specialties; requiring reservations in advance. $ *Average main: €16* ✉ *Höhenstrasse 145* ☎ *0512/303065* ⊕ *www.seegrube.at* ☯ *Closed weekends.*

$$$ MEDITERRANEAN Fodor's Choice ★ 🍴 **Sitzwohl Restaurant-Bar.** Stylishly modern, with a functional yet intimate atmosphere, Sitzwohl has built up a solid reputation for superb cuisine, with an emphasis on Mediterranean and Tyrolean dishes. Chanterelle mushroom stew with dumplings or black gnocchi with wild salmon and fennel are favorites here. **Known for:** attentive and quick service; some of the best food in the city; great produce from deli next door. [$] *Average main: €20* ✉ *Stadtforum, City Forum, Gilmstrasse* ☎ *512/562888* 🌐 *www.restaurantsitzwohl.at* 🕒 *Closed Sun.*

$$ THAI 🍴 **Thai-Li.** This Thai kitchen has quietly fashioned a reputation as one of the best and most popular dining spots in the Old Town, just along from the Golden Roof. Thai-Li is short on elbow room, but long on excellent food presented with elegance and efficiency. **Known for:** very affordable menu; possibly the best Thai food in Tyrol; classic curry dishes. [$] *Average main: €14* ✉ *Marktgraben 3* ☎ *0512/562813* 🌐 *www.thaili.at* 🕒 *Closed Mon.*

$$ AUSTRIAN 🍴 **Weisses Rössl.** This is Innsbruck's oldest restaurant, and the hunting pedigree of the area is reflected by the array of antlers adorning the walls in the authentically rustic dining rooms. Be aware that this is not a vegetarian's natural habitat, but meat lovers will enjoy the solid local standards, such as *Tiroler Gröstl,* a tasty hash, and Wiener schnitzel (veal, or pork if you prefer, cutlet), both of which taste even better on the outside terrace in summer. **Known for:** Innsbruck's most historic eatery; classic Austrian meat-heavy staples; lively atmosphere. [$] *Average main: €15* ✉ *Kiebachgasse 8* ☎ *0512/583057* 🌐 *www.roessl.at* 🕒 *Closed Sun.*

## WHERE TO STAY

$$ HOTEL Fodor's Choice ★ 🏨 **Adlers.** One of Innsbruck's newer hotels, Adlers eclipses all with its panoramic vistas, and every room in the striking, supermodern building has floor-to-ceiling windows. **Pros:** best view in the city; handy for train station; spacious rooms. **Cons:** no on-site parking (but €15 a day parking close by); windows don't open; a little way from the prettiest part of town. [$] *Rooms from: €122* ✉ *Bruneckerstasse 1* ☎ *0512/56–31–00* 🌐 *www.deradler.com* 🛏 *75 rooms.*

$$ HOTEL Fodor's Choice ★ 🏨 **Goldener Adler.** In the heart of the Old Innsbruck's pedestrian area, this is said to be one of Europe's oldest hotels, and since 1390 it has welcomed nearly every king, emperor, duke, or poet who passed through Innsbruck. **Pros:** perfect location; atmosphere of living history; friendly and helpful staff. **Cons:** no spa; no on-site parking; old-fashioned feel not for everyone. [$] *Rooms from: €140* ✉ *Herzog-Friedrich-Strasse 6* ☎ *0512/571–11110* 🌐 *www.goldeneradler.com* 🛏 *37 rooms* 🍽 *Breakfast.*

$$$$ HOTEL Fodor's Choice ★ 🏨 **Grand Hotel Europa.** Opposite the train station, this five-star hotel has provided lodging to the celebrated and wealthy in richly appointed, extremely comfortable rooms since it opened in 1869. **Pros:** spacious rooms; wonderful restaurant; opposite train station. **Cons:** on a busy square, although this adds to the city vibe; a little way from the center of the old town; nearby underground parking lot a bit of a walk away. [$] *Rooms from: €260* ✉ *Südtirolerplatz 2* ☎ *0512/5931* 🌐 *www.grandhoteleuropa.at* 🛏 *127 rooms* 🍽 *Breakfast.*

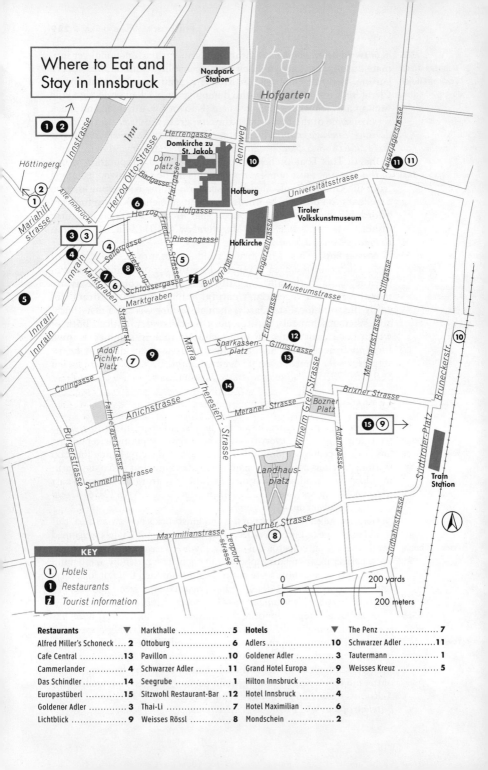

# Where to Eat and Stay in Innsbruck

## KEY
- ① Hotels
- ❶ Restaurants
- 🛈 Tourist information

**Restaurants** ▼

| | |
|---|---|
| Alfred Miller's Schoneck | **2** |
| Cafe Central | **13** |
| Cammerlander | **4** |
| Das Schindler | **14** |
| Europastüberl | **15** |
| Goldener Adler | **3** |
| Lichtblick | **9** |

| | |
|---|---|
| Markthalle | **5** |
| Ottoburg | **6** |
| Pavillon | **10** |
| Schwarzer Adler | **11** |
| Seegrube | **1** |
| Sitzwohl Restaurant-Bar | **12** |
| Thai-Li | **7** |
| Weisses Rössl | **8** |

**Hotels** ▼

| | |
|---|---|
| Adlers | **10** |
| Goldener Adler | **3** |
| Grand Hotel Europa | **9** |
| Hilton Innsbruck | **8** |
| Hotel Innsbruck | **4** |
| Hotel Maximilian | **6** |
| Mondschein | **2** |

| | |
|---|---|
| The Penz | **7** |
| Schwarzer Adler | **11** |
| Tautermann | **1** |
| Weisses Kreuz | **5** |

**12**

$$ ⊡ **Hilton Innsbruck.** Built in the 1970s as part of a 14-story complex
HOTEL that sits rather uncomfortably in this historic city, the Hilton neverthe-
less offers wonderful views and a full range of classic comforts. **Pros:**
fantastic views; huge breakfast buffet; city center location. **Cons:** not
very much personality; chain-hotel feel; architecture is out of place.
$ *Rooms from: €190* ⊠ *Salurner Strasse 15* ☎ *0512/59350–2220*
⊕ *www.hilton.com* ➷ *176 rooms* ⦿ *Breakfast.*

$$ ⊡ **Hotel Innsbruck.** With an ideal location in the heart of Innsbruck,
HOTEL there's an efficient and functional slant here rather than any wow fac-
tor—until you look out the window. **Pros:** lovely sauna area (including
indoor pool); great location; family run. **Cons:** often has large groups;
can be difficult to navigate; business feel rather than Tyrolean charm.
$ *Rooms from: €160* ⊠ *Innrain 3* ☎ *0512/59868–0* ⊕ *www.hotelinns-
bruck.com* ➷ *109 rooms* ⦿ *Breakfast.*

$$ ⊡ **Hotel Maximilian.** The clean, modern lines within the vaulted interior
HOTEL of a historic building are immediately striking in this hotel, a couple of
FAMILY minutes from the center of the old town. **Pros:** great location; free Wi-Fi
Fodor'sChoice throughout and lots of English-language channels on TV; striking mod-
★ ern luxury. **Cons:** some will feel the Tyrolean character has been aban-
doned along the way; no parking on-site; some rooms on the small side.
$ *Rooms from: €160* ⊠ *Marktgraben 7–9, Innenstadt* ☎ *0512/59967*
⊕ *www.hotel-maximilian.com* ➷ *46 rooms* ⦿ *Breakfast.*

$$ ⊡ **Mondschein.** Among the city's oldest houses stands this pink hotel,
HOTEL built in 1473, a warm and welcoming family-run Best Western facing
the River Inn a few minutes from the center of the old town. **Pros:**
very friendly staff; on-site parking; convenient, riverfront location.
**Cons:** some rooms can be noisy; courtyard rooms are dark and some
areas are looking tired; on-site parking is pricey. $ *Rooms from:
€129* ⊠ *Mariahilfstrasse 6* ☎ *0512/22784* ⊕ *www.mondschein.at*
➷ *34 rooms* ⦿ *Breakfast.*

$$ ⊡ **The Penz.** The ultramodern steel-and-glass architecture of this luxury
HOTEL hotel, designed by the renowned French architect Dominique Perrault,
is a striking contrast to the old town and has a purposeful, business
feel that will make traveling executives feel right at home. **Pros:** sleek
design; great breakfast; popular rooftop bar. **Cons:** no spa or sauna;
some may find it all a bit sterile; beware of the rooms above the
noisy delivery entrance. $ *Rooms from: €200* ⊠ *Adolf-Pichler-Platz
3* ☎ *0512/575657–0* ⊕ *www.thepenz.com* ➷ *94 rooms* ⦿ *Breakfast.*

$$ ⊡ **Schwarzer Adler.** The vaulted cellars of this 500-year-old building
HOTEL were once stables for Emperor Maximilian's horses; now they host
Fodor'sChoice glittering events in atmospheric surroundings, and the hotel attracts
★ those in search of a romantic experience. **Pros:** lovely spa; romantic
ambience; every room is different. **Cons:** only one elevator; some rooms
face busy street; smoking still seems to be allowed in the bar. $ *Rooms
from: €140* ⊠ *Kaiserjägerstrasse 2* ☎ *0512/587–109* ⊕ *www.deradler.
com* ➷ *47 rooms* ⦿ *Breakfast.*

$ ⊡ **Tautermann.** This solid red-shuttered house, a friendly family-run
HOTEL hotel, is within a five-minute walk of the city center, but is in a quiet
FAMILY area and offers a great value to anyone traveling on a budget. **Pros:** very
quiet location on the fringes of the city; inexpensive rates; free parking.

Cons: located up a steep hill; furnishings a little dated; no elevator. ⓢ *Rooms from: €90* ✉ *Stamserfeld 5* ☎ *0512/281–572* ⊕ *www.hotel-tautermann.at* ⇆ *32 rooms* ⍁ *Breakfast.*

**$$** 🏨 **Weisses Kreuz.** Quirky, endearing, and in an unrivaled position over
HOTEL  ancient stone arcades in the pedestrian heart of the old town, this hotel
FAMILY  begs you to fall in love with it—and you might, as long as you put
character and atmosphere above slick service and cutting-edge ameni-
ties. **Pros:** oozing with history and character; family-friendly; couldn't
be more central. **Cons:** parking is a short walk away; not all rooms
are air-conditioned; touristy neighborhood can be noisy in evenings.
ⓢ *Rooms from: €105* ✉ *Herzog-Friedrich-Strasse 31* ☎ *0512/59479–0*
⊕ *www.weisseskreuz.at* ⇆ *40 rooms* ⍁ *Breakfast.*

# NIGHTLIFE AND PERFORMING ARTS

## PERFORMING ARTS

It's said that Tyrol has more bandleaders than mayors. Folklore shows
at the **Messehalle** and other spots around the city showcase authentic
Tyrolean folk dancing, yodeling, and zither music. The tourist office
and hotels have more details.

**Festwochen der Alten Musik** (*Festival of Early Music*). Between mid-July
and late August, the Festival of Early Music highlights music from the
14th to 18th centuries, performed by many of Europe's finest musicians
in such dramatic settings as Innsbruck's beautiful Schloss Ambras and
the Hofkirche. In summer there are frequent brass-band (*Musikkapelle*)
concerts in the Old Town. During the Renaissance and in the Baroque
era, Innsbruck was one of Europe's most important centers for music,
and this is the oldest existing festival to celebrate such early music.
✉ *Burggraben 3* ☎ *0512/5710–32* ⊕ *www.altemusik.at.*

**Internationaler Tanzsommer Innsbruck.** The world's premiere dance com-
panies have been visiting Innsbruck between the last week in June and
mid-July for this international dance festival since 1992. The world-
renowned Dance Theatre of Harlem and the Sao Paulo Dance Com-
pany, as well as Maracana, Brazil's Grupo Corpo, and Sankai Juku all
feature regularly. Visitors can join in dance workshops, too. Tickets are
available through the tourist office or the festival office. ✉ *Burggraben
3* ☎ *0512/561–561* ⊕ *www.tanzsommer.at.*

**Kongresshaus.** The original congress house was built by Archduke Leo-
pold V in 1629 as the first freestanding opera house north of the Alps,
and in the 19th century it was converted into the Dogana, or customs
house. Destroyed during World War II, its remains were used to create
this modern congress and events center in 1973. Concerts take place in
the modern Saal Tirol. ✉ *Rennweg 3* ☎ *0512/5936–1120.*

**Tiroler Landestheater.** Innsbruck's principal theater is said to be the oldest
German-speaking theater. It was built in 1654 as the court opera house,
but totally renovated in the classical style in 1846 and modernized and
extended in the 1960s. Both operas and operettas are presented in the
main hall, usually starting at 7:30 pm; plays and dance in the Kam-
merspiele start at 8. Obtain tickets at the box office or at the city's main
tourist office. ✉ *Rennweg 2* ☎ *0512/52074–4* ⊕ *www.landestheater.at.*

**12**

## NIGHTLIFE

**Blue Chip.** For dancing, this basement club on Landhaus Square is a leading hot spot and a magnet for students on Wednesday and the weekend. DJs are highly rated, usually playing house music, hip-hop, and R&B. ⊠ *Wilhelm-Greil-Strasse 17* ☎ *0512/565050.*

**Casino.** The jazzy casino next to the Hilton Innsbruck offers blackjack, baccarat, roulette, poker, and plenty of slot machines, as well as a bar. You must present your passport to enter the casino. Special meal-plus-gambling-chips packages are available in conjunction with the Hilton. ⊠ *Salurner Strasse 15* ☎ *0512/587040–0* ⊕ *www.casinos. at/en/innsbruck.*

**Jimmy's Bar.** This upstairs bar is wildly popular and has built up a jazz-loving clientele. In the winter it's something of an après-ski hangout. You can expect lots of events here, from guest DJs to jam sessions and party nights. ⊠ *Wilhelm-Greil-Strasse 17* ☎ *0512/650–5454579.*

**Krahvogel.** Known for its wide choice of beer—the drink of choice here rather than cocktails—Krahvogel is also something of a gastropub, with regional and international cuisine on offer. It's on one of Innsbruck's busiest shopping streets and attracts a good cross-section of customers, from tourists to local office workers and students. ⊠ *Anichstrasse 12* ☎ *0512/580149.*

**Piano Bar.** Tiny, and exuding old-world charm, this bar is a favored hangout of local artists and has occasional live music. Devotees insist it has the best steaks in Austria, and the Wiener schnitzel is good, too. It has a nice patio with an outdoor dining area. ⊠ *Herzog-Friedrich-Strasse 5* ☎ *0512/571010* ⊕ *www.cafepiano.at.*

**Tapabar.** For Latin rhythms, Tapabar is the go-to place. On Wednesday there are flamenco lessons and occasional live performances that are a good warm-up for long nights of dancing. You can sample some excellent homemade tapas, too. ⊠ *Marktplatz, Innrain 2* ☎ *0512/586398–43.*

## SPORTS AND THE OUTDOORS

### GOLF

**Golf Course Innsbruck-Igls.** Breathtaking views of surrounding mountains from the concentric, partly hilly fairways on an ascending plateau make this a special experience. About 9 km (5½ miles) outside Innsbruck, this club has two courses, an 18-hole championship course at Rinn and a 9-hole course at nearby Lans. Founded in 1935, it's among Austria's oldest. It's open April through November. ⊠ *Oberdorf 11, Rinn* ☎ *05223/78177* ⊕ *www.golfclub-innsbruck-igls.at* 🏌 *Rinn: €75 for 18 holes weekdays, €80 on weekends; Lans: €60 for 18 holes weekdays, €65 on weekends* 🏌 *Rinn: 18 holes, 6622 yards, par 71; Lans: 9 holes, 5056 yards, par 33.*

### HIKING

Both easy paths and extreme slopes await hikers and climbers. From June to October holders of the Innsbruck Card can take free, daily, guided mountain hikes. The tourist office has a special hiking brochure.

## HORSEBACK RIDING

**Reitclub Innsbruck.** Horseback riding can be arranged through Reitclub Innsbruck, which is based in the village of Igls outside Innsbruck. ⊠ *Römerstrasse 50, Innsbruck-Igls* ☎ *0516/5505* ⊕ *www.reitclub-innsbruck.com.*

## ROCK CLIMBING

**Alpine Auskunft.** Whether you're an experienced climber or new learner, the man to contact for rock climbing in Tyrol is Mike Rutter at Alpine Auskunft. He has advice on everything from suitable climbing areas to guides and courses. ⊠ *Maria-Theresien-Strasse 55* ☎ *0512/587828* ⊕ *www.alpine-auskunft.at.*

## SKIING

Around Innsbruck you'll find everything from the beginner slopes of the Glungezer to the good intermediate skiing of Axamer Lizum and Patscherkofel to the steep runs and off-piste skiing of Seegrube. Your Innsbruck Card includes transportation to the ski areas and reduced prices on a number of ski lifts. A variety of combination ski passes are available that give access to lifts at resorts around Innsbruck and throughout Tyrol. For example, the OlympicWorld Ski Pass gives access to nine mountains, with 300 km (186 miles) of trails, including Nordkettenbahn-Seegrube, Patscherkofel, Axamer Lizum, Muttereralm, Kühtai, Rangger Köpfl, Glungezer, Schlick 2000, and Stubai Glacier. The tourist office can give you more information and also sells all necessary tickets.

**Ski & Snowboardschule Innsbruck.** You can book all skiing needs, including lift tickets, equipment, and lessons here. You can also hire instructors through the Innsbruck Ski School to meet you at your hotel or one of the ski areas, or the school can arrange transportation (at extra cost). It can also arrange days out, with instruction, at farther-flung resorts such as St. Anton, Ischgl, or Solden. One-on-one tuition starts at €195, with each additional person €20. The school is based at Die Boerse Ski and Snowboard store in Innsbruck. ⊠ *Leopoldstrasse 4* ☎ *660/21–44–660* ⊕ *www.skischule-innsbruck.com.*

**Snowboard Börse.** This is a good place to rent ski and snowboard equipment, particularly as it's on-site at the Innsbruck Ski School, making for one stop for all your skiing needs. It's tucked into an alley just south of the Triumphpforte. ⊠ *Leopoldstrasse 4* ☎ *0512/581742–0* ⊕ *www.dieboerse.at.*

## SWIMMING

Around Innsbruck there are plenty of lakes, but in town you have little choice other than pools, indoors and out.

**Freischwimmbad Tivoli.** Come here to swim under the sun with a panoramic view of the mountains. ⊠ *Purtschellerstrasse 1* ☎ *0512/502–7081.*

**Hallenbad Amraser Strasse.** If the weather goes south, try this turn-of-the-20th-century indoor swimming pool with an Art Nouveau look. ⊠ *Amraser Strasse 3* ☎ *0512/502–7051.*

**Hallenbad Höttinger Au.** This is a popular indoor swimming facility, also boasting a counterflow pool and sauna and sunbeds. ⊠ *Fürstenweg 12* ☎ *0512/502–7071* ⊕ *www.innsbruck.info/en/.*

## SHOPPING

**12**

The best shops are along the arcaded Herzog-Friedrich-Strasse in the heart of the Altstadt; along its extension, Maria-Theresien-Strasse; and the adjoining streets Meraner Strasse and Anichstrasse. Innsbruck is the place to buy native Tyrolean clothing, particularly lederhosen (traditional brushed leather shorts and trousers) and loden (sturdy combed-wool jackets and vests). Look also for cut crystal and woodcarvings; locally handmade, delicate silver-filigree pins make fine gifts.

**Christmas Market.** For sheer holiday delight, nothing tops the traditional Christmas Market, which features wooden and glass handicrafts, Christmas-tree decorations, candles, and Tyrolean toys and loden costumes. The market stalls are set up around the giant, illuminated Christmas tree next to the Goldenes Dachl museum, in the heart of the Altstadt, and are open from mid-November until Christmas Day. ⊠ *Herzog-Friedrich-Strasse 15.*

**Galerie Thomas Flora.** The droll graphics by Tyrolean artist Paul Flora on sale here provide much to smile at, and maybe you'll even find something to take home. ⊠ *Herzog-Friedrich-Strasse 5* ☎ *0512/577402.*

**Hubertus Loden Steinbock.** This is an outstanding source of dirndls, those attractive traditional costumes for women, with white blouses, dark skirts, and colorful aprons. It also has children's clothing. ⊠ *Sparkassenplatz 3* ☎ *0512/585092.*

**Rathausgalerie.** Innsbruck's swish, central, glass-roofed indoor mall is home to luxury boutiques and world-famous brand names. Here you can shop, eat, and drink in style. ⊠ *Maria-Theresien-Strasse* ⊕ *www.rathausgalerien.at.*

**Rudolf Boschi.** Reproductions of old pewterware, using the original molds when possible, are among the items you'll find here, along with locally produced, hand-decorated beer mugs with pewter lids. A second location, nearby, has mostly prints. ⊠ *Kiebachgasse 8* ☎ *0512/589224* ⊕ *www.boschi.at.*

**S'Culinarium.** At *the* shop to buy Austrian wine and liquor (Austria produces some very decent wine these days and always has produced wonderful schnapps and rum) you can try everything before you buy, and the talkative, friendly owner will be happy to advise. Some of the famous Rochelt schnapps may still be available, but supplies are limited since owner Gunter Rochelt's death. ⊠ *Pfarrgasse 1* ☎ *0512/574903* ⊕ *culinarium-signor.at.*

**S'Speckladele.** The smallest shop in Innsbruck is definitely work a visit. With room for only two clients at a time, it sells delicious *Speck* (bacon) and other smoked meats produced by local organic farms. Enjoy a sandwich; you'll be tempted to take something home, but import rules on meat products are strict, so check before you buy, or consume your purchases before you go home. ⊠ *Stiftgasse 4* ☎ *0512/588816.*

**Swarovski Crystal Gallery.** This dazzling gallery, in the old town near the Golden Roof, features mostly crystal from the world-renowned maker, whose headquarters is in nearby Wattens, east of Innsbruck. ⊠ *Herzog-Friedrich-Strasse 39* ☎ *0512/573100* ⊕ *innsbruck.swarovski.com.*

**Tiroler Heimatwerk.** Make this your first stop for high-quality souvenirs. The extremely attractive shop carries textiles and finished clothing, ceramics, carved wooden chests, and some furniture, but don't expect a bargain. You can also have clothing made to order. ⊠ *Meraner Strasse 2–4* ☎ *0512/582320* ⊕ *www.tiroler.heimatwerk.at.*

# EXCURSIONS FROM INNSBRUCK

Few cities have such an intimate blend of history, culture, nature, and spectacular scenery than these, all closely accessible from Innsbruck. The variety of excursions and activities in this area is endless.

## NORDPARK

The closest ski area to Innsbruck, Nordpark is famous for ferociously steep runs.

FAMILY **Alpenzoo.** Take the funicular from the city center to see this unusual collection of Alpine birds and animals, including many endangered species. ⊠ *Weiherburggasse 37A, Innsbruck* ☎ *0512/292–323* ⊕ *www.alpenzoo.at* ☜ *€9; combined ticket with park-and-ride from city €11.*

FAMILY **Nordpark Funicular.** Travel from the city center to the Hungerburg Plateau, from where you take the Nordkettenbahn Cableway to the top of the mountain for a staggering view of Innsbruck. ⊠ *Rennweg, Innsbruck* ☎ *0512/293344* ☜ *Funicular round-trip €6.80; cable-car round-trip €27.*

## SCHLOSS AMBRAS

A Renaissance castle in the hills above the city, Schloss Ambras is one of Tyrol's most popular attractions.

**Schloss Ambras.** When Archduke Ferdinand II was begrudgingly allowed to marry the commoner Philippine Welser, the couple was forced to live outside the city. He had an existing 10th-century castle virtually rebuilt from scratch for his bride, and it was completed in 1556, becoming Schloss Ambras. He made sure it had every luxury, including a sunken bath. Amid acres of gardens, it is also home to a collection of armaments and portraits. ⊠ *Schloss Strasse 20* ✛ *The castle is 3 km (2 miles) southeast of the city. By public transportation, take Tram 3 or 6 to Ambras (a short walk from the castle) or Rte. 1 on the Sightseer from Maria-Theresien-Strasse* ☎ *01/525–24–4802* ⊕ *www.khm.at/ambras* ☜ *Apr.–Oct., €10; Dec.–Mar., €7* ☉ *Closed Nov.*

## THE STUBAITAL VALLEY

The delightful Stubai Valley, less than 40 km (25 miles) long, is one of the most beautiful valleys in the Tyrol, with no fewer than 80 glistening glaciers (including the Stubai Glacier) and more than 40 towering peaks. The gondola lift up to the glacier is spectacular, and you can venture onto the glacier on marked walks. The higher slopes are open for skiing most of the summer, too. If you just want to look, you can see the whole Stubaital in a full day's excursion from Innsbruck.

The narrow-gauge electric Stubaitalbahn can take you from the center of Innsbruck (on Maria-Theresien-Strasse and in front of the main train station), as well as from the station just below the Bergisel ski jump, as far as Fulpmes, partway up the valley. You can take the bus as far as Ranalt and back to Fulpmes, to see more of the valley, then return on the quaint rail line.

**Autobusbahnof.** Buses leave from Gate 1 of the Autobusbahnhof, just behind the train station at Südtiroler Platz, about once an hour, and the tram-train leaves from there, too. ✉ *Maria-Theresien-Strasse, Innsbruck* ☎ *0512/5307–102.*

12

# TYROL

The area north of the Kitzbüheler Alps and south of the German border is a distillation of all things Tyrolean: perfectly maintained ancient farmhouses with balconies overflowing with flowers; people who still wear the traditional lederhosen and dirndls as their everyday attire; Alpine villages and medieval castles; and wonderfully kitschy winter resorts such as Kitzbühel and St. Johann.

The upper Inn Valley, from Innsbruck stretching up to the Swiss border, is beautiful countryside, particularly the narrow valleys that branch off to the south. Most visitors take Route 171 west from Innsbruck along the banks of the Inn, rather than the autobahn, which hugs the cliffs along the way. This is a region of family-run farms perched on mountainsides and steep granite peaks flanking narrow valleys leading to some of Austria's finest ski areas.

■ TIP→ Many of the Tyrol's finest folk musicians come from the beautiful Zillertal (Ziller Valley) so if you go, ask about live music programs.

## HALL IN TIROL

*12 km (7 miles) east of Innsbruck.*

A few minutes by road east of Innsbruck is what many say is the most beautiful town in Tyrol—ancient Hall, wonderfully preserved and with a historic center actually larger than that of Innsbruck. The town has a history of great prosperity—salt mining in the Middle Ages made it the most important commercial hub in the region at the time (the High German word *Hal* means salt mine). The town received its municipal charter in 1286, but even greater prestige was to come nearly 200 years later when the provincial mint was moved to the town.

### GETTING HERE AND AROUND

From Innsbruck, take Highway A12 east. There is frequent bus service between Innsbruck and Hall on Route 4 (every 15 minutes), with a journey time of about 30 minutes. The Postbus system has frequent services linking Hall with the rest of Tyrol and beyond. Hall is also on the rail network.

### ESSENTIALS

**Visitor Information Hall in Tirol.** ✉ *Wallpachgasse 5, Hall in Tirol* ☎ *05223/45544* ⊕ *www.hall-wattens.at.*

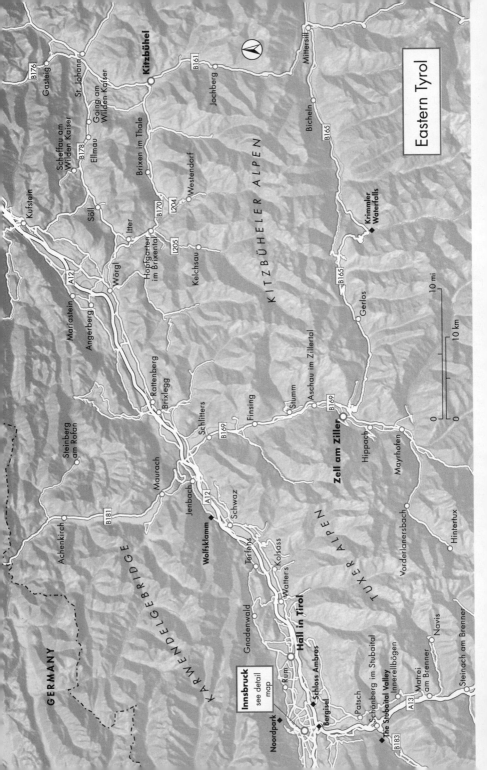

Eastern Tyrol

GERMANY

Kitzbühel
Gasteig
B176
St. Johann
Going am Wilden Kaiser
Scheffau am Wilden Kaiser
B178
Ellmau
Söll
Kufstein
Itter
Wörgl
A12
Mariastein
Angerberg
Brixen im Thale
Westendorf
B170
L204
Hopfgarten im Brixental
L205
Kelchsau
Jochberg
B161
Bicheln
Mittersill
B165
KITZBÜHELER ALPEN
Krimmler Waterfalls
B165
Gerlos
10 mi
10 km
0

Steinberg am Rofan
Achenkirch
B181
KARWENDELGEBIRGE
Maurach
Jenbach
A12
Schwaz
Wolfsklamm
Terfens
Kolsass
Rattenberg
Brixlegg
Schlitters
B169
Finsing
Stumm
Aschau im Zillertal
B169
Zell am Ziller
Hippach
Mayrhofen
Vorderlanersbach
Hintertux
TUXER ALPEN

Gnadenwald
Watters
Hall in Tirol
Schloss Ambras
Rum
Innsbruck
see detail map
Noordpark
Bergisel
Patsch
Schönberg im Stubaital
Innerellbögen
The Stubaital Valley
Matrei am Brenner
Navis
Steinach am Brenner
A13
B183

12

## EXPLORING

**Burg Hasegg and Hall Mint.** Built to protect the salt mines and trade on the River Inn, Burg Hasegg was enlarged into a showpiece castle by Duke Siegmund and Emperor Maximilian I. Meanwhile, the first silver coin in Tyrol, the thaler (say it quickly and you'll realize it was the root of the modern word, dollar), emerged from the mint in the center of Hall. In 1567, Ferdinand II moved the mint to Burg Hasegg, and thereafter the fortunes of the mint and the castle became intertwined. In the 18th century, 17 million Maria Theresa thaler were minted here and became a valued currency throughout the world. Today, you can visit the mint museum—even mint your own coin—and climb to the top of the Mint Tower for splendid views. ✉ *Burg Hasegg, Hall in Tirol* ☎ *0680/553–2117* 🌐 *www.muenze-hall.at* 🎫 *€6; €4 for mint only* 🕒 *Closed Sun. and Mon. in Nov.–Mar.*

**Damenstift.** Archduchess Magdelena, sister of Ferdinand II, founded the Damenstift Abbey, home of the silent order of Carmelite nuns, in 1567–69. The church front, with its four full-length fluted pilasters, is an example of the transition from the Renaissance to the Baroque style. Very few nuns remain, mostly elderly, but it is interesting to witness their silent and extensive devotions (visitors are welcomed by the nunnery). ✉ *Unterer Stadtplatz, Hall in Tirol* 🎫 *Free.*

**Pfarrkirche St. Nikolaus.** The Waldaufkapelle is the best-known part of this 13th-century church—it's home to Florian Waldauf's rather gruesome collection of 45 skulls, said to be those of B-list saints. Waldauf, something of a fixer for Emperor Maximilian I at the beginning of the 16th century, began scouring Europe for relics to purchase, and eventually opened his prized collection to the public. Now each skull rests on an embroidered cushion and, incongruously, has also been given a headdress—the result is a horribly fascinating museum. ✉ *Pfarrplatz, Hall in Tirol* ☎ *05223/57914* 🌐 *www.pfarre-hall.at* 🎫 *Free.*

Fodor's Choice ★ **Wolfsklamm.** This is an exhilarating and spectacular, but very safe, climb up through a gorge beside a raging torrent from the village of Stans, to the northeast of Hall, to the Benedictine monastery of St. Georgenberg. The climb, on walkways hewn from the mountainside and across bridges spanning the tumbling river and beside waterfalls—all protected by railings—takes about 90 minutes and features 354 steps. At the top the monastery's sumptuously decorated Baroque church, precariously perched on a rocky peak, is worth a few minutes of your time. There is a decent restaurant there, too, with a terrace dizzily located above a sheer drop of several hundred feet. ✉ *Stans* ☎ *05242/71435* 🌐 *www.silberregion-karwendel.com.*

## WHERE TO STAY

$$ HOTEL 🏨 **Garten Hotel Maria Theresia.** Built in solid, substantial, flower-bedecked chalet style, this is a family hotel to the core, and the family that runs it is the epitome of true Tyrolean innkeeping and hospitality. **Pros:** very good value; family run and very friendly; excellent food. **Cons:** away from the prettiest district of Hall; bit of a walk to the town center; the bells of a nearby church may disturb some. [$] *Rooms from: €100* ✉ *Reimmichlstrasse 25, Heiligkreuz, Hall in Tirol* ☎ *05223/56313* 🌐 *www.gartenhotel.at* 🛏 *24 rooms* 🍴 *Breakfast.*

$$ **Gasthof Badl.** For a short stay, this gasthof can fit the bill at a budget
HOTEL    price, offering a warm welcome and rooms that are sparkling clean,
FAMILY   with all the comfort you need for an overnight stay. **Pros:** extremely
friendly and family run; excellent value; great views on the river side.
**Cons:** close to an autobahn, so can be noisy; not in the center of town;
friendly dogs roam the grounds, which some guests might not like.
$ *Rooms from: €110* ✉ *Haller Innbrucke 4, Ampass, Hall in Tirol*
☎ *5223/56784* ⊕ *www.badl.at* ⇄ *25 rooms* ⦿ *Breakfast.*

$ **Rettenberg Hotel.** Close to Hall in Tirol and very handy for Innsbruck,
HOTEL    this comfortable hotel remains a place where you can feel part of a small
community and actually meet locals in the bar. **Pros:** reasonable prices; lots
of local character; on-site spa, pool, and bowling alley. **Cons:** rooms at the
front can be noisy in the morning; smoking still allowed in the bar; main
slopes are car or bus ride away. $ *Rooms from: €59* ✉ *Mühlbach 6, Kol-*
*sass-Weer* ☎ *05224/68124* ⊕ *www.kolsass.at* ⇄ *45 rooms* ⦿ *Breakfast.*

# ZELL AM ZILLER

*60 km (40 miles) southeast of Innsbruck.*

Zell is the main town of the Zillertal, one of the many beautiful Alpine
valleys of the Tyrol, and a real working community rather than just a
resort town. It is notable for its traditional 500-year-old Gauder Fest,
and has also developed into a center of summer activities. You can
choose to stay in one of a dozen hotels or bed-and-breakfast pensions
at surprisingly reasonable cost. Although Zell is considered the valley's
main town, the bigger-name resort, especially for skiing, is Mayrhofen,
a little farther up the valley and somewhat more expensive. In Zell,
families enjoy the Fun-arena, which has water glides and a roller coaster
for kids, while adults can try rafting or paragliding.

### GETTING HERE AND AROUND

From Innsbruck, take Highway A12 or Route 171. The B169 will lead
you to the Ziller Valley. Kids—and quite a few adults—will love the
old steam engine of the Zillertalbahn pulling a few historical cars from
Jenbach train station up the Zillertal to Zell, and then on to Mayrhofen,
twice a day.

### EXPLORING

Fodor's Choice   **Gauder Fest.** The more than 500-year-old Gauder Fest is held on the first
★    weekend in May. Thousands of visitors, many of them in traditional
costume from Tyrol and other parts of Austria, pack the little market
town of Zell am Ziller for the colorful skits, music, and singing—and
great quantities of *Gauderbier,* a strong brew created for the occasion.
You can hear some of the country's best singing by the valley residents
and listen to expert harp and zither playing, for which the valley is
famous. Tradition runs strong here, so even if you can't make it in
May, there are other festival opportunities: witness the Perchtenlaufen,
processions of colorfully masked well-wishers going the neighborhood
rounds on January 5; the annual Almabtrieb is celebrated in the last Sep-
tember and first October days, when the cows, decorated with wreaths
and bells, are herded back from the high Alpine pastures into the lower
fields and barns. ✉ *Zell am Ziller* ⊕ *www.gauderfest.at.*

**Krimml Waterfalls.** The tiered Krimml falls plunge down in three stages, with a total drop of 1,247 feet, making it the highest waterfall in Austria and one of Austria's most popular natural attractions. A path ascends through the woods beside the falls, with frequent viewing points. By car or bus, it's 35 minutes from Zell am Ziller over the Gerlos Pass. ✉ *Krimml* ☎ *06564/7212* 🌐 *www.wasserfaelle-krimml.at* 🎟 *€8.80 (includes parking and water park); €3 to just walk the path beside the waterfall* 🕒 *Closed Nov.–Apr.*

### WHERE TO EAT

$$ AUSTRIAN FAMILY 🍴 **Hotel Gasthof Bräu.** The core of this frescoed building in the town center dates from the 16th century, but subsequent renovations have brought the five-story structure up to date. The three-room restaurant offers a menu with an emphasis on fish and game, and many ingredients come directly from the owner's own farm and fish ponds or from other local suppliers. **Known for:** beautifully decorated wood-paneled parlors; locally grown produce; beer from nearby family brewery. [$] *Average main: €16* ✉ *Dorfplatz 1* ☎ *05282/2313–0* 🌐 *www.hotel-braeu.at* 🕒 *Closed Apr. and mid-Oct.–mid-Dec.*

### SPORTS AND THE OUTDOORS

#### ZIP-LINING

FAMILY **Arena Skyliner.** A development of the Flying Fox zip-line concept, the Skyliner has four lines where you can hurtle along at 50 kph (31 mph) and get a bird's-eye view of the area (on Line 3 you are more than 200 feet above the ground). The meeting point is at the top station of the Gerlosstein cable car. Minimum and maximum weight restrictions apply—40 kilos (88 pounds) and 120 kilos (265 pounds), respectively. ✉ *Dorfplatz 3a* ☎ *0664/44–19–283* 🌐 *www.zillertalarena.com/en/arena/sommer/arena-skyliner.html* 🎟 *€37.50.*

## KITZBÜHEL

*12 km (7 miles) south of St. Johann, 71 km (44 miles) northeast of Gerlos.*

Kitzbühel is indisputably one of Austria's most fashionable winter resorts, although the town boasts a busy summer season as well. "Kitz" offers warm-season visitors a hefty program of hiking, cycling, and golf, along with outdoor concerts and plays and a professional tennis tournament in July. In winter, many skiers are attracted by the famous Ski Safari—a carefully planned, clever combination of chairlifts, gondola lifts, draglifts, and runs that lets you ski for more than 145 km (91 miles) without having to walk a single foot. Kitzbühel is in perpetual motion and is busy December through mid-April, notably at the end of January for the famed **Hahnenkamm World Cup** downhill ski race. At any time during the season there's plenty to do, from sleigh rides to fancy-dress balls. ■ **TIP→ In summer visitors are offered free guest cards, which provide free access or substantially reduced fees for various activities, such as tennis, riding, and golf.** The best swimming is in the nearby Schwarzsee.

### GETTING HERE AND AROUND

From Innsbruck, take the autobahn A12 or B171 west to the town of Wörgl, then the B170 to Kitzbühel. From here you can travel south on the B161/B108 on the Felbertauernstrasse and through the Felbertauerntunnel to Matrei in OstTirol and Lienz.

### ESSENTIALS

**Visitor Information** Kitzbühel. ✉ *Hinterstadt 18* ☎ *05356/66660* 🌐 *www.kitzbuehel.com/en.*

## EXPLORING

**Alpine Flower Garden Kitzbühel.** Take the *gondolabahn* (cable car) up the Kitzbüheler Horn to this lovely garden at 6,500 feet. Amid glorious mountain scenery you will see hundreds of varieties of Alpine flowers in their native habitat, including varieties from other parts of the world. Guided tours are offered daily at 11 from June to early September. ✉ *Kitzbühel* ☎ *05356/62857* 🌐 *www.kitzbuehel.com/en* 🎫 *Free; cable car: one way €19.60, round-trip €24.50.*

**Church of St. Catherine.** Built around 1350, this church houses a Gothic winged altar dating from 1515. ✉ *Kitzbühel.*

**St. Andrew's Parish Church.** With parts of the town dating back to the 14th century, Kitzbühel is quite scenic. Much of the town's affluence came from the proceeds of copper and silver mining, but among its best sights are its churches. St. Andrew's parish church (1435–1506) has a lavishly Rococo chapel, the Rosakapelle, as well as the marvelously ornate tomb (1520) of the Kupferschmid family. ✉ *Kitzbühel.*

## WHERE TO EAT

$$$ AUSTRIAN Fodor's Choice ★

🍴 **Hallerwirt.** In the small village of Aurach about 5 km (3 miles) south of Kitzbühel, Hallerwirt is known for its great Austrian cuisine and charm. Old wooden floors and a ceramic stove in the parlor lend a period flair to this 400-year-old farmhouse. **Known for:** warm welcome from the owners; charming surroundings; use of local produce. [$] *Average main: €18* ✉ *Oberaurach 4, Aurach bei Kitzbühel* ☎ *05356/64502* 🌐 *www.hallerwirt.at* 🕒 *Closed Mon., Tues., and mid-Nov.–early Dec.*

$$$$ INTERNATIONAL Fodor's Choice ★

🍴 **HeimatLiebe.** After a day of hiking or skiing at Kitzbühel, put yourself in the hands of head chef Andreas Senn and enjoy his Tyrolean cuisine par excellence at this Michelin-starred destination restaurant. The gourmet cuisine, skillfully blending traditional methods with contemporary ideas and international influences, has brought accolades on both the chef and the restaurant. **Known for:** romantic ambience; exquisitely creative cuisine; multicourse tasting menu. [$] *Average main: €40* ✉ *Grand Spa Resort A-Rosa, Ried Kaps 7* ☎ *05356/656600* 🌐 *resort.a-rosa.de/english/kitzbuehel/fine-food/gourmetrestaurant-heimatliebe/* 🕒 *Closed Sun., Mon., and May–mid-Dec. No lunch.*

$ CAFÉ

🍴 **Praxmair.** Après-ski can't begin early enough for the casually chic crowds that pile into this famous pastry shop for its *Krapfen* (something like jelly doughnuts and available throughout Austria in January and February). For locals, the Praxmair is a meeting point for regular get-togethers, cabaret performances, and small events. **Known for:** bustling atmosphere; live après-ski music; tasty pastries. [$] *Average main: €10* ✉ *Vorderstadt 17* ☎ *05356/62646* 💳 *No credit cards* 🕒 *Closed Apr. and Nov.*

**12**

$$$$
AUSTRIAN
Fodor's Choice
★

✕ **Tennerhof.** Expect elegant dress and quiet conversations at this high-class restaurant, where Stefan Lenz and his creative team have been awarded 15 Gault Millau points and a Michelin star. Freshly picked herbs from the garden accompany almost every dish, from soup to sorbet, and imaginative dishes might include roasted goose liver with mango ravioli and a reduction of cacao. **Known for:** cozy Tyrolean atmosphere; local produce from the on-site garden; great wine menu. $ *Average main: €30* ⊠ *Griesenauweg 26* ☎ *05356/63181* ⊕ *www.tennerhof.com* ⊘ *Closed Mon., Tues., Apr.–mid-May, and mid-Oct.–mid-Dec.*

## WHERE TO STAY

$$$$
HOTEL
Fodor's Choice
★

⊞ **Golf-Hotel Rasmushof.** It's hard to imagine a better choice for a Kitzbühel stay than this superluxurious but relaxed former farmstead, with unrivaled year-round proximity to outdoor activities. **Pros:** fabulous location; breathtaking views; ski-in ski-out in winter. **Cons:** pretty pricey for the area; away from the town center. $ *Rooms from: €346* ⊠ *Hermann Reisch Weg 15* ☎ *05356/65252* ⊕ *www.rasmushof. at* ↝ *60 rooms* ⦿ *Breakfast.*

$$$
B&B/INN
Fodor's Choice
★

⊞ **Hotel Villa Licht.** This luxurious bed-and-breakfast is an adorable Hansel-and-Gretel chalet where hospitality and attention to detail are paramount. **Pros:** a short walk from town center; very quiet; lots of free parking. **Cons:** no restaurant, although plenty are close at hand; stays of at least six days required in high season; need to book well in advance. $ *Rooms from: €210* ⊠ *Franz Reisch Strasse 8* ☎ *05356/62293* ⊕ *www. villa-licht.at* ↝ *17 rooms, 3 apartments* ⦿ *Breakfast.*

$$$$
HOTEL
Fodor's Choice
★

⊞ **Tennerhof.** Adored by the rich and famous, from the Duke of Windsor to Kirk Douglas, this Alpine Shangri-la is at once rustic and glamorous, with gold chandeliers hung over country cupboards and silk-covered sofas next to shuttered windows. **Pros:** aristocratic flair; great breakfast; lovely garden. **Cons:** a little way from the town center and the ski lifts; can be a bit too fancy for some; expensive. $ *Rooms from: €322* ⊠ *Griesenauweg 26* ☎ *05356/63181* ⊕ *www.tennerhof.com* ⊘ *Closed Apr.–mid-May and mid-Oct.–mid-Dec.* ↝ *40 rooms* ⦿ *Breakfast.*

## NIGHTLIFE

**Fünferl.** Located in the center of town, this place is full of character and has many dedicated fans. It's good for late-evening cocktails and attracts a somewhat more mature and relaxed clientele who prefer conversation to partying. ⊠ *Franz-Reisch-Strasse 1* ☎ *05356/71300–5.*

**Jimmy's.** A modern bar, occasionally with a DJ, Jimmy's might not be the most atmospheric bar in town, but it's a popular rendezvous point at the start of the evening before moving on elsewhere. ⊠ *Hinterstadt 22* ☎ *05356/644–09.*

**Kitzbühel Casino.** Few casinos can be located in such a charming and historic building as this, in the center of town. It offers baccarat, blackjack, roulette, and one-armed bandits. There's a restaurant and bar, and no set closing time. A valid passport or driver's license is needed to enter. ⊠ *Hinterstadt 24* ☎ *05356/62300* ⊕ *www.casinos.at/en/kitzbuehel.*

**Londoner.** Young people flock to this popular watering hole, one of the biggest-name bars in town. It gets packed by fans and racers alike on big ski-race days, and can be just too crammed to get in. ⊠ *Franz-Reisch-Strasse 4* ☎ *05356/71428.*

**Stamperl.** This is an established local favorite—it's been going strong for nearly 45 years—and in winter it's very popular with the après-ski crowd; try to nab a seat on the heated terrace. It serves decent Tyrolean food until 10 pm. ⊠ *Franz-Reisch-Strasse 7* ☎ *05356/62555.*

**Take Five.** The dance-club crowd moves from place to place, but check out this hot spot in the center of Kitz. It has three bars and a spacious VIP area, and aims for a sophisticated atmosphere. ⊠ *Hinterstadt 22* ☎ *05356/71300–30.*

## SPORTS AND THE OUTDOORS
### GOLF
With 19 courses within an hour's drive, Kitzbühel may properly lay claim to being the golf center of the Alps. The Golf Alpin Card offers special deals (five green fees for €325, four for €260, and three for €199); it's available at some hotels and golf clubs, or from the tourist office.

**Golf Eichenheim.** Heady views of soaring Alpine peaks surrounding the course are mixed with leafy fringed fairways to give this 18-hole PGA-rated venue a unique appeal. The name, meaning "Oak Home," reflects the surroundings, and a round includes the opportunity to appreciate rare flora and fauna. If you work up an appetite, the clubhouse includes a gourmet restaurant. ⊠ *Eichenheim 8–9* ☎ *05356/66615–560* ⊕ *www.eichenheim.com* ⚐ *Apr. and May, €75; June and Oct., €80; July and Sept., €95–€100; 9 holes €40* ⚑ *18 holes, 6092 yards, par 71.*

**Golfclub Kitzbühel.** A pretty course, the 9 holes of the Golfclub Kitzbühel wind between ancient trees and water hazards with a fabulous backdrop of Alpine grandeur. The slightly hilly terrain is set around the Grand Spa Resort A-Rosa, and resort guests receive a discount. There are plenty of water hazards, with two of the greens located on islands. The course, built in 1955, is open from May to October and has a handicap limit of 36. ⊠ *Ried Caps 3* ☎ *05356/63007* ⊕ *www.golfclub-kitzbuehel.at* ⚐ *€86 for 18 holes, €53 for 9 holes* ⚑ *18 holes, 6135 yards, par 70.*

**Golf-Club Kitzbühel-Schwarzsee.** Amazing views to the Wilder Kaiser mountain range and the Kitzbuheler Horn peak nearby help to make this 18-hole course a treat for the senses. The par-72 course is varied, with wide fairways. A big surprise is sprung at the par-3 16th hole—called the Mousetrap—which is played over a small ravine. The course is open from May to October, and holders of the Kitzbühel Guest Card get a 30% discount on weekdays and various multiround deals. ⊠ *Golfweg 35* ☎ *05356/66660–70* ⊕ *www.kitzbuehel.com/golf-schwarzsee* ⚐ *May and June, €82 for 18 holes, €43 for 9 holes; July–Oct., €89 for 18 holes, €48 for 9 holes* ⚑ *18 holes, 6675 yards, par 72.*

**Rasmushof Golf Club.** This May-through-October golf course is also the location of the final slope of the famous Streif run of the fearsome Hahnenkamm World Cup downhill race. Part of the Rasmushof Hotel, it's also the course closest to the town center. The greens and fairways are in full view of the glorious old building's balconies, and hotel guests receive special rates. ⊠ *Hermann Reisch Weg 15* ☎ *05356/65252*

⊕ *www.rasmushof.at* ☎ *€25 for 9 holes on weekdays, €31 on weekends; €35 for 18 holes on weekdays, €41 on weekends. Hotel guests: €19 per day for unlimited play* ⅄ *9 holes, 3060 yards, par 54.*

**SKIING**

Kitzbühel is one of Austria's leading resorts and home to the Hahnenkamm World Cup Downhill, one of the most daunting events on the ski-racing calendar. There are many easy slopes, too, and the ski network here is vast and spectacular, with many lovely mountain huts scattered over the slopes offering excellent food and drink to break the ski day—56 at the last count. There are 170 km (106 miles) of slopes and 53 ski lifts. Intersport Kitzsport has a number of shops in town with the latest equipment for rent, as does Sport 2000. There are 11 ski schools with more than 500 instructors at peak times. The tourist office website has full information.

# SÖLDEN

*176 km (109 miles) southwest of Kitzbühel.*

Sölden's addition to its already massive lift network is the "Black Blade," which carries eight at a time more than 9,800 feet to the Rettenbach glacier, completing the only lift system in Austria to boast skiing on three mountains more than 9,800 feet high. The view from any of the three peaks provides a panoramic 360-degree view of the mountains. Sölden's reputation as a wild, après-ski party town is well deserved, meaning that if you are searching for a tranquil, romantic ski holiday, or have small children, you may want to try the village of **Hochsölden**—on the slopes above town, where things are quieter—or search elsewhere.

**GETTING HERE AND AROUND**

From Innsbruck take the A12 west. Then take the B168 south to the Ötztal; after about 40 km (25 miles) you will reach the town of Sölden.

Leaving Sölden you can backtrack on the B168 north to the A12, or if you feel like some real hairpin Alpine driving, go south into Italy over the Timmelsjoch Pass.

**ESSENTIALS**

**Visitor Information Sölden/Ötztal.** ✉ *Rettenbach 466* ☎ *05254/510–0.*

## WHERE TO STAY

**$$$$**
**HOTEL**
🏨 **Aqua Dome Hotel and Spa.** Here you'll not only find what is reputed to be the finest spa in Tyrol, but also elegant guest rooms with balconies and stunning mountain views. **Pros:** amazing spa; great food; nonalcoholic drinks in the minibar are complimentary. **Cons:** spa busy on weekends; too sprawling for some; in winter, some distance from the ski slopes. 💲 *Rooms from: €372* ✉ *Oberlängenfeld 140, Längenfeld* ☎ *05253/6400* ⊕ *www.aqua-dome.at* 🛏 *200 rooms.*

**$$$$**
**HOTEL**
🏨 **Central.** Huge arches and heavy wood beams set the mood at this five-star hotel that's substantial both in size and character, and it has superb spa and fitness amenities. **Pros:** wonderful personal service; on-demand shuttle to the slopes; fabulous spa. **Cons:** slopes are not within walking distance; not all rooms have great views; church bells can give

early wake-up call. [$] *Rooms from: €450* ✉ *Auweg 3* ☎ *05254/2260–0* 🌐 *www.central-soelden.at* ⏱ *Closed May–mid-July* 🛏 *121 rooms.*

$$$ HOTEL 🏨 **Hotel Ritzlerhof.** Spectacularly located in the village of Sautens, on a shelf in the hillside high above the Oetz Valley, the Ritzlerhof is single-mindedly purposed toward meditational levels of peace and relaxation. **Pros:** idyllic location; heated indoor and outdoor pools; lots of peace and quiet. **Cons:** for winter stays, the ski lifts are not nearby; no bars or nightlife close by; for some, the remoteness might be a little too much. [$] *Rooms from: €278* ✉ *Ritzlerhof 1, Sautens* ☎ *05252/62680* 🌐 *www.ritzlerhof.at/en* 🛏 *44 rooms.*

$$$ HOTEL 🏨 **Liebe Sonne.** Skiers will be right next to the Giggijoch chairlift to Hochsölden at this sprawling yellow complex; the famous lift is also open all summer to give hikers and mountain bikers a flying start to their day. **Pros:** spacious rooms; close to the ski slopes; on-site stables for horseback riding. **Cons:** can sometimes be too busy; expensive Wi-Fi; lacking in Tyrolean tradition and decor. [$] *Rooms from: €280* ✉ *Dorfstrasse 58* ☎ *05254/22030* 🌐 *www.liebesonne.at* ⏱ *Closed May and June* 🛏 *60 rooms* 🍴 *Breakfast.*

$$$ HOTEL Fodor's Choice ★ 🏨 **Nature-Hotel Waldklause.** It's hard to tell where this hotel ends and the countryside begins—floors are natural stone, rooms smell of applewood paneling, and some exterior walls are built around trees. **Pros:** environmentally friendly; guests can use the nearby Aqua Dome spa for free; beautiful natural environment. **Cons:** not close to the mountain lifts; some rooms overlook a recreation area, not the mountains. [$] *Rooms from: €300* ✉ *Unterlangenfeld 190, Längenfeld* ☎ *05253/5455* 🌐 *www.waldklause.at* 🛏 *55 rooms.*

## NIGHTLIFE

The nightlife here varies from nonexistent to wild, depending on the season. In winter the more than 85 bars, discos, pubs, and eateries are packed, and many nightspots have live bands, but expect cover charges of around €5.

**Bierhimml Partyhaus.** This is the most popular music bar in the area, with a never-ending selection of beers and decent food. ✉ *Dorfstrasse 9* ☎ *05254/50112.*

**Fire & Ice.** In this very popular bar, the partying lasts from 3 pm to 3 am, thanks to the great dance floor. ✉ *Dorfstrasse 58* ☎ *05254/2203.*

## SPORTS AND THE OUTDOORS

### CLIMBING

**Wildspitze.** The Ventertal valley burrows far into the Ötztal Alps, ending in the tiny village of Vent, a popular resort center. In summer the village is transformed into a base for serious mountain climbers experienced in ice and rock climbing, who want to attempt the formidable Wildspitze (12,450 feet) or other, even more difficult neighboring peaks. Hiring a professional local guide is strongly advised. To reach Vent from Sölden, turn off at the road marked to Heiligenkreuz. ✉ *Vent.*

### RAFTING

**Vacancia Outdoor Tirol.** Everything you need to enjoy the area's wild waters can be found here, including guided rafting trips. It also organizes canyoning, glacier walks, and special outdoor adventures for kids. In winter you can secure skiing gear, lessons, and more children's programs. ⊠ *Dorfstrasse 11* ☎ *05254/3100* ⊕ *www.vacancia.at.*

### SKIING

Sölden is one of Austria's top skiing and snowboarding areas, with great snow and a long season thanks to its high-altitude slopes and two skiable glaciers. There are 150 km (93 miles) of slopes, with the top station at 10,660 feet, served by 33 lifts. The tourist office website has full information on ski instruction and equipment rental.

## ST. ANTON AM ARLBERG

*88 km (54 miles) northwest of Sölden.*

St. Anton is a particularly lovely town in summer, which has also become a fashionable season, but it really swarms with visitors at the height of the ski season. It is known as a cult destination for good skiers and boarders from around the world because of its extensive slopes full of character and challenges, and its huge amount of off-piste opportunities. But it's also a high-profile destination and attracts the wealthy, the prominent, and, occasionally, the royal. Therefore, accommodations are not cheap, but there is a wide range of options, and if you shop around you can find somewhere to stay, particularly outside the center of the action, at a bearable price.

Thanks to an amazing system of cable cars, gondolabahns, chairlifts, and T-bars, St. Anton grants skiers access to the Arlberg region's more than 300 km (186 miles) of marked runs. If you decide to take to the slopes, remember that skiing remains a serious business in St. Anton; this is a resort where skiers come in search of the steep and the deep, so choose your itinerary with care. Be aware of the different trail classifications in Europe—easy runs are marked blue on the trail map, medium is red, and difficult is black—but in places such as St. Anton, a blue might be a red elsewhere and a red might easily be a black.

### GETTING HERE AND AROUND

If you come from the east—from Innsbruck and Landeck—you either take Autobahn A12, then the B516, or you come on the B171. From the west from Bregenz you travel on Autobahn A14, which at the city of Bludenz becomes the B516. Near the village of Klösterle in summer you have to decide: continue on the B516 through the 14-km (8½-mile) Arlbergtunnel or travel over the pass on the B197 1½ km (1 mile) to St. Anton. If you're not in a hurry, go over the pass every time. This is high Alpine country and the surrounding views are fabulous.

### ESSENTIALS

**Visitor Information** St. Anton am Arlberg. ⊠ *Dorfstrasse 8* ☎ *05446/2269–0* ⊕ *www.stantonamarlberg.com.*

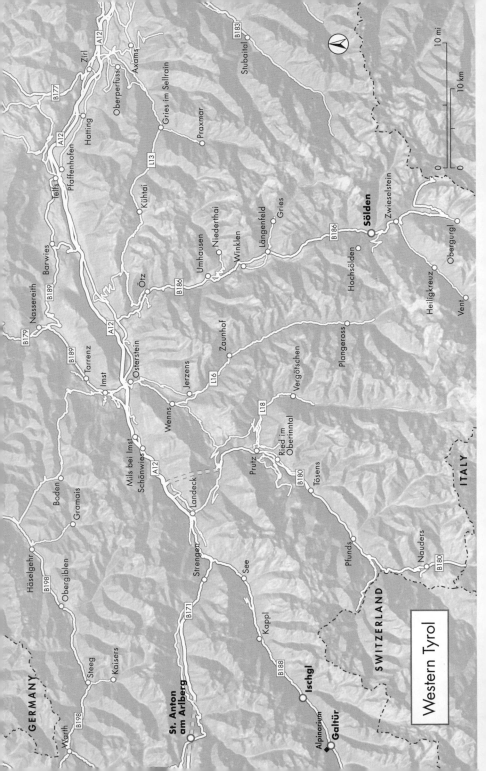

Western Tyrol

## WHERE TO STAY

**$$$**
HOTEL
Fodor's Choice
★

☷ **Anton Aparthotel.** If you're not looking for a quaint Tyrolean hotel, this wood-and-glass house—modern, casual, and almost Zen-like in its simplicity—could be the answer, thanks to its location in front of the slopes and steps from the main ski lifts. **Pros:** contemporary architecture that some will find refreshing; hip vibe; central location. **Cons:** modern look not for devotees of the traditional; draws a party crowd and, inevitably, party noise; need to book far in advance. $ *Rooms from: €260* ✉ *Kandaharweg 4* ☎ *05446/2408* ⊕ *www.hotelanton.at* 🛏 *14 rooms, 3 apartments* ¶❍¶ *Breakfast.*

**$$$**
HOTEL

☷ **Brunnenhof.** A homely and intimate 300-year-old farmhouse in nearby St. Jakob, painted a distinctive yellow, the Brunnenhof has character in abundance. **Pros:** cozy and romantic; reasonable off-season prices; quiet location. **Cons:** shuttle bus needed to get to the skiing; not for those who like to be in the middle of everything; taxi or car needed to get to any nightlife. $ *Rooms from: €230* ✉ *St. Jakober Dorfstrasse 53* ☎ *05446/2293* ☾ *Closed May, June, Oct., and Nov.* 🛏 *9 rooms, 1 apartment* ¶❍¶ *Breakfast.*

**$$$$**
HOTEL

☷ **Hotel Raffl's St. Antonerhof.** The Raffl family has created a distinctive and memorable hotel filled with antiques and art of all kinds. **Pros:** great location for skiers; fabulous cuisine; supreme luxury. **Cons:** closed in summer; very expensive; early booking is essential. $ *Rooms from: €680* ✉ *Arlbergstrasse 69* ☎ *05446/2910* ⊕ *www.antonerhof.at* ☾ *Closed mid-Apr.–Nov.* 🛏 *36 rooms.*

**$$$$**
HOTEL

☷ **Schwarzer Adler.** The beautifully frescoed facade of this ancient inn, which has been offering hospitality for nearly 450 years, hints at what you'll find inside: open fireplaces, Tyrolean antiques, and colorful Oriental carpets. **Pros:** very helpful and friendly staff; best bar in St. Anton; lovely building. **Cons:** in the lively center, so can be noisy occasionally; not cheap. $ *Rooms from: €416* ✉ *Dorfstrasse 35* ☎ *05446/22440* ⊕ *www.schwarzeradler.com* ☾ *Closed mid-Apr.–May, Oct., and Nov.* 🛏 *77 rooms.*

## NIGHTLIFE AND PERFORMING ARTS

For some visitors to St. Anton the show, not the snow, is the thing. Most of the bars are in the pedestrian zone.

**Horny Bull.** Formerly the Bar Kandahar, this place is still a popular après-ski spot in late afternoon and early evening. It becomes a typical restaurant around dinnertime, then morphs into one of the area's best nightclubs, with live music and guest DJs. ✉ *Sporthotel, Dorfstrasse 48* ☎ *05446/30260.*

**Krazy Kanguruh.** A favorite après-ski gathering spot, the Krazy Kanguruh is located right on the slopes: that means you'll have to ski down to get back to town, which could be tricky after a few drinks. Skiers have been partying here since 1965, and a trip to St. Anton is not complete without at least one visit here. ✉ *Moos 113* ☎ *05446/2633.*

**Mooserwirt.** Raucous, mind-boggling, and legendary, the Mooserwirt, on the piste side above St. Anton, has carved a reputation as one of skiing's most famous—or notorious—après-ski haunts. By all acounts, owner Eugen Scalet decided to "kill the cows and milk the tourists" by turning his parents' farmhouse into one of the world's rowdiest après-ski bars. It's said to sell the second-largest amount of beer annually of any bar in Austria. It has a boutique (soundproofed) hotel next door—the ultimate ski-in, ski-out destination. ⊠ *Unterer Mooserweg 2* ☏ *05446/3588* ⊕ *www.mooserwirt.at.*

## SPORTS AND THE OUTDOORS
### SKIING

The *Skihaserl,* or ski bunny, as the beginner is called, usually joins a class on St. Anton's nursery slopes, where he or she will have plenty of often-distinguished company. Once past the Skihaserl stage, skiers go higher in the Arlberg mountains to the superlative runs at Galzig and the 9,100-foot Valluga above it. Check with your hotel or the ski-pass desks at the base of the Galzigbahn gondola about an **Arlberg Skipass,** which is good on cable cars and lifts in St. Anton and St. Christoph on the Tyrol side and on those in Zürs, Lech, Oberlech, and Stuben in Vorarlberg, as well as the resorts of Warth and Schrecken, to which Lech is now linked via a gondolabahn. For complete details on St. Anton's skiing facilities, contact the town's tourist office.

**Skischule Arlberg.** This is considered by some to be the Harvard of ski schools and its location is certainly fitting, since Arlberg is known as the cradle of skiing. The world's first properly organized ski school was opened here by ski pioneer Hannes Schneider. ⊠ *St. Anton am Arlberg* ☏ *05446/3411* ⊕ *www.skischool-arlberg.com.*

# ISCHGL AND GALTÜR

*67 km (42 miles) southeast of St. Christoph.*

**Ischgl,** the best-known resort in the Paznaun Valley, has become as renowned for its party scene as for its excellent skiing—it links with the Swiss resort of Samnaun and has a wealth of high-altitude runs. In summer it's a popular health resort, with activities including hiking, climbing, and mountain biking. There are many high-profile events here, both in summer and winter, including big-name rock concerts, mountain biking, and culinary events, and one of Europe's leading snow sculpture (as opposed to ice sculpture) competitions.

Slightly higher up the valley is **Galtür,** equally popular as a winter-sports area, summer resort, and a base for mountain climbing. Although Galtür is a starting point for practiced mountaineers, many of the climbs up the Blue Silvretta are easy and lead to the half-dozen mountain huts belonging to the Alpenverein. Galtür and the Silvretta region inspired Ernest Hemingway's novella *Alpine Idyll*; the author spent the winter of 1925 here, and the town still remembers him fondly.

You can get to Idalp, at 7,500-feet, via the 4-km-long (2½-mile-long) Silvretta gondolabahn. The enchanting Paznaun Valley follows the course of the Trisanna River for more than 40 km (25 miles). The valley runs into the heart of the Blue Silvretta mountains, named for the shimmering ice-blue effect created by the great peaks and glaciers, dominated by the Fluchthorn (10,462 feet) at the head of the valley.

### GETTING HERE AND AROUND

From the B516 just west of Landeck, take the B188 into the Paznauntal (Paznaun Valley). After about 40 km (25 miles) you'll reach Ischgl. Another 13 km (8 miles) gets you to Galtür. Returning, you can either double back, or, if it's nice weather and you feel like some serious Alpine driving, head to the Silvretta-Hochalpen-strasse (Silvretta High Alpine Road). It takes you on many hairpin curves up to 7,000 feet and then down into the Montafon Valley in Vorarlberg. The cost for driving on the pass is €15 per car.

### ESSENTIALS

**Visitor Information** Ischgl. ✉ *Dorfstrasse 43, Ischgl* ☎ *05444/52660* 🌐 *www.ischgl.com/en.*

## EXPLORING

**Alpinarium.** Following an avalanche of catastrophic proportions on February 23, 1999, which took 31 lives and destroyed many centuries-old homes and guesthouses, the community of Galtür undertook a massive building project that resulted in the Alpinarium, a memorial, museum, conference center, café, indoor climbing hall, library, and, most significantly, a 1,132-foot-long wall built of steel and concrete designed to prevent such an accident from occurring again. On summer Saturdays, 10–4, the *Bauernmarkt* (farmers' market) sets up in front of the Alpinarium, bringing produce, cheese, meat, and specialty products. ✉ *Hauptstrasse 29c, Galtür* ☎ *05443/20000* 🌐 *www.alpinarium.at* 🎟 *€8* 🕒 *Museum closed Mon.*

## WHERE TO STAY

$$$$ HOTEL 🏨 **Hotel Madlein.** Quirkiness reigns supreme at this luxurious hotel, from the minimalist lobby to the Zen-influenced guest rooms (although some retain Tyrolean wood paneling), and the two nightclubs. **Pros:** unique atmosphere; exlusive celebrity vibe; escalator access to ski lift. **Cons:** expensive; lacking in Tyrolean feel; with two nightclubs, can feel very bustling. [$] *Rooms from: €420* ✉ *Madleinweg 2, Ischgl* ☎ *05444/5226* 🌐 *www.madlein.com* 🛏 *79 rooms.*

$$$ HOTEL 🏨 **Hotel Rössle.** The oldest guesthouse in Galtür (as shown by a tax return record from 1600), the centrally located Rössle hotel overflows with Tyrolean charm. **Pros:** plenty of atmosphere; top-notch dining; quiet village surroundings. **Cons:** the lifts are a short ski-bus ride away; the nightlife of Ischgl involves a taxi ride; church bells can be intrusive. [$] *Rooms from: €250* ✉ *Am Dorfplatz, Galtür* ☎ *05443/82320* 🌐 *www.roessle.com* 🛏 *40 rooms.*

$$$$ HOTEL 🏨 **Post Ischgl.** In the middle of the town's pedestrian area, an imposing facade fronts this 200-year-old haven of luxury and Tyrolean charm, with attractive rooms and a highly rated restaurant serving international and local cuisine. **Pros:** close to shops, bars, and restaurants; a luxurious atmosphere; excellent food. **Cons:** lively bar-nightclub means it can be noisy in ski season; in winter high season you can book only by the week; smoking still seems to be tolerated in the bar. [$] *Rooms from: €370* ✉ *Dorfstrasse 47, Ischgl* ☎ *05444/5232* 🌐 *www.post-ischgl.at* 🛏 *83 rooms* 🍴 *Breakfast.*

$$$$
HOTEL
Fodor's Choice
★

**Trofana Royal.** This is Ischgl's flagship hotel, elegant and romantic, and the only five-star property in town. **Pros:** great location; large, impressive nightclub; fabulous food. **Cons:** very expensive; the hotel's popular après-ski bar can mean some noise; smoking seems to be allowed in the lounge. $ *Rooms from: €520* ✉ *Ischgl 334, Ischgl* ☎ *05444/600* ⊕ *www.trofana.at* ⊃ *112 rooms.*

### NIGHTLIFE AND PERFORMING ARTS

Ischgl has such a rousing nightlife that during the ski season it would be difficult not to find the après-ski and nightlife action.

**Kuhstall.** In the center of town, Kuhstall (meaning cowshed) in the winter is a rocking, ultrapopular après-ski bar, rustically themed. ✉ *Sporthotel Silvretta, Dorfstrasse 74, Ischgl* ☎ *05444/5223* ⊕ *www.kuhstall.at.*

**Niki's Stadl.** An Ischgl après-ski institution, this place is traditional, raucous, bizarre, and a must-visit. It regularly provides a mix of Europop and Tyrolean après-ski cheesy oompah-rock. ✉ *Piz Buin Hotel, Dorfstrasse, Ischgl* ☎ *05444/5300* ⊕ *www.nikis-stadl.com.*

**Trofana Alm.** It might feel like an ancient timbered converted barn, but Trofana Alm is actually one of the most successful and slick après-ski bars in the Alps. Open from 3 pm, it switches at 7 pm from dance venue to romantic candlelit restaurant, then at 11 it's back to full-on nightclub and disco. ✉ *Trofana Royal Hotel, Dorfstrasse 91, Ischgl, Ischgl* ☎ *05444/602.*

# VORARLBERG

The Western Alps are a haven for those who love the great outdoors. It's also a region that provides getaway space and privacy—Ernest Hemingway came to Schruns to write *The Sun Also Rises*. In spring, summer, and fall, travelers delight in riding, tennis, swimming, and hiking the Montafon Valley, which is dominated by the "Matterhorn of Austria," the Zimba peak (8,671 feet), and is probably the most attractive of Vorarlberg's many tourist-frequented valleys. When the snow arrives, skiers head to the hills to take advantage of the Arlberg mountain range, the highest in the Lechtal Alps.

## SCHRUNS-TSCHAGGUNS

*10 km (6 miles) southeast of Brand, 60 km (39 miles) southeast of Bregenz.*

Author Ernest Hemingway spent many winters at the Schruns–Tschagguns skiing area in the Montafon Valley. Today neither of the towns—across the Ill River from each other—is as fashionable as the resorts on the Arlberg, but the views over the Ferwall Alps to the east and the mighty Rätikon on the western side of the valley are unsurpassed anywhere in Austria. In winter the heavy snowfalls here provide wonderful skiing. In fact, many believe the fully integrated ski area to be seriously underrated. The snow record is good, the runs are interesting, and a renaissance of the area's winter status is on the horizon. Many skiers head for Hochjoch-Zamang—the main peak at **Schruns**—to have lunch

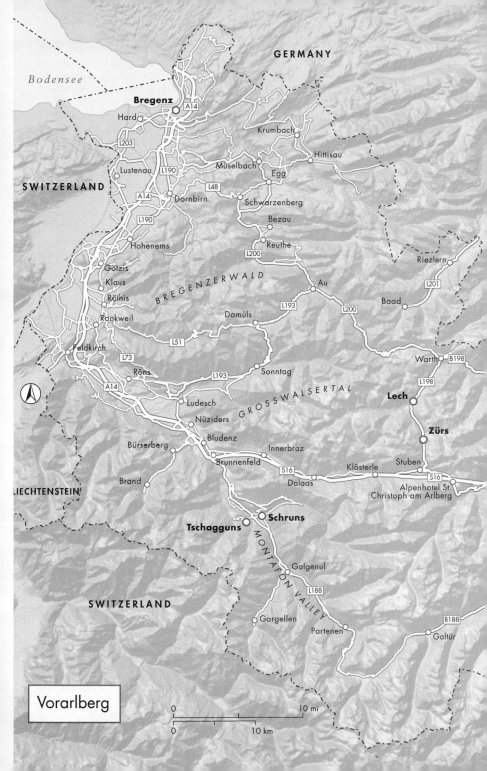

on the spectacularly sited sun terrace of the Kapell restaurant. Then it's on to Grabs-Golm over the river in **Tschagguns.** Others prefer the Silvretta-Nova run at Gaschurn and St. Gallenkirch. In summer, the heights are given over to climbers and hikers, the mountain streams to trout anglers, and the lowlands to tennis players.

#### GETTING HERE AND AROUND

From Bregenz take the Autobahn A14 south. Soon after Bludenz take the B188 to the Montafoner Tal (Montafon Valley). After about 8 km (5 miles) you reach Schruns–Tschagguns. If you want to experience Alpine driving after your visit to town, continue south on the B188 to the Silvretta-Hochalpenstrasse (Silvretta High Alpine Road) to the Bielerhöhe at 7,000 feet, and then over many hairpin curves into Tyrol and the Paznaun Valley. The cost of using the pass is €15 per car. Attempt the drive only in ideal weather conditions and if you have good brakes; in winter the pass is closed.

**Tourist Information** Montafon Valley. ✉ *Montafoner Strasse 21, Schruns* ☎ *050/6686* 🌐 *www.montafon.at.*

### WHERE TO EAT AND STAY

$$ AUSTRIAN 🍴 **Gasthof Löwen.** Guests started eating here more than 500 years ago, and they've been coming back ever since. The old dining room has wood-paneled walls and is the perfect setting in which to enjoy a *Zwiebelrostbraten* (steak with onions) and a good red wine. **Known for:** traditional atmosphere; live folk music; solid Austrian fare. [$] *Average main: €15* ✉ *Kreuzgasse 4, Tschagguns* ☎ *05556/72247* 🌐 *www.loewen-tschagguns.at* 🕒 *Closed Mon. and mid-June–mid-July.*

$$$ HOTEL 🏨 **Löwen.** In the heart of Schruns this hotel looks (and is) huge, but inside the modern take on a traditional Austrian abode works well, with the rustic dark-wood theme of the exterior carried over elegantly into the comfortable rooms with balconies. **Pros:** spacious and luxurious; enormous spa, which includes a women-only section; glorious scenic setting. **Cons:** atmosphere can feel a bit formal; large size means no sense of intimacy; some feel it lacks Austrian tradition. [$] *Rooms from: €300* ✉ *Silvrettastrasse 8, Schruns* ☎ *05556/7141* 🌐 *www.loewen-hotel.com* 🕒 *Closed mid-Apr.–mid-May and mid-Oct.–mid-Dec.* 🛏 *85 rooms.*

$$$$ HOTEL 🏨 **Montafoner Hof.** There's a lot of local flavor in this popular and welcoming family-run hotel in Tschagguns, where the owner's hunting credentials are reflected in the delicious traditional food in the restaurant. **Pros:** Austrian hospitality at its finest; comfortable atmosphere; wonderful food. **Cons:** restaurant not great for vegetarians; some rooms not renovated; as in many Austrian hotels, smoking habit still persists. [$] *Rooms from: €350* ✉ *Kreuzgasse 9, Tschagguns* ☎ *05556/71000* 🌐 *www.montafonerhof.com* 🕒 *Closed Apr., May, and end of Nov.–mid-Dec.* 🛏 *48 rooms* 🍽 *Breakfast.*

### SPORTS AND THE OUTDOORS

#### FISHING

The local mountain streams and rivers are full of fish. Licenses are available; ask the regional tourist office in Bregenz for detailed information on seasons and locations.

## SKIING

Schruns is one of the skiing centers of the Montafon region, which also includes the Bartholomäberg, Gargellen, Gaschurn-Partenen, St. Gallenkirch/Gortipohl, Silbertal, and Vandans ski areas. They are together covered with a Montafon Ski Pass and comprise 65 lifts and 208 km (129 miles) of groomed runs. Ski pass prices are attractive here, €102 for a two-day adult pass, for example, with discounts for seniors and children. For details contact Montafon Tourism.

**12**

# ZÜRS

*42 km (26 miles) northeast of Schruns-Tschagguns, 90 km (56 miles) southeast of Bregenz.*

The chosen resort of the rich and fashionable on this side of the Arlberg, Zürs is little more than a collection of large and seriously plush hotels. Perched at 5,600 feet, it's strictly a winter-sports community; when the season is over, the hotels close. But Zürs is more exclusive than nearby Lech and even more fabulous, in an ultradiscreet fashion, than Gstaad or St. Moritz in Switzerland. Royalty and celebrities don't come here to promenade or to be seen. They come to enjoy a hedonistic lifestyle behind the often anodyne facade of their five-star hotel, and to ski on perfectly

### CHAMPAGNE ON THE SLOPES

Accessible by the Trittkopf cable car, at the highest point of the Flexen Pass, you'll find the Flexenhäsl (Little Flexen House), a very special little hut that can seat only 20. Here you can order up mouthwatering tidbits such as scampi with garlic butter and *Hirschwürstel* (venison sausage) with fresh horseradish sauce, washed down with a bottle of chilled Dom Pérignon. In the evening join in for piping-hot fondue *chinoise*. Reservations are essential (☎ 05583/4143).

groomed slopes, anonymous in helmets and sunglasses. Full board is required in most hotels, so there are relatively few "public" restaurants in town and little chance to dine around. But the hotel dining rooms are elegant; in some, jacket and tie are required in the evening. High standards were always part of the history of Zürs—the hotel Zürserhof was built by the aristocratic hotelier Count Tattenbach in the 1920s, and the first ski lift in Austria was constructed here in 1937.

### GETTING HERE AND AROUND

If you are coming from the west on the B516, make sure to take the B197 toward the Arlberg Pass after passing Klösterle (do not go into the Arlberg Tunnel). A few miles past Stuben follow the sign to the left toward Zürs/Lech on the B198. The Arlberg Pass is sometimes closed in winter after heavy snowfall, but the road to Zürs/Lech is rarely closed, with sections protected by avalanche balconies. Coming from the east from Innsbruck in winter, you may have to go through the Arlberg Tunnel and then use the B197/B198.

### ESSENTIALS

**Tourist Information Zürs.** ✉ *Lechtal Strasse* ☎ *05583/2245* ⊕ *www.lech-zuers.at.*

### WHERE TO STAY

$$$$ HOTEL [H] **Sporthotel Edelweiss.** Housed in a 19th-century building, the Edelweiss has become a Zürs institution. **Pros:** rooms gorgeously decorated; gourmet restaurant; stylish luxury. **Cons:** can get very lively; room decoration might be too busy for some; very expensive. [$] *Rooms from: €520* ✉ *Lechtal Strasse 79* ☎ *05583/2662* 🌐 *www.edelweiss.net* ⏲ *Closed mid-Apr.–Nov.* 🛏 *63 rooms, 3 apartments.*

$$$$ HOTEL [H] **Sporthotel Lorünser.** The hospitable elegance of this hotel draws royalty, including Princess Caroline of Monaco and Princess (formerly Queen) Beatrix of the Netherlands. **Pros:** discreet elegance; continued top quality; right by the slopes for skiing. **Cons:** closed in summer; very expensive; might be too over-the-top for some. [$] *Rooms from: €692* ✉ *Nr. 112* ☎ *05583/22540* 🌐 *www.loruenser.at* ⏲ *Closed mid-Apr.–early Dec.* 🛏 *74 rooms* 🍴 *All-inclusive.*

$$$$ HOTEL [H] **Zürserhof.** When celebrities seek privacy, they ensconce themselves in this world-famous hostelry resembling five huge interlinked chalets, a family-run house that has managed to preserve a certain intimacy. **Pros:** exclusivity and privacy; top luxury fit for a royal; wonderful food. **Cons:** high prices; it might be too formal for some; even here, smoking is allowed in one area of the bar. [$] *Rooms from: €920* ✉ *Nr. 75, 6763* ☎ *05583/2513–0* 🌐 *www.zuerserhof.at* ⏲ *Closed mid-Apr.–Nov.* 🛏 *104 rooms* 🍴 *Breakfast.*

### SPORTS AND THE OUTDOORS

#### SKIING

There are four main lifts out of the village: take the chairlift to Hexenboden (7,600 feet) or the cable car to Trittkopf (7,800 feet), with a restaurant and sun terrace; two chairlifts head up to Seekopf (7,000 feet) and the Zurzersee, where there is another restaurant. This mountain often gets huge snowfalls. ■ **TIP→ Skiers need to be particularly aware of avalanche conditions—check with the tourist office or your hotel before you hit the off-piste slopes.**

## LECH

*4 km (2½ miles) north of Zürs, 90 km (56 miles) southeast of Bregenz.*

**Fodor's Choice** ★ Just down (literally) the road from Zürs, Lech is a full-fledged community—and one of the most fashionable in the Alps. But there are more hotels in Lech than in Zürs, better tourist facilities, bigger ski schools, more shops, and more nightlife. Hotel prices are nearly as high. Celebrities, captains of industry, and royalty are often found in this very pretty Alpine village. Be sure to check with the hotel of your choice about meal arrangements; some hotels recommend that you take half-board, which is usually a good deal.

### GETTING HERE AND AROUND

From Zürs go north on the B198 for 4 km (2½ miles) to Lech. In summer you can continue north on the B198 down to the town of Warth and Reutte in Tyrol, near the German border. You can't get to Zürs or Lech via rail; take the train to Langen am Arlberg station, then transfer to a bus or taxi.

12

### ESSENTIALS

**Tourist Information Lech.** ✉ *Dorf 2* ☎ *05583/2161–0* 🌐 *www.lech-zuers.at.*

### SAY KÄSE, PLEASE

In the last two decades, cheese making has undergone a magnificent revival in the region. Farmers produce more than 30 varieties of *Käse*—from Emmental to beer cheese, Tilsit to red-wine cheese, and *Bergkäse* (mountain cheese) in dozens of varieties. Look for discreet *KäseStrasse* signs along the road, pointing you toward the region's elite cheese makers, or for the word *Sennerei*, which means Alpine dairy (🌐 *www.kaesestrasse.at*).

### WHERE TO STAY

$$$$ HOTEL Fodor's Choice ★ 🏨 **Gasthof Post.** A gemütlich atmosphere enfolds in this blue-shuttered Relais & Chateaux chalet hotel, with murals, flower boxes, and a wood-paneled interior of extravagant luxury. **Pros:** refined, comfortable luxury in historic setting; antiques artfully displayed throughout the hotel; huge spa with in- and outdoor pools. **Cons:** very expensive; it gets very booked up, so reserve well in advance; hotel atmosphere not for everyone. [$] *Rooms from: €530* ✉ *Dorf 11* ☎ *05583/22060* 🌐 *www.postlech.com* 🕒 *Closed May–mid-June, Oct., and Nov.* 🛏 *46 rooms, 2 apartments* 🍴 *Breakfast.*

$$$$ HOTEL 🏨 **Pfefferkorn's Hotel.** A cozy yet spacious wood-paneled lobby makes you feel welcome the minute you enter the Pfefferkorn, and this warm-wood Alpine style continues into many of the guest rooms. **Pros:** warm atmosphere; very attentive staff; great location close to the main lifts. **Cons:** rooms near the street on the lower floors can be noisy; some rooms may feel a little dated; very popular with nonresidents in the evening, so can lack intimacy. [$] *Rooms from: €526* ✉ *Dorf 138* ☎ *05583/25250* 🌐 *www.pfefferkorns.net* 🕒 *Closed May, June, Oct., and Nov.* 🛏 *29 rooms.*

$$$$ HOTEL 🏨 **Romantik Hotel Krone.** Across the street from two of the main lifts, this family-managed five-star hotel started life as a tavern in 1741 and is now providing hospitality of an altogether more luxurious variety. **Pros:** in winter, it's ski-in ski-out here; excellent cuisine; impressive spa. **Cons:** the hotel is very close to the main street, so nighttime revelry can intrude; worth requesting a room on the slope side, as morning deliveries can be noisy; smoking is allowed in the Krone Bar. [$] *Rooms from: €480* ✉ *Dorf 13* ☎ *05583/2551* 🌐 *www.romantikhotelkrone-lech.at* 🕒 *Closed mid-Apr.–mid-June, Oct., and Nov.* 🛏 *56 rooms* 🍴 *Breakfast.*

### NIGHTLIFE AND PERFORMING ARTS

Lech has a lively après-ski and nightlife scene—not nearly as overt as in nearby St. Anton or Ischgl, but partying is important to most Austrian ski villages, even ones as upscale as Lech. Prices vary from place to place, but in general a mixed drink will cost €12–€16.

**Burg.** The bar in the Burg hotel in Oberlech features live music most nights. ✉ *Oberlech 266* ☎ *05583/2291* 🌐 *www.burghotel-lech.com.*

**Goldener Berg.** The bar at the Goldener Berg is usually a hot après-ski spot, often with live music. ✉ *Goldener Berg, Oberlech 117* ☎ *05583/2205.*

**Krone Bar.** The bar in the Romantik Hotel Krone is open, and remains quite lively, until 2 or 3 am. ⊠ *Dorf 13* ☎ *05583/2551* ⊕ *www.romantikhotelkrone-lech.at.*

**Pfefferkörndl.** This is a popular bar in Lech for a mid-evening drink. It stays open until about 2 am, and is good for speciality coffee, too. ⊠ *Pfefferkorn's Hotel* ☎ *05583/2525–429.*

**Tea Dance.** The tradition of tea dancing (literally a dance at teatime, popular since Victorian times, especially at smart ski resorts) carries on après-ski at the ice-bar of the Tannbergerhof—but nowadays it's more disco than foxtrot. ⊠ *Dorf 111* ☎ *05583/2202–0* ⊕ *www.tannbergerhof.com.*

**Umbrella.** You can join the snacks-and-drinks crowd as early as 11 am at the outdoor and famed Umbrella bar at the Petersboden Sport Hotel at Oberlech. ⊠ *Oberlech 278* ☎ *05583/3232* ⊕ *www.petersboden.com.*

## SPORTS AND THE OUTDOORS
### SKIING

Lech is linked with Oberlech and Zürs, with more than 30 ski lifts and cable cars, all accessed by the regional ski pass. This also allows skiers to take in the entire region, including Stuben, St. Christoph, and St. Anton, as well as Warth and Schrocken, newly linked by lift to Lech. The St. Anton area is also now linked to Zürs thanks to a gondola system, negating the need to take a ski-bus. The area as a whole includes more than 90 cable cars and lifts (many of them with heated seats) and 300 km (186 miles) of groomed pistes. In addition, there is a large network of cross-country trails.

The slopes in Lech are spread between 4,757 feet and 9,186 feet above sea level, including the runs of Rüfikopf, Madloch, and Mohnenfluh. Some 400 skiing instructors can help you master the craft here. Snowboarders have their own Fun Park, and there is a floodlit toboggan run and horse-drawn sleigh rides.

**Lech-Zürs Tourist Office.** For complete information on skiing facilities contact the Lech-Zürs Tourist Office on the main street in the center of Lech. ⊠ *Lech* ☎ *05583/2161–0* ⊕ *www.lechzuers.com/lech-zuers-tourist-office.*

# BREGENZ

*150 km (90 miles) west of Innsbruck, 660 km (409 miles) west of Vienna, 120 km (75 miles) east of Zurich, 193 km (120 miles) southwest of Munich.*

Lying along the southeastern shore of the Bodensee (Lake Constance) with the majestic Pfänder as its backdrop, Bregenz is where Vorarlbergers themselves come to make merry, especially in summer. Along the lakeside beach and public pool, cabanas and cotton candy encourage starched collars to let loose, while nearby an enormous floating stage is the open-air site for performances of grand opera and orchestral works (Verdi, Rimski-Korsakov, Strauss, and Gershwin are just some of the composers who have been featured). Bregenz is the capital of

Vorarlberg, and has been the seat of the provincial government since 1819. The upper town has maintained a charming old-world character. The lower city is a vibrant part of town with pedestrian streets, shops, the train station, restaurants, and offices.

**GETTING HERE AND AROUND**

**12**

Fly into Zurich airport and take a Euro City Express train directly from the airport to Bregenz Main Station. The trip takes about 1½ hours. From Innsbruck you come through the Arlberg tunnel, from Germany on the autobahn, and from Switzerland on the autobahn via St. Gallen. From Vienna it takes about 7½ hours by car, from Munich about 2½.

Taxi fares in Bregenz start at about €8, so taking one even a short distance can be expensive. Call to order a radio cab. The city of Bregenz also runs a very efficient public bus line.

**Bus Information Bus.** ✉ *Rathausstrasse 4* ☎ *5574/4959-0* ⊕ *www. bregenz.travel/en/tourism/planning-a-trip/getting-around-in-bregenz/ bregenz-by-city-bus.*

**Taxi Companies City Taxi.** ☎ *05574/65400* ⊕ *www.citytaxi-bregenz.at.*

**ESSENTIALS**

**Visitor Information Visitor Information.** ✉ *Poststrasse 11, Dornbirn* ☎ *05572/3770330* ⊕ *www.vorarlberg.at.*

# EXPLORING

## TOP ATTRACTIONS

Fodor's Choice ★ **Bregenzer Festspiele.** Bregenz is pleasant at any time of year, but a great time to visit is during the Bregenzer Festspiele (Bregenz Music Festival) in July and August. Acclaimed artists from around the world perform operas, operettas, and musical comedies on the festival's floating stage, part of the Festspiel und Kongresshaus (Festival Hall and Congress Center) complex. In front of the stage, the orchestra pit is built on a jetty, while the audience of 6,800 is safely accommodated on the 30-tier amphitheater on dry land—a unique and memorable setting for a concert. Reserve your tickets and hotels in advance, as performances and rooms sell out early. ✉ *Platz der Wiener Symphoniker 1* ⊕ *www. bregenzerfestspiele.com/en.*

**Martinsturm.** This tower (1599–1602) has the largest onion dome in Central Europe, and was the first Baroque construction on Lake Constance. It has since become a symbol of Bregenz. ✉ *Martinsgasse 3b* ⊕ *www. bregenz.gv.at/kultur/martinsturm* ☒ *€3.50* ⊙ *Closed Mon. in Oct.–Apr.*

FAMILY Fodor's Choice ★ **Pfänder.** A cable car takes you up to this 3,491-foot peak overlooking Bregenz, one of the most famous lookout points in the region, from which you can see four countries—Austria, Germany, Liechtenstein, and Switzerland—and almost 240 Alpine peaks. It's a breathtaking view, with the city directly below on the shores of the Bedensee and the lake stretching for 64 km (40 miles) into the hazy distance. On your left lies the Rhine valley, and you can see the hills of Liechtenstein and Switzerland. Just across the water from Bregenz you'll notice the ancient and fascinating German island-city of Lindau in Bavaria, once a free state (a status it lost in 1802). The Pfänder restaurant is open June–mid-September. Children will enjoy a 30-minute circular hike to a small outdoor zoo with deer, Alpine goats, and wild boar. ⊠ *Bregenz* ☎ *05574/421600* ⊕ *www.pfaender.at/en* ☜ *Cable-car round-trip €12.70* ⊙ *Closed 2 wks in mid-Nov.*

## WORTH NOTING

**Adlerwarte.** At the Birds of Prey show at the Pfander, eagles, hawks, falcons, and owls demonstrate their prowess in free flight. Shows at 11 am and 2:30 pm happen at the Eagle Observatory in May through September. ⊠ *Bregenz* ☎ *0664/905–3040* ☜ *€5.90.*

**Altes Rathaus** (*Old City Hall*). Amble on along Martinsgasse to Graf-Wilhelm-Strasse and the brightly shuttered Altes Rathaus, the old town hall. The ornate half-timber construction was completed in 1622. ⊠ *Rathausstrasse and Anton-Schneider-Strasse.*

**Beckenturm.** From the hill outside the church there is a wonderful view of the southwestern wall of the Old City, including the Beckenturm, the 16th-century tower once used as a prison and named after bakers imprisoned there for baking rolls that were too skimpy for the town fathers. ⊠ *Bregenz.*

**Bodensee White Fleet.** The lake itself is a prime attraction, with boat trips available to nearby Switzerland and Germany. Don't forget to bring your passport. The Bodensee White Fleet ferries offer several trip options. You can travel to the "flower isle" of Mainau or make a crossing to Konstanz, Germany, with stops at Lindau, Friedrichshafen, and Meersburg. The longest round-trip excursion is the Drei-Länder Rundfahrt, which includes stops in Germany and Switzerland. The ferries have different operating schedules, with most routes restricted to the summer months. The Mainau excursion runs from May to mid-September. The fleet does not shut down completely in winter, however; there are festive sailings for Christmas and New Years. ⊠ *Vorarlberg Lines Bodenseeschiffahrt, Seestrasse 4* ☎ *05574/42868* ⊕ *www.bodenseeschifffahrt.at* ☜ *Single trips starting from €5.10.*

**City Wall.** Remains of the ancient city wall are to the right of the tower on Martinsgasse. The coats of arms of several noble Bregenz families can still be seen on the house standing next to the wall's remains. ⊠ *Martinsgasse.*

**Gasthof Kornmesser.** To the right of the Nepomuk-Kapelle along Kornmarktstrasse is the Gasthof Kornmesser, built in 1720 and a gorgeous example of a Baroque town house. It is now a restaurant serving hearty Austrian dishes at very reasonable prices. ⊠ *Kornmarktstrasse* ⊕ *www.kornmesser.at.*

**Gesellenspital** (*Journeymen's Hospital*). Behind the Altes Rathaus on Eponastrasse stands the former Gesellenspital; remnants of a fresco still visible on its wall depict St. Christopher, St. Peter, and a kneeling abbot. ⊠ *Eponastrasse.*

**Herz-Jesu Kirche.** Off Belrupstrasse, the Herz-Jesu Kirche was built in 1908 in brick Gothic style. The stained-glass windows by Martin Hausle are especially bright and colorful. ⊠ *Bregenz.*

**Kunsthaus.** Vorarlberg has had its own modern art museum since 1997. Designed by Swiss architect Peter Zumtho, the steel-and-concrete building with etched-glass panels creates a feeling of space and light. The innovative feature of 8-foot openings between each story allows sunlight to enter the translucent glass through the ceiling. This design marvel bathes each gallery in natural light in spite of concrete walls. ⊠ *Karl-Tizian-Platz* ☎ *05574/485–940* ⊕ *www.kunsthaus-bregenz.at* ☜ *€9* ⊙ *Closed Mon.*

**12**

**Künstlerhaus Thurn und Taxis.** Owned by the princely Thurn und Taxis family until 1915, this building, erected in 1848, now contains a modern art gallery. The **Thurn und Taxispark** contains rare trees and plants from around the world. ⊠ *Gallusstrasse 8* ☎ *5574/427–51* ⊕ *www. kuenstlerhaus-bregenz.at.*

**Martinskirche.** Next to the Stadtsteig, explore the interior of this tiny church with its fine 14th-century frescoes. ⊠ *Martinsplatz.*

**Montfortbrunnen** (*fountain*). Every year on Ash Wednesday, the Montfortbrunnen, in the center of Ehreguta Platz, is the scene of the ritual washing of wallets and change purses, when carnival jesters clean out their empty pockets and spin tales about the events of the previous year. The fountain honors the minnesinger Hugo von Montfort, a poet who performed songs of courtly love, who was born in the city in 1357. ⊠ *Ehreguta Platz.*

**Nepomuk-Kapelle.** Behind the post office is the distinctive circular Chapel of St. John of Nepomuk, built in 1757 to serve the city's fishermen and sailors. It has a richly decorated altar, and today the town's Hungarian community celebrates mass here. ⊠ *Kaspar Moosbrugger Platz.*

**Parish Church of St. Gallus.** The small parallel streets running uphill from Ehreguta Square roughly outline the boundaries of the town in the Middle Ages. Hidden around the corner of the building at the beginning of Georgen-Schilde-Strasse are the **Meissnerstiege** (Meissner steps), named after a local poet, that lead from the Old City to the parish church of St. Gallus. At the bottom of the steps, follow Schlossbergstrasse up the hill to the church, which combines Romanesque, Gothic, and Rococo elements. The interior is decorated simply with pastel coloring instead of the usual excessive gilding. Empress Maria Theresa donated the money for the high altarpiece. You'll notice the monarch's features on one of the shepherdesses depicted there. ⊠ *Schlossbergstrasse.*

**Post Office.** The town's Neoclassical main post office was built in 1893 by Viennese architect Friedrich Setz. Because of the marshy conditions, the post office is built on wood pilings to prevent it from sinking. ⊠ *Seestrasse 5.*

**Seekapelle** (*Lake Chapel*). Next door to the Rathaus is the Seekapelle (Lake Chapel), topped with an onion dome. The chapel was put up over the graves of a band of Swiss citizens whose 1408 attempt to incorporate Bregenz into Switzerland was rejected. ⊠ *Rathausstrasse.*

**Stadtsteig.** Go left from Belrupstrasse onto Maurachgasse. Walking up Maurachgasse, you'll reach the Stadtsteig guarding the entrance to the Old City, which bears the emblem of a Celtic-Roman equine goddess (the original is now housed in the Vorarlbergmuseum). Inside the gate are the coats of arms of the dukes of Bregenz and the dukes of Montfort, the latter crest now the Vorarlberg provincial emblem. ✉ *Maurachgasse.*

**Theater am Kornmarkt.** Just after the alley simply marked "theater" along Kornmarktstrasse you'll reach this theater, originally constructed in 1838, when Bregenz was still an important commercial port, due to its role as a grain storehouse; in 1954 the granary was converted into a 700-seat theater. ✉ *Kornmarktstrasse* 🌐 *www.landestheater.org.*

**Vorarlbergmuseum (formerly Vorarlberger Landesmuseum)** (*Provincial Museum*). Next door to the Theater am Kornmarkt, this museum houses relics from Brigantium, the Roman administrative city that once stood where Bregenz is today. Gothic and Romanesque ecclesiastical works are also on display. Guided tours are offered on weekends. ✉ *Kornmarktplatz 1* ☎ *05574/46050* 🌐 *www.vorarlbergmuseum.at* 🎫 *€9; guided tour €5* 🕓 *Closed Mon. in Sept.–mid-July.*

## WHERE TO EAT

$ CAFÉ — 🍴 **Café Götze.** Locals frequent this small, unpretentious café, also a bakery, because it's known to have the best pastries in town. The location halfway between the waterfront and the Old City is convenient. **Known for:** gorgeous displays of cakes; wonderful chocolates; elegant gift-wrapping for souvenirs. [$] *Average main: €8* ✉ *Kaiserstrasse 9* ☎ *05574/44523* 🌐 *www.conditorei-goetze.com* 💳 *No credit cards* 🕓 *Closed weekends.*

$$ ECLECTIC — 🍴 **Gasthof Goldener Hirsch.** Allegedly the oldest tavern in Bregenz and close to the Old City, this rustic restaurant offers delicious traditional food and drinks in lively surroundings. Many say it's the most authentic Austrian eatery in town, great for *Tafelspitz* (slow-cooked beef with horseradish). **Known for:** lots of history; a fantastic Tafelspitz and pasta dishes; reasonable prices. [$] *Average main: €12* ✉ *Kirchstrasse 8* ☎ *05574/42815* 🌐 *www.hotelweisseskreuz.at/de/goldener-hirschen* 🕓 *Closed Tues. and 2 wks in Sept.*

$$$$ INTERNATIONAL — 🍴 **Maurachbund.** Heino Huber, rated one of Austris's top five chefs, runs this elegant restaurant with a focus on home-style Austrian cuisine with a sophisticated twist. All ingredients are locally sourced if possible, and fish figures heavily. **Known for:** understated elegance; menu full of local produce; alfresco dining on the peaceful terrace. [$] *Average main: €30* ✉ *Maurachgasse 11* ☎ *05574/45029* 🌐 *www.maurachbund.at* 🕓 *Closed Sun.*

$$ AUSTRIAN — 🍴 **Wirtshaus am See.** This striking half-timbered house with a steep gabled roof is in an idyllic position right on the shore of Lake Constance, next to the floating stage used for the Bregenz Festival. With a fabulous lake view, diners can watch the steamers from the nearby harbor go by while enjoying classic Austrian dishes with an accent on fresh fish. **Known for:** terrace dining on beautiful lakefront setting; fresh fish right from the lake; excellent breakfast. [$] *Average main: €16* ✉ *Seepromenade 2* ☎ *05574/42210* 🌐 *www.wirtshausamsee.at* 🕓 *Closed Jan. and Feb.*

## WHERE TO STAY

**$$** 🏨 **Mercure Bregenz.** Adjacent to the Festival Hall and housing the casino,
**HOTEL** the look and atmosphere here is typical of the Mercure chain: function-
ally modern with every comfort. **Pros:** lovely waterside location and
lake views; excellent breakfast; conveniently close to the train station.
**Cons:** chain-hotel feel; surrounded by parking lots; can be very busy due
to the casino. $ *Rooms from: €170* ✉ *Platz der Wiener Symphoniker*
☎ *05574/46100–0* ⊕ *www.mercure.at* ↪ *94 rooms* ⏾ *Breakfast.*

**$$** 🏨 **Schwärzler.** On the edge of town, the Schwarzler has the feeling of
**HOTEL** being in the country. **Pros:** spacious lobby and rooms; very attentive
staff; bicycles available for use by guests. **Cons:** on the edge of town so
far from town center; rooms on the street side can be noisy; during the
week it can feel like a business hotel. $ *Rooms from: €150* ✉ *Landstrasse*
*9* ☎ *05574/4990* ⊕ *www.s-hotels.com* ↪ *75 rooms* ⏾ *Breakfast.*

**$$** 🏨 **Weisses Kreuz.** This traditional, family-run, turn-of-the-20th-century
**HOTEL** house is in a great central location, on the edge of the pedestrian zone,
and is noted for its friendly staff. **Pros:** traditional center of hospitality
in Bregenz; excellent restaurant; central location. **Cons:** front rooms
look out onto a busy street; creaky floorboards; some rooms overlook
a garage and office buildng. $ *Rooms from: €150* ✉ *Römerstrasse 5*
☎ *05574/4988–0* ⊕ *www.bestwestern.com* ☽ *Closed Christmas wk*
↪ *44 rooms* ⏾ *Breakfast.*

## NIGHTLIFE AND THE PERFORMING ARTS

Fodor's Choice **Bregenzer Festspiele** (*Bregenz Music Festival*). The big cultural event in
★ Bregenz is the Bregenzer Festspiele, held mid-July to late August, with
the main stage a huge floating platform on the lake. For information
and tickets, contact the festival office. Tickets are also available at the
Bregenz tourist office. In the event of rain, the concert performance
is moved indoors to the massive Festival Hall and Congress Center
adjacent to the floating stage (it can accommodate at least 1,800 of
the 6,800 seats usually available for performances on the floating lake
stage). ✉ *Platz der Wiener Symphoniker 1* ☎ *05574/4076* ⊕ *www.bre-
genzerfestspiele.com.*

**Bregenzer Frühling.** The cultural year starts with the spring music and
dance festival that runs from March to May. Information and tick-
ets are available through the tourist office in Bregenz. ✉ *Bregenz*
☎ *05574/4080* ⊕ *www.bregenzerfruehling.at.*

**Casino.** There's much activity at this gambling house, which opens at
3 pm and closes at 3 or 4 am. It offers table games, poker, and slot
machines. The dress code demands appropriate clothing (no sports-
wear) and that men wear a jacket (some are available to rent if you
come casual). Bring your passport. ✉ *Platz der Wiener Symphoniker 3*
☎ *05574/45127* ⊕ *www.bregenz.casinos.at.*

**Music Pavilion.** Outdoor concerts are held during the summer months
in this horseshoe-shape pavilion at the end of the promenade on the
lake. ✉ *Bregenz.*

**12**

## SPORTS AND THE OUTDOORS

### BICYCLING

It's possible to cycle around Lake Constance in two to four days, traveling all the while on well-marked and -maintained paths (don't forget your passport). If this sounds too strenuous, parts of the route can be covered by boat. Rental bikes can be hired at local sports shops or at the train stations in Bregenz or Feldkirch; the tourist office can provide you with maps and details. Another cycling path, popular with families, follows the Rhine—a 70-km (43-mile) stretch from Bregenz south to Bludenz. Parts of the route are possible by train.

### SKIING

**Pfänder.** There is some modest skiing on the Pfänder mountain, in Bregenz's backyard, which has a cable tramway and two drag lifts. The views are stunning from atop the peak, stretching as far as the Black Forest and the Swiss Alps. ⊠ *Steinbruchgasse 4* ☎ *05574/42160* ⊕ *www.pfaenderbahn.at.*

### WATER SPORTS

With the vast lake at its doorstep, Bregenz offers a variety of water sports, from swimming to fishing to windsurfing.

**Segelschule Lochau.** You can learn to sail here, although a minimum of two weeks is required for a full course. ⊠ *Alte Fähre im Yachthafen, Marina, Lochau* ☎ *05574/52247* ⊕ *www.segelschule-lochau.com.*

# TRAVEL SMART
# VIENNA AND
# AUSTRIA

# GETTING HERE AND AROUND

## ▌ AIR TRAVEL

Flying time from New York to Vienna is eight hours; it's nine hours from Washington, D.C., and two hours from London. Airline and Airport Links.com has links to many of the world's airlines and airports. The Transportation Security Administration has answers for almost every security question that might come up.

### AIRPORTS

Austria's major air gateway is Vienna's Schwechat Airport, about 19 km (12 miles) southeast of the city. Salzburg Airport is Austria's second-largest airport, about 4 km (2½ miles) west of the center. Just south of Graz, in Thalerhof, is the Graz Airport. Two other airports you might consider, depending on where in Austria you intend to travel, are Bratislava's M. R. Stefanik international airport in neighboring Slovakia, and Munich Airport International in Germany, not far from Salzburg. Bratislava is about 80 km (50 miles) east of Vienna and is the hub for Ryanair, a budget carrier with low-cost connections to several European cities. Frequent buses can take you from Bratislava airport to central Vienna in about an hour. Consider Munich if your primary destination is western Austria, Salzburg, or Innsbruck.

**Airport Information Graz Airport (GRZ).**
☎ *0316/2902–172* ⊕ *www.flughafen-graz. at.* **M. R. Stefanik Airport (Bratislava, BTS).** ☎ *044/702–402–0722 from outside of Slovakia* ⊕ *www.airport-bratislava.sk or www.bts.aero.* **Munich Airport International (MUC).** ☎ *49/899–7500 from outside Germany* ⊕ *www.munich-airport.de.* **Salzburg Airport (SZG).** ☎ *0662/85800* ⊕ *www.salzburg-airport. com.* **Schwechat Airport** (*VIE*). ☎ *01/70070* ⊕ *www.viennaairport.com.*

## GROUND TRANSPORTATION AND TRANSFERS

The City Airport Train (CAT) provides service from Schwechat to downtown Vienna for €19 round-trip (€11 one way). Tickets are available at the CAT counter in the arrivals hall; the trip takes about 16 minutes. Travel into the city on the local S-Bahn takes about 25 minutes and costs €4.40 (ticket machines are on the platforms). City bus No. 2 runs every 10 minutes between both the city center and Salzburg's main train station and the airport; transfers cost €2.30. A taxi ride from the airport will be about €20. Schwechat Airport's website has information for all ground transfers.

**Ground Transportation Contacts CAT.**
☎ *01/25–25–0* ⊕ *www.cityairporttrain. com.* **S-Bahn.** ⊕ *www.schnellbahn-wien.at.* **Schwechat Airport.** ☎ *01/7007–0* ⊕ *www. viennaairport.com.* **Vienna Bus.** ☎ *01/7909– 100* ⊕ *www.wienerlinien.at.*

## FLIGHTS

Austria is easy to reach from the United States. Austrian Airlines, Austria's flagship carrier and a Lufthansa subsidiary, flies nonstop to Vienna from the United States, departing from New York's JFK airport and Washington Dulles. From Canada, Austrian flies direct from Toronto. Its membership to the Star Alliance means that cities serviced by United Airlines have good connecting service to Austria. Austrian Airlines has an excellent network of domestic flights linking Vienna to regional cities like Salzburg and Graz. It's also possible to travel from North America with major U.S. carriers—including American, Delta, and United—but you'll be routed through a major European hub, such as London, Amsterdam, or Frankfurt, to Vienna. Leave plenty of time between connections (a minimum of three hours is ideal), as transfers at major airports inevitably take some time. Many international carriers also offer service to Vienna after stopovers at major European airports.

In addition to the major international carriers, European budget airlines, including Ryanair and FlyNiki, offer low-cost flights from major cities around the Continent. These airlines are not normally recommended for connecting with transatlantic flights because of the occasional hassle of changing airports, but they provide a low-cost way of getting around. They travel between Vienna, Graz, Linz, Klagenfurt, Salzburg, Innsbruck, and major hubs in Europe, Asia, Africa, the Caribbean, the United States, and Canada. More recently, German charter carrier Condor also added flights between Vienna and Las Vegas to its schedule, as did Canadian charter airline Air Transat (⊕ *www.airtransat.ca*), with planes flying from Montreal and Toronto to Vienna.

Within Austria, Austrian Airlines and its subsidiary Austrian Arrows, operated by Tyrolean Airways, offer service from Vienna to Linz, Salzburg, Klagenfurt, and Innsbruck; they also provide routes to and from points outside Austria.

## ▌ BUS TRAVEL

Austria has an extensive national network of buses run by the national postal and railroad services. Where Austrian trains don't go, buses do, and you'll find the railroad and post-office buses (bright yellow for easy recognition) in even remote regions carrying passengers as well as mail. You can get tickets on the bus, and in the off-season there is no problem getting a seat; on routes to favored ski areas, though, reservations are essential during holiday periods. Bookings can be handled at the ticket office (there's one in most towns with bus service) or by travel agents. In most communities bus routes begin and end at or near the train station, making transfers easy. Increasingly, coordination of bus service with railroads means that many of the discounts and special tickets available for trains apply to

buses as well. There are private bus companies in Austria, too. Buses in Austria run like clockwork, typically departing and arriving on time, even, astonishingly, in mountainous regions and during bad weather. Most operators on the information lines *below* speak English and, impressively, many of the drivers do, too.

**Bus Information Blaguss Reisen.** ☎ 01/610900 ⊕ www.blaguss.at/en. **Columbus.** ☎ 01/534–110 ⊕ www.columbus-reisen. at. **Dr. Richard Reisebusse.** ☎ 01/331–00–335 ⊕ www.richard.at. **Post und Bahn.** ☎ 05/1717 customer service for postbuses and trains ⊕ www.postbus.at, www.oebb.at.

## ▌ CAR TRAVEL

Carefully weigh the pros and cons of car travel before choosing to rent. If your plans are to see Vienna and one or two other urban destinations, you're better off taking the train, avoiding hassles, and saving money. Bear in mind that in addition to the not inconsiderable cost of renting, you'll have to pay for gasoline (which costs more than twice what it does in the United States) and frequent tolls. In addition, you might find yourself dealing with heavy traffic on the main roads. Added to that is the constant headache of finding a place to park. Central Vienna is completely restricted and the situation is not much better in the smaller cities.

On the other hand, if you have the time and your plan is a more leisurely tour of the country, including back roads and off-the-beaten-track destinations, then car rental is certainly an option. You'll have more freedom—and roads are mostly very well maintained, even in rural districts and mountainous regions. Bear in mind that if you're traveling in winter, your car should be fitted with winter tires and you should also carry snow chains. Even in summer you can come across sudden winterlike conditions on the high mountain passes.

Vienna is 300 km (187 miles) east of Salzburg and 200 km (125 miles) north of Graz. Main routes leading into the city are the A1 Westautobahn from Germany, Salzburg, and Linz and the A2 Südautobahn from Graz and points south.

## GASOLINE

Gasoline and diesel are readily available, but on Sunday stations in the more out-of-the-way areas may be closed. Stations carry only unleaded (*bleifrei*) gas, both regular and premium (super), and diesel. If you're in the mountains in winter with a diesel, and there is a cold snap (with temperatures threatening to drop below -4°F [-20°C]), add a few liters of gasoline to your diesel, about 1:4 parts, to prevent it from freezing. Gasoline prices are the same throughout the country, slightly lower at discount and self-service stations. Expect to pay about €1.38 per liter for regular gasoline and slightly less for diesel. If you are driving to Italy, fill up before crossing the border, because gas in Italy is even more expensive. Oil in Austria is expensive, retailing at €14 or more per liter. If need be, purchase oil, windshield wipers, and other paraphernalia at big hardware stores. The German word for "receipt" is *Quittung* or *Rechnung*.

## RENTING A CAR

Rates in Vienna begin at about €80 per day and €100 per weekend for an economy car with manual transmission. This includes a 21% tax on car rentals. Rates are more expensive in winter months, when a surcharge for winter tires may be added. Renting a car is cheaper in Germany, but make sure the rental agency knows you are driving into Austria and ask for the car to be equipped with the Autobahnvignette, an autobahn sticker for Austria. The answer will usually be that you have to buy your own vignette, which you can get from service stations near the border. Get your sticker, also known as a *Pickerl,* before driving to Austria *(See Rules of the Road section).* When renting an RV be sure to compare prices and reserve early. It's cheaper to arrange your rental car from the United States, but be sure to get a confirmation in writing of your quoted rate. Extremely big savings can often be made by renting from a company that has partnered with your chosen airline—airline websites will have the link—or use ⊕ *Arguscarhire. com,* which has connections with a range of car rental companies and often comes up with the best prices.

The age requirement for renting a car in Austria is generally 19 (the minimum age for driving a car in Austria is 18), and you must have had a valid driver's license for one year. There is no extra charge to drive over the border into Italy, Switzerland, or Germany, but there may be some restrictions for taking a rental into Slovakia, Slovenia, Hungary, the Czech Republic, or Poland. If you're planning on traveling east, it's best to let the agency know beforehand.

In Austria your own driver's license is no longer sufficient. An International Driver's Permit (IDP; $20) is required. These international permits are universally recognized and can be obtained in person or by mail from AAA (⊕ *www.aaa.com*).

## ROAD CONDITIONS

Roads in Austria are excellent and well maintained—perhaps a bit too well maintained, judging by the frequently encountered construction zones on the autobahns. Secondary roads may be narrow and winding. Remember that in winter you will need snow tires and sometimes chains, even on well-traveled roads. It's wise to check with the automobile clubs for weather conditions, because mountain roads are often blocked, and ice and fog are hazards.

## ROADSIDE EMERGENCIES

If you break down along the autobahn, a small arrow on the guardrail will direct you to the nearest emergency (orange-color) phones that exist along all highways. Austria also has two automobile clubs, ÖAMTC and ARBÖ, both of which operate motorist service patrols. Both clubs charge nonmembers for emergency service.

## CAR RENTAL RESOURCES

### LOCAL AGENCIES

| | | |
|---|---|---|
| Megadrive Autovermietung GmbH, Erdbergerstrasse 202, A-1030 Vienna | 01/054–124 | www.megadrive.at |
| Autoverleih Buchbinder at all major Austrian airports | 0810/007–010 | www.buchbinder-rent-a-car.at |

### MAJOR AGENCIES

| | | |
|---|---|---|
| Alamo | 877/222–9075 | www.alamo.com |
| Avis | 800/331–1212 | www.avis.com |
| Budget | 800/527–0700 | www.budget.com |
| Hertz | 800/654–3131 | www.hertz.com |
| National Car Rental | 800/227–7368 | www.nationalcar.com |

**Emergency Services ARBÖ.** ☎ *01/891–21–0* ⊕ *www.arboe.at.* **ÖAMTC.** ☎ *0810/120–120* ⊕ *www.oeamtc.at.*

No area or other code is needed for either number.

## RULES OF THE ROAD

Tourists from EU countries may bring their own cars into Austria with no documentation other than the normal registration papers and their regular driver's license. A Green Card, the international certificate of insurance, is recommended for EU drivers and compulsory for others. All cars must carry a first-aid kit (including rubber gloves), a red warning triangle, and a yellow neon jacket to use in case of accident or breakdown. These are available at gas stations along the road, or at any automotive supply store or large hardware store.

The minimum driving age in Austria is 18, and children under 12 must ride in the back seat; smaller children require a car seat. Note that all passengers must use seat belts.

Drive on the right side of the road in Austria. Unmarked crossings, particularly in residential areas, are common, so exercise caution at intersections. Trams always have the right-of-way. No turns are allowed on red.

When it comes to drinking and driving, the maximum blood-alcohol content allowed is 0.5 parts per thousand, which in real terms means very little to drink. Remember when driving in Europe that the police can stop you anywhere at any time for no particular reason.

Unless otherwise marked, the speed limit on autobahns is 130 kph (80 mph), although this is not always strictly enforced. If you're pulled over for speeding, though, fines are payable on the spot, and can be heavy. On other highways and roads the limit is 100 kph (62 mph), 80 kph (49 mph) for RVs or cars pulling a trailer weighing more than 750 kilos (about 1,650 pounds). In built-up areas a 50-kph (31-mph) limit applies and is likely to be taken seriously. In some towns special 30-kph (20-mph) limits apply. More and more towns have radar cameras to catch speeders. Remember that insurance does not necessarily pay if it can be proven you were going above the limit when involved in an accident.

■TIP→ If you're going to travel Austria's highways, make absolutely sure your car is equipped with the Autobahnvignette, a little sticker with a highway icon and the Austrian eagle, or with a calendar marked with an M or a W. This sticker, sometimes also called a Pickerl, allows use of the autobahn. It costs €82.70 (valid for one year) and is available at gas stations, tobacconists, and automobile-club outlets in neighboring countries or near the border. Some rental cars may already have them, but you need to check. You can also purchase a two-month vignette for €24.80, or a 10-day one for €8.50. Prices are for vehicles up to 3.5 tons and RVs. For motorcycles it's €32.90 for one year, €12.40 for two months, and €4.90 for 10 days. If you're caught without a sticker you may be subjected to extremely high fines. Get your Pickerl before driving to Austria from another country. Besides the Pickerl, if you are planning to drive around a lot, budget in a great deal of toll money: for example, the tunnels on the A10 autobahn cost €11, the Grossglockner Pass road will cost about €34 per car (you can buy a ticket for €10 for a second ride over the pass in the same calendar year and in the same car if you show the cashier the original ticket). Driving up some especially beautiful valleys, such as the Kaunertal in Tyrol, or up to the Tauplitzalm in Styria, also costs money—around €23 per car for the Kaunertal.

## ▌ SHIP AND BOAT TRAVEL

For leisurely travel between Vienna and Linz, or eastward across the border into Slovakia or Hungary, consider taking a Danube boat. **DDSG Blue Danube Schifffahrt** offers a diverse selection of pleasant cruises, including trips to Melk Abbey and Dürnstein in the Wachau, a grand tour of Vienna's architectural sights from the river, and a dinner cruise, with Johann Strauss waltzes as background music. **Brandner Schifffart** offers the same kind of cruises between Krems and Melk, in the heart of the Danube Valley.

Most of the immaculate white-painted craft carry about 1,000 passengers each on their three decks. As soon as you get on board, give the steward a good tip for a deck chair and ask him or her to place it where you will get the best views. Be sure to book cabins in advance. Day trips are

also possible on the Danube. You can use boats to move from one riverside community to the next. Along some sections, notably the Wachau, the only way to cross the river is to use the little shuttles (in the Wachau, these are special motorless boats that use the current to cross).

For the cruises up and down the Danube, the DDSG Blue Danube Steamship Company departs and arrives at Reichsbrücke near Vienna's Mexikoplatz. To reach the Reichsbrücke stop, you walk two blocks from the Vorgartenstrasse stop on the U1 subway toward the river. The DDSG stop is on the right side of the Reichsbrücke bridge. There is no pier number, but you board at Handelskai 265. Boat trips from Vienna to the Wachau run daily from May to September. The price is €23.70 one way and €28 round-trip. There are other daily cruises within the Wachau, such as from Melk to Krems. Other cruises, to Budapest, for instance, operate from April to early November. The website has dozens of options and timetables in English. For cruises from Krems to Melk, contact Brandner Schifffahrt. *For more information, see the "Danube River Cruises" box in Chapter 7.*

**Cruise Lines Brandner Schifffahrt.**
☎ *07433/259–021* ⊕ *www.brandner.at.* **DDSG/ Blue Danube Schifffahrt.** ☎ *01/58880* ⊕ *www.ddsg-blue-danube.at.*

## ▌ TRAIN TRAVEL

Austrian train service is excellent: it's fast and, for Western Europe, relatively inexpensive, particularly if you take advantage of discount fares. Trains on the mountainous routes are slow, but no slower than driving, and the scenery is gorgeous. Many of the remote rail routes will give you a look at traditional Austria, complete with Alpine cabins tacked onto mountainsides and a backdrop of snowcapped peaks.

Austrian Federal Railways trains are identifiable by the letters that precede the train number on the timetables and posters.

The IC (InterCity) or EC (EuroCity) trains are fastest. EN trains have sleeping facilities. The EC trains usually have a dining car with fairly good food. The trains originating in Budapest have good Hungarian cooking. Otherwise, there is usually a fellow with a cart serving snacks and hot and cold drinks. Most trains are equipped with a card telephone in or near the restaurant car.

The difference between *erste Klasse* (first class), and *zweite Klasse* (second class) on Austrian trains is mainly a matter of space. First- and second-class sleepers and couchettes (six to a compartment) are available on international runs, as well as on long trips within Austria. Women traveling alone may book special compartments on night trains or long-distance rides (ask for a *Damenabteil*). If you have a car but would rather watch the scenery than the traffic, you can put your car on a train in Vienna and accompany it to Salzburg, Innsbruck, Feldkirch, or Villach: you relax in a compartment or sleeper for the trip, and the car is unloaded when you arrive.

Allow yourself plenty of time to purchase your ticket before boarding the train. IC and EC tickets are also valid on D (express), E (*Eilzug*; semi-fast), and local trains. For information, unless you speak German fairly well, it's a good idea to have your hotel call for you. You may also ask for an operator who speaks English. You can reserve a seat for €3.50 (€3 online) up until four hours before departure. Be sure to do this on the main-line trains (Vienna–Innsbruck, Salzburg–Klagenfurt, Vienna–Graz, for example) at peak holiday times.

For train schedules from the Austrian rail service, the ÖBB, ask at your hotel, stop in at the train station and look for large posters labeled "*Abfahrt*" (departures) and "*Ankunft*" (arrivals), or log on to the website. In the Abfahrt listing you'll find the departure time in the main left-hand block of the listing and, under the train name, details of where it stops en route and the time of each arrival. There is also information about connecting trains and buses, with departure details. Working days are symbolized by two crossed hammers, which means that the same schedule might not apply on weekends or holidays. A little rocking horse sign means that a special playpen has been set up on the train for children.

There's a wide choice of rail routes to Austria, but check services first; long-distance passenger service across the continent is undergoing considerable reduction. There is regular service from London's St. Pancras station to Vienna via Brussels and Frankfurt; the fastest journey time is 13 hours, 55 minutes. An alternative is to travel via Paris, where you can change to an overnight train to Salzburg and Vienna. Be sure to leave plenty of time between connections to change stations. First- and second-class sleepers and second-class couchettes are available as far as Innsbruck. Although rail fares from London to these destinations tend to be much more expensive than air fares, the advantages are that you'll see a lot more of the countryside en route and you'll travel from city center to city center.

**Information ÖBB (Österreichische Bundesbahnen).** ☎ *05/1717* ⊕ *www.oebb.at.*

# ESSENTIALS

## ∎ ACCOMMODATIONS

You can live like a king in a real castle in Austria or get by on a modest budget. Starting at the lower end, you can find a room in a private house or on a farm, or dormitory space in a youth hostel. Next up the line come the simpler pensions, many of them identified as *Frühstückspensionen* (bed-and-breakfasts). Then come *Gasthäuser,* the simpler country inns. Fancier pensions in cities can often cost as much as hotels; the difference lies in the services they offer. Most pensions, for example, do not staff the front desk around the clock. Among the hotels, you can find accommodations ranging from the most modest, with a shower and toilet down the hall, to the most elegant, with every possible amenity. Increasingly, more and more hotels in the lower to middle price range are including breakfast with the basic room charge, but check when booking. Room rates for hotels in the rural countryside can often include breakfast and one other meal (in rare cases, all three meals are included). It's worth remembering that in Austria the cheaper option will usually still bring high standards. Most village *gasthofs* take great pride in providing sparkling cleanliness and a warm welcome—and you'll often find they have spacious rooms of great character.

Lodgings in Austria are generally rated from one to five stars, depending mainly on the facilities offered and the price of accommodations rather than on more subjective attributes like charm and location. In general, five-star properties are top of the line, with every conceivable amenity and priced accordingly. The distinctions get blurrier the farther down the rating chain you go. There may be little difference between two- and three-star properties except perhaps the price. In practice, don't rely heavily on the star system, and always try to see the hotel and room before you book. That said, lodging standards are generally very good, and even in one- and two-star properties you can usually be guaranteed a clean room and a private bath.

These German words might come in handy when booking a room: air-conditioning (*Klimaanlage*); private bath (*Privatbad*); bathtub (*Badewanne*); shower (*Dusche*); double bed (*Doppelbett*); twin beds (*Einzelbetten*).

All hotels listed *in this guide* have private bath unless otherwise noted. *Prices in the reviews are the lowest cost of a standard double room in high season.*

Most hotels and other lodgings require you to give your credit-card details before they will confirm your reservation. If you don't feel comfortable emailing this information, ask if you can fax it (some places even prefer faxes). Get confirmation by email or in writing and have a copy of it handy when you check in.

Be sure you understand the hotel's cancellation policy. Some places allow you to cancel without any kind of penalty—even if you prepaid to secure a discounted rate—if you cancel at least 24 hours in advance. Others require you to cancel a week in advance or penalize you the cost of one night. Small inns and B&Bs are most likely to require you to cancel far in advance. Most hotels allow children under a certain age to stay in their parents' room at no extra charge, but others charge for them as extra adults; find out the cut-off age for discounts.

The Vienna Tourism Board has a hotel assistance service.

**Contacts. Vienna Tourist Information.**
☎ *01/24555* ⊕ *www.wien.info.*

### APARTMENT AND HOUSE RENTALS

Rentals are an important part of the accommodations mix in Austria, with one-, two- or four-week rentals becoming increasingly popular. Most of the

## ONLINE BOOKING RESOURCES

| | | |
|---|---|---|
| Barclay International Group | 800/845–6636 | www.barclayweb.com |
| Interhome | 800/882–6864 | www.interhome.us |
| Villas and Apartments Abroad | 212/213–6435 | www.vaanyc.com |
| Villas International | 415/499–9490 or 800/221–2260 | www.villasintl.com |

rental properties are owned privately by individuals, and often the main rental organizers are simply the local tourist offices. For rental apartments in Vienna, check out ⊕ *www.apartment.at* or ⊕ *www.netland.at/wien*.

### CASTLES

Schlosshotels und Herrenhäuser in Österreich, or "Castle Hotels and Mansions in Austria," is an association of castles and palaces that have been converted into hotels. The quality of the accommodations varies with the property, but many have been beautifully restored and can be a memorable alternative to standard hotels. The website is in English and has plenty of photos. The association also lists a smattering of castles in the Czech Republic, Hungary, Slovenia, Croatia, and Italy.

**Information Schlosshotels und Herrenhäuser in Österreich.** ☎ *062/459–0123* ⊕ *www.schlosshotels.co.at.*

## ■ COMMUNICATIONS

### INTERNET

Most hotels in Austria have worked hard to upgrade their Internet offerings, and the majority will offer some form of Internet access for your laptop, sometimes still via a LAN line, but often with Wi-Fi. Occasionally these services are offered free of charge; sometimes you have to pay. Hotels that don't offer Internet access in the rooms will usually have a computer somewhere in their business center or lobby available for guests to check email. Outside of hotels there are some, but not many, Internet cafés (ask at your hotel). A good number of regular cafés offer Wi-Fi to customers.

### PHONES

The good news is that you can now make a direct-dial telephone call from virtually any point on earth. The bad news? You can't always do so cheaply. Calling from a hotel is almost always the most expensive option; hotels usually add huge surcharges to all calls, particularly international ones. In some countries you can phone from call centers or even the post office. Calling cards usually keep costs to a minimum, but only if you purchase them locally. Cell phone calls are nearly always a much cheaper option than calling from your hotel.

When calling Austria, the country code is 43. When dialing an Austrian number from abroad, drop the initial 0 from the local Austrian area code. For instance, the full number to dial for the Hotel Sacher in Vienna from America is 011 (international dial code) –43 (Austria's country code) –1 (Vienna's full city code is 01, but drop the 0) and –514–560 (the hotel number). All numbers given *in this guide* include the city or town area code.

### CALLING WITHIN AUSTRIA

As the number of cell phones has risen in Austria, the number of coin-operated pay telephones has dwindled. If you find one, a local call costs from €0.14 to €0.60, depending on whether you call a landline or a cell phone. Most pay phones have instructions in English.

When placing a long-distance call to a destination within Austria, dial the local area codes with the initial zero (for instance, 0662 for Salzburg). Note that calls within Austria are one-third cheaper between 6 pm and 8 am on weekdays and from 1 pm on Saturday to 8 am on Monday.

# Local Do's and Taboos

## CUSTOMS OF THE COUNTRY

Austrians are keen observers of social niceties, and there are strongly embedded cultural norms for guiding behavior in all sorts of public interactions, ranging from buying a piece of meat from the butcher (be extremely polite) to offering your seat on the metro to an elderly or physically challenged person. In general, always err on the side of extreme politeness and deference (particularly to age).

## GREETINGS

Greetings are an important part of day-to-day interaction with strangers. On entering a shop, it's customary to say *Grüss Gott* or *Guten Tag,* "good day," to the shopkeeper. Don't forget to say *Auf Wiedersehen,* "good-bye," on leaving. Austrians do like their academic titles. PhDs go as "Frau/ Herr Doktor;" those who have a master's degree are addressed as "Frau/Herr Magister."

## OUT ON THE TOWN

In busy restaurants at lunchtime it's not uncommon to have to share a table with strangers. You're not expected to make conversation across the table, but you should at least offer a tip-of-the-hat *Grüss Gott* when sitting down and a farewell *Auf Wiedersehen* on leaving. When your neighbor's food arrives, turn and wish him or her *Mahlzeit,* literally "mealtime," the Austrian-German equivalent of "bon appétit." When it comes to table manners, there are a few departures from standard American practice (beyond how one holds a knife and fork). Toothpicks are sometimes found on restaurant tables, and it's normal to see people clean their teeth after a meal, discreetly covering their mouth with their free hand. Austria is a dog-loving society, and you will often find dogs accompanying their masters to restaurants.

If you have the pleasure of being invited to someone's home for a meal, it's customary to bring a small gift, like a bouquet of flowers, a box of chocolates, or a bottle of wine.

## DRESS (OR UNDRESS) CODE

Austrians tend to be far more comfortable with public nudity than Americans. Women routinely remove their tops on public beaches and in saunas at hotels. Resorts with saunas are usually used in the buff by both sexes, and a towel is optional. In many spas it will cause offense if you wear a swimsuit in the sauna, bringing frowns from other users or even intervention by the management.

## LANGUAGE

German is the official language in Austria. One of the best ways to avoid being an Ugly American is to learn a little of the local language—Austrians are usually delighted if you at least try to speak German. In larger cities and most resorts you will usually have no problem finding people who speak English; hotel employees in particular speak it reasonably well, and many young Austrians speak it at least passably. However, travelers do report that they often find themselves in stores, restaurants, and train and bus stations where it's hard to find someone who speaks English—so it's best to have some native phrases up your sleeve. Note that all public announcements on trams, subways, and buses are in German. Train announcements are usually given in English as well, but if you have any questions, try to get answers before boarding.

For information about phone numbers inside and outside of Austria, dial 118–877. Most operators speak some English; if yours doesn't, you'll most likely be passed along to one who does.

### CALLING OUTSIDE AUSTRIA

It costs more to telephone from Austria than it does to telephone to Austria. Although nearly everyone now uses their cell phone for all calls, international or otherwise, it is still possible to make inexpensive calls from some post offices, and you can get helpful assistance in placing a long-distance call; in large cities these centers at main post offices (*Hauptpostamt*) are open around the clock. To use a post office phone you first go to the counter to be directed to a certain telephone cabin; after your call you return to the counter and pay your bill. Faxes can be sent from post offices and received as well, but neither service is very cheap.

To make a collect call—you can't do this from pay phones—dial the operator and ask for an *R-Gespräch* (pronounced air-geh- *shprek*). Most operators speak English; if yours doesn't, you'll be passed to one who does.

The country code for the United States is 1.

**U.S. Phone Access Codes from Austria AT&T Direct.** ☎ *888/333-6651 in the U.S., 0800/293-3336 for 24/7 support within Austria ⊕ www.att.com.* **Verizon Wireless.** ☎ *800/500-55-0999 within Austria.*

### CALLING CARDS

If you plan to make calls from pay phones, a Telecom Austria calling card is a convenience. You can buy calling cards with a credit of €10 or €15 at any post office or Telecom Austria shop, and they can be used at any public phone booth. Insert the card, punch in your access code, and dial the number; the cost of the call is automatically deducted from the card—note that the "credits" displayed is not usually the amount of money left on the card, but a different sort of counter. A few public phones in the cities also take American Express, Diners Club, MasterCard, and Visa credit cards.

### MOBILE PHONES

In Austria a cell phone is called a *Handy*.

If you have a GSM cell phone, you can probably use your phone abroad. Roaming fees are generally being dramatically reduced by most phone companies. As soon as you switch your phone on after arriving you are likely to get a message from your provider telling you exactly how much it will be to call home or to receive calls. It's almost always cheaper to send a text message than to make a call, because text messages have a very low set fee.

If you just want to make local calls, consider buying a new SIM card (note that your provider may have to unlock your phone for you to use a different SIM card) and a prepaid service plan in the destination. You'll then have a local number and can make local calls at local rates. If your trip is extensive, you could also simply buy a new cell phone in your destination, as the initial cost will be offset over time.

■ TIP→ **If you travel internationally frequently, save one of your old cell phones or buy a cheap one on the Internet; ask your cell phone company to unlock it for you, and take it with you as a travel phone, buying a new SIM card with pay-as-you-go service in each destination.**

If you want to use your own cell phone in Austria, first find out if it's compatible with the European 1800 GSM standard. Once in Austria, stop by a cell phone store, usually identifiable by the word "Handy" in the name, and purchase a prepaid SIM card (make sure your existing SIM card is unlocked). Prepaid cards start at around €15. Local calls are then billed at about €0.15 to €0.20 a minute. If you don't have a phone but want to use one here, look into buying a used phone. Rates are reasonable. Buy the prepaid card in the same way you would as if you were bringing in your own phone.

When dialing an Austrian "Handy" from abroad (generally 0676, 0699, or 0664), dial 00–43, then the number without the 0.

**Contacts Cellular Abroad.** ☎ 800/287–5072 ⊕ www.cellularabroad.com. **Mobal.** ☎ 888/888–9162 ⊕ www.mobal.com. **Planet Fone.** ☎ 888/988–4777 ⊕ www.planetfone.com.

## ▍EATING OUT

When dining out, you'll get the best value at simpler restaurants. Most post menus with prices outside. If you begin with the *Würstelstand* (sausage vendor) on the street, the next category would be the *Imbiss-Stube,* for simple, quick snacks. Many meat stores serve soups and a daily special at noon; a blackboard menu will be posted outside. Many cafés also offer lunch. *Gasthäuser* are simple restaurants or country inns. Austrian hotels have some of the best restaurants in the country, often with outstanding chefs. In the past few years the restaurants along the autobahns, especially the chain Rosenberger, have developed into very good places to eat (besides being, in many cases, architecturally interesting). Some Austrian chain restaurants offer excellent value for the money, such as the schnitzel chains Wienerwald and Schnitzelhaus and the excellent seafood chain Nordsee. You can also grab a quick sandwich made from a wide variety of scrumptious whole-wheat breads at bakery chains such as Anker, Felber, and Mann. With migration from Turkey and Northern Africa on the rise, thousands of small kebab restaurants have set up shop all over Austria, offering both Middle Eastern fare and sometimes pizza at a reasonable rate. The latest fad is the Asian noodle lunchbox, available at many sausage vendors.

▍**TIP→ In all restaurants be aware that the basket of bread put on your table isn't free.** Most of the older-style Viennese restaurants charge €0.70–€1.25 for each roll that is eaten, but more and more establishments are beginning to charge a per-person cover charge—anywhere from €1.50 to €5—which includes all the bread you want, plus usually an herb spread and butter. Tap water (*Leitungswasser*) in Austria comes straight from the Alps and is some of the purest in the world. Be aware, however, that a few restaurants in touristy areas are beginning to charge for tap water.

Austrians are manic about food quality and using agricultural techniques that are in harmony with the environment. The country has the largest number of organic farms in Europe, as well as some of the most stringent food-quality standards. An increasing number of restaurants use food and produce from local farmers, ensuring the freshest ingredients for their guests.

### MEALS AND MEALTIMES

Besides the normal three meals—*Frühstück* (breakfast), *Mittagessen* (lunch), and *Abendessen* (dinner)—Austrians sometimes throw in a few snacks in between, or forego one meal for a snack. The day begins with an early continental breakfast of rolls and coffee. *Gabelfrühstück,* normally served a little later in the morning, is a slightly more substantial breakfast with eggs or cold meat. Lunch is usually served between noon and 2, although in some country districts where work, particularly agricultural, might start very early in the morning, you will see people eating lunch from 11 am. An afternoon *Jause* (coffee with cake) is taken at teatime. A light supper would traditionally be eaten between 6 and 9, but tending toward the later hour, and dinner in the evening, as the main meal of the day, is increasingly the norm. Many restaurant kitchens close in the afternoon, but some post a notice saying *durchgehend warme Küche,* meaning that hot food is available even between regular mealtimes. In Vienna some restaurants go on serving until 1 and 2 am; a tiny number also through the night. The rest of Austria is more conservative.

Unless otherwise noted, the restaurants listed *in this guide* are open daily for lunch and dinner.

## PAYING

*Prices in the reviews are the average cost of a main course at dinner or, if dinner is not served, at lunch.*

*For guidelines on tipping see Tipping below.*

## RESERVATIONS

Regardless of where you are, it's a good idea to make a reservation if you can. In some places it's expected. We mention reservations specifically only when they are essential (there's no other way you'll ever get a table) or when they are not accepted. For popular restaurants, book as far ahead as you can (often 30 days), and reconfirm as soon as you arrive. (Large parties should always call ahead to check the reservations policy.)

## WINES, BEER, AND SPIRITS

Austrian wines range from unpretentious *Heurigen* whites to world-class varietals. Look for the light, fruity white *Grüner Veltliner*, intensely fragrant golden *Traminer*, full-bodied red *Blaufränkischer*, and the lighter red *Zweigelt*. Sparkling wine is called *Sekt*, some of the best coming from the Kamptal region northwest of Vienna. Some of the best sweet dessert wines in the world (*Spätlesen*) come from Burgenland. Austrian beer rivals that of Germany for quality. Each area has its own brewery and local beer, to which people are loyal. A specialty unique to Austria is the dark, sweet Dunkles beer. Look for Kaiser Doppelmalz in Vienna. Schnapps is an after-dinner tradition in Austria; many restaurants offer several varieties, and it is not uncommon for the management to offer a complimentary schnapps at the end of a meal. One of the most popular types is nicknamed a "little Willy," made from the William pear.

## ■ ELECTRICITY

The electrical current in Austria is 220 volts, 50 cycles alternating current (AC); wall outlets take Continental-type plugs, with two round prongs.

Consider making a small investment in a universal adapter, which has several types of plugs in one lightweight, compact unit. Most laptops and cell phone chargers are dual voltage (i.e., they operate equally well on 110 and 220 volts), so require only an adapter. These days the same is true of small appliances such as hair dryers. Always check labels and manufacturer instructions to be sure. Don't use 110-volt outlets marked "for shavers only" for high-wattage appliances such as hair dryers.

## ■ EMERGENCIES

On the street, some German phrases that may be needed in an emergency are: *Hilfe! (hill-feh)* (Help!), *Notfall (note-fall)* (emergency), *Rettungswagen* (ambulance), *Feuerwehr (foy-ur-wear)* (fire department), *Polizei (poll-it-sigh)* (police), *Arzt* (doctor), and *Krankenhaus* (hospital).

**Foreign Embassies Consulate of the U.S./ Passport Division.** ⊠ *Parkring 12a, 1st District* ☎ *01/313-3975-35, 01/313-390 for after-hours emergencies* ⊕ *at.usembassy.gov.* **Embassy of the United States.** ⊠ *Boltzmanngasse 1b, 9th District/Alsergrund* ☎ *01/31-339-0* ⊕ *at.usembassy.gov.*

**General Emergency Contacts Ambulance.** ☎ *144.* **Fire.** ☎ *122.* **Police.** ☎ *133.*

## ■ HEALTH

Travel in Austria poses no specific or unusual health risks. The tap water is generally safe to drink—in fact, Austrians are obsessed about water quality, and Austria has some of the purest in the world. If in doubt, buy bottled water—available everywhere. The only potential risk worth mentioning is tick-bite encephalitis, which is only a danger if you're planning to do extensive cycling or hiking in the backcountry.

**OVER-THE-COUNTER REMEDIES**

You must buy over-the-counter remedies in an *Apotheke (app-oh-take-uh)*, and most personnel speak enough English to understand what you need. Try using the generic name for a drug, rather than its brand name. You may find over-the-counter remedies for headaches and colds less effective than those sold in the United States. Austrians are firm believers in natural remedies, such as homeopathic medicines and herbal teas.

**SHOTS AND MEDICATIONS**

No special shots are required before visiting Austria, but if you will be cycling or hiking through the eastern or southeastern parts of the country, get inoculated against encephalitis; it can be carried by ticks.

# ▮ HOURS OF OPERATION

In most cities banks are open weekdays 8–3, Thursday until 5:30 pm. Lunch hour is from 12:30 to 1:30 pm. All banks are closed on Saturday, but you can change money at various locations, such as American Express (which has an office in Vienna open on Saturday from 9 to noon) and major train stations, open around the clock; changing machines are also found here and there in the larger cities.

Gas stations on the major autobahns are open 24 hours a day, but in smaller towns and villages you can expect them to close early in the evening and on Sunday. You can usually count on at least one station to stay open on Sunday and holidays in most medium-size towns, and buying gas in larger cities is usually not a problem.

Pharmacies (called *Apotheke [app-oh-take-uh]* in German) are usually open from 9 to 6, with a midday break between noon and 2 pm. In each area of the city one pharmacy stays open 24 hours; if a pharmacy is closed, a sign on the door will tell you the address of the nearest one that's open. Call ☎ *01/1550* for names and addresses (in German) of the pharmacies open that night.

In many villages and small towns shops still keep the custom of half-day closing one day a week, usually Tuesday or Wednesday, so don't be surprised to find an apparent ghost town on those days. Shops usually close at 12:30 pm and place the sign *Ruhetag* (rest day) in the window or door. Hotels sometimes follow suit—they will be open, but the front desk will not be manned and, typically, a welcome note will be left with your key. It is also common in country areas for shops to close from midday on Saturday until Monday morning.

**HOLIDAYS**

All banks and shops are closed on national holidays: New Year's Day; Jan. 6, Epiphany; Easter Sunday and Monday; May 1, May Day; Ascension Day; Pentecost Sunday and Monday; Corpus Christi; Aug. 15, Assumption; Oct. 26, National Holiday; Nov. 1, All Saints' Day; Dec. 8, Immaculate Conception; Dec. 25–26, Christmas. Museums are open on most holidays, but are closed on Good Friday, Dec. 24 and 25, and New Year's Day. Banks and offices are closed on Dec. 8, but most shops are open.

# ▮ MAIL

All mail goes by air, so there's no supplement on letters or postcards. Within Europe a letter or postcard of up to 20 grams (about ¾ ounce) costs €0.80; to the United States or Canada, it's €1.70. Up to 50 grams costs €2.10 for Europe and €2.75 for the United States or Canada. If in doubt, mail your letters from a post office and have the weight checked. The Austrian post office also adheres strictly to a size standard; if your letter or card is outside the norm, you'll have to pay a surcharge. Always place an airmail sticker on your letters or cards. Shipping packages from Austria to destinations outside the country can be expensive.

You can also have mail held at any Austrian post office; letters should be marked *Poste Restante* or *Postlagernd*. You will be asked for identification when you collect mail.

## SHIPPING PACKAGES

For overnight services, Federal Express, DHL, and UPS service Austria; check with your hotel concierge for the nearest address and telephone number.

# ∎ MONEY

## ATMS AND BANKS

Your own bank will probably charge a fee for using ATMs abroad; the foreign bank you use may also charge a fee. Nevertheless, you'll usually get a better rate of exchange at an ATM than you will at a currency-exchange office or even when changing money in a bank. And extracting funds as you need them is a safer option than carrying around a large amount of cash.

∎TIP→ PIN numbers with more than four digits are not recognized at ATMs in many countries. If yours has five or more, remember to change it before you leave.

Called *Bankomats* and fairly common throughout Austria, ATMs are one of the easiest ways to get euros. Cirrus and Plus locations are easily found throughout large city centers and even in small towns. Look for branches of one of the larger banks, including Bank Austria, Raiffeisen, BAWAG, or Erste Bank. These are all likely to have a bank machine attached somewhere nearby. If you have trouble finding one, ask your hotel concierge. Note, too, that you may have better luck with ATMs if you're using a credit card or debit card that's also a Visa or MasterCard rather than just your bank card.

## CREDIT CARDS

It's a good idea to inform your credit-card company before you travel, especially if you're going abroad and don't travel internationally very often. Otherwise, the credit-card company might put a hold on your card owing to unusual activity—not a good thing halfway through your trip. Record all your credit-card numbers—as well as the phone numbers to call if your cards are lost or stolen—in a safe place, so you're prepared should something go wrong. Both MasterCard and Visa have general numbers you can call (collect if you're abroad) if your card is lost, but you're better off calling the number of your issuing bank, since MasterCard and Visa usually just transfer you to your bank; your bank's number is usually printed on your card.

If you plan to use your credit card for cash advances, you'll need to apply for a PIN at least two weeks before your trip. Although it's usually cheaper (and safer) to use a credit card abroad for large purchases (so you can cancel payments or be reimbursed if there's a problem), note that some credit-card companies *and* the banks that issue them add substantial percentages to all foreign transactions, whether they're in a foreign currency or not. Check on these fees before leaving home, so there won't be any surprises when you get the bill.

∎TIP→ Before you charge something, ask the merchant whether or not he or she plans to do a dynamic currency conversion (DCC). In such a transaction the credit-card processor (shop, restaurant, or hotel, not Visa or MasterCard) converts the currency and charges you in dollars. In most cases you'll pay the merchant a 3% fee for this service in addition to any credit-card company and issuing-bank foreign-transaction surcharges.

Dynamic currency conversion programs are becoming increasingly widespread. Merchants who participate in them are supposed to ask whether you want to be charged in dollars or the local currency, but they don't always do so. And even if they do offer you a choice, they may well avoid mentioning the surcharges. The good news is that you *do* have a choice. And if this practice really gets your goat, you can avoid it entirely thanks to American Express; with its cards DCC simply isn't an option. However, many establishments in Europe prefer MasterCard or Visa to American Express because of the high commission that the latter charges.

**Reporting Lost Cards** American Express. ☎ 800/327–2717 in U.S., 336/393–1111 collect from abroad ⊕ www.americanexpress.com. **Diners Club.** ☎ 800/234–6377 in U.S., 303/799–1504 collect from abroad ⊕ www.dinersclub.com. **Discover.** ☎ 800/347–2683 in U.S., 801/902–3100 collect from abroad ⊕ www.discovercard.com. **MasterCard.** ☎ 800/307–7309 in U.S., 800/627–8372 collect from abroad ⊕ www.mastercard.com. **Visa.** ☎ 800/847–2911 in U.S., 303/967–1096 collect from Austria ⊕ www.visa.com.

## CURRENCY AND EXCHANGE

Austria is a member of the European Union (EU) and its currency is the euro. Under the euro system there are eight coins: 1 and 2 euros, plus 1, 2, 5, 10, 20, and 50 euro cents. All coins have one side that has the value of the euro on it and the other side with a country's own national symbol. There are seven banknotes: 5, 10, 20, 50, 100, 200, and 500 euros. Banknotes are the same for all EU countries.

At this writing, the euro continues to hold strong against the U.S. dollar, and one euro was worth about $1.17.

Although fees charged for ATM transactions may be higher abroad than at home, Cirrus and Plus exchange rates are excellent, because they are based on wholesale rates offered only by major banks. Otherwise, the most favorable rates are through a bank. You won't do as well at exchange booths in airports or train and bus stations, in hotels, in restaurants, or in stores, although you may find their hours more convenient than the banks'.

■ **TIP→ Even if a currency-exchange booth has a sign promising no commission, rest assured that there's some kind of huge, hidden fee (oh, that's right. The sign didn't say "no fee"). And as for rates, you're almost always better off getting foreign currency at an ATM or exchanging money at a bank.**

## ❚ PACKING

Austrians, particularly the Viennese, are dapper dressers. Packing "musts" include at least one nice shirt and sport coat for men and a casual but stylish dress or shirt and skirt combination for women. These will see you through nearly any occasion, from a decent dinner out on the town to a night at the opera. Note that Austrians dress nicely for the opera and the theater. Men should bring a nice pair of dress shoes, because this is a wardrobe staple to which the locals pay particular attention. As a general rule of thumb, the more expensive the shoes, the more respect you're likely to get. High on the list, too, would be comfortable walking or hiking shoes. Austria is a walking country, in cities and mountains alike. And because an evening outside at a *Heurige* (wine garden) may be on your agenda, be sure to take a sweater or light wrap; evenings tend to get cool even in the summer. Music lovers might consider toting those rarely used opera glasses; the cheaper seats, understandably, are usually far from the action (and standby tickets will have you craning your neck at the back). However, opera glasses are usually available for a modest fee.

If you are heading into the mountains, bring sunscreen, even in winter. Sunglasses are a must as well—make sure that they block lateral rays. Boots that rise above the ankle and have sturdy soles are best for hiking. Consider packing a small folding umbrella for the odd deluge, or a waterproof windbreaker. Mosquitoes can become quite a bother in summer around the lakes and along the rivers, especially the Danube. Bring or buy some good insect repellent.

### SHIPPING LUGGAGE AHEAD

Imagine globe-trotting with only a carry-on in tow. Shipping your luggage in advance via an air-freight service is a great way to cut down on backaches, hassles, and stress—especially if your packing list includes strollers, car seats, and so on. There are some things to be aware of, though. First, research carry-on restrictions; if you absolutely need something that isn't practical to ship and isn't allowed in carry-ons, this strategy isn't for you. Second, plan to send your bags several days in advance to U.S. destinations and as much as two weeks in advance to some international destinations. Third, plan to spend some money: it will cost at least $100 to send a small piece of luggage, a golf bag, or a pair of skis to a domestic destination, much more to places overseas. Some people use Federal Express to ship their bags, but this can cost even more than air-freight services. All these services insure your bag (for most, the limit is $1,000, but you should verify that amount); you can, however, purchase additional insurance for about $1 per $100 of value.

Contacts **Luggage Concierge.** ☎ 800/288–9818 ⊕ www.luggageconcierge.com. **Luggage Free.** ☎ 800/361–6871 ⊕ www.luggagefree.com.

## ▌PASSPORTS AND VISAS

U.S. citizens need only a valid passport to enter Austria for stays of up to three months.

▌**TIP→** Before your trip, make two copies of your passport's data page (one for someone at home and another for you to carry separately). Or scan the page and email it to someone at home and/or yourself.

## ▌RESTROOMS

Vienna has a scattering of public toilets that are suitably clean and cost about €0.50 to use. Metro stations invariably have decent public facilities. Public toilets are less common outside the big cities, but you can usually use the facilities of hotels and restaurants without too much fuss. It's courteous to purchase something in a bar or restaurant beforehand, but this is rarely a problem and nothing that can't

usually be resolved with a smile and a *Danke.* Gas stations along highways usually have restrooms attached, and these are generally open to the public whether you purchase gas or not. Cleanliness standards vary, but are usually on the acceptable side.

## ▌SAFETY

Austrians are remarkably honest in their everyday dealings, and Vienna, given its size, is a refreshingly safe and secure city. That said, be sure to watch your purses and wallets in crowded spaces like subways and trams, and to take the standard precautions when walking at night along empty streets. The number of pickpocketing incidents has increased over the years. Be particularly careful if you're traveling with a bicycle. Here, as everywhere else, bikes routinely go missing. Always lock your bike firmly.

## ▌TAXES

The Value Added Tax (V.A.T.) in Austria is 20% generally, but this is reduced to 10% on food and clothing and certain tourism services. If you are planning to take your purchases with you when you leave Austria (export them), you can get a refund. Wine and spirits are heavily taxed—nearly half of the sale price goes to taxes. For every contract signed in Austria (for example, car-rental agreements), you pay an extra 1% tax to the government, so tax on a rental car is 21%.

When making a purchase, ask for a V.A.T. refund form and find out whether the merchant gives refunds—not all stores do, nor are they required to. Have the form stamped like any customs form by customs officials when you leave the country, or if you're visiting several European Union countries, when you leave the EU. After you're through passport control, take the form to a refund-service counter for an on-the-spot refund (which is usually the quickest and easiest option), or mail it to the address on the form (or the envelope with it) after you arrive home. You receive the total refund stated on the form, but the processing time can be long, especially if you request a credit-card adjustment.

Global Refund is a Europe-wide service with 225,000 affiliated stores and more than 700 refund counters at major airports and border crossings. Its refund form, called a Tax Free Check, is the most common across the European continent. The service issues refunds in the form of cash, check, or credit-card adjustment.

**V.A.T. Refunds** Global Refund. ⊕ *www.globalrefund.com.*

# TIME

The time difference between New York and Austria is six hours (so when it's noon in New York, it's 6 pm in Vienna). The time difference between London and Vienna is one hour; between Sydney and Vienna, eight hours (when it's noon in Sydney, it's 4 am in Vienna); and between Auckland and Vienna, 10 hours (when it's noon in Auckland, it's 2 am in Vienna).

# TIPPING

Although virtually all hotels and restaurants include service charges in their rates, tipping is still customary, but at a level lower than in the United States. In very small country inns such tips are not expected but are appreciated. In family-run establishments, tips are generally not given to immediate family members, only to employees. Tip the hotel concierge only for special services or in response to special requests. Maids normally get no tip unless your stay is a week or more or service has been special. Big tips are not usual in Austrian restaurants, since 10% has already been included in the prices.

# TOURS

Guided tours are a good option when you don't want to do it all yourself. You travel along with a group (sometimes large, sometimes small), stay in prebooked hotels, eat with your fellow travelers (the cost of meals is sometimes included in the price of your tour, sometimes not), and follow a schedule. But not all guided tours are an if-it's-Tuesday-this-must-be-Belgium experience. A knowledgeable guide can take you places that you might never discover on your own, and you may be pushed to see more than you would have otherwise. Tours aren't for everyone, but they can be just the thing for trips to places where making travel arrangements is difficult or time-consuming (particularly when you don't speak the language). Whenever you book a guided tour, find out what's included and what isn't. A "land-only" tour includes all your travel (by bus, in most cases) in the destination, but not necessarily your flights to and from or even within it. Also, in most cases prices in tour brochures don't include fees and taxes. And remember that you'll be expected to tip your guide (in cash) at the end of the tour.

Among companies that sell tours to Austria, the following are nationally known, have a proven reputation, and offer plenty of options. The classifications used here represent different price categories, and you'll probably encounter these terms when talking to a travel agent or tour operator. The key difference is usually in accommodations. Note that each company doesn't schedule tours to Austria every year; check by calling.

**Super-Deluxe Abercrombie & Kent.** ☎ 800/554–7016 ⊕ *www.abercrombiekent.com.* **Travcoa.** ☎ 888/979–4044 ⊕ *www.travcoa.com.*

**First-Class Brendan Tours.** ☎ 800/687–1002 ⊕ *www.brendanvacations.com.* **Trafalgar Tours.** ☎ 866/513–1995 ⊕ *www.trafalgartours.com.*

**Budget Cosmos.** ☎ 800/276–1241 ⊕ *www.cosmos.com.*

## SPECIAL-INTEREST TOURS
### BIKING

The Austrian national tourist information website, ⊕ *www.austria.info,* includes excellent sections on hotels that welcome cyclists, as well as some of the better-known tours and routes.

You can no longer rent a bike at train stations in Austria. The cost of renting a bike (21-gear) from a local agency is around €35 a day. Tourist offices have details (in German), including maps and hints for trip planning and mealtime and overnight stops that cater especially to cyclists. Ask for the booklet "Radtouren in Österreich" or go to the website ⊕ *www. radtouren.at.* There's also a brochure in English: "Biking Austria—On the Trail of Mozart" that provides details in English on the cycle route through the High Tauern mountains in Salzburg Province and neighboring regions in Bavaria (⊕ *www. mozartradweg.com*).

E-bikes are becoming increasingly popular and are widely available for rent. Small electric motors make cycling up hills easy and increase the range of routes you can tackle in a day. You still have to pedal and can choose how much input you want the motor to make. A network of battery stations—at shops, gas stations and even mountain huts—means you can exchange a waning battery for a fully charged one at suitable intervals.

■ TIP→ **Most airlines accommodate bikes as luggage, provided they're dismantled and boxed.**

**Contacts Austria Radreisen.**
☎ 07712/5511–0 ⊕ *www.austria-radreisen. at.* **Backroads.** ☎ 800/793–6583 ⊕ *www. backroads.com.* **Butterfield & Robinson.** ☎ 866/551–9090 *from the U.S., 800/678–1477 from other countries* ⊕ *www.butterfield.com.* **Euro-Bike Tours.** ☎ 800/575–1540 ⊕ *www. eurobike.at/en.* **Mountain Bike Hotels.** ☎ 0810/101818 ⊕ *www.austria.info.* **Pedal Power.** ☎ 01/729–7234 ⊕ *www.pedalpower. at.* **VBT (Vermont Biking Tours).** ☎ 800/245–3868 ⊕ *www.vbt.com.*

### ECOTOURS

Austria is a popular vacation spot for those who want to experience nature—many rural hotels offer idyllic bases for hiking in the mountains or lake areas. The concept of the *Urlaub am Bauernhof* (farm vacation), where families can stay on a working farm and children can help take care of farm animals, is increasingly popular throughout Austria. There are numerous outfitters that can provide information on basic as well as specialty farms, such as organic farms or farms for children, for people with disabilities, or for horseback riders.

**Contacts Austrian Tourist Board.** ☎ 212/575–7723 *in the U.S., 416/967–3381 in Canada* ⊕ *www.austria.info.* **Naturidyll Hotels.** ☎ 01/867–3660–16, 0800/80–18–400 *reservations* ⊕ *www.naturidyll.at.*

**Information on Farm Vacations Farmhouse Holidays in Austria.** ⊕ *www.farmholidays. com.* **Tirol/Das Land der Berge.** ☎ 05/9292–1172 ⊕ *www.bauernhof.cc.*

### HIKING AND MOUNTAIN CLIMBING

With more than 50,000 km (about 35,000 miles) of well-maintained mountain paths through Europe's largest reserve of unspoiled landscape, the country is a hiker's paradise. Three long-distance routes traverse Austria, including the E-6 from the Baltic, cutting across mid-Austria via the Wachau valley region of the Danube and on to the Adriatic. Wherever you are in Austria, you will find shorter hiking trails requiring varying degrees of ability. Routes are well marked, and maps are readily available from bookstores, the Österreichische Alpenverein (ÖAV: Austrian Alpine Club), and the automobile clubs.

If you're a newcomer to mountain climbing or want to improve your skill, schools in Salzburg province will take you on. Ask the ÖAV for addresses. All organize courses and guided tours for beginners as well as for more advanced climbers.

Tourist offices have details on hiking holidays; serious climbers can write directly to ÖAV for more information. Membership in the club (€55, about $74) will give you a 30%–50% reduction on the regular fees for overnights in the 275 mountain refuges it operates in Austria and for huts operated by other mountain organizations in Europe. Membership also includes accident insurance for vacations of up to six weeks. Memberships for young people up to age 25 and for senior citizens have a reduced price.

**Contacts** Inn Travel. ☎ +44 1653/617001 *from outside U.K.* ⊕ *www.inntravel. co.uk.* **Österreichischer Alpenverein.** ☎ *0512/59547* ⊕ *www.alpenverein.at.*

# ▌RESOURCES

## ONLINE TRAVEL TOOLS

**"About Austria".** This is a nice general overview of facts and figures, useful German phrases, and some mouthwatering recipes. ⊕ *www.aboutaustria.org.*

**Austria Tourist Office.** ⊕ *www.austria.info.*

**Die Falter.** It's mostly in German, but this site has excellent movie and restaurant reviews and comprehensive coverage of the city's "alternative" scene. ⊕ *www. falter.at.*

**Die Presse.** In German only, this is the website of the city's leading serious newspaper. ⊕ *www.diepresse.at.*

**Jirsa Tickets Wien.** This is the place for prebooking event tickets online. ⊕ *www. viennaticket.at/de.*

**MuseumsQuartier.** Visit this website for the scoop on what's happening in Vienna's trendy museum quarter. ⊕ *www.mqw.at.*

**Salzburg.** ⊕ *www.salzburg.info.*

**Train Information.** ⊕ *www.oebb.at.*

**Vienna.** ⊕ *www.wien.info.*

**Wien Online.** Vienna's official government website, in German and English, for daily events in parks and public spaces, religious and cultural holidays, etc. ⊕ *www. magwien.gv.at.*

**Wienerzeitung.** This Vienna newspaper site has an English translation. ⊕ *www. wienerzeitung.at.*

# INDEX

## PHOTO CREDITS

# NOTES

# NOTES

# NOTES

# NOTES

# NOTES

# NOTES